Kealey '72
Tor.

D1105276

THE NEW WORLD OF

Henri Saint-Simon

THE
NEW WORLD
OF
Henri Saint-Simon

FRANK E. MANUEL

HARVARD UNIVERSITY PRESS

Cambridge, Massachusetts

1956

© Copyright 1956 by the President and Fellows of Harvard College

Distributed in Great Britain by
Geoffrey Cumberlege, Oxford University Press, London

———————————————

Library of Congress Catalogue Card Number 56–6519
Printed in the United States of America

To
CRANE BRINTON

THIS VOLUME IS PUBLISHED WITH ASSISTANCE FROM
BRANDEIS UNIVERSITY

CONTENTS

CONTENTS

Contents　xi

THE NEW WORLD OF
Henri Saint-Simon

Introduction

READING SAINT-SIMON TODAY is in some respects like reading Rousseau. So many of his grandiloquent periods have been assimilated by the slogan-makers of modern political ideologies that it is well-nigh impossible to apprehend them intellectually in their original meaning without hearing the overtones of later usage. By emphasizing selected passages in the diffuse congeries of Saint-Simon's writings one can make him out to be an early exponent of fascism, socialism, or democratic planning, a theoretician of finance capitalism, a technocrat, or just another utopian advocating rule by an intellectual élite. Like his contemporary Hegel, he has been claimed as a respectable ancestor by both the Right and the Left. The Pereires, aggressive nineteenth-century French financiers and organizers of the *Crédit Mobilier*, paid for the edition of his collected works, and their descendant set aside a fund in perpetuity for the care of his grave in Père Lachaise. On an obelisk in Moscow his name is inscribed among the fathers of the Communist revolution.

In the decades immediately following his death, when Europe was a battleground of rival theoretic systems, utopias, and ideologies, the few original works of Saint-Simon available in print were read primarily as antecedents of some later philosophy. The Saint-Simonians who delivered the series of lectures in 1828–1830 published as the famous *Doctrine de Saint-Simon* were expounding — and they said so — not a literal interpretation of his ideas but their own development of the doctrine. Indeed, Saint-Simon's philosophy was sometimes less a foundation for their beliefs than a springboard for an entirely different or at least significantly variant body of ideas. The Saint-Simonians at times caught the essence of his thought far better than later commentators, but they altered the theory at will and when they republished the original texts they even modified the phraseology without compunction, since a "progressive" doctrine like Saint-Simonism was not hidebound by specific first formulations. By attaching his name to their ideological proliferations, the Saint-Simonians who called themselves "disciples of the master" made it impossible for the uninitiated to distinguish between Saint-Simon's original conceptions and the glosses and interpretations of the epigoni.

To compound the confusion, during the heyday of their notoriety in the early 1830's, the Saint-Simonian cultists were torn by schisms, each of whose leaders proclaimed that his own extravaganzas were in the true spirit of Saint-Simon. Since the Saint-Simonians enjoyed an international reputation and their missions and propaganda penetrated to small groups throughout Europe, as well as to isolated individuals in North and South America, the master's name became widely identified with bizarre notions such as the search for the Female Messiah and the practice of "free love."

"I am this Saint-Simon, dead, living, and being born; past, present, and future; this Saint-Simon eternally progressive, manifested in time under the name of Enfantin, in space under the form of Enfantin; it is by me and in me that Saint-Simon advances towards God. It is by my son and in my son that I shall rise there, bearing Saint-Simon, when by death I shall be more lovingly united with him in my son," wrote the Père Enfantin in his *Physiologie religieuse*.[1] No thinker could survive such mystical lucubrations among disciples and emerge with a reputation unscathed.

With the commentaries on Marx and Engels, a characteristic set of intellectual problems was born. What was the influence of Saint-Simon on Marx? Was he a pre-Marxist, a forerunner of "scientific socialism," or was he no Marxist at all? The ideas themselves were forgotten as each new polemicist tried to prove by piecing together a few aphorisms here and there, often completely out of context, that Saint-Simon was or was not a pre-Marxist or a socialist. The problem was an "appearance problem" typical of much of late nineteenth- and early twentieth-century German scholarship. Saint-Simon's writings were ransacked for the genesis of Marxist concepts which were in themselves as ambiguous and complex as Saint-Simon's doctrine. What could be proved at most was that Saint-Simon did or did not conform to a commentator's views of Marx or of socialism. In the process the class theory of Saint-Simon, which can stand on its own feet, was ignored. Becoming a precursor, he ceased to be a man.

Marx and Engels themselves had differed in their final estimate of his worth as a thinker, Marx tending to dismiss him rather cavalierly along with Owen and Fourier as a utopian (the view popularized by the Communist Manifesto), while Engels later paid homage to his original genius as a social philosopher and declared that almost all the ideas of later socialists were contained in embryo in his theories.[2] Lenin called Saint-Simon's prophetic visions of capitalist development "guesswork, the guesswork of a genius, but guesswork all the same." [3]

Auguste Comte and the Positivist School also introduced obfuscatory elements into the appreciation of Saint-Simon. Again the issue was "to what extent" — an ill-defined notion in any case — Saint-Simon had influenced the young Auguste Comte. Was Saint-Simon a forerunner of Posivitism or should his right to the role be denied? Since Auguste Comte participated in the preparation of Saint-Simon's periodicals from 1817 through 1824, the problem could even be inverted into a study of Comte's influence on Saint-Simon. Whichever way the question was turned, it ended as a partisan array of Positivists versus Saint-Simonians, a battle which somehow endured for decades after both the Positivist Religion and the Saint-Simonian cult had become historical movements without visible descendants. Professor Henri Gouhier's profusely documented and in many respects admirable study on *La Jeunesse d'Auguste Comte* fires the most recent salvo in this sham war which has been waged for more than a century.[4] Through a one-sided selection of texts it is possible to demonstrate that many if not all of Saint-Simon's ideas had contemporary parallels. Comte is then depicted as an original genius who did not need Saint-Simon as a source for his thought, while Saint-Simon was merely an eclectic who soaked in the intellectual atmosphere around him.[5] Saint-Simon himself in the appendix to the second *cahier* of the *Catéchisme des industriels* (1824) very obligingly provided the future historian with a long list of thinkers whom he credited with having actively influenced him. The discovery of contemporary analogues does not reduce to nullity a seminal force of Saint-Simon's magnitude. To label him a pre-Positivist, as Professor Gouhier does, is to write from a perspective that is not likely to yield a comprehension of his total system or an appreciation of his originality. For Auguste Comte himself, of course, Saint-Simon eventually was nothing more than a "depraved juggler."[6]

Leading nineteenth-century social theorists varied sharply in their estimates. John Stuart Mill recalled that Saint-Simon was considered a clever "original";[7] Carlyle admired and translated him;[8] to Nietzsche he was a fanatic in the same class with Savonarola, Luther, Rousseau, and Robespierre.[9] Modern sociologists have either raised him on an intellectual pedestal or treated him with contempt. Durkheim considered him the founder of Positivism and of sociology.[10] Pareto disdained him as a buffoon.[11] Mosca lauded him as a brilliant forerunner of his own theory of the élite.[12] In very recent years he has awakened interest in diverse areas of knowledge: Toynbee returned to the original texts for parallels to illustrate his own theories of philosophical history;[13] Schumpeter, though aware of weaknesses, appreciated his "pungent sense of reality."[14]

On the whole, Saint-Simon has been written about far more often than he has been read and understood for his own sake in the locus of his creation. He was both an innovator and a copier. He had great insights and he also wrote a good deal of nonsense — a combination not infrequent in the history of human thought. And he had more to say than has usually been grasped by those studying him primarily as an introduction to something else.

The manner in which his works were made available to later generations has served to multiply the misconceptions. His Empire writings, now bibliophilic rarities, were either published in limited private editions or remained in manuscript until decades after his death. The Restoration works were periodicals issued irregularly in a variety of strange formats, followed by excerpts, circulars, lithographed public letters, and reëditions with emendations, a bewilderment to any bibliographer. Posthumous editions of Saint-Simon's works, composed of selections only, were always prepared with bias. First, by the Saint-Simonians — Rodrigues in 1832 and 1841,[15] Hubbard in 1857,[16] Lemonnier in 1859,[17] and the supposedly definitive edition by former members of the cult in 1865–1878.[18] When Bouglé published excerpts in 1925, he tried to make another kind of precursor of Saint-Simon — the father of respectable late nineteenth-century sociology.[19] French writers in search of native ancestors for modern communism have lately revived him, and their distortions make the pious Saint-Simonians seem meticulous scholars by contrast — as, for example, the excerpts edited by Dautry,[20] bent upon metamorphosing Saint-Simon into a Marxian materialist by chopping up individual texts. By comparison Volgin's Russian edition of 1948 is a balanced selection, introduced with a straightforward preface.[21] Markham's English translation of "selected writings" of Saint-Simon, though excellent for its limited scope, does not pretend to present a full-blooded impression of his work.[22]

Even the complete first editions and the manuscripts which M. Alfred Pereire has deposited in the Bibliothèque Nationale do not solve the problems of expounding Saint-Simon's thought. He was always digressing, backtracking, repeating himself with slight modifications, contradicting himself, lapsing into paradoxes, coining brilliant phrases in the midst of turgid, involved, often ungrammatical paragraphs. Ideas were not logically developed or expanded, but were rephrased over and over again.

Much of the misunderstanding which has been visited upon Saint-Simon arises from his neologisms. When he invented a new word such as *industriel*, he did not use it consistently in its first meaning, but shifted the sense, catching the reader unawares by a new definition. Sometimes he employed common words in so individual a way that they became a private language. *Deism* to him was orthodox revealed religion. Many of his slogans and epigrams entered the vocabulary of nineteenth-century socialist thought and in the course of time acquired very different connotations from those in the Saint-Simon texts. Incautious students coming upon these phrases have all too frequently understood them as if they had already acquired their later import.

Many of Saint-Simon's productions have more psychological significance for the understanding of his character than they have genuine intellectual merit. A segment of his work was commonplace political pamphleteering which did not deserve to outlive the day-to-day issues and partisan conflicts of the Bourbon restoration. And since his style was rather pedestrian, even his contemporaries did not count him among the more vigorous and influential popular propagandists espousing the cause of the middle class against "feudal reaction." Today, most of these long-winded arguments convey little to anyone not interested in the polemics of the period.

But there are other writings of far more lasting quality. Saint-Simon really had a *doctrine*, elaborated over a quarter of a century of haphazard publication from 1802 to 1825. An underlying pattern of ideas is discernible in his works, and though it changes in detail from time to time, it remains intrinsically the same. To an exposition of these ideas a major portion of this book is dedicated. Unfortunately in no single work is there an orderly presentation of his thought, even though he considered it a "system," let alone a logical or reasoned defense of the brilliant, though often categoric affirmations he made about science, history, man, and society. The purpose of the present study is not to emphasize the divergences in Saint-Simon's viewpoint from one period of his life to another — these could be annotated all too easily — but to highlight what was relatively constant in his writing. A systematization of his *idées maîtresses* necessarily disguises some of the confusion of the original texts. He was a man of intuitions who did not have the patience to develop coherently an idea he borrowed or invented. It took the mature Auguste Comte of the *Système de Politique Positive* to compose with precision and to string out in volume after volume of involved prose what Saint-Simon had tossed off casually.

Saint-Simon's "industrial doctrine" ended in a vision of the good society, a social order administered by working industrialists, scientists, artists, and engineers, all in the service, not of the state, but of "the most numerous and the poorest classes." Because he grasped the essence of the new industrialized society before it became bewildering in its complexity, Saint-Simon's work is a revelation of western social ideals in modern times. Though it is doubtful that his ideas profoundly altered the historic process, in the nineteenth century many of his formulations became common coin, even among men who had never heard his name or read his books. One of his observations on the nature of intellectual influence applies to the fate of his own doctrine:

"General ideas may be compared to musk. One does not have to see or touch it in order to sense the odor. As soon as a new general idea is emitted human thought becomes subject to its influence." [23]

The reconstruction of Saint-Simon's biography presents problems analogous to the interpretation of his works. He himself wrote many autobiographical sketches, none of which jibes with any other, since he blithely reorganized his life history from time to time to fit political and intellectual exigencies of the moment. To these inconsistencies must be added the legends of Saint-Simonian hagiographies and anti-Saint-Simonian pasquinades. As a summary of his life and work there is some merit to the transparently archaistic periodization of the Saint-Simonians, making his trials and labors a "symbol of perfectibility":

"In a period of thirty-four years comprising what may be called the *pre-*

paratory works of *Saint-Simon*, that is to say, all those which preceded the *Conception of the New Christianity*, seven years he consecrated to the acquisition of pecuniary resources and seven years to the acquisition of scientific materials; ten years to the renovation of philosophy and ten years to the renovation of politics." [24]

Even the signature of his name did not remain constant; he varied the more antique Henry with Henri; usually he eliminated the Claude. He suppressed the aristocratic *de* in his surname, revived it, then dropped it again. After 1815 he rarely used the title Count. At one period he omitted the Saint, leaving plain Simon; or he adopted an entirely new name, that of the virtuous Bonhomme. Henri Saint-Simon is the form most frequent during his last years.

Among contemporaries he was a controversial figure. At one time or another he was called a wicked sensualist, a madman, a genius, a naïve fool, a wit, a conscious mystifier, a hard-headed analyst of public affairs, a philanthropist, a philosopher, an innovator, an atheist, an embezzler, a religious prophet. Since his death, Marx's epithet "utopian socialist" has tenaciously clung to him. He surely was not a Saint-Simonian. In a manuscript written during his waning years he bestowed upon himself the title "Founder of the Industrial Doctrine."

PART I

THE PHILOSOPHICAL APPRENTICESHIP

1

Hero of the American Revolution

IN THE MID-EIGHTEENTH CENTURY the House of Saint-Simon mourned the passing of the last of the great courtiers, arrogant defender of the prerogatives of the French nobility, and witnessed the birth of a philosopher, herald of the new world industrial society.

The Duke Louis de Rouvroy, of the Rasse branch of Saint-Simon, had strutted about the court of Louis XIV and the Regent, and at his death in 1755 left voluminous secret memoirs, a mordant record of the corrosion of aristocratic France through the infiltration of the *bourgeois* spirit. Scornful and vitriolic when stripping some *parvenu* noble of a spurious ancestry, the duke was naïvely credulous about the glories of his own house, which he proudly traced back through the counts of Vermandois to Charlemagne.[1] Skeptical modern research has failed to establish such antiquity for the Saint-Simon line, and scholars maintain it was founded in the fourteenth century by valiant though insignificant knights mentioned in the chronicles of the Hundred Years' War.[2] Early nineteenth-century representatives of the family not only credited the duke's account, but as *émigrés* of the Revolution showed themselves rather partial to the pretentious genealogy elaborated for them by a Spanish priest in 1808.[3] This remarkable testament accepted direct descent from Charlemagne as a foregone conclusion and then pursued the thread back to an even more remote ancestor, the Gallic nobleman Marcus Maecilius Avitus, who in 455 wore the imperial purple at Rome — a family tree which reduced the Capets or any reigning house in Europe to insignificance.

Guardian of the family honor, throughout his life the duke applied himself with indefatigable zeal to the advancement of his relatives, not forgetting those of allied branches of the great house. Under the Regency Louis-François de Rouvroy, a young son of the Sandricourt line of Saint-Simon, became the special object of his solicitude. "We are of the same house," wrote the duke, "though separated for more than three hundred years. I have always loved my name. I have never neglected to elevate all those who bore my name in my time." Dolefully he added, "I have not always been successful." [4]

The Sandricourts are depicted in the memoirs as intelligent, but miserly, retiring, obscure, and rooted in the rich lands of Picardy. The duke was quick to perceive that young Louis-François de Rouvroy needed patronage if he was to make his mark at court. A colonelship in the provincial regiment of Berry was the first commission bestowed upon the stripling through his relative's shrewd intervention. When Louis-François de Rouvroy showed capacity and will, he was rewarded with a brigadiership, amid the outcries of a host of young rivals. Presented everywhere by the ubiquitous duke, the favorite's prestige was fast mounting.

His rapid promotion inspired in the Sandricourts nothing more glorious than a desire to contract a profitable marriage for their son. The duke, somewhat out of countenance, tried to stay their impatience, arguing that ever more lucrative and worthy prospects awaited his young *protégé* as he progressed in his career. But the Sandricourts, beyond persuasion, so pressed the duke for a bride that he reluctantly surveyed the terrain, finally producing Mademoiselle de Richebourg, a noble name and a fortune. The affair was under sober consideration, when the country bumpkins descended upon the duke with a boorish objection that the safe preservation of their territorial rights in Picardy demanded an alliance with the nobility of the robe, a guarantee in case of litigation. The duke had hardly recovered his composure when Louis-François de Rouvroy himself, rashly ignoring his patron's displeasure, brought news that a marriage with Louise-Marie-Gabrielle de Gourgue, daughter of a *maître-des-requêtes*, had already been arranged. [5] The duke's horrified remonstrances against this degradation of the family name made no impression, for he was speaking to a lover. When Madame de Sandricourt reappeared to rail against the duke's attempted interference, he endured his country relative with studied indifference. To send the lady off with a neat thrust, the duke's mother transmitted to her scandalous rumors concerning the future daughter-in-law, as whispered about by the Gourgue servants. The intransigence of the Sandricourts on this occasion led to a complete rupture between the families. In a few days the young couple were married without the ducal blessing. [6]

These were the paternal grandparents of Claude-Henri de Saint-Simon.

To the duke's malicious satisfaction the union of Louis-François de Rouvroy with Louise-Marie-Gabrielle de Gourgue was not a happy one. [7] The nuptials were celebrated in 1717, and in a few years the beloved were, after the manner of the age, no longer beloved. The contemporary tale-bearer Mathieu Marais recorded a singular story about the young Madame de Sandricourt.

A woman (Madame de Sandricourt), beloved of the Chevalier Marle and having an affair with him, told him that she was lacking something in her pleasure; that he was not absolutely like another; that it would be very easy to alter him with a small cut of the knife which she herself would give him, and that he would suffer no more ill than in the cutting of a child's umbilical cord. The chevalier, in love, believed her, placed himself in her hands, and she made him a circumcision which put him all in blood, which made him faint, and of which he was long sick.

"Love, love," concluded the scandalmonger, "when you hold us, one may say adieu to prudence." [8] In later years this eccentric creature lived at Saint-Germain, occupying herself with chemistry. Some believed that she sought the philosopher's stone, others had her brewing medicines for the poor. In 1754 Madame de Sandricourt was found asphyxiated in a laboratory with her assistant.[9] The Gourgue was a strange personage to have fallen in with the earthy Sandricourts of Picardy. Her husband nursed his discontent in the family château of Berny-en-Santerre, became embittered, and finally vented his spleen against the enemy in the War of the Austrian Succession. A son, Balthazar-Henri, Count de Saint-Simon, was born in 1721, at a time when Madame de Sandricourt was outraging the memoir writers.

The Duke de Saint-Simon's passion for his family induced him to further the fortunes of another young relative, member of the Rouvroy branch this time. After careful manoeuvring he procured the rank of colonel for Henri, Marquis de Saint-Simon, before he was fifteen. The duke invited the youth to accompany him on the famous mission to the king of Spain in 1721 when the infanta's hand was sought for Louis XV. Henri so prospered under this tutelage that in 1734, during the Italian campaign, he was already a brigadier. But the duke's meticulous arrangements to safeguard the dignity of his house were again thwarted by wayward affections. Under warm Italian suns, Henri became infatuated with the Signora Blanche-Louise Zacaria, seductive forty-year-old widow of the Marquis Gastona de Botta, and he married her after eight days of courtship. Though the Bishop of Metz and all the other Saint-Simons, incensed at the misalliance, intrigued to break bonds of matrimony contracted "in an excess of passion which left [the marquis] no more liberty than a drunken man," [10] in the eyes of the church the evil was irreparable. The young marquis had his "Litta" for four years, and in the fifth he died. The Italian temptress had given birth to their only daughter, Blanche-Elisabeth, in 1737.

On June 25, 1758, the offspring of these two misalliances in the House of Saint-Simon were married to each other — Blanche-Elisabeth, a maid of twenty-one, Balthazar-Henri, Count de Saint-Simon, a benedict of thirty-six. While Blanche-Elisabeth was an only child, her husband had eight brothers and sisters, not all of whom were without distinction. The eldest brother, Maximilien-Henri, is called a madcap in the archives of the Ministry of Foreign Affairs.[11] He quit the army, settled near Utrecht, and devoted his life to hyacinths, gathering some two thousand varieties in his garden at Haarlem.

His work, *Des jacinthes, de leur anatomie, reproduction et culture*, presented novel observations on the cultivation of plants. For the rest, he wrote military history and translated the classics and Ossian.[12] Another brother, Charles-François-Siméon de Saint-Simon Sandricourt, joined the church and was elevated to the bishopric of Agde. Author of sundry works of erudition, in 1785 he became an associate member of the Royal Academy of Inscriptions and Belles-Lettres.[13]

Balthazar-Henri de Saint-Simon entered the army, as might any scion of an impoverished eighteenth-century noble family. Participation in profitable industrial and commercial enterprise was spurned by the aristocracy of blood, and the *bourgeois* merchants, lawyers, and manufacturers eagerly snatched up land which the nobles relinquished for ready cash. The heritage of patrician families diminished from generation to generation. The king was besieged with requests for money and offices to support the station of his penurious nobles, and the military establishment became a patchwork of gradations, with empty spectacular titles created to appease the demands of young sons with influence whose patrimony did not yield sufficient income. The father of Balthazar-Henri de Saint-Simon had at least performed military duty; the Crown did not require the active services of the son. Though he retained hereditary civil and military titles, and even acquired new posts, they were sinecures with no functions attached to the emoluments they drew. The sustenance of the nobility in the last decades of the old régime had become a ludicrous economic whirligig. In 1783 Balthazar-Henri died in straitened circumstances, having poured back into the royal treasury large sums of money to purchase new sinecures and honors for his six sons. His wife Blanche-Elisabeth lived on into the next century, her reason gone, her fortune shrunk by the events of the Revolution.

The offspring of this union between two branches of the House of Saint-Simon — three females and six males — were a sickly and hapless brood. Of one son a story is told that he left his bride the night of their marriage, absconding with her dowry to Naples, where he consumed it wantonly with an actress of the San Carlo Theatre. Claude-Henri-René died a year after his birth in 1762. Eudes-Claude-Henri, Hébert, and André-Louis became Knights of the Order of Malta, a common practice by which the younger sons of noble families received honorific office with one of the small seigneuries the order possessed in France. The Revolution interrupted their careers and sent them packing to foreign lands. A daughter, Adélaïde-Blanche-Marie, married a Saint-Simon of the Montbléru branch and barely escaped the scaffold during the Terror. Only the second child and eldest son, Claude-Henri, Count de Saint-Simon Sandricourt, born at Paris, October 17, 1760, was to mount to fame.[14] Molting the shriveled skin of the class to which he was born, he stepped forth as champion of a new industrial society. What historical disparagement for the proud Duke de Saint-Simon — the sole perpetuator of the family renown an atheist, a philosopher, a publicist for the Third Estate, a land speculator, a beggar.

In his autobiographical writings Claude-Henri de Saint-Simon was not voluble about his early life. Though he once boasted of a rigorous metaphysical training directed by d'Alembert,[15] for which there is not a scrap of evidence, he also deplored the pedagogical methods of which he had been the victim, complaining that they retarded the development of his thought. "I was overwhelmed with masters, who did not permit me time to reflect on what they taught; with the result that the scientific seeds which my mind received could not sprout until long years after having been sown."[16] The desultory education of Saint-Simon left its tell-tale mark.

As an old man, surrounded by enthusiastic disciples, he mused over his boyhood exploits. Olinde Rodrigues, hierophant of the Saint-Simonian cult, recorded these anecdotes and passed them on to the next generation of devotees. The Englishmen Hubbard and Booth incorporated them in their biographies, bequeathing them to Saint-Simonian posterity.[17] From the hallowed pages of Saint-Simonian legend a stubborn boy emerges. At thirteen he refuses his first communion, threatening, if he is forced, to partake of the gifts without conviction in their efficacy — thus have the teachings of the Encyclopedists borne fruit. His father, unsuccessful at imposing discipline at home, imprisons his son in Saint-Lazare for his contumely. Saint-Simon overpowers his jailor, snatches the keys, and makes his way to the home of an aunt, through whose intercessions the prodigal is returned to his father's house. Like Alcibiades, he lies in the path of a wagoner's cart, preferring to be crushed rather than cede the way. With a penknife he stabs the buttocks of one of his tutors who tries to whip him and he runs away from home.[18] Bitten by a mad dog, he cauterizes the wound himself, preparing to blow out his brains with a pistol at the first symptoms of hydrophobia. Every morning a servant wakes him with the words, "Arise, Count, you have great deeds to perform today." [19]

Among his miscellaneous manuscripts Saint-Simon has left satires on the education of the nobility in the last years of the old régime which reflect his own experience. In a few telling paragraphs he conveys the psychological confusion of a young noble nurtured at one and the same time on anticlerical witticisms, on respect for royalty, and on the cynical realism of "society," where influence alone counted.[20] The revolutionary virus had been introduced into the youth through the medium of the classics and the *philosophes*.

Let us recollect the education which we received. They began by fixing our attention on the history of the Greeks and the Romans. Our young hearts were excited over the virtues of the Gracchi and the Brutuses. Our still tender souls were pierced by the republican dagger. They inspired in us the most democratic sentiments. When we passed from the study of ancient languages to French, Jean-Jacques, Voltaire, Helvétius, Raynal, d'Alembert, all the Encyclopedists not excluding Diderot (who wanted to hang the last of the kings with the gut of the last of the priests) were the authors they put in our hands.

Our education attained its goal. It made us revolutionaries.[21]

When Saint-Simon was sixteen he was appointed to a second lieutenancy; his father deferred acceptance of the commission until the following year, "to render him more worthy of entrance into the King's service and for fear of leaving him to himself too soon." [22] His advance in the regiment of Touraine was rapid and on June 3, 1779, he was promoted to a captaincy. But life in the French army had little of glamor after the humiliation of 1763, and high-spirited young nobles, chafing at the tedium of the military regimen, sought escape from their ennui in debauch. Saint-Simon squandered his money recklessly and often complained of his meagre 1200-franc allowance.

When Spain first joined France in the War for American Independence, there was discussion of a descent upon England, but this was abandoned for a plan of strategy which involved striking at Britain simultaneously in all her colonies throughout the world — India, America, Gibraltar, and the Antilles. By the fall of 1779 the American army had suffered defeat, and Spain was futilely besieging Gibraltar. In order to snatch the Antilles while the British were engaged on the American continent, the three poorly-equipped regiments of Touraine, Agenois, and Gâtinois were designated for duty overseas. Quartered with his regiment in Brittany under the Marquis de Bouillé, Claude-Henri de Saint-Simon was so enthusiastic at the prospect of action that he wrote to the Minister of War offering to serve in the American expedition without remuneration.[23]

After a turbulent voyage, during which the soldiers were obliged to help man the ships, the three regiments landed at Cap François in San Domingo. In this luxuriant, disease-ridden colony the French troops, ravaged by fevers, languished until the spring of 1780.[24] When in April they finally ventured forth upon the seas in an attempt to storm St. Lucia and Barbados, their sallies were repulsed by the English admiral Rodney and they were forced to ensconce themselves again in their original stronghold.

In the summer of 1781 de Bouillé's troops, marooned for months in the Antilles, finally received orders to reinforce Rochambeau and Lafayette in America. Saint-Simon's contingent landed in Virginia, after a perilous journey during which their vessel, stuck on a sand-bar in Chesapeake Bay, was almost wrecked.[25] Cornwallis's forces were disposed between Yorktown and Gloucester on the York River. Claude-Henri de Saint-Simon's regiment of Touraine, brigaded along with the rest of the detachment of his cousin, the Marquis Claude-Anne de Saint-Simon, one of the leading French officers of the expedition, was assigned a position on the allied right. The regiment of Touraine was ordered to construct a battery threatening the enemy ships which hovered on the James River, to distract Cornwallis's attention from the menace on the other flank. Claude-Henri de Saint-Simon, in command of the cannoneers, directed the transportation of the siege guns, which had to be dragged through swamp land from the mouth of the river to the place of encampment before operations could begin. The French quartermaster, Blanchard, has mentioned Saint-Simon briefly in his account of the actual Battle of Yorktown. In the course of inspection Blanchard entered a trench where a battery of mortars had been set in position to fire on an enemy redoubt. "In this trench I met M. de Saint-Simon, who commanded it. I had had occasion to write a very firm letter to him a few days before; we exchanged amicable explanations. A few enemy deserters came to us and told us that our fire greatly inconvenienced the English." [26] Nothing else of note is reported of Saint-Simon's conduct at Yorktown. After some confusion arising from the presence in the same detachment of the Marquis de Saint-Simon as well as the Baron Claude de Saint-Simon, Claude-Henri de Saint-Simon was belatedly elected to the Society of the Cincinnati in recognition of his services in the War for American Independence — the last French officer to be accorded the distinction.

The entire length of Saint-Simon's much-vaunted American sojourn was two months. Preoccupied with the exigencies of a military campaign, he had only a limited opportunity for general observation of the country, still less for conversation with those American fathers who were guiding the destinies of the fledgling state. The account of Saint-Simon's meeting with Franklin, whose honest simplicity and republican virtues were said to have delighted the young count, is apocryphal and can no more be corroborated than his supposed audience with Rousseau.[27] But Saint-Simon did see the ragged American troops, those farmer-soldiers who fought without either the restraints or the discipline of European mercenaries, and their performance left a lasting impression upon him. The spectacle of an army without an aristocratic officer class was a complete novelty. A similar society of farmers and artisans and merchants existed nowhere else in the world.

Emboldened by their success at Yorktown, where they had trounced the British in the most decisive encounter of the war, the French contingent — without a respite — set sail for the West Indies in high hope, to storm the enemy in another of her colonial citadels. Dropping anchor at Saint Kitts, one of the Lesser Antilles, de Bouillé's troops leveled the English fort of Brimstone Hill in a surprise foray.

Two long letters written by Saint-Simon to his father from encampments in the West Indies in 1782 are the first important revelations of his character during this formative period of his life. They show at an early age a keenly perceptive, analytical mind absorbed in psychological if not philosophical problems.[28] The letters corroborate the Saint-Simonian tradition which represented his father as harsh and irascible.[29] At moments of psychic strain in later life, Saint-Simon's deep-seated rancor against his father would break out into an open attack upon his memory, even decades after the old count's death. The neurotic tensions of his mature years can be traced back to the family relationships described in his letters — the authoritarian father over sixty and ailing, the son alternately rebellious and contrite, overcome with a feeling of guilt and pleading for love and forgiveness. The whole Saint-Simonian system might be interpreted as an expression of the philosopher's revolt against the aristocratic societal order — symbolized by the father — in which he was born and which oppressed him, and a longing for the utopia of a new system founded upon a love which he had been denied. At the same time there is discernible in Saint-Simon's character an authoritarian streak in imitation of his father which manifested itself throughout his life in a rigid adherence to absolute principles and in his completely domineering attitude towards his friends and those who worked for him. Like a pendulum he swung from one extreme to another, from outbursts of overflowing affection to insistence upon unquestioning submission to his will. Saint-Simon's ambivalence towards his father is one of the clues to his personality. He hated the patriarchal social order and he reveled in its destruction, yet he longed for a new hierarchy, under another father. Perhaps in the end he came to believe that he was that father himself, the restorer of order, the lover of all humanity.

On the twentieth of February, 1782, a young soldier of twenty-two wrote from Brimstone Hill, Saint Kitts, to his father, the elderly courtier of a monarchy that was doomed.[30]

You would not believe, dear papa and friend, how uneasy I am about your health and that of my mother and all my brothers and sisters. It is a year since I have had any news from you. I cannot attribute it to laziness on my part, because for a very long time I have not neglected a single opportunity to write you.

My circumstances have changed completely since that letter which I wrote you from Yorck [Yorktown]. At that time the Marquis de S. [Saint-Simon] began to treat me a little better. He is about to depart for France on the frigate which will bring news of the success of our arms at Saint Kitts. . . Since my cousin is leaving, none of the reasons which prompted me to serve in the 7th Regiment of Touraine any longer apply. Much, on the contrary, moves me to leave it. Among other reasons, the suspicion that this unit, which has only recently been employed in two expeditions, may not be used in many more. Prudence prohibits me from writing to you about them. But I believe that when you learn about them, you will strongly approve what I am doing.

Consequently, I requested M. le Marquis de St. Simon to ask M. de Bouillé to take me on as his aide-de-camp, which he was glad to do. He even promised to use me on the staff of his army which will total eight to nine thousand men when his troops are joined with those from San Domingo. This will give me a better chance to learn my profession than if I remained attached to the seventh in a rank which, moreover, affords very few opportunities to distinguish oneself.

. . . I hope, my dear papa and friend, that the order which I have put into my private affairs during the last year will have made you forget my past blunders. The Marquis de Saint-Simon will be in a position to tell you about my conduct as he has seen it, in order to make you give me back the friendship which my youth in part caused me to lose. Nothing is dearer to me in the world and you may be sure that I shall in the future neglect nothing to keep and increase it.

Of the details of his wild youth we have no knowledge, nothing but his own testimony. While the plea for forgiveness from the prodigal son is touching, there was always a calculating streak in Saint-Simon and he quickly came to the point.

My expenditures, even since I put them in good order, must appear to you to be very heavy and even above your means. I am perfectly aware of the fact, but I also know your way of thinking and I know that you will never consider money when it may be useful to the advancement of your children. This campaign will be very helpful to me and thus also to all my brothers, for I believe you do not doubt the affection which I bear them.

He mapped out for himself a glorious military career in whose sun his whole family would bask. If he was to succeed he had to maintain a standard of expenditure befitting a Saint-Simon. That was the way to preferment.

Everything is so exorbitant in this country that I think it will cost you ten thousand silver francs this year merely to keep me at the same level as other persons of my grade with whom I am going to serve, without permitting myself any extravagance.

There had been a rupture with his father so violent that some other member of the family had had to act as intermediary between them. After his heroic soldiering he expected to be forgiven.

I hope that now I shall be able to deal directly with you. A third party, whoever it may be, only serves to cool your friendship for me, which I am trying my best to merit.

You must have received the detailed account which I sent you of our campaign, from our departure from the Cape to our arrival at Port Royal. You have seen how taxing it was on sea as well as on land, but thanks to the care which you bestowed upon my physical education I bore up perfectly well and I even feel better than ever. I only wish that the care you took of my moral education had succeeded as well. But *mea culpa*. I do not want to occupy myself in regretting things past, only to try to repair the damage as best I can.

Saint-Simon then proceeded to render a reasonably good circumstantial account of the siege of Brimstone Hill in Saint Kitts, one that is in accord with the narratives of modern historians.[31] Either out of ignorance or in deference to the naval commander, he did not comment on de Grasse's tactics, though naval historians have been less kind to the French admiral who let the English under Admiral Hood slip through his fingers when he enjoyed a marked superiority in ships and men. Hood's attempt to land troops at Saint Kitts and take de Bouillé from the rear was considered by Admiral Mahan to be the most daring stroke of the war. In April of 1783 de Grasse paid dearly for allowing Hood to escape and join Rodney's fleet unscathed.

Having described the battle, the young Count turned again to what had been troubling him for months, his family's utter neglect. The depiction of his abandonment, his loneliness and sadness at not hearing from his father and brothers might have been written by a soldier anywhere in the world.

I had forgotten to tell you that M. de Vaudreuil rejoined our squadron on January 30 with only two ships. He brought letters for everybody. I believe I am the only one in the army who did not receive any. You must feel how hard this is on a son who desires above all else to merit the title of your friend and who is resolved to force you to bestow it upon him by his conduct. If finally, my dear papa and friend, a few peccadilloes have caused me to lose your esteem entirely and have extinguished in your heart the paternal feelings which I always knew were there, I beg at least my brothers and sisters to treat me with somewhat less severity and to write me about our dear sick one whose condition I fear may have grown worse. They have had the right to reproach me for my laziness, but they punish me very severely for it. . . . Eude has reached an age when he ought to join the service immediately. If I should dare to take the liberty of giving you advice it would be to send him to this country. I know from experience that one year of war here will teach him more than ten years of peace in France. It will surely cost you much more but you will be recompensed by the advancement which this will procure him both now and later and by the fact that, in view of the action which we are going to see, it will be impossible for him to commit those follies common to young men entering the world.

His own heroic participation in the battle of Saint Kitts was described with the nonchalance of a veteran. He had commanded a detachment of infantry cannoneers.

I got out of it all right except for a few bruises from bomb bursts, but these are not worth talking about. I had a few men in my detachment who were not quite as lucky. There were seven killed and eleven wounded.

But I feel, my dear papa and friend, that the pleasure of talking to you by letter, though in no wise a substitute for seeing you, carries me away to the point of making me forget the frigate which is about to set sail. Please forgive my scribbling. One is not very much at one's ease in camp. Please return your esteem and your friendship to a son who loves you tenderly and you will make him the happiest of men. I do not ask that you intercede on my behalf for my preferment, but I am working with good heart to merit your occupying yourself with it. . . .

Nine months later, on November 10, 1782, from Fort St. Pierre in Martinique Saint-Simon again wrote to his father. He had in the interim received news from his family.

Despite the fact that I received your letter I am not yet completely reassured about your health, and I am afraid that, in the early stages of convalescence, the condition in which I left your spirits may seriously affect your physical state. I think I ought to tell you candidly that the cure of the latter depends upon the former. Therefore, my dear friend, permit me to beg you to worry as little as possible, and to try to distract yourself with the numerous and agreeable society which you abandoned for the good of your children and in which you will occupy a place of distinction as soon as you reënter it. Once again my sister Louise has written me a charming letter. With heartfelt effusion which brought tears to my eyes she wrote me of her regrets at not having always behaved towards you in a manner which pleased you. I am convinced that she has already repaired her faults and that she will bring you a thousand times more joy than she has caused you grief. I really believe that she needs, above all in the beginning, in view of her great sensitivity, the feeling that she shares equally in your paternal goodness, in order to have in you that trust which now makes me as happy as one can be at eighteen hundred leagues from the best of friends. . . .

The general [Bouillé], who is always showering his kindness upon me, has just ordered me to leave for Domingo, where in my capacity as chief billeting officer I shall make an exact reconnaissance of the roads, visit the fortifications, prepare the quarters for the troops, and in general put myself in a position to serve as a guide for the troops that will be sent to its aid in case the island is attacked. M. de Bouillé works with incredible energy to put all the colonies in a state of defense.

Everything seemed to be going well. He had been named aide-major general of the army, was favored by de Bouillé, and he respected and admired his commanding officer. He was entrusted with important functions and great battles were in the offing. But the old question of preferment still rank'ed. There was a young count, another aide-de-camp of de Bouillé's, who had been awarded the stipend of a lieutenant-colonelcy despite the fact that he had not yet heard a gun fired. It was bitter for a Saint-Simon, a veteran of four campaigns "who had been wounded," to be outstripped. "But be assured, my dear friend, that however great the injustice with which the court treats me I am not the less grateful for all the intercessions which you are surely making in my behalf. . . I conclude with a kiss and with great regret, but we are setting sail." [32]

Rodney, sensing the vital importance of San Domingo to the French and foreseeing a move to reinforce the island, set out to intercept the advance party. In the famous Battle of Les Saintes which developed on April 12, 1783, between Rodney's forces and the fleet of Admiral de Grasse — a decisive victory for the British — Saint-Simon, who was aboard the frigate *Ville-de-Paris*, was taken prisoner. A story he delighted in retelling in after years describes his shock when, stunned by a shell and feeling the brains of a fallen compatriot strewn over his face, he mistook them for the contents of his own skull. "Can a living man touch his own brains?" he asked himself. The pallor of the young count made the English sailors think that life had departed from him, and they were preparing to drop him over the side of the ship. After moments of indescribable anguish, during which Saint-Simon could hear all but was powerless to make known that he was alive, the "corpse" managed to raise an arm. The gesture caught the eye of one of the English, by miraculous chance the very man whose life Saint-Simon had once saved in America, sparing him an ignominious death as a spy. The Englishman now graciously returned the kindness, and for a sea burial Saint-Simon exchanged an English prison in Jamaica and his ultimate release. In later life when every action of his youth became a portent of his future mission, he looked upon his unique capacity to introspect while he lay prostrate in the midst of battle as proof of his nascent scientific curiosity. Had any man before him ever experienced such an emotion — feeling his own brains? [33]

In the writings of his adult years the American Revolution assumed broad ideological significance, and Saint-Simon reinterpreted his American experience as an heroic adventure which helped establish the first free industrial society in the modern world. He read back into his military participation in the war an awareness of the political implications of his soldiering which is not apparent in his letters as a young officer intent upon advancement.

It was in America, it was while fighting for the cause of industrial liberty, that I first conceived the desire to see this plant of another world flower in my country. . . .

I realized that the revolution in America signalled the beginning of a new political era, that this revolution would necessarily bring about major progress in general civilization, and that in a short time it would cause great changes in the social order which then existed in Europe.[34]

He contemplated his personal role in the American Revolution with self-satisfaction. "I was present at the siege of York [sic], I contributed rather significantly to the capture of General Cornwallis and his army; I can thus consider myself as one of the founders of liberty in the United States, because it was this military operation which determined the peace and established irrevocably the independence of America." [35]

The interlude between the time Saint-Simon regained his liberty and the outbreak of the French Revolution was a period of restless wandering, of craving for grandiose accomplishment, and of zest for physical creation. The young Saint-Simon dedicated himself to a life of action. Though his projects, pretentious for his mediocre resources, were abortive, the energizing drive behind them was not dissipated and found sublimated expression in his later theoretical formulations.

Saint-Simon's first exploit in engineering is described by his own account. He presented to the viceroy of Mexico a scheme for a canal across the Isthmus of Panama. Though this was not the first ever proposed, since 1700 no plans for an interoceanic canal had been seriously revived.[36] Saint-Simon based his plan upon a deepening of the river *in Partido*, the branches of which he thought had outfalls into both oceans. The entire project was once regarded as spurious, because the river he alluded to could not be located, but an early map of the Kingdom of Guatemala indicates a belief at the time that a river *in* or *de Partido* did exist.[37] Whatever its merits, the project failed to capture the viceroy's fancy, and Saint-Simon made his way back to France.[38]

Named assistant quartermaster of the Aquitaine regiment, stationed at Mézières, in January 1784, Saint-Simon resumed his army career and executed his military duties with conscientiousness. He may even have followed courses at the School of Engineers which made Mézières one of the great centers of scientific education in eighteenth-century France. The Marquis de Chastellux, Inspector of the Army, noted that he was a "good officer . . . much zeal and intelligence." [39] The comment is rather startling in the register of army reports of the declining régime, which abound in accusations of neglect or faint praise like "joli sujet." In recognition of such diligence, the marquis proposed a pension of 1500 livres, which was awarded him for his services in the American Revolution. Saint-Simon's dossier at the War Archives shows an officer of unwonted docility. Striking in view of past and future performance is the record of his attendance at confession. The sincerity of his religious devotion may be questioned, but he was quite capable of external conformity in the spirit of the age. His life at this time was not extravagant, for his family was poor by aristocratic standards, and his own allowances, amounting to about 4000 livres, were not overgenerous. Though the family fortune ran to 100,000 francs income a year, it was in his mother's name; his father had died in February 1783 leaving him no inheritance.

Saint-Simon was not strictly obliged to remain with his regiment, and when the boredom of garrison routine weighed too heavily upon him, he looked for adventure in strange callings. In an army cluttered with supernumerary officers, it was not unusual for a patronized noble to take himself off to foreign parts where he pursued the king's business or his own pleasures at will.

In 1785 Saint-Simon set out for Holland on a diplomatic mission of the greatest secrecy. A plot was afoot to unite the French and Dutch forces in an attack upon the English possessions in India. According to the Marquis de Bouillé, the purpose of the cabal was to "return the provinces which the English had conquered to the princes of the country, and to procure for both nations factories and commercial establishments open to all the peoples of the world." [40] The affair became an episode in the complex internecine political strife between the Orangist faction and their opponents, with England the protagonist of the House of Orange, and France throwing her weight to the other side of the balance. The Marquis de Bouillé had conditionally accepted command of the proposed expedition; for some mysterious preliminary groundwork Saint-Simon, his former aide, was despatched to Holland. No record exists of Saint-Simon's role in the venture, apart from his own cryptic remarks in autobiographical sketches that he was to have been "employed honorably in it," and that "Vergennes's pusillanimity" prevented its success.[41] It is known that his uncle, Maximilien-Henri, Marquis de Saint-Simon, spared time from his hyacinth gardens at Haarlem to serve as an active French agent. In the midst of the secret negotiations, the Revolution of 1787 broke out in Holland, the anti-Orangist francophile party was completely defeated, all ties between Holland and France were severed, "and the great project of the conquest of India went up in smoke." [42]

In 1786 Saint-Simon returned to France, where he was overwhelmed with the boredom of military life. "To pass the summer in garrison, the winter paying court, was a way of life which offered no nourishment to my desire for glory." [43] Hardly a year elapsed before the restless young noble, with the complaisance of the War Department, was traveling again, bent upon the realization of imposing plans. Since, by 1787, of 36,000 officers only 13,000 were active, His Majesty's ministers were not interested in impeding the extraregimental designs of another idle soldier by insisting upon punctilious observance of imaginary duties. They did not hesitate to free Saint-Simon of his ties, nor did they balk at the creation of one more anomaly where so many existed already. On July 22, 1788, when Saint-Simon was named colonel attached to the infantry he was already abroad. An official order made everything smooth: "The King . . . wishes to retain him in the service with the rank of colonel, without assigning him to any regiment, which will leave him more at ease to attend to his business in Spain." [44]

Saint-Simon threw all his energies into a new Spanish enterprise.[45] It was his hope that he might retain rank both in the service of France and of Spain, since there was a grandeeship of Spain attached to the family name. When Saint-Simon appeared in Madrid he found the philosophical statesmen Jovellanos, the Count de Aranda, and Floridablanca in control, and everyone excited about liberal reform. An adventurer of genius, Francisco Cabarrús, a Frenchman from Bayonne, had founded a new central bank, the Banco San Carlo. No mere money-maker, though he promised shareholders fantastic profits, Cabarrús envisaged his bank as an instrument of *progreso* in the service of the public weal — strange language for Spain.[46] The man was a daring speculator in Saint-Simon's style. He thought in terms of extensive road systems, networks of canals, and large-scale mining operations; he dreamed of the expansive industrialization of dying bureaucratic Spain. In a report to stockholders published in Amsterdam in 1786 Cabarrús described his newest "welfare" project, the building of a canal from the mountains of Guadarrama to Seville which would revolutionize internal communications in the peninsula and afford Madrid, situated in the midst of a dry plateau, access to the sea via the Guadalquivir River.[47] The Spanish reformers were wildly enthusiastic about the plan, and in their letters were already congratulating themselves on the acquisition of the grandest canal in Europe.[48] Under the direction of French engineers, the Le Maur brothers, actual construction was begun, though digging operations were constantly interrupted by battles between the gangs working on the canal and the peasants of the areas through which it was cut.[49]

While the Spanish archives are silent on Saint-Simon's role in the canal project, his autobiography leaves the impression that this was a joint venture elaborated by Cabarrús and himself, which is not entirely in harmony with the facts since it was initiated before his arrival in Spain. For his part Saint-Simon offered to recruit a legion of six thousand foreigners, of whom two thousand would always remain in garrison while the other four thousand were at work on the canal. Clothes and hospital expenses alone would be defrayed by the government; the workers would care for other needs from their pay, to be furnished by the enterprise itself. But the canal, like so many other projects proposed to resuscitate the moribund Spanish economy, came to naught.

Although his efforts ended again in frustration, Saint-Simon's Spanish journey was in no sense an isolated chapter in his existence. Two of the personages he met in Spain were to become major influences in shaping the course of his future life. The Count de Cabarrús was the father of Madame Tallien, and when she became the light of the Directory, the doors to high political circles were open to Saint-Simon. Cabarrús's influence was probably far more profound than the casual reference to him in the autobiography would indicate. He was a prototype of the grand projector whom Saint-Simon the philosopher later elevated to the apex of the new industrial society —the banker who utilized the credit system to inaugurate vast enterprises which energized the whole social organism. In Spain, too, began Saint-Simon's stormy friendship with Count de Redern, the Saxon ambassador.

Thus far Saint-Simon had avoided France. He had fought in the American Revolution, participated in sundry schemes in Mexico, Holland, and Spain. When he finally returned home in 1789 his native land was in turmoil. There was now opportunity for an astute entrepreneur to display his talents and to reap his measure of glory.

2

Victim of the Terror

WHEN A FRENZY OF SUSPICION seized the nation during the Terror, a noble of the Saint-Simon family could hardly escape the ubiquitous eye of the revolutionary committees. The very sound of the name aroused aristocratic and religious associations which rendered the bearer suspect.

Members of the Saint-Simon family were notorious traitors to the Revolution. The former commander at Yorktown, the Marquis Claude-Anne de Saint-Simon, as deputy of the nobles from Angoumois arrogantly flaunted the prerogatives of his estate before the Constituent Assembly. He vigorously protested against the perusal of letters addressed to him and he took the civic oath reluctantly after a circumspect statement of the reservations with which he accepted its articles.[1] On July 1, 1790, this M. Saint-Simon, identified in the official *Moniteur* as a *ci-devant Marquis*, begged leave to absent himself from the sessions of the assembly;[2] and once outside of Paris, he joined the ranks of the *émigrés*. Leaving his papers to be sequestered by the revolutionaries, the marquis made his way into Spain, to seek his fortune at the court of another Bourbon.[3] Claude-Henri's two brothers, as well as an uncle, the bailiff of Saint-Simon, were less conspicuous than this cousin, but they too were stigmatized *émigrés*, who had taken refuge in Malta with the order to which they belonged.[4] An outspoken enemy of the Revolution cast deep shadows upon other members of his family.

A sister of Claude-Henri, the widow Adélaïde-Blanche-Marie Saint-Simon, aroused the suspicions of the state in the person of the watchful citizen Dubois, who despatched a letter to the section of *Halle aux Blés*, noting the profound affection she bore the House of Orleans and the insolent air she assumed with revolutionaries. The informer further divulged that she held clandestine meetings in her house. Immediately, on December 9, 1793, two citizens were detailed from the section's Committee of Vigilance to enhance their civic virtue by bringing a conspiring noblewoman to justice. Careful search of all her drawers and closets revealed nothing contrary to the principles of the Revolution except a few brochures and newspapers in the library. These were confiscated and sent on to a higher committee. Legality was punctiliously observed in these revolutionary investigations; the report was drawn up on the spot and attested to by all present, including a servant, who assumed the responsibility of guarding his mistress.

Six months later, when the Terror was at its height, another report accused the widow Saint-Simon as the sister of an *émigré* and emphasized the discovery of the royalist brochures, allegedly characteristic of her opinions. Her profession, "ex-noble living on an income." Her sin — the Orleanist conspiracy was always feared — friendship with the woman Egalité (the Duchess of Orleans), whose lady-in-waiting she had been under the monarchy. Fortunately for Adélaïde Saint-Simon she was not summoned to defend herself before the committee of her section until after Thermidor, on December 23, 1794. The *sans-culottes* interrogated her sharply about possible relationships with her two *émigré* brothers and her counterrevolutionary uncle. She pled ignorance both of their flight and of their supposed return to France. She admitted having been a lady-in-waiting to the woman Egalité, but in 1791 she had left her post and had severed all ties with the Orleanist house and their intimates. Her answers were eminently correct. The revolutionaries decided, however, that in view of the law concerning *émigrés* and in view of the law concerning the relatives of *émigrés*, it was incumbent upon them to place her under guard. When she called the section committee's attention to her illness her custodians gallantly consented to continue watching her at home. The Revolution was gracious to her.[5]

Another cousin of Claude-Henri, the former Baron Claude de Saint-Simon, lived in the section of *l'Unité*, where the revolutionary committee carefully followed in its deliberations his most minute diurnal activities. One day he was arrested on his way out of an "aristocratic club," was detained for some time in the prison of Les Madelonnettes, and only liberated because of insufficient derogatory evidence. The good revolutionaries of the section were not appeased; they knew him to be a brother of the *émigré* Marquis de Saint-Simon, aide to de Bouillé, a commander of the enemy troops; further, they were advised that the former baron had remained behind in Paris only to collect an 80,000-franc income which his brother had once enjoyed. *Sans-culottes* chafed at seeing the people despoiled of so much gold; moreover, they did not want the former baron to contaminate their section. Hence the decision of the revolutionary committee:

"Relatives of *émigrés* can be tolerated only if they loudly proclaim their attachment to the Revolution. When did the Baron appear in the section office? Never. Who ever heard him make patriotic motions? No one. The law is clear with respect to the former Baron de Saint-Simon. The formalities of a denunciation are not even necessary. He is of the first class of suspects, infinitely dangerous in every sense."[6]

Upon the discovery of a ribbon with a *fleur de lys* among his effects, the baron was again apprehended and taken off to the annex of the Abbaye. Though jailed, he too was spared by the Revolution. On October 9, 1794, the Baron de Saint-Simon regained his freedom after attestations of his civic virtue were delivered by various citizens of the general assembly of the section of *l'Unité*.

The fate of Claude-Henri's uncle, Charles-François Saint-Simon, former Bishop of Agde, was tragic. During the Revolution he tried to hide his identity, living as an inconspicuous abbé in the parish of Saint-Sulpice in Paris. In a letter which the seventy-year-old cleric sent to the revolutionary committees after his arrest, he protested that he had not administered the sacraments since 1764, but an ex-noble and an ex-priest, a relative of *émigrés*, was a counterrevolutionary cut to the cloth. Jacobin suspicions were confirmed when titles of nobility were discovered under a stone in his attic. The record denounced him as an *hypocrite* who had never publicly proclaimed his adherence to the principles of the Revolution.

While the abbé languished in prison, friends sent letter after letter to the Committee of Public Safety calling upon them to remember the solemn vow of the Convention to honor old age, reminding them of the philosophic temper of the prisoner who had taken the civic oath, pleading that the Committee should not stain the purity of the Revolution with the blood of one who had always hated the privileges of the nobility and the church. When there was no response, the abbé himself wrote in a trembling hand, hailing the Revolution as the regeneration of the human species. He rejoiced in his old age to see the first torch of a new light which would soon be universal and again he swore by his civic oath.[7] On July 26, 1794, a day before the end of the Terror, he was executed.[8]

His church, unmindful of the anticlerical letters the abbé composed in prison, has bestowed beatification upon him. The *Articles pour la cause de Mgr. de Saint-Simon, évêque d'Agde et de ses compagnons, victimes pour la foi catholique du tribunal révolutionnaire de Paris, 1793–1794* describe him as a martyr-priest, driven from his episcopal palace in the early years of the revolution by an unruly mob of provincial Jacobins. His death on the guillotine is commemorated with a pathetic image: ". . . he revealed such firmness and self-composure one might have imagined that here was a priest about to offer up a . . . *sacrificium vespertinum*."[9]

Of the entire family, the revolutionary career of Claude-Henri de Saint-Simon was by far the most romanesque, the subject of a weird tale of mistaken identity. In the confusion of the times the identification of a suspect was a major problem of revolutionary justice. The victims, taking advantage of new customs, often succeeded in bewildering the secret committee investigators. Nobles and priests sought to eradicate traces of their former station by assuming common, even vulgar, names. Scoundrels registered themselves as illustrious characters from classical antiquity. And there was a general tendency to drop Christian names as superstitions of the old régime, a practice which sorely aggravated the police agent's lot.

On November 19, 1793, the person of Claude-Henri de Saint-Simon was seized on a warrant for the arrest of a certain Simon — a surname which figured prominently in the records of the police and of the revolutionary tribunals. Dossiers have been preserved for Citoyen Simon, Chevalier Simon, Samuel Simon, Simon Simon, Isaac Simon, François Thomas Simon, Charles Simon, Victor Simon, Pierre Simon, Pitr Simon, Fritz Simon, Henri Simon, Michel Simon, and the unfortunate Darchial Simon, for whom there is an order of liberation on October 10, 1794, after his head had long since been dropped into the basket.[10] When the great Condorcet was arrested on March 27, 1794, he was hiding under the simple alias of Pierre Simon.[11] Here was a list of suspects who in themselves might well have represented all the counterrevolutionary conspiracies which agitated Jacobin France. Mighty was the revolutionary will, but it was not free from the play of caprice in a sea of Simons.

The order of arrest which struck down Claude-Henri de Saint-Simon had emanated two days previously from both the Committee of Public Safety and the Committee of General Security — an indication that this was no casual affair. The only ground set forth in the warrant was the enigmatic "purpose of general security." [12]

After a few months' detention at Sainte-Pélagie, on May 3, 1794, Saint-Simon was transferred to the Luxembourg, antechamber of death.[13] There he was kept "au secret." With the threat of the guillotine imminent, he followed the practice of many a victim of revolutionary justice and wrote in self-defense to the members of the Committee of General Security of the National Convention. Saint-Simon's spelling tended ordinarily to be eccentric and his distraction multiplied the number of errors. The *apologia* is nevertheless written with a firm hand. It is carefully phrased, preserves the customary legal form, and is supported by ample documentary proof of his contentions. Often the prisoner grows arrogant, almost irate, in his proclamation of revolutionary virtue.

I believe that I have been arrested in place of another, because the name *Simon* noted in the committees' order of arrest is not precisely the one I bore before I called myself Bonhomme, and the description "Simon living on his income" which is found in the police order does not at all fit me. But if it is truly I whom the committees intended to arrest, then I hope that an exact account of my conduct since 1789, based upon proofs, which I am about to submit, will show that from the beginning and during the whole course of the Revolution I have been one of its warmest partisans.

What followed was the self-portrait of an earnest provincial revolutionary.

I was a soldier before the Revolution and in that capacity I defended the cause of liberty in the American War. I was wounded. I assure you that since then my master has been my country and I so little cherished the favors of the court that, wearied by the idleness to which imbecile prejudices condemned former nobles in France and not having a cent's worth of patrimony, I left my estate to go to Spain, usefully to employ my time and my powers. I was at the head of a considerable enterprise when the first lights of liberty were kindled in France. I immediately returned. I remained at Falvy, a commune of the district of Péronne, from the month of November 1789 until October 1790, and from this date up to the time of my arrest I lived constantly at Péronne, except for the months of May, June, July, and August 1791, which I spent in Cambrai.

Saint-Simon then proceeded to detail numerous acts of charity towards his Picard countrymen, demonstrating to the committee that his virtuous deeds were inspired by purely altruistic motives.

Acts of goodness have often been acts of perfidy, but they cease to be suspect when he who performs them has other proofs of patriotism to produce; having renounced public office it cannot be imagined that I intended to gain votes when I confided the distribution of my gifts to public authorities. I always followed this practice. Any present which I could make to my brothers came to them through the municipality or the Popular Society. Thus, in conjunction with the municipality, at a time when food supplies were very dear, I maintained them at a low price in Péronne by putting on the market a substantial quantity of grain below the current price. Proof of this is under seal in the apartment which I occupied when I was arrested, number 55 Rue de la Loi.

Saint-Simon further claimed that he had stopped wearing the cross of Saint-Louis two years before it was suppressed,[14] and that he had deposited at Péronne certificates of his numerous army commissions and his military medals. The municipality had divided these mementoes into two groups: the papers and parchments were burned in Saint-Simon's presence; the "Order of Cincinnatus" and the gold pieces of the cross of Saint-Louis were preserved in the registry. If added testimony were necessary the committee had only to remember that from the very outset of the Revolution he had severed all ties with the aristocracy, including members of his own family. "I was honored by the hatred which the former nobility nursed against me."

Having set forth his revolutionary principles and conduct, Saint-Simon tried to remove the last vestige of suspicion by explaining how he supported himself. He was no idler living on inherited wealth. He was a man of affairs whose enterprises were inextricably intertwined with the fate of the Revolution.

Since the Revolution began my regular occupation has been the purchase and management of national lands for a Saxon whom I persuaded to transfer his fortune and his domicile to France. He had entrusted me with the task of finding him investments and I had bought national lands exclusively. This operation was advantageous to the Republic because it brought to France foreign capital which was never taken out again since income from this capital was reserved for payments to the national treasury. My relations with this foreigner were scrutinized last October (old style) by three deputies of the Committee of Public Safety before whom I was denounced. And after scrupulous examination of our correspondence they withdrew the order of arrest which had been issued against me. I own no other goods but national property on which I have made a down payment from the fruits of my labor.

The sale of national lands was the life blood of the Revolution, for the income fed the armies of the Republic. A man who cast his lot with the Jacobins by daring to purchase the confiscated properties of the nobility and the church was performing an act of civic virtue.

Is it not obvious that my interest and my very existence itself are irrevocably bound up with the preservation of the Revolution? Having shown myself to be one of its earliest, most constant, and most vocal partisans, I would be one of the first victims of a counterrevolution. I have therefore the right to believe, after this brief exposition, that I shall not be judged as a suspect in any event. And I hope to receive from national justice and the goodness of the Committee of General Security that freedom which I have done nothing to forfeit.

Numerous documents from Falvy, Marchélepot, Cambrai, and Péronne — towns near his ancestral estates — lent credence to his story.

When the municipal officers of Falvy heard that their former lord, the virtuous Claude-Henri de Saint Simon, was in danger, they recalled his revolutionary acts and the modesty of his behavior, and they wrote a memorandum to rescue him. The General Council of the commune could certify that he had given specific evidence of patriotism in their town from the month of November 1789, when he returned from a trip to Spain (a confirmation of his own account), until October 1790. His holiday speeches delivered in the churches of the commune had demonstrated a burning devotion to Liberty and Equality. He had renounced the titles and privileges which he had enjoyed by hereditary right long before a decree of the Constituent Assembly rendered them void. Without a trace of egotism, he had refused the office of mayor which his fellow townspeople were eager to bestow upon him, indicating the danger of electing former nobles and priests before the end of the Revolution. Although it was a matter of common knowledge that his father had died without leaving him a penny, he had lent financial aid to the local *sans-culottes*.

A transcript record of the assembly held at Falvy on February 7, 1790, to organize a commune in accordance with the municipal law of December 14, 1789, further elaborated the details of his self-effacement. When Saint-Simon, the *seigneur*, was offered the chairmanship of the body, he rose to deliver a lesson in revolutionary egalitarianism:

I am flattered, Gentlemen, to have been chosen for the honor of presiding over you. Only one thing beclouds the joy which I feel. I am afraid that in naming me you meant to tender your respects to your *seigneur* and that my personal qualities did not at all determine your votes. There are no more *seigneurs*, Gentlemen. All of us here are absolutely equal. And in order to prevent the title of count from leading you into the error of believing that I have rights superior to yours, I hereby declare that I renounce forever this title, which I consider far inferior to that of citizen, and I ask, to establish my renunciation, that it be inserted in the records of the assembly.

Supported by this document, Saint-Simon could write with pride, even with a trace of irony, to the grim Committee of General Security: "The misfortune of having been born in a proscribed caste will not be prejudicial to me before impartial judges. This act was involuntary. I repaired it."

When the citizens of Marchélepot heard of his plight they too had corroborating evidence forwarded to Paris. They remembered his address on May 12, 1790, advocating the suppression of noble titles. Never were his speeches considered demagogic attempts to court popularity or to win an election, for he continually admonished the townspeople against filling their offices with ex-nobles and priests. Saint-Simon had composed the memorandum which the canton sent to the Constituent Assembly calling for the abolition of all noble privileges, and the men of Marchélepot preserved the florid bit of prose. The ex-count, a dabbler in the writings of the *philosophes*, was well versed in the current conceptions of Law, Reason, Justice, General Will, and Supreme Being, and he could turn a pompous phrase in the style of the period. He was progressing with the Revolution:

Staunch with admiration at the sight of each article of the Constitution, filled with a noble pride when we realize that our will created the great code of Justice and Reason, imbued with a most lofty respect towards the National Assembly which one small part owes to the great whole upon which it depends, the electors of the canton of Marchélepot have unanimously decided to consecrate the first moments of the political existence which it has given us to congratulate it upon the sublime usage which it has made of the supreme power and of the general will whose organ it is. We dedicate the most sovereign contempt to those devout worldlings who dare to call God to the aid of their riches, feigning to fear for religion at the time when twenty-five million men present a great example to the universe, reminding it that the Eternal One created them all without distinction in his image; they should finally cease to insult the majesty of his omnipotence by impious distinctions of birth and seeking to obey but those among them who approach nearest to his divine perfection, they should declare that all citizens are equally admissible to all dignities, charges, and public offices, according to their capacity, and without any other distinction than that of their virtue and of their talents.

The citizens of Cambrai, too, made persistent efforts to establish Saint-Simon's loyalty to the Revolution and to secure his release from prison. In his *apologia*, Saint-Simon referred rather vaguely to an earlier examination of his papers and his exoneration the previous October, and the Péronne archives indicate that in September and October 1793 there were in fact local denunciations against him despite his known acts of civism. When he was being questioned at Péronne, the Cambrai Society of Friends of the Republic, which he had helped found in 1791, hastened to send the printed form of a certificate of civism stamped with the red cap of liberty. The tiny locality of Bussu joined the citizens of Cambrai in his defense, recalling that he had bought horses to cultivate the lands of men who had been summoned to the colors.[15] At Cambrai testimonials were not casually distributed and the local historian Eugène Bouly has noted pointblank refusals of these life-giving documents only a few days before Saint-Simon's request was granted. Even in the certificate of Saint-Simon's civism, the printed words "since the beginning of the Revolution" were scrupulously scratched out and the phrase "during the time that he remained in Cambrai" was substituted. In December of 1793 and throughout 1794 various revolutionary committees of Cambrai made earnest pleas to save the man who had always conducted himself as a "true son of the Revolution."

An old citizeness whom Saint-Simon had been supporting with a pension ever since her nephew was killed in a fight with aristocrats scrawled a cross upon a document testifying that her imprisoned benefactor had heeded the revolutionary commandment to respect old age. Another document, stamped with the symbol of the Masonic eye and sent up by the Cambrai Committee of Vigilance, confirmed Saint-Simon's general account of himself and praised him as one of the most zealous members of the Popular Society, enduring its dangers and suffering its hardships. The townsmen were particularly mindful of his services to the Revolution on June 20, 1791, at the time of the king's flight to Varennes, when Saint-Simon had been called upon to take over from a suspected officer the command of the National Guards in Cambrai. He had reluctantly agreed to accept the post for twenty-four hours, but only after a solemn oath to preserve the ideals of the Revolution had been administered to the guards. The shabby condition of his troops, in contrast with the well-equipped royal Swiss regiment which was stationed there, made his act the more courageous. The committee recalled the threats which had then been hurled against him by aristocratic officers.

At Péronne itself, the capital of the district, Saint-Simon had maintained a residence on Rue St. Sauveur, and its inhabitants were by now so confident of their neighbor's civism that with revolutionary speed, three days after his arrest in Paris, the municipality, the Committee of Vigilance, and the Popular Society all united to forward the necessary certificate to the departmental offices of the Somme. Never had he appeared on any of the lists of *émigrés*. To make certain that the subject of their panegyric was the prisoner, they appended a description: age, thirty-three; height, 5′ 5″; hair and eyebrows, brown; aquiline nose; medium round chin; ordinary forehead; full face.

Saint-Simon was well known throughout the district for his public performance of civic acts. On September 20, 1793, only two months prior to his arrest, he had officially dropped his aristocratic name in a solemn ceremony before the bar of Péronne as excerpts from their minutes proved:

The citizen Claude-Henri de Saint-Simon, former noble living in this city, presents himself to the Council and declares that he wishes to wipe out the blemish of his original sin by a republican baptism. He asks us to change a name which recalls an inequality proscribed by Reason long before it was denounced in our Constitution. He petitions that the Council give him a new name. The Council orders him to pick one. He announces his choice, "Claude-Henri Bonhomme." The Council, after hearing the citizen Sauvage who represented the procurator of the commune, decides that the former Saint-Simon shall henceforth be called citizen Bonhomme and that he shall be listed under this name in the census of the commune.

According to the record, Bonhomme thanked the men of Péronne for granting him the right to cast off his tainted name. But he felt that in addition he had to accumulate positive acts of virtue to counterbalance the weighty sins of his forefathers. Reminding the Péronne Council that for two years he had been responsible for the support of an old woman in Cambrai and that he had faithfully discharged his duties to her, he besought his fellow citizens to grant him an opportunity to demonstrate his worth anew. Romans all, the French revolutionaries had revived the ancient custom of adoption and in the Constitution of '93 had inserted a clause bestowing the rights of citizenship upon anyone who took unto himself a foster child or a parent. When he was being detained in prison well into 1794 the men of Péronne copied the records of all the meritorious acts which he had performed two months before his arrest and sent them on to Paris.

From his own account and from the numerous testimonials of civism which arrived from Falvy, Marchélepot, Cambrai, and Péronne, it would appear that Saint-Simon lived a revolutionary idyll in the provinces. Dwelling among his brothers of the soil from 1789 to the day of his arrest, he taught them good doctrine when they faltered in the ways of the Revolution; in times of famine he supplied them with grain; in moments of danger before the enemy he bravely stood at the head of the National Guard; at the sight of old age without a staff he wept and provided sustenance.

The reality beneath this mask of sober republican virtue was far more complex, for Saint-Simon's revolutionary career was not confined to the display of civic courage on solemn occasions in his native Picardy. His was a personality which could function effectively, even exuberantly, in two worlds, and up to the time of his arrest in Paris he had led a turbulent double life. In the provincial towns where he maintained residence he was a *sans-*

culottes who delivered revolutionary speeches; in Paris he lived as a cynical manipulator, keeping up an establishment on the Rue de la Loi close by the former Palais Royal. If sometimes he listened to the political conversations of the constitution-makers, his main interest lay elsewhere. He frequented low dives, and he consorted with a motley crew of international bankers, speculators, foreign spies, Dantonists, and Hébertists of the extreme left. They led licentious lives in sharp contrast with the Incorruptible One who dominated the Committee of Public Safety. They were debauched and venal. The speculators bribed the wildest Jacobins to win special favors for their business ventures. In the end Robespierre moved against the whole crew and he was able to throw many of their heads into a common basket by using the police agent's technique of guilt by association — especially with the *émigré* conspiracy directed from abroad.

In his letter written from prison to the Committee of General Security, Saint-Simon had made reference to his means of livelihood — the purchase of national lands — without, of course, giving them any inkling of the scope of his operations. Appearing in his own name or concealing his interest behind straw men, Saint-Simon had left his mark on land transactions involving millions of francs throughout the northern provinces of France. On that memorable day in Cambrai, at the time of the king's flight to Varennes, when he had displayed revolutionary ardor in the presence of the hostile Swiss guards, he had had to use guile and all his powers of persuasion to force the resumption of the sale of national lands, which had been halted by the terrified citizens of the province. From the archival records and his own later testimony Saint-Simon emerges as one of the great speculators of the revolutionary period.[16]

It was Count de Redern who provided the resources for Saint-Simon's initial plunges. Redern, who had become Prussian Ambassador to the Court of St. James, had taken leave in 1790 to go over to Paris in a private capacity in order to look after his securities consisting of government bonds and shares of the India Company. While there he encountered his friend Saint-Simon, whom he had grown fond of in Madrid. Though Saint-Simon had no money himself, he was gestating a vast financial scheme for the purchase of ten millions worth of national properties, based upon a modest capital investment at the outset. He had already solicited a M. Doesan, a M. de Marigny, and even the great Lavoisier, without any definitive success.[17] It appears that Count Médavy, on the eve of his emigration, had placed 25,000 francs in his hands, but this was a trifling sum for Saint-Simon's ambitious designs. Redern was the capitalist he needed to launch his venture, and the ambassador, for his part, seems to have been eager to invest his money in something more profitable than the securities of a tottering government. Acting for himself and for his sister, the Countess Stolberg, Redern entered into an agreement with Saint-Simon in accordance with which the investors, upon dissolution of the company, would receive interest figured at 5 percent annually and a 25 percent blanket increment on the funds invested; any remaining assets would be divided equally between the investors on the one hand and Saint-Simon on the other. In addition, Saint-Simon as the director of the enterprise would draw an annual stipend of 12,000 francs. Redern left his securities (yielding an income of some 25,000 francs) in the hands of Perregaux, the Swiss banker who in time came to have an almost official status vis-à-vis the revolutionary governments, with broad instructions to turn over such amounts as Saint-Simon might need to further his manipulations. The total amount invested by the Redern family may have run to over half a million francs — the precise amount later was a bone of contention between the partners. Saint-Simon claimed that there were also other investors, including his mother.

Saint-Simon expected substantial returns, especially through transactions in his native Picardy where he knew the land and the people, but he did not anticipate that the *assignats* would fall as precipitously as they did, opening for him stupendous prospects. As he himself later explained, once the church lands in an area were put up for sale, title to extensive abbey domains could be acquired by the down payment of a mere twelfth of the total purchase price. The local administrators of national properties were not assiduous in the regular collection of the other payments. Often they could be put off or bribed. When a payment did have to be made, the money could be obtained by selling a small portion of one's original purchase at a very high price in depreciated paper *assignats*, which were then accepted by the government officials as hard money at their original value. In this way Redern's securities were exchanged for titles to vast land holdings in the departments of the Somme, Nord, Pas-de-Calais, Seine, Oise, Seine-et-Oise, Eure-et-Loir, and Aisne. To conceal the breadth of the enterprise, the traces of Saint-Simon's transactions were confused by complicated sales and resales back and forth among a group of strange characters, including a Lieutenant-Colonel Bernard O'Neill and a Marchélepot postmaster named Torchon, who in addition to his other activities had sneaked the future Louis XVIII across the border to safety.[18] By the time Saint-Simon was arrested, the holdings of the "company" — which was not registered — had reached a value of three to four millions.

It required energy, imagination, and daring to come out on top in this mad whirl of the *assignats*. Saint-Simon the adventurer and speculator took chances. All his life he played for high stakes. As soon as his work became routinized, fell into a groove, he grew restless and broke loose. This was as true of his soldiering and his career in business as it was of his philosophical projects.

During the Revolution Perregaux was advised by Saint-Simon of most of the deals — they dined together from time to time — and the banker helped him to find reliable fronts. Saint-Simon kept dashing back and forth between Paris and Péronne, his two major bases of operation. There are hints in a letter to Perregaux dated June 30, 1792, that at one point he planned a hasty trip to London.[19] In the early critical days of the Prussian invasion, when many Frenchmen, including Saint-Simon, expected the enemy to cut through Dumouriez's citizen army in six weeks, he was preoccupied with making suitable arrangements to cover up Redern's interests. There would have been a major scandal if the Prussian ambassador to England had been unmasked as the backer of one of the great land-purchasing schemes of the French Revolution.

Not the man to hide his light under a bushel, the flamboyant Saint-Simon could not cloak all his activities with anonymity. The most extravagant rumors about the enterprises of this great noble turned speculator, aside from his real estate deals, were noised about Paris.[20] One project, which involved a proposed joint purchase with Talleyrand of Notre Dame de Paris in order to smelt down its roof, failed, the story goes, only because the wagonloads of *assignats* he sent in payment were insufficient to appease the administrators of national property.[21]

Saint-Simon's business deals are out of harmony with the lament of the simple passionate revolutionary. And they are not the only discordant notes. As an army colonel, in the full flush of youth, he might have been expected to rush to the defense of *la patrie* and to take a command with the armies of the Republic when it was threatened by foreign invaders. The documents indicate that he was probably a malingerer. On March 15, 1793, an Assembly of Citizens held at Péronne had designated the Citizen Saint-Simon for military service by a plurality of 233 votes and had ordered him to proceed to Ghent as a member of the contingent which the commune was obliged to furnish for the Belgian theatre.[22] The notice he received two days later to pick up his arms and equipment was not honored and he managed to keep out of the army throughout the war.

Saint-Simon's arrest in Paris on November 19, 1793, was not the first time he had fallen under grave suspicion. As far back as 1790 there had been an anonymous attack against him as a relative of *émigrés*, and in June 1793 his name was before the Committee of Public Safety.[23] Again on September 6, 1793, he was denounced to the revolutionary committee at Péronne in the course of an investigation conducted by special representatives sent from Paris by the Committee of Public Safety. In his absence, seals had been put on his papers and on those of Daniel Coutte, the local notary, who worked with him on many of his clandestine business affairs. When an examination of the records revealed nothing worthy of the commissioners' attention, the papers were returned to him on the twentieth of September, an act of restitution which he formally acknowledged by signing himself Simon, *tout court*, without the Saint. This was the very day when, to symbolize an absolute break with his dark aristocratic past, he changed his surname to Bonhomme, with all its affected overtones of traditional peasant simplicity, and petitioned the commune to designate an elderly citizen for him to adopt and support.[24] Such cautious prophylactic acts of revolutionary loyalty were not effective against the feverish temper of Péronne in the fall of '93. A special Committee of Surveillance was established, and on October 8, after a harangue by André Dumont, the commissioner sent down from Paris, a formal public purge session was organized during which every one of the local inhabitants was interrogated individually about his civic virtue. The rescrutiny of Saint-Simon's revolutionary record did not satisfy the inquisitors, and an order for his arrest as an ex-noble was issued.[25] On the same day, however, the order was withdrawn and a certificate of civism was awarded him.[26]

For decades after his death the impression persisted at Péronne that Saint-Simon had consorted promiscuously with all manner of people — common artisans, farmers, and members of a disreputable declassed local nobility who had joined him in piling up new fortunes during the revolutionary chaos. The staid Picard antiquarian Gustave Ramon, the last to examine the revolutionary archives of Péronne before their loss in the first World War, could not transcribe the record of Saint-Simon's affairs without expressing his priggish consternation at the company and carryings on of this scion of the ancient House of Saint-Simon. Ramon suggests that two of Saint-Simon's close associates, the Marquise de Folleville and Daniel Coutte, may have extended their intimacy beyond the bounds necessary for the conduct of their complex purchases, sales, and resales of national property. "*Coûte que coûte, il me faut Coutte!*" the wanton marquise is reputed to have quipped.[27] Most of Saint-Simon's Péronne agents somehow managed to survive the Terror, and during the dark days of his poverty and psychological breakdown these provincial friends of his revolutionary period did not abandon him. It was Madame de Folleville and Coutte who saved his life in 1812.

The specific warrant under which Saint-Simon was seized in Paris, part of a raid on international speculators and spies, probably was not directed against him, but was meant for one of the Simon brothers, Belgian bankers. In the fall of 1793 there was a mounting fear among the Jacobins that all counterrevolutionaries, from ex-priests and ex-nobles through their loyal servants who uttered royalist sentiments, and the speculators, bankers, and foreign spies, were tentacles of one vast conspiracy. The watchdogs of the Revolution could no longer rest content with individual accusations of treachery. If interconnections could be established among the enemies of the Revolution in various strata of society, the committees could move against the common danger simultaneously on all fronts. The order of arrest of November 17, 1793, was no routine police action. It was a full-scale attack launched against the international bankers, speculators, and spies, with a twofold purpose: to draw into the net the Dantonists and Hébertists who had been consorting with the speculators, as well as to crush the foreign agents. The original general order called for the arrest of de Batz, Benoît, Proli, Dubuisson, Simon, Duroy, and Boyd.[28] As it turned out, in the process of rounding up the accused it was not difficult to throw a web around the international clique and their revolutionary hangers-on who frequented the dens of the Palais Royal. Proli, reputed to be the bastard son of the Prince de Kaunitz, actually was a spy in the service of Austria.[29] A secret report to the committees had accused him of relations with the foreign bankers Walckiers and Simon of Brussels, both supposed agents of the Austrian emperor.[30] Proli was also associated with a certain Charles-Jean Goury de Champgrand, a former officer and friend of the Duke of Orleans. According to one witness, Proli had his eye on Champgrand's daughter Sophie — Saint-Simon's future wife. De Batz, who was named first in the order of arrest, was believed to be at the heart of the royalist conspiracy in control of a network of agents throughout France. It was he, they suspected, who had directed the plot to rescue Capet when he was lodged in the Temple, an attempt foiled only by the vigilance of a police inspector who was — to increase the confusion of this tale of many Simons — also named Simon. Benoît was a Dantonist; Dubuisson, a dramatist implicated with Proli; Duroy was a banker, and so was Boyd, an Englishman suspect as one of Pitt's agents. Perregaux, also linked with Proli, was ordered under arrest a month later on December 14, when he was conveniently at Basel, like so many of the other well-informed financiers who operated at the height of the Terror.

The conspiring bankers and spies had been denounced before the revolutionary committees by two prominent Jacobins, Chabot and Basire, who had themselves often been guests at the wild parties run by the speculators and who in the end were caught in Robespierre's seine.[31] All of this lends credence to the ingenious hypothesis of Albert Mathiez that Desfieux, of the scum of the same gang, the man who was instrumental in arresting Saint-Simon, intentionally mistook his identity when the police were actually looking for the Belgian banker Henry Simon, the Simon intended in the November 17, 1793 warrant.[32] Desfieux himself had been under a cloud for more than a month. He had been coupled with Proli by Fabre d'Eglantine and had been identified as another creature of the Walckiers and Simon of Brussels ring; shortly before he had been arrested and interrogated by the everpresent police inspector Simon about his relations with Proli. Desfieux's release had been arranged only through the intervention of the Hébertists, who were still powerful in the government. His appearance at the local committee headquarters of the section of *1792* at six o'clock in the morning of November 19, ready for revolutionary service, hardly seems fortuitous. Since he had known most of those accused in the order of arrest, he was, Mathiez surmises, anxious to participate in acts of revolutionary virtue against his old associates in order to save his own skin. The circumstantial account of the manner in which he led the two agents of the central committees in search of Saint-Simon, a record he wrote himself in a brash half-literate scrawl, bolsters this theory. Since Henry Simon, the Belgian banker, was by this time safe in Basel on business, Desfieux, bent on producing a victim, led the way to another speculator of the group with a similar name.

The police first visited a lodging house on the Rue de la Loi, whose proprietor, one Armand, showed them that according to his register Citizen Saint-Simon, now Bonhomme, had departed for Péronne twelve days previously. Desfieux was not hoodwinked. He prowled about the section making inquiries until he finally discovered that his prey had in fact returned from the provinces two days before and was living in another house (number 55) on the same street. When the police did not find him at home, they put seals on his second-floor apartment and posted a guard. In the early afternoon Saint-Simon himself put in an appearance at section headquarters where he announced boldly: "I heard that I was being sought after and I have come to the committee to find out what they want me for. Here I am." After reading the order of his arrest, the police escorted him to his home, where they searched his papers, finding many records of sales of public lands. Some of his documents were sent to the Committee of General Security, the rest were placed under seal with his other effects, and Saint-Simon himself was remanded to jail. In signing the record of his arrest, he persisted in the use of his revolutionary name Bonhomme.

There is a characteristic anecdote about the arrest, which has it that when Saint-Simon began to feel himself threatened as an aristocrat, he procured a passport and made preparations to escape. He was actually descending the stairs of his Rue de la Loi lodgings when the emissaries of the revolutionary tribunal were coming up. In answer to their inquiry he told them that Citizen Simon lived on the second floor. Then he sprang on his horse and sped away at a gallop. He had reached the outskirts of Paris when he learned that the landlord of the house where he lived had been arrested for complicity in his escape. Immediately he returned and offered himself to the tribunal to exculpate the man.[33] The tale is not completely at variance with the known facts of the arrest.

His display of revolutionary zeal did not save Desfieux from the guillotine. During the process of crushing the foreign conspiracy the chief informers met their death. Two days after Saint-Simon's imprisonment, Robespierre was already demanding the execution of Desfieux along with Proli and Dubuisson. On March 21, 1794, a swarm of Hébertists, Desfieux among them, was brought to trial and identified with the international bankers and extravagant philosophers like Anacharsis Cloots. In early April, 1794, another combination was effected: the Dantonists were tried for treason and Fabre d'Eglantine, Chabot, and Basire, who had originally denounced the financiers and spies, were accused of corruption and beheaded.

It is an irony of revolutionary history that the politicians of various stripe who attacked the international bankers and speculators as traitors to the Revolution perished in their own purges, while many of the bankers and speculators, with an admirable capacity for survival, eluded the guillotine to prosper under the Directorate, the Empire, and the Restoration. The astounding circumstance in Saint-Simon's revolutionary fortunes is not that he was apprehended, whether or not by mistake, but that a speculator, a former noble, a man involved in the society of Palais Royal intriguers, a relative of notorious *émigrés*, a business partner of a Prussian ambassador, managed to escape death when he was already lodged in the prisons of the Terror.

The eleven months of his confinement left a lasting imprint upon Saint-Simon's mind. Whenever he wrote or thought about the Revolution, this terrible duress weighed heavily upon him. He could not forget the anarchy and capriciousness of the Revolution and he hated it even when he praised some of its works.

During moments of great stress Saint-Simon revealed an oddly prudent streak, and in the antechamber of death he behaved with circumspection. The prisons of the Revolution were not highly disciplined institutions. There were never enough old jails to accommodate the transient population of suspects, and houses of detention were improvised from convents and mansions. The turnover of prisoners was great and the political coloration of the watchmen shifted with the course of the Revolution. The treatment of prisoners was influenced by the character of the turnkey in charge. Popular revolutionary figures had free access to the inmates, for no one dared refuse entrance to a hero of Valmy or to a powerful tribune. Conflicting parties in the commune of Paris did not neglect that section of the population which happened to be behind bars. The prisoners were a desperate group, invaluable allies if the political rivalries ever broke into an open struggle. Robespierre's committees were cognizant of the intrigues in the prisons, for every clique of incarcerated conspirators had its stool pigeons, who used the time-honored tricks of agents of provocation, nurturing a plot in its early stages in order to reap a rich harvest of suspects.

The conspiracy of the Hébertists was one of the last with which Robespierre dealt before his own fall. Swept away by egalitarian ideas, these extremists toyed with the agrarian law, were frenzied in their attacks on every form of religion, even Robespierre's pure worship of the Supreme Being, and associated themselves with men who preached against the sanctity of property. Some of their number, Desfieux among them, even advertised doctrines of free love. They promised more bread and more blood. And they had a mob of *sans-culottes* from the Paris commune following them.

In prison Saint-Simon just escaped being drawn into the Hébertist conspiracy. General Ronsin, one of their leaders, introduced himself into Sainte-Pélagie by intimidating the keepers and threatening them with revenge if they balked his will. After he had established the proper contacts he promised liberation to anyone who would join the insurrection of the people of Paris against Robespierre. At his side was a spy from the Committee of Public Safety, Jaubert,[34] and when the Hébertists were later brought before the bar of revolutionary justice the procurator Fouquier-Tinville could thunder the names of all those whom Ronsin had approached during his visits to the prisons. The general apparently had selected as possible recruits the group of speculators and their associates among the revolutionary section leaders. There were Pereyra, Desfieux, Cazerou, Dubuisson, the brothers Frey, and Bonhomme. Emanuel Frey was brought forth to testify at the trial and he pinned down Desfieux, Pereyra, and Dubuisson as partisans of Ronsin. Bonhomme was reckoned among the antagonists of the plot and he lived.[35]

The society of the prisons was a fantastic collection of great nobles and their ladies, crooks, lackeys, scientists, crackpot philosophers, defeated politicians draped in the pose of noble Romans. In the shadow of the guillotine they debated abstract problems of science and human destiny. They contracted amorous liaisons and experienced religious conversions. Men went mad under the tension of waiting for each new list of the doomed.

Saint-Simon had hallucinations. Charlemagne, his illustrious ancestor, appeared to summon him to a life of glory. "Since the world began no family has had the honor to produce both a hero and a philosopher of the first rank. This honor has been reserved to my house. My son, your success as a philosopher will equal mine as a soldier and a statesman," and then he vanished.[36] The account of the apparition first appeared in an autobiographical fragment written under the Empire. It cannot be dismissed as a momentary aberration, for it became one of his repetitive megalomaniac fantasies. He was to be the new Charlemagne come to end the chaos of western European society, of which the Revolution was a symptom, to unify it as his celebrated ancestor had done a thousand years before. From time to time Saint-Simon experienced moments of conscious existence when illusion and reality were hardly distinguishable.

Before Thermidor, all the provincial attestations of Saint-Simon's civism had availed nothing. On August 23, 1794, the men of the Popular Society of Péronne renewed their plea for his freedom. As one of the first revolutionary societies they had a right to demand justice.

"When the Tyrant sowed terror and death everywhere, strong in our conviction of Saint-Simon's innocence we did not fear to proclaim it. We were not even heard. Justice is now the order of the day, and we demand it for a persecuted patriot." Five days later the representative of the people

Boissy d'Anglas placed his signature on this document beneath a personal testimonial that though Saint-Simon bore the same name as the ex-deputy and *émigré* his cousin, he had never maintained relations with him. On the same day, August 28, 1794, the precious act of liberation was issued. "In consideration of the demands and pleas concerning the Citizen Saint-Simon called Bonhomme, detained at the Luxembourg, the Committee orders that he be set at liberty and that the seals on his papers be lifted."

Saint-Simon now would establish his center of operations in Directorate Paris, far from the annoying surveillance of local revolutionaries, though for a time he continued to maintain relationships with the town officials of the Péronne district, piling up a treasury of certificates of residence and civism against possible rearrest.[37]

3

Masquerade of the Directorate and the Consulate

AFTER A YEAR of forced inactivity, Saint-Simon flung himself into his real estate operations with renewed energy. Legally, the company of Redern and Saint-Simon had defaulted on their purchases of national property, but their holdings had not been liquidated, even under the Terror. During the months of Saint-Simon's imprisonment, Count de Redern hibernated in Florence, where he had sought refuge after his resignation from the London embassy in the summer of 1792. While in Florence he had received a request from a M. Roux, who in Saint-Simon's name asked for a trusteeship of their properties. Redern complied with alacrity, since the holdings of other foreigners were being sequestered.

In 1794 Redern's petitions in defense of his property won support from a high diplomatic official, François Barthélemy, French Ambassador to Switzerland, who ventured to write in his behalf on the day after Thermidor. Barthélemy, who had been attached to the French embassy in London when Redern was Prussian ambassador to the Court of St. James, volunteered an account of the odd behavior of Saint-Simon's partner. Barthélemy called Redern a Saxon, not a Prussian, even though he was born in Berlin. He thought his choice as envoy to England from the king of Prussia most curious because he had never been in sympathy with Prussian antirevolutionary policy. To Barthélemy's utter astonishment, Redern had gone about proclaiming revolutionary sentiments. Every court day he would openly debate the merits of the French Revolution with King George before the assembled diplomatic corps. At first Barthélemy, puzzled by Redern's temerity, thought he was a *provocateur* who secretly agreed with the English sovereign, but he soon proved his adherence to the principles of the Revolution by supplying Barthélemy with secret intelligence. Barthélemy also knew of Redern's trip to Paris early in the Revolution and of his investment in the purchase of church lands. In court circles Redern was an object of either ridicule or wrath. "One must say that Redern's soul was endowed with great courage and zeal to brave at this point all the prejudices of the government he served as well as that to which he was accredited." [1] It would be unjust, he concluded, if Redern lost a fortune which he had entrusted to France at a time when cowardly Frenchmen and foreigners were panicked into exporting their capital. Ambassador Barthélemy's testimony, which was sent through regular diplomatic channels, may have saved the company when it was without a director.

By 1796 Saint-Simon had so successfully reëstablished his own relations with government officials that he secured permission for Redern to return to France as a worthy foreigner who had aided the cause of the Revolution. The break in their transactions had turned out to be eminently profitable, for after Thermidor they obtained full rights to the holdings on which they had made only trifling down payments, by clearing up their debts with *assignats* which had now become almost worthless.[2]

Under the Directorate, the company's investments shifted from church lands in the provinces to real estate in and around Paris.[3] The Goncourts have dramatized the wild spectacle of the frenzied trading in the capital during this period. "One half of Paris sells the other! The whole of former Paris is put up for auction. Everywhere national goods are for sale. Everywhere the sale of effects and properties in the name of and for the profit of the Republic! It is the liquidation of the guillotine.

"Sale of the condemned, of the *émigrés*, of the confiscated, of the ruined! Paris! a market where the voice of the criers is never silent. Who wants hotels, who wants furniture?" [4] Swimming with the current, Saint-Simon bought up the mansions which had once been inhabited by the great nobles of France, now either dead or in exile. In addition he involved himself in all sorts of minor industrial and commercial deals — he tried his hand at manufacturing cheap body linen and revolutionary playing cards in which Geniuses, Liberties, Equalities, and Laws replaced the traditional monarchical symbols; [5] he became a wine merchant; he formally received a commercial license from the section of the *Halle aux blés*.[6] As a culmination of his schemes, he planned the erection of a vast new business center near the Hôtel des Fermes and the Hôtel du Roulage which was to rival the Palais Royal.[7] He was reported to have organized a system of stagecoaches between Paris and Bordeaux [8] (though later he denied the story, explaining that a M. Dumorey, to whom he had rented space for his stagecoaches in the new business center, had merely featured Saint-Simon as a place-name).[9]

In September 1797 a rumor spread through Paris that the stagecoach company which had emblazoned the name Saint-Simon on its vehicles was a cover and a network for royalist reactionaries and that Saint-Simon had been rearrested as an enemy of the Republic.[10] The story was a fabrication, like many of the tales which were embroidered about his picaresque personality. In the Paris newspapers he inserted an angry denial both of the charge and of the account of his arrest. Nobody could impugn his revolutionary purity. "In view of my opinions and my political conduct since 1789, I am not 'arrestable' for any reason, either for a real or for an apparent cause. I have only the enemies of the Revolution to fear, a Revolution to which I know no single man in France who is more strongly attached than I." [11] This was by no means the last time that he aroused political suspicions. In 1799 the Directorate police agents were on his trail again,[12] but in an age when political rivals habitually spied on each other, this did not represent a singular interest in the activities of so bizarre and prominent a personage.

When Redern first reappeared in Paris early in 1796, he found his partner living in lavish style. According to Saint-Simon, Redern was welcomed as a beloved brother and separate apartments were set aside for him, along with the sisters and brothers of Saint-Simon who were living in the Chabanais mansion and in adjoining buildings.[13] Redern later took issue with this description of their relationship, commenting acidly that when the mansion was crowded he was packed off to the apartment of a M. de Combis, who happened to be absent from Paris and who was shocked on his return to find the foreign ex-diplomat ensconced in his chambers.[14] Saint-Simon's 1807 vignette of their friendship during these Directorate years was an idyll of the true love of David and Jonathan in a setting of domestic bliss.

Each day our affection for each other grew stronger. We continually talked about our desire to spend our lives together. M. de Redern had gone into all the details for the execution of our plan. "We shall pass," he said, "the winter in Paris. You will keep house. I want for myself only the valet whom I have brought with me, a little jockey, a cabriolet, and a horse. We shall buy some well-built-up estate and we shall pass the summer in the country. If there is a wing or a detached pavilion, I shall move into it." Happy period of my life. I loved. I was loved.[15]

They had a common purse, according to Saint-Simon, more than twenty servants, and the best table in Paris. For Saint-Simon had not only acquired possession of the palaces and furniture of the guillotined nobility — he had even hired the grand servitors. His *maître d'hôtel* was Monoyer, formerly in the Duc de Choiseul's employ; his chief cook was Le Gagneur, who had made the suppers of the Maréchal de Duras famous; his major domo was Tavernier, who had served the Cardinal de Bernis in Rome. In later years of penury Saint-Simon wistfully evoked the memory of the *punch aux oeufs* and the delicate truffles which had once adorned his table. As hosts to the great men of the Directorate — Ségur, Muraire, Monge, Lagrange — either partner issued invitations indiscriminately.[16]

Shortly after Redern's return, his sister, the Countess Stolberg, insisted upon withdrawing from the enterprise; whereupon a new contractual arrangement providing for equal partnership was drawn up on February 25,

1796 and the original 1791 agreement was thrown into the fire. The Countess Stolberg was awarded properties yielding an annual income of 30,000 francs and the company was left with an annual income of at least 115,000 to 120,000; their total holdings were worth millions. The Stolberg settlement may well have been a ruse on Redern's part for the safeguarding of his original investment, which was thereby returned intact, along with a substantial increment. About 20 percent of the company's assets were thus removed from the common treasury in favor of the Redern family.

Whatever his private misgivings, Redern had not yet voiced any dissatisfaction with his friend's conduct of their business. Their relationship remained intimate and warm, and when Redern departed on a trip to Germany in June 1796, his boon companion journeyed with him as far as Basel. Later Redern dated the birth of his first suspicions from the period of his absence abroad. For months he received no communications from his partner or the Saint-Simon sisters, with whom he corresponded. Two years later he found among the company's effects a trunk in which were scattered pell-mell his own unopened letters to Saint-Simon and intercepted letters to the sisters. In the meantime the Countess Stolberg wrote him that she had not been receiving the income payments agreed upon. Returning to Paris in September 1797, he began to be seriously troubled by the profligacy of Saint-Simon's expenditures and the recklessness of his business ventures. He found their fortune sunk more and more deeply in strange new enterprises, their income reduced to 81,000 francs. The retail wine business and the system of stagecoaches featuring Saint-Simon's name were especially distasteful to him. Considerable portions of their solid rural land holdings had been sold and some 400,000 francs had been borrowed to finance new undertakings — principally real estate in Paris and the communes to the west of the capital. The whole company seemed shaky and unsound. Redern was worried lest they might have to default when further payments on their purchases fell due: it spelled bankruptcy.

He was now outspoken about his desire to withdraw from active participation in the company. He assured Saint-Simon, however, that as long as he could salvage a reasonable income for himself, he wished him to have the means of following through on his new interests. Saint-Simon later recalled his friend's precise words. ". . . I shall restrict myself to a guaranteed annual income of 15,000 francs on the properties we hold in common, and I shall leave you free to dispose of the whole of what remains. This arrangement will satisfy me completely, if it makes you happy." [17]

The proposal was not acted upon. In the ensuing weeks, Redern became thoroughly annoyed with the visibly sloppy administration of his manager, and increasingly uneasy that all of their properties were being jeopardized by his wild plunges. In order to liquidate the partnership before its remaining assets were dissipated, Redern intervened and on October 22, 1797, took over personal direction of the business. Saint-Simon interposed no objection; he announced that the whole enterprise belonged to Redern, and told him to proceed with its dissolution in whatever manner he saw fit. (In 1796, whether to elude creditors or in fear of a capricious government, Saint-Simon had made a written declaration that all the property acquired was Redern's.) As he delved into the financial history of the company, Redern was increasingly bewildered. Many documents relative to their transactions were missing. Moreover, Saint-Simon had not established any clear distinction between his personal and his businesss expenditures. While stray records were being collated, Redern tried to convince Saint-Simon that he should retire to the country on a pension of five hundred francs a month, an absurd pittance for the Directorate *bon vivant*.

The old proposal for a division of their joint property was not revived; instead they now reached an understanding for an unequal allocation of their 80,000 franc income which would guarantee Redern an income of 45,000 francs, while 35,000 francs would be reserved for Saint-Simon. Redern felt that by charging his personal expenditures to the company, Saint-Simon had already forfeited his right to a substantial portion of the principal. When Saint-Simon's share was designated, he requested for some inexplicable reason that the titles to half his properties be placed in Redern's name, the titles to the other half in that of Béhague, a friend and agent.

On the surface Saint-Simon seemed uninterested in all these tiresome commercial details — suddenly he was aglow with grand projects for the reorganization of society. Early in 1798 he departed for Brussels, which he had chosen as the seat of a "reforming noviciate," [18] and he began to write letters to Perregaux proposing the establishment of a business house and a bank "such as had never before existed." Redern's seizure of control of the company he accepted as a "bath of contrariety" in which his soul, which had begun to grow soft, was being immersed. Back in Paris again he played with the fantasy of a romantic escape to the valley of Montmorency, where he would proceed to reëducate himself as a prelude to the formulation of a new moral system. He had visions of living the simple life in the company of his sheep dog, and of drawing his ideas directly from nature. The Rousseauist revery did not last long. On July 9, 1798, he unveiled his first grandiose project for universal reorganization at a dinner party for his banker friends, among them both Perrégaux and Redern. For four or five hours he bored his listeners with a proposal that they pool 1,200,000 francs and acquire all the houses around the Hôtel des Fermes. The magnitude of the undertaking would so startle the stock exchange that their consortium would soon dominate it. With Paris as a springboard they would by leaps and bounds gain possession of the major financial markets of the world, and once in control they would inaugurate a new moral order.

His world regeneration through a real-estate scheme was a fiasco which left Saint-Simon in a sour mood. He began to grumble that Redern had treated him shabbily in assigning him properties yielding only 35,000 francs. For his part, Redern was so disquieted by his friend's mad obsessions that he decided not to delay the final wind-up of the company's affairs any longer. His calculation of Saint-Simon's personal expenditures was staggering: 320,993 francs (inclusive of administrative costs) for the period January 1791 through October 1793; a complete lacuna for October 1793 to May 1795; 5,627,943 francs in assignats in varying stages of depreciation for personal expenses from May 1795 to February 1796; 303,481 francs in hard specie for the period February 1796 to October 1797. Redern divided the property into two equal parts, and subtracted from Saint-Simon's portion his personal expenditures, that is, the costs of the house. When the accounting was completed, there remained to Saint-Simon of his once magnificent estates half of the Hôtel des Fermes and a half of their possessions in the Bois de Boulogne.

Saint-Simon protested that the household expenditures were an integral part of their enterprise. As the moving spirit of the business during the Revolution, he claimed for his portion two-thirds of their jointly-owned properties, particularly since part of the profit due the Redern family had already been siphoned off to the Countess Stolberg. He tried to repudiate the 1796 agreement under which the remaining properties were to be divided equally. Redern's position was bolstered by the arguments of his lawyer, Poirrier, a relic of the *ancien régime* who was deaf to anything but the legalities of the case. Ultimately, after protracted wrangling over the liquidation details and bitter mutual recriminations, Saint-Simon accepted about 150,000 francs in cash plus an annuity of 1800 francs for one of his mistresses who had borne him a child, in a final settlement before a Paris notary on August 4, 1799.[19] Saint-Simon later explained away his momentary acquiescence in this arrangement on a variety of grounds: his disgust with the whole affair, his growing indifference to business in view of his new scientific mission, his realization that the legalities were on Redern's side since he had signed away his titles. Redern saw Saint-Simon's ready acceptance of the cash settlement in another light. Saint-Simon, he said, had begun to despair of the whole political and social order of France. He foresaw a catastrophe and he was telling friends that "there would soon be no more property titles even as there were no more titles of nobility."[20] The spirit of Babeuf's communist egalitarianism was in the air.

Despite these annoying business quarrels and the ugly termination of his friendship with Redern, Saint-Simon basked in a dazzling summer light throughout the Directorate. This was the epoch of his great worldly success. In tumultuous reaction against the reign of Robespierre the virtuous one, a gang of cynics and debauchees had assumed control of the state. Speculators in falling *assignats*, former nobles, and ex-Jacobins who had survived, now joined in one wild spree. In this turbulent atmosphere Saint-Simon breathed freely. There were no prescribed forms and there were no restraints. The government was notoriously, frankly corrupt, controlled by Barras the Rotten, the old scribe Abbé Siéyès, and the financier Ouvrard. The general spirit of licence expressed itself in the extravagant foppish costuming of the *incroyables* and the diaphanous gowns of the women. If one should believe De Lépine, author of *Le Dieu malgré lui*, a pasquil written to discredit the cult, Saint-Simon himself was "an emulator of the Marquis de Sade," and directed the wild orgies and depravities of the *jeunesse dorée.*[21] "His contemporaries speak of his relations with prostitutes, his friends refer to the refinements of his lubricity, his guests describe his intimate suppers unsurpassed by those of the *oeil-de-boeuf*. They report that in his excesses he made a studied attempt to outstrip the famous regent and his cardinal, that he reproduced better than they the pagan saturnalia, the mysteries of the *Bonne-Mère*, and their imitations of the orgies of the ancients."[22] Michaud's popular biographical dictionary added gambling to the list of Saint-Simon's vices, and then crowned the portrait of the debauchee "by system rather than taste": "He innoculated himself with all the maladies of the age in order later to determine their physiology."[23]

A pastel of Saint-Simon painted by Madame Labille-Guiard in 1796 gives the impression of a well-nourished individual with a round face and a high broad forehead.[24] The lips are delicately shaped and sensual, the nose long, firm, and aquiline, the eyes large and soft, keenly intelligent, the eyebrows gracefully arched. The pampered face has a vaguely feminine air. A rather quizzical smile is compressed between the lips. From a M. de Fourcy, who as a young man knew Saint-Simon, Michelet derived a perceptive word picture which can serve as a companion piece.

He was a handsome man, very gay, with an open and jovial face, admirable eyes, a fine long nose, Don Quixotic. He lived in and around the Palais-Royal with the cynical libertinism of a *grand seigneur sans-culotte*. His toilet was in the manner of Anaxagoras Chaumette. No tie, or a very low one which fell at random. . . .[25]

In his unpublished memoirs, to which Weill had access, Fourcy left a further account of the philosopher who so fascinated him that he could not tear himself from his company.

His speech was often characterized by a rather obscene cynicism, but he could treat serious matters seriously. Our conversation usually turned on the evils of our social order. . . . I do not remember ever having heard him express an opinion about the role of women in his social organization. All I can say is that he had anything but indifference for this half of the human species and that he expressed his feelings about them in terms that were not very Platonic. Nevertheless, his very keen taste for physical beauty in no wise prevented him from appreciating the qualities of the heart. The most beautiful woman, he said, holds no attraction for me, if her features fail to show me an expression of goodness. . . . He made a noble use of his money, well or ill acquired, and he spoke of it in a tone of disdain which proves that he possessed his wealth without being possessed by it. "Go ahead," he would say to those whose efforts in the promotion of a useful enterprise he encouraged, "and when it is only money that is lacking, come to me. I have some of that." . . . He was not one of those philosophers of whom Rousseau spoke, who are smitten with a vast love for humanity in order to dispense with loving their neighbors.[26]

The image of the Directorate as a chaotic interlude between the brutality of the Terror and the seizure of power by Napoleon has so imposed itself that the brilliant scientific efflorescence of the age, the intellectual passion in the schools, has sometimes been obscured.[27] Michelet, for all his hyperbole, caught its essential spirit as no other writer has done since. The Directorate abounded in extravagant charlatans and great scientists with bold new conceptions, and often the charlatans could not be readily distinguished from the geniuses. There was no rigid academic hierarchy in the schools, but a wonderful fluidity, for all the educational establishments were new, not fettered with the dead weight of precedent.

. . . the Ecole Normale summons from everywhere in France all those who already teach or will teach tomorrow.

Twelve chairs are inaugurated at the Ecole Normale, twelve chairs at the Museum of Natural History. On December 4 the three schools of medicine. Finally the Ecoles centrales (or lycées) on February 25, '95.

Stupendous creations, astounding in their grandeur, but even more in the spirit of life, the heart which one feels beating everywhere. . . .

Teaching, until then disdained, appears in its true worth as a magistracy. One sees the Convention summon all the geniuses of the age to its schools. At the Ecole Normale, one sees the Lagranges and Laplaces teaching mathematics. Men like Bernardin de St. Pierre, Volney, etc., were called to teach morals, literary and historical studies.

Students were paid at the Ecole Normale, the Ecole Polytechnique, the Ecole de Médecine; they received an annual stipend of 1200 francs, and they came to study with a new verve. For the most part they were impetuous men, furious workers, men like Bichat and Biot, Cuvier and Dupuytren.[28]

During the day Saint-Simon was absorbed in his business ventures, at night he played host to the new science, a Baron d'Holbach. Alien to no circle, he drew his friends from all ranks of society. The old social stratification had been exploded and French society had not yet settled into a new one. Men were received by the *parvenus* of the Directorate not because they could trace their lineage back to a remote ancestor, but for some shining quality of their intellects or charm of their persons. For the first time in the modern world men were judged by their talents without consideration of

social status. Society was mobile. The government of the Directorate, confused and disorganized, imposed no formal structure upon society. Each
man developed his capacities without restraint: the industrialist manufactured, the banker speculated, the scientist experimented, and the artist
created. In some respcts this was the prototype of Saint-Simon's good society,
a world which allowed for a free play of human capacities.

In Saint-Simon's salon, scions of the old nobility, government officials,
bankers, industrialists, scientists, mystics, and artists were intermingled.
Though successful scientists predominated, his circle never lacked eccentrics [29] — men like Clouet the chemist, a worker's son, who lived a Spartan
life and allowed himself only one hour of sleep a day, and who in revulsion
against Napoleon's ascendancy fled to Guiana to live the natural life;[30] or
Coëssin, the mystic, who later founded a cult which rivaled the Saint-Simonians; or Larévellière-Lépeaux, a leader of the new theophilantropic sects.
Saint-Simon listened to their conversations and gleaned a stray idea here and
there. Echoes of these evenings reverberate in many of his works. No subject
was barred from discussion, and Saint-Simon for his part unfolded grand
projects for the reorganization of the sciences and the social system.

Saint-Simon dabbled in all the sciences, acquiring a hodge-podge of
universal knowledge which was superimposed on the meagre classical education of his youth. Immediately after the final dissolution of his partnership
with Redern, he concentrated on developments in the mathematical and
physical sciences in and around the Ecole Polytechnique,[31] and he patronized
the young Poisson, one of the most brilliant mathematicians of the age, whom
Lagrange and Laplace considered their heir.[32] With Poisson as director,
he opened a free school, where courses duplicated exactly the program at the
Ecole Polytechnique, except that he employed brilliant young students as
professors. The school served several purposes at once: it provided stipends
for impecunious young scientists and at the same time offered public education in the sciences gratis. The introduction of science into general education
became one of Saint-Simon's major goals and he worked towards its fulfillment throughout his life. When he paid for the publication of a Dr.
Burdin's *Cours d'études médicales* he was subsidizing a work which became
one of the standard French texts for instruction in medicine and was soon
translated into several European languages.

Saint-Simon thought the Redern settlement would suffice for his own
reëducation, for that necessary interlude during which he would acquire
enough concrete scientific knowledge to perfect the system which he knew
was gestating within him. He had actually taken rooms opposite the Ecole
Polytechnique and had especially invited the scientists to his house to sop
up their learning.

Good cheer, good wine, great eagerness in my relations with the professors,

to whom my purse was always open, procured for me all the facilities I could desire.

I had great difficulties to overcome. My brain had already lost its malleability. I was no longer young. But on the other hand I enjoyed a great advantage. Long voyages, converse with a great number of capable men whom I had sought out and met, an early education directed by d'Alembert, an education which wove so tight a metaphysical thread that no important fact could escape me. . . . I analyzed the knowledge which I found in the heads of the scientists with whom I stood in familiar relationships.[33]

By the turn of the century he began to abandon the mathematicians as he became more interested in the schools of medicine, and his friends were doctors and physiologists — Prunelle, Dupuytren, Burdin, Bichat, Blainville, Cabanis, and Bougon.[34] This desertion of the Polytechnicians for the doctors, a shift from what he called the *brutiers*, the mathematical scientists, to the life scientists of the new century, was a change pregnant with meaning for his intellectual orientation.

On occasion Saint-Simon, the man of many faces, undertook brief excursions into active politics, toying with clandestine diplomatic negotiations and new constitutional schemes which floated around the Barras coterie. Perhaps his most curious venture was his participation in the Lille peace negotiations in August 1797, where an attempt was made to close the Anglo-French War.[35]

The bankers and the owners of national lands were heartily sick of the war, and when peace negotiations were temporarily suspended because of long delays involved in transmitting further instructions from Paris, a number of unofficial French representatives, as if by chance, came forward to placate the English. There is no evidence that these citizens acted as agents for England or that they received gifts for the information they conveyed. The diplomatic correspondence between Lord Malmesbury and Lord Grenville, relaying their reports, described them as emissaries of good will eager for peace, men who expected no other reward. At this period Saint-Simon was still on close terms with the Perregaux group of bankers, whose private interests transcended national boundaries. In the Lille conversations with the first secretary to Lord Malmesbury, Mr. George Ellis, whom he knew personally, Saint-Simon was the spokesman for a French peace faction among the financiers.[36]

On August 10, 1797, Saint-Simon analyzed for Ellis the French domestic situation. The English were accurate reporters, and Ellis's account affords a rare glimpse of him as a man of political affairs in action. Saint-Simon opened by lightly tossing off a series of paradoxical reflections: he hoped the English had not despaired, even though Paris had begun to feel that peace was more unlikely than ever. The Directory was "intractable" and it would require a new revolution to get rid of it, but nobody wanted another revolu-

tion. On the other hand, the continuance of the war was just as intolerable. In the end, Saint-Simon consoled the English negotiators, there would be peace because the Directory had no other alternative, and he counseled the British to follow a policy of patient waiting.

Saint-Simon was well enough informed about Directory politics to describe with circumstantial detail the squabbles which had taken place over the peace issue within the inner circle, and his account delighted the British Foreign Office. "Mr. Ellis's friend has the merit of furnishing one of the most *interesting* and certainly the most entertaining dialogues that ever made part of a negotiation," wrote Pitt.[37] When Talleyrand broached the idea of disengaging France from her commitments to Spain and Holland as a preliminary to peace, Saint-Simon reported to Ellis, Rewbell had threatened to throw a portfolio at his head. The English had come to believe that the Directors were prolonging the war in order to bolster their waning influence at home. Saint-Simon scoffed at Ellis's analysis because it imputed a rational and systematic policy to the men who ruled France. "You do them too much honor," he said, as he reeled off a series of incisive character sketches which left no doubt about their several capacities. Carnot, the only one among them capable of a consistent course of action, was in favor of peace. As for the rest, they persevered in advocating a contrary policy only to oppose the councils and their own ministers. Rewbell was a "brutal Attorney," Barras "the most profligate of mankind," Larévellière-Lépeaux "means well, but he is a strange mixture of weakness and obstinacy." Barthélemy was the "least efficient of the whole set" because he was unaccustomed to power and timorous about using it. As for the councils, though there were individual men of genius among them, when they acted collectively they were as irresponsible as a bunch of schoolboys. The entire government was so "null and insignificant" that a counter-revolution would occur at once, except that half the nation's lands were in the hands of the new property-holders, who therefore had a vested interest in upholding the existing order. The taste for equality, which was universal in the great cities, also made the return of the monarchy with its distinctions of rank and title impossible. And so the Directory was the only body worth dealing with.

Here was Saint-Simon rational, calculating, effective in action — a man to inspire confidence in the cautious Ellis and in Malmesbury, who wrote to Grenville: "He is a shrewd, sensible, strong-headed man; and there can be little doubt but that he spoke his own genuine sentiments, and those of the public in general." [38] But nothing came either of Saint-Simon's intervention or of the peace negotiations. Though the record is silent about their relationships at the Lille pourparler, it is of interest that the plenipotentiary extraordinary of the king of Spain was none other than Saint-Simon's old friend the Count de Cabarrús, founder of the Banco San Carlo.

In a few weeks the political impasse of the Directorate which Saint-

Simon had described with such disdain to the English was broken by the *coup d'état* of 18 fructidor (September 4, 1797), a sort of preliminary to the more fundamental constitutional change of 18 brumaire. In the memoirs of Thibaudeau, a member of the Council of Five Hundred, there is a passing reference to Saint-Simon's participation in the private, behind-the-scenes debates on the revision of the constitution after the *coup d'état*.[39] His name and his outlook were coupled with Barras's cousin, the Count de Lauraguais, another member of the old nobility who had adopted the libertine manner of the age and who dabbled in chemistry and politics with the abandon of a senescent playful *grand seigneur*. The constitution-making project with which Saint-Simon was identified turned in a Napoleonic rather than in a libertarian direction. The Council of Ancients would be suppressed, he told the republican Thibaudeau with the shocking frankness which he affected, and executive power would be centralized. One spoke of the forthcoming elections only to while away the time. Saint-Simon and Lauraguais claimed in their conversations that they had communicated their ideas to Barras and Napoleon, both of whom had adopted them. Saint-Simon's general political orientation as reported by Thibaudeau would have been eminently acceptable at this time to the reigning *idéologue* circle of Madame de Staël and Benjamin Constant, as well as to Talleyrand and Barras. In due course, many of the intellectual and philosophical constitution-makers were destined to get far more than they had bargained for in their espousal of strong, centralized executive authority. As for Saint-Simon's authoritarian position, it was nearer to the political viewpoint he normally supported than was the libertarianism of his speeches in 1789. His sojourn in the Luxembourg cured him of any sympathy with the levelers, if indeed he had ever had any. Enlightened despotism was as attractive to him as it was to the *philosophes* from whom he derived, as long as the absolute power was employed to put his social and philosophical theories into effect.

Of all the strange episodes of Saint-Simon's life during this period, the most difficult to comprehend is his marriage to Alexandrine-Sophie Goury de Champgrand on August 7, 1801. She was born in 1773, the daughter of Charles-Jean Goury de Champgrand, a veteran of the Seven Years' war and author of miscellaneous books on hunting. Sketches and descriptions in later years depict her as petite, with bright eyes and an intelligent face.[40] Under Robespierre her father, suspected of relations with the foreign agent Proli, was imprisoned a few days after Saint-Simon. During a search of Champgrand's apartment, the Prince Jules-Armand-Camille de Rohan-Rochefort, nephew of the notorious Cardinal Rohan who had figured in the case of the diamond necklace, was discovered in hiding. There was probably a liaison between the Rohan and Sophie Champgrand, though stalwart defenders of Sophie's reputation maintain that the pair had been wed in secret since the groom was afraid to appear before the civil authorities. On

June 10, 1794, Prince Jules was guillotined as a participant in the de Batz conspiracy, and in 1797 a child born of the union with Sophie Champgrand died. Old Champgrand spent ten months in prison,[41] and eventually lost the national properties which he had accumulated earlier in the Revolution. In 1799 he ended his days a broken man, having tried his hand at divers Palais Royal activities including the operation of a gambling house.[42]

After her father's death Sophie Champgrand, overwhelmed by tragedy, found refuge in the home of the popular composer Grétry. She wrote music and Garat sang her songs at the lavish parties of the Directorate *parvenus*. Sophie Champgrand knew well the society of bankers, speculators, playwrights, musicians, actors and actresses, having attended their spectacular balls and partaken of their ostentatious extravagance. In later life she moralized that hardly any of the *nouveaux riches* with whom she had been acquainted preserved their fortunes — Perregaux was one of the exceptions.[43] She was equally familiar with the company of the great scientists and has left charming pen portraits of Cuvier, Laplace, and the mathematician Poisson.[44] Her published recollections preserve absolute silence about her husband of the Consulate.

There are contradictory accounts of her relations with Saint-Simon. According to the Saint-Simonian cult, the marriage had its origins in an act of friendship and humanity. Saint-Simon invited the destitute daughter of an old comrade-in-arms to live with him in order to provide a roof over her head. When the indelicacy of her situation was pointed out, he married her, guaranteeing her an annuity of 10,000 francs a year, and she presided over his salon.[45] A different version derives from two bosom friends of hers under the Restoration, Madame Elise Gagne and Madame Virginie Ancelot, who filled in the lacunae in her printed memoirs with piquant details on domestic life with Saint-Simon, gathered in the course of intimate boudoir and salon conversations.

Sophie Champgrand married Saint-Simon in 1801 when she was twenty-eight, still mourning for her beloved Rohan and her son. In Saint-Simon she had hoped to find the security of a man of wealth. Instead she had cast her lot with an eccentric whose bizarre ideas were leading him to madness. One day when she respectfully asked her husband about his mania for collecting *assignats* which had become worthless, he gravely replied that it was his intention to use them in setting fire to Notre Dame (the cathedral story keeps cropping up in different forms).[46] In Madame Ancelot's Restoration salon she described in a subdued reticent voice how Saint-Simon tried to cross the threshold of her room in violation of his solemn promise that theirs would be a marriage of convenience in which her sole duty was to perform the functions of a salon hostess. She was thoroughly frightened when he propounded to her his theory of race miscegenation and other fantastic schemes for the reorganization of mankind. At the time she regarded his plans apprehensively as indications of approaching insanity, though in later years she alluded to them with gentle mockery and not without a trace of sympathy.[47]

To their house on the Rue Vivienne Sophie Champgrand introduced a clan of popular actors, actresses, playwrights, composers, singers, and painters. Alexandre-Vincent Duval and Grétry, both witnesses at the Saint-Simon marriage ceremony, were adventurers, facile artists, witty talkers. Duval had fought in the American Revolution, sketched the heads of members of the National Assembly at the height of the Revolution, and made fun of the Revolution under the Directorate in a lively comedy entitled *Les Suspects,* in which the inhabitants of an isolated village vied with one another for what they supposed to be the honorific office of *suspect.* Grétry composed some fifty operas, most of which fell flat. He was also a *philosophe* with pretentious socio-historical conceptions *à la Saint-Simon* which he strung out in a prolix, three-volume work entitled *De la vérité; ce que nous fûmes, ce que nous sommes, ce que nous devrions être* (1803). Saint-Simon in later life made varying estimates of the role of the artist as a "capacity" in the new social order. His recollection of their table conversation was not flattering: he thought they ate a lot and talked little sense.[48]

De Lépine's compendium of scurrilous revelations about Saint-Simon's life includes the story that when he despaired of siring a child he asked his friend Laya, author of *Ami des lois,* to impregnate his wife.[49] The Michaud biography, in a variant version, has Saint-Simon make the request of a great mathematician in order that the child might inherit its father's genius, but adds that the progeny failed to live up to expectations.[50] The tales do not entirely lack verisimilitude, since crude ideas about eugenics were fashionable.

According to Sophie's biographer, Saint-Simon proposed divorce in 1802 after less than a year of marriage when he became convinced that she would not join him in projects of social reform. A letter announcing his decision deplored the narrow and commonplace education which prevented her from soaring with him beyond all hitherto known bounds of human experience. The first man in the world, he concluded, could only have as a wife the first woman.[51] Sophie acquiesced, apprehensive that her husband was on the road to ruin; if she had enjoyed his wealth any longer, her tender and sympathetic nature would not have allowed her to abandon him in the days of his poverty.[52] Divorce by mutual consent was still a rather simple matter under the Consulate and they had their day in court. At the formal session, M. de Saint-Simon voiced nothing but praise for the devotion of his wife and wept so copiously at their parting that the officer of the court, mistakenly believing Sophie to be the petitioner, pleaded with her to withdraw the suit.[53]

During the final divorce proceedings on June 24, 1802, Sophie refused alimony for she, the new woman, was prepared to earn her own living, a job she accomplished far more successfully than her ex-husband. She struggled along with her pen until a handsome young Russian, M. de Bawr, wooed and won her. When he lost his fortune and shortly thereafter was killed in an accident, Mme. de Bawr resumed her literary activities. In 1818 she was awarded a pension of 600 francs because of the purity of her Bourbon sentiments, a sum increased to 2100 in 1825 when loyalty became rarer.[54] There is no record that she ever crossed Saint-Simon's path again.[55] When Sophie died an old woman in 1860, she left numerous works of literature — plays, novels, and histories—and a gentle memory among her friends. Sophie Champgrand is the only woman who occupied a well-defined position in Saint-Simon's life, though there were numerous casual mistresses and in his final years a housekeeper. The absence of enduring heterosexual love relationships in his existence is a psychological datum consonant with the rest of his personality.

In his old age Saint-Simon explained the marital episode to Olinde Rodrigues retrospectively as a deliberate act of his planned scientific apprenticeship.

I used marriage as a means of studying the scientists, something that to me appeared necessary for the execution of my enterprise, for to improve the organization of the scientific system it was not enough to be thoroughly acquainted with the status of human knowledge, it was also necessary to know what effect the cultivation of the sciences produces on those who are devoted to it. It was necessary to appreciate the influence which this occupation exercises on their passions, on their minds, on the whole of their moral beings as well as on their different parts.[56]

In Saint-Simonian tradition, the divorce took place because Saint-Simon had found the perfect woman elsewhere. She was none other than the formidable Madame de Staël, author of *De la littérature considérée dans ses rapports avec les institutions sociales* (1800), a work in which the philosopher recognized a soulmate. There is a tale that after M. de Staël's death in 1802 Saint-Simon dashed to Coppet and broke in upon the presence of the Baroness with a salutation which came right to the point: "Madame, you are the most extraordinary woman in the world, as I am the most extraordinary man. Between us, we would, without doubt, have an even more extraordinary child." [57] She refused him, and he retired in despair. The incident was embroidered with all manner of fantastic detail by nineteenth-century writers: according to one anecdote Saint-Simon had proposed that they spend their first night in a balloon.[58]

Nothing supports the story of an attempted liaison with Madame de Staël, except an undated letter whose authenticity is not absolutely confirmed. Saint-Simon is supposed to have written Madame de Staël an extravagant eulogy as a prelude to their meeting and the ultimate union of their two intellects. The romanesque proposal is characteristic of his studied flamboyant gestures. After commiserating with her over her unhappiness, for she "who had constantly labored for the amelioration of the lot of humanity" deserved a better fate, he introduced himself as a literary colleague who had not yet published his thoughts (which dates the letter not later than 1802). They had common ideas, he knew, only his were "clearer and more vigorously interwoven" than hers. This lover of intrigue neither signed his name nor appended an address, and he begged her to keep his letter secret. To receive an answer he promised to appear in person at her door. When the news that Madame de Staël had been exiled from France by Napoleon was brought to him in the midst of his writing, he interrupted his intricate planning of their momentous encounter to denounce the First Consul. "This Bonaparte who exiles you, this Bonaparte who says that women are good only for mending socks, has he produced ideas as useful as yours for the progress of the human spirit? No." The act of expulsion had enflamed his ardor. He must now follow her wherever she would go. The story of her sufferings had transported him to celestial regions where he had read a mystic message: "Communicate your thoughts to each other as promptly as possible for your mutual happiness and for the happiness of humanity." [59]

It is possible that the grotesque missive was never sent. Though Saint-Simon traveled to Geneva in 1802 there is no evidence that he succeeded in penetrating the charmed circle further along the Lake of Geneva at Coppet. The numerous Saint-Simonian anecdotes which have sprung up around their purported meeting find no corroboration in the voluminous records of Madame de Staël's tempestuous career.

If the Saint-Simonian story has any factual basis, courageous, foolhardy Saint-Simon was offering himself for an alliance with the woman who broke one of the subtlest intellects of the generation on the whirling wheel of her conversation and her passion. Saint-Simon's courting of Madame de Staël for a union of their two minds on behalf of the progress of the human species which both espoused so passionately was not in her manner; in Madame de Staël's relations with men it was she who did the choosing. Few of those she sought out escaped her. There was more than a superficial affinity between Madame de Staël and Saint-Simon. Both had the capacity to suck in ideas from the atmosphere, to alter them, often to distort them, and then to come forth with new combinations, epigrammatic formulae, impressive syntheses. This giant female intellect scattered ideas abroad with an open palm. Her achievement was crowned with more immediate success than his, but it was of the same character. No single great work remains from either of them, though they changed a climate of opinion and molded a generation.

Throughout his life Saint-Simon treated Madame de Staël's writings with a respect which he accorded few of her contemporaries. In the early years of the Restoration he had some relations with Benjamin Constant, his more successful rival for the possession of Madame de Staël's mind and body, and they seem to have behaved in a rather formal and chilly manner towards each other. Saint-Simon's extravagances were easy targets for the Constantian wit.

During Europe's brief respite from war following the Peace of Amiens in 1802 Saint-Simon had set off on a journey in search of new philosophical conceptions. He found nothing novel in the way of general ideas in "Pitt's homeland." In Germany he was less moved by the beauties of the romantic poets than by the prospect of the nascent scientific and philosophical movement, which captured his imagination. "I brought back from this voyage the certainty that general science was in its infancy in this country since it was still based on mystical principles, but I conceived hope for the progress of general science when I saw the whole German nation passionate in a scientific direction." [60]

In the early years of the century, Saint-Simon published his first philosophical tracts and began to draft projects of social reorganization, many of which did not see the light until more than a century later. Despite his sojourn abroad, his ideas do not bear the imprint of contemporary foreign intellectual movements, but seem to stem directly from the French *idéologues*. Though the mark of the dilettante who has prospered is stamped upon them, they are graced with a touch of genius and they sparkle with novelty. The colonel of the Aquitaine regiment, the speculator who survived the revolutionary turmoil sweeping over the European world was reborn a philosopher.

4

Leaflets to Humanity

WHEN SAINT-SIMON THE DECLASSED ARISTOCRAT was trying to establish relations with her, Madame de Staël was the most famous woman in Europe, the center of a coterie of *idéologues* who had once expected to use Napoleon as a figurehead in order to rule France.[1] On the morrow of the eighteenth of brumaire, 1799, Madame de Staël's group were under the illusion that they had raised a pliable Marcus Aurelius to the throne and that through him the Institute would govern. The scientists and the *idéologues*, a great aristocracy of talent, a new ruling class, would fill the councils of the state and control the educational system which determined its character. To their utter consternation, as soon as Napoleon seized power, he summoned former nobles and ex-Jacobin politicians to his side and alienated himself from the *idéologues*, in their eyes an act of dark betrayal. When they discovered their folly, they became his mortal enemies, shooting ironic barbs at him, denouncing him, plotting his overthrow. Napoleon soon learned that there was no wrath like that of an intellectual spurned — especially if the intellectual was a woman of the pen. *De la littérature* became the irate manifesto of the intellectuals against the man who had excluded them from power. Its central proposition on the surface seemed innocuous, a restatement of Condorcet's idea of progress five years after its grand formulation in the *Esquisse d'un tableau historique des progrès de l'esprit humain*. But in the tense political atmosphere, the doctrine of human perfectibility was no mere philosophical abstraction; it was a battle-cry of *philosophes* and *idéologues* against the tyrant. Throughout, Madame de Staël proclaimed her alignment with the philosophers Turgot, Ferguson, Kant, Condorcet, and, she added with a snide thrust, the Talleyrand of the report on education to the National Assembly, against the military hero. She looked upon the personal despotism of the First Consul as a denial of the moral perfectibility of man and an affirmation that man needed the mailed fist to maintain order and to curb his anarchic tendencies. Her treatise was a none too gentle reminder to Bonaparte that military glory was sterile and that only the philosophers could shed lustre upon an age.

The theory of "universal progress of knowledge by the simple effect of the passage of time" which Madame de Staël propounded recognized no breaks or interruptions. "In reviewing the revolutions of the world and the succession of centuries there is one primary idea which I never lose sight of, that is the perfectibility of the human species. I do not think that this great achievement of moral nature has ever been abandoned. In centuries of light as well as centuries of darkness, the gradual advance of the human spirit has never been interrupted." [2] In examining the contemporary state of knowledge (in a work nominally devoted to a history of literature) she came to the conclusion that "our veritable riches are the sciences." [3] What she called the "philosophy of the positive sciences," a neologism she used numerous times in this treatise, was at the heart of all human progress in morals and in politics. She adopted Condorcet's idea that the law of probabilities would make the predetermination of political action feasible. "La politique is still a science to be created," but ultimately the "combination of experience and axioms will yield results so positive that one might succeed in reducing all the problems of the moral sciences to mathematical series, to deductions and proofs." [4] In a preface to a second edition she announced that scientific progress would inevitably induce moral progress "because in augmenting the power of man it becomes necessary to strengthen the checkrein which prevents man from abusing it." [5]

Napoleon had cannily separated the physical scientists from the moral scientists, retaining the former as his supporters, rejecting the latter as idéologues. This was Madame de Staël's major grievance since it excluded her group, and in revenge her shafts were aimed unerringly at the First Consul. "The profound meditations which the combinations of the exact sciences require distract the scientists from interesting themselves in the events of the world; and nothing serves absolute monarchs better than men so profoundly preoccupied with the physical laws of the world that they abandon the moral order to whoever wants to seize it. No doubt the discoveries of the sciences must in the long run give new vigor to the lofty philosophy which judges peoples and kings, but this distant future does not at all terrify the tyrants. We have seen several of them protect the sciences and the arts. All have feared the natural enemies of protection itself, the thinkers and the philosophers." [6]

The enmity between the First Consul and the de Staël circle grew more violent with each new Napoleonic triumph. The idéologues actually hoped for his defeat at Marengo. The Concordat with the Catholic church and the peace treaties of 1801–1802, which rallied a substantial body of public opinion behind Napoleon, only embittered the idéologues in the Tribunate and the Institute. At times mercurial Madame de Staël longed for a reconciliation, even made overtures to him, but she confessed that she felt "like a goose" in Napoleon's presence, and realized that she failed to charm him — an unforgivable inadequacy on his part.[7]

In January 1802 Napoleon took the offensive and eliminated the outstanding intellectuals of the de Staël coterie from the Tribunate — Cabanis, Daunou, Ganilh, Jean-Baptiste Say, even her beloved Constant. The savants fought back with epigrams. Napoleon sneered *idéologues*, and they retorted *idéophobe*. Genius had power too, warned the philosophical Amazon; he would "break her" if she tried to impede his course, threatened the First Consul.

The Concordat was a bitter pill for the *idéologues*, for many of them had had visions of the science of the Institute recognized as the new religion. Madame de Staël had hoped at least for a liberal Protestant establishment, never a revived Catholicism. This acceptance of the arch-enemy of the *idéologues* led to an absolute breach; thereafter, Madame de Staël intrigued with jealous malcontents among Napoleon's generals who might be willing to risk another *coup d'état*. For Napoleon the Concordat was nothing more than an enlistment of the "holy gendarmerie" and the "professors of passive obedience" on his side. On August 2, 1802, the Consulate for life was proclaimed and two days later Napoleon's right to name his own successor. Within a brief period the climate of opinion was transformed and the institutions of society were changed from a loose, almost anarchic régime in which irreligious scientists were a spiritual force to a monarchical government called a Consulate, which looked for support to the traditional Catholicism of France. Madame de Staël and her *idéologues* had been routed.

Viewed against this background, Saint-Simon's first writings were in a sense throwbacks to the intellectual climate of the Directorate when the reign of the scientists still seemed a reality. He had no profound personal animus against Napoleon, hence he clung to the earlier illusion of the *idéologues* that the First Consul might still be the agent of the new scientificism rather than a tyrant for whom all talents were mere glorifiers of his name.

Saint-Simon wrote four short works during the period from 1802 to 1804, the first socio-philosophical compositions of a man over forty. Two of them were published anonymously at the time, a series of letters *A la Société du Lycée*, printed in Paris in March 1802, and a tract entitled *Lettre d'un habitant de Genève à l'humanité*, which appeared in a Geneva edition in 1802,[8] and then was reissued in an expanded version as *Lettres d'un habitant de Genève à ses contemporains* in Paris, 1803.[9] The manuscript *Lettre aux Européens* cannot be dated with precision, though it indubitably belongs to the early years of the century. Copies of an *Essai sur l'organisation sociale* are known to have been circulated in Paris among Napoleonic officials in 1804.[10]

The first projects of Saint-Simon have a common character — they are the schemes of an expansive man of action planning the reorganization of world science and world society in the grand manner, as he would a business speculation, with *élan*, with a sense of urgency, with optimist confidence in early, quick, and assured success. The universal "religious" order of the *Lettres d'un habitant de Genève* and the social hierarchy of the *Essai sur l'organisation sociale* are titanic molds into which, on the morrow of a revolutionary cataclysm, a fluid society could be cast by a great entrepreneur turned social reformer. For the most part these tracts are written conversations and they sound as if they were sketches of ideas which he had mulled over with friends many times. When the conversational tone is dropped the style becomes bombastic and abounds in mixed metaphors and long Latin periods with faulty grammatical construction. The writing lacks a uniform tone and shifts abruptly from the language of the apocalypse to dry epigrammatic psychological analyses of individual and group behavior in the great French tradition of the seventeenth and eighteenth centuries. Those who know the later flowering of Saint-Simon's ideas can recognize the seed-plant in these flimsy brochures, despite all their glaring structural defects.

The *Lycée républicain* (which in the summer of 1802 dropped its revolutionary name to become the respectable *Athénée*) was a school for higher adult education, open to all male subscribers paying 96 livres a year, and to women subscribers at half-rates. The *Société du Lycée* was composed of the founders of the school, and Saint-Simon's pamphlet, his first known publication, represents actual correspondence with them.[11] Although the *Lycée* curriculum included courses both in literature and science, and its roster of professors was distinguished with such names as Cuvier, Hassenfratz, and Fourcroy, interest in science among the subscribers had waned, and there was not even a permanent chair of mathematics on the faculty. Most of the auditors confined their attendance to the popular lectures on literature, especially those delivered by Laharpe, who was vociferously recanting his earlier revolutionary views and adapting himself to renascent Catholicism.

According to the minutes of the *Lycée*'s administrative committee, Saint-Simon, who was a subscriber, created an incident on January 26, 1802, at the end of one of Laharpe's lectures, when he dashed to the head of the class, seized the professor's chair, and demanded to be heard on several subjects concerning the arts and sciences. His outburst only provoked laughter among the fashionable audience. The staid administrative committee took the performance more seriously, and to prevent a repetition of such follies on the part of overzealous students, decreed that henceforward there be posted in all the public rooms a notice of its rule that it was forbidden to usurp the professor's place and speak without proper authorization.[12]

Ridicule did not cut Saint-Simon too deeply at this period. He wrote out his ideas in public letters (soon a favorite medium for his halting intellectual efforts) and asked the *Société du Lycée* to transmit copies to all its members. On February 1, 1802, the administrative committee noted tersely Saint-Simon's offer to deliver several lectures on the sciences and the arts. After deliberation, the committee refused him an auditorium and decided that it was against the rules to circularize the membership with his communications.

Nettled at the unwillingness of the *Lycée* administrators to provide him with a forum, Saint-Simon proceeded to publish his letters privately. In an opening jibe, he criticized the committee's inflexibility: if a rule of the Society prevented members from corresponding with one another, the regulation was a bad one and should be abolished. Then, plunging *in medias res*, he dramatically proclaimed the need for a general theory of the sciences, "a general metaphysics," as if the idea had never before flashed through the mind of man.

Each one of our professors begins his course with an exposition of the metaphysics of the part which he treats. The union of these particular metaphysics should form a general metaphysics; or rather, to present the idea in another manner, it would be desirable that our professors should agree upon a general metaphysics, to which the particular metaphysics of the parts which they treat might be related. I have a few insights on a general metaphysics. I shall speak on particular metaphysics in the following order: Mathematics, Physics, Chemistry, Physiology, Literature, and the Arts. I shall then present my insights on a general metaphysics.[13]

In the light of the vast theoretical structure which later evolved out of these platitudes, it is clear that he was already groping for a unitary scientific system and a philosophy of science that would correlate all knowledge. He simply could not express himself with lucidity.

A second letter announced that he was in travail with a brand new conception which would be born in another ten days, though he was uncertain whether its form would be oral or written. His excitement was that of the stammerer who cannot say what he thinks he means. He could only repeat over and over again that he had grasped a novel idea, and that it was of the greatest consequence to the human species that it be communicated to his contemporaries. Printing his half-digested notions was rationalized into a moral imperative.

I think that a man in whose head a new conception is formulated must assure himself by all the means in his power whether that conception is new for others, and that he must inform them of it as promptly as possible if the result of his examination leads him to believe that he has thought of things of which others are ignorant. . . . A new conception is a good fortune for the man in whose head it is formed; it is a good fortune for the Society to which he communicates it. It is a good fortune for humanity. I hope to have a new conception.[14]

A distinguished member of the Institute with whom he had discussed his ideas had encouraged him despite the indifference of the *Lycée* administrators. Both of them realized that in effect his plan meant putting into execution Bacon's project for a total systematization of knowledge. They were aware that the idea was bold and that d'Alembert and Diderot had failed in the undertaking, but, added the anonymous scientist, "I am not convinced that it is impossible." He had urged Saint-Simon to perfect his ideas, to construct the "vast edifice of a general theory," and to publish his work. Then he would have no need for the protection of any society.[15]

Heeding his friend's advice, Saint-Simon pompously heralded a scientific genesis in his last letter to the *Société du Lycée*: "I begin." What followed was a fizzle — but he did propound an overwhelming question. What was the key to historical progress in mathematics from the quantitative judgment of the first animals through Newton? Mathematics was a universal phenomenon; every animal practiced it, from the dog who chose the larger of two pieces of meat of unequal size through the great abstract thinkers. Primitive man's mentality was not far above that of the animal directly beneath him on the scale of intelligence, and yet man had made such impressive strides in this one science. What was the nature of mathematical progress? If the secret of the history of mathematics were unraveled, then the future of science would be within man's grasp, subject to acceleration at will. Newton was the last thinker who had made a major contribution to the science of mathematics. His ideas about the attraction of bodies in direct ratio to their weight and in inverse ratio to the square of their distances were surely "the finest known," but they were susceptible of extensive improvement, and Saint-Simon promised to treat of the matter in a forthcoming letter.

Of any further correspondence on this perplexing question there is no trace in manuscript or printed form. Incidents such as the altercation with the administrators of the *Lycée* helped to establish Saint-Simon's reputation in the learned circles of Paris as a buffoon of science.

The next year in the *Lettres d'un habitant de Genève à ses contemporains*, he jumped from inarticulate reflections on the nature of mathematical progress to a "practical" scheme of world reorganization which would create an ideal environment for the advancement of science in all its branches. In the manner of a daring speculator unfolding a new "combination," he presented to the various classes of society a plan to remedy all the evils of the world. Napoleon was sent a copy along with a signed letter addressed from the *Rue derrière le Rhône à Genève*, since renamed *Rue du Rhône*.[16] Deferentially Saint-Simon, who had rebounded from his earlier hostility towards the First

Consul, placed himself under his protection, entreated him to read the work upon which he had been meditating his life long, and extolled him as the only contemporary whom he considered worthy of passing judgment upon it. In a postscript he earnestly requested the secretary who might chance to open the letter to deliver it forthwith into Napoleon's hands. From the First Consul there was no reply; the archives of his police had dossier upon dossier full of all kinds of crackpot projects for the reorganization of society. The silence did not alienate the irrepressible Saint-Simon, who for more than a decade manoeuvred to catch Napoleon's ear — always in vain.

The opening sections of the tract summoned all men to commit themselves to a new social order by subscribing to an international fund with headquarters at Newton's tomb. Each contributor would be allowed to vote in the election of the three greatest mathematicians, physicists, chemists, physiologists, writers, painters, and musicians in the world. For the first year the president of the Royal Society would be honored as head of the fund; in succeeding years the largest contributor would be vested with this office, bait for the rich men. The president would be empowered to divide the international fund among the elected geniuses. Women would have the franchise and might be among those chosen.[17] Reëlection was permissible. Through the fund the scientific and artistic geniuses of the world, instead of living in poverty, would be endowed with money and esteem. Their election would be contingent upon their surrender of all other emoluments and offices, leaving them absolutely free to develop their capacities and talents untrammeled by any consideration extraneous to the good of humanity as a whole. Genius would thus be emancipated from dependence upon any fraction of humanity to the detriment of the totality. Though the scientists would vie with one another for the glory of election to the top rank, their competition would be ennobled by the universality of their purpose, love of humanity, for no man whose work did not breathe with this passion could conceivably draw the votes of the international subscribers. Through the marvelous alchemy of the fund the strong self-love of the geniuses would be transmuted into a love for mankind.

The contemplation of this imminent felicitous harmony of interests moved Saint-Simon to ejaculate: "How beautiful it is to work for the good of humanity! What a noble goal! Has man a means of approaching nearer to divinity?" [18] With what fervor these elect of humanity would compete, surpass one another in their labors, abandon the beaten paths of knowledge, and strive forward towards the progress of the human spirit! How different would be the free and independent genius from the academicians whose spirits were enslaved, who fancied themselves the sole repositories of truth while combatting every new opinion. Saint-Simon had a way of whipping dead horses. The Revolution had abolished the royal academies founded by the Bourbons; he was still denouncing them. Academicians had always opposed progress because they were named for life and depended upon their governments for sustenance. The chair of the academician enervated; the academician, bondsman of a single power, produced nothing. History would demonstrate the evils of academies. England, with two scientific societies but no academies, had discovered and adopted more truths than any other country in Europe. In France the academy was the creation of despotic Richelieu, who had hoped to use it as an instrument for the propagation of his own ideas. Italy, swarming with academies, produced only trash. All human progress in the past could be attributed to the achievements of perseceuted genius working alone.

Eloquently Saint-Simon bewailed the hardships of the genius, his bitter trials, the sterile labors to earn a living which wasted his youth. His description is redolent of the new romantic sensibility and its laments for the lot of the genius unrecognized by his fellowmen. In this work Saint-Simon was far more zealous in the preservation of the scientific genius's unsullied independence than in his later writings. The *Lettres d'un habitant de Genève* saw an absolute contradiction between the nationalist or private loyalties of a scientist and his service to humanity. Saint-Simon bemoaned the fate of his scientific idol, the great Newton, who in becoming a master of the mint ceased to be a citizen of the world and was thenceforward nothing more than an Englishman.

An imaginary interlocutor interrupted his rhetoric with the two disturbing questions flung in the face of every utopian: "Will the project be adopted? If the project is adopted will it heal the present ills of humanity, ills about which prudence prevents me from speaking?" [19]

In reply Saint-Simon gave an ingenious demonstration that the plan was at once feasible and a panacea for the evils of mankind. In the spirit of the eighteenth-century doctrine of economic harmonies, he set out to prove that his project fulfilled the basic desires of all classes in society and was prejudicial to the interests of none. As a straightforward disciple of the French sensationalist school, he felt it incumbent upon him to show that the natural selfish hedonism of all men had been taken into account before he had ventured to publish his proposal.

Society was divided into three classes: property-holders, nonproperty-holders, and a floating intellectual class, and for each of them he mustered separate and distinct arguments appropriate to their class character.

No elaborate proof would be needed to convince the intellectual class — the scientists and the artists — for they were the direct beneficiaries of the projected international fund. They might hesitate for a moment, skeptical of its success, but they would soon be won over. Since as intellectuals they had a deep feeling for humanity as a whole, they would be moved by a desire to preserve posterity from the evils which had encumbered their own lives.

To the property-holders his reasoning was more devious. The nobility had been wiped out and the ruling class in France now consisted solely of property-holders led by their First Consul. To them he issued a solemn reminder and warning that they were a numerical minority in the midst of great masses of nonproperty-holders. Their present power and their status in society they owed primarily to one circumstance, their alliance with the intellectuals. If they had any doubt on the subject they had only to recollect the days of the Terror, a period when the intellectuals abandoned them and for a time aligned themselves with the nonproperty-holders, the rabble. "The propertied classes command the nonpropertied, not because they possess property, but they possess property and command because taken collectively they have a superiority of intelligence over the nonpropertied classes." [20] This was a novel justification of the right of property, quite different from either the traditional Christian or the Lockian. The right to rule, vested in a class of society endowed with property, is here derived not from divine ordination or from the extension of man's person in labor or from constitutional tradition, but from the superior wisdom which the class of property-holders had acquired from the intellectuals attached to them. Rightful power and just ownership were dependent on knowledge, which Saint-Simon defined as science. In one passage he even tried to persuade the propertied class to accept a permanent secondary rank in the social hierarchy, ceding primacy to a sacerdotalism of scientists.[21]

In the *Lettres d'un habitant de Genève*, the scientists were thus an anomalous class, bearers of the seeds of progress and at the same time capable, if they fell into an alignment with the class of nonproperty-holders, of becoming a destructive social force. His advice to the property-holders on the tactful handling of these difficult intellectuals has a faint trace of irony. "Avoid, gentlemen, all quarrel with these men, because you will be defeated in all the battles in which you permit them to engage you; you will suffer more than they during the hostilities, and the peace will be disadvantageous to you; grant yourself the merit of doing with good grace what sooner or later the scientists, the artists, and the men of liberal ideas, united with the non-propertied classes, would make you do by force. . . ." "Obey history or be crushed by it." [22]

Saint-Simon was convinced that every nation in Europe in turn would undergo the revolution which France had just experienced, and he plainly told the property-holders of the continent that no power in the world could ward it off. But though some form of crisis was inevitable, if property-holders in other countries were prudent, if they lost no time in instituting the new scientific hegemony of the international fund, they could prevent cataclysms, they could avoid anarchy — the greatest of all scourges — and pave the way for the revolution through slow changes. Throughout, Saint-Simon's diagnosis of social realities was brilliant, his remedy puerile: "Subscribe, all of you, it is the only means you have of preventing the evils with which you are menaced." [23]

While the property-holders were urged to contribute to the international fund, they were not to render the scientists dependent upon them. The financial support of science was a necessity of the class interest of the property-holders, the only means of safeguarding their temporal power, but it bestowed upon them no additional privileges. The advancement of science was a transcendent ideal for the whole of society, which towered above all existing class interests and superseded the interests of any single generation. The immediate effect of many scientific inventions was to impose severe hardship upon contemporaries, but it was in the nature of things that one generation endure evil in order that future generations might enjoy the delights of a new creation. The good of humanity was not to be measured by the utilitarian standard of any one country or one age. The criterion of the good was redefined as the good of humanity throughout all time. Saint-Simon gave poignant expression to the new version of immortality formulated by the *philosophes*, by Turgot and Diderot and Condorcet — eternal life in the memory of all future generations of mankind.

For the nonpropertied masses whose support of the international fund he solicited along with that of the property-holders, Saint-Simon wove subtle arguments of another character. They ought to realize, from the contrast between the condition of the lower classes in England and in Russia, that living standards were proportionate to the level of science in a country. To the masses for whom science at the time appeared to be a remote, indifferent occupation, a subject of philosophic curiosity to a few learned men, he pointed out that scientists actually produced works of practical use to the people in their daily lives. Though most of the revolutionary scientists had been working technicians who participated in the war production mechanism, the idea of the scientist as a practical inventor, though presaged by Bacon, was in 1803 not a widespread conception. Inventions, Saint-Simon argued, increased man's power in his struggle against nature. Scientists, slowly emancipating man from errors of the imagination, had in turn made astronomy, physics, and chemistry sciences of observation which yielded practical advantages for all of mankind in new inventions. "Physiology," or the moral sciences, would soon reach the mature status of an exact science, and when that happened, benefits would overflow to the mass of the people who now bore the brunt of the social ills of a disorganized society.

Each class in society had its appointed function. While the masses were obliged to labor with their hands, they could insist that the upper classes labor with their intellects. It was to the interest of the nonpropertied class to accept a position subordinate to scientists and property-holders and to subscribe to the international scientific fund because in the progress of all the sciences, and more specifically social science, lay the sole prospect for the amelioration of their condition. If the elect of humanity, the scientists, were universally acclaimed the foremost men in the world, then the most elemental drives for human action would be transformed, the rich and the mighty of the earth would forsake their struggles for power and seek prestige in good works in order to win the greater glory. The masses were now slaughtered in wars over issues which were alien to them, conflicts among potentates for the possession of territory. If the powerful could have their martial instincts curbed and switched to scientific endeavors, the people would be spared these massacres. What more cogent argument to encourage popular subscriptions for the fund?

When he came to discuss voting for the scientific elect, the memory of revolutionary contests gave him pause. Though nominally he provided for popular balloting, he had a word of advice for the masses. They should rely on the judgment of the élite. "I shall tell you, my friends, the course which I shall follow in making my [choice]. I shall ask the mathematicians I know who, in their judgment, are the three best mathematicians, and I shall name the three mathematicians who have obtained the majority of voices among the people whom I have consulted." [24] Nonproperty-holders had to suppress their passion for equality and their desire to wield power. For them, too, he conjured up images of the grim days of the Revolution, when they elected nonproperty-holders to office and imposed upon themselves the burden of supporting these representatives through heavy taxes. In their own interests, it was better that the masses leave temporal authority to property-holders, rather than risk again the impractical schemes of the Revolution.

If his plan were adopted, the old society of three estates would be replaced by a new order of three classes living in gentle harmony with one another. "I believe that all classes of society will be benefited in this organization: the spiritual power in the hands of the savants; the temporal power in the hands of the men of property; the power to name those called upon to fill the functions of the great chiefs of humanity in the hands of the whole world; as salary for the governors, esteem." [25]

While the appeals addressed to the three classes of society were firmly rooted in the current doctrine of self-interest, the social mechanism he had invented so directed this driving force that men's energies were inevitably poured into channels beneficial to humanity. The passion for glory and power remained constant, but it could only be satiated by the vote of a humanity grateful for good works. "This conception affords the solution to a problem which from time immemorial has been the subject of study among moralists: To so situate man that his personal interest and the general interest are always located in the same direction." [26] The warrior ceased to be the ideal type, only the scientist was glorified. "No more honors for the Alexanders, long live the Archimedes." [27]

In the last section of the *Lettres d'un habitant de Genève* the rationalist style was abruptly terminated. The idea of world leadership by scientific geniuses, the elect of humanity, was metamorphosed into a formal organized religion of science. In a romantic artifice, Saint-Simon intoned as the prophet of the new religion. "Is it an apparition? Is it only a dream? I do not know, but I am certain that I experienced the sensations which I am about to describe to you." [28] He had a vision that Rome would renounce its false claims, and the ecclesiastical hierarchy would abandon its pretensions to interpret the word of God. The Lord of the Religion of Science spoke a new language. "I had forbidden Adam to make the distinction between good and evil and he disobeyed me. I drove him out of Paradise, but I left for his posterity a means of appeasing My wrath. Let it labor to perfect itself in the knowledge of good and evil and I shall ameliorate its lot. A day will come when I shall make a paradise of the earth." [29] Through the perfection of science man would recover the pristine happiness which he had lost when he fell from the state of innocence. Redemption would come not through Christ, but through Science. The clergy had betrayed their trust, for they had failed to lead men towards God along the path of scientific progress; they had ceased to be wiser and more learned than their flocks and had surrendered their spiritual dominion to the temporal power. Therefore God had called Newton to his side. The reformed religion, named the Religion of Newton, had only one commandment, "All men shall work," [30] and the central function of the Supreme Council of the Religion of Newton was the organization of the world to implement this unique commandment in the spirit of science and human progress. False distinctions between man's physical and moral natures were wiped out in a new unitary conception. The prime religious virtues no longer were chastity and continence, the preachments of the old religions, but the expansiveness of creative talent and boundless love for one's neighbors. Under the Religion of Newton a general peace would forthwith be imposed upon western Europe and the nations would find a goal for their dynamic activism in the conversion of the heathen of Africa and Asia to the new science.

The epilogue on the Religion of Newton is in the temper of the theophilanthropic cults of the Directorate. The creaky artifices of structure, worship, and hierarchy have the same charm or dullness, according to taste, as in all utopias. Humanity is divided into four sections: English, French, German, and Italian. There is an elaborate system of councils, with religious chiefs and ceremonials. Temples are decorated by the artists with vivid images of the infernal resting-place awaiting the dark sinners against the new religion, those who impede the progress of the arts and the sciences.

Any of the faithful who find themselves less than one day's walk from a temple will descend into the mausoleum of Newton once a year through an opening reserved for this purpose.

Children will be brought there by their parents as soon as possible after birth.

Whoever fails to fulfill this commandment will be considered by the faithful an enemy of the Religion.

If Newton judges it necessary, in order to fulfill My intentions, that the mortal who has descended into his mausoleum be transported to another planet, he will do so.

In the environs of the temple, laboratories, shops, a college will be built. Luxury will be reserved for the temple. Laboratories, shops, college, dwellings for members of the councils and dwellings kept for the deputations from other councils will be built and decorated in a simple manner. The library will never contain more than five hundred volumes.[31]

Like the Masonic ritual and the celebrations of the "national holidays" during the Revolution, the majesty of the spectacle was to inspire social virtues among the adepts. Dogma and catechism were of no significance. The Religion of Newton was utilitarian, scientific, and humanitarian. Indirect reference to Napoleon and the special honors reserved for the founder of the new religion were a naïve attempt to cast the First Consul in the role of Constantine.[32]

The Religion of Newton was still-born. Napoleon's Concordat with the Papacy was a far more satisfactory religious legitimization of his power.

The *Lettre aux Européens*, a brief work of this period which remained in manuscript for more than a century, was another plea for subscriptions to support the leading intellectuals in a European institute, and it preserved the same three-class division of contemporary society which Saint-Simon had featured in the *Lettres d'un habitant de Genève*. The temporal world as an arena of conflict between the property-holders and the workers was a conception which he later abandoned, at least in the stark, incisive form of the early tracts. Those who insist on seeing in Saint-Simon a precursor of the Marxist theory of the class struggle have only to turn to these texts for documentation. His fundamental purpose, however, in depicting the class war in society was the reverse of Marx's; instead of heralding a proletarian revolution he was issuing prophetic warnings to the property-holders to mend their ways, to adopt his antirevolutionary prophylactic measures in order to prevent the masses from rising. In the *Lettre aux Européens*, as in the published tracts, the crux of the social problem lay in the skillful manipulation of the third class, the savants. The *Lettres d'un habitant de Genève* had already severed rigidly the spiritual from the temporal powers in the good society. The manuscript *Lettre aux Européens*, stressing this separation, formulated for the first time one of his persistent reflections on the character of ideal ruling classes — the doctrine of the mutually exclusive capacities of men of theory and men of action.

The class of property-holders, being the one which must provide members for public administration, will see with a secret pleasure the approach of the moment when the line of demarcation between theory and practice will be definitively traced, because thenceforward no savant will be able to be part of the government. Indeed, the same individual cannot unite in the same degree of superiority the double capacity of speculation and of action. Does one want to be transcendent? [33]

The intellectuals should be supported, honored, allowed absolute freedom in their researches, perhaps raised to the magnificence of a priestly class, but they should by all means be kept distant from practical affairs of state. The property-holders, with the experience of the French Revolution vivid in their memories, should be willing to pay any price to discourage the savants from political action. A promise on the part of the scientific élite that they would eschew public office in the temporal sphere was to be exacted as a condition precedent to their admission to learned bodies. The formal isolation of the scientists from the struggles of temporal society, from the conflict between the property-holders and the nonproperty-holders, was intended, among other purposes, to preserve the purity of their researches, for in any ultimate historical reckoning the driving impetus behind human progress was the unfettered inventive power of the savant.

Saint-Simon's image of society in a state of constant class conflict is astonishing in so devout a Newtonian. Most eighteenth-century contemplators of Newton's world-machine had been struck by its wondrous, smooth-flowing mechanism, and had drawn their society as a reflection of the perfect balance of the order of nature. Saint-Simon gazed at the same Newtonian world-machine and while he too saw the physical universe in a state of balance, he was impressed with the tension, not the harmony of its parts. His societal image was congruent with this perception of conflict in nature. "Societies, like everything else in the universe, are preserved only by the play of forces which combat each other. The opposition between the governors and the governed, or what is the same thing, between the property-holders and the men without property, is the result of this great law of nature." [34]

In the war between the classes, the weight of numbers would bestow upon the nonproperty-holders overwhelming preponderance, were it not for the tremendous accretion of power on the side of the property-holders when they were supported by the intellectuals. The strength of the intellectuals resided in their unique capacity to devise the scientific principles which alone made the governing action of the minority of property-holders effective over the great mass of nonproperty-holders. This was the lesson of the *Lettre aux Européens*, a renewed admonition to property-holders. "On the one hand, an inferior physical force [the property-holders], but ordered by a moral force [the intellectuals], on the other a physical force [the nonproperty-holders] a hundred times greater but ignorant and without motive power. The laws in the hands of the property-holders are instruments which allow them to manipulate the inferior class. If they do not know how to modify the action of these instruments or to simplify them or to recast them in order to make them flow into new molds, they will expose themselves to revolutions, that is to say, to the men without property." [35]

In what is probably the last work of this period, the *Essai sur l'organisation sociale*, Saint-Simon clothed his ideas in a more circumspect form dictated by the new spirit of stringent intellectual censorship imposed towards the end of the Consulate. In May 1804 a close friend of Saint-Simon's with whom he shared an apartment, Rigomer Bazin, an *enragé* of 1793, later jailed as a republican, had tried to publish abroad a manuscript entitled *Esquisse d'un nouveau plan d'organisation sociale par un philanthrope*, which appears to have consisted of the *Essai sur l'organisation sociale*, along with excerpts from the *Lettres d'un habitant de Genève* and a *Discours adressé aux Anglais et aux Français*. The attempt was foiled by the Napoleonic police. They accused Saint-Simon of writing a work against the government, signaling its emphasis on the "perfectibility of the human spirit" (a subversive doctrine identified with the *idéologues*), its proposal to turn over to a subscription fund offerings destined for priests of the Catholic church, and its suggestion that to end the war France should withdraw from Italy, Holland, and other conquered lands on the continent while England restored the freedom of the seas. Saint-Simon got off with a denial that he intended to have the work published without official authorization.[36] But his encounter with the law was chastening. He expurgated the controversial sections from his manuscript and circulated only that portion known as the *Essai*.

Saint-Simon's earlier works had embodied overt proposals for direct social action; the new plan was disguised as a utopia in the pattern of Johann Valentin Andreä's *Christianopolis* and Francis Bacon's *New Atlantis*. Its leading idea was akin to the seventeenth-century dream — the organization of the world under the spiritual direction of a college of scientists — but this was the work of an activist, not a utopian. Though nominally the *Essai* was addressed to an "enlightened people inhabiting an imaginary isle with a radius of ten leagues," the literary subterfuge was transparent; actually he meant this blueprint for immediate implementation by the great Napoleon or any other historical agent. Long after the *idéologues* had broken with Napoleon, Saint-Simon still appealed to him as a modern philosopher-king who would reorganize society in the spirit of the new science.

While the mechanics of this utopian organization are artificial, contrived, they are consistent with his basic theory of society and are profoundly at variance with the concepts of the better-known contemporary liberal constitution-makers like the Abbé Siéyès or Benjamin Constant, who worked exclusively within the restrictions of the Montesquieu division among legislative, executive, and judicial powers. From the earliest days of his philosophical apprenticeship Saint-Simon thought of society as an organization of capaci-

ties rather than powers, hence his entire stress was different from that of the
followers of the eighteenth-century mechanists. Government was not a power
set over society; it was an expression of the vital forces of society, its great
geniuses and men of action performing their normal functions. The officials
of Saint-Simon's good society occupied their positions in order to act positively for the progress of the human species, not merely to preserve a system
of checks and balances.

Each year his blessed little isle would elect thirty scientists — the five
most distinguished physicists, mathematicians, astronomers, chemists, physiologists, and *littérateurs* (by this term he meant rationalist philosophical
writers like himself). The thirty would coöpt five artists and ten active
industrialists (he did not hit upon his neologism *industriel* until the Restoration, but used the clumsy phrase *personnes choisies dans la carrière de l'industrie*). Meeting together, the total of forty-five elect would be known as a
Parliament of Improvements and would be presided over by the mathematician who polled the most votes. Under the direct influence of Condorcet,
Saint-Simon at this period allowed mathematics to dominate all the natural
and social sciences.[37] Support of the scientific elect and the financing of their
research projects were derived from voluntary contributions of the people,
who upon casting their ballots contributed a sum of money proportionate to
their means (*à leurs facultés*).

This predominantly intellectual parliament exercized specific functions: it
fired officials who abused their authority, directed public education, presented
rewards to those who contributed to the progress of the arts, sciences, and
industry, kept a roster of all those who accomplished works useful to society.
Parliamentary salaries were not equal: for some inexplicable reason the
artists received double the amount of the scientists and the industrialists
double the amount of the artists.

The educational system was organized to stimulate the emergence of
superior talents. At the conclusion of their general education young people
were free to inscribe themselves as members of an occupation of their
own choosing. Annually each occupational group elected its five outstanding
members, who then undertook to classify the rest of their colleagues into
three categories of descending excellence. The elect wore badges of distinction and were allowed to designate women of their favor to be honored with
similar decorations. Women formed separate classes or work groups. There
was great mobility in this early postgraduate work system, since people could
switch from one type of occupation to another at will.

Direction of the temporal order of society was vested in a group Saint-
Simon called *proprietors*, men with independent incomes. The class of
proprietors who enjoyed "active power" was further restricted to those who
held diplomas certifying their capacity, documents issued by their schools.
They filled the traditional legislative, executive, and judicial offices without

salary. Though the plan seemed to bestow all the traditional "powers" upon property-holders, their influence on the island should not be exaggerated, because their governmental role — an administrative one — was of secondary importance. The Parliament of Improvements, which controlled the instruments of education, was the real heart of the society.

Saint-Simon saw no reason why the same institutional framework could not be adapted to larger territories by pyramiding the component units. Like a child playing with his blocks, he neatly arranged divisional parliaments and a supreme world parliament in a proper hierarchy.

Saint-Simon proudly established a filiation between his ideas and the last of the *philosophes*, the Marquis de Condorcet.[38] In the *Essai sur l'organisation sociale* he owned that he had been directly inspired by the Condorcet prediction that ultimately all enlightened peoples would advance their geniuses to the forefront of society. Condorcet in turn had credited Francis Bacon with the origins of the conception almost two hundred years before. The *New Atlantis* depicted a utopia ruled by a sacerdocy of scientists from various branches of learning who busied themselves with devising new techniques and inventions for the use and pleasure of mankind. Two early translations of this work had appeared in French, one in the seventeenth and another in the early eighteenth century.[39] The Encyclopedists and the *idéologues* had popularized Bacon's theories, and at the turn of the century new translations of his complete works were being published in France [40] — their historic moment for general intellectual communication having arrived. At his death in 1795 Condorcet had left a manuscript commentary on Bacon entitled *Fragment sur l'Atlantide, ou efforts combinés de l'espèce humaine pour le progrès des sciences*, which was published posthumously in 1804 along with a new edition of his *Esquisse d'un tableau historique des progrès de l'esprit humain*. In the *Fragment sur l'Atlantide* Bacon's utopian dream was crystallized into a program for immediate action, with procedures for the election of a supreme body of scientists who would in concert execute projects which no single scientist or group of specialists could venture upon.[41] To preserve the freedom of the scientists from the constraints of individual or state patronage he proposed that they be supported by international subscriptions, a mechanics reminiscent of the *Lettre d'un habitant de Genève* of 1802.[42] Saint-Simon was reverting to Bacon's original idea when he constituted the select scientific geniuses a high priesthood of humanity, a religious conceit which Condorcet would have contemned. The influence on Saint-Simon's thought of the *Esquisse* itself, which was first published in 1795, is apparent, for he discussed and annotated it profusely. He may have had access to the manuscript of the *Fragment sur l'Atlantide* during his Directorate days, when he wined and dined scientists who had been Condorcet's friends, or he may have heard it discussed in table-talk, even if he had not read the 1804 edition prior to the composition of the *Essai sur l'organisation sociale* that same year. Whatever the source for Saint-Simon's conception of the reign of an intellectual élite, he believed that it would be the fundamental principle of the "science of social organization" when it became positive.

The general spirit of the utopian *Essai sur l'organisation sociale* is not out of harmony with the *Lettres d'un habitant de Genève* and was preserved in all his later schema for the reorganization of society, whether in the manuscript of the early Restoration where he named his new order the Baconian society, or in the more developed plans for a society administered by three professional chambers in *l'Organisateur* (1819), or by four in the *Catéchisme des industriels* (1824). What he chiefly vacillated about from one blueprint to another was the relative position of the proprietary industrialist and the scientist. During the course of his life's work he took every possible stand on this issue: he elevated the scientists to supremacy, he tried them as equals of the industrialists, and he raised the industrialists above the scientists. He also tergiversated about the religious question: he was never quite certain whether his scientists were to become a full-fledged sacerdotal power or not. Finally, he shifted his opinions from time to time about the method for recognizing genius and excellence of capacity in the various productive and creative areas. In the *Lettres d'un habitant de Genève* and the *Essai sur l'organisation sociale* he included an element of election — the mass of the people who contributed at least a nominal sum would be called upon to designate the geniuses to direct their destinies. Later he was more reluctant to allow the people to make choices in a field where they had no competence, the determination of scientific expertness or capacity. It was flagrantly contrary to his basic conception to leave such decisions to the uneducated masses who were unqualified to make them. The intellectual élite alone was capable of judging itself and this idea became the key to his technique of coöption. Under the Restoration he would accept election of the experts in the first instance by members of their respective professions and then expand the ruling scientific bodies like the French academies through designations by the existing membership. Popular voting was eliminated.

Management of the state apparatus was not a fundamentally different problem from the exercise of any other talent; hence Saint-Simon's decision to entrust the direction of temporal affairs to the proprietors, who had demonstrated their capacity to organize business enterprises. The administered industrial society — his most general social conception of later years — was an insight whose embryonic form can already be detected in these early tracts. The act of voting by popular ballot had no special sanctity for a man who had witnessed the elections of the Revolution and the Napoleonic plebiscites. Purely political forms exerted no fascination upon one who had seen so many different constitutions transformed and corrupted from their original intent in a brief period. In the historical process of mankind, the achievements of the scientists alone seemed to be accumulating a lasting storehouse of knowledge which was impervious to the vicissitudes of politics. If the scientists could only gain possession of the moral center of society, the educational system, they would save mankind from chaos.

The prevailing tenor of Saint-Simon's first works is more Baconian than Platonic — though both thinkers left their mark. The wise experts rule, each in his respective sphere, harmony of the social parts being achieved by the infusion of the Baconian ideals of science and utility. The later Saint-Simonian gospel of production harnessed to a humanitarian purpose, the amelioration of the physical and moral condition of the species, is not yet the moving spirit of the whole social organism, though the proclamation of the universal obligation to work is a decisive initial step in that direction.

Saint-Simon himself never referred to his Consulate writings in later years and only a few copies of the original editions and manuscripts have survived. Olinde Rodrigues first republished the *Lettres d'un habitant de Genève* in 1832, eight years after the master's death. The manuscript *Lettre aux Européens* and the *Essai sur l'organisation sociale* were not printed until 1925. The letters *A la Société du Lycée* were unnoticed for years and have only recently been identified as Saint-Simon's first publication. For all their piquant novelty, these projects for the apotheosis of scientific genius and plans for the reorganization of world society at the time of their composition attracted the attention of nobody except the Napoleonic police.

5

The Savant in Arms

DURING THE YEARS 1804 to 1806 Saint-Simon squandered the remainder of his fortune. In this shadowy period of his life the Maecenas was reduced to beggary. From Geneva in 1802 he had addressed his contemporaries with an unmistakable air of aristocratic condescension. By 1806 he was destitute, abandoned by the friends who had fed upon him during the days of his lavish entertainments. With malicious delight De Lépine has dramatized his degradation: "Look at the Count, descendant of Charlemagne, issue of the Vermandois. Look at him beg in the Tuileries and receive a penny in his hat with an humble bow of the head." [1]

The account of his poverty penetrated the imperial household and on October 14, 1806, through the intervention of Count Louis-Philippe de Ségur, one of his former guests at the Hôtel de Chabanais, he was named to a clerk's post in the Mont-de-Piété. When he listed the objects which the poor of Paris brought to this government pawnshop, he was addressed as "Monsieur," a distinction which the other employees did not enjoy. The record of his service is inscribed on a bronze bust which stands in the entrance of the establishment. "Hired as a clerk at a salary of 1,000 francs, he was paid, by the end of the year 1806, at the rate of 1250 francs. This salary was reduced to 1200 francs in 1807 by a general order."

In his autobiography Saint-Simon left an affecting description of the wretchedness of his workingman's existence, and the final appearance of a savior. For six months he spent nine hours a day in drudgery as a copyist, leaving the philosophical studies which now completely possessed him for the night, when he returned home.

I spit blood, my health was in a most deplorable state, when chance brought me together with the only man I could call my friend. I met Diard, who had been attached to me as a servant from 1790 to 1797. I had not been separated from him until the period of my break with Count de Redern. Diard said to me: "Sir, the place which you occupy is unworthy of your name as it is of your capacities. I beg you to come to my house. You can use everything that belongs to me. You will work at your ease and you will do yourself justice." I accepted the proposition of this good man. I have been living in his house for two years (1806 to 1808) and since that time he has taken care of all my needs with alacrity, even the considerable expense of the work which I have printed.[2]

During the period of his dismal penury Saint-Simon had had no regular place to live, and had kept moving about Paris from one furnished room to another. Of the extant letters posted to him during the Empire hardly two bear the same address. After Diard rescued him, he was able on occasion to afford a retreat in one of the little inns on the outskirts of Paris.

Working under the protection of his former servant he published a succession of thin volumes in quarto, all privately printed and distributed by the author; they are now rare bibliophilic treasures. In 1807 there appeared the one-volume edition of the *Introduction aux travaux scientifiques du xix*[e] *siècle*;[3] in 1808 a two-volume expansion of his ideas under the same title. The half-unintelligible *Histoire de l'homme* bore no publication date. In 1808 he also issued a series entitled *Lettres de C.-H. de Saint-Simon* addressed to the Bureau of Longitudes and to the Institute. In 1810 he introduced a project for a new encyclopedia with a sketch and a prospectus: the *Esquisse d'une nouvelle encyclopédie ou introduction à la philosophie du xix*[e] *siècle, ouvrage dédié aux penseurs. Premier aperçu* and the *Nouvelle encyclopédie par C.-H. de Saint-Simon, première livraison servant de prospectus.* Sundry other projects with and without formal titles and many miscellaneous manuscripts from this period were never published — though selections and extracts have appeared in recent years.

In these Empire writings Saint-Simon turned away from bold schemes for the immediate reorganization of European society, a field which Napoleon had invaded and possessed with overwhelming force, to contemplate the creation of a grand philosophic system, a "general science," a broad theory which would at once encompass in its sweep the physical sciences, the whole of philosophy, and all the known facts about man and society since the beginning of recorded history. A few months before his death he interpreted for his favorite Olinde Rodrigues the intent which underlay the rather enigmatic Empire works.

"I wanted . . . to try, like everybody else, to systematize the philosophy of God. I wanted to descend in sequence from the phenomenon universe to the phenomenon solar system, from there to the terrestrial phenomenon, and finally to the study of the species considered as a dependency of the sublunar phenomenon, and to deduce from this study the laws of social organization, the original and essential object of my research."[4] What he sought, he told his disciple, was one "positive coördinative law" for his philosophy.

This quest for a unitary system was a relatively new departure in French thought at the time. With rare exceptions the philosophers of eighteenth-century France, in rebellion against Descartes, had been markedly hostile to the *esprit de système*. The great systematizers of the Age of Reason — Leibnitz, Wolff, Kant — had been Germans, and though their works were known and discussed by the *idéologues* at the turn of the century, they made no converts, and their influence on French philosophy did not become significant until after Saint-Simon's death.[5] The great *Encyclopédie*, that characteristic enterprise of the French *philosophes*, was, as Saint-Simon recognized, a popular dictionary of arts and sciences, only loosely held together by a thin preliminary *Discours* which could hardly be considered an adequate systematization of knowledge. Writing in the opening years of the nineteenth century, Saint-Simon was an early expression of the passion for "system" which possessed France once again and was destined to raise so many baroque theoretical edifices in the next fifty years.

Though Saint-Simon had acquired a smattering of science from *idéologue* acquaintances, even in prosperity he had remained on the periphery of their coteries. Without money his eccentricity was no longer tolerable, and in the days of his poverty he was not admitted into their company. Yet for all his alienation from the official School, his philosophic imagination was profoundly stirred by the scientific effervescence in the new universities and institutes of the Revolution and the Empire which bore the imprint of the *idéologues*.

Practitioners of science were a respected élite in French society of the period and Napoleon himself was flattered to be elected a member of the First Class of the Institute.[6] Perhaps the most dramatic explosion of scientific creativity took place in medicine, biology, and psychology, but it was also a brilliant age in astronomy, mechanics, and chemistry. The experimental activity concentrated in the city of Paris produced a flood of learned papers which hazarded provocative if sometimes dubious conclusions in every field of knowledge. The *idéologues* posed basic problems in many sciences even when they jumped at solutions prematurely. Their method always aspired to be rigidly scientific, exact, free from preconceived ideas and any dependence on religion or metaphysics. Saint-Simon applied to their researches the term *positive science*, which Madame de Staël had popularized in *De la littérature*.

After the eighteenth of brumaire, the Concordat, and the *idéologue* rupture with Napoleon, intrepid social scientists like Dr. Cabanis were more inhibited in their speculations than were the physical sicentists. The Class of Moral and Political Sciences in the Institute, which had become a stronghold of *idéologue* political opposition to the Napoleonic régime, was finally dissolved by the First Consul in 1803, and under the Empire the whole area of study became suspect.[7] Ultimately all contemporary controversial subjects were prohibited in the Institute by decree, but in the brief eight years of its free existence, 1795–1803, the Class of Moral and Political Sciences left its mark upon the methodology and subject matter of all the social sciences.

Saint-Simon fancied himself the grand coördinator, the systematizer of the discoveries both in the natural and in the social sciences made by the *idéologue* specialists dispersed among the various classes and sections of the Institute.[8] They had gone astray by failing to synthesize their researches and it was his historic mission to draw these scattered scientific troops together again in pursuit of a common objective, the "positive coördinative law."

The work plan Saint-Simon sketched for himself in the foreword to the *Introduction aux travaux scientifiques du xixe siècle* (1807) announced four major works in preparation, the whole forming one universal system: 1. on the "physics of inorganic bodies," the "physics of organic bodies," and philosophy; 2. a critique of Condorcet's *Esquisse d'un tableau historique des progrès de l'esprit humain*, to be followed by an *Esquisse d'un nouveau plan historique* by Saint-Simon, in nine parts instead of Condorcet's ten epochs; 3. a plan for a new encyclopedia which was to be a substantial improvement upon the efforts of Diderot and d'Alembert; 4. an "examination of the manner in which the conceptions expounded in the three preceding works were formed, interrelated, and clarified in the mind of the author." [9]

Though in later years Saint-Simon was no longer confident that the new systematic philosophy would be constructed in final form during his lifetime, he never abandoned the conviction that his grand design was a basic and urgent necessity for a comprehension of the world and for effective action in society. Throughout his life the *idée fixe* persisted that scientists and philosophers must collaborate to create a unity out of all knowledge in order to save mankind from chaos.

Men were athirst for a total system and he, Saint-Simon, had invented the "general idea" of the system before anyone else in the world. Pathetically conscious of his own ignorance of positive science and his impotence to carry out alone the monumental plan, he kept appealing frantically to prominent *idéologue* scientists for their aid and collaboration. The official scientists of the Napoleonic government institutes and universities regarded his synthesis of universal knowledge as the scheme of a crackpot, and the newspapers made his plans the subject of witty *feuilletons* for the entertainment of their readers. Among the scientists of the Institute, men like De Lacépède, the famous naturalist and president of Napoleon's Senate, did not even bother to cut the pages of his copy of the *Introduction aux travaux scientifiques du xixe siècle*.[10] Alexis Bouvard, Director of the Bureau of Longitudes, sent back a brief note, curtly informing him that the work had been duly deposited in the library of the Observatory.[11] When Saint-Simon, who had proclaimed a scientific revolution, saw his work thrust aside, unnoticed by the eminent scientists whose criticism and coöperation he was beseeching, the utter neglect provoked in him a feeling of aggressive violence against the hirelings of the imperial institutes and universities who had disdained him. With wild abandon he slashed away at the scientific potentates of the age. He had invented an encyclopedic conception superior to Bacon's, a cosmology which improved upon Newton, and an epistemology which had far outstripped the doctrines of Locke, and yet the obdurate fools barred him from the fellowship of scientists.

Bouvard's indifference to the *Introduction aux travaux scientifiques du xix*e *siècle* only goaded Saint-Simon into further efforts to obtain recognition through more arresting formulations of his ideas and scathing indictments of the official scientists. However slow they might be to appreciate the true merit of his works, they would at least be unable to ignore him. The *Lettres de C.-H. de Saint-Simon*, the *Histoire de l'homme*, and the *Nouvelle encyclopédie*, have more significance for a study of Saint-Simon's combative psychological nature than they have intrinsic intellectual merit.[12] Disjointed sketches and drafts pulled out of the sheaves of manuscript he had been accumulating, they are primarily emotional outbursts on paper, though once in a while in the mounds of chaff a gem can be found which makes the search rewarding.

The *Lettres de C.-H. de Saint-Simon*, directly addressed to the Bureau of Longitudes and Bouvard its director, included an autobiography and a reprint of volume II of the *Introduction aux travaux scientifiques*, which Bouvard had received so impassively.[13] In the main body of the letters, the constant refrain of the bold thesis that science needed a "dynamic conception of the universe" [14] rather than a static one was as far as his theory got before it lost itself in the morass of dogmatic generalities about solids and fluids which exhude a vague pre-Socratic odor but which always border on nonsense. The plan of the "system" as reformulated in the *Lettres de C.-H. de Saint-Simon* now revolved around three "conceptions," a conception of the universe, an encyclopedic conception, and a methodological conception.[15] The astronomy and the physics of his "cosmological conception" are the scientific dreams of an autodidact who first acquired a smattering of knowledge in these fields when he was over forty. There is the same megalomaniac obsession that he alone has discovered a general theory for astrophysics and other sciences which would reduce the ordinary academic practitioners to the position of mere aides and collaborators.

In the *Lettres de C.-H. de Saint-Simon*, Newton, Lalande, Bouvard, and Laplace had their "errors" mercilessly exposed.

"Good sense makes it clear that since the solar system is nothing but a secondary phenomenon, it can only have a limited duration. It is evident therefore that the researches of scientists should tend to discover the causes which must lead to the destruction of the solar system. . . .

"Newton, great physicist, great geometer, and great astronomer, did not know how to generalize or how to coördinate his thoughts. Philosophical values were entirely unknown to him." [16]

Bouvard of the Bureau of Longitudes, Lagrange, and Laplace were all deficient in the power of philosophical generalization. To develop a French school of science free from subordination to the British — and at the height of Napoleonic power he was cunning enough to appeal to chauvinist prejudice in his scientific battles — they needed Saint-Simon. And he was not reluctant, despite the violence of the insults with which he was bespattering them. "It has pleased nature to accord me what you lack. With enthusiasm I offer to coöperate in your work." [17] His specific plans for the elevation of the French school of science were all of the same general character: prize essay contests on astronomy and on the limited duration of the solar system. As a concrete symbol of the superiority of the French philosophical school over the English particularizers, he proposed to have hewn out of stone a vast monument to Descartes, with the inscription *Au Fondateur du Système du Monde*.[18]

The chilly formal response to his generous offer of coöperation which he received from Bouvard on August 29, 1808, drove him into a frenzy. He was told that his works were not within the competence of the Bureau of Longitudes and that scientists and the public would have to judge their merit.[19] In reply he lashed out that the French scientists were merely following the English like sheep. They were traitors to France and subversive of the Imperial principle of centralized authority. "Descartes had monarchized science. Newton republicanized it; he anarchized it. You gentlemen are anarchist scientists. You deny the existence, the supremacy of the general theory." He renewed his offer of coöperation and then with paranoid petulance hinted that if he were rejected he had "ways" of avenging himself.[20]

In the eighth and last letter, forming the second brochure of the correspondence, he turned to the Institute, complaining of Bouvard's rebuff, illustrating the subservience of the Bureau of Longitudes to English science by harping on the absence of a single copy of Descartes's works in their library. In passing he shouted wild hosannas to Napoleon, even louder and more extravagant than the cringing pronouncements of the official scientific sycophants of the Empire. No one paid much attention to his ravings.

The earlier letters to the Bureau of Longitudes had stretched out a helping hand to the errant scientists. But now Saint-Simon was done with such conciliatory overtures. In the *Histoire de l'homme* he unsheathed his sword and lunged at his scientific adversaries with a loud war cry and a keen appetite for battle. Many words of the original manuscript were capitalized and drawn in large black letters, as if in a strident tone Saint-Simon were hammering each point over and over again, like a man who would be heard above the babble of trifling scientific controversy.[21] When the manuscript was published, he interpolated blank pages in between the printed text in order that the scientists to whom he communicated his new cosmology might conveniently send him their comments.[22] For savants who were not interested enough to express an opinion he added a curt note: "Those persons who will not want to take the trouble to help me with their advice are requested to send back to me the copies they receive." [23]

Obsessed with the idea that he and he alone was unraveling the secret of the universe, he was in a state of terror lest his truth be stolen from him. Therefore he insisted that every copy bear his autograph. "This precaution appeared necessary," he explained, "to eliminate fraud on the part of printers or booksellers who might be tempted to publish my ideas without my participation." [24]

In the *Histoire de l'homme* he launched his attack on the French school of astronomy with a eulogy of violence in debate, delivered with theatrical rodomontades. The idea of a cohesive body of opinion called a "French astronomical school" was of course a figment of his scientific dream world.

> Successes obtained by moderation, by prudence, by skill are in my eyes shameful successes. I prefer more danger and more glory. I am going to raise the issue directly and frankly. I am going to put in evidence the errors of the French astronomical school by combatting the prejudices with which its chief [Laplace] is imbued and on which he has set his dunce cap.
>
> Great Corneille! I invoke your powerful genius to come to my aid. Let it serve as my guide. Let it make secure my steps as I descend from the summit of thought to the low regions inhabited by the astronomer Laplace.
>
> And you, Bacon, whose genius was more scientific but less heroic than that of Corneille, give me the weapons to fight with success against all my contemporaries, and to make the French and English schools return to the path which you had traced for them and which they have completely lost sight of.[25]

The summons to past geniuses to act as his "protectors" was a characteristic affectation of the classical revival. More significant psychologically is this self-tormented man's challenge to the whole world. He is ready to take on all comers to prove his truth. Yet aside from its neurotic aspect, the blast at his contemporaries has an element of profound meaning which a more balanced scientist would not have dared formulate. There are scattered passages in the *Histoire de l'homme* which leave one with the same ambivalent feelings as does a Nietzschean diatribe. A brutal truth is there, however strangely cloaked.

> The cowardly scientist and the cowardly soldier are equally despicable. The doors of the temple of glory open only for the brave. The soldier exposes himself to the danger of physical wounds and the scientist runs the risk of moral wounds. The result is the same, for both lead to the grave when they are too severe.
>
> Only men with a passion for glory are in a position to debate well. The passionate scientist is completely identified with the proposition which he advances and his opinions necessarily take on the character of his personality. To see things otherwise means not seeing them as they are. To wish they were other-

wise means to wish that they should change their nature, which is a fantastic idea. If the scientific discussions which have taken place in the last century have been polite it is because for a century there has been no important scientific discussion.

The last important scientific discussion, the last one in which general ideas were treated, was the debate between the Cartesians and the Newtonians, and this discussion was very lively and very much mixed up with personalities.

The degree of warmth of discussions has always been and will always be proportionate with the importance of the question which one treats and the discovery which one examines.[26]

The *Histoire de l'homme* is an apology for the dialectic, discursive, argumentative method of arriving at scientific truth. Great ideas could emerge only in ferocious discussion and the French school of scientific thought had been sterile ever since it became official, polite, and sedate. Saint-Simon was prepared to rekindle the flames of controversy, for the good fight was never impersonal. The elimination of personality from science stifled passion and resulted in a mere defense of outworn ideas. Saint-Simon pictured himself as a noble who had laid aside the sword of his class to resume the combat with ideas, the scholar in arms, the hardy warrior who fought without quarter. He disdained aesthetic embellishment for his ideas, the formal presentation that was for petty scribes and feeble *littérateurs*. He was for Corneille and against Racine, for the vigor of the idea, not its elegant phrasing. Corneille was the teacher of kings and men of genius, Racine the favorite of sultans, bigots, and courtesans. Corneille was for the strong, Racine for the weak; Corneille for the proud, Racine for the sensitive and soft. "It would be proper to send my wife and my subordinates to performances of Racine, while I attend alone performances of Corneille." [27] Nurtured on the Roman ideal of glory as transmitted by the poets of French neoclassicism, he proclaimed, "The end of my works, the object of my hopes, is to obtain the favors of living and speaking glory. . . . I am of the religion whose great prophet was Corneille." [28]

To strike down his phantom windmills, the "rival systems of Laplace and Lalande," in one fell swoop he raised aloft a new cosmological theory. Succinctly it stated:

The universe is space without bounds filled with matter. Half of the matter is in a state of solidity, the other half in a state of fluidity. . . . The hemisphere of the universe of which the solar system forms a part is the one in which matter tends to solidify. . . . Phenomena, whether one considers them as a whole or whether one considers them separately, may be conceived as a strife between solids and fluids. In the beginning fluids exercise a preponderant action over solids. Having passed the midpoint of its process the action of the solids becomes dominant, and the superiority of solid action becomes more and more absolute until the cessation of the phenomenon.[29]

He found empirical proof for his system in the skies, while gazing at the stars in the observatory of the Bureau of Longitudes with its director M. Bouvard. "I say that in the boreal hemisphere matter tends to solidification and that it tends to fluidification in the austral hemisphere."[30] Laplace had not understood this, neither had Lalande, Humboldt, nor M. Hassenfratz of the *Athénée*.

While his specific astronomic observations were an autodidact's meanderings in darkness, his grasp of the relationship between a cosmology and the rest of human knowledge has meaning. "The system of human knowledge has always been based upon astronomic knowledge, and astronomic knowledge will always serve as its basis. Indeed, the conception of a system of the world is, by the nature of things, the most important which can exist. All other considerations are only secondary considerations. All other ideas are only consequences of this general idea. Now, from this fact it follows that the perfection of a conception of the system of the world necessarily involves the perfection of the whole mass of human knowledge."[31]

For man-to-man combat he chose from among the host of imperial scientists, all of whom he regarded as his enemies, the great Laplace, the creator of a rival cosmology. The descendant of Charlemagne could cross swords only with a scientist of stature. He conjured up a Quixotic fantasy in which after a mortal struggle with Laplace, who for some unknown reason his sick mind designated as his arch-persecutor, the astronomer would be humbled and exposed to universal ridicule, and he reveled in the spectacle of Laplace subjected to the same indignities which were being heaped upon him.

During the last ten years I have acquired ever new rights to scientific esteem, and all the time my social position has deteriorated. It is M. Laplace who has poisoned these ten years of my life, and at this moment I challenge M. Laplace, to obtain from him reparation for the evil he has done me. . . . To Laplace we owe the most absurd reasonings the human mind has ever produced. . . . Let all the fools in the world get on their knees, let them bow their heads respectfully to M. de Laplace and let them proclaim him their general. . . . I demand that asses' ears should be attached to the fool's cap of M. de Laplace and that said Laplace should be exposed, thus capped, to the jeers of the pupils of the *lycées*.[32]

When these daydreams of vengeance against the powerful scientists appeared in print they did not improve his status with the official savants.

Saint-Simon's universal system had many chambers and he fluttered from one to another leaving behind a trail of unfinished brochures. In 1810 he temporarily abandoned his excursion into astrophysics to concentrate upon part three of the system as it had been outlined in the *Introduction aux travaux scientifiques du xixe siècle*, a grand project to mobilize the total scientific resources of the western world in one Herculean effort — a new encyclopedia. With sketches, prospectuses, and diagrams he solicited subscriptions to his encyclopedia, which was to be published simultaneously in French, English, German, and Italian, from a continent locked in bloody war.[33]

"The philosophy of the eighteenth century was critical and revolutionary, that of the nineteenth will be inventive and organizational," was the epigram he coined for the original sketch of the encyclopedia.[34] The new encyclopedia would have none of the destructive anticlerical characteristics of Diderot's enterprise; it would, on the contrary, become the mainstay of the throne and the altar. Since the clergy no longer enjoyed special privileges, no effort need be wasted on combatting them.[35]

To Napoleon he sent a manuscript *Projet d'encyclopédie*, a complete administrative blueprint for the organization of the "enterprise," a perfect plan that only awaited imperial implementation.[36] The initial act was to be the convocation in Paris of an international assembly of scientists devoted to "general science," each of whom would independently prepare his own total plan for the encyclopedia. To safeguard the organic unity of the encyclopedia, the plan had to be the creation of a single individual working in isolation. Unlike the great *Encyclopédie* of the eighteenth century which was a mere dictionary of ideas, the new encyclopedia had to be endowed with "organic dispositions" and the unity inherent in this requirement could only be achieved by one man. To choose the ideal encyclopedic plan from among the drafts submitted by the great savants, the whole body of general scientists would constitute themselves a jury. After a review of one another's performances, they would select the optimum outline and appoint its author the general editor of the whole encyclopedia. Then the separate disciplines in the arts and the sciences would repeat the same procedure among themselves, so that in the end one organic plan would be voted for each area of specialization and its author would be named section editor under the director general of the encyclopedia. The over-all plan and the subplans would thus achieve integral interrelationship among all the sciences and their derivation from a single unitary principle, as well as organic treatment of the individual sciences.

From the fountainhead of his new *idée fixe*, the nineteenth-century organic encyclopedia, benefits unforeseen would pour over France and the world. Since the new encyclopedia would be international, the union of the scientists of England and France would be the first step in a rapprochement between the two countries, putting an end to their hostilities and inaugurating an era of universal peace. "All the peoples in the world have an interest in the success of my undertaking, for the discovery of the political combination which could conciliate the interests of the French and the English is their only favorable opportunity. The French and English share the world and all humanity will groan under oppression while these two giant peoples are at war." [37]

The idea of synthesizing a new encyclopedia was in his private estimate a discovery whose "dimension and importance is superior to all those which have ever been made; one which future generations will never surpass." [38] Before this colossal structure the achievements of Newton shrank. "Plato, Descartes, and Kant presented vague speculations which were not of very great utility." Only Aristotle and Bacon, who had taught a "positive philosophy," were worthy enough to be considered his precursors. And even Bacon's plan could not hold a candle to his grand encyclopedic tree in which all the arts and the sciences grew organically out of a common trunk labeled General Science and then embraced and intertwined one with another like living branches. Diagrams and lithographs prepared as advertisements graphically illustrated the superiority of his "organic" conception over the Englishman's "mechanical trisection of knowledge." [39]

A published prospectus, the *Nouvelle encyclopédie*, bid for Napoleon's patronage with a vision of the glory which the grand project would bestow upon the imperial throne. "What a magnificent spectacle Paris will present when the most illustrious scientists in the world are gathered there and the scientific workshop labors under the orders of the Great Napoleon on the organization of the system of human knowledge." [40]

Saint-Simon's fulminations against the scientists and his genuflections to the emperor were alike consigned to oblivion. From time to time the newspapers deigned to mention his works, only as a pretext for comedy. In 1808 a literary feuilletonist of the *Courrier de l'Europe et des spectacles* made fun of the scholar in arms. "While our warriors are on the march everywhere in pursuit of the enemy of France and of peace, M. de Saint-Simon prefers for them another war. Once he was ambitious for the glory of arms; today he seeks another glory." [41] The commentator mocked his ignorance of mathematics, his philosophizing about sciences of whose most elementary principles he was uninformed, and ended by calling him deranged. In a review of the *Nouvelle encyclopédie*, the *Journal de l'Empire* of April 21, 1810, joined the general mockery of Saint-Simon's account of the apparition of Charlemagne and the story of his direct descent from the emperor. The wit thought it required some courage to proclaim oneself a "Carolingian."

His posterity was quite a miserable lot, and his blood could not have reached M. de Saint-Simon but through sorry channels. With all his worthless descendants, is it surprising that after a thousand years, finding one worthy of him, the Emperor came down from the heavens on a beam to embrace him? We know how hard Charlemagne, who loved letters, tried to learn to read fluently. Why not admit it — Voltaire's organs of application could not long endure Newton. Ours are too weak to study M. de Saint-Simon. Once in Egypt kings proposed enigmas to wise men. M. de Saint-Simon — he is of royal blood — wishes perhaps to renew this custom. But we must counsel him to imitate the Pharaohs and to give us the key to the enigma.

During this period when he was an object of popular ridicule, a touching correspondence was exchanged between Saint-Simon and a less prominent draftsman of a universal system, Hyacinthe Azaïs.[42] Saint-Simon had initiated the relationship in a valiant effort to compose their differences on the fundamental nature of "the system." Azaïs wrote back on July 2, 1809, that he was flattered by the proposal that they meet because he felt certain their discussion would wind up in common agreement on all fundamentals, but unfortunately he was ill and he had to go to the country. If Saint-Simon wanted the most recent version of his ideas he had only to turn to his *Bases du système universel*, which was anchored in irrefutable truths. Saint-Simon responded by despatching to Azaïs copies of his works; to which Azaïs rejoined with a flattering estimate of their profundity and essential soundness. Azaïs could not, however, refrain from remarking that whereas Saint-Simon's life seemed to have been agitated, he for one had always led a quiet, solitary existence, with the result that his work had "unity, simplicity, and consequently truth." But his terrible exertions in the construction of the universal system had naturally exhausted him, hence he was in no state to endure a discussion until the autumn. If Saint-Simon so desired, he could in the interim publish his observations on Azaïs's work. Unfortunately the two systematizers never arranged for a meeting on the unitary universal truth. Azaïs stuck to his principle of expansion and contraction, Saint-Simon to universal gravity.

His old friend of revolutionary days, Coëssin, who later developed a mystical system and set up a cult of his own, wrote Saint-Simon to assure him that he was actively gathering subscriptions for the projected universal encyclopedia and that mutual acquaintances were joining him in the drive, in order to assure an "uninterrupted exposition of his ideas." [43] These French system-makers of the early nineteenth century were at first rather benignly tolerant of one another's visions. Violence was generated by the disciples, the epigoni, when the systems descended into the marketplace; then the battle of the monisms waxed hot. Charles Fourier and Saint-Simon, the major protagonists of the struggle among intellectuals in the thirties and forties, a secret war that raged from Paris to Moscow on the borderlands of polite society, were not aware of each other's existence when their first revelations were being printed simultaneously in Napoleonic France.

6

A Psychological Self-Portrait

OVERWHELMED BY THE CRUSHING BLOWS of his contemporaries, Saint-Simon tried time and again to defend himself both as a person and a scientist against his detractors. In 1810 he prepared *apologiae* for his life which illuminate the powerful psychological drives that kept this middle-aged philosopher, hovering on the brink of insanity, from complete disintegration.

"My intention, dear Victor, in dedicating my work to you is to drive you to be great." [1] As self-appointed spiritual guardian of his orphaned nephew Victor, who was serving with the the armies of Napoleon, he prefixed his *Nouvelle encyclopédie* with a long dedicatory letter expounding the romantic doctrine of creativity and justifying his tempestuous way of life. In a second letter the same year he told Victor that a genius had to be an enthusiast, a passionate believer, even a frenzied zealot. "Only those enter the temple of glory who are escapees from the madhouse." [2] The essence of life itself was a desperate striving for fame, the Renaissance noble's quest for *gloria* for its own sake. Though men destroyed themselves in pursuit of this passion, he hoped to inspire his cherished nephew with its intoxicating zest.

There were only two types of greatness worth emulating, military genius and scientific genius, and both distinctions were reserved for men of noble blood like themselves. The memory of his aristocratic ancestry was resurrected to bolster his failing self-confidence; the grandeur of his family name was a last straw to clutch.

I quit the sword to take up the pen because I felt that it was in the scientific direction that nature was driving me to greatness. . . . The study of history will teach you that the greatest things that have been done or said have been done or said by gentlemen. Our ancestor Charlemagne, Peter the Great, the Great Frederick, and the Emperor Napoleon were born gentlemen and the thinkers of the first order like Galileo, Bacon, Descartes, and Newton were also gentlemen. [3]

My nephew, one must be modest in prosperity and proud in adversity. Our pride must equal our misfortunes. It must be boundless.[4]

In the depths of his despair he clung to the traditional account of his imperial origins.

We once possessed the empire of the west. We were first reduced to the kingdom of France, then to the lands of Vermandois. Dispossessed of this sovereign state we fell back into a secondary position, but we were still in the first rank of the governed. . . . Today we no longer have any relationship with the throne. We have descended from the pinnacle of greatness to the deepest abyss of obscurity. The Revolution has pushed us into the last ranks of the governed. And the memory of our past grandeur has become an obstacle to our advancement. Under the circumstances, nephew, one must exert oneself two-fold, three-fold. One must be proud to the point of arrogance.[5]

These megalomaniac rantings were not the only expression of his nature. There was a subtler, more analytic side which revealed itself even in his most extravagant outbursts. Though so much of his behavior seems at least on the surface to indicate a schizoid lack of contact with his environment, at moments he showed signs of a very different character — a complete, painful awareness of public disdain for his person and his writings. An autobiographical fragment of 1810 which remained manuscript for half a century is an arresting revelation of the inner depths of his complex being. He drew his own psychological profile. Superficially he was imitating the great *idéologue* practitioners of introversion and self-dissection, an art which culminated in their most distinguished disciple, Stendhal. Actually, the portrait was not genuine, and at moments even Saint-Simon appeared to be acutely conscious of its artificiality.

The new encyclopedia for which he had just written a prospectus was his fourth attempt at a philosophical "enterprise" and the previous three had been failures. People, he realized, had lost faith in him. "There exists in society, there must exist with the reader a sort of prejudice against me. ..."[6] To solace himself and to retrieve the confidence of the world he produced an ingenious piece of rationalization. Though his life had been a succession of defeats, after each failure he rose again, and never did he recede to his original point of departure — that was his psychological thesis.[7] He was a man of fifty and penniless. His "moral position" was even worse and every bit of advice he received was discouraging. And yet, at his stage in life, when most men were prepared for retirement, he, undaunted, was embarking on a new philosophical career. Characteristic images which mark the manic-depressive keep cropping up in his autobiography. He compared his experiences to a surging sea in which there were mountainous waves and deep troughs. (The cyclical image of disintegration and resurgence persists in his philosophy of history.) At the time of writing this fragment he was in a state of euphoria. "Well, in this position I rejoice. I am happy. I am feeling my powers; and this sensation is more agreeable to me than any other I have ever experienced in my life. I see without uneasiness the difficulties which I have to overcome. I smile at those which might present themselves." [8] He had made a discovery which in his mind accounted for this new infusion of energy. It had dawned upon him that his defeats had been due not to any individual weaknesses of his own but to the "imperfections of human nature." He was not at fault since his frailties had their origins in human physiology. True, he had led a shameful life. Feelings of guilt crowded in upon him. He might have sunk beneath their weight but for the comforting realization that his foibles were shared by other men. Indeed, his very failings, if properly appraised, elevated him to the company of men of genius. One would be in complete error if one believed that the few moralists "who have forthrightly posed the great problem, who have occupied themselves with rectifying the line of demarcation between good and evil, who have tried to indicate with more precision than their predecessors the goal towards which mankind should move, and to trace the routes which might lead there . . . were models of wisdom and purity in their private lives." [9] The more a soul was exalted, the more it was accessible to the passions. The philosopher, from the very nature of his mission, had to lead a turbulent existence. Since experimentation was the key to "positive progress," the man conducting research in *haute philosophie* had to subject himself to a great variety of experiences, even "to commit many acts which verge on madness." [10]

Science, the experimental method, cleansed Saint-Simon of his sense of failure and shame and guilt by suffusing the past decades of his distraught and debauched life with a fresh light, the sun of the new philosophy. He grew so enthusiastic over the idea of the essentially experimental character of his own existence that he pronounced it the perfect model for any genius who would aspire to scientific and philosophical achievement. In a set of four precepts a new "Baconian" ethic, alien to both the Greeks and the Christians, was evolved for the philosopher's way of life.

1. To lead the most original and active life possible during the vigorous years.
2. To take careful cognizance of all theories and all practices.
3. To pass through all classes of society. To place oneself personally in the most variegated social situations, and even to create situations which have never before existed.
4. Finally, to utilize one's old age to summarize the observations on the effects which have resulted from these actions on other people and on one's self, and to establish principles based upon these summaries.

To the man who has behaved in this manner humanity owes the greatest esteem. He is a man who should be classed as the most virtuous since he has labored in the most methodical manner for the progress of science, sole veritable source of wisdom.

No. My actions should not be judged in accordance with the same principles as those of other people, because my active life has been a series of experiments.[11]

In a few pages Saint-Simon outlined the principles of a new moral order. Individual actions could be evaluated only in a historical context, in harmony with a new relativist conception of the world. An act was not a finite, isolated performance subject to a Christian judgment of good and evil, but had to be weighed upon the scale of history, Saint-Simon's history. The illustrations which he brought to bear in defense of this revolutionary outlook are cogent. He contrasted the different motivations which could be attached to the same act — for example, a man's manipulation of an animal. Though outwardly two acts were identical, their moral import might be poles apart. What would be an act of cruelty on the part of one man would be an act of virtue in a scientist conducting a physiological experiment and thus contributing to progress and to the solace of humanity. Similarly he contrasted the purposes of men who frequented gambling dens and whorehouses. If a man were not a scientist, he was on the road to perdition. "But if this man is working on a philosophical theory, if the goal of his researches is to rectify the line of demarcation which separates various acts into good and evil, if he is trying to discover the means of curing those maladies of the human intelligence which make us follow paths away from happiness, I would say this man is passing through a career of vice in a direction which will necessarily lead him to the highest virtue." [12]

The passage, transparently autobiographical, was an apology offered by the Directorate debauchee become a *philosophe* to explain his strange companions and eccentric habits. In an attempt to refurbish his tarnished reputation, Saint-Simon laid down the doctrine of "participant observation." "I made my best efforts to understand as precisely as possible the manners and opinions of the various classes in society. I have sought out, I have seized every occasion to become acquainted with men of all sorts of character and types of morality. And although such researches have injured my public reputation I am far from regretting having made them." [13] Saint-Simon grew so enamored of his self-portrait in the costume of the first great experimental social scientist that he returned the gibes of public disapprobation with contempt. "My esteem for myself has always increased in proportion to the harm which I have done to my reputation. . . . " [14]

In middle age he had consecrated himself to a life of science. But this proud noble was not content to become an humble worker in the vineyard of scientific discovery. He was genius, who had appeared at the precise historic moment when the greatest truth of all time was about to be revealed to mankind. He had a new system of science and society; not just another system, another hypothesis, but the only true one. It was the broadest and most universal. Beneath its canopy all other scientific labors would be ranged in their proper subordinate places. He was convinced that he had found the way to universal happiness for all mankind, to an unending expansion of human knowledge, and to infinite progress. The whole of past history had been a prolegomenon to this climactic event.

Like many another Messiah, he too had his terrible moments of doubt. Had he really succeeded? But these misgivings did not hold him in their toils for long, for he knew that he had found the secret. His own life process with its ups and downs was a symbol of the whole history of mankind. It too had been a slow overcoming of hardship, a progression from momentary defeats to final victory. His contemporaries judged him by his overt acts, by the licence of his conduct during the Directorate. If they could only understand the progressive, scientific nature of his personal development, they would turn to him who had lived many lives and shake off the crabbed official scientists who lacked the imagination to grasp the essential problems of the physical and moral universe. If men would only listen he could be their savior.

7

The Climacteric

THE GRAND TOURNEY WITH HIS ENEMIES the imperial scientists which crowded his fantasy with bloody images had never materialized. He had flung down the gauntlet — but nobody picked it up. The men worthy of crossing swords with him had not deigned to recognize his existence. He had become the butt of rather heavy-handed journalistic humor by literary men whom he despised. But if the scientists could turn their backs on him there was one man who could not, the Count de Redern, the former bosom friend and business associate who had listened to the first expositions of his philosophy, now a man of substance living in the provinces. A duel with Redern was on even before Laplace had abandoned the field.

The public quarrel with Redern over the liquidation of their partnership devoured Saint-Simon's energies for six years, from 1807 to 1813, a dissonant *obbligato* to his philosophical studies, the sketches, drafts, and *brouillons* for a new system to regenerate mankind. The demon which had driven him to scientific combat with Laplace now fired his litigious contest with the former Prussian ambassador. Throughout the embroilment, discovering a scientific key to the universe and squeezing a more favorable settlement out of Redern were twisted together in Saint-Simon's mind. What impelled him to prolong the wrangling, he assured himself and the world, was not the pursuit of filthy lucre, for which the scion of Charlemagne could have nothing but disdain, but the hope of obtaining money enough to sustain him in his scientific labors, to finance his encyclopedic projects, to hire learned collaborators, to establish magnificent educational foundations for the benefit of humanity.

In the confused and contradictory record of the dispute, Redern appears by far the more meticulous contestant in arraying financial details and dating the various transactions which defined their business relationship.

He was by nature punctilious and he ended up in possession of whatever written contracts survived their disorderly association. Saint-Simon had turned his back on commercial affairs during the passion of his scientific apprenticeship. Negligent about bookkeeping and accounts even in the heyday of his speculations, he preserved none of the relevant papers. Throughout the period of his imbroglio with Redern he was in a profoundly disturbed psychic state and his memory was often befuddled. His account of the sequence of their formal agreements and his chronology of Redern's comings and goings are therefore not reliable.

While Saint-Simon was quite capable of outright and deliberate distortion of fact, he deluded himself as often as he deceived others, for he had an exaggerated tendency to project his own feelings into other people. He dramatized his relationship with Redern, grafted upon it overtones of sentiment which his friend did not always experience. Redern bent in the other direction, formalizing and desiccating the friendship in his public recollections. When the issue hangs upon past motives for action, it loses itself inextricably in a psychological labyrinth. Saint-Simon's description of their revolutionary ventures as a mere preparation for a prospective "philosophical enterprise" hardly bears conviction, but neither does the impression which Redern sought to convey that they had simply been engaged in a cold, impersonal, business deal. At one time their friendship had an emotional quality which Redern in later years chose to forget, when he had installed himself as the respectable lord of the Château de Flers and Saint-Simon had sunk into eccentric, perhaps dangerous beggary.

As for the concrete issues in the case, whether Saint-Simon or Redern should have been allotted a greater portion of their total acquisitions, whether personal expenses should or should not have been deducted in the final settlement, whether Redern's capital or Saint-Simon's directorial capacities were more essential, there is no criterion for passing a historical judgment. The legalities of the fight, in terms of Napoleonic law, were overwhelmingly on Redern's side. Since Saint-Simon had signed the dissolution agreements, he had no further recourse. On the other hand, as Saint-Simon maintained, Redern could have been paid off with a "bootful of assignats" upon his return from Florence in 1796 and instead he had been welcomed as a brother.[1] During the crisis in Saint-Simon's life, Redern was not generous. In his utter desperation Saint-Simon was prepared to resort to any means to secure for himself at least a meagre allowance while he continued his great work.

After Redern had sold his Paris real estate holdings to Périer, he retired to Normandy and bought the Château de Flers as his seat. He was hardly settled on his lands when in 1807 Saint-Simon disturbed his bucolic tranquillity with an annoying letter. After a tedious recapitulation of their financial history Saint-Simon asked for a reopening of the affair. At no point, he concluded, did he consider as final the arrangement by which he accepted 150,000 francs in cash for his interest in the company. In his heart he still believed that his old friend Redern was witholding "une poire pour le soif. . . . You have an annual income of 200,000 francs. . . ; it would be easy for you to procure for me the means of ending my career in ease." [2] Subsequent letters combined protestations of affection — "I still love you, despite the astonishing severity of your treatment" [3] — with a bristling resolve to compel a review and veiled threats about ruining Redern's reputation.

In a reply stiffly written in the third person, Redern brutally rebuffed him. The Lord of Flers rejected the title of friend, refused him a new arbitration, and broke off correspondence. "His threats are out of place and are as indifferent to me as his person. His own reputation deprives him of the power of injuring that of others. It is not mine that he will affect." [4] Whereupon Saint-Simon had the exchange of letters printed as the *Correspondance entre M. de Saint-Simon et M. de Redern*, prefaced with an introduction and a circular letter to Napoleonic dignitaries in which he complained of his despoilment and demanded redress. Incidentally he applied for a "scientific post," on the ground that his cosmological works entitled him to a position in the Bureau of Longitudes. [5]

The imperial bureaucrats — Boissy d'Anglas among them — were treated to sentimental excursions on his past friendship with Redern. Their affection was unprecedented. "I do not know whether there has ever existed between two men ties similar to those which bound M. de Redern and myself." The uniqueness of their relationship made it impossible to resort to the public courts in any adjudication of the affair. "The laws can only judge known cases. They cannot pronounce on disputes arising from a new order of relations." [6]

Among other accusations, Redern had alleged that Saint-Simon was a libertine, an immoral man. This Saint-Simon steadfastly denied before the newly respectable Napoleonic hierarchy. "The taste for pleasure has never been my dominant passion. It is the desire to make scientific discoveries; it is the ambition to distinguish myself by useful works; it is, in a word, the passion for glory which over the past ten years has estranged me from my relatives, my friends, and my affairs." [7]

Saint-Simon beseeched the Napoleonic officials, many of whom had once been his guests, for a personal interview during which he might exculpate himself from the false accusations which had been spread abroad about his character and his beliefs. He cried Justice and assumed the role of a naïve savant hoodwinked by the wily Prussian. Count de Redern had abused his friendship and his confidence, taking advantage of his carelessness in financial matters, a negligence which had been rendered pardonable, even honorable, by his scientific labors. Saint-Simon marshalled argument after argument with subtle detail, twisting fact where expedient, waxing eloquent, cannily appealing to the nationalist prejudices of his hoped-for readers.

The first polemical assault by Saint-Simon was embarrassing enough to force Redern into complicated private negotiations in which Senator Boissy d'Anglas, a common friend of the Directorate, acted as intermediary. The principals never met. Redern finally offered Saint-Simon an annuity of 1200 francs; this he disdainfully rejected in public, then blithely proceeded to draw 100 francs a month through Redern's Paris agent. The pittance quieted him, though not for long.

A few years later, during his attempt to create a new psychological image of himself in the minds of his contemporaries, while he was industriously spinning the web of his universal system, the two sources of income which had kept him alive were suddenly dried up. First his servant Diard died and then, in the middle of 1811, Redern cut off his monthly allowance. The crisis of 1806 repeated itself in a more acute form — again he was on the verge of starvation.

In 1808 the Count de Redern had married Madame Henriette de Mont-pézat, widow of the Count de Molijac and daughter of Jacques-Timothée de Tremolet, Marquis de Montpézat, an ancient Languedoc house which traced its genealogy back to the thirteenth century. The new Countess de Redern, a woman of about thirty-eight, was deeply attached to the old régime. Later, under the Restoration, she gave fervid expression to her royalist sentiments in literary performances which earned her a measure of fame, the *Retour de Louis XVIII* and the *Mort du Duc de Berry*. The origin of her husband's newly-acquired fortune was a blot on the escutcheon of this noblewoman and the person of Saint-Simon an ugly reminder to the Count de Redern that he had profited from the misfortunes of the nobility and the church. Saint-Simon's notoriety made any contact between them demeaning, for the former Prussian diplomat was now trying desperately to acclimatize himself to provincial French society and to become a respected lord of the manor in the department of the Orne.

The Count de Redern had applied for naturalization as a French citizen by virtue of having rendered outstanding services to the state.[8] The forges he was operating in the Orne were a signal contribution to the Napoleonic war effort. Though informed officially that he should restrict his request to the enjoyment of civil rights in France and abandon his attempt to become a full-fledged citizen, he continued to seek imperial favor. In the Orne he was a hard-working squire who built a model farm on his lands and propagated the newest scientific ideas on agriculture throughout the district.[9] But for all his good deeds he was not a popular figure in the locality, for though his iron works were useful to the Napoleonic military establishment, they were not welcomed by the small local forgemasters, who resented the competition of this Prussian noble fast achieving a virtual iron monopoly in the region.

COUNT HENRI DE SAINT-SIMON, *about* 1796

Pastel by Mme. Labille-Guiard
Collection of André Le Mallier

Saint-Simon's father, BALTHAZAR-HENRI
Marble bust by Le Roux de Thionville
Collection of André Le Mallier

Saint-Simon's mother, BLANCHE-ELISABETH

Marble bust by Le Roux de Thionville

Collection of André Le Mallier

HENRI SAINT-SIMON, 1 8 2 5. *After Engelmann*
Bibliothèque Nationale. Viollet, Paris

The Count de Redern was no simple, sedate German aristocrat; he too seems to have been bitten by a desire for expansive industrial activity and he did not always prudently evaluate his limitations. He had purchased a chemical factory at Choisy near Paris and had invested in a scheme for the acquisition of a hundred thousand acres of land in Kentucky.[10] By 1810 he had so overextended himself that he was on the verge of bankruptcy. The discontinuance of Saint-Simon's annuity was one of his first economies.

Early in 1811 Redern's citizenship request was being reconsidered and numerous officials joined in support of his petition, among them Senator Barthélemy, the prefect of the Orne, and the mayor of Flers. His police record was impeccable, his political opinions pure, his affection for the French nation and the person of His Majesty widely known. He had married a Frenchwoman, his mother had been French, and, as it turned out, his father had been naturalized a Frenchman in 1769 — a circumstance difficult to explain.

In the midst of these financial tribulations and the prolonged naturalization proceedings, Saint-Simon resumed his harassment, resolved to constrain Redern to recognize his existence, to break the barrier of silence even if it meant confronting him at Flers. Saint-Simon had been ruminating over his estrangement from his friend and had prepared manuscripts in which he elevated their dispute to a philosophical level. Their association became a prototype of the symbiotic relationship existing between the two dominant forces in society, the men of action and the theorists. In high flown psycho-philosophical terms he reviewed the drama of their friendship. Two individuals of the same age, born with two different aptitudes, one for the practical life, the other for contemplation, were, when they first met, preordained to form a relationship. As long as they continued to reëxamine principles which were already generally accepted they would remain friends. Thereafter it was inevitable that they should quarrel, each one going his own way, until finally, in their mature years, they were destined to become reconciled and to synthesize the knowledge they had acquired in their divergent careers. The meaning of their friendship had far wider implications than any mere private relationship, for it held the solution to one of the overriding problems which beset mankind. At this precise historic moment in the evolution of philosophy an integration of all the positive sciences was about to take place. For this task two different aptitudes were necessary, a brilliant imagination and a sound judgment, two rare spiritual qualities which could never be found in one man. Saint-Simon and Redern, with their contrasting temperaments, were the chosen pair. United, they could elaborate a new philosophical system and reorganize the spiritual power of society. Their renewed friendship would yield noble fruits for humanity. What glory would be their common reward upon the completion of their masterpiece, *L'histoire du passé et de l'avenir de l'intelligence humaine.* Saint-Simon fluctuated between moments of exalted Platonic mysticism as he contemplated the new being created by the fusion of their two natures and cries of anguish and despair at his abandonment.

I cannot express to you how happy I find myself since I have conceived of the formation of a moral being composed of your soul and mine, united in a manner to form a homogeneous whole. . . . Yesterday I spent a day of delight. I was in a state difficult to describe. It was an ecstasy during which I experienced the full realization of ourselves. There was in my feeling something transcendent, something divine. . . . Take, my friend, your part of the joy of our common being . . . . Read in the great book of the future. Discover the remedy of the ills which afflict all of humanity and particularly European society at this moment.[11]

The auto-intoxication of Saint-Simon's first letters was followed by darkest gloom. Renewed entreaties to Redern in the autumn of 1811 were pathetic — Saint-Simon was in the early stages of a major psychological crisis. There is a distraught letter from Paris dated October 14, 1811:

I did not sleep last night. I no longer sleep. But despair has not overtaken me. No ugly feeling pollutes my soul. Tomorrow I depart. In a few days my fate will be decided. It is you who will decide it, you who were my friend, you whom I love despite the severity of your behavior towards me. It will be decided by you, who have the necessary capacity to judge the value of the sketch of my work, a sketch in which I recognize a thousand imperfections, a part of which I feel myself capable of rectifying when I am in a calmer state but the largest part of which can only be corrected by a person who possesses faculties which are the opposite of mine.

These reflections give me hope. A more positive feeling strengthens my soul. It is the resolution which I have taken, no matter what your conduct towards me may be, not to harbor any grievance against you, or rather not to harbor it any longer, because I do not pretend that I never had any. Bread and indispensable books, a room, that is all I ask of you. Imagine how miserable I shall be in Alençon until I have received your reply.[12]

The next day he had reached a decision.

Today I depart. Tomorrow I shall be in Alençon. It is time that this end. For three nights I have not closed an eye and I pass the time repeating to myself involuntarily, "What will become of me! What will become of me!" I have already said this to you many times. I repeat it again and I shall write it to you when I reach Alençon. Bread and books, that is all that your old friend asks of you, admitting that he has been guilty towards you, his family, the whole world, but feeling that he has the means of repairing all his misdeeds towards you, towards his family, towards the whole world if you give him the indispensable books and bread.[13]

On October 23, 1811, he wrote from Alençon, after having received Redern's brusque reply, "Your letter afflicts me profoundly. The rest of my life will be devoted to repairing my misdeeds. Never will I renounce the desire and the hope of finding my old friend again, but I shall be very careful to avoid any action which might displease him." [14]

A month later, when a package of his manuscripts had been returned by Redern, who refused to read them, he wrote again, with a pitiful, obsessive insistence. Redern would yet have occasion to regret this cruel rejection.

I have received the package which you sent back to me. Your refusal to read the beginning of my work is the most painful thing that could have happened to me. I shall continue this work and it will reach a point, I hope, where I shall have attained my goal — to change your attitude towards me. When it shall have reached this point your new friends will inform you and you will regret that you were so stubborn as to remain inaccessible for so long to one who would be most miserable if he merited the judgment which you have of him. I am going to leave Alençon. I have not done there a single act which might vex you.[15]

There is something masochistic about the protestations of affection for Redern. Saint-Simon was fast approaching a psychic breakdown. The frantic letters of this period were published not by Saint-Simon but by Redern, who callously included them as an appendix to a memorandum on the affair which he printed privately in 1812. This crusty man, untouched by the lamentations of his former friend, used them to point up logical contradictions between the outbursts of love and the scurrilous accusations with which Saint-Simon filled his memoranda. Redern did not imagine that a reader might be affected by them, as he coldly accumulated the positive evidence that Saint-Simon was unbalanced, a subject for ridicule.

When Senator Barthélemy on Redern's behalf warned Saint-Simon that if he remained in the Orne he would get nothing, but that if he returned to Paris provision would be made for him, Saint-Simon went off to the capital, accepted five hundred francs from an intermediary, and in the spring of 1812 turned up in Alençon again. He was not unsuccessful in fanning the flames of provincial resentment against the foreign Count de Redern. A M. Louis Dubois, secretary of the Orne prefecture and a translator of Odericus Vitalis, joined with the local doctor Bougon in espousing Saint-Simon's cause. A letter from Saint-Simon on June 20, 1812, was a reluctant declaration of war by a rejected suitor. "It is against my will that I am doing you harm. It is because you forced me to it, for I love you and I should like to divide with you the joys which will be the reward of the long and difficult work to which I have devoted myself and of the success which I achieved in the analysis of a few major ideas." [16]

Redern, though unmoved by Saint-Simon's transports of exaltation and agony, was deeply worried about more mundane things, what his neghbors might say to the Countess concerning his relations with his old partner, what barbed remarks might upset her. On May 31, 1812, while absent on business,

he had dutifully written to prepare her for an onslaught of provincial scan-
dalmongers. Madame de Redern was in a state of nervous excitation over
Saint-Simon's intrigues with local notables, and the Count wrote again on
July 1, 1812, to comfort her with philosophy, to minimize the significance of
an abusive memorandum which he believed Saint-Simon had circulated
privately among the eager gossips of the district.

> What disturbs me very much is your stomach trouble; it is this beastly
> memorandum of M. de Saint-Simon which is causing it. This man has kept you
> in an agitated state ever since he arrived in Alençon. Really, my dear, it is nothing
> to be troubled over. These are passing things. They bother one for a moment and
> that is all. If you see M. de Fermon try to find out when M. de Saint-Simon
> communicated his fine production to him. I am persuaded that even while he was
> offering to sell me his memorandum he had taken the precaution to circulate it
> secretly. The secrecy demanded of M. de Fermon renders it probable and the
> character of M. de Saint-Simon even more so.[17]

According to Saint-Simon, he had prepared a memorandum on the
dispute and had sent Redern a copy through an intermediary, promising
not to circulate the damaging broadside if Redern proved tractable and
agreed to reopen the affair, submitting it to arbitration. The memorandum,
though printed, had not been published.[18] In it Saint-Simon presented the
quarrel between himself and his former partner as "essentially philosophic." [19] When they had made their money they had a dispute about the
wisest method of utilizing it, each one choosing a course harmonious with
his character. Redern had given himself up to practical philosophy. Saint-
Simon launched upon a philosophical career. Redern thought that he had
discovered the principles of absolute good and had only to apply them.
Saint-Simon thought that the general theory of philosophy and science was
lagging far behind particular studies and needed the attention of scholars.
Saint-Simon now appealed to his partner to abandon his false direction —
immersion in practical affairs — which was only doing harm to himself, to
Saint-Simon, and to all their friends. If he would but return to participate
in the execution of their original philanthropic project! "Redern is very
methodical but his principles are wrong. A private person has only one
way of being directly useful to the species: that is to work towards the
progress of the sciences and the arts." [20]

This summons to the path of philosophic and philanthropic virtue was
then peppered with scurrilous accusations: Redern had been a traitor to
Prussia, for he drew his money out of his native land; he married a woman
who could bear no children; he was so stingy that he had refused to help
his own relatives; people in the Orne did not love him, especially since he
was trying to grab up the property of his neighbors; he was brutal towards
the poor; he was a member of the occult sect of the *illuminati*, believing

in "direct and continuous relations between himself and God"; his avarice was inherited from his father, whose penny-pinching was proverbial in Prussia.[21]

In the body of the bewildering memorandum vicious personal attacks were interlarded with sweeping *aperçus* on the history of education in western Europe. In the fifteenth century education was still predominantly theological; then Latin and Greek authors became the core of the curriculum. Under Louis XV physical and mathematical sciences were introduced and literature became a pastime. In his own day he witnessed physics, chemistry, and natural history occupying an ever more significant role in general studies. The next stage would be the introduction of physiology, the last of the great sciences, into the educational system. In the works of the famous anatomist Vicq-d'Azyr he found the psychological explanation for the reluctance of contemporary education to admit the new science of physiology. "Without doubt it is repugnant to man to see his extermination so close at hand. He flees this spectacle and he chooses to ignore himself rather than to afflict himself with so much horror." [22] It was Saint-Simon's lofty mission to overcome this squeamishness through the establishment of an educational institution in which physiology would take its place beside the other physical sciences and literature. Then popular education would be completely "positive" and the whole structure would be crowned with a positive philosophy. Psychology too would figure among the positive studies, not the "conjectural psychology" of the standard metaphysical systems but "physiological psychology," an integral branch of general physiology.[23]

There was always method in his madness. This digression on educational philosophy was not as irrelevant to the affair as may appear at first glance, for if Redern joined him in materializing his educational project, their whole controversy would speedily come to an end. "Is there a delight equal to that of contributing to the progress of the sciences and to the amelioration of the lot of the species?" [24]

With sharp forensic logic he demanded of Redern a clear public statement of their motives in forming the original business enterprise. If it had been founded for "philosophical purposes," as he, Saint-Simon, contended, then Redern was obliged to follow through and join in the reorganization of the world educational system. If it had been set up for private ends, as Redern maintained, then both of them were disgraced — two nobles, one the descendant of the Vermandois and the other a son of the Grand Marshal of the Prussian court, engaging in sordid financial speculations. In that event Redern had only one way to purge himself, the settlement on Saint-Simon of so substantial a sum of money that he would be able to organize the educational project without Redern's further assistance.

Even though the legalities were in Redern's favor, justice was not. Everyone seemed to have emerged from the company rich except Saint-Simon:

their former agents now enjoyed annual incomes ranging from thirty to a hundred thousand francs. Saint-Simon again invoked the shades of Perregaux to support his case, quoting the banker's opinion that if Redern had been handed an income of 25,000 francs upon his return to France, it would have been munificent treatment. Saint-Simon pointedly recalled the fact that Redern was the Prussian ambassador in England in 1791 and 1792, an important official of the enemy of France. How could he have expected profit from his French investments at a time when he was working to crush France beneath "Germanic supremacy"? [25] (Saint-Simon did not miss a shot.) The whole of Redern's fortune which was not part of his direct inheritance rightfully belonged to Saint-Simon, but he was generous; he was willing to have the three senators, Barthélemy, Boissy, and Le Couteulx, arbitrate. If Redern rejected his offer he would try him before the bar of public opinion. Who would emerge victorious, Redern with his avaricious passion for lucre or he, Saint-Simon, with his passion for science and glory? Saint-Simon's peroration was an abusive challenge: "M. de Redern, honest men as a rule refuse to play the role of judge in their own case. Are you an honest man or a rascal? Do you consent to submit the operations. . . to an arbitrator?" [26]

Redern refused to be cowed by Saint-Simon's menacing tone. Financially he was in no position to make any settlement on his ex-partner. Moreover, as he had indicated to the Countess, he believed that Saint-Simon had already besmirched his name, and that no worse damage could follow his continued rejection of any proposal to arbitrate their dispute. Instead of surrendering, he counterattacked.

On July 13, 1812, from Caen, he sent home to his wife half of the two hundred copies of a long forty-four-page memorandum which he had printed with the expectation that if they were judiciously distributed throughout the Alençon district his opponent would be crushed and the scandal would subside. Redern's letter to his wife breathed an air of self-righteousness. "All this has brought back to me a thousand incidents which I do not like to remember, and the more M. de Saint-Simon obliges me to reëxamine the affair, the more I find it dirty and ugly. All the worse for him. What harm this man has done to himself and what happiness fortune had intended for him. He is more of a threat to himself than to others." [27]

Redern's documented *Mémoire sur mes anciennes relations d'affaires avec M. de Saint-Simon* carefully recapitulated the financial history of their company, described his munificence to Saint-Simon, and then fired away with a barrage of indictments which included blackmail and embezzlement.[28] Saint-Simon, without authorization, had tried to draw 1200 francs on Redern's Paris account. He had made attempts at extortion from a number of his former business associates. In self-defense Redern denied that his father was really a Prussian, since he had spent the last twenty years of his life in Saxony. Neither was it true that Redern had once been a member of the mystic *illuminati*, as vengeful, atheistic Saint-Simon had charged.[29] For Saint-Simon's purported scientific mission Redern had nothing but mockery and contempt. "M. de Saint-Simon has come from Paris to Alençon to summarize his scientific ideas. His science was properly evaluated at Paris. The same will happen just as promptly at Alençon. After having reëducated himself, he intends to reform mankind. He means to launch all the inhabitants of the Orne on the study of physiology and physiological psychology: a new science whereby he would explain our intellectual functions mechanically, with the result that the soul would be thrust aside along with the *idea of God.*" [30]

When word of Redern's *Mémoire* reached him, Saint-Simon struck the pose of outraged innocence. He berated Redern for publishing a reply to a memorandum still held secret, and thus damaging both their reputations by a public airing of their differences. Since Redern was the aggressor, in justice to his own case Saint-Simon had to cast aside his reticence. With all the power that frenzy could muster, he let fly at his old comrade in a manuscript *Réponse de M. de Saint-Simon à M. de Redern* (with the printed *Mémoire introductif* appended) for which the Baron de la Magdelaine, prefect of the Orne, refused publication authority.[31] On August 12, 1812, a much revised version of seven pages was published in Alençon, with or without permission, to be followed by a *Réponse, Seconde lettre* of four pages on August 18. Despite the official prohibition the earlier, more vituperative manuscript *Réponse* was privately circulated. After a lengthy description of their luxurious life in common under the Directorate, when Redern had first returned from abroad, Saint-Simon resumed his attack.

"You found our truffles excellent. You praised our *punch aux oeufs.* Was it with the hope of not paying your part that you found the cheer so good! You say that we did not keep house together. On this fact over which we are arguing, do you want to refer to the Count de Ségur, His Excellency Count Muraire, to Counts Boissy, Lagrange, Monge. They were our guests rather frequently. They were invited sometimes by you, sometimes by me. Is it your custom to invite people to dinner elsewhere than in your own home? It is good that the inhabitants of the Orne should know the customs which you have brought to France from Germany."

This manuscript reply was adorned with new circumstantial details about the last crucial stages of their financial settlement, all the facts sharply at variance with Redern's reconstruction. The deceased banker Perregaux, who could not testify for either partner, was resurrected as a central figure in the negotiations. Convinced of Redern's injustice Perregaux had tried to arrange an informal agreement among his former clients through an impartial businessman arbitrator, since lawyers of the *ancien régime* of the M. Poirrier type were in his judgment prejudiced parties where a complex financial enterprise involving revolutionary transactions was at stake. Perregaux had suggested

Crétet who had since become Minister of the Interior. Redern was adamant against any arbitration; in full possession of the vital documents, he stuck by the technicalities of their signed agreements. After Crétet cursorily examined the position of the contending parties he advised Saint-Simon to accept whatever Redern offered because the legal forms were against him. Therefore Saint-Simon took 150,000 odd francs in cash and left Redern 150,000 in annual income. However Redern might balance the books and manipulate the accounts, whatever the complicated legalities, in these two simple figures honest men would recognize the gross injustice of the partition. As for Poirrier, Redern's lawyer, he loomed in Saint-Simon's mind as a second villain in the drama of his despoilment. The lawyers became his *bête noire* and later he wreaked literary vengeance upon them in devastating passages on their parasitic character.

The solution to the impasse which Saint-Simon proposed in 1812 was an old refrain, a reopening of the settlement under a prominent arbitrator, one of the great Napoleonic officials — Ségur, Muraire, Barthélemy, Boissy d'Anglas, Le Couteulx — men who had once feasted at their board. If Redern would acquiesce in a reconsideration of the finances of their relationship, Saint-Simon for his part would bind himself to a series of strange personal commitments. After a characteristic *mea culpa* about his past profligacies he announced an infantile resolution to turn over a new leaf. He also promised not to molest his contemporaries with his ideas until they had ripened — a revelation of agonizing doubts about the worth of his scientific writings, despite his bombastic proclamation of their world-shaking significance.

Saint-Simon declared his resolve to retire to a garret and to await Redern's reply. "There I shall live on bread and cheese. In that condition I shall await the happy day when your soul, now possessed by pecuniary ideas, will be awakened by the voice of honor." And then the corrosive longing for vengeance, the desire to make Redern suffer as he was suffering, broke through. He showed his claw. "I tell you that I shall remain in my garret for as long as it may be necessary to complete your dishonor." In a final outburst of rage he threatened that when he was through with Redern not a gentleman in the Orne would rub shoulders with him.

The published replies were condensations which added nothing to the earlier indictment. Warding off the serious charge of atheism with which Redern had sought to discredit him in decent post-Concordat society, Saint-Simon scribbled a parting thrust at the end of the second printed letter. "Your religious principles have permitted you to rob me. My supposed atheism led me to place everything in your hands. You will admit that it is better to have as a friend an atheist like me than a devout person like you." [32]

Saint-Simon stirred up a tempest as he wandered about the country towns, acting peculiarly, outraging the *bourgeois* with his eccentricities, a living ghost out of the Lord of Flers's shameful past. Friends of Redern kept track of him and advised the Count, who was at Varennes, of Saint-Simon's movements and strange behavior. In turn Redern relayed the news to his wife at Flers. When a rumor spread that Saint-Simon had fallen sick, Redern assured her that he was only feigning illness to arouse local sympathy. "Be informed by a person worthy of confidence that M. de Saint-Simon is walking about and that he appears to be enjoying excellent health. This confirms me in the belief that he has been putting on a show. He let his beard grow. This ornament made him look even more bizarre, but it disappeared as soon as he was assured that someone would pay his expenses." [33]

In a letter of December 3, 1812, Redern explained to his wife why he had previously sent Saint-Simon money and now cut him off.

I gave help to M. de Saint-Simon, but never did I obligate myself to give him an annuity. The relations which had existed between us had only been broken for a few years. He had not yet attempted against me what he has since tried to do at Alençon. He found himself in great poverty without anyone of his family or his acquaintances feeling duty-bound to aid him. He was in dire need, on the point of starving to death or living by embezzlement. One of his sisters whose words were always truthful and whose actions were always guided by justice, had already judged before me to what degree he was base and evil. Her modest revenue was less than insufficient for her and her son. M. de Saint-Simon had over a long period of years piled up wrong upon wrong in his relations with her. I am sure that nonetheless she would have helped him if she had seen him in need. She died. I paid homage to her memory in doing what she herself would have done if she had been alive. At that time I had neither debts, nor forges, nor expenses for others than myself.[34]

Redern refused to arbitrate and he disappeared from the life of Saint-Simon. For a number of years he cut a public figure as author of memoranda opposing the importation of foreign iron, a member of the Council of Manufactures, and a candidate for deputy from the Orne. But he tasted the bitterness of political failure and financial ruin. In 1820 his vast enterprises crashed about him. To escape his creditors he fled to Brussels, and from there to Holland, where he was imprisoned. He took to practicing hypnotism, underwent a religious conversion, and in Munich, where he finally sought refuge, he was forced to disguise himself as a Professor Voigt-Reinhardt. After many years he was allowed to return to France, where he resumed his philosophical studies and in his old age published a weighty *Considérations sur la nature de l'homme en soi-même et dans ses rapports avec l'ordre social* (1835), in which snide references to Saint-Simon can be detected. He died in 1841, having done penance for the suffering which he had caused the Philosopher of Humanity.[35]

Saint-Simon departed from Alençon in defeat, leaving behind a sack of manuscripts as security for the debts he had accumulated. He was indeed a curious creditor who accepted these aphorisms, notes for universal systems, and scientific visions as collateral — and strangely enough the disordered papers have been preserved. Saint-Simon's peregrinations throughout the northern departments during the months that followed have left only vague traces, and the philosopher later kept a discreet silence about this dismal period of his life. He moved homeward in the direction of his native Picardy, and at Péronne he collapsed.

For a month he writhed in a feverish state, unable to put two consecutive ideas together.[36] A prolonged depression followed. During the breakdown friends of his revolutionary days in Péronne — the faithful notary Coutte, the frivolous Madame de Folleville, and Danicourt — nursed him and saved him from total derangement. They called the local physician Capon, who diagnosed the case as a manifestation of change of life. "Men also have their climacteric periods," he told Saint-Simon, "You have reached the most marked of these crises, and you will come to the same end as your mother if you do not take the necessary steps to prevent it." His prescription was straightforward. "Isolate yourself completely from society for a year, in order to avoid occupying your mind with too many ideas at the same time. For that purpose you should withdraw to a very calm sanitarium." Knowing his patient, he added, "That is to say, one that is not a house of pleasure. Bathe often and follow precisely the regimen prescribed in my written consultation." He warned him that if he failed to follow his instructions rigidly, he would go stark mad.

Madame de Folleville came to console him. "You have great resources and even though you are no longer young you can still accomplish something." Danicourt promised to try to reopen the "affaire" with Redern's agent, in order to provide Saint-Simon with some means of support. But it was the notary Coutte who really took upon himself the responsibility for Saint-Simon's care. When Coutte first communicated with the Saint-Simon family, Hébert, a younger brother, rented a furnished lodging for him in a building overlooking the hectic Palais Royal, his old Paris haunt. After visiting the place Coutte warned his sick friend that if he stayed in these rooms he was a lost man, for such noisy areas had been absolutely proscribed by the Péronne physician. Coutte sought out Dr. Burdin, whom Saint-Simon had befriended during his prosperous period; the doctor kept him at his house for eight days, studied the patient, and approved of the treatment ordered at Péronne. Dr. Burdin further arranged for a consultation with the great Dr. Pinel, one of the pioneers in the modern treatment of insanity, without revealing Saint-Simon's identity.[37] When Pinel also confirmed the diagnosis and the remedy, Dr. Burdin secured his admittance into a private sanitarium for nervous and mental diseases, Belhomme's on Rue de Charonne.[38] The establishment had a strange history, having once been a convent inhabited by the nuns of Picpus. Belhomme himself was not a physician but a cabinet-maker who had accidentally gotten involved in the lucrative business of housing the deranged. The house had been open during the Revolution, and was said to have served from time to time as a hideout for aristocratic suspects. There is evidence that after mulcting them of their money Belhomme would inform on his noble patients to the revolutionary committees. Dr. Pinel had regular access to the house and made scientific observations there for many years, though his estimate of Belhomme's behavior was not complimentary; he accused the keeper of retarding the cure of his patients for his own profit.

However badly others may have fared, Saint-Simon seems to have recovered his wits in this hospital. By February 8, 1813, he was able to write coherently to his sister Adélaïde describing his illness, praising the generosity and solicitude of his Péronne friends, and begging her not to withhold consent to an annual allowance of 2000 francs which the rest of the Saint-Simon family had agreed to. Her approval was necessary because the money was being withdrawn from the estate of their mother, in trusteeship since she had been declared mentally incompetent. Saint-Simon complained to his sister that the pension of 2000 francs a year was little enough to cover his minimal expenses. In order to economize and to procure for himself a few little niceties, he had told Belhomme that he would content himself with bread and cheese in the morning, and a piece of boiled meat at dinner, if the price of board were cut to 1000 francs a year. "It must be a matter of indifference to my brothers and sisters that I am economizing 500 francs on my stomach to use this sum otherwise. I have condemned myself to eat alone and to live on meagre fare, a thing which my brothers and sisters would certainly not have asked of me." Coutte had paid the entrance fee to Belhomme's, and in order to reimburse him and cover his board for the next quarter, Saint-Simon needed 731 francs immediately, a paltry sum which their mother's estate could well afford since the price of grain was rising. He was willing to sign any papers the family submitted to him and to consent to a deduction of the annuity from his portion of the inheritance when they had the misfortune to lose their mother. He begged Adélaïde to visit him. In his melancholy state, abandonment by his family gave him cause to worry about his sanity.

As the cloud lifted from his brain, he became elated with the brilliant vision of a new life about to dawn. Both Coutte and the Péronne doctor had encouraged him in the belief that he would emerge from his distraction more vigorous than ever. "An individual cannot undergo a moral revolution without experiencing a great physical crisis," Coutte had reassured him in the psychological manner of the *idéologues*.[39] A climacteric followed by a total reorganization of the personality is a frequently attested medical phenomenon. Throughout his illness Saint-Simon had an extraordinarily keen insight into the changes which were taking place in his psyche.

A second letter to his sister Adélaïde on February 12, 1813, shows him well on the upswing of his psychological cycle, free from depression, busy elaborating a new rationalization of his life. He would demonstrate to his sister that a fine future could be the natural consequence of his past. Not all fruits ripened at the same time, and those of winter kept the longest. "I was destined by my organization to be a fruit of winter. Do not reproach me with not having ripened earlier. . . . Realize that at my age most men are no longer good for anything, while I am just getting to the period when my real powers are developing." [40] He beseeched her not to heap reproaches upon him for they upset him. His nerves were raw and he was shielding himself from possible blows — family censure of his past conduct. Now he was starved for affection, and he asked only that they love each other and work together to rehabilitate the family name and fortune.

Within a day after a visit from Adélaïde, he was busy concocting an intricate new scheme for the reëstablishment of the House of Saint-Simon. If only his family forgave him his transgressions and they all labored in harmony again as loving brothers and sisters, Adélaïde's children would be vouchsafed a secure status in the world. "You and I can still strew a few flowers on the remaining paths which we have yet to travel in our life's course," he wrote her. [41] The old venom against his father — even though he had been dead for twenty years — broke out again, as he contemplated the "detestable" alienation of the lands of Saint-Simon which had been a part of their mother's inheritance. Vermandois was the cradle of their ancestors. There the Saint-Simons would always have an advantage over their rivals, whether in soliciting the hand of a rich heiress, or in seeking election to a legislative body. If the family pooled their resources, they could repurchase the Saint-Simon properties cheaply and reassemble an estate even grander than the old duchy.

The prospect set him afire and in a state of wild enthusiasm he devised a scheme to repossess the lands of Saint-Simon. The central point of the plan was his old fixation, another attempt to approach Redern through intermediaries. He no longer coveted a fortune for himself, for experience had taught him that a simple, frugal, and calm life rendered him happier than an existence crowded with business affairs. Neither did he require money for his scientific labors; he had reached the conclusion that collaborators impeded rather than helped him. [42] He was beginning to show signs of standing on his own feet emotionally and intellectually.

The implementation of Saint-Simon's plan involved the summoning of a family council of the House of Saint-Simon. By early June 1813 he was busy formulating proposals for presentation to them, anxiously preparing for the encounter with the assembly of his estranged relations. The agenda for the meeting was drawn up under two headings: the provision of an annuity for himself and the rehabilitation of the name of Saint-Simon. The key person in the family upon whom he relied for the execution of his scheme was his brother-in-law, Joseph de Montmorency, to whom he hoped to have the guardianship of his mother transferred after the elimination of the present incumbent. Once appointed, Montmorency was to invest Madame de Saint-Simon's money in purchasing the seat of the original Duchy of Saint-Simon; the rest of the family were then to combine in buying adjacent lands. Montmorency was also to use his prestige in finally bringing the refractory Redern to terms. While the scheme was still a fantasy of his own excited imagination, Saint-Simon was already drafting grandiose projects for the expenditure of the money he sanguinely hoped to acquire from a redivision of Redern's wealth. The family would win renown with an impressive engineering feat, draining the swamplands of the Somme. He would leave his relatives fat inheritances.[43]

There is no record that the House of Saint-Simon ever gathered in formal conclave to assess his grand design.

Later in the same year Saint-Simon left Belhomme's and in lodgings in Paris he managed to piece together two of his strangest writings, the *Mémoire sur la science de l'homme*, the most important of his Empire works, and the even more eccentric *Travail sur la gravitation universelle*, both of which were laboriously copied by hand for limited circulation. Penniless again, hardly recuperated from his depression, he tried frantically to arouse the scientific conscience of Europe to its sacred mission, to end the European crisis. In these works he had written down the great truths which if comprehended by the emperor and the leaders of European science would call a dramatic halt to the massacre of millions of men on all the battlefields of Europe. "All Europe is slaughtering itself," he cried out to the scientists of the world, "what are you doing to stop this butchery? Nothing. What am I saying! It is you who perfect the means of destruction." [44]

His neurotic state seemed to intensify his forebodings about the fate of a continent abandoned to inner strife without any principle of organization. He summoned the learned societies of Europe to send delegates to Rome to elect a new scientific Pope. The matter was urgent.

In fact, since the fifteenth century the institution which had united the European nations, which put a checkrein on the ambitions of peoples and kings, has grown steadily weaker. It is now so completely destroyed that a general war, a terrible war, a war which threatens to devour the whole of the European population, has been in progress for the last twenty years and has already harvested several million men, who should be thought of as no more than the advance guard of the armies which are going to be put in the field. . . .

Only you can restore peace to Europe. Only you can reorganize European Society. Time presses, blood is flowing. . . .[45]

How, he kept asking himself, through what device, what felicitous turn of phrase, could he capture the distracted attention of the rulers of mankind and rivet it upon his system? On December 8, 1813, he wrote to the Baron Degérando, whose works had illuminated the sessions of the Institute, pleading for advice: "Should I not give this work a scientific character? Should I impress upon it a circumstantial stamp? Should I finish the episode and the project of the proclamation? Should I suppress the episode and the dedication? What form should I give to this work to render it agreeable to the Emperor and useful to the state?" [46]

Manuscript copies of the *Travail sur la gravitation universelle* were sent to scientists throughout Europe (including Dr. Pinel), many of them accompanied by a pitiful letter.[47]

Be my saviour; I am dying of hunger. My position deprives me of the means of presenting my ideas in proper form. But the value of my discovery is independent of the method of presentation which circumstances have forced me to adopt in order to fix public attention more promptly. Have I succeeded in finding a new philosophical path? That is the question. If you take the trouble to read my work I am saved.

Consecrated as I have been for a number of years to the search for a new philosophic path, I necessarily had to hold myself aloof both from the School and from society and now, after having made the most important discovery, I am in a state of absolute isolation.

Exclusively absorbed with the general interest, I have neglected my personal affairs to the point where this is my precise position. For more than three weeks I have been living on bread and water. I work without a fire, and I have sold my clothes up to my last shirt in order to pay for the expenses of having my work copied to make it known. I await your aid with the impatience of a man clutching a branch which hangs over the deepest abyss.[48]

To Napoleon, whom he addressed on the advice of Cambacérès, he wrote in more formal style.

I am a cousin of the Duke de Saint-Simon, author of the *Mémoires sur la Régence*; I was a colonel in the Aquitaine regiment at the outbreak of the Revolution. I am dying of hunger. Political events have ruined me, a passion for science has reduced me to poverty. I have for fifteen years been engaged on a work which would soon be finished if I had a means of livelihood.

MM. les chevaliers Cuvier and Hallé are acquainted with the beginning of my work. They believe that it contains important new ideas. I beg Your Majesty to accord me help. It is the Prince Arch-Chancellor who has emboldened me to solicit the beneficence of Your Majesty directly.[49]

The emperor, engaged in warding off the combined allied armies of Europe, never was informed of Saint-Simon's solution to the world crisis set forth in the *Travail sur la gravitation universelle*, not even when it was disguised as a practical war measure with the outlandish subtitle, *Moyen de forcer les Anglais à reconnaître l'indépendance des pavillons.* When Saint-Simon failed to hear from the emperor, he bombarded the ministers with petitions intended to convince them of their duty to set his work before the eyes of His Majesty. In utter desperation he besought the ministers for interim aid from their own pockets while the emperor was reaching a decision on his work. He begged, but without humility, for he, the only worthy descendant of Charlemagne, had a right to a mere rich man's purse. He needed money to continue his scientific labors for humanity, to fulfill his great mission, to lead Europe out of chaos. In a letter at once naïve and bristling with an indefinable aristocratic irony, he addressed the high officials of the mightiest of European bureaucracies.

Government is a necessary evil. It is good only in the sense that it prevents the greatest of all evils which is anarchy. Intelligent men should always pose as their goal the reduction of governmental power to action necessary for the main-tenance of order. Now, my lord, if a thinker cannot hope to obtain the means of subsistence from any other source except the government, he will find himself obliged to use his intellectual powers more in flattering the government than in discovering new and useful ideas. Rich and enlightened men should employ a part of their income to grant independence to thinkers moving in a correct philosophic direction. In that way I spent my fortune as long as I possessed it. You are, my lord, enlightened and rich. I am a thinker wholly occupied in prescribing the means of reorganizing European society. Thus the demand for pecuniary aid which I make of you is entirely honorable both for you and for me.[50]

The emperor, deaf to the voice of Saint-Simon, went down to defeat. The *Mémoire sur la science de l'homme* remained in manuscript until 1858, when it was reverently resurrected by Enfantin and published in conjunction with one of his own masterpieces. Half a century after its composition, the work was accorded a favorable reception, for by that time Saint-Simonism had become a semi-official ideology of the Second Empire. Napoleon III sent a personal letter of acknowledgment to the *Père* of the Saint-Simonian cult, and *Le Siècle* on January 10, 1859, called it "one of the most admirable works which the illustrious philosopher left to posterity." The Vatican, belatedly aware of the dangerous and heretical propensities of Saint-Simon, placed it on the *Index Librorum Prohibitorum*.

Saint-Simon was eventually rescued by a small pension for which his family made provision, though they never resumed relations with him. Under the Bourbon Restoration they preferred to keep this black sheep away from the respectable royalist door of the House of Saint-Simon. His later activities were a disgrace to their aristocratic name, an affront to staunch upholders of the throne and the altar.

PART II

THE UNIVERSAL SYSTEM

8

In Search of a Monist Principle

FROM 1807 THROUGH 1813 Saint-Simon produced some half dozen opuscules. Their contents were repetitious, their form disorganized, their factual data often fanciful; even their purported direct quotations from scientists and philosophers were inaccurate. These are the outpourings of a man who suffered from intermittent fits of mental disorder, and any attempt to make rigidly consistent the many peculiar and variant formulations of his ideas would be absurd. Yet in the history of thought these writings cannot be dismissed, because for all their exasperating confusion they constitute the first version of a socio-philosophical system which gained broad acceptance on the European continent. It was in the fevered brain of Saint-Simon that Positivism had its hectic inception. The most important of his Empire works, the *Introduction aux travaux scientifiques du xixe siècle* and the *Mémoire sur la science de l'homme*, divested of their more blatant extravagancies, contain theories of scientific development, of philosophical history, and of religion which were bold first attempts to solve the perturbing problems of science and society confronting Europe after the Revolution, when the inadequacies of the world outlook of the Enlightenment struck men with force. The works of this period are particularly significant in the history of Positivism, just as the works of the Restoration are of paramount interest in the history of Marxism. Professor Gouhier's study has argued learnedly that Auguste Comte did not need Saint-Simon to develop his great philosophical structure, that Saint-Simon's ideas were commonplaces by the time he met his most famous disciple in 1817. Any such bald formula must disregard those vital passages of the *Mémoire sur la science de l'homme* of 1813, written when Comte was still a boy, which compress the essence of Positivism into capsule form.

Saint-Simon conceived of himself as a rebel against the simple mechanism, the atomism, the critical and destructive character of eighteenth-century thought. His system would create a new conception of unity and organic growth for mankind. But for all his reaction against the *philosophes*, he was still steeped in their psychology and their epistemology. His Empire writings are typical works of intellectual transition; the old conceptions had not yet worn off, the novel ideas had not yet assumed coherent form.

As a total coördinated system, Saint-Simon's positive philosophy was a dismal failure. He kept hailing "the system" and it never appeared, but there is more intellectual validity in his *ébauches* than the cursory reader is likely to discern. It was the misfortune of the man who was always weaving theories about the need for order, for systematization, for the integration of all the physical and moral sciences, that he could draft a logical, orderly paragraph only with the greatest difficulty. He was a conversationalist who could not learn how to write. He needed a collaborator, some one to unify his flashes of insight on organic unity, to draw out their significance, to develop them with illuminating detail. Saint-Simon did not have Bentham's psychopathic horror of the printed word; alas, he had the opposite vice and would publish even the half-digested notions which occurred to him in the night. With the Restoration he would find a series of young men to help with the exposition of his ideas while they were still in a formative stage, and a brilliant group they were — Augustin Thierry, Auguste Comte, Olinde Rodrigues, Léon Halévy. During the Empire he was alone, isolated, secretly tormented by a sense of inadequacy at the very moment when he was proclaiming his genius most vociferously. Yet the "system" could not be contained within him; it had to find expression, whatever its external habit. Although at times his Empire writing was compulsive like that of a deranged man, there was always a core of brilliant rational conceptual patterns which reformed themselves even after the most violent attacks of mental disturbance. The "system" reasserted itself.

Precisely what did Saint-Simon mean by a system?

In the *Introduction aux travaux scientifiques du xixe siècle*, he accepted Condillac's simple definition from the opening section of the *Traité des systêmes* (which has been described as a treatise against systems):

"A system is nothing but the disposition of the various parts of an art or a science in such an order that they mutually sustain one another and that the later parts are explained by the earlier. Those elements which explain others are called *principles*, and the system is the more perfect as the principles are smaller in number. It is even desirable that they be reduced to one." [1]

The monist element of the definition had not been the nub of the Condillac philosophy, and his orthodox *idéologue* followers were leery of a first principle as smacking of metaphysics and religion, but in Saint-Simon's dream of science the quest for a single principle became obsessive. Once discovered, the monist principle would demonstrate the essential unity of the phenomenal world in all its manifestations. Dr. Cabanis, in papers delivered before the

Institute, had dilated upon the interrelationship of the physical and the moral in man and had mused about the essential unity of science, as his master Bacon had done almost three hundred years before.[2] Saint-Simon was afire with an ambition to outstrip the *idéologues*, to prove the actual unity of all material and spiritual existence in a world governed by one law, one irreducible principle.

In the period of the Empire Saint-Simon believed that he had solved the riddle of the universe, that he had found the principle. Since Newton had synthesized physics with a simple, mathematical law of gravity, why could not the other natural sciences and the sciences of man be unified by the identical principle correctly interpreted? Saint-Simon's apotheosis of Newton and Newton's law in the *Lettres d'un habitant de Genève à ses contemporains* came at the end of over a century of Newtonian faddism during which the *Principia* passed through more than twenty editions, including popular versions marked "for the ladies." Intellectuals of the age had been fascinated by the sublime simplicity and perfection of the one law which was applicable to all physical phenomena. Not much mental stretching was required for a self-taught latter-day *philosophe* like Saint-Simon, brought up in the crude materialist school of the eighteenth century, to make the law of gravity cover moral and spiritual phenomena as well. The sensationalists had shown that the real origin of ideas was in matter, and matter obeyed Newton's law; why then should ideas be exempt from its dominion?

Saint-Simon's fixation upon the law of gravity was not unique. When Charles Fourier in 1808 used the phrase "passionate attraction" to describe his new system, he declared that the laws of passionate attraction conformed at every point with those of the Newtonian material attraction and he too was proclaiming the "unity of the system of movement for the material world and for the spiritual world."[3] In the late eighteenth and early nineteenth centuries literally scores of thinkers were hawking about similar catch-alls to explain the social universe and the physical universe and their overwhelming complexities with a word or a concept or a law or a principle.[4]

In 1808, simultaneously with the announcement of his vast project for a series of works coördinating all knowledge, Saint-Simon reaffirmed the Newtonian law as the single principle governing the entire world: ". . . universal gravity is the sole cause of all physical and moral phenomena. . . ."[5] When completed, his system would demonstrate that science was deducible step by step from this first principle, and would show how it actually operated in practice in the various branches of knowledge, physical and moral. To Saint-Simon the monist belief that all sciences must have the same underlying principle was the logical conclusion of any conception of order and law in nature. If the individual sciences had different fundamental principles, nature would be in a state of anarchy. To imagine that moral phenomena had a cause distinct from that of physical phenomena showed a complete absence of philosophical understanding. Saint-Simon was disturbed lest the newer sciences like physiology, which still lacked a broad "general theory," fall into grave error at the outset by failing to adopt the same basic Newtonian law as the more developed physical-astronomic and chemical sciences. For Saint-Simon, philosophical understanding rested on the perception of oneness in nature; by definition a philosopher could not dispute the existence of a unifying principle. If one principle failed to embrace and explain the subsidiary laws in all the sciences, something would be grievously lacking either in the perfection of the principle or of the universe.

In the *Travail sur la gravitation universelle* (1813), Saint-Simon, shaken by the carnage of the Napoleonic wars, urged immediate practical application of the principle to abate the European crisis. "I have given this first sketch of my project on the reorganization of European society the title of *Travail sur la gravitation universelle*, because the idea of universal gravity must serve as a base for the new philosophical theory, and the new political system of Europe must be a consequence of the new philosophy." [6] In the same work Francis Bacon was resurrected to address the members of the French Institute on the crying need for a monist principle:

Gentlemen, there are a hundred and sixty of you, all men of great merit. You have both talent and erudition. You hold regular meetings. You are divided into classes and sections with distinct scientific functions. You have presidents and secretaries. And nevertheless you do not form a scientific corporation. You are only assembled scientists and your works have no unity. They are but a series of ideas bracketed together, because your ideas are not linked to any general conception, because your society is not organized systematically. . . .

Do you want to organize, gentlemen? Nothing would be easier. Choose an idea to which others can be related and from which you would deduce all principles as consequences. Then you will have a philosophy. This philosophy will certainly be based on the idea of Universal Gravity, and all your works will, from that moment on, assume a systematic character.[7]

Saint-Simon was always drawing parallels between the birth of Christianity and the inauguration of the "new system" in the nineteenth century. The crisis of the ancient world had witnessed a transition from many gods to one God. What did this signify, what was the clue to the development? The movement of thought from the many to the one. This was exactly what the modern intellectual revolution would achieve, the adoption of one principle, gravity, integrating a vast number of disparate and hitherto unrelated scientific laws which had been accumulating since the inception of the scientific revolution.

Like the eighteenth-century *philosophes*, Saint-Simon was by no means emancipated from the monist spirit of Christianity. His application of the law of "universal gravity" to all phenomena, the conceit of an eccentric,[8] was only an exaggeration of a widespread belief among his contemporaries. The search for a monist principle was a symptom of that bewilderment before an inexplicable universe which dazed Christian Europe when the full enormity of the Voltairean revolution had been realized. For a thousand years mankind had lived with unquestioning faith in the existence of a unifying principle in the world. The first full understanding of its destruction gave birth to scores of artificial and highly self-conscious attempts to substitute for the old religion a scientific principle or a moral principle or an emotional principle dressed up as God. The throne of the absolute could not be left untenanted.

9

The Religion of Science

THE IDEA THAT "THE SYSTEM" would have to be a religious system had been fermenting in Saint-Simon's brain from the inception of his philosophical career. His first published brochure in 1802 had proclaimed the founding of the Religion of Newton; and his last work, the *Nouveau Christianisme,* launched a movement of religious reformation throughout the world.

According to Saint-Simonian tradition, as a youth Saint-Simon had a violent quarrel with his father over receiving the sacraments, and there is scant evidence that he was ever a practicing Catholic for long. After 1789 the speeches he delivered on solemn national holidays to the villagers of his native province bristled with diatribes against the usurpations of priests, who, he taught, should be considered "born enemies of the Revolution." [1] In the conduct of life of the Directorate *bon vivant* there was no place for traditional religious devotion. Nevertheless, Saint-Simon was always acutely sensitive to the social implications of the multifarious religious movements which swept through France during his lifetime, even though he was himself not touched by the emotions they inspired.

Eighteenth-century attitudes underlie all the religions of Saint-Simon, for this is the world in which he was formed as a boy and a man. Though the *philosophes* had undermined the power of the Catholic church, there were few outright atheists among them. Rebelling against the institutions and practices of existing revealed religions, they could not conceive of a society enduring without some religious belief. Their English master John Locke had refused toleration to atheists — their oaths and covenants would have been meaningless. The idea of God was retained because, as Hume understood so well, men knew no other way of naming the unifying principle of the natural and moral order.

With the momentary triumph of anticlericalism in the early stages of the Revolution and the sudden institutional breakdown of the Catholic church, men were confronted with a religious vacuum. The first impact of this novel condition shocked the revolutionaries into a realization that the abhorrent society of atheists might become a fact. Could there be a godless society? What was to come after Catholicism? [2] The solutions which sprang up overnight were as numerous as the mystery cults sweeping the Mediterranean basin in the first centuries of the Christian era. In a decade a profusion of state-sponsored religions was spawned: a reformed Catholicism administered by a juring clergy, a worship of Reason, a cult of the Supreme Being, a *Culte Décadaire*,[3] a weed patch of theophilanthropic cults. Except for the denatured official Catholicism, they all had a crucial element in common — they represented in one form or another a deflection of love from the God of the Christians to mankind and a transfer of interest from the future of the immortal soul to man's destiny on earth. Their ceremonials were an admixture of Masonic ritual and Roman civic religious performances, with a residue of orthodox Catholic practice. The fervid patriotism of the revolutionaries assumed quasi-religious garb as the great popular celebrations, organized by the state for the first time in modern history, imitated the majesty of religious observance. Saint-Simon knew intimately leaders of the revolutionary cults, which in turn enjoyed governmental sanction for a brief moment as substitutes for the old religion, and he could not escape their influence.

While most of these synthetic religions tended to be rationalistic in tenor, there was another trend in the religious life of France which derived directly from the mystics of the prerevolutionary decades, particularly from the *illuminati*. Saint-Simon lived in many different social worlds during the revolutionary era, he learned the aphoristic language of the mystics, and on occasion he adorned his religious doctrine with apocalyptic visions written in their affected style.

After the turn of the century the *émigré* thinkers made a valiant attempt to resurrect and reinvigorate the old Catholic faith of France by an appeal to "sentiment." In this counterrevolutionary crusade the theocratic school was influenced by a romantic spirit which had drawn from diverse sources; and their writings in turn swelled the stream of a romantic religious revival of Catholicism. The idea of a society bereft of religious sanction was as terrifying to men at the turn of the century as it had been to the prerevolutionary *philosophes*. Madame de Staël calling for a new religion to fill the spiritual void and the Counts de Bonald and Joseph de Maistre demanding a strengthened papal Catholicism cleansed of eighteenth-century rationalism were expressing their common dread of a godless world.[4]

For a quarter of a century Saint-Simon lived with the problem of finding a new absolute to replace the Catholic monotheism which he condemned as outmoded. When in 1808 he used the phrase *unité systématique* to define his theory, he admitted that he and the contemporary traditionalists of the Catholic revival were aiming for the same goal. While he could not accept the Catholic thinkers' *exaltation pour le déisme* (which in his private language meant revealed religion), he recognized that he and they were both inspired by a passion for unity expressed in a religious form.[5]

Saint-Simon's own solution to the religious dilemma of the age was syncretic. It was a combination of ideas derived from two thinkers who were almost three hundred years apart, the Elizabethan Francis Bacon and the contemporary *idéologue* François Dupuis. Bacon's influence, the more remote, was evident in the mechanics of the new religion rather than in its spirit. The sacerdocy of scientists on *New Atlantis* was reincarnated in the scientific priesthood of the Religion of Newton; the ritual prescribed in the *Lettres d'un habitant de Genève* bore more than passing resemblance to the practices of the scientists in Salomon's House in Bacon's utopia.[6] To François Dupuis, whose voluminous work, *L'Origine de tous les cultes ou religion universelle*, first published in 1795, enjoyed widespread reputation among the *idéologues* and was abstracted and commented upon by no less a figure than Destutt de Tracy, Saint-Simon owed a more direct debt, his conception of religion as the generalized expression of the state of science at a given epoch of human development.[7]

Dupuis's study in comparative religion purported to prove that the myths, fables, tales, dramas, and epics of the pagan religions as well as Christianity were conscious dramatizations of the planetary movements and allegorical descriptions of heavenly constellations composed by priests. The prerevolutionary *philosophes* had regarded sacred writings as a compendium of nonsense, or at best as works of the imagination. Dupuis saw the phenomenon of religion too widespread throughout the world and the myths of various religions too patently similar to be mere universal delirium. They had to have a rationale, for all phenomena in nature, including myths, were founded on reason. "The moral world, like the physical world, has fixed laws whose reign can be recognized even in the greatest aberrations." [8] The myths of all religions were, he concluded, merely expressions of physical science, the ancient, hieratic knowledge of astronomy and physics preserved by priestly bodies.

Christianity was the most difficult religion to integrate into his system. While the origins of the oriental and north European pagan cults were lost in the dim past and hence amenable to the broadest conjectures, Christianity had been born in historic times when documents were available. Yet here, too, Dupuis maintained that like the cults it overthrew, Christianity was in its essence a formulation in allegorical terms of the truths of astronomy and physics. In many ways his theory leveled a more devastating attack on traditional Christianity than had the *philosophes*.

We shall destroy with one and the same blow the errors of the people and those of the new philosophers and we shall strip Christ of his two natures at the same time. The people made of him at once a God and a Man; the philosopher today makes of him nothing more than a Man. As for us, we shall not make of him a God at all; still less a man than a God, for the Sun is further from human nature than it is from the divine nature.

Christ will be for us what Hercules, Osiris, Adonis, and Bacchus were. He will share in common with them the worship which all peoples of all countries and all ages have rendered to universal nature and to its principal agents; and if he seems to assume a mortal body, like the heroes of the ancient poems, this will be only the fiction of a legend.[9]

Although nobody today takes seriously the Dupuis work with its pretentious scholarly apparatus, it helps to make Saint-Simon's Religion of Newton and his later redefinitions of Christianity comprehensible. The religions of antiquity, Christianity among them, were for Dupuis primarily solar religions, because the sun then appeared to be the principal, life-giving agent in the world. Since Newton had revealed a new scientific principle which explained all phenomena both in the heavens and on earth, since gravity was the one cause of all movement throughout the universe, what more fitting than for Saint-Simon to transform gravity into the central principle of a new religion, even as the sun once had been made the key figure in the older cults. Religion was a universal and eternal manifestation; while the ancients, who knew no better, had sun cults, Saint-Simon, like a modern Chaldean priest, would bestow upon humanity a Religion of Newton appropriate to its mature scientific development.[10]

Under Dupuis's guidance, Saint-Simon defined his religion as that ideal expression of the human spirit which afforded the optimum formal order for contemporaneous scientific knowledge. Instead of viewing religion as locked in mortal combat with the new science, he came to regard religion in its innermost essence as a synthesis and distillation into a unity of the whole body of scientific thought. What he demanded of the institutional leaders of contemporary religion was that they cease to conceive of it as a set of fixed and changeless dogmas and regard it instead as a spiritual form evolving throughout the ages. In 1813 he put into Chancellor Bacon's mind his own ideas on the relations between science and the Christian religion.

"Religion was not and could not be, in the eyes of a man with as good a head as Bacon's, anything but the general theory of science. Now the sole purpose of a theory is to relate facts to one another. Fifteen hundred years had passed since this theory [Christianity] had been organized. It was not astonishing that it should find itself inadequate to dispose in the best arrangement the knowledge which mankind possessed fifteen hundred years later, and it was impossible for it to relate facts which had been discovered only after its establishment." [11] Religion had to keep pace with science, and since religion had a tendency to lag, periodic renovations were in order. True religion was the philosophy of science of the age.

In the *Introduction aux travaux scientifiques du xixe siècle*, religion, discussed in a different context, appeared as a utilitarian social function, particularly necessary for the masses, rather akin to the footman's God of

Voltaire.[12] Saint-Simon was not even certain that the idea of God would always be necessary in the age of science. Physicism, his new name for the religion of science, could ultimately dispense with the idea of God. For the transitional epoch he nevertheless considered it expedient to preserve God.

"I say that I think I have proved that the idea of God does not at all need to be employed in physical sciences, but I do not say that it should not serve a purpose in political combinations, at least for a long time. This is the best method one has found to motivate lofty legislative dispositions." [13]

More and more he identified religion as a political instrument, a governmental technique for the effective maintenance of power over the people. "Religion is the collection of the applications of general science by means of which enlightened men govern ignorant men. . . ." [14] And since religion was an agency of the state, it had to be refurbished from time to time like all other institutions which tended to become set in their ways and blind to new truths.

"Every religion in the beginning is a beneficent institution. Its priests abuse it when they are no longer restrained by the check of opposition, when they have no more discoveries to make in the scientific direction which they received from their founder. It then becomes oppressive. When religion has been oppressive it falls into disrepute and its ministers lose the public esteem and the fortune which they had acquired." [15]

In 1808 Saint-Simon suddenly became aware that the dominant Christian revealed religion (which he insisted on calling Deism) had fallen into a hopeless state of decadence. This represented a grave immediate danger for the social order. The former anticlerical became agitated lest the official Catholic religion crumble completely before his own Physicism was in a position to assume its full responsibilities in the world. He dreaded the hiatus, the period during which society might be left without religious sanction or support. In the *Introduction aux travaux scientifiques du xixe siècle*, he expressed the hope that after Napoleon's death the spiritual power would be separated from the temporal and vested in a "Pope and a clergy of physical scientists." [16] Saint-Simon seemed absorbed with the preservation of a sacerdotal body as an institutional form, as a social safeguard against the menacing flood-tide of anarchy.

For the critical transition period before the acceptance of Physicism, he finally came upon a religious formula which could prevent the total breakdown of popular belief. His physician friend from Alençon, Dr. Bougon, had suggested the coexistence of two systems: one for the educated and another for the masses, Physicism for the élite and Deism for the ignorant. His perennial historical analogy to the crisis of the nineteenth century, the period from Socrates to Christ, provided justification for a two-headed religion in one society. As Saint-Simon read history, in the centuries after Socrates the upper classes were already monotheists, while the lower classes remained polytheists. A similar duality would now be repeated. He therefore found himself converted to Napoleon's religious policy of making concordats with the various creeds or "deist sects," since the opportune moment for the proclamation of Physicism had not yet arrived.[17] He confessed that he had only recently appreciated the need for a double standard in religion, he who had once belonged to the militant antireligious school. The emperor had enlightened him. As a consequence of this new comprehension of the complexity of the religious problem, he had resolved to adopt a circumspect attitude towards public expressions on the subject of religion.

My conduct is in conformity with my opinions. I am working to perfect Physicism, but I do not publish my ideas. I communicate them only to persons sufficiently enlightened to look at things from this viewpoint without there resulting any inconvenience for society. I do not put my works on sale. I do not have them discussed in the newspapers. I have them printed, but I order only a very small number of copies, and I place them in safe hands alone. Finally, I overtly respect Deism as the public doctrine which is and should yet be for a long time. I say that this is my present behavior and I am telling the truth. But I do not say that this has always been my conduct. Until the period when the dispositions of the emperor removed the cataract which was blinding me, I followed a completely contrary course.[18]

The *Nouvelle encyclopédie* (1810) reiterated the principle of the double standard in religion. "Philosophy prohibits the belief in God to the man who devotes himself to lofty scientific researches but it prescribes a profession of faith, of belief in God when he publishes his discoveries. For those persons who cannot rise to the combination of the great abstractions cannot stop believing in God without there resulting the greatest inconveniences for themselves and for the social order." [19]

Saint-Simon's new conception of religion was expressed most fulsomely in a letter of 1810 to his nephew, Victor Saint-Simon. In this epistolary sermon three ideas stand out: religion is an eternal attribute of human consciousness; the forms of religion are subject to variation in time; a society without religion is inconceivable.

Religion, my nephew, has always served and will always serve as the basis for social organization. This truth is incontestable; but it is not more certain than the axiom: for man there is nothing absolute in the world. There exist for him only relative things.

From these two principles taken together I deduce the consequence that while religion has always existed and will always exist, it always modified itself and it will always modify itself in such a manner that it always has been and always will be in harmony with the level of enlightenment.

Let us pass to another type of reflection. Let us examine the matter from the standpoint of experience. The study of history will prove to you, my nephew, that humanity has always found itself in a scientific, moral, and political crisis when the religious idea was being modified.

Let us finally consider the present state of affairs. We shall see that they are in a state of scientific, moral, and political crisis, and that this crisis is determined by the modification which is taking place in the religious idea.

In accordance with the insights, the reasoning, and the observations which I have just presented to you, I advise you, my nephew:

1. Always to profess a great respect for religion.

2. To keep yourself alert to adopt and to propagate the first good modification of the religious idea which is produced.

3. To become a zealous partisan of the first religious innovator who, marching along the road opened by Luther and pushing the reformation further than he did, will know how to extend in the religious sphere the domain of reason and to restrict within narrower limits revealed ideas. [To become a zealous partisan] of the innovator who will introduce into the seminaries the study of the sciences of observation, and who will reduce to as low a level as possible the teaching of the theological sciences; of the innovator, finally, who will succeed in putting an end to the existing division in the Church and who will strive to reconstitute the Papacy, the conclaves, and the councils, giving them an organization in harmony with the present state of enlightenment.[20]

To silence those "superficial and superstitious minds" who accused him of atheism, Saint-Simon published his credo. "To the tribunal of the emperor I shall summon them. At the foot of the throne they shall listen to me make my profession of faith. I believe in God. I believe that God has created the universe. I believe that God has submitted the universe to the law of gravity." [21] This was his overt profession of orthodoxy.

Whatever the motives behind Saint-Simon's great show of caution in discussing Physicism in public, he had been far from discreet in commenting privately upon the idea of traditional revealed religion to his scientific colleagues, most of whom held official posts in imperial institutions. In the spirit of *idéologue* materialism, he described the idea of God as nothing more than a generalization of the faculties of human intelligence. He arrayed a few hackneyed atheistic arguments purporting to show contradictions inherent in the idea of God and he affirmed the manifest superiority of Physicism, the new godless religion.

What is this idea called God without revelation? A sterile idea. Every scientific discovery has made evident another one of the errors of the supposed system of revelation. . . .

The idea of God lacks unity, because before presenting this idea to those who do not understand it one must first prove that there are two natures of things: one moral, the other physical, that one also calls things either material or immaterial. One says that God is of one of these two natures and that He is of only one of these two natures. In that event there cannot exist any relationship between Him and the things which are not of His nature.

The idea of God being vicious all the applications which have been made of this idea have had to be vicious. . . .

Physicism has none of these inconveniences of Deism.
This conception possesses the character of unity above all else. . . .[22]

In the *Mémoire sur la science de l'homme* of 1813, which remained in manuscript until long after his death, all forms of revealed religion were treated in the same critical tone, but he was wary as ever of any abrupt public breach with official religion. Still trying to devise techniques for effecting a smooth passage from Deism to Physicism, he clung to Dr. Bougon's idea that for periods of transition there had to be both an esoteric and an exoteric religious doctrine.

The belief of those who are working towards the perfection of the scientific system should not be the same as that of the mob. Persons devoted by profession to the cultivation of the sciences should believe that the universe is governed by a single law. They should study this general law and the secondary laws which derive from it for their own happiness, for that of the scientists, and for the maintenance of order in society. The mob should believe that the universe is governed by an all powerful being, that this being, that this God made himself man, that he revealed to his apostles what is important for man to know.

Scientists should modify the language of revelation in such a manner that they always put into the mouth of God the best scientific *résumés* which they have obtained as a result of their works.[23]

In the *Travail sur la gravitation universelle*, written the same year, the dissolution of religious bonds loomed before him as the greatest of all evils, even more horrible than religious wars. He prepared a Proclamation of the First Pope of the New Scientific Theory, a truncated cry in the dark, for his manuscript broke off in the middle of a sentence.

"Europe still preserves a bitter memory of the Thirty Years' War. Wars of religion are, they say, the most cruel. Truly they are cruel, but not as cruel as the war which has as its goal the breaking of the religious bond, since this destruction plunges the human species back into the state of nature which is a state of continuous war. And indeed. . . ."[24]

Both the coördinative principle of universal gravity and the rather mechanical Religion of Science were among his most sterile conceptions. They are more significant as expressions of his inner passionate longing for a haven of certainty in the midst of his distractions than as creative ideas. The search for "the system" and his faith in science remained characteristic features of his thought, but in later years they were clothed with more brilliant vestments than these arid and jejune excursions into godless theology. During the Empire period there was intellectual vitality in his theory of the evolution of the sciences, in his reflections on the nature of the science of man, in his idea of perfectibility, and in his over-all concept of the historical process. The Science of Man rather than religion was the world into which he had piercing insight.

10

Towards a Positive Science of Man

WHEN SAINT-SIMON APPLIED THE TERM "POSITIVE" to science in general or to his system in particular, he meant the elimination of mysterious origins and final causes. He nowhere analyzed the problem of causality itself. Positive, real science, as he understood it, implied abandonment of any attempt to dwell upon essences. This was the spirit of *idéologue* scientists, still under the tutelage of their philosophical mentor, the Abbé Condillac. Laplace had assumed this position in the opening pages of the *Exposition du système du monde* (1796): ". . . First causes and the intrinsic nature of beings will remain eternally unknown to us." [1] Cabanis had been equally explicit in proclaiming that man could not comprehend the essence of anything. It was an article of faith among the *idéologue* scientists to exhibit a militant indifference to the first cause of phenomena as long as they could study their laws. Universal gravity was a law of general science for Saint-Simon in the Condillac-Cabanis sense, neither a first cause, nor an essence, nor a definition of the nature of things.

At the beginning of the nineteenth century many of the major scientific disciplines had not yet emerged as "positive sciences," exact and experimental, free from reliance on authority, from superstition, metaphysics, and mysticism. In 1807 only astronomy, physics, and chemistry were universally recognized as exact sciences, and chemistry itself had but recently received its basic theory from Lavoisier. The grouping of the scientists in the first two Classes of the Institute — before the Napoleonic reorganization of 1803 — is probably the best index of current opinion on the proper distribution of the various fields of knowledge, though it was by no means generally approved in Europe.[2] The life sciences had no sharply demarcated boundaries, not even botany and zoology, let alone human physiology. Lamarck's famous paper on the transformist theory, delivered on May 11, 1800, at the Museum of Natural History, an early attempt to provide zoology with a conceptual framework, was hardly accepted as sound scientific doctrine.[3] As for the social sciences, the terms physiology, psychology, analysis of ideas and sensations, anthropology, ideology, political economy, political arithmetic, the science of government, *art social*, morals, moral sciences, and science of man were employed indiscriminately, with no consensus as to their meaning, to describe different facets of the study of man and society.[4]

The construction of a total system of positive knowledge required as a preliminary condition a more precise definition of the various sciences, especially those new sciences which dealt with man. From the very beginning it was vital to demonstrate the close interrelationship of all the sciences, for the establishment of that interrelationship would facilitate the final acceptance of the idea that all were subject to a single law. Hence Saint-Simon's passionate interest in a plan for a new encyclopedia, which he represented in a lithograph as a tree of all the sciences, with branches and shoots merging into a trunk labeled General Science.[5] D'Alembert's *Discours préliminaire* to the *Encyclopédie* which had divided all knowledge in accordance with Bacon's scheme in the *Novum Organum*[6] and had mechanically distributed the sciences under three separate headings — those of memory, reason, and imagination — had blindly neglected to emphasize their manifold interconnexities. The Diderot *Encyclopédie* was not sufficiently "organic" — that was its fatal error.

It is difficult to know just what this word "organic" connotes in Saint-Simon's writings.[7] The adjective had become current in the scientific and the philosophical vocabulary of a good number of late eighteenth-century European writers. In Herder's *History of Man* it often appeared in phrases like "living, organic power," a "principle . . . innate, organical, genetic."[8] Saint-Simon invested it with a meaning rather distinct from that of the German philosophers, for whom it had vague mystical overtones. In his philosophy of science praise for the "organic" implied an attack on the eighteenth-century *philosophes* because their encyclopedia had chopped up knowledge into discrete compartments instead of integrating it. He wanted somehow to express the essential wholeness and unity of knowledge, to reveal the common elements in the sciences and their dependence upon one another. He was a man of the transition between the rationalist metaphysical systematizers and the new philosophical romanticism, and he lived in both intellectual worlds. On the one hand he sought desperately for a first principle from which by reasoning alone every scientific fact both in the physical and social sciences could be deduced in the "geometric manner." On the other hand he longed to represent the sciences as an organic reality, a whole which was perhaps more than the sum of its constituent parts. His two philosophical personalities were never successfully fused. Like many of the *idéologues*, he was less of a "positive" scientist than he imagined.

When he viewed the world organically it was not only the essential unity of the sciences which he sought to communicate, but a sense of their common growth and natural evolution. In the new metaphor which his school of thought made common coin the sciences were related to one another as the parts of a living organism, and like other living beings, they evolved organically. The Institute reorganized by the Revolution and the great educational establishments of the Directorate and the Empire had divided the sciences into classes, and scientific specialists in each class deliberated in separate bodies. From the beginning of his philosophical career, Saint-Simon was possessed by the belief that this was not the way of knowledge, that science was thus being broken up into bits and pieces. All of his early "projects" were aimed at persuading the major scientists in the several fields to coöperate with one another in common enterprises for the progress of science as a living whole. (Helping to work out the details of his system was perhaps the worthiest enterprise they could undertake.)

The very organization of the Institute in 1795 was a partial realization of the Bacon-Condorcet conception [9] which Saint-Simon had adopted in his first projects and it is therefore not necessary to seek further than the actuality of the scientific hierarchy in France for the origin of some of his ideas. But there is a basic difference as well as a similarity. The official classification in the Institute highlighted the dichotomy between the mathematical-physical sciences and the moral and political sciences, while for Saint-Simon the heart of the matter was the interrelationship and interdependence of all the sciences.[10] To the concept of the unity of science most of the secretaries of the Institute Classes gave lip service in their inaugural addresses, while in their work they proceeded to concern themselves with restricted areas of research. Saint-Simon, who was not burdened by a scientific profession, was free to dream of the abstraction of general science.

The idea of integral coöperation among scientists of the highest echelons remained one of Saint-Simon's *idées maîtresses,* and it became the rock upon which his theory of the role of an intellectual élite in society was built. Saint-Simon anticipated that one of the early achievements of coöperation among scientists would be an accelerated development of that new Science of Man which in his day was still lagging behind in a rather amorphous state. The *Lettres d'un habitant de Genève* had already included a number of passages which forecast the imminent emergence of the social sciences into the status of full-fledged exact sciences (he did not use the word "positive" until 1807). There too he first hinted at the idea of the hierarchy of the sciences by describing the successive emancipation from superstition and metaphysics of the astronomical (including physics), the chemical, and the physiological sciences, an embryonic version of the Positivist theory:

The period of which I speak (the most memorable in the history of the development of the human spirit) is the one when astronomers drove out the astrologers from their midst. I must make another remark on this subject. Since that time astronomers have become good modest people who no longer try to appear to know what they are ignorant of. And you [the people] on your part have stopped making of them the impertinent request that they read your destiny in the stars.

Since chemical phenomena are more complicated than astronomical phenomena, man did not busy himself with them until long afterwards. In the study of chemistry man fell into the same errors that he had committed in the study of astronomy. But ultimately the chemists got rid of the alchemists.

Physiology is still in the unfortunate position through which the astrological [sic] and chemical sciences have passed. The physiologists have now to expel from their midst the *philosophers*, the *moralists*, and the *metaphysicians*, just as the astronomers drove out the astrologers and the chemists the alchemists.

. . . . The main function of philosophers, moralists, and metaphysicians is to study the relationship between phenomena that are called physical and those called moral. When they become successful in this branch of their work it should be called physiology. But they also try to tie all the observed facts together into a general system. I am convinced that this will not be possible until physiology reaches the stage which I described with reference to astronomy.[11]

In the *Introduction aux travaux scientifiques du xixᵉ siècle* (1808), the *Travail sur la gravitation universelle* (1813), and the *Mémoire sur la science de l'homme* (1813), he elaborated these sketchy ideas on the development of new positive sciences with greater detail. The most complete exposition appeared in a number of lengthy passages of the *Mémoire*.[12] Saint-Simon there set down what Dr. Burdin, attached to the Armies of the Republic, is supposed to have said to him in a conversation in 1798 during the Directorate.[13] The two men no doubt had once had many discussions on the nature of science, the course which it had followed in the past, and what might be expected of its future progress, even before they had met again during Saint-Simon's psychic breakdown in 1812–1813. Though Burdin's medical works, which were published with Saint-Simon's aid in 1803, make some reference to philosophical conceptions,[14] most of what we know of his theories was transmitted by his friend. It is reasonable to assume that Saint-Simon interjected many of his own ideas in the report of their historic colloquy when he recorded it fifteen years later. Putting his own thoughts into the mouth of Socrates or Bacon or some other eminent historical personage was a favorite literary device with him. There was already a feeble echo of the Burdin doctrine in the letters *A la Société du Lycée* and the *Lettres d'un habitant de Genève*. But whoever is the originator of the following propositions, they are among the earliest formal expressions of European Positivism.

"All sciences began by being conjectural. The great order of things has ordained that they shall all become positive. Astronomy began by being astrology; chemistry was in its origins nothing but alchemy; physiology, which for a long time floundered about in charlatanry, today rests on observed and verified facts; psychology is beginning to base itself on physiology and to rid itself of the religious prejudices on which it was founded." [15]

Why were the sciences conjectural at the beginning? Simply because there were not enough verified facts which had been examined and tested over a long period of time to make them positive. The theories of the sciences were then mere presumptions, guesses. In the future, with more experimentation and observation, all knowledge was destined to become positive.

The physical sciences did not pass from their conjectural to their positive states simultaneously. They made their appearance in a set order which was by no means fortuitous. To ferret out the law of this succession was important, because if the controlling principle of the order were discovered it could become the key to future scientific progress. The particular order of emergence was based upon the essential nature of each of the sciences.

"Astronomy [the term included physics and mechanics] being the science in which one looks at facts in their simplest and least numerous relationships, is the first which had to acquire a positive character. Chemistry had to follow astronomy and precede physiology, because it considers the action of matter in relationships which are more complex than astronomy and less detailed than physiology." [16]

Thus the simplest came first in the series, followed by the more complex. This was the kind of formula which appealed to common sense. Men apparently had to accustom themselves to the more elementary scientific phenomena before they could tackle really complicated manifestations of nature like man and society. Burdin's doctrine bears an intellectual affinity to eighteenth-century ideas about the great chain of being, which saw in nature a hierarchy from the simplest objects of creation to man, the most complex.[17] Hypotheses about the evolution of the species, which were current in France and England during the last decades of the eighteenth century, also had a number of component ideas identical with Burdin's theory of the evolution of the sciences, the most striking of which was the common notion of progression in time from the simple to the complex.[18] Even as man was the ultimate achievement of the evolutionary process, the science of man was about to climax the whole development of positive science. Burdin named the science of man physiology — which for him encompassed what are now the disciplines of anatomy, physiology, psychology, and history.

"Physiology does not yet deserve to be classed among the positive sciences; but it has only one step to make before it raises itself completely above the level of the conjectural sciences. The first man of genius who appears in this scientific field will found the general theory of this science upon observed facts. Almost all one has to do to formulate the general theory of physiology is to pull together the works of Vicq-d'Azyr, of Cabanis, of Bichat, and of Condorcet, because these four authors treated almost all the important physiological questions, and they based all the theories they produced on observations which had been verified." [19]

When the theory of physiology was perfected as a consequence of a successful synthesis of the outstanding French anatomist, psychologist, physiologist, and philosophical historian, it would become a full-fledged positive Science of Man.[20] The application of this new science would immediately revolutionize the basic institutions of European civilization.

1. The teaching of physiology will be introduced into public education. I base my conjecture in this respect on the observation that each of the physical sciences has been introduced into public education as soon as it became positive.

2. Morals will become a positive science. The physiologist is the only scientist who is in a position to demonstrate that in every case the path of virtue is at the same time the road to happiness. The moralist who is not a physiologist can only demonstrate the reward of virtue in another world, because he cannot treat questions of morality with enough precision.

3. Politics will become a positive science. When those who cultivate this important branch of human knowledge will have learned physiology during the course of their education, they will no longer consider the problems which they have to solve as anything but questions of hygiene.

4. Philosophy will become a positive science. The weakness of human intelligence has obliged man to establish in the sciences a division between general science and individual sciences. General science or philosophy has as its elementary facts the general facts of the individual sciences, or, if you like, the individual sciences are the elements of general science. This science, which can never have any other character than that of its elements, was conjectural as long as the individual sciences were. It became semiconjectural and semipositive when some of the individual sciences became positive, the others still remaining conjectural. Such is the present state of affairs. It will become positive when physiology is based in its entirety on observed facts, because there exists no phenomenon which cannot be observed either from the viewpoint of the physics of inorganic bodies or the physics of organic bodies, which is physiology.

5. The religious system will be perfected. Dupuis in his work on the origin of cults has demonstrated to the point where it is obvious that all the known religions were based on a scientific system, and that any reorganization of the scientific system will bring in its train the reorganization and improvement of the religious system.

6. The clergy will be reorganized and reconstituted. A religious system is divided into two parts: one is the passive part and the other is the active part; or rather one is the theoretical part and the other is the practical part. The coördination of principles constitutes the first, the organization of those who apply the principles constitutes the second part. These two parts are intimately related to each other, are dependent each on the other, in such a manner that the improvement of the principles brings with it an improvement in the education of the clergy and a better composition of the clergy produces a perfection in the intrinsic value and in the coördination of the principles. But it is always a perfection of the principles which initiates and reinitiates any movement which, for a period of time of greater or less duration, then becomes alternating and reciprocal. The clergy will therefore necessarily reorganize itself when the system of ideas, the religious

principle, is reorganized. But we have seen above that the passive religious system was nothing but the materialization of a scientific system (as Dupuis has shown). Thus the reorganization of the clergy can only mean the reorganization of the scientific corps, because the clergy must be the scientific corps. The clergy can only be useful, can only have strength, as long as it is composed of the most knowledgeable men, as long as the principles which it knows are unknown to the common people.[21]

Here was the crux of the Positivist faith and its characteristic form of reasoning. Most of Saint-Simon's philosophic ideas are contained in embryo in this Burdin conversation. Since the other sciences had developed in accordance with a set pattern, why not the life sciences? From its origins, his Positivism was based on the dogmatic assertion that the method of the physical sciences was applicable to the social sciences. The burden of proof seemed to lie on those who believed that the social sciences would follow some path divergent from that of the other positive sciences whose progression in a series had been so orderly.

Saint-Simon foresaw "an epoch when the philosophy which will be taught in the schools will be positive." [22] Thus in 1813 he already had the conception of a "positive philosophy," [23] with a connotation not unlike its meaning in Auguste Comte's *Cours de philosophie positive* (1830–1842), though in Saint-Simon it was still primarily a descriptive phrase, not a detailed system. The same holds true for his *aperçus* about positive politics and positive religion, which Comte elaborated into the *Système de politique positive* (1851–1854), a full-blown Positivist system of religion and morals. The germ of all these ideas was sown in the same *Mémoire sur la science de l'homme.*

"One realizes that systems of religion, of general politics, of morals, of public education are nothing but applications of the system of ideas, or, if one prefers, that it is the system of thought considered from various angles. Thus it is obvious that after the completion of the new scientific system there will be a reorganization of the systems of religion, of general politics, of morals, and of public education, and that consequently the clergy will be reorganized." [24]

The final step in the positive reorganization of society would be the elimination of national boundaries and the creation of a European Union.

"One realizes that national organizations are individual applications of general ideas on the social order and that the reorganization of the general system of European politics will bring in its train the national reorganization of the various peoples who, by their political union, form that great society." [25]

Saint-Simon did not use the term sociology — it is Comte's neologism combining Latin and Greek roots in a clumsy name — preferring variants like the science of man, the science of society, physiology, social physiology, the science of politics. He would have attacked the modern segmentation of the science of man into separate disciplines. He did not differentiate among the branches of the social sciences, and his terminology was consistently loose and even vague throughout his writings. At times he reverted to the term "moral sciences" in the eighteenth-century sense, and subsumed under it everything related to man and society.

Saint-Simon never wrote anything about the character of the individual physical sciences worth serious analysis, and this immediately distinguishes him from his disciple Auguste Comte. Some of his brochures published privately during the Napoleonic period contain passages which are arrant nonsense, especially when he spins out scientific theories at random like an alchemist trying all sorts of combinations. The rational element in these portions of his work is too thin to deserve exposition. We know that these theoretical eccentricities exist; relating them, as one might, to the scientific beliefs of the day would not be rewarding. On the whole the wildest of his pseudo-scientific lucubrations have to be ignored.

But from the murky confusions of Saint-Simon's writings in the period before 1814 one idea stands out with striking clarity — that the dominant preconceptions of the Science of Man were to be biological and not mathematical. In effect this meant that the science of society would be evolutionary and historical rather than mechanistic. In this respect Saint-Simon gave expression to one of the fundamental shifts in thought from the eighteenth to the nineteenth century. In 1802, in his project for a world-wide election of the outstanding priest-scientists, the mathematicians were ensconced at the apex of the scientific hierarchy as they would be in a Newtonian eighteenth-century world. Very much in the spirit of Condorcet, he still thought of mathematics as the foundation of all sciences, including the social sciences. Condorcet's tenth epoch of the *Esquisse* and his other fragments on the progress of science always envisaged some form of mathematics — statistics or calculus — as the key method of the social sciences. The widespread application of the calculus of probabilities to moral phenomena, he anticipated, would lead to momentous developments in the study of man and society. By 1813 Saint-Simon had made an abrupt departure from this subordination of social sciences to the method of mathematics. He attacked the *brutiers*, the inorganic scientists, for their failure to deal with the moral crisis of the times, proof to him that they had nothing to contribute to a science of man. His parting thrust at the mathematical scientists, "those sorry calculators ensconced behind their rampart of X and Z," was full of disdain. He pushed them angrily from the eminence to which they had been raised in the *Lettres d'un habitant de Genève*.

. . . My blood boils, rage possesses me. . . . What right have you at this point to occupy the position of scientific advance guard? The human species is involved in one of the severest crises it has ever experienced since the beginning of its existence. What efforts have you made to terminate this crisis? What methods have you adopted to reëstablish order in human society?. . . . In all the armies you are found at the head of the artillery. It is you who supervise the works in laying a siege. What are you doing, I ask again, to reëstablish peace? — Nothing. — What can you do? — Nothing. The knowledge of man is alone capable of leading us to find ways of conciliating the interests of peoples and you do not study this science. You have taken only one of its observations — that by flattering those who have power one obtains their favor and shares in their munificence. Leave the direction of the scientific workshop. Allow us to warm its heart which has become frozen under your presidency and allow us to recall its entire attention to works which may bring back general peace by reorganizing society. Leave the presidency. We are going to fill it in your place.[26]

Having thus dismissed the mathematical scientists as base sycophants who cravenly served the most destructive elements in European society, Saint-Simon now placed his reliance on the life sciences, which in the last decades of the eighteenth century and under the Empire had experienced a remarkable efflorescence. He proclaimed the closer affinity of the science of society with biological phenomena rather than with mechanics. Society was a living organism, not a machine.[27] The proper handmaidens for the new science of society would be physiology and psychology, not mathematics.

11

The Law of Alternativity

NAPOLEON HAD POSED THE PROBLEM to the Institute: "Render me an account of the progress of science since 1789; tell me what its present state is, and what means should be employed to make it achieve great progress."[1] In due course his official scientists had transmitted their rather pedestrian fawning reports.[2] They were unworthy of the great Napoleon, wrote the outraged Saint-Simon; the transcendent question of the age merited a more profound analysis. Napoleon's command involved penetrating to the innermost secret of the history of modern science — an idea he had hinted at in the letters to the *Société du Lycée* — for only an understanding of the basic law of scientific development in the past would make it possible to respond adequately to the Napoleonic challenge, to predict, to prescribe the direction science should follow in the future. To Saint-Simon this succinct question was more than a mere scientific inquiry; it was central to the whole idea of progress, because the scientific revolution, the great seminal force of modern times, was the prime mover which sparked all other revolutions. Since the official scientists had failed their emperor, Saint-Simon undertook to step into the breach. By 1808 he saw in Napoleon not only a military leader but the scientific chief of humanity. "In one hand he holds the infallible compass; in the other the exterminating sword against the opponents of the progress of knowledge. About his throne the most illustrious scientists of the earth should group themselves, even as the most valiant captains."[3] Saint-Simon would illuminate the future of science for Napoleon by revealing the true principle of its historical evolution.

In sketching the history of modern science Saint-Simon began with the Arabs. To Konrad Oelsner,[4] a contemporary German philologist and historian who wrote in French, he owed his appreciation of the influence of Arab science upon the European mind and his emancipation from the stereotyped attack against the Middle Ages in d'Alembert, Condorcet, Cabanis, and the other *philosophes* and *idéologues*. His was an early, though by no means unique, appreciation of the role of the Arabs in the diffusion of scientific ideas. Oelsner had once told him: "The Europeans (forming the scientific advance guard of the human species) followed the direction given by Socrates up to the period when the Arabs conceived of looking for the laws which order the universe, making an abstraction out of the idea that an animate cause governs it. The Arabs guided the human spirit in the land of discovery until the fifteenth century, the time when the Europeans drove them out of Spain and surpassed them intellectually in their effort to discover the one law to which the universe was subject." [5] Thereafter Europeans built upon the Arab discoveries, particularly in astronomy and medicine, and became the central figures of world science.

Saint-Simon's account of the modern European scientific revolution which was outlined in the *Introduction aux travaux scientifiques du xixᵉ siècle* and the *Mémoire sur la science de l'homme* was a popularized, not too well-informed history of the contributions of individual scientific geniuses from Copernicus on, written by a man with no technical scientific or philosophical training. There are numerous traces of adaptations from the historical appraisals of scientists and philosophers written by Turgot and Condorcet. But in differentiating among the scientists in his roster, in typing them, he introduced a novel conception. These geniuses were not all men of the same cut; they were divided into two fundamental classes: those who reasoned *a priori*, or as he said "synthetically," and those who reasoned *a posteriori*, or "analytically." By these terms he distinguished between the philosophical generalizers, men who prepared grand systems of scientific and philosophical thought, and the particularizers, the specialists who performed a series of isolated experiments. It is not difficult to identify the rather commonplace origin of this terminology, twisted in singular fashion by Saint-Simon. The *a priori* and *a posteriori* were obviously a derivation from Bacon's ideas, probably in the form used by d'Alembert in the *Discours préliminaire* of the encyclopedia. Saint-Simon revered Bacon as the initiator of the modern scientific revolution for his epochal discovery of the distinction between these two methods of thought.[6] From the *Discours* itself he probably borrowed also the terms "synthesis" and "analysis." As for his actual description of the thought processes implicit in these two methods, they bear a certain remote resemblance to Galileo's *metodo compositivo* and *metodo risolutivo* (Though Saint-Simon often expressed great admiration for Galileo, he never quoted any of his works directly and very likely never read them.)

What Saint-Simon did was to elevate these two contrasting methods to the level of a broad conceptual pattern of scientific development. The terms synthesis and analysis became in his writings more than mere labels for two different scientific procedures; they were adopted as characterizations of whole epochs in the progress of the modern scientific revolution. Scientific geniuses could not, either accidentally or in accordance with the exercise of

their own free choice, follow one or another method. There was a predetermined oscillation of phases in the history of modern science, during which
one or the other methodology predominated and bound the individual discoverer. This was the underlying law of the history of science: the necessary
alternativity of the *a priori* and the *a posteriori* methods in successive ages.

While Saint-Simon credited Bacon with the original insight into the
existence of this law, the first *a priori* synthesis achieved in modern times was
Descartes's, because he was the one "to proceed to the organization of a new
scientific system." Descartes appeared in the series of geniuses as the epoch-
making synthesizer of the discoveries of Copernicus, Galileo, and Kepler.
The Cartesian synthesis, the system of vortices, aroused in Saint-Simon an
extravagant admiration. In his mind it was the first great attempt to substitute observation and reason for theology and faith. In the *Introduction aux
travaux scientifiques du xixe siècle* Descartes was eulogized as the philosopher
who had embraced the world of nature and the world of man in one theoretical system, not the ultimate one to be sure, but the first in modern times.
The eighteenth-century *philosophes* had tended to discredit Cartesian rationalism in the name of the Baconian method of scientific observation.
Though by this time the controversy was dead, Saint-Simon fancied himself the rehabilitator of Descartes. (Ironically enough, in 1750 Descartes had
found refuge among the theologians of the Sorbonne.[7]) For Saint-Simon
absolute or exclusive devotion to one or the other method of science was not
the issue. Each was "relative" to its period of development. The idea of historical relativity both in the method of science and in the character of religion
is one of Saint-Simon's bold intuitions. He actually used the word *"relatif"*
in this new sense. Descartes was pursuing the appropriate scientific method
for his historic moment. Saint-Simon, the nineteenth-century Descartes, had
come after more than a century of particularizing analytic science to resume
the method of synthesis on a higher level. Today in the *Musée de l'homme* in
Paris their two skulls are fittingly displayed side by side as specimens of
genius.

Saint-Simon's estimate of Newton underwent a sharp change from 1802
to 1807. He pushed Newton as an individual off the pedestal to which he had
raised him in the *Lettres d'un habitant de Genève*, even though he doggedly
stuck by the law of gravity as the one universal principle of all science. The
rationale behind his glorification of Descartes at Newton's expense was a
realization that the English scientist was not as lofty a synthesizer as Descartes, that his method was essentially that of a lowly particularizer.[8] For all
Saint-Simon's scientific determinism, his belief in the operation of the iron
law of alternativity of synthesis and analysis to which all scientists were subject, he could not avoid betraying a predilection for the synthetic genius over
the analytic. Even though the methods of each were dictated by history, the
synthesizer performed the grander role. The transfer of allegiance from

Newton to Descartes was also politically expedient. In 1807, during the full fury of French military nationalism under Napoleon, it ill behooved the philosopher who sought the emperor's ear to find his idol among the citizens of perfidious Albion. Amid various disjointed pieces, puerilities about the changing proportion of solids and fluids in the universe in the second part of his *Introduction aux travaux scientifiques du xixe siècle*, he launched an open attack on Newton. "I have put myself into a rage against Newton in order to propel my thoughts. I see that the influence exercized by the shades of Newton is very harmful for the progress of science and I cry out with all my strength to my contemporaries, and to my countrymen in particular. It is time to change the route. It is on the *a priori* route that at the present time there are discoveries to be made." [9] But this rage was directed only against the protracted influence of the Newtonian method in the nineteenth century; in Newton's own day the *a posteriori* method had been fitting and proper. After Descartes, Locke and Newton were still the greatest scientists of modern times. In an imaginary conversation Locke and Newton discuss the necessity of tearing down the Cartesian system, because in their day it had outlived its usefulness as a scientific hypothesis.

"We must destroy the edifice constructed by Descartes. We must carefully preserve the materials which were employed in its construction. We must add new materials to those which will result from this demolition. We must labor at the discovery of new facts and postpone the construction of the edifice until the supply of materials is complete. In a word, it is necessary to stop approaching things *a priori* and to consider them *a posteriori*. We must for the moment abandon the synthetic movement and adopt the analytic movement." [10]

The passage does more than illustrate the alternativity principle; it points up another image, the characteristic upward spiral of the advancement of science as it moves through the cycles of synthesis and analysis. Locke-Newton not only tear down the old edifice, they add "new materials"; the accumulation of scientific data is constant through all the vicissitudes of history.

The eighteenth century, in Saint-Simon's judgment, had continued to labor in the shadow of the two analytic English scientists. In one section of the *Introduction aux travaux scientifiques du xixe siècle* he saw the whole of eighteenth-century science as neatly epitomized in four works (all of them French): two particularizing even further on Newton's discoveries, Lagrange's *Théorie des fonctions analytiques* and Laplace's *Traité de mécanique céleste*, and two particularizing further on Locke, Condillac's *Traité des sensations* and Condorcet's *Esquisse d'un tableau historique des progrès de l'esprit humain*. [11] The official scientific schools of France, he feared, were in his own day continuing to specialize and particularize more and more, a method that had grown sterile. Whatever grain of reason there was in his psychopathic attack on Laplace in the *Histoire de l'homme* was implanted in this theory of scientific development. The age of synthesis had dawned again and if the scientists wished to heed Napoleon's call they would collaborate with Saint-Simon on a new universal theory, abandoning the English school and returning to the great French tradition — back to Descartes.

Saint-Simon had thus found a way of settling the eighteenth-century controversy between the followers of Descartes and the followers of Locke-Newton, between those who espoused the superiority of the deductive method and those who extolled the virtues of induction. He accepted both methods and maintained that the scientific process, working itself out through the centuries, required the alternativity in time of the *a priori* and *a posteriori*. Since Descartes had generalized, the first genius who appeared after him had to particularize. Since Newton particularized, the first genius who appeared after him would generalize. And there was no doubt about his identity!

Saint-Simon made a rather feeble attempt to explain why this alternativity of the two methods was inherent in the nature of things, incidentally exhibiting one of the quirks of his thought processes. Like Fourier and so many other systematizers of the period he was addicted to reasoning by facile analogy. To illustrate the universality of the alternativity principle he resorted to homely analogies from nature. He compared it, for example, with the heartbeat: "To generalize, to particularize, are actions as necessary to the life of the mind as those of the systole and diastole are to physical life. These are faculties which the human brain exercizes alternately for equal lengths of time." [12] Or he drew the analogy of the pump: "When the piston is in the upper section of the pump, it must be lowered; when it is in the lower section it must be raised. It is its alternative movement from high to low and low to high which keeps the pump going." [13] He conjured up an image in which the man of the mountain represented synthesis, and men of the plain, analysis: "The domain of science may be considered like a country in the midst of which a great mountain rises. From the summit of this mountain a single man can cover the whole country. From the plain at least two persons are needed to grasp the totality of the objects which a single person discovers from the summit. If one supposes that Descartes put himself on the summit and that Newton and Locke put themselves in the plain, one will realize that the School [of Science] had only one guide in the seventeenth century and that it had two in the eighteenth. . . ." [14]

He sought to prove the necessary alternativity of scientific method by a comparison with the psychological reactions of an individual, one of his favorite analogies:

Our eyes grow tired when we look at things for a long time from the same point of view. We then stop discovering among them new relationships. We even stop perceiving clearly those relationships which we had once seen.

For almost a hundred years the School [of Science] considered things from an *a priori* viewpoint. The School was tired. The scientific eyes of humanity no longer had the faculty to perceive new relationships. Science had stopped making progress. Many principles were set forth but men drew no consequences from them. Systems were multiplied. The scientific workshop labored with ardor towards the organization of an ideal world and it neglected the study of the existing world. Men were occupied exclusively with metaphysics and they lost sight of the physical world completely. They no longer observed facts. At this point Locke and Newton started to write.[15]

By the nineteenth century the same fate had overtaken the Locke-Newton school which had once desiccated the Cartesians. The time had come for another change, a new start to refresh the collective scientific eye. His *Introduction aux travaux scientifiques du xixᵉ siècle* was written to point the way.

In the *Mémoire sur la science de l'homme*, he credited none other than Socrates himself, the founder of science, with originating the whole conception of the alternativity of scientific methods. The manner in which he presented the conceit is fanciful, but this *aperçu* on the exhaustion of a scientific methodology and the need for a dramatic shift to a polar methodology has in recent years received more extensive and sometimes more pompous development.

. . . [I]n order to organize his scientific system, that is to say, in order to coördinate his ideas on the organization of the universe and solidly to base his knowledge on the composition and the process of phenomena, man must move to the coördination of his ideas with alternativity, *a priori* and *a posteriori*. The power of his intelligence is extremely limited, so that his attention grows weary from always contemplating things from the same point of view and his only method of accelerating his progress is to change his direction. Thus, when after having made his efforts to descend from the idea of a single cause ruling the Universe to the most specific effects, he feels that his attentiveness is so wearied that he no longer finds anything new, that his abstract and concrete ideas are mixed together to the point where he can no longer disentangle them — then the best he can do is to change direction, to adopt one completely contrary, that is to say *a posteriori*, to rise from a consideration of particular facts to the more general facts and to return in the most direct manner to the general fact.[16]

In 1813 Saint-Simon was in one of his less rational periods, but he still clung to his belief in the alternativity of the two methods of science. In the *Travail sur la gravitation universelle* his rather free analogical associations allowed him to identify the *a priori* method with a study of the little world of the inner man, the microcosm, and the *a posteriori* method with an absorption in the outer or great world, the macrocosm.[17] Once Saint-Simon had caught an analogy, had made a comparison or had discovered a set of opposites, he stretched the insight to the uttermost bounds of credibility and often beyond. The nature of the *a priori-a posteriori* dichotomy had its origin in the very fibres of our nervous system — in the fact of breathing. *A priori* knowledge was connected with breathing in, *a posteriori* knowledge with breathing out; the former was active, the latter was passive. This led him to equate the development of *a priori* science from Plato to the Arab Caliphs — roughly eleven centuries — with an identical stretch of *a posteriori* or Aristotelian thinking in the eleven ensuing centuries. There was thus a sort of breathing process of world science; inhaling and exhaling had lasted for approximately equivalent periods, establishing an equilibrium. The conclusion of this phantasmagoria was that the time had come for humanity to take a new deep *a priori* scientific breath, to create a system of general science.[18]

He also tried to play the same game with the general character of the individual sciences. Fundamentally they could all be reduced to those in which an *a priori* element prevailed and those in which the *a posteriori* prevailed, both types being derivatives of the two basic sciences originally known as astronomy and medicine (an idea that came directly from d'Alembert's *Discours préliminaire*). This was of course somewhat contradictory of his main thesis of the alternativity of synthesis and analysis, but anyone who pursues his analogies to their bitter end must wind up in confusion.[19]

One thing was clear. A new synthesis was about to be revealed to mankind, a synthesis after the manner of Socrates, the teacher of both Plato and Aristotle. When Saint-Simon, the great schizophrenic, did not fancy himself the modern Descartes or the modern Charlemagne he thought of himself as the reincarnation of Socrates, not envisioning a metempsychosis in the "Pythagorean sense," but in what he called a positivist sense. He put words of prophecy into the mouth of Socrates: "When I say to you that I shall reappear in two thousand years I mean that since the moral circumstances of the age must be at that epoch about the same as they are today, there will then be a man in whom sensations more or less similar to those which I feel will converge. . . ." [20]

Since the law of scientific development operated irrespective of the will of the individual scientist, none of the scientists and scientific philosophers who preceded Saint-Simon had ever self-consciously adopted a scientific method. When men like Locke and Newton went about particularizing rather than generalizing they were merely obeying their "scientific instinct" of what was historically useful.[21] This last phrase is worth pondering over. In the full flower of eighteenth-century rationalism, a "scientific instinct" would have been considered a contradiction in terms. But after the turn of the century a strengthening of romantic and historical and utilitarian conceptions altered the intellectual climate of Europe. Even the scientist in his laboratory, who in the eighteenth century would have been conceived as performing an individual act of free will, indulging perhaps in "curiosity" (d'Alembert's analysis of a scientist's motivation in the *Discours prélim-*

inaire), was found to be subject to historical laws, to the dictates of underlying utilitarian forces expressed in history. And how did he respond to these
forces? Through instinct. The whole rational process of science was thus becoming adulterated with other phenomena. Saint-Simon had perhaps merely
breathed stray influences in the air, but whether he was aware of it or not,
he was proclaiming the domination of history and utility over rational science
and the search for abstract truth. In Saint-Simon's doctrine relativism, utili-
tarianism, and historicism all fortified one another as they did throughout
the nineteenth century.

A scientist's creativity — his method and even his subject matter — were
determined by his placement in the historical series. The accomplishment of
the individual scientist did not depend upon his genius alone, for it was
subordinate to the anonymous historical process. "Indeed, are the constitutions and the conceptual power of men like Lagrange and Laplace inferior
to those of Newton? I do not believe it at all. But I think that they are subject to a law of circumstances which has left them no other use for their
powers than the improvements which we owe to them. At the end of the sixteenth century they would have been Bacons, at the beginning of the seventeenth Descartes, at the beginning of the eighteenth Lockes and Newtons;
and if today these same men were no more than twenty, I would answer
that before having finished half their careers they would alter the route of
the School [of Science]." [22] The man who continued to think *a posteriori* at
the tail end of an analytical period was really wasting his own and humanity's
time.

The advancement of science in order to be meaningful and useful to
mankind must follow along in an orderly fashion, in a proper sequence of
discoveries. Premature scientific insights, ideas far ahead of the general scientific level, have no significance — they are usually lost, like some of the early
Greek scientific ideas. The individual genius makes the discoveries, but they
must occur at the appropriate historical epoch to be fruitful; otherwise the
same discoveries will have to be made anew by other men at a later date.

The series of reports on the status of scientific development which he
wrote under the Empire, particularly the *Introduction aux travaux scientifiques du xix*^e^ *siècle*, and the *Mémoire sur la science de l'homme* were an
autodidact's passionate, pretentious attempt to identify the character of the
historical hour in science, to formulate its task. It was vital to be aware of the
realities of the scientific moment in the history of science before the corps
of world scientists proceeded with their century's labors. If haphazard scientific investigation continued, men would spend themselves on the wrong
projects. At each period in the history of science there was an area of knowledge where the main effort of world science had to be exerted. The nineteenth century was to be the age of the Science of Man. In this field there
was a historical imperative which demanded the concentrated efforts of all

scientists laboring to achieve a synthesis of the findings of the most advanced physiologists, psychologists, and philosophical historians.

The law of the alternativity of the analytical and synthetic movements of science solved the problem posed by Napoleon: to assure the progress of science, the new synthesis had to be undertaken — that was the mission of nineteenth-century savants. For this synthesis Saint-Simon had provided the framework. Fitting the details into his system was a vast enterprise which could only be accomplished by a collaborative effort of the leading scientists of all nations. "To prepare a good Encyclopedia is a labor which requires the participation of the foremost scientists in the world, twenty years of work and a hundred millions. This project is worthy of being presented to the emperor. It is the only fitting reply to the question he posed to the Institute. It is a fruit of the grain which he sowed." [23]

In the period of the Empire Saint-Simon was not interested in the popularization of his works. That continuous appeal to public opinion had been the great failing of eighteenth-century thought which was, after all, adequate only for the making of a destructive Revolution. The mission of the nineteenth century was to be constructive, to reorganize "the system of morals, the religious system, the political system, in a word, the system of ideas, from whatever viewpoint one examines them." [24] For the purpose of construction scientists had to work in secret because the mob could contribute nothing to their investigations. This was the reason, he said, for circulating his memoranda only among the leading scientists.[25] Science had to remain esoteric; there was danger in premature revelation, particularly where the explosive Science of Man was involved.

The alternativity in time of the two scientific methods is Saint-Simon's first use of the cyclical principle, which became a characteristic feature of his later works on the philosophy of history. It is perhaps far-fetched to identify this scientific alternativity with a historical dialectic; yet even in its simplest form, it has some of the concepts associated with dialectics. Saint-Simon wrote in the *Mémoire sur la science de l'homme* that science first pursued one method, then it had to adopt a method which was "completely contrary"; but in the process of this alternativity science was rising to an ever higher level of development.[26] This is not Hegel, and Saint-Simon did not use the word dialectic, but it may fortify the believers in a *Zeitgeist* to find a French *philosophe*, working in isolation in Paris during the years 1807–1813, formulating a law of scientific development which has at least shadowy resemblances to the system expounded in Berlin by the German philosopher in his *Vorlesungen* of 1822–1823, which was not published until 1837.

12

Man Before History

SAINT-SIMON'S PHILOSOPHY OF HISTORY did not fully mature until the Restoration, but his esoteric Empire works contained novel reflections which, never again repeated in the same form, were the seed from which his later doctrine flowered.

Saint-Simon had expounded in the letters to his nephew Victor the view that a man's moral character was to be judged neither by his daily behavior in the immediate circle of his friends, nor by his charity towards the stranger who crossed his path, nor by his attitude towards abstract justice and truth. Saint-Simon was not interested in whether a man was "good" by natural habit, "virtuous" in the spontaneous expressions of his soul. Such definitions of the moral man had preoccupied the eighteenth-century *philosophes*, who were primarily absorbed by the dilemmas of individual conduct. This focus on the individual was as characteristic of Diderot and Voltaire as it was of Rousseau. Saint-Simon, who had the reputation among contemporaries of being a libertine, sought the crux of the moral issue elsewhere. To him the momentous moral act was the perception of one's right place in the historical process and the decision to follow its dictates. A man's primary duty was therefore to understand the nature of the historical epoch into which he was born. As a necessary preliminary to discovering what his role should be in the stream of history, man had to comprehend the general direction of its flow.[1]

The whole conception of moral conduct thus had its source in a philosophy of history. Failing to analyze correctly the vital forces at play in the epoch in which he lived, a man could act neither rationally nor morally. There was no such thing as moral conduct in the abstract. The same public act might be virtuous in one period of civilization and in another pernicious. Morality — even as science — had no meaning out of a historical context. Private acts, as such, had no great significance at any time. As he had written to his nephew Victor, in his historic role of philosopher Saint-Simon rather playfully considered it his duty to make a social experiment of his life, to

indulge himself in all manner of strange experiences, with the avowed
purpose of drawing conclusions at the end of his days for the betterment
of mankind. It was a matter of relative indifference that he injured his
fellow-men during the course of his field work in social science. A man's
conduct was to be assessed not by its effect upon his neighbors, but by its
impact on the grand sweep of history. Saint-Simon even tried to prove that
the great progressive figures of history, those who contributed most to the
acceleration of the historical process, tended to be sensualists, while the
wicked ones, the leaders of antihistorical forces, were usually "severe moralists." Thus there was, paradoxically, almost an inverse ratio between traditional morality on the private level and morality on the stage of history.

"Did not Luther love the pleasures of the table and women? The
greatest men, those who contributed most to the progress of the human spirit,
did they not in general have a taste for pleasure? The men who have done
the most evil, the most bloody men, have they not been severe moralists?
Have we not had in Robespierre and in Billaud de Varennes models of
economy and of continence?

"I can prove that I have been despoiled by a man with whom I lived
for more than ten years on terms of the greatest intimacy, by a man whom
I had enriched, and who is certainly one of the most austere moralists of the
present generation." [2]

Hegel adopted precisely the same position in his *Philosophy of History*
with respect to "world-historical individuals." "It is even possible that such
men may treat other great, even sacred interests inconsiderately; conduct
which is indeed obnoxious to moral reprehension. But so mighty a form
must trample down many an innocent flower — crush to pieces many an
object in its path." [3]

Saint-Simon's morality, although it represents a departure from eighteenth-century universalism, was nevertheless not relativist in the sense that
all action could be explained, understood, and perhaps condoned. The
moral act was absolute at any particular historical moment. A moral man
first had to undertake a study of world history, to trace the mainsprings
of proper conduct in his age. Only then could he determine what his course
of action in life should be. Saint-Simon, like so many of his followers, was
intoxicated with history. Throughout his writings the proposition is self-
evident that if a man failed to choose the right side in the great conflicts of
his time, he would be guilty of the most heinous crime against humanity,
for he would thereby be impeding the movement of progress.

There is of course a pervasive confidence in all his works that the partisans of the true historical destiny of man, those with faith in perfectibility,
will ultimately triumph. Of the generality there is hardly a single instance
of doubt or even an isolated expression of ambivalence. But the determinism
is not absolute in every detail. While the general law of progress is laid

down, the particularities are not preordained. The idea of general universal determinism coupled with individual freedom within a limited human sphere was a standard solution to the problem of the freedom of the will. Medieval theologians had resorted to it; Diderot's encyclopedia article seems to accept it; and later nineteenth-century moralists like de Tocqueville found it a convenient answer to the dilemma. Man is a free creature for Saint-Simon and he can either accelerate or retard the evolution of society. This is in fact both the scope and definition of his freedom. As a generality, the good men are identifiable as those who contribute to the speeding-up of the historical process and the evil as those who cause it to drag. There is an implied virtue in the historical process achieving its next station on the ascent to felicity as fast as possible. D'Alembert's law of least action had highlighted the wondrous efficiency of physical action in nature if allowed to complete a process unimpeded. This feeling underlies Saint-Simon's conception of history. The historical process moved its inevitable way, but individual man had a limited power to affect the tempo. There is no fixed timetable in history and Saint-Simon did not venture to prophesy when specific changes would take place. The doctrine even allowed for setbacks when the antiprogressive elements in society were, for a variety of ephemeral reasons, temporarily in power, but these minor deviations in the flow of the mainstream could not alter its general direction.[4] The images of the war of good men with antihistoric forces never lose their Christian overtones in Saint-Simon or in other philosophers of history.

The moral man could not be a mere contemplator of the historical process; he had to add action to his discernment of the true course of history. Mere knowledge of the historical trend would produce an indifferent man, incapable of either good or evil. He would be a neutral, a creature who might just as well not have been born. The moral man must labor passionately in the direction of progress. Without the blueprint of a philosophy of history moral man would wander about blindly and aimlessly, not knowing where to turn, how to fight for the historically determined new epoch. He would be slashing away in the dark. The current of the historical process would not, however, turn completely awry even without human awareness and consciousness of the nature of the moment in the great progress. History did not have to be apprehended by man in order to proceed with its benefactions. Mankind somehow had managed to conform to a fundamental pattern of progressive development even before individual men awakened to what was taking place. Perfectibility, based on the sense of utility, had operated instinctively in past ages, before the dawn of historical awareness.

But the new historical consciousness of modern times could significantly alter the tempo of progress, and that was no mean power. The work of the philosopher, and above all the philosopher of history, was itself action which influenced the world in a profound sense. "The philosopher places himself at the summit of thought. From there he views the world as it has been and as it must become. He is not only an observer. He is an actor. He is an actor of the first rank in the moral world because it is his opinions on what the world must become which regulate human society." [5]

Saint-Simon's conception of the relations of man and history was expressed with rare precision in one of the manuscripts he left behind in Alençon in 1812. He proclaimed himself at once an activist and a determinist, a posture he assumed in common with both Calvin his antecedent and Marx his successor.

In the development of the sciences and arts the human spirit follows a predetermined course which is superior to the greatest intellectual forces, which appear only as instruments destined to produce successive discoveries at given times.

Although this force derives from us, it is no more in our power to escape its influence or to master its actions than it is to change at our pleasure the primitive impulse which makes our planet circulate around the sun.

Secondary effects alone are subject to dependence on us. All we can do is to obey this law (our veritable providence) with understanding, taking into account the course which it prescribes for us instead of being blindly pushed by it, and, let it be said in passing, it is precisely in this that the greatest philosophical improvement of the present epoch will consist. [6]

Had it been developed and more brilliantly stated this could have been the manifesto of nineteenth-century historicism. It remained a fragment in a sack of papers in pawn at Alençon. [7]

Man's history on earth not only had a plan, it had purpose. It was not a mere sequence of accidents or a wild juggling of atoms which formed ever new configurations without meaning. Nature's goal was the increasing happiness of mankind on earth. There had been progress in the universalization of happiness since the beginning of time. Saint-Simon set himself the task of identifying the signs of this progress in the chaos of history, of seeking out its hidden laws, and of teaching mankind tactical measures for accelerating progress and hastening the coming of the New Day. The key to the attainment of future general progress — not merely scientific progress — lay in an understanding of the true nature and direction of history. There was an essential history, stripped of accident, which could be revealed by scientific study, and he called it "philosophical history." [8] The factual narrative of the rise and fall of states, empires, and their rulers — traditional history — had no significance. Saint-Simon clung to the deluded opinion that he was the discoverer of the hitherto unknown science of history or philosophical history, the only serious history.

He sturdily contended that history was not a branch of literature and that it could not be written by belletrists without formal scientific training.

The purpose of history was to yield laws of mankind's development and the literary men were not competent to deduce such generalizations, since they had fixed their attention on "political, religious, and military facts." [9] In 1813, speaking as Bacon, he reviewed and rejected virtually all contemporary historical studies. "In fact history in a scientific sense has not yet come out of its swaddling clothes. This important branch of our knowledge is nothing but a collection of more or less well-established facts. These facts are not tied together by any theory. They are not linked in an order of consequences. . . . There are thus far only national histories whose authors have proposed as their principal purpose to extol the qualities of their compatriots and to depreciate those of their rivals. No historian has yet placed himself in a general vantage point. No one has yet written the history of the species. . . ." [10]

History as it had been practiced up to the middle of the eighteenth century was nothing but a "biography of power, in which nations figured only as instruments and as victims. . . ." [11] It was about 1750 that the English historians, and above all Hume,[12] began to adopt a broader outlook and to consider history as the progress of a civilization. From time to time Saint-Simon also spoke well of the Abbé Raynal's popular *Histoire philosophique et politique*, of the Scottish historian William Robertson, and of the Scottish moralist Adam Ferguson. He never mentioned Voltaire's histories, since they would have represented a false historical conception, but there are many passages in Saint-Simon's writings where the influence of the *Essai sur les moeurs* is visible. Among French contemporaries he saw in Lemontey, Raynouard, Daru, Volney, and Daunou precursors of the "integral reformation" of history in a philosophical sense, but even they were not emancipated from the faults of the particularist approach.[13] Most of the antiquarians whom Napoleon had put into the historical sections of the reorganized Institute left him cold, as well they might, and he ignored them. Dacier's report to the emperor on the state of history and ancient literature had cautiously avoided any broad hypotheses and had been mainly a catalogue of works of erudition.[14] Levesque in 1808 had announced to the emperor that history as a branch of knowledge was undergoing a training period "in order some day to celebrate in a worthy manner the greatest of reigns and the greatest of nations." [15] To Saint-Simon such sycophancy perverted the nature of historical science. In so bleak a setting he could well consider himself a great philosophical historian.[16]

For enlightenment on special historical problems he expressed his debt in his Empire works to Konrad Oelsner for an understanding of the Arabs; although he quarreled with Charles Villers's study on the Reformation, he was influenced by it. He was less explicit in acknowledging his dependence upon the revised historical judgment of the middle ages for which the traditionalists were responsible even though they wrote no formal histories.

Saint-Simon, who was by no means a scholar or a prodigious reader, apparently was unacquainted with the German philosophies of history elaborated by Herder, Kant, or Lessing; neither does he seem to have been aware of Vico.[17] He made no specific references to Turgot, though many of his own views on progress paralleled strikingly the famous discourses delivered before the Sorbonne in 1750.[18] Among the philosophers of history he considered Condorcet alone his precursor, though he thought of him less as an original thinker than as a continuator of Locke, Price, and Priestley. While he often attacked ideas in the *Esquisse* with his accustomed aggressiveness, he judged Condorcet a worthy opponent. There are extant manuscript summaries of the *Esquisse* decorated with marginalia which carry on a running debate with its author and label specific ideas as meriting adoption or refutation.[19] As far as Saint-Simon was concerned, with the exception of Condorcet, there had been no real philosophical history before him, and his works in this most vital area of knowledge basic to the Science of Man were breaking new ground.

Universal history in his mind was Europocentric, and he rarely took cognizance of the existence of other societies beyond Europe, the Near East, and North Africa. Prehistory and early recorded history he shunned[20] because the paucity of materials would have forced him to resort to conjectures and he was a "positive" historian — though, despite his own admonitions, at times this mercurial philosopher hazarded the wildest hypotheses about the origins of mankind on the "plateau of Tartary."

In his Empire writings Saint-Simon made several attempts at a periodization of the total historical process. To a philosopher of history fascinated by the life sciences, one of whose major achievements in the eighteenth century had been a classification of the species, the establishment of appropriate chronological divisions was a first prerequisite of scientific history. Historical epochs were conceived as the equivalents of biological species. Both were organisms, and the accurate, precise definition and description of epochs was the initial step in scientific history as contrasted with rambling literary history. Saint-Simon's contempt for contemporary historiography was due in large measure to its failure to emancipate itself from the arbitrary compartments of dynastic history and to recognize natural, organic units of time.

His own first efforts under the Empire at drafting a philosophy of history based upon a sound periodization were rather crude. Though he admittedly derived from Condorcet, he considered himself a world-shaking innovator, and it would not have been meet for him to accept the ten epochs of the *Esquisse* as the correct classification scheme. He experimented haphazardly with a variety of other divisions, four, five, and nine, ultimately fixing on the number three, quite unconscious of the mystic-religious drive which had led him there.

In the Empire fragments, both those published and those which remained in manuscript, the most common motif was a hackneyed comparison between the life cycle of the individual and that of the species, a parallel development which could be interpreted to yield predictions about the future history of mankind.[21] The great world of humanity was a magnified image of the microcosm man, and the history of the species recapitulated the history of the individual. Many passages written in this spirit have the oracular ambiguity and suggestiveness of all such theories and it is possible to read into them greater profundities than Saint-Simon probably intended. He wrote in the second *aperçu* of his manuscript *Projet d'encyclopédie*: "It appears to us possible to conceive of the individual history of man generalized and of the history of humanity particularized as being one and the same history; the facts composing the material of the history of a man, of two men, of several men, of all men, are the same facts." [22]

This overworked analogy brought forth intellectual fruits of dubious quality. In the fragment entitled *Théorie de l'histoire de l'espèce humaine*, included in the *Introduction aux travaux scientifiques du xixe siècle*, the Egyptians were likened to children playing with giant blocks, the Greeks to adolescent poets and artists, the Romans and the Saracens to manly warriors struggling against their rivals and against nature. Contemporary humanity had reached the age of a man of forty, when it was appropriate to devote oneself to a rational summary of experience. Though Saint-Simon was not quite certain of the precise longevity of the human species, he was partial to the idea that mankind had arrived at the half-way mark of its destined span — it was middle-aged. The *Nouvelle encyclopédie* featured a five-epoch periodization, an outgrowth or variant of the earlier one. History was divided into stages which represented the progressive expansion of the human intellect, its acquisition through time of a series of new capacities. While in the first version man lost as well as added talents, as he advanced from the childish playful Egyptian stage to maturity and old age, the later theory emphasized an accumulation of new arts and sciences with each epoch. The first period, vaguely identified as the pre-Egyptian, had man in a stage not far above the brute, busy devising conventional signs; the second period was dominated by Egyptian civilization, an age in which idolatry was the central idea and the novel talent the perfection of mechanical arts and trades; the third period was polytheist, the age of the Greeks, who perfected the fine arts; the fourth period was monotheist, the age of the Romans and Christianity, when men simultaneously discovered the truths of moral and political science and embodied them in a humanitarian doctrine; the fifth period he named physicism, the modern age when men were discovering the unitary scientific principle of all phenomena.[23]

In all his schema, however they varied, Saint-Simon abolished the traditional Christian era as the fundamental bench-mark in universal history, because it was artificial, not associated with a revolution in the history of human knowledge. In a letter of 1807 to the Arabist Konrad Oelsner he proposed Mamoun instead of Christ as the pivotal figure;[24] his 1813 fragments suggested Socrates as the only theorist important enough to bisect man's historical experience.

The *Travail sur la gravitation universelle* settled on a tripartite periodization of history, his definitive number.[25] In an imaginary, prophetic discourse, Saint-Simon had Socrates trisect universal history into three main epochs of thought: a pre-Socratic period called the "epoch of the preliminary works"; a second period initiated by Socrates and destined to last for twenty to twenty-five centuries, called the "epoch of the organization of the conjectural system"; and finally the "epoch of the positive system." [26] A triadic division of the historical process had been fundamental to Vico, was hinted at in Turgot, and would become central to the philosophy of Comte. At least elements in Saint-Simon's triad are identical with Comte's law of the three states which he considered a discovery with universal repercussions when he wrote his opuscule of 1822.

Perhaps the most important of Saint-Simon's underlying preconceptions in the Empire works was a deep-rooted conviction that the substance of history, its very fabric, had been conflict. Since he was not a systematic philosopher, he never defined the abstract nature of conflict and he nowhere set forth the thesis in so many words that conflict was the immanent, quintessential character of the historical process; but the idea was implicit in all his writings. Progress had thus far been achieved only through the engagement of opposing forces. Conflict had assumed multifarious forms, had manifested itself in a variety of ways. Saint-Simon isolated crucial types of conflict in the mass of visible and covert antagonisms. Traditional Christian historiography had described the all-pervasive conflicts of this world in terms of the war between good and evil as interpreted by the church. For the anti-Christian *philosophes* of the eighteenth century the historic conflict was the war between science and religious superstition or moral virtue and vice. Saint-Simon was not satisfied with these abstract — he would say "metaphysical" — definitions. He endowed conflict with what he considered to be a scientific meaning; for him it was the warring of real elements in society. Though clashes and oppositions other than those he emphasized occurred in nature, they were fortuitous; they were incidental to, not causative factors in history.

In studying conflict, Saint-Simon often perceived novel patterns in the world which exerted a profound influence upon European thought. At one time or another he focused his philosophical eye upon the conflict of classes, of ideas, of scientific methods, of social systems, of nations, even of races. At different periods in his life he gave these conflicts varying weights in explaining the progress of mankind. One of the knotty problems raised by his scattered writings is to relate these conflicts to one another, to establish the primacy of one and the subordination of the others. Saint-Simon's manner of presentation does not facilitate a solution to these questions, and finally as a last resort one is driven to accept the fact that his philosophy of history has variant versions which cannot be conciliated. The theory of race conflict, at least, can be dismissed as relatively minor in his philosophy: interpreting the whole history of France as a war between the Frankish invaders and the native Gauls appealed far more to Augustin Thierry than it did to Saint-Simon, even though he was willing to concede the idea some validity.[27] The conflict of rival thought systems and the conflict of classes are manifestly the paramount antagonisms in history which he appreciated and studied.[28] The interplay of these two types of conflict, however, poses some of the most fundamental and thorny issues in his philosophy of history.

Similar generalizations about the nature of history were current in the thought of the previous generation and among other contemporary philosophers. Kant used the concept of antagonism to define and explain the character of historical change in his brief excursion into the philosophy of history in 1784.[29] There is no evidence that Saint-Simon knew Kant's article any more than he was acquainted with Fichte or Hegel. But one does not have to seek a specific intellectual origin for this historical orientation in the early nineteenth century. The French Revolution with its titanic clash of ideas and men, that great cataclysm of Saint-Simon's manhood, made it difficult to view history other than as a "shock" of massive forces whose inherent nature was antagonistic. While Saint-Simon had accepted the faith that the course of history proved the existence of progress and that the nineteenth century would be a new high point of mankind's development, it seemed equally patent to a veteran of the American Revolution and a former prisoner of the Terror that the wished-for ascent to happiness was taking place amid convulsions and upheavals.

In the *Introduction aux travaux scientifiques du xixe siècle* he jotted down a few aphorisms for a theory of revolutions. "The human spirit progresses only through crises; its greatest advances have been preceded by bloody revolutions."[30] He decried them as great evils, as he always had since his imprisonment, but in 1807, in contrast with the doctrine he later enunciated, he believed that revolutions were inevitable evils. Their profound source he had already hinted at in his first pamphlets: whenever the rulers of society ceased to have a marked superiority of real positive knowledge over their subjects, insurrection would burst forth irresistibly. Napoleon's government was strong, immune to revolution, because the genius of the emperor and the concentration of knowledge in the entourage of governors surrounding his throne made the mass of the people appear ignorant by comparison, a desirable chasm between rulers and ruled, almost a "pathos of distance." All revolutions had an egalitarian tendency and to the extent that they pushed men of knowledge to the fore from the lower ranks of society their effect was progressive. What was calamitous was the incapacity of former revolutionaries to abandon their "exaltation for the idea of equality" once the revolutionary period was over.[31]

Saint-Simon's psychological nature fed upon crises; he sometimes invented them and dramatized his own existence around them. His philosophy of history followed suit. This does not establish, even remotely, any simple causal relationship between his personality and his theory; it does affirm a parallel and poses a problem worth pursuing.

This was the general tenor of his philosophy of history in sketches written under the Empire — an early and incomplete formulation which was expanded and made more systematic in his Restoration publications. The goal of mankind was being approached through time and the optimism of the eighteenth century was vindicated, but the good had been emerging in conflicts, in struggles, and in great travail. Progress had been universal, but thus far violence — the attack of one force and the resistance of another — had been its inevitable concomitant. Saint-Simon forgot neither the images nor the terminology of his years of soldiering. His depictions of the historical process were pockmarked with "sieges of historic forces," the "breakthrough" of new elements, "hand-to-hand combats" of classes, and the "defeat" of whole societies and civilizations. History was not a river which flowed gently.[32]

13

The General Nature of Perfectibility

DURING THE CONSULATE AND THE EMPIRE, perfectibility, at once descriptive of the historic process and of the historic goal, was defined by Saint-Simon primarily as scientific progress. The concept was not as restrictive as appears at first sight because the sciences were crowned by the Science of Man, which could be applied to the eradication of moral vice in the same way that the science of medicine was enlisted to cure physical disease.

Saint-Simon was not convinced that there was equal or parallel progress in every one of the multifarious expressions of human capacity. While all man's rational talents were inevitably destined to develop, certain faculties had to deteriorate with time — indeed, they had already shown signs of decline. As mankind grew older, for example, there was a tendency for the maturing rational faculties to crowd out the imaginative faculties, which would thus regress to ultimate impoverishment. The future of the imagination had been widely debated during the seventeenth- and early eighteenth-century "quarrel between the ancients and the moderns." While a few die-hard progressionists in the dispute had upheld the modern title to superiority in all fields, imaginative as well as rational scientific, a substantial body of opinion had agreed upon a compromise, bestowing laurels upon the ancients for their excellence in the arts and upon the moderns for their discoveries in science. Turgot had accepted this position in his famous Discourses at the Sorbonne in 1750 and this is probably the version in which the theory of progress was transmitted to Saint-Simon.

Condorcet had been so completely absorbed in the advancement of physical science and its technological applications that he barely posed the question of what would happen to the creative arts of the imagination in the glorious tenth epoch of "indefinite progress." Condorcet had in passing affirmed the inevitability of artistic as well as scientific progress; this straw man Saint-Simon attacked with a show of independence, upholding the supremacy of the Greek imagination in the traditional manner of French neoclassicism. Since under the Empire Saint-Simon was consistently equating the process of universal history to a single human life cycle, he was bound by the logical implications of his analogy. The mature man — modern civilization — might become more rational, but he was visibly losing those powers of the youthful imagination which are revealed in great poetry. The physiological doctrines of his favorite Dr. Bichat coincided neatly with this particular formulation of the idea of progress. Each man, wrote Bichat in his *Recherches physiologiques sur la vie et sur la mort* was endowed with a fixed quantum of vitality. This "vital principle" would find expression in the various human faculties in different degrees, never in all the faculties to the same degree. By extension of the analogy to the history of mankind, the ancients, who were weak in works of science, had great imaginative capacity, but in their descendants the imagination waned in the precise measure that the power of reason increased.[1]

One of Saint-Simon's scientific fantasies depicted the world as a struggle between fluids and solids. In the human brain this conflict expressed itself as strife between reason or the action of solids and imagination or the action of fluids. As humanity grew older, the solidification process was extended and the powers of reason were augmented at the expense of the fluid element, the imagination. Though man could now separate the elements and play with thunder he would never again create an Iliad or an Apollo Belvedere. Preceding ages of man had been capable only of simulating reason; they never formulated a general system of knowledge and their ideas were always interpenetrated with chimeras of the imagination. By the same token, future generations would seem to be "imagining," while in fact they would only be exercising the power of "rational reminiscence."[2] Cabanis in his treatises read to the Institute gave a physiological explanation of the predominance of imaginative faculties in youth and reflective faculties in age: there was in the passage from youth to age a diminution of the movement of body fluids; the solids became more dense.[3] This dialectic of the solids and the fluids was a fairly common idea at the time and Saint-Simon adopted it as one of the basic explanations for all change.

Many passages in Vico's *Scienza Nuova* dwell on the idea of a simultaneous impoverishment of the imagination and a strengthening of rationality as man moves through the three stages of his development, but this is a less likely source for Saint-Simon's thought than either Fontenelle or Madame de Staël, who had independently arrived at the same general conception. The similarity of Saint-Simon's formula and Madame de Staël's in *De la littérature* is too patent to be overlooked. "The fine arts are not infinitely perfectible. Moreover, the imagination which gave birth to them is far more brilliant in its first impressions than even in its most felicitous recollections."[4] This had led her to a pessimistic view of the future of works of the creative imagination, a general thesis which the stilted poetry of her philosophical age supported. "Philosophy is extending itself over all the arts of the imagination and over all the works of reason; and man in this century has only curiosity for the passions of man. . . . Poetry of the imagination will make no more progress in France; philosophical ideas will be put into verse. . . ."[5]

Whatever quibbles Saint-Simon might have with Condorcet on the perfectibility of the imagination, he always ranged himself by his side in defense of the general idea of progress, in sharp opposition both to Rousseau and to the theocratic school.[6] While Joseph de Maistre, the most profound of the traditionalists, in revulsion against the optimism of the *Esquisse*, was thundering away to postrevolutionary Europe: "The human species retrogresses!" Saint-Simon was one of the first to point out a curious parallel between the attack of the Catholic theologians against modern civilization and of the Rousseauists whom they abominated: both had a doctrine of the fall instead of the progress of man.

The difference was not yet too great in the eighteenth century between the opinion of the *philosophes* and that of the theologians, with respect to the first steps taken by the human intelligence. The theologians said, they still say: Adam and Eve were happy in a terrestrial paradise before they had eaten the apple; and the *philosophes* said: in the savage state man was happy; it is only since the invention of political, civil, and religious institutions that man has known misfortune. That was the profession of faith eloquently drafted by Rousseau and coldly expressed by d'Alembert; Condorcet himself is not as distant from this viewpoint as one might imagine in his *Esquisse d'un tableau historique des progrès de l'esprit humain*.[7]

Saint-Simon's identification of Condorcet's and d'Alembert's position with Rousseau's in this passage does seem to have some justification in fact. The equation of the *philosophes'* "state of nature" and the Christian Garden of Eden is a provocative idea, one which Carl Becker developed as the central theme of his *Heavenly City of the Eighteenth-Century Philosophers*.[8] But under the Empire the analogue between Christian and philosophical primitivism must have sounded like a shocking paradox.

Saint-Simon's use of the descriptions of primitive peoples in the literature of travel and discovery to illustrate the idea of progress anticipated later nineteenth-century anthropologists. He knew something of the work of Bougainville, Cook, and La Pérouse and he drew upon their accounts of various tribes in South America and the South Sea Islands to establish a progression of steps from the most primitive to a fully civilized state of society.[9] His belief that each one of these tribes actually represented a specific stage in the progressive history of civilization — a stage through which European man had already passed — was for him positive evidence that there had been no fall, either from the state of nature or from the state of innocence in Eden. On the contrary, there had been a steady ascent, and the anthropological record was living proof of the various social forms through which all the civilized races of man had progressed at one time in their history.

His conviction that progress was inevitable was so absolute that he compared it to a mathematical series. He could shift his position about the tempo of progress in a given epoch or about the tactics for accelerating it, but he never, except at moments of extreme mental illness, lost faith in the perfectibility of man. The path of progress might be cyclical and the periods of transition cataclysmic, but the general direction was preordained, at least for as long as the physical conditions of the planet remained the same.[10] Both Saint-Simon and his disciples were willing to entertain the possibility of unpredictable geological or astronomic catastrophes which would affect the human species in an unforeseen manner. The Laplace nebular hypothesis was still a novelty and Saint-Simon grasped the idea as a portent of future astronomic revolutions which might reverse the upward climb of mankind. In the *Travail sur la gravitation universelle* (1813) he ventured a hypothesis of his own about the ultimate catastrophe awaiting humanity sometime in the far distant future. He forecast a gradual desiccation of the globe, during which mankind would fall backward through a series of stages until it relapsed into the condition of the brute. In embroidering upon this vision of regression, he conjured up dismal philosophical fantasies: the moral reflections on the history of mankind of the last man after he had drunk the last drop of water; the pain of his realization that with him all mankind was disappearing from the face of the earth.[11] Such passages are expressions of Saint-Simon's pathological morbidity during the period of his psychic breakdown and should not be considered seriously as an intrinsic part of his theory.

During the Consulate and the Empire Saint-Simon picked up a few new hypotheses from the bolder life scientists and shoved them as grist into his progressionist mill. Lamarck, following upon the theses propounded by earlier eighteenth-century naturalists and by contemporary physiologists and psychologists (including Dr. Cabanis with whose major work Saint-Simon was familiar) had propounded his transformist theory of the evolution of the species before the Institute in 1800.[12] Saint-Simon no doubt had discussed many of the current theories in this field with his medical friend, Dr. Bougon. These daring ideas — which he only partially understood — gave rise to all manner of wild speculations in his fragment entitled "The Difference between the Intelligence of Man and the Animals."[13] There he arrived at the conclusion that "if the human species should disappear from the earth, the best organized species after him would be perfected."[14] Saint-Simon's candidate for the post was odd: he believed that after man, the beaver rather than the ape would take over — possibly because he was the "industrial" of the animal world. These reflections of Saint-Simon are only simulacres of far more reasoned evolutionary hypotheses current among the *idéologues*. They are Saint-Simon in the rough.

Saint-Simon's total view of the evolutionary process from the solidification of the planet out of a fluid comet through the emergence of man, a curious hodge-podge of contemporary scientific theories, is interesting primarily because of its emphasis upon the dynamism of the natural order, which was reflected in his philosophy of history. Once solidified, the planet kept growing more dense until "pretty little phenomena" called organic bodies were formed upon its surface. The size of these bodies was dependent upon the amount of fermentation which had preceded their coming into being. Fish, the largest animals, were the first to take shape. When the plateau of Tartary appeared out of the water it was the first dry land and on it new animals were created. The emergence of America caused a deluge and brought forth another class of animals. These organic bodies were evidence of the continuous struggle between solids and fluids. Man's superiority over animals was only the result of his internal and external structure; there was no soul. "Thought is material attraction, the result of the movement of the nervous fluid. . . . Why attribute his moral superiority to another cause? The line of demarcation between the intelligence of man and the instinct of animals was not clearly drawn until after the formation of conventional signs, spoken or written." [15] Man had been placed in a superior position in the universe, he had oppressed other animals, and had hindered the development of their faculties in order to further his own advancement; but he was no unique creature among organic bodies.[16]

The equality among men proclaimed by the Revolution was a fiction; the same physiological gradation noted among animals prevailed among the various races, accounting for the dominance of the European and the inferiority of the negro. A good physiologist, advised Saint-Simon, would devote himself to an investigation of the steps by which man rose from the lower animals, through the less perfect species of humanity to the highest existing specimen. Profound consideration of these changes would give insight into the future physiological perfection of man.[17]

His friend, the physiologist Dr. Blainville, one of the few contemporary scientists who had deigned to comment on the manuscript of the *Science de l'homme* which was sent to him, took issue with Saint-Simon on his hierarchy of animal life. He denied that the beaver was closest to man in structure and would take over control of the world if the human species disappeared. On physiological grounds Dr. Blainville still opted for the ape.[18]

The general character of Saint-Simon's doctrine of progress as a continuation of the Turgot-Condorcet thesis can perhaps best be illumined by drawing contrasts with the conception of progress developed by the German thinkers, particularly Herder and Kant, in the last decades of the eighteenth century. Such a comparison lays bare at its very origins the nineteenth-century differentiation between French *civilisation* and German *Kultur* and their relationship to human perfectibility. Even when the theorists use similar terminology the substance of the ideas evolved on opposite sides of the Rhine is not the same. Saint-Simon's Empire writings are in the direct French tradition, untouched by German influence.

In the French philosophies of history of the Condorcet-Saint-Simon type there is a pervasive feeling that man has already climbed far up the ladder of progress since his first emergence into a state of civilization. Condorcet was able to sketch the character of fully nine antecedent epochs before he ventured to gaze into the glorious tenth epoch of the future. In Saint-Simon's early writing (the *Introduction aux travaux scientifiques du xixe siècle* of 1807–1808) mankind's condition in the nineteenth century was equivalent to that of a middle-aged gentleman who had reached the forties. These Frenchmen had known the brilliant intellectual society of eighteenth-century Paris, and though they prophesied an even more dazzling golden age in the future, the attainments of their own contemporary civilization did not appear puny in their eyes.[19] Kant and Herder, isolated for long years in small towns in the midst of the Slavic East Prussian peasantry, were not powerfully impressed with the advancement achieved by the human species. Kant could not suppress "a certain disgust when contemplating men's action upon the world stage," [20] and Herder, who in general was more buoyantly optimistic, nevertheless felt that "man is raised, upon the whole, but a short step above the brute." [21]

There is also a different emphasis in the content of the idea of progress among the philosophers of the two nations. Condorcet on the whole was thinking in utilitarian terms. Progress was the perfection of technological instruments to supplement man's natural capacities, the increase of the food supply, the lengthening of the life-span, the eradication of disease, the perfection of the techniques of government administration, the end of human slavery, a growing egalitarianism among men in a nation and the general raising of the cultural level throughout the world (approaching the high standard of the Atlantic community of Englishmen, Frenchmen, and North Americans), the establishment of equality between the sexes, an improvement of social security in health and old age through the activities of insurance companies which utilized the calculus of probabilities in making their computations, a clarification of terminology in all the sciences, the creation of an international language, the development of coöperative enterprises to discover new laws of science, make morals scientific, and apply the scientific findings in projects of public utility. Saint-Simon likewise thought almost exclusively about affecting the social environment directly through better education, a social system which would recognize scientific, engineering, and industrial capacities, a popularization of science, better governmental administration with the elimination of nonuseful classes like soldiers, lawyers, and bureaucrats. To Condorcet and Saint-Simon progress depended above all upon changes in the environment, in social institutions and practices. Nothing revolutionary, at least in the beginning of the new epochs of progress, happened to the essential nature of man. At most Saint-Simon and Condorcet hoped that through habit and education man would learn to master his asocial, destructive passions, to channelize them into socially useful activities. Various propaganda techniques, including even a suitable type of music, might be devised for this purpose. Serving the elementary needs of the great mass of the people was the first criterion of progress for Saint-Simon and an approximation of universal equality was the moral goal for Condorcet. Happiness would be generated quickly, they both believed, once the priests and tyrants and noble idlers were eliminated or reformed and the right social order was instituted.

Condorcet adopted Bacon's *New Atlantis* as his ideal, and thought of reigning congregations of coöperative scientists as a practical possibility. Saint-Simon vacillated as to whether the scientists would become the priests of a new order with rule over the whole of society or whether they would share their authority with industrialists. In any event, in the good society of the future there would be an élite of talented scientists and industrialists. The goal towards which mankind had been tending from the beginning was an enjoyment of terrestrial happiness through the satisfaction of its material wants and an unending search for scientific facts and theories which would both stimulate new desires and appease them. Ultimately the scientific truths would reveal to the administrators of society (they were hardly to be considered rulers) how to make sure that man remained mild, productive, scientific, unwarlike, an orderly internationalist. Human misery and unhappiness might not disappear completely from the earth, but, as Condorcet said, they would clearly become the rare misfortunes rather than the common experience of the race.

The Baltic Germans measured progress in very different terms. They were Protestant pietists — Herder more profoundly than Kant. They were not obsessed with mechanical or environmental changes, but were absorbed in the transformation of man's essential nature, the development of his rationality, his sense of justice, the moral humanity which distinguished him from the brute. They speculated about the ultimate perfection of the man within, and judged that humanity had still a long and arduous road to travel. As for the superficial comfort, the ease and polish of society, both Herder and Kant were too intoxicated with Rousseau to regard with anything but suspicion the façade of elegance and material well-being behind which man concealed himself.

To the Frenchmen man was simply a higher form of animal life. Their

twin goals, more science and more sensual happiness, were readily obtain-
able. Their vision of the future was altogether human. To Herder the end
of man was "so high, so extensive, so infinite. . . ." [22] He saw the gradual
alteration of something within man, the unfolding under Divine guidance of
what so distinguished him from the beasts, until he fulfilled himself in a
new man, entirely different in his inner nature.

The Germans saw progress as God's manifestation in time and their
unshakable faith in man's perfectibility was based upon an appraisal of
Divine intentions during the process of creation. It would have been blasphemy to imagine that the perfect God should have troubled to create a
man doomed to remain stunted, undeveloped, imperfect for all eternity.
Obviously Nature or Nature's God, who observes the law of parsimony,
would not have endowed man with rationality if He did not mean it to
become the instrument of his perfectibility in time. Condorcet did not invoke
God at all, and Saint-Simon, though he eventually proclaimed a religion of
humanity, really never recognized a deity like Herder's immanent God.

In Cordorcet and Saint-Simon the whole historical process was rather
mechanical, and progress was a world in external movement: roadbuilding,
financial manipulation, canal digging, landscaping highways, popularizing
the arts. At worst, evil or misguided men might be able to slow down the
tempo of this beneficent activity. There was some question whether progress
would take place amid bloody revolutions (if the ruling powers were obsti-
nate and failed to perceive the light fast enough) or whether governments
would institute the necessary basic reforms and allow for a peaceful advance.
But in any case there was no mystery in the forces accelerating or impeding
the attainment of a Golden Age. To the Germans, the core of progress was
not the change in the material conditions of life, but the history of man's
moral conquest of his instinctual nature and the triumph of his rationality.
Progress was the development of artistic perception and love of mankind. It
was an individual metamorphosis. The contrasting tempers of the two
philosophies are poignantly revealed in their analogies and metaphors:
Herder was struck with the idea of progress as he watched a caterpillar
transform itself into a butterfly; Condorcet and Saint-Simon thought of
progress as a mathematical series.

Saint-Simon and Condorcet were content to know that history had
demonstrated the inevitability of indefinite progress. They did not pretend to
tackle the problem — which to them would have smacked of the metaphysical and hence would have been suspect — of why nature or society
manifested this characteristic. While Herder at moments of soul-searching
doubted the very existence of perfectibility in our chaotic world he could not,
once he accepted the idea as dogma, divorce it from the teleology of nature.
The teleology was immanent and visible in zoology, botany, and most of all
in human physiology. It was obvious that man had been given a certain

type of brain and had been made to walk in an erect posture in order that he might ultimately be ruled by Reason.[23] To Herder everything in the system of nature was explainable as part of a best possible Leibnitzian world. Even death had a proper and salutary purpose.[24]

Condorcet may have thought of the Age of Reason as the highest stage in the historical development of mankind, while Saint-Simon, after the Revolution, adopted the traditionalists' condemnation of the *philosophes* as destructive agents directly responsible for the horrors of the Revolution; but both of them were equally impressed with the totality of the scientific works which had accumulated by the end of the century. The piling up of scientific discoveries since the renaissance of science under Arab initiative had proceeded irrespective of political vicissitudes. Condorcet and Saint-Simon focused their eyes on the mathematician's study and on the laboratories; they were fully conscious of the technological applications of science in society. The search for scientific truth, from whatever motives or forces it may have sprung, had passed muster before the bar of utility, and it was directly related to the everyday real world. The progress of science was the key to the idea of moral progress in Condorcet and Saint-Simon because science was useful.

To the German philosophers, the motive drives behind an individual's conduct and the force explaining mankind's development in time were quite distinct from each other. The individual man, ruled mostly by brute instinct, was paradoxically in his very nature an impediment to the perfection of mankind. God was slowly unfolding man's rational nature — perhaps revealing its potentialities to one man in a million — in despite of man's baser passions.

To the Frenchmen, the individual was moved by self-love, self-interest, and fellow-feeling or benevolence in various proportions. Both of these drives had in actuality helped to further progress. The love of glory or power — an aspect of self-love — would continue to be a strong motive force, and once comprehended there was to Condorcet and to Saint-Simon nothing deplorable in the fact that progress was dependent upon such passions. In itself love of power was neither good nor bad, unless it took on monstrous forms. What humanity needed was a good system and a sound doctrine, a social order which would make it possible to channelize individual drives into paths leading to the "good of mankind." Once the good social order — an organic scientific-industrial society with a way open for all talents — was established, individual capacities and faculties would naturally express themselves in ways beneficial to mankind. Only if the social order did not provide for the satisfaction of basic desires would self-interest be manifested in destructive ways. Man's essential nature remained the same, but whether his manifest nature was benevolent or vicious depended on the order of society.

The Germans were primarily moral preachers to individuals wrestling with their refractory natures which were obstructing the manifestation in time of that human perfectibility predestined by God and history. Condorcet and Saint-Simon were first and foremost social reformers with "systems," organizers of progress.

PART III

IN THE SERVICE OF
THE GOOD BOURGEOIS

14

The Reorganization of Europe

WITH THE FIRST RESTORATION Saint-Simon, recuperated from his melancholia and provided with a small annuity which took care of his primary necessities, again moved into the public limelight. In a new life both his theory and his fortune underwent a metamorphosis. The *a priori*, universal system-maker of the Empire, the new Descartes, the new Bacon, the new Socrates, assumed for a time a more modest habit and appeared to the entrepreneurs, the economists, the bankers, and the merchants of France as a paid publicist, a pamphleteer for the good *bourgeois*. He had always respected the sober virtues of the men of industry and in his earliest plans for the reorganization of society (1802–1804) he had reserved posts for them by side of or just below the scientific elect. Men of property who accepted his commandment that all must work in some capacity were the stable element in society — a counterpoise to the revolutionary rabble. For them he would now formulate sound political policy. In 1814 he conveniently forgot his youthful advocacy of the Revolution and his adulation of the emperor, and, like so many of his contemporaries, rearranged his recollections to include only his persecutions under the Terror and at the hands of the Napoleonic police.

A new generation of industrialists and financiers had emerged during the Revolution and the Empire, men who had not known the humiliation of the *bourgeoisie* under the old régime, who had manufactured equipment and clothes for the soldiers of Napoleon, and had been awarded titles of nobility for their industrial efforts. Now they were rid of the tyrant who, though he had honored them with prizes at exhibitions, had lorded it over them and finally had brought them to the brink of ruin. The new men of commerce and finance and industry, who came out of the revolutionary epoch with enhanced social status and expanded factories into which the latest machinery had been introduced,[1] clung fiercely to the position they had attained and tried to solidify it. Continuous prosperity, security in the enjoyment of their wealth, required a régime of trade free from governmental restrictions and heavy taxes. Between them and the disinherited noble turned philosopher a strange relationship was fashioned.

In 1814 Saint-Simon finally discovered a collaborator in Augustin Thierry, whom he had met in the fall of 1813 and who had been relieved of his professorship of history at Compiègne upon the return of the Bourbons.[2] Though the young man was not the towering scientific partner whom he had dreamed of under the Empire, for a while the historian was eminently satisfactory, especially since the scope of the universal system was temporarily reduced to a practical social program. From this date until his death Saint-Simon never again worked alone. He always had by his side a bright youth called a secretary, a "pupil," or an "adopted son," who would take dictation, correct manuscripts, and prepare drafts based upon notes of the master's discursive monologues.

With the First Restoration the philosopher and his "adopted son" Thierry unfolded a complete political system, comprising both a foreign policy and a domestic party platform for the guidance of liberals, industrialists, and all men of good will who were not too deeply attached either to Napoleon or to the Bourbons, people who were committed to preserving the liberties of the Revolution while steering France along a middle course between mob violence and despotism.

Since the European peace settlement was uppermost in men's minds, the solution to the international crisis took immediate precedence. The first fruit of Augustin Thierry's collaboration with Saint-Simon was a lively pamphlet entitled *De la réorganisation de la société européenne*, intended as a directive for the princes gathered at the Congress of Vienna. On October 27, 1814, it was singled out for censorship by the Bourbon officials and, after judicious emendations had been made, managed to see a second edition, one of the most successful publications of Saint-Simon's lifetime.

On the morrow of Napoleon's abdication, the overriding problems of European reorganization, of the future of the continent, of war and of peace, had brought forth a swarm of political pamphlets to direct the kings and their ministers to the proper solutions and settlements. Metternich, Castlereagh, Alexander I, and Talleyrand, untouched by the outpouring of paper plans, balanced interests and powers in the traditional eighteenth-century manner, although even they gave lip service to fashionable shibboleths about the "regeneration of Europe." Saint-Simon's little pamphlet was one more tract in the deluge of unsolicited counsel from the publicists of Europe, and had it not issued from his pen it would have quickly passed into oblivion.[3]

The pompous predictions with which he introduced his plan hardly required clairvoyance. Saint-Simon forecast that the assembled diplomats, who thought in the restricted terms of the balance of power which had been the dominant international system of Europe since Westphalia, would achieve no lasting peace, despite their apparent agreement upon formal conventions and treaties. Ever since the breakdown of the medieval system of society, war had become the habitual condition of a continent divested of a common body of moral principles.[4] Treaties had served only as temporary truces and nothing better was to be expected from the Vienna Congress. The basic reason for its inevitable failure lay in a false conception of the nature of European organization. Saint-Simon was particularly suspicious of England's role in the peace settlement, for in past centuries this island had cannily dominated the whole world through manipulation of the balance of power principle. No secret negotiations or skillful manoeuvres among diplomats would end English hegemony or the continental wars through which she maintained it. England either had to abandon this mischievous role and become an integral part of the continent or there would be everlasting strife.

Though operating on a higher level, the several states of contemporary Europe were comparable to individual members of a society which had not yet assumed corporate form. They were like men who lived by a series of independent, discrete contractual relations among themselves while fancying that they were in an organized social state.[5] "To expect Europe to be at peace as the result of treaties and congresses is to expect a social body to subsist on conventions and accords. On both sides a coactive force is necessary which would unite the wills, concert the movements, render interests common and engagements solid."[6] The nation-state was not a mere succession of accords among individuals, for it had always required a cohesive element, a general will, patriotism, to bestow upon the union real solidarity, to make of it more than an agglomeration of isolated units governed by mutual agreements. Similarly the European system would remain formalistic and attain only passing effectiveness unless the same general spirit animated the modern European community of nations as had once inspired medieval society. The concept of the "organic" was applied to the European crisis.

Saint-Simon's eulogy of the common consciousness of the middle ages bore abundant evidence of his thoroughgoing, uncritical acceptance of the romantic myth of the theocratic school.[7]

"Before the end of the fifteenth century, all the nations of Europe formed a single body politic, at peace within itself, armed against the enemies of its constitution and its independence.

"The Roman religion, practiced from one end of Europe to the other, was the passive bond of European society. The Roman clergy was its active bond. Spread everywhere, depending only upon itself, compatriot of all peoples while having its own government and its own laws, it was the center from which emanated the will which animated this great body — it was the impulse which made it act."[8] Whatever the objective validity of his roseate medieval image, Saint-Simon pleaded for the rebirth of that pre-Reformation European consciousness, for without it there could be no common society and no peace. The alternatives were an organic Europe or chaos.

After passing in review a number of earlier projects of perpetual peace, particularly the Abbé de St. Pierre's, he condemned them one and all as ineffectual, for they suffered from the common fault of advocating a mere federation of independent princes, not a "homogeneous" system with a corporate will (*volonté de corps*). While the Abbé de St. Pierre had proposed a European council of powers with mutual guarantees of one another's territories and had provided for sanctions — the violator of the peace was to come under a general ban — his plan was patently inadequate to meet the grave problems besetting Europe. In the abbé's project the states not only agreed to respect one another's boundaries, but committed themselves to suppress internal rebellions; instead of a European system of peoples there was thus created an alliance of princes to preserve one another on the throne. When the states met together in the abbé's Council of Europe, their envoys would represent isolated units, and no force or power would speak for Europe as a whole, for the totality of the continent, in the sense that the Papacy had once symbolized the unity of Catholic Europe. There could be no authentic common decisions in any body where representation was de-rived from nothing more general than individual interest. A national society could not exist if its governing body were composed solely of emissaries of conflicting groups. Similarly European society would collapse or dissolve in an endless round of internecine struggles if it remained a mere collection of individual states. With the same passion that he had argued a few years previously for an integration of the scientific disciplines, he now pleaded for the integral unity of the European states.

In place of the abbé's project [9] and the diplomatic play at Vienna, Saint-Simon came forward with a far more ambitious and comprehensive plan. Europe required an organization based on four cardinal principles, prerequisites for a corporate existence:

1. Every political organization instituted to bind together several peoples, while preserving to each its national independence, must be systematically homo-geneous, that is to say, all its institutions must be the result of a single conception and consequently the government, at every level, is obliged to have similar forms.

2. The general government has to be completely independent of national governments.

3. Those who constitute the general government should be influenced by their position to have only general views and to occupy themselves particularly with general interests.

4. They should be strong with a power which resides in themselves, and which owes nothing to any alien force: this power is public opinion.[10]

In search of appropriate constitutional forms with which to clothe these principles, Saint-Simon was "directed by the science of politics" to adopt the organization of Great Britain, the most successful and effective state unit on the continent. Neither Montesquieu nor contemporary Englishmen would have recognized their ideal instrument of government in Saint-Simon's analysis of the British system. What he saw in the British constitution was a marvelous amalgam of three elements: the Commons, who represented individual interests in their society, the local and the professional interests; the Crown, which from its very unitary character could only represent the general interest, the wholeness, the will of Britain; and the Peers, who represented an intermediate moderating influence to balance the other two views, each of which if given absolute free rein could not act soundly. Upon Europe he would settle the identical tripartite system. First, there would be a general chamber of men chosen from each state (one deputy per million inhabitants who could read and write), primarily on the basis of professional aptitude, by the chief professional classes, the businessmen, scientists, magistrates, and administrators. He would require a minimum annual income qualification (25,000 francs) for most members to assure their independence, though some would also be selected from the impecunious professionals of outstanding talent, who would be allotted the same income from an international budget. Then, a peerage of Europe would be named by the European king, with income qualifications far higher than those of the deputies — they would need 500,000 francs a year. As for the king of the European system, he hedged on a final solution, deferring it to a second volume which never appeared; but he knew the office would be hereditary.

This central government for Europe would levy taxes and undertake vast international public works, starting with a canal system that would join the Danube to the Rhine, the Rhine to the Baltic. The Grand Parliament of Deputies would not accept intra-European territorial boundaries as definitive, but would entertain pleas from any group which aspired to cut itself off from an existing state and become autonomous. The Parliament would adjudicate such national issues not in the interest of governments, but of peoples. The European Council — another name for Parliament — would direct a common educational system based upon positive science and would tolerate all religions as long as they adhered to certain common moral principles.

One of the most effective ways to establish real cohesion among the nations of Europe was to undertake a crusade against the backward areas of the world. Saint-Simon had early been impressed with the medieval crusades as the external movement which had forged the internal unity of Europe and had ended its internecine strife, and he was sanguine that a similar remedy would effect the same cure on the bellicose continent of the nineteenth century.[11]

"Without external activity there can be no internal tranquillity. The surest method of maintaining peace in the confederation will be ceaselessly to direct its efforts outside of itself and to occupy it without a let-up on great internal public works. To people the globe with the European race, which is superior to all other races, to open the whole world to travel and to render it as habitable as Europe, that is the enterprise through which the European parliament should continually engage the activity of Europe and always keep up the momentum." [12]

The doctrine of European race superiority is an old idea with Saint-Simon. What is striking in this remarkable passage is the advocacy of breathless activity, expansive business ventures, militant colonization throughout the world, as a sublimation of the European warlike instincts which, if turned inward, would be suicidal. The necessity of spending the aggressive spirit both of power-lusting individuals and warrior nations in productive activity is an insight which he reiterated many times in his works. Such acute psychological observations are the salt of his writing.

Saint-Simon could not content himself merely with the launching of a utopian project for integral European union. He had to demonstrate to his own satisfaction that it was eminently practicable in the light of existing power relationships and state interests. In the same sense that an appeal to individual self-interest or class interest underlay most of his early social plans for the individual state, his European project could only prove workable if it were consistent with an appeal to national interest.

Europe meant primarily western Europe, and even in this orbit he thought exclusively in terms of France, England, and Germany; eastern Europe still lay beyond the pale of civilization. Therefore to win the argument that his plan was realistic he had to demonstrate that at least England and France would be driven to adopt it in the furtherance of their own national good. As a consequence his European system was solidly anchored in an Anglo-French alliance. Since these two nations held between them a clear preponderance of power in the world, once they had opted for the European system the success of the plan was a certainty. Twentieth-century Frenchmen have referred back to this prophecy of the *entente cordiale* after centuries of Anglo-French hostilities.[13] The specific forensic points in his appeal to English and to French national interest are in themselves not too startling. They narrow down to a thinly veiled threat that unless England and France both moved in unison in this direction, each of their governments individually would be overthrown by revolution. It was his mission to alert rulers to the danger. To the recently restored Bourbons he ventured the rather snide observation that thus far there had been a perfect historical parallel between each of five periods of the English Revolution of the seventeenth century and five periods of the French Revolution as they had succeeded one another through 1815. If the Bourbons were not circumspect, a stage equivalent to the final expulsion of the Stuarts would repeat itself in France, a circumstance he hoped to prevent because Europe had had its fill of wars and revolutions.

The work is replete with emotional arguments, with pleas to the humanity of Europeans that they end their internecine civil strife and create a new common spirit, a "European patriotism." [14] One conception dominates the whole plan of European reorganization: the idea that integral unity can be achieved only if all the participant states are endowed with identical social and political systems and with common moral ideologies — a postulate that Kant had already dwelt upon. There could be no European society if half the régimes remained monarchical, military absolutisms, and the other half parliamentary systems in which the scientific and industrial classes occupied preponderant positions. Since only equals, states of like natures, could be united into one Europe, the creation of an industrial society in each country was a condition precedent to any reorganization of the continent. The notion that in one world civilization there might be a coexistence of sundry governmental, social, and moral systems was absurd to Saint-Simon. Such a heterogeneous agglomeration had characterized European society since the Reformation, with disastrous consequences.

Concluding, he expressed a polite regret that his project had not been conceived by one of the great European sovereigns, for then its chances of acceptance might have been greater. Alas, that was not in the nature of things. Since rulers had to administer affairs of state from day to day they could operate only in terms of the "old combinations" and were incapable of rising above their immediate interests to an over-all view of the European crisis. Therefore he, Saint-Simon, had to perform the task, *faute de mieux*. The manifold practical difficulties involved in winning general European approval for his project neither overwhelmed him nor dampened his optimism. He ended on a note of prophetic illumination, expressed in ecstatic phrases which have long since become a part of the vocabulary of pacifist internationalism.[15]

There will doubtless come a time when all the peoples of Europe will feel that they must regulate matters of general interest before descending to matters of national interest. Then evils will decrease, troubles will be quieted, wars will be extinguished. That is the direction in which we are continually moving. That is where the current of the human spirit is sweeping us. But what is more worthy of the prudence of man, to be dragged there or to run there?

The imagination of the poets placed the Golden Age in the cradle of mankind, in the ignorance and brutality of early times. It is rather the Iron Age which should be relegated there. The Golden Age of the human species is not behind us, it is before us. It lies in the perfection of the social order. Our fathers did not see it at all. Our children will one day arrive there. It is for us to clear the path.[16]

The press reception of this ambitious plan for European reorganization was equivocal, but tolerant and courteous. He heard none of the sneers which had greeted his earlier publications. His views were now considered seriously even when the final judgment was negative.

Rigomer Bazin, the revolutionary publicist who in 1804 had attempted to get one of Saint-Simon's early plans of social organization published abroad and had involved himself with the Napoleonic police in the process, gave the pamphlet a thoroughgoing analysis in *Le Lynx, coup d'oeil et réflexions libres sur les écrits et les affaires du temps*, which he edited. This was a "periodical book" similar to Saint-Simon's later journalistic ventures and like them it was shortlived, lasting for a scant two years from 1815 to 1817. After some thirteen pages of summation consisting largely of quotations, Bazin presented a skeptical critique of his old friend's project.[17] A European federation was an impossibility, came the verdict. The historical analogy of the middle ages which had been adduced by Saint-Simon and Thierry was not a valid precedent, because far from having served as a unifying force, Papal pretensions to supremacy had excited endless wars and revolts. Rigomer Bazin further attacked the plan in the name of a romantic conception of the nation. Unlike men, nations could not contract permanent unions with other nations and become members of a stronger supersociety without losing that identity, that *moi*, which defined their nature. Saint-Simon's machinery for the European Parliament he considered top-heavy, without a sound base among the people. Bazin was especially derogatory of the idea that an Anglo-French federation should form the nub of the great European society, since he did not at all agree that the two countries had common interests and an essentially common spirit; on the contrary, he denounced England's Machiavellianism in always opposing France in European politics, and directed a withering attack on England's feudal and oligarchic society. Saint-Simon had passed over the glaring defects in the English system; why should France bind herself to those antiquated institutions?

For all his critical comments, Bazin appreciated Saint-Simon's clarity in laying bare the status of the great powers. "He evaluates the present with a broad sweep. He foresees the future with a rare sagacity. Afflicted by the misfortunes which still threaten us, he seeks a remedy." Yet this was precisely where Saint-Simon had failed. Like an alchemist he had prescribed an old specific, and while the illness of Europe was diagnosed correctly, the remedy was inadequate.

Le Censeur, the outstanding liberal periodical of the First Restoration, adopted a similar position. The reviewer praised the nobility of Saint-Simon's sentiments and the philanthropy of his ideals, but indicated that the whole project was somewhat extravagant, premature in its anticipation of the slow march of the centuries.[18] Perhaps this was a carry-over of the derisive attitude towards Saint-Simon among serious people who had heard of his Empire extravaganzas, for the general ideas formulated in *De la réorganisation de la société européenne* were by no means alien to the liberals of the period. Though Benjamin Constant could not refrain from mingling his characteristic ironies with niggardly praise for Saint-Simon, the tenor of his own more brilliant *De l'esprit de conquête* was in the same current of opinion. Many essays in *Le Censeur* of 1815 seem to be echoing and paraphrasing Saint-Simon, or at least joining in the common chorus of ideas. An article entitled "Sur la situation de l'Europe, sur les causes de ses guerres, et sur les moyens d'y mettre fin" reads: "[O]nly free peoples can be united in a confederation. It is moreover necessary that they have analogous constitutions in order that they may proceed in a uniform manner to the creation of a central government which should hold them united. The confederation should occupy itself with great works of general utility, establish great communications, open canals, cut isthmuses, thrust colonies in the midst of barbaric peoples to hasten the diffusion of civilization and extend commercial . . . relations." [19]

The solution to the problem of European reorganization which the Congress of Vienna devised was far from the spirit of Saint-Simon and his liberal compatriots. Under attack, the absolute monarchs of the east hoped to save Europe from disintegration with a Holy Alliance — which only prolonged the crisis. Czar Alexander, to whom a copy of *De la réorganisation de la société européenne* had been sent, preferred the more mystical outpourings of Mme. de Krüdener.

15

The Baconian Society

THE DOMESTIC POLICIES advocated by Saint-Simon and Thierry were a logical counterpart of their foreign policy. Liberal, constitutional, mercantile England had become the *beau idéal*. Since there was no formal party organization to which they could adhere in the amorphous political situation of the First Restoration, they became members of the anticlerical, antifeudal, liberal group whose leaders were Jean-Baptiste Say, Benjamin Constant, Charles Comte, and Charles Dunoyer. Saint-Simon tended to phrase his ideas in an uncompromising manner and his style was more flamboyant than that of the cautious directors of *Le Censeur*, but he was tolerated in their circle, and this important journal not only reviewed his tracts, but opened its pages to the announcement of the numerous political schemes which he devised in rapid succession. During the First Restoration they published a *Lettre de M. le Comte de Saint-Simon sur l'établissement du parti de l'opposition* which called for the organization of a two-party system in imitation of the English,[1] a *Projet d'une association des propriétaires de domaines nationaux*,[2] and long excerpts from his *Prospectus d'un ouvrage ayant pour titre: Le Défenseur des propriétaires de domaines nationaux ou recherches sur les causes du discrédit dans lequel sont tombées les propriétés nationales, et sur les moyens d'élever ces propriétés à la même valeur que les propriétés patrimoniales*,[3] through which Saint-Simon hoped to consolidate a political party around the core of national property-owners, whose titles were threatened by the *émigrés* aiming to reverse the whole revolutionary land settlement.

Napoleon's sudden reappearance threw Saint-Simon and Thierry into the same quandary as the other liberals. During the Hundred Days the publicist team continued to issue tracts in which they accommodated themselves as best they could to the changing fortunes of the battlefield. On March 15, 1815, they published a *Profession de foi des auteurs de l'ouvrage annoncé sous le titre de Défenseur des propriétaires de domaines nationaux, de la Chartre et des idées libérales, au sujet de l'invasion du territoire français par Napoléon*, in which they attacked Napoleon "who for ten years desolated France with all the excesses of a military despotism," and exhorted the army to rally in support of Louis XVIII. Instead of being chastised, Saint-Simon was rewarded by the new "liberal" Napoleonic régime, and on April 10, 1815, through the intervention of Lazare Carnot whom he had known under the Directorate,[4] he was appointed a librarian in the Bibliothèque de l'Arsenal. With this solid source of income as a mainstay, he forthwith proceeded to address lofty political advice to the emperor. A manuscript plan, *Sur l'organisation du droit public*, called upon Napoleon to establish public chairs of scientific politics which would end the crisis of European society and graciously offered his own candidacy for one of the posts.[5]

On May 18, 1815, less than two weeks before the festivities of the Champ de Mai, at which the French people's approval of the new Napoleonic constitutional régime embodied in the *Acte Additionnel* was to be proclaimed, Saint-Simon and Thierry published a brochure entitled *Opinion sur les mesures à prendre contre la coalition de 1815*.[6] They took seriously the plebiscite which was being conducted, espoused the thesis that in this period of virtual interregnum the people had the right to lay down basic constitutional principles for the government not only in domestic but in international affairs. Their tract forthrightly posed the question as to what should be the proper orientation of French foreign policy in the light of the national interest, since France could not stand alone assailed by all the European powers and she had to choose a friend. After reviewing a roster of the nations they quickly eliminated Austria, Russia, and Prussia, concluding that the Anglo-French alliance which they had been advocating for over a year was the only solution to the dilemmas of foreign affairs. Their avowed purpose in writing the new tract was to persuade the people of France to insist upon acceptance of the idea of an Anglo-French alliance as a condition precedent to the grant of new constitutional powers to the emperor. All this on the eve of Waterloo.

Saint-Simon's incumbency at the Bibliothèque de l'Arsenal was cut short when the Bourbons regained their throne and Pasquier, the new minister of Louis XVIII, quickly discharged him and invited back his predecessor.[7] In August 1815 Saint-Simon made a request for a passport, perhaps out of fear of Bourbon reprisals.[8]

During this bewildering period of kaleidoscopic political change, when régimes rose and fell within a few months, Saint-Simon was gravitating ever closer towards that stable social element upon whom all governments seemed to depend. He was successfully making his way into the society of liberal industrialists and bankers, some of whom he had known under the Directorate and Consulate. Jacques Laffitte, who had started out as an employee in the Perregaux bank, with which Saint-Simon had done business during the Revolution, had become a financial power in his own right. In the last years of the Empire the great merchant-manufacturers of France had been grouped in official bodies, the Napoleonic consultative councils of industry and commerce, and in unofficial organizations such as the *Société d'encouragement pour l'industrie nationale*. They had sponsored inventions, new techniques of scientific agriculture, the introduction of machinery, and, along with the new technology, projects of educational reform which, they expected, would provide them with a more intelligent labor force. Virtually the same names appear on the records of all the philanthropic societies and agencies for the diffusion of the new industrial outlook — Ternaux, Périer, Delessert, Alexandre de Laborde — and they would later be featured on the lists of subscribers to Saint-Simon's publication ventures. There are even indications that during the Hundred Days Napoleon himself was moving towards the creation of a new governmental system in which bankers, manufacturers, industrialists, and scientists would sit in councils of state as representatives of their occupations and professions. Though it is doubtful whether Saint-Simon's plans had any direct influence on these projects which Carnot espoused in imperial circles, he sensed an affinity between the Napoleonic hierarchic conceptions and his own. In the early years of the Restoration Saint-Simon assured his salon audiences that the emperor had been a propagator of his ideas.

During the last of the Hundred Days a group of *bourgeois* industrialists with and without noble titles, economists, and philanthropists, as if turning their backs upon Napoleon and the fate of the French armies, occupied themselves with the reform of the primary schools.[9] In June 1815 among the founders of the *Société de Paris pour l'instruction élémentaire* was Saint-Simon; along with Charles Comte, Charles de Lasteyrie, Alexandre de Laborde, Jean-Baptiste Say, and Dr. Blainville he was interested in experimenting with the Bell and Lancaster system of "mutual education" in order to raise the literacy standards of the poor without too vast an expenditure of funds. To these "philanthropists" higher standards of education meant more competent industrial workers in France, and a more prosperous commercial society. As always, England was the prototype. Saint-Simon, who had long before independently arrived at the idea that the educational system was the key to the general character of a civilization, took a personal interest in the experimental school which the Society was operating in Popincourt, visited the establishment, made a survey, and in 1816 submitted a report entitled *Quelques idées soumises par M. de Saint-Simon à l'Assemblée générale de la Société d'instruction primaire*. He found the attendance record bad and the teacher harassed by the contradictory instructions of eight different committee members. The educational experiment would not succeed, he predicted, because they had selected an area where the children were the most bedraggled and worst reared in Paris. Saint-Simon had not yet become the defender of the lowest classes in society. He suggested that instead of these working-class children the Society first sponsor the education of the middle classes and artisans, because this was the social stratum most amenable to enlightenment. Of the basic soundness of the Bell and Lancaster system he was convinced. If reading and writing could be taught in eighteen months, the general educational level of Frenchmen would be raised and the productive potentialities of the nation would be enormously increased. To fix the curriculum for the remaining years of schooling, he reverted to his favorite procedure whenever he was in doubt, a prize essay contest to determine the optimum plan.

With the Second Restoration the *émigrés* swarmed into France resolved to resurrect prerevolutionary society. State control was once again to be concentrated in the royal family, their noble administrators, and the church. But the great industrialists and bankers of France, who had acquired a consciousness of their power during the past quarter of a century, no longer were content to occupy a secondary status in the realm. Bankers like Casimir Périer, Delessert, and Laffitte, industrialists like Ternaux and Richard Lenoir, were proud of their executive capacities, of their productive and creative role in society, and they refused to humble themselves before an *émigré* aristocracy returning to France in the train of the foreign occupation forces with all its inherited prejudices against commerce and industry intact.[10] These industrialists wrote no pamphlets or political tracts, neither were they social theorists. But as the ultra-Royalists increased their economic levies to the detriment of the new *bourgeoisie*, the idea gained strength among the industrialists that instead of proffering unheeded advice to an obscurantist, hostile government, they should themselves assume direction of the state. Held in a position of subordination, forced to yield an indemnity of a milliard to the do-nothing *émigrés* and to acquiesce in many projects harmful to their economic interests, they planned with slow certainty to rid themselves of the Bourbon régime, though in a quiet, unspectacular manner, as befitted solid citizens.

In the eighteenth century the *bourgeoisie* had patronized the revolutionary anticlerical publicists who undermined the church and the state. For the industrialists of 1815, who were intimidated by a powerful clerical reaction and troubled by bitter revolutionary memories, antireligious propaganda could not be utilized safely as an ideological weapon. New defenders of the industrialists against the prerogatives of the nobility had to present their point of view in arguments disassociated from the religious question which touched the very fabric of the social structure. Therefore respectable liberal economists, the founders of a new science, became the favorite chief protagonists of the Restoration *bourgeois*. Political economy came into fashion, particularly during the financial crisis of 1817.[11] At times the economists, crying aloud for the supremacy of the industrialists, were too radical for the cautious men whose cause they were espousing, and often it was difficult to convince the industrial and financial leaders that they were destined to be the lords of the age; but for the most part the doctrines of *laissez-faire*, stated without reference to underlying moral problems, were eminently acceptable theory for the *bourgeois*.

During the first years of the Restoration, Saint-Simon was an exponent of the doctrines of these liberal economists. Jean-Baptiste Say, himself an entrepreneur, had spread Smithianism in France and at one time Saint-Simon would not have been loath to consider himself a simplifier and journalistic popularizer of Say's ideas.[12] If he had stuck to his last he would have earned his keep and been forgotten among a host of other publicist defenders of the cause of the *bourgeoisie*.

His relations with Jean-Baptiste Say were intimate in the early years of the Restoration. There is an undated note to a friend enclosing tickets to Say's public lectures, in which Saint-Simon extolled the "public spirit" in England in contrast with the total absence of any such sentiment in France. If French bankers, merchants, and industrialists had any sense of social obligation, they would all have subscribed to Say's lectures and dramatically appeared *en masse* at the opening of the course. By this demonstrative act they would have expressed their adherence to institutions which spread abroad "good principles." [13] It was Saint-Simon's new purpose in life to stimulate public spirit among the industrialists in their own interest, despite their apathy. Jean-Baptiste Say reciprocated his esteem and always had a kind, encouraging word to write about Saint-Simon's Restoration publications and the manuscript drafts he submitted to him for criticism. On the morrow after Waterloo, on August 1, 1815, a sketch of one of Saint-Simon's projected works on the Anglo-French alliance, a scheme to which he perennially reverted, won Say's approval as far as the soundness of the principles enunciated was concerned. The economist was less sanguine about the chances of any general acceptance of the idea. To those who did not understand political economy his ideas would appear dubious or false. Since only about two dozen minds in France comprehended these things, they had to begin by educating the public. Say himself was working diligently on a Catechism of Political Economy with questions and answers, and he promised to bring Saint-Simon a copy.[14] The use of a secular catechism as a method of propagating his doctrine appealed to Saint-Simon, and in the twenties he adopted the form, calling one of his own periodicals the *Catéchisme des industriels*. In one sense Saint-Simon's career in the next period of his life was a fulfillment of the mission described by Jean-Baptiste Say — educating the public to an appreciation of the values of an industrial society.

Among Saint-Simon's extant unpublished manuscripts there is a finished project entitled *Aux Anglais et aux Français qui sont zélés pour le bien public*.[15] Though this plan cannot be dated with precision, it clearly belongs to the early years of the Restoration and probably is the one referred to in Jean-Baptiste Say's letter. The idea of an Anglo-French union was here developed with great detail. It is one of Saint-Simon's most minutely outlined projects, the nearest to a utopia of anything he composed during these years; it was intended, however, as a realistic proposal for the integral unification of the two greatest western powers, a fusion of two states which would then become the nucleus of a community of western Europe and later of the whole world. Ideas which had been merely suggested in *De la réorganisation de la société européenne* were presented in this tract as a specific program of action to be implemented immediately.

The Anglo-French union would be endowed with a common spiritual power even while the two countries retained separate temporal powers. The spiritual power would have broad functions; it would institute a common system of education, establish prizes for the encouragement of scientists, enforce a uniform doctrine based on the ideals of work, positive science, and Christian charity. Under the direction of the spiritual power, all the works of man would be divided into three categories, those which were useful, those which were harmful, and those which were of an indifferent character, and each man would be recompensed according to his works judged by the standard of utility. Sermons under the direction of the spiritual power would be devoted to a presentation of the virtues of science and work. To achieve spiritual unity at the top the educational system would be crowned by an *école normale* common to both nations and staffed by the members of the "spiritual legislative council." The educators of the new society were to be its spiritual power. A supreme body in this sphere, the "legislative council of the spiritual power," would be comprised of twenty-four scientists drawn from both countries, twelve organic specialists and twelve inorganic. The council would perpetuate itself by filling its own vacancies.

There was also a "spiritual executive power" to enforce the decisions of the council of scientists and it would be staffed by rich men who received no salary, only lodgings. Whereas the legislative council of the spiritual power would sit for no longer than one month a year, the executive was a continuing power. Saint-Simon here, as in many later works, betrayed a deep-rooted suspicion of excessively protracted parliamentary debates. While he was not absolutely opposed to the discussions he wished to limit their duration. Until the chief nations recognized this Anglo-French union its seat would be in London; thereafter the locus would be shifted back and forth across the channel at regular intervals.

During a transition period the traditional religious state cults would continue to operate as before and those spiritual leaders who helped effect the translation of powers to the educators would be recompensed. Once the new scientific spiritual power was established, religious teachings would be allowed only on a private basis, without governmental subvention.

The temporal powers of the two countries were to be organized separately, though they were linked "organically" by the spiritual power. The English Parliament would be replaced by a legislative council of sixteen farmers, sixteen manufacturers, sixteen merchants, and eight bankers. The upper stratum of these industrial classes would participate in the first election; thereafter the council would fill its own vacancies. Membership was specifically restricted to active industrialists, who upon retirement from business were obliged to withdraw from the council. Saint-Simon here expressed his enduring fear of a permanent bureaucracy devoted exclusively to the functions of government. Four of the retired industrialists, however, would be appointed to serve as a liaison between the temporal and the spiritual power.

This temporal legislative council drew up the budget — its central function. Few European theorists were as convinced as Saint-Simon of the crucial character of this operation in the modern state. In addition to the budget, the council passed laws aimed at the increase of production and "the amelioration of the moral and physical welfare of society." The temporal executive was vested in a president and six councilors chosen by the legislative body and subject to removal. The temporal legislative body was allowed only fifteen days to a month each year for its deliberations.

At first glance this industrial society appears to be nothing more than government by a rich oligarchy, but Saint-Simon introduced a number of elements which distinguish it. The oligarchy had to function in terms of an ideal of maximum production; the *rentier*, the hoarder of capital, was to be "encouraged" by law to invest his money in new ventures. Though Saint-Simon did not set up *equality* as an abstract social ideal he was wary of enduring fortunes in the same hands. While his society was ruled by the rich, he expected the movement of enterprise and capital to be so fast that this class would be composed of constantly changing individual members. Though he never went as far as his later disciples in advocating the abolition of inheritance, he did insist on a high degree of social mobility in his society.

"Under the industrial régime which will be essentially one of equality it is not at all desirable that the same families should conserve their wealth for many generations. All men should work either to enrich their children loyally or to impoverish them honorably. Capital must be kept in a continual state of movement. It would be monstrous if those who possess the instrument and do not use it should enjoy greater esteem than those who are capable of employing it well." [16]

The French temporal power would evolve constitutional techniques which were somewhat different from those of the English — Saint-Simon was enough of a disciple of Montesquieu and the nascent romantic nationalists to be willing to make allowances for differences of climate and of national character. He was not certain which of the two national temporal powers would institute their new régimes first. Under the existing system the *industrials*[17] of England and of France had different balances of advantages and disadvantages. The French industrials had greater provocation to oust the ruling groups of their society than did the English, but they were less well educated and they had an enemy at their gates in the shape of German feudalism. The English industrials enjoyed a commercial monopoly and status in the realm, which tended to keep them satisfied and dampened any incentive to assume direct control of society. Hence his general conclusion that the spiritual power of the Anglo-French union was likely to become established before the temporal.

Saint-Simon was as interested in the mechanics necessary to insure the institution of the industrial society as he was in its final organizational forms. His proposed method of action in this manuscript plan was a discreet combination of persuasion and "force" — though he never advocated the direct use of violence. Under the heading of moral suasion he included propaganda to prove both to princes and peoples that his plan would increase the general welfare. The scientists particularly had to preach the new doctrine with the zeal of the apostles, a task made difficult by the dependence of most of them on government salaries. It was therefore necessary for the industrials to support them with at least a threat of force.

"The chiefs of industrial enterprises in England and in France should declare to the English and the French governments that if, at a date which they will fix, the governments refuse to consent to the establishment of a scientific and industrial constitution for the two nations, they and their workers will stop paying taxes. They should announce to them that if they consent to the change in social organization necessitated by the progress of civilization they would be well treated and recompensed insofar as possible for the losses that they will suffer; and that in the contrary circumstances they would be accorded no damages."[18] If nineteen-twentieths of the population of both countries — the industrials — made this demand of their governments simultaneously, nothing could resist them. It was shameful for the industrials to endure the yoke of the phrase-makers, the swashbucklers, the rich idlers.

The Anglo-French union was, Saint-Simon was quick to emphasize, only the core of the industrial society. The combination of the two most powerful industrial units would serve as a solid rallying point for the industrials of the world. The secure Anglo-French industrial society would act as protector for the industrials of other countries whenever they would have the strength and the enlightenment to effect the transition to a new régime in their own areas. Ultimately the whole globe was destined to adopt the same industrial-scientific doctrine and to organize itself in accordance with its principles.

The constitution of the new industrial society as Saint-Simon outlined it in this manuscript fulfilled all the conditions necessary for the happiness of the human species in accordance with his analysis of the nature of man, his main sources of conduct, and his basic requirements. All men had a passion to increase their moral and physical well-being. By placing at the head of society the men with capacity for works of "positive utility," this passion would be satisfied. Men had a passion for equality. By placing at the top of the social ladder the most distinguished scientists and industrialists, irrespective of their class origins, this passion would also be satisfied, insofar as possible, because it would allow for social mobility. The most illustrious scientists and industrialists normally emerged from the lower ranks of society and free opportunity would adequately appease their passion for status. The rich had a passion for esteem. By awarding them posts of conspicuous display their passion would be satiated. Public tranquillity was guaranteed because the supreme power in society was vested in those classes who had the most direct interest in peace — the rich, the scientists, and the industrials. One of the ends of government was to administer public affairs as cheaply as possible. Since the most important functionaries were the rich they would naturally economize because it was they who paid taxes, and offices were unsalaried. Finally, the good was equivalent to the acceptance of positive, utilitarian judgements. The constitution elevated those with positive capacities and knowledge and subordinated metaphysics; it awarded primacy to "doers," not to "talkers."

Saint-Simon devised an organizational instrument, a society which in the course of recruiting its membership would become a sort of living nucleus of the new societal order in the very body of the old. When this society expanded enough it would virtually become the new industrial régime. The society has a most provocative name, the *Société Anglo-Fran-çaise*, or the *Société Baconienne* — explicit recognition of the theoretical inspiration of his social conception in the works of the great Elizabethan. Membership in the society was open to any Englishman or Frenchman who signed the pledge: "I accept the general principles which have been set forth in the prospectus of the society." Each member had to contribute annually in accordance with his means. Subscriptions could be sent to leading banking houses and industrial firms. With these funds he was prepared to begin the publication of positivist treatises, instruments of propaganda for the Baconian Society which was in turn the agency for the realization of the Anglo-French union and ultimately of a world industrial society.

In a long series of publications during the Restoration Saint-Simon developed variations on the theme outlined in the manuscript on the Baconian Society. This version was a transitional schema midway between the grandiose plans of the Consulate and the programs of the later Restoration.

16

"All for Industry"

AMONG THE WEALTHY RESTORATION *BOURGEOIS* Saint-Simon, the constant propagandist for "new ideas," cut a rather anomalous figure, a descendant of one of the most ancient houses of France who had opted for the new social classes against the *émigrés*. It was doubtless flattering to *bourgeois* self-esteem to sponsor a Saint-Simon as their paid publicist. In a number of respectable *bourgeois* houses he was received despite his shady libertine reputation. He was considered a "clever original" —the phrase quoted by John Stuart Mill who met him in Jean-Baptiste Say's salon.[1] More cautious bankers and industrialists would see him in their offices when they were reluctant to invite him to their homes. Among them he at first won a far more sympathetic hearing than he was ever accorded by the pompous official scientists of the Empire, and he reciprocated with enthusiasm for the role of the industrialists, the seminal class of the historic moment. This does not mean that they all accepted his daring theories, even when they helped finance his publications. To some of them a subscription for one of Saint-Simon's periodicals was an act of charity to a hapless character; others, and not the least among them Ternaux and Laffitte, took him seriously. They argued with him about the merits of his propositions, including those which they considered too extravagant for tactical use in their battle against the *émigrés*. In later years a fellow-publicist of the liberal group, Charles Dunoyer, made light of Saint-Simon's original contribution to the propagation of the "industrialist" viewpoint.[2] There were controversies over who actually coined the nouns *industriel*[3] and *industrialisme*, neologisms which Saint-Simon thought he had invented, problems in historical semantics which cannot be resolved with absolute certainty and which have limited significance. A class of merchant-manufacturers who usually did their own financing were pushing to the fore of French Restoration society and a new terminology was being created to define their achievements and to articulate their class desires. In this process Saint-Simon was a historic midwife.

Saint-Simon was a great conversationalist, a far better talker than a writer. The flashes of insight which captivated his listeners when they heard them spoken, often seemed either platitudinous or ridiculous in cold print. His incapacity to develop the structural framework of his ideas was no handicap in café monologues, salon debates, intimate discussions with young favorites. Henri Gouhier has called him a "professor of energy," an epithet which deprives him of consideration as a creative thinker. Saint-Simon compared himself with another philosopher twenty-two hundred years before his time who left no written record in his own hand and whose genius expressed itself in sharp dialogue with young men in the marketplace.

There are a few eyewitness accounts of Saint-Simon the fascinating conversationalist of the early Restoration, the aging aristocrat who as the central figure of a group riveted the attention even of cynics and skeptics when he delivered himself of lengthy discourses on the approaching triumph of the industrial society. A young man who had once observed Saint-Simon in action at the Café Procope recalled his father's later description of the scene.

"Every evening M. de Saint-Simon would be at the café from eight to ten. He usually sat at a marble table facing the counter. He was tall, built like an athlete, but he appeared broken up by the fatigues of the American War. He had a superb head which Girodet would have liked to take away with him to make a study of it. His manners were exquisite, his conversation entrancing. . . . His speech seemed logical and belied the opinion one formed of him in reading his works, which were enthusiastic to the point of madness." [4]

Saint-Simon was always on the look-out for bright young men to bear his message to distant parts of the world. Hippolyte Auger's memoirs have an account of his meeting with the Russian Michael Lunin in the salon of Madame Lydie Roger. Saint-Simon had come expressly for the purpose of converting the brilliant young foreigner and he expounded his ideas in great detail, dilated upon his projects, congratulated himself on the success of his work, and especially on his direction of men of talent. He predicted future greatness for his pupils Augustin Thierry and Auguste Comte. His conversation was a continuous repetition of the basic tenets of his doctrine in its most recent version. Mankind could only reach its new destiny if sentiment, science, and industry were joined together for the progress of society. Lunin impressed him, and he regretted the imminent departure of the fiery Russian visitor. "Another man of intelligence escapes me," he said, "Through you I was beginning a relationship with a people whom skepticism has not yet denuded, among whom I could sow the seed of the doctrine of the future." Though Lunin offered to correspond with him,

Saint-Simon was not sanguine about this method of communication. He had enough insight into himself to know that he was really great only in the heat of conversation, in the give and take of personal contact. "One never understands oneself better than when one argues. Objections are the price of victory." Saint-Simon penetrated into the esssential nature of the young men who attracted him. He sensed the restless spirit of the Russian who was destined to become enmeshed in the quixotic uprising of the Decembrists and to end his years in Siberia. Saint-Simon warned him against involvement in party politics, a waste and a diversion of the main effort of mankind which should be concentrated upon hastening the coming into being of the new industrial society. The absorption of the young liberals in political forms and constitutions was an evil, but he knew all too well that Lunin would be ensnared by them like all men of his age and temperament everywhere throughout the world. At one point in the monologue Madame Roger broke in to twit Saint-Simon with the objection that after all he too was playing politics. To which he rejoined:

Madame, if I am in politics, it is without wanting to be. It is unavoidable, but a deterrent, a barrier on the road of progress. Do you call progress the errors of today, which succeed the errors of yesterday and prepare the errors of tomorrow? The old *nous* is not dethroned. The most absurd of beliefs places the golden age in the past. It is the future alone which holds it in store. Giants will return, not giants in stature, but giants in the power of reasoning. Machines will replace the arms of men. The seven-league boots of the fairy tale are ordered for humanity by the great captain of the army of workers. Industry is the only politics of peace, because peace is the only politics of nations, even if governments continue for a while longer to make us grasp the full odiousness of their present methods by the odiousness of their results.

Saint-Simon was worried by contemporary Russian expansionism (the cossacks had marched through Paris), another distraction from the central problem of European society. His parting words to Lunin were a prophecy:

"If you forget me, do not forget our French proverb: He who embraces too much cannot hold on well. Since Peter the Great your sovereigns have been losing themselves in extension. Rome ruined itself through conquest. The spirit of Christ harvested the field fertilized by blood. The saber has perpetuated slavery. The instrument of labor will establish liberty, the inalienable right of man on earth." [5]

To a whole group of young *bourgeois* who had been drawn from the provinces to Paris for their studies, Saint-Simon in his middle fifties was a grand figure of the *ancien régime* — an impression he did nothing to discourage. When he captured the imagination of intellectuals or artists he possessed them completely with his system, at least for a time. In the early years of the Restoration he was beginning to make converts. Professor

Eugène Péclet's letter from the south of France exudes warmth and enthusiasm, the eagerness for news by a member of an intimate circle of
friends who is temporarily absent from the "little band." When he received
one of Saint-Simon's letters he had actually "jumped around his room like
a madman." He announced his firm decision to teach in accordance with
Saint-Simon's system. If he were ever received into the Academy he intended to deliver his inaugural address on the influence of the sciences on
industry, a typically Saint-Simonian subject. Though in his passionate
search for general ideas he had also read Hoëné-Wroński, another contemporary system-maker, he had found him incredibly hard sledding —
"a mine where there is a little gold, but very difficult to extract." The Paris
friends of Saint-Simon's circle had not been profuse with their letters, he
complained. "Thierry, it seems to me, might have spent half an hour less
fashioning his cravat," and sent along some news. "I hope that when I am
an academician he will have somewhat more respect for my illustrious person." [6]

A secretary employed by Saint-Simon in 1816 has left an anonymous
account of the founding of *l'Industrie*, his first important venture as an
official publicist for the new party of liberal industrialists.[7] Saint-Simon had
proposed to a group of prominent bankers and manufacturers that each
month he would publish a volume of three to four hundred pages, comprising articles on the arts and the sciences, edited in consonance with their
viewpoint, if they on their part would open for him a credit account of
10,000 francs monthly to cover the expenses of editing and printing. After
the initial contacts were established, Saint-Simon addressed a letter to the
leading lights of all the professions, the bankers, the merchants, and the
purchasers of national property, soliciting subscriptions for his great project.

I undertake to free you from the supremacy exercized over you by the
courtiers, by the idle, by the nobles, by the phrase-makers.

I promise to employ only legal, loyal, and inoffensive methods. I promise,
moreover, to obtain for you in a short period of time the greatest degree of public
esteem and a dominant influence over the direction of public affairs. I am opening
subscriptions in order to procure the means of multiplying my writings and dis-
seminating them widely. As soon as industrial opinion is crystallized, nothing
will be able to resist it.

You see, gentlemen, that already houses of the first rank have accorded me
their aid.

A long list of bankers and manufacturers and deputies and scientists
who had already subscribed included the outstanding personalities of France.
There were Périer and Ardoin and the Banque Perregaux, Talma and Lafayette, Arago, Cuvier, Delessert, Jean-Baptiste Say, and Ternaux. The
beginning of the enterprise was auspicious. Saint-Simon removed to a more
comfortable apartment on the Rue de l'Ancienne Comédie, and he was able

to pay both Augustin Thierry and the anonymous secretary regular salaries. Every Thursday he assembled his editorial board and some friends for a meal. There were the Scheffer brothers, artists, the financial authority, M. de St. Aubin, Doctor Bougon, his Alençon friend who was now a physician-in-waiting to the Duchess of Berry, Professor Magnien of the Collège Bourbon, and one of the Didot's. Each month the anonymous secretary went to M. Laffitte and drew the 10,000 francs agreed upon.

Saint-Simon's work habits were as eccentric as ever. He ordinarily spent the hours before noon at his desk, then devoted the remainder of the day to walks, to visits, and to other pleasures. His morning began a little early, "often very near to midnight," his harrassed secretary later complained. "As soon as the silence and peaceful seclusion of the night permitted M. de Saint-Simon to grasp an idea which he did not wish to lose, the bell rang and got me out of bed to take a pen. He dictated and then sent me off to bed again, except that he called me again as often as his inspiration came to demand it." Saint-Simon's ideas were often so jumbled and confused that he was incapable of expounding them with clarity. "Thus it happened," wrote the secretary, "that almost every time we resumed our work, after having me read what he had dictated at the previous session, he tore it up or threw it into the fire, telling me to take another sheet." [8]

Early drafts of his propaganda plans for the industrial society appeared under many different names. One was called an *Entreprise des intérêts généraux de l'industrie ou Société de l'opinion industrielle*.[9] In a statement of purpose he promised to support everything and anything that favored production and elevated the social prestige of producers and bestowed glory upon them. The Society, for which he solicited members, would bolster the self-confidence of producers as a class, a sentiment he thought needed strengthening, would draw up a plan of political action for them, would inspire them with the will to act. To guide producers through the bewildering controversies of the day the Society would decide upon and announce the course of conduct most favorable to industry in every particular issue. The Society would also put an end to the battle of the alternative systems of social reorganization proposed by reformers, by affording the public an opportunity — through its agency — to choose the one they considered most appropriate to their needs.

Saint-Simon's most succinct statement of his ideas, often in epigrammatic form, first appeared in the prospectuses, circulars, and lithographed letters which ushered in a new publication. He was most successful in jotting down the kernel of an idea, in grasping a whole aspect of social evolution in a phrase, in striking a slogan which ultimately penetrated everywhere on the continent. His long expositions of the doctrine tended to lose themselves in digressions, repetitions, and contradictions.

An 1817 Prospectus of *l'Industrie* opened with his social manifesto, his credo. First, a sharp break with the *philosophes*: "The eighteenth century did nothing but destroy, we shall not continue its work." Then a positive commitment to the idea of social happiness and utility: "What we undertake . . . is to lay the foundations for a new construction, to pose and to treat the question of the common interests of men which have thus far, so to speak, been left untouched; to make politics, morals, and philosophy — instead of dwelling forever upon idle useless contemplations — return at last to their veritable goal which is the constitution of social happiness; to see to it in a word that liberty shall no longer be an abstraction nor society a fiction." [10]

Throughout the year 1817 a whole series of circulars were addressed alternately to businessmen and to scientists, with the hope of forming a "coalition" between these two main branches of the industrial society. Though the two classes were by nature distinct, as he realized since his reading of the physiologist Bichat (one was practical, the other theoretical), a real collaboration between them had to be achieved before the inauguration of the industrial society. And he was prepared to act as their go-between. Thus while consorting with industrialists and abandoning the hope that he would be admitted to the intimacy of the great scientists of the age, he was not underestimating the potency of this class in society. He merely recognized the equivalent vitality of the new industrial class in the social structure.

Under the Empire Saint-Simon, with a part of his being still rooted in the aristocratic, classical tradition, had announced that all his labors were in pursuit of living glory. During the early years of the Restoration he made a desperate effort to integrate himself with the utilitarian values of the *bourgeois* which in a profound sense were alien to his psychological nature, though they were fundamental to his philosophy. Publicly he submitted his ideas before the utilitarian bar of the industrial society for judgment and reward, like any man selling his wares in the marketplace. "We have conceived of a philosophic enterprise which we believe useful. We seek to derive from it esteem, ease; we frankly admit it. We ask this of industry: let it grant us all this if it thinks our products are useful to it. Let it reject us if it thinks that we are of no use to it." [11]

Sometime during 1817 Saint-Simon lost Augustin Thierry as a collaborator and he acquired in his stead Auguste Comte, an unemployed young man who had been expelled from the Ecole Polytechnique. The "anonymous secretary" suggests that it was the cloudiness of his thought which finally repelled and alienated Augustin Thierry, despite Saint-Simon's pressing insistence that he continue their work. The account of their breach in the Thierry family tradition emphasized reasons of another character. There is an anecdote that when Saint-Simon told Augustin Thierry he could not imagine an association without someone in control, he was answered, "And I cannot conceive of an association without liberty." [12] More than any clash of temperaments, however, a basic dissension over ideas drove the romantic and individualist Thierry from Saint-Simon's side. Their separation took place without a violent quarrel, and at crucial episodes in the old man's life Thierry manifested his devotion.

Even though Saint-Simon's name was always featured on the fly-sheet of *L'Industrie,* his two brilliant young disciples were important associates, not mere secretaries. Over the precise measure each one contributed to a final draft of their work controversy has raged for more than a century, particularly among the partisans of Auguste Comte and Saint-Simon, without any resolution. By what abstract criterion can one apportion the two streams of a common effort? Even when Auguste Comte prepared the manuscripts, as he did for the *cahiers* of volume three of *L'Industrie,* was he an independent thinker or was he still primarily a draftsman for the conceptions which Saint-Simon, who had difficulty in writing, poured forth in hours of conversation by day and night and which surely had held the young man entranced until 1819, as his correspondence with friends bears witness in unrestrained eulogies of the middle-aged philosopher. While a part of the collaborative effort was Thierry's and Comte's, the heart of the doctrine was still Saint-Simon's.

The character of the four volumes of *L'Industrie,* which after a long string of announcements finally appeared at irregular intervals between 1816 and 1818, is far from uniform. Not only is there a different ideological emphasis in each one of them, the very level of communication, the underlying purpose of the work changed from volume to volume, on occasion even from *cahier* to *cahier.*

When *L'Industrie* first appeared in 1816 it bore an incredibly prolix and windy title: *L'Industrie littéraire et scientifique liguée avec l'industrie commerciale et manufacturière, ou Opinions sur les finances, la politique, la morale, et la philosophie dans l'intérêt de tous les hommes livrés à des travaux utiles et indépendans.* The promised volumes were never printed on schedule and long months passed during which announcements, circulars, and prospectuses again took the place of solid material. Part I of the first volume of *L'Industrie* opened with a highly technical study of the French credit system, of the problems of state bondholders, and of the advantages of a public debt cautiously administered, written by Saint-Aubin. It was a tedious work, entitled *Sur les finances* and subtitled *De la conduite que tout gouvernement et particulièrement le gouvernement français doit tenir à l'égard de ses créanciers nationaux,* [13] and not likely to attract the attention of anyone but an expert on banking or public finance. The first edition of this volume in 1816 did not bear Saint-Simon's name on the fly-sheet; the second edition in 1817 did. Part II of the first volume, called *Politique,* was subtitled *Des nations et de leurs rapports mutuels; ce que ces rapports ont été aux diverses époques de la civilisation; ce qu'ils sont aujourd'hui; quels principes de conduite en dérivent.* After an attempt to define a nation and national welfare, it linked the prosperity of the modern nation with its industry and insisted upon the unity of the European political system. The influences of Crèvecoeur, Adam Ferguson, John Millar, Benjamin Constant, and Sismondi, all of whom favored the civil industrial society over the military society, are explicit throughout in numerous quotations and references. The author of this second part of volume one was identified on the title-page as A. Thierry, "adopted son of H. Saint-Simon."

With the publication of the second volume of *L'Industrie* in 1817 Saint-Simon sounded a strident note in sharp contrast with the rather staid academic phrases of the preceding *cahiers*. In a pugnacious statement of the object of the "enterprise" Saint-Simon declared himself set to attack those men in society who were parasites, do-nothings, "thieves in other words," [14] men who lived on the work of others. He reduced his theory of the state to a simple formula: to govern as little and as cheaply as possible; and he repeated a call for the direct meeting and coöperation of industrialists and scientists, without government mediation, a dominant motif of his preparatory circulars and prospectuses. A feature of the second volume of *L'Industrie* was a series of *Lettres de H. Saint-Simon à un Américain*, in which he used a rather idyllic portrait of hardworking, simple, frugal, industrial America, free from privileged castes, to dramatize the contrast with status-ridden Europe, weighted down by noble idlers. He dwelt on the grandeur of free America, on the wisdom and moderation of the founders of American liberty, on the spirit and manners of the American people at the time of the Declaration of Independence. He eulogized ideal American types like William Penn, "essentially peaceful, industrious, economical" — the dominant character of the American nation.[15] The letters prophesied the universal application of the principles of the American experience. ". . . [T]he time has come for the general revolution, the revolution common to all civilized peoples . . . ," he proclaimed in the sixth letter.[16]

To flatter his financial supporters he included in the second volume excerpts from Laffitte on the national budget, Casimir Périer on government loans, and the "opinions" of an anonymous merchant. The central theme remained the same, clothed and reclothed with new epigrams: "Government is a necessity, that is to say a necessary evil." Then followed a thorough, serious treatise by Count J. A. Chaptal, the former Napoleonic minister, entitled *Des progrès de l'industrie agricole et manufacturière depuis trente ans*. In broad strokes Chaptal sketched the history of the introduction of machinery into France and developed at great length the thesis — a favorite with Saint-Simon — that science and industry were closely interrelated, illustrating his point with numerous examples of the immediate practical application of chemical discoveries. At the time the Chaptal work was by far the best account of the early stages of the industrial revolution in France. The final piece in the volume was an anonymous essay, *Les trois époques ou considérations sur l'état de la France depuis 1787*, which outlined a philosophical history of the French Revolution based on a periodization into revolutionary, warrior, and industrial epochs.

The liberal press accorded these first volumes of *L'Industrie* an ambivalent reception. Mahul's bibliographical review was the most favorable: "Among many sound ideas this work includes a few that are hazardous, or perhaps too bold, justified nevertheless by the author's rectitude and the sincerity of his intentions." [17] *Le Censeur Européen*, successor to *Le Censeur*, quoted long passages and expressed fundamental agreement with the underlying proposition that it was highly desirable for government to be as cheap and as inconspicuous as possible; but the reviewer doubted that the elaborate costly structure of the state would ever wither away. Men were too afraid of each other to dispense with strong government. They were driven by a lust for power, vanity of office, and a desire to profit from the exercise of authority. "Try and persuade a minister, a state councillor, a prefect, or a university official that the public welfare does not need to have them wield great power and to enjoy incomes of 10, 20, 30, 40, 100 thousand francs. You would have to be endowed with extraordinary powers of eloquence to make yourself heard without exciting violent movements of impatience." [18] In the abstract the reviewer agreed with Saint-Simon's analysis of the real interests of industry in a well-regulated government, but unfortunately the industrialists did not have an *esprit de corps*. *Le Censeur Européen* upbraided them for not being class-conscious. It was an unfortunate fact that the industrialists were not moved by philosophical conceptions, even those which furthered the interests of their own class. "The men who control industry have no ideas or they have erroneous ones. The men who have ideas own no industries." [19] Therefore they dismissed his proposal for a joint effort of organized savants and united industrialists as illusory. On the whole the editors of *Le Censeur Européen*, who were Saint-Simon's competitors for the favor of the liberal industrialists, tended to be facetious about the pretentious title of his publication and about Saint-Aubin's financial treatise; Augustin Thierry's articles were reviewed more positively.[20] Benjamin Constant wrote Saint-Simon with a superior air: "Your ideas are fine, but I see difficulties about putting them into practice. I do not believe that the clash of systems can be terminated forever. I do not even believe that it would be good for humanity. . . ." [21] Jean-Baptiste Say was more kind. He praised the style and called Saint-Simon a true friend of the public weal.[22]

Saint-Simon planned to tackle virtually every aspect of public economic and social policy. The manuscript outline of a work *De l'organisation sociale*[23] ran the gamut of all the problems being debated in his society:

On the budget, on the food supply of the people, on means of limiting the population, on the relations which have existed, on those which exist, and on those which will exist between the two great classes of which society is composed, on the French Revolution, on the relations between the armed class and the class deprived of arms at various epochs, on the national guard and the professional army, on the Abbé de Saint-Pierre's project for perpetual peace, on the social contract, on women, on artists, on politics, on parliament, on the selection of deputies, on royalty, on democracy, on public education, on egotism, on the Institute, that is to say, on the scientific corps, on morals, on the bank, on the tariff system, on the happiness of the human species, philosophical considerations on the present state of political affairs, and finally a report on the method we have followed in the exposition of our ideas in the first volumes of this work and on the path which we intend to take in those which follow.

Some of these topics were covered in *L'Industrie* and later individual brochures, others were sketched out in manuscripts, still others never grew beyond the heading stage. The mortality among Saint-Simon's projects was always high.

17

Revolt of the Subscribers

WHEN THE FIRST TWO VOLUMES of *L'Industrie* met with partial success Saint-Simon immediately resolved to broaden the scope of his enterprise. Modest journalistic acclaim was not for him. With a blare of trumpets a prospectus announced that he was about to raise the curtain on a brand new conception. An impresario of ideas, he was creating an atmosphere of suspense. In June 1817 he dispatched a circular letter to all his fellow journalists in Paris, giving them advance notice of the momentous event, advising them to stand by in anticipation: "Gentlemen, I believe that I have found a good idea. I hasten to communicate it to you. In my opinion it is a duty for every one of us to inform his colleagues as promptly as possible of the discoveries which he may make." He promised that the third volume of *L'Industrie* would show the world how to organize a "system of terrestrial morality." The restrained liberal publicist of the early volumes cast off his mask and revealed the old monist still in search of an absolute. The passion for unity which prior to 1814 had expressed itself in the apotheosis of Newton's law now seized upon a uniform moral law, one and indivisible, to be imposed upon all mankind. "The philosophers of the nineteenth century will make people feel the necessity of submitting all children to the study of the same code of terrestrial morality, since the similarity of positive moral ideas is the only bond which can unite men in society. . . ." [1]

In this great enterprise there would be jobs aplenty for his fellow publicists. All men of the pen, from philosophers to songwriters, would be enlisted in the crusade to render ideas positive and morality terrestrial, their common efforts culminating in that old Saint-Simon reliable, an encyclopedia of positive ideas. It required hardihood, to say the least, to address an invitation to collaborate to his literary colleague Chateaubriand, the pillar of the Catholic romantic reaction.

On June 7, 1817, the *Journal des Débats* published an article mocking his prospectus; later in the month a M. Benaben, writing in *Le Constitutionnel*, joined the general sport. Retorting that it was in bad taste for the journalists to comment publicly on a private letter, Saint-Simon launched into a brief exposition of the new system of terrestrial morality which had to be developed for the nineteenth century. M. Benaben then offered a tongue-in-cheek apology for his breach of etiquette and proceeded to tear this relativist conception apart: morals were absolutes, and the notion of a new morality for the nineteenth century was as absurd as a geometry for the nineteenth century.[2]

In July and August 1817 there appeared another set of circulars advertising the forthcoming third volume of *L'Industrie*, which seems to have been long in incubation. In September 1817 the first three *cahiers* of the third volume were finally published; in October, the fourth and fifth *cahiers*. This third volume of *L'Industrie* turned out to be far the most provocative of the whole series. Auguste Comte by this time had become an intimate collaborator and his solid polytechnical training helped the philosopher to phrase and to order his ideas.

The first *cahier* reverted to Saint-Simon's 1810 conception that a new encyclopedia of science was needed to effect the transition to an industrial society. The "celestial" had to be replaced by the "terrestrial," the vague by the positive, the poetic by the real.[3] The confused state of contemporary French science was evidence of the lack of cohesion even among men of the same profession. In order to have real communion, it was not sufficient that academicians meet from time to time in solemn assembly; scientists had to share "general ideas about all the sciences"; only then would they be able to inaugurate an epoch of boundless prosperity for mankind. He returned to his old philosophical hunting ground, firing away at the most flagrant contradiction of modern society — the artificial division of the educational system between the clergy and the scientists. How ludicrous that despite all the advances made by positive science in modern times, a progress symbolized by the achievements of the Institute, the educational system of France was still in the hands of the theologians. The anomaly had to end — in favor of the Institute, a conclusion which was a direct affront to the clerics who had repossessed both the university and the lower schools.

In his discussion of temporal affairs, Saint-Simon roamed even farther from the tidy reservation of permissible *bourgeois* opinion. Debates about ideal political forms for society which were agitating his contemporaries were beside the point for Saint-Simon. In the second *cahier* he proclaimed a theory of historical relativism for the institutions of the state, a prelude to the even more dangerous pronouncements about moral relativism which followed later. The doctrinaires of abstract political thought were refuted: "It is no longer a problem of discussing endlessly how to know which is the best of governments. There is nothing good, there is nothing bad, absolutely speaking. Everything is relative — that is the only absolute. Everything is relative above all to the times, insofar as social institutions are concerned." [4]

Though his theory was shocking, his tactics remained conservative. The contemporary period was transitional and there was nothing men could do about that fundamental fact. The statement of the modern political problem was in essence: "What are the means of passing imperceptibly and without conflicts from the social régime which has existed up to the present to the one which will certainly be established later?" [5] The solution derived from the formulation of the issue; it involved the creation of a régime with a mixed character, so that the new elements would be able slowly to swallow up the old until the transition had been accomplished. The parliamentary régime answered to this requirement, since it was constituted of one part royalty and one part commonalty.

Preparatory philosophical indoctrination of the people in the virtues of the new industrial forms was advisable prior to their adoption. Even in the service of the passion for humanity men could be led astray if they took premature violent measures. Saint-Simon had effectively cured Auguste Comte of his youthful revolutionary Jacobinism. The second *cahier*, which the young collaborator drafted, was unambiguous about the order of precedence of philosophical and institutional innovations. "One cannot change institutions until opinions have been changed. Every social régime is founded upon a philosophical system. . . . The only revolution appropriate for us is a philosophical revolution, the change in system of ideas; the political revolution, the change in institutions, can only come later." [6] The order, he believed at this time, could never be inverted. The centuries required to convert mankind to monotheism were a warning against the folly of expecting precipitous action. Although the tempo of modern times had become accelerated, "the day [is yet] far distant for those men who are burning to see the dawn of the age of felicity for which mankind has hoped for so long. . . . [L]et us not force the course of events. We cannot. Let us resign ourselves." [7]

But even though the trend of events and the general tempo were determined, Saint-Simon did not wind up in a doctrine of quietism or indifferentism. There were consolations for those philosophical progressionists imbued with a faith in the future of mankind. The solace he offered them was not unlike the prospect held out by Condorcet at the tail end of his *Esquisse*. The men who were dedicated to laboring for the new system would already savor in their lifetime the delights of the future golden age. "[O]ne must not believe that all men of the same century are contemporaries. There are those who live in past centuries. Others are of the centuries of the future. Those who discern the correct state of affairs and the goal to which it must lead us, those who participate in the works which have to be done in our period of transition, will live as if they themselves were under a new régime.

As for the others, they will perhaps be less happy; but they will always enjoy the continual and progressive perfection of the human species." [8]

In the third *cahier* of the third volume of *L'Industrie* he continued to develop the theme of the suitable tempo of social change. The desire for innovation was inherent in man; it was so basic a part of his nature that progressive improvement was inevitable. It was impossible, as the philosophers of the Catholic parties hoped, to stifle this love of innovation. Since it could not be fought, it had to be comprehended. The extremists who believed that once an abstract new idea had been conceived it had to be put into effect immediately, were equally unrealistic, childish, crying for the moon. There were bounds to the practical applicability of general conceptions, however praiseworthy. ". . . Each epoch has limits which are impossible to cross, and to seek to pass beyond them means retarding the progress of civilization instead of accelerating it. . . . One century prepares the following century and if all too often there are troubles, disorders, revolutions, it is always because one epoch has tried to leap over the other, and because the power of time was misjudged. . . . Let us try to see what is possible and to do it; but let us not seek, let us not try more. . . ." [9]

Saint-Simon was appealing to the historical moderates, the gradualists, the men of the center to show courage and energy and to control the impulsive forces in society. But Saint-Simon preaching moderation was still a firebrand by Restoration standards. He was impolitic enough to announce that the philosophy of theism (by which he meant revealed religion) had lost almost "the whole of its dominion." Then this "moderate" reflection on the state religion of France was followed by the disastrous fourth *cahier* which brought down upon him a crushing repudiation by his most illustrious subscribers.

The burden of the essay *Sur la morale* was that political institutions were the embodiment of idea systems, that politics were always derivative from the prevailing system of morals in a given historical epoch.[10] His intent was not subversive; he was trying to preach another lesson in political moderation, to prove in a circuitous way that revolution was wicked and that the constitutional monarchy was the appropriate transitional régime for his day and age. Since politics stemmed from morals, if he could demonstrate that morals were not universal absolutes but relationships that varied historically, then he would have shown, by his peculiar brand of reasoning, that political forms too were relative and would have laid the basis for the argument that constitutional monarchy was for the time being the best of all possible régimes.

But Saint-Simon had a way of digressing, and after a dictum, "No society is possible without common moral ideas," [11] he proceeded to sketch a world history of morals: the Greeks before Socrates had no system of morals because they considered all barbarians enemies; Christianity created a morality of brotherly love and in its essence it had endured for eighteen hundred years; now the day of the Christian moral outlook was passing. The whole system of moral ideas had to be refashioned and established on a new basis.

In a word, we must move from celestial to terrestrial morality. Without here discussing the inconveniences one experiences in founding morals on theology, it is sufficient to note that in fact ideas of the supernatural are almost everywhere destroyed, that they will every day continue to lose their hold and that the hope of paradise and the fear of hell can no longer serve as a basis for the conduct of men. The human mind has advanced since the establishment of Christian morality and as a result of this progress the facts are that the epoch of theology is past beyond recall, and that it would be folly to try to continue to base morals on prejudices whose absurdity is becoming more obvious every day. The theogonies have played their role and henceforth they can no longer serve any purpose. Christianity made morals advance significantly. It would be unjust and absurd to deny it. But one must recognize with the same good faith that its reign is over and that the period during which it was useful is already in the distant past. The era of positive ideas is beginning. One can no longer give morals any other motives but those of palpable, certain, and present interests. This is the spirit of the age, and more and more this will be forever the spirit of future generations. This is the great step forward which civilization is about to make . . . the establishment of terrestrial and positive morality.[12]

This brazen attack on Catholicism was delivered with an insouciance which had not been witnessed since the early years of the century. Formally Saint-Simon drew a sharp distinction between the doctrine and the institutions. Church institutions had to be preserved, he preached, while they were being infused with the new conceptions of positive morality. His approach was precisely the reverse of most forays against Catholicism, which hammered against institutional abuses and steered clear of entanglement with dogmatics.

We must fashion the new moral ideas. But should we establish new moral institutions? It is clear that we should not, for the simple reason that we must wait for the ideas to be formed before thinking of organizing them. Thus it would be madness to try to suppress at present the moral institutions which still exist, that is to say the religious institutions. They tried it in our Revolution, but what happened? These institutions were reconstituted and after many misfortunes we reverted to the point of departure. The same is true for the sacerdotal power as it is for royalty. It is still impossible to wipe it out. This is a task destined for our descendants, a task which will be accomplished by itself, peacefully, if we are wise enough to conform to the course of the human spirit, and do not try to skip a generation.[13]

In the political temper of France in 1817, this fourth *cahier* of volume three of *L'Industrie* was either incredibly naïve or snidely humorous.[14] Saint-Simon was capable of so inextricable a combination of both that it is hard to determine which was the dominant tone. No longer shouting *"Écrasez l'infâme!"* in the eighteenth-century manner, he contented himself with a dispassionate diagnosis of the status of Catholicism and a verdict that since the patient was slowly dying it was best to let him alone rather than to use violent measures against him.

Restoration Catholicism could accept no such analysis of its position and made it uncomfortable for prominent citizens who might venture to associate themselves with this prognosis. Saint-Simon's proper subscribers had never expected him to meddle in religious affairs under the cover of a book or periodical called *L'Industrie*. The leaders of the industrial and financial circles dared at most to advocate a division between church and state, an arrangement under which the secular and sacerdotal powers would be kept far apart. Here was "their" publicist carrying the attack against Catholicism and reviving, even though in rather novel dress, the anticlericalism of the *philosophes*. The industrialists were satisfied to be tolerated and left alone, ignored by the church of the White Terror; they saw no advantage in rousing this formidable antagonist.

The original favorable reception of *L'Industrie* turned into horrified denunciations. On October 30, 1817, a group of the subscribers addressed a letter to the Minister of Police publicly disclaiming responsibility for Saint-Simon's opinions. They told of his solicitation the previous year, of his avowed intent to publish works on the progress of industry and commerce, of his unfortunate pecuniary situation, and of their act of pure generosity in aiding him.[15] The Duke de la Rochefoucauld-Liancourt, who had been among the most prominent of the original subscribers and who figured at the head of the list, wrote Saint-Simon an irate letter:

 . . . . How great is my astonishment and pain, when upon opening today the *cahiers* in quarto which you have just published and which I had not yet had time to cut, I find enunciated there principles which are entirely alien to the title of the work, principles which I do not permit myself to qualify here, principles which have not been, which are not, nor will ever be mine. I have reason to be personally wounded when I find such principles, such assertions in the work, when you promised me not to write anything which could not be approved by the friends of order and of the government under which we live. Therefore, I have the honor to request, Sir, that you no longer consider me a subscriber to your work . . . for it is profoundly painful to me to see my name at the head of a work which enunciates principles I denounce with all my strength as disruptive of the whole social order, as incompatible with liberty as I conceive it and as I love it.[16]

The majority of industrialists and bankers, frightened by the White Terror, could not brook even an oblique attack on the official religion of France.

Laffitte and Ternaux, however, did not join their colleagues in public repudiation of Saint-Simon.

With the feeble fourth volume of *L'Industrie* which appeared in 1818 Saint-Simon vainly attempted to rehabilitate his reputation among the industrialists.[17] In the preface he tried to wheedle his way back into grace with a partial recantation of his improper principles. "We are reproached with having in our third volume abandoned the thread of our first direction. This direction was then good. Hence we find even in this reproach a sort of praise and encouragement which consoles us for the past in warning us for the future. We even like to believe that after reading this volume, the public will return to a more indulgent opinion of the preceding volume." [18]

He left off attacking the clergy and opened up full blast against the legal profession and the evils of its political importance in France. Then he produced novel reflections on the role of agricultural banks and the central position of credit in expanding the economy of a nation. Saint-Simon was flexible about the techniques of persuasion. He had no intention of overthrowing the government, and the purity of his ideal would not be stained by temporary concessions to the *status quo*. A journalist had to hold the public ear, and if people were alarmed by his formulations, he had to lead them to the inevitable goal along another path.

L'Industrie ceased publication in 1818. The retraction of subversive opinions in the first issue of the fourth volume had failed to allay the apprehensions of the timid. The Catholic reaction was gaining momentum, and no *bourgeois* would risk the appearance of his name on a list of subscribers to a periodical which had once used sacrilegious language. The ex-noble publicist was not reliable; he was erratic and unpredictable.

Saint-Simon had devoted himself to the cause of industry and the industrialists had denied him, even as had the scientists a decade earlier. His new principle of social organization announced in *L'Industrie* "had created a great public sensation," he later wrote in his *Histoire de ma vie politique*,[19] but unfortunately not of a character to sustain its regular appearance.

18

The Trial

AT FIRST Auguste Comte had been paid three hundred francs a month, but when Saint-Simon fell into one of his frequent states of penury after public repudiation by the subscribers, the young polytechnician remained by his side both for philosophical reasons and the prospect of future reward. He wrote to his confidant Valat:

"I still do political economy for him, and although my work is gratis, I am almost certain that if he should, which is very possible, happen to get himself out of his terrible pecuniary straits, I shall not have lost anything by waiting. He is a man of more than fifty. Well, I can tell you that never have I known a young man as ardent and as generous as he. He is an original being in every respect." [1]

Comte was fascinated by the passionate, aging thinker. He called him "Père Simon" and said he was loved like a son. [2] Their association had given a new orientation to the brilliant young man who up to that time had been toying with revolutionary ideologies. [3] ". . . I have learned by this relationship of labor and friendship with one who sees furthest into philosophical politics a thousand things which I would have sought for in vain in books, and my mind has made more progress in the last six months of our relationship than I would have made in three years if I had been alone. . . . He is the most estimable and the most amiable man I have ever known in my life." [4]

After the fiasco of volume three of *L'Industrie*, Auguste Comte drafted two letters to Saint-Simon whose precise meaning and significance are obscure. Alfred Pereire, who published them in 1912, has evolved the theory that they were part of a literary artifice which Saint-Simon was proposing to use in effecting a transition from the unfortunate volume three to volume four of *L'Industrie*. [5] The paradoxical style of the letters, which were to be addressed publicly to Saint-Simon by an anonymous correspondent, was meant to hoodwink outraged subscribers and to obliterate the memory of the terrible words "terrestrial morality." Though this may well have been their purpose in part, the hypothesis does not completely explain a serious undercurrent in Comte's argument which is not disguised by the bantering tone of the letters. After a brief period during which Auguste Comte had been influenced by revolutionary egalitarianism, he had come to accept, far more absolutely than Saint-Simon himself, the élitist conception that politics was an area of specialization for experts, publicists, theoreticians, and that public opinion or mere popular desire in this field was as preposterous as an ordinary man's pretension to teach the shoemaker his art or the astronomer his science. This was the burden of one of Comte's first essays, *Séparation générale entre les opinions et les désirs* rejected by *Le Censeur Européen* in July 1819. With uncompromising logic Comte demonstrated the futility of any premature propagation of new ideas, because mere mass "opinion" was not too important in the historic process. The two anonymous letters of 1819 reveal the persistence of this conception in Comte's thinking. They widen the chasm between pure hard theory and the popularization of ideas.

Systematically Comte's letters tried to prove to Saint-Simon that he did not even have a remote chance of winning general support for his doctrine among any of the major social classes in French society. The journalists would surely not risk their reputations by sponsoring his ideas, however profound they might be. The scientists were equally egotistic and indifferent to general conceptions. As for the industrials, they were "too occupied with their personal affairs to give much time to reading," and besides they had no taste for intellectual pursuits. They did not know how to combine their particular interests with the general interest, they were cravenly submissive to the government, and they were less concerned with reforming abuses than with turning them to their own profit. "Thus you should not hide from yourself that your writing will be read by only a small number of merchants and manufacturers, that among the small number, very few will sense its utility, and that the tiny pinch of those who approve it will not support you, for fear lest they compromise themselves." [6] The large landowners and nobles whom Saint-Simon attacked in *L'Industrie* were his natural enemies, along with the lawyers whom he had antagonized, and he could expect nothing from them. This left only the ministers of state. If he had devised new techniques for the accretion of arbitrary power while preserving constitutional forms, they would have rewarded him handsomely, but since his revelation of the true laws of the body politic was contrary to their interests, they would ignore him. They would not even bother to arrest him, depriving him of the honor and advantages of official persecution.

Since this was the dismal fate which awaited him if he continued as a publicist, Auguste Comte proposed, as a logical consequence of his realistic analysis of contemporary French society, that they adopt a completely different philosophical direction. They should forthwith abandon all political activity and concentrate their common labors on the elaboration of a scientific system in pure theory, firm in the conviction that society would ultimately be constrained to accept their doctrine. Saint-Simon's impatient emphasis upon the practical application of his theory at this early stage of its development was an error. With subtlety Comte demonstrated that the premature publication of an action program based on Saint-Simon's system was in flagrant contradiction with the very precepts of his doctrine. Since there was no positive knowledge among the mass of the people, because the positive system of science had not yet been accepted, Saint-Simon should have expected to be judged with prejudiced passion. Against these class prejudices, as he himself so well understood, there could be no argument. His theory was the most brilliant ever conceived, but he had exploited the poorest and most difficult lode in his mine. He might, for example, have developed the philosophical bases of political economy, thereby rendering the science of politics positive. This could have been achieved by elaborating upon a single general principle which Saint-Simon had already proclaimed in *L'Industrie:* "Property is the most important institution of all, and it should be constituted in a manner most favorable for production." In the same spirit he might have founded the theory of a positive morality by developing the abstract laws of useful social action. He might have established the essential unity between positive politics and positive morality — anything except this foolhardy attempt to put his "idea" into action before it was finished. He had followed his fundamental idea "in its political consequences instead of in its scientific consequences" — this was the fatal error.[7]

The letters contain in embryo the whole basis of the future philosophical dispute between Saint-Simon and Auguste Comte, the problem of the primacy of the scientist or the industrialist, the issue of the precedence of theory or practice. But the letters do not present a novel viewpoint unexplored by Saint-Simon. In effect the voice of Comte was attacking Saint-Simon the pamphleteer for the industrials of the Restoration in the name of Saint-Simon the universal positive philosopher of the Empire.

The intellectual divergence between Saint-Simon and Auguste Comte, if there was a fundamental one at the time, did not as yet obtrude into their personal relationship, which continued warm and intimate for at least two more years, before a gradual estrangement set in.[8] The letters were not published, though their author wrote them as publicity pieces, not private communications. Comte may have been in dead earnest in proposing their new departure and he may have offered the draft of the two letters to Saint-Simon as a journalistic maneuver to explain the policy switch. Saint-Simon may even have weighed the advantages of accepting his disciple's proposal. That he finally rejected it is obvious from the direction of his next periodical.

The new publication of the philosophical team had to be financed in large part by Saint-Simon himself. The agreement drawn up by a Society of Men of Letters, which assumed formal responsibility for the new venture, called *Le Politique*, was a device to protect the major shareholders from any harebrained schemes of their chief editor.[9] In this enterprise Auguste Comte became a recognized shareholder and editor. Other shareholders were Saint-Simon's old friend Coutte, and a M. La Chevardière, who was chosen one of the editors, as well as director of the journal for a period of a year, with powers of review over the contents of the publication. If he believed that an article was likely to create trouble, he could call a board meeting at which a majority decision — Saint-Simon was not allowed to participate in the vote — would prevail. Saint-Simon undertook to bear the costs of the first four numbers of *Le Politique*, and the serious involvement of the other shareholders was not to begin until after they had accumulated three hundred subscriptions. A final article of their understanding provided that legal liability for each contribution belonged to its signatory and would not implicate the whole group with the Restoration police. This plan put the maximum onus on Saint-Simon and protected the other three editor-shareholders from prosecution. Though there was an arrangement for signing articles only with an initial, Saint-Simon was quick to inform his public about the authorship of his own contributions. Glory was more vital to him than security.

Le Politique, far from harkening to Comte's advice, descended into the very thick of the fight to wrestle with the specific political issues of 1819. By advocating day-to-day policies of the *bourgeois* industrialists, Saint-Simon hoped to win back adherents whom his philosophical and moral principles had alienated. He was consistently wary of violating the sanctity of royalty itself. His sole purpose, he explained, was to save the Bourbon monarchy from condemning itself to that terrible punishment invented by the Egyptians, who bound together a corpse and a living man. The cadavers of modern France were the clergy, an ignorant class devoid of science, and the nobility, a useless class living on sinecures.

The tone of *Le Politique ou Essais sur la politique qui convient aux hommes du xixe siècle* (1819) was even more popular and less sophisticated than that of the later volumes of *L'Industrie*. There was throughout a clean-cut division between "we" and "they" — the industrials and the do-nothings:

"What do they want?
"What do we want?
"They want 1788, we want 1789.
"They want privileges.
"We want civil, judicial, and political equality.
"They want to exclude us from everything except taxes.
"We want to admit them to everything when they shall be capable." [10]

Le Politique discussed the election laws, duels, ministerial responsibility. The editors used simple publicist devices like writing a piece on the need for government economy entitled *Le Projet de Finances de Benjamin Franklin*.[11] They played intimate editorial games, writing "letters to the editors" under transparent pseudonyms. Auguste Comte was a M. B——— identified as a former student of the Ecole Polytechnique. The editors congratulated M. B——— for his excellent study on the budget. Saint-Simon was clearly M. A———, a member of the Society of the Cincinnati and one of the great purchasers of national property.[12] They reported their quaint little jokes: the mother of one of their workers employed as a bookbinder had read *Le Politique* and liked it, but said that it was not at all *politique* because it was too frank.[13]

The forced humor of *Le Politique* failed to create a ripple in the stream of publicist literature then inundating France. One critic expressed regret that Saint-Simon had not expounded his ideas in a "somewhat less absolute fashion." Lanjuinais, the liberal politician, wrote him a favorable note.[14] But independent industrialists preferred the laissez-faire doctrine to be expounded in less bald a manner. *Le Politique*, which was to have been a "continuous work," not a regular periodical, in order to escape the heavy stamp tax, did not manage to survive more than twelve issues. The industrialists and bankers were not assuaged by the new tone of relative caution which Saint-Simon had adopted.

Throughout 1819 and 1820 brochure followed brochure dealing exclusively with immediate problems of constitutional government. In June 1819 Saint-Simon tried to bring the subprefect of Péronne to justice over the illegal collection of taxes and he posed the basic constitutional issue of bureaucratic responsibility.[15] In 1820 he wrote a pamphlet *Sur la loi des élections* in which as a publicist artifice he had twelve industrialists address their compatriots. It was his old refrain that only the richest industrialists should comprise the corps of electors because riches were an index of capacity. He was particularly eager to eliminate the half-million antiindustrials, the officials, their subordinates, and their servants, who in number amounted only to a sixtieth of the nation, though their actual powers were disproportionately great. These political pamphlets were generally turgid and had none of the dash or brilliance of Benjamin Constant or even of lesser liberal journalists of the day.

If *Le Politique* died obscurely, the next venture of Saint-Simon and August Comte, *L'Organisateur*, a series of letters which first appeared in November 1819, won instant notoriety. Saint-Simon started off with a dramatic conceit which immediately riveted attention; in later years it came to be known as the Parable.[16] Let France suddenly lose the leaders of productive industry, he speculated playfully, its creative scientists, artisans, and writers, and it would become an inferior among nations, deprived of its genius and most vital forces. Should, however, the royal family and thousands of unproductive churchmen, functionaries, and military men die, the loss would not appear disastrous. With ghoulish humor, Saint-Simon rubbed in the contrast.

Let us suppose that France keeps all of the men of genius which it possesses in the sciences, in the fine arts, and in the trades, but has the misfortune to lose on the same day Monsieur, the brother of the King, Monseigneur the Duke d' Angoulême, Monseigneur the Duke de Berry, Monseigneur the Duke d' Orléans, Monseigneur the Duke de Bourbon, Madame the Duchess d' Angoulême, Madame the Duchess de Berry, Madame the Duchess d' Orléans, Madame the Duchess de Bourbon, and Mademoiselle de Condé.

Let us suppose that at the same time [France loses] all the great officers of the crown, all the ministers of state (both those with and those without departments), all the councillors of state, all the *maîtres-des-requêtes*, all the marshals, all the cardinals, archbishops, bishops, grand vicars and canons, all the prefects and subprefects, all the employees in the ministries, all the judges, and, in addition to these, the ten thousand richest landowners among those who live as nobles.

This accident will certainly afflict the French for they are good people, because they would not be able to look with indifference upon the sudden disappearance of so large a number of their compatriots. But this loss of the thirty thousand individuals, reputed to be the most important in the State, would only cause them grief in a purely sentimental sense, for it would not result in any political evil for the State.

First for the reason that it would be very easy to fill the places which became vacant. There exist a great number of Frenchmen in a position to exercise the functions of brother of the king as well as Monsieur does; many are capable of occupying the positions of prince as fittingly as Monseigneur the Duke d' Angoulême, as Monseigneur the Duke de Berry, as Monseigneur the Duke d' Orléans, as Monseigneur the Duke de Bourbon. Many Frenchwomen would be as good princesses as Madame the Duchess d' Angoulême, as Madame the Duchess de Berry, as Mesdames d' Orléans, de Bourbon and de Condé.

The antechambers of the château are full of courtiers ready to occupy the positions of great officers of the crown. The army possesses a great number of military men who are as good captains as our present marshals. How many clerks are as good as our present Ministers of State? How many administrators are more capable of conducting the affairs of the departments than the prefects and subprefects presently in office? How many lawyers are as good jurisconsults as our judges? How many priests as capable as our cardinals, as our archbishops, as our bishops, as our grand vicars, and as our canons? As for the ten thousand proprietors who live like nobles, their heirs will require no apprenticeship to do the honors of their salons as well as they.[17]

Not only could the posts of the deceased nobles and cardinals and bureaucrats be readily filled; their present occupancy of these positions was injurious to the public weal. They maintained their position through the propagation of superstitions hostile to positive knowledge, and they usurped posts which rightly belonged to the creative men of society. These idlers drew three to four hundred millions from the nation in the form of pensions, sinecures, and other emoluments.

Reprinted twice in December 1819 as *Extraits de L'Organisateur*, this macabre hypothesis struck the popular fancy and was beginning to stir widespread interest. On January 8, 1820, the police finally took notice, seized the copies available at the publisher's, and had the author summoned before a judge. On the way upstairs to the magistrate's chambers in the Palace of Justice, Saint-Simon fell and had to be transported home, where the preliminary inquiry was pursued despite a rather painful injury. The case was sent to the Court of Assizes and the appearance of the accused was fixed for February 3, 1820. When Saint-Simon defaulted, he was found guilty, given a three-months prison sentence, fined five hundred francs and ordered to pay costs, but he was then granted the right to appeal to a jury trial.[18]

Within ten days, on February 13, this rather trifling, run-of-the-mill charge of having committed a literary offense against the royal family, assumed grave proportions when Louvel assassinated the Duke de Berry and the profligate heir apparent became a posthumous national hero. A few months before, Saint-Simon's Parable had specifically and by name envisaged the possibility of the duke's sudden demise. To show that he was unregenerate, Saint-Simon issued the fourteenth and last letter of *L'Organisateur*, in which, though he called the assassination an atrocious crime, he warned the Bourbons against using the incident as a pretext for the curtailment of press liberties. In a separate series of printed letters to his jury, Saint-Simon not only refused to recant, but stuck firmly by his doctrinal position that there was an urgent need for the institution of the industrial-scientific society.[19] When on March 20 Saint-Simon, a declassed noble of sixty, wearing his "Order of Cincinnatus," stood trial for an offense against the Bourbons, the prospects for acquittal looked dim.

The formal charge against him was that under the guise of a "supposition" he had inserted in his work passages offensive to the royal family.[20] To counteract the apparent violence of the Parable his lawyer Legouix made every effort to point up the essentially pacifist and conservative character of Saint-Simon's total doctrine.

"This system contains nothing subversive of the social order for it aims only at reconstituting it. It rests, it is true, on new principles which are perhaps too little known at this time, but the bases of society always remain the same. . . ."[21]

How could he possibly be considered an anti-Bourbon subversive? Under Robespierre he had been imprisoned for thirteen months, during eight of which he had been kept *au secret*. To Napoleon he had boldly written signed letters which spoke the severe language of justice and truth, with the result that a "hundred eyes of the police" scrutinized his every move.

His work forecast a pacific revolution in the domain of science and theory as a result of the workings of judgment and reason. He had never contemplated fast changes, either those of a day, or a year, or a century. It was not his intent to foment revolutionary transformations in society precipitously. All he wanted was to be the first to point out that they were taking place. Fully aware that there was still a vast area to traverse before his system would come into effect, he proposed no "brusque transition," only a "gentle, easy one, appropriate to the men and circumstances of today." [22] It seemed peculiar, Legouix pointed out to the jury, that two editions of *L'Organisateur* had been sold out before the charge was brought. Moreover, the passages on which the government rested its case had been lifted out of context. The accusation could never be sustained in the light of his whole doctrine, which had consistently repudiated the use of force.

The jury, after deliberating for an hour and a half, found him not guilty of any offense against the royal family. Whereupon the prosecutor arose to announce a new charge against him: attacks against the constitutional principles of the monarchy in his pretrial defense pamphlet, the *Lettres de Henri Saint-Simon à MM. les jurés.* Since his lawyer Legouix had also signed this plea to the jurors he too was included in the new accusation. When Legouix protested to the court that he had acted only as lawyer and had appended his name to the plea merely as a formality, Saint-Simon intervened to assume total responsibility for the content of the letters himself and then launched into an extemporaneous defense of his principles. He was outraged that his theories should be associated with Louvel. "What connection can there be between my work and the crime of Louvel, between me and an assassin?" The prosecutor had charged that "Louvel had been fanaticized by principles and doctrines similar to those which M. de Saint-Simon professes." To which Saint-Simon replied that Louvel had been fanaticized not by ideas but by Bonapartism, by the political "party spirit." Turning to the prosecutor he defied him to question his loyalty. "I daresay that he is not more attached to the Bourbons than I." [23] He was the Bourbons's best friend. It was he who had first apprised them of dangers to the dynasty resulting from the foolhardy policy of the First Restoration in 1814, even as he was now warning them of new impending disasters. He was the honest counsellor of the king, not the flatterer. "You will weigh, gentlemen of the jury, what are my veritable intentions. I have left to my lawyer the defense of what concerns the head, but I alone speak for my heart." [24]

With more candor than rhetoric, he thanked the king's prosecutor for having brought his name before the people, whose ear he had long striven to gain. For the king he had a final bit of advice: unless royalty allied itself with the commons, abandoning both the ancient and the Napoleonic nobility, another revolution would overwhelm the dynasty. And he, of all men, had reason to dread such a catastrophe.

Unmoved by his paradoxical arguments, the prosecutor again remanded Saint-Simon to the *juge d'instruction*; but there the case petered out.

For a brief moment the trial brought him the public attention which he had long been seeking. Most of the Paris newspapers gave circumstantial accounts of the court session.[25] The liberal *Le Censeur Européen*, on the day of the trial, attacked his prosecutors and indicated that there was nothing novel in Saint-Simon's ideas — a reflection which no doubt displeased him far more than the scorching denunciation by his enemies.[26]

Saint-Simon thirsted for fame, and when fame eluded him he clutched even at notoriety. Any attention to his doctrine was good. His bold stance at the trial had added to his stature and, what was equally important, to his self-esteem. After 1820 his conceptions grew more venturesome again, more universal than circumstantial in their implications. He felt less bound to the transient interests of the industrialists and saw himself the independent prophet of the new industrial-scientific society. In *L'Organisateur* he had already become more than a mere paid publicist for the industrialists. His system had begun to unfold itself in a vigorous style. His doctrine was taking final shape. After the trial he emerged with a full consciousness of the fact that he had founded a movement around a system which he called *politique positive*. His circulars of the early eighteen-twenties were less advertisements for his books than attempts to sell subscriptions which were to be considered acts of commitment to the movement and its doctrine. He needed to be supported, but not in a pretentious manner. Though head of the movement, he was prepared to continue his frugal existence. He wrote of his needs in a circular advertising *L'Organisateur*, dated March 26, 1820, six days after the trial:

"For many years I have made all the sacrifices within my means in order to demonstrate that the scientific method can be used in the formulation of the political system.

"My enterprise is not a speculation. I desire neither honors nor riches. It is my ambition to be useful to my country without rising out of the class of simple citizens and without receiving in exchange for my labor more than a salary necessary to provide for my elementary living expenses." [27]

The publicity achieved during the trial allowed him to assume the role of benefactor of humanity with a semblance of verisimilitude, a public-spirited Roman who had a claim upon the rewards of the citizenry. He vaguely threatened his contemporaries with a suspension of his project if they showed no greater alacrity in assuring him a livelihood. Without their aid the continuation of his labors would be impossible. "They alone would be able to propagate and to multiply the fortunate results of my ideas far more than I could as an isolated individual, even if I had the richest private fortune. For this reason, it seems to me a matter of primary and great utility that through the association of various forces, my work should become identified with a great number of enlightened persons and should thus become a sort of common property bearing fruit for our state of knowledge."

Once he had addressed himself exclusively to scientists, then to industrialists, now he let the barriers down and was appealing to all humanity — "anyone convinced of the advantages of my system." If they were believers they would understand the necessity of contributing to his movement both their money and their scientific works. With a few prompt subscriptions he would be able to continue publication, but if they really wanted to increase the number of readers exposed to the "positivist doctrines" they ought to help him decrease the price of the copies. Hence his special offer.

"I invite all those who feel called upon to found the philosophy of the nineteenth century to take a subscription for the first three volumes of *L'Organisateur* at 50 francs in their quality as founders of positive politics." In this way he would be able to lower the general sales price to 25 francs instead of 40 francs. He was not excluding the impecunious from his orbit; those too poor to subscribe would receive a free copy if they wrote to him. Two hundred prominent scientists and artists received this statement of the urgency of his need and of the "inconveniences" to society if the exposition of his system suffered any long delay.

Though aware that his friends considered him a utopian, a fantast, that they regarded his project as "impractical," he was not fazed by their skepticism. If they only read his public letters, particularly the one which he had addressed to the eligible electors in November 1820, and if they paid particular attention to his postscript, they would be forced to agree to the formation of a "nucleus of believers," they would adhere to his proposals for terminating the European revolution during the course of the year 1821. Images of the colossal, which had been characteristic of his Empire writings but were absent during the early years of the Restoration, reappeared. His vision of the future of the movement needed the Alps for illustration: he hoped the nucleus would "grow with the same speed as a snowball pushed from the summit of Saint-Bernard down the steep slope of that mountain." [28]

From September 1820 to June 1822 he issued a new series of brochures entitled, in its two-volume edition, *Du système industriel*. Professor Gouhier believes that the new project, in which Auguste Comte was still an active participant, was financed by the same group of industrialists, bankers, merchants, prominent liberal deputies, and scientists who had figured among the first group of supporters of *L'Industrie*. Many of the letters comprising *Du système industriel* were republished as separate brochures and distributed as propaganda leaflets for the industrial cause.[29] *Du système industriel* is alive with a sense of personal dedication to the industrial society. Once again the megalomaniac element has become accentuated. "I have received the mission of releasing political power from the grasp of the clergy, the nobility, and the judicial order, to entrust this power into the hands of the industrials. I shall fulfill this mission no matter what obstacles I may encounter, and even if the royal power, blind to its true interests, should try to oppose it." [30]

After a hiatus of more than a year there followed another collection of pamphlets, the *Catéchisme des industriels,* which ran from December 1823 to June 1824. A new group of essays in 1825 was entitled *Opinions littéraires, philosophiques et industrielles.* In its opening sketch Saint-Simon reformulated his conception of the special dual function which he discharged as a philosopher — at once the critic of the old system and the organizer of the new. "Philosophy is the science of generalities. The principal occupation of philosophers consists of conceiving of the best system of social organization for the epoch in which they live, of ensuring its acceptance by the governors and the governed, of perfecting this system insofar as it is possible, thereafter of overthrowing it when it has reached the extreme limits of its perfection, in order to construct a new one with materials gathered everywhere by men devoted to specialized intellectual pursuits." [31] In these essays the doctrine assumed its penultimate form; he was on the eve of the *Nouveau Christianisme,* the strange last work originally intended as part of the *Opinions.*

In many respects he repeated himself in these letters, *cahiers,* and "opinions" of the twenties, but if one looks for novelty, fresh insights, grand hypotheses, vast generalizations, these too can be found. When the ideas of *Du système industriel,* the *Catéchisme des industriels,* and the *Opinions littéraires, philosophiques et industrielles* are collated with the earlier propositions of *L'Industrie* and *L'Organisateur,* a complete social theory emerges.

In the next chapters there is a distillation of the mature essence of his thought, the totality of his system as it developed during a decade of his writing under the Restoration, up to but not inclusive of his final religious phase, which warrants separate definition. Saint-Simon himself never completed the writing of a single book or formal treatise; he was an "inventor of ideas." To others he always left the lesser task of presenting his doctrine methodically.

PART IV

A NEW THEORY OF SOCIETY

19

Epochs Organic and Critical

AFTER 1814 Saint-Simon never again reverted to his prognosis of old age and extinction for the human species, an inevitable fate had he remained wedded to a literal parallel between ontogeny and phylogeny. In the ebullience of the *vita nuova* which followed his psychological recovery, he depicted human society as bubbling over with fresh, creative energy. Mankind was young and vigorous again, no longer confronted by the dismal prospect of a slow relentless decline. The monocyclic philosophy of history of the Empire writings was reformulated to hypothesize three successive life cycles for humanity spiraling one above the other towards infinite perfectibility. Full of optimism, he thought of his own period as the up-swing of the newest cycle, the dawn of the industrial-scientific civilization.

The version of his philosophical history which was communicated to his disciples and through them entered the main current of European thought was expounded in the second volume of *L'Industrie* (1817) and in *L'Organisateur* of 1819. Manuscript fragments of the 1820's recapitulate and sometimes sharpen but do not fundamentally alter the earlier published accounts. A grand definitive survey of the history of European civilization, which was intended to supplant Condorcet's *Esquisse*, remained uncompleted. The drafting of a text was left for Auguste Comte, but the quarrel between master and pupil intervened and Saint-Simon was by then too old to undertake the major effort alone. When it was finally written, Comte's own grandiose philosophical structure assimilated Saint-Simon's philosophy of history to the point where a new independent creation emerged. In the *Doctrine de Saint-Simon*, the brilliant succinct series of lectures delivered by his loyal disciples after his death, the development of ideas, despite certain innovations he would have disavowed, more nearly preserves the spirit of the original work of the master.

In *L'Industrie* Saint-Simon divided universal history at two crucial points, the first sometime around the third and the fourth centuries A.D., the second around the eleventh and twelfth, breaks or cut-off dates which resulted in three major divisions. The first had a polytheist ideology and a societal order based on slavery; the second, an ideology called "theological" and a feudal system; the ideology of the third, which had not yet attained fullness, was scientific or positive and its social system was industrial. Each of these three systems or social organizations could be viewed in either its spiritual or temporal aspect. These were the units, the elements of the science of history. Having isolated these units from the fluidity of historical experience, he could study them as a natural scientist would examine the phenomena of his special discipline.

A system — and the term came to mean an organic civilization in his language — did not spring into being full-grown, like Athena from the head of Zeus. Even as any other organism, a system was born, matured, and finally knew senescence and extinction. The first historical system of mankind had already passed through its complete life cycle; the second was on its deathbed; the third was soon to attain full vigor. The three cycles did not succeed one another as discrete self-contained historical entities, but overlapped substantially in time, since a new system was born simultaneously with the flowering of the old. As soon as the elements of a new system achieved any strength it flexed its muscles and proceeded to engage the old system in mortal combat. There was thus constant change and tension from the maturation point of one system to the maturation point of another.

The periods of overlapping between systems, the centuries of transition between the bloom of two organized civilizations, had a temper essentially different from the systems themselves. Intermediary periods, particularly their tail ends, were years of destructive "criticism," of violent antagonism between hostile spiritual and temporal forces in society. In recorded history mankind had already lived through one such age of crisis during the disintegration of the ancient world; in Saint-Simon's own day society was in the throes of a similar epoch of transition — men were now witnessing the last death gasps of the medieval system.

The Saint-Simonian school later developed a fixed terminology to distinguish between the organized systems and the periods of transition, naming them "organic" and "critical" epochs. Saint-Simon himself had not consistently labeled them "organic" and critical," though he used the adjectives in his general descriptions of their characteristics. In the exposition of the *Doctrine de Saint-Simon* the disciples insisted on their derivation from the master's theory.

The alternativity principle which under the Empire had been the crux of his theory of modern scientific development was adapted to new purpose in the Restoration philosophy of history. Universal history unfolded itself in an alternativity of organic and critical epochs, as the history of modern science had oscillated between synthetic and analytic periods. The organized society was assimilated to a synthetic period of science and the critical epoch to an analytic period of science. The perception of systems as organisms and the historic process as a rhythm were for Saint-Simon vivid physical analogies which became dogmas never subjected to proof or demonstration. Facile analogies to the physical sciences were fertile sources for the Positivist philosophy; they were also the origin of its weakness and puerility.

Among the expositions of Saint-Simon's philosophy of history — and the minor variants are too numerous to be detailed — the best developed and the keenest was his juxtaposition of the transition periods in ancient and modern times. The second volume of *L'Industrie* illuminated the contemporary crisis by comparing it with the spiritual and political turmoil in the Mediterranean world during the imperial epoch of Rome.

The philosophical revolution which then took place consisted in the passage from polytheism to theism. Once this revolution was completed, once theism was organized, a corresponding political revolution resulted, which consisted of the passage from the ancient social order which had existed among the Greeks and the Romans to the one which was later established among modern peoples. . . .

The transition which is now taking place is composed, like the preceding one, of two elements: one philosophical, the other political. The first consists in the passage from the theological system to the terrestrial and positive system; the second, in the passage from a régime of arbitrary rule to a liberal and industrial régime.

The philosophical revolution has long since begun, because we should trace its origins back to the study of positive sciences introduced into Europe by the Arabs more than ten centuries ago. To complete this revolution we have to accomplish only one more thing: we must finish the comprehensive work necessary for the organization of a positive system, whose elements now exist isolated.

The transition in its political form can be said to date from Luther's Reformation. Although this political transition has been less catastrophic than the political transition from polytheism to theism, it has already produced great misfortunes; it was the issue behind the Thirty Years' War, the two English revolutions of the seventeenth century, and the French Revolution.[1]

Since the period of transition prior to the birth of the medieval system had been a stormy one, the analogy, at first sight, seemed to augur ill for the present age. Would the moderns too be confronted with a similarly protacted time of troubles? Saint-Simon reassured and comforted his contemporaries. They need not sink into despair at the contemplation of the fall of the Roman Empire, for although the two periods of transition were similar in their general implications, there were concrete historical circumstances which explained the turbulence of the crisis in antiquity.

"First, those nations which were somewhat enlightened were in a minority in comparison with the peoples who were totally barbarous. And even among the enlightened, the class of men who were possessed of the corpus of acquired knowledge was a very small minority. The mass of mankind were in a state of gross ignorance. Hence it was impossible to oppose the terrible invasions of the northern barbarians, who came pouring over the west precisely during the period of the transition, at the very time when the battle of the two systems brought confusion into the ideas of men and anarchy into society." [2]

The evils resulting from the bad timing of the barbarian invasions had been further aggravated by the character of the ideological conflict in ancient times.

". . . The very nature of the two systems which [then] confronted each other was essentially unfavorable to the possibility of an [easy] transition. Each one of them was too absolute, too rigid, to make a gradual passage between them feasible. One had to embrace completely either polytheism or monotheism. It was impossible to adopt one of the two systems without abjuring the other in its entirety. No one saw a middle way and in fact there was none. Thus even if a man of genius could then have conceived of a plan to effect the transition gradually, it would have been chimerical to think of putting it into execution." [3]

Saint-Simon had good tidings for mankind; in contrast with this *guerre à outrance*, he believed that an easy childbirth was possible for the new ideology. The calamities which had already taken place during the recent epoch of transition were the result of ignorance in the comprehension of philosophical history. Misfortunes had not been averted "because until now we never knew where civilization was at. As a result we always desired more than was possible. Because, in a word, no one had ever recognized that we were in a transitional stage." Now that Saint-Simon had revealed history to mankind, the unforeseen — dark source of political chaos — had been banished.

"Having recognized that we are in a period of transition, we make for ourselves a plan according to which the transition takes place in the quickest, the easiest, and the most peaceful manner; thus we cut all the evils short." [4]

Saint-Simon described the historical process in the same manner that one of his medical friends would diagnose an illness and prescribe remedies. He was powerless to eliminate historical transitions, because they were in the nature of the process, but knowledge made it possible to alleviate the sufferings of mankind, the historic patient, and to hasten his cure. In the present epoch, men would not have to repeat the travail of the ancient world, since the progress of the human spirit had placed them in a position to perceive clearly where they were, whither they were tending, and consequently to steer their course in the most advantageous manner. "Consciousness of our condition" [5] — therein lay the means of our salvation.

The ninth letter of *L'Organisateur* was a felicitous application of his theory to the last great clash of historic systems.[6] More than a mere statement of the axioms of his philosophy of history, it was a detailed analysis of the strategy and tactics of the warring spiritual and temporal forces since the high middle ages.

For the past eight centuries Europe had been the battleground of two systems of civilization. During this long process one system had been steadily losing its grip over the minds of men, while the other had been gaining strength. In its heyday the medieval system had been a combination of two vigorous powers, one of which Saint-Simon variously called spiritual, papal, or theological, and the other temporal, feudal, or military. Throughout the centuries a "constant simultaneity" had prevailed in the origins, maturity, and decadence of the two powers, spiritual and temporal, which constituted the system. While the first beginnings of this medieval system dated back to the early propagation of Christianity and the irruption of the barbarians into Europe, like any organism the system had required time to ripen, to assume a definitive shape. It had not attained maturity until about the eleventh or twelfth century.

According to Saint-Simon's periodization, the medieval system was born not after the complete breakdown of the old Roman imperial polytheist system, but at the very moment when the ancient world had reached its "integral development." And the same phenomenon of new birth recurred at the climax of the medieval society. As soon as the feudal theological system was firmly established, the "germ of its destruction was born" [7] — a mighty phrase which was to echo through decades of Marxist historical writing. In the very centuries when the medieval system was in full fruition, the eleventh and the twelfth, the embryonic elements of a rival system came into being. These elements were the establishment of the free communes and the transmission of Arabic science.

The temporal power of the new system, the industrial class of the communes, manifested the first signs of independent existence, that is, freedom from the power of the military, when it wrested communal liberties from the nobles. The creation of a novel type of property in the midst of feudal relationships was the key to the birth of the new class. Industrial property, or movable property (the production of free artisans in cities), at first had a hard struggle merely to achieve recognition as distinct in character from landed property. Soon it became an open rival. While the military feudal nobles remained the heads of the temporal order in medieval Europe, in the very bosom of their society men of industrial and commercial property managed to survive and in time to flourish.

Science, destined to be the spiritual power of the new system, had been introduced into Europe by the Arabs, whose teachings were accorded a special status in the universities. Observatories, dissection rooms, and cabinets of natural history became the havens of the nascent positive spirit. Thus in the intellectual centers of the old theological system an interest in Arabic

science was nurtured — two future popes had studied "the sciences of observation" under Arabic professors at Cordova.

Saint-Simon's exposition of the historical process since the eleventh
century focused attention alternately on one or the other of the two systems,
the modern or the medieval, the one that was growing or the one that was
dying. True philosophical history of the past eight centuries was essentially
the account of their conflict, the battle of the systems; it was a narrative of
the successive stages and crises in the protracted struggle. During the first
four or five centuries of the war, from the eleventh to the sixteenth, the new
system was too feeble to risk engagement in "direct combat." A philosophical
analysis of this period therefore had to consider two layers of historical
reality, a superficial "visible part," the splendor of the feudal and theological
powers on display in feudal tourneys, on crusade, and at religious performances, and crucial events transpiring beneath the surface manifestations
of society, the secret history of the industrial scientific forces gathering
strength.

The philosopher or the political scientist had to distinguish between the
statement of the issues in a conflict as formulated by contemporaries who
were dazzled by surface appearances and the real underlying meaning of the
history. Thucydides had already made that distinction between the two
levels of historical perception very sharply, but the principle had not been
observed until the rebirth of philosophical history in the eighteenth century.
The differentiation between the visible symptom and the deep-rooted nature
of a disease is analogous to this historical method, and both Thucydides and
Saint-Simon lived in the shadow of important discoveries in medical science.
Throughout his works, Saint-Simon was adapting what he understood to
be the methods of medical analysis and practice to the study of history.

Although many centuries passed before the scientific industrial forces
could openly challenge the old system, Saint-Simon saw more than one
symptom of weakness in medieval society even at its very zenith. Most
glaring was the bitter rivalry between the spiritual and the temporal powers
within the system. Though the middle ages was an organic epoch, the
harmony between its two ruling classes was far from perfect. Internal
conflict was inevitable because the medieval system, like the ancient one, was
based on powers and powers were necessarily competitive in character — "it
is natural that each of them should pretend to the totality of domination." [8]
What appeared to be simply a struggle for mastery between two forces within
the system in reality had far graver implications. If read aright, this competition was a sign of deep-rooted imperfection in the medieval system which
spelled its final destruction. Though the modern system also had two elements, science and industry, it would escape this debilitating inner struggle
because they were capacities, each of which had a natural role and a unique
function, and because neither had pretensions to universality. The distinction

between powers and capacities later played an important role in Saint-Simon's delineation of the character of the élite in the new industrial society.

Dissensions within the medieval ranks encouraged the nascent industrial and scientific forces to make forays into the enemy camp, and eventually to press their advantage in a full-scale offensive. Saint-Simon's philosophical history boldly sketched the conflict of the systems as an international two-front war. The spiritual class of the modern order, the scientific capacity, went after the theological power with its cudgels, at the same time that the commons attacked the medieval temporal power in their sector. "Each capacity fought body to body with its opposite number," [9] using essentially the same strategy. While the commons managed to split the feudal power, making an alliance with one fraction of it, the scientists drew arguments for the overthrow of the theological system from one group of theologians themselves.

It was in the sixteenth century that Luther and his coreformers thrust into the open the latent conflict between the old system and the new. They broke the absolute hegemony of the medieval spiritual power, and "free examination" began to extend its sway over ever wider intellectual areas. The same basic spiritual revolution occurred simultaneously everywhere on the continent, though there were local variants in the class alignments in different countries. For example, during their retreat in France the clergy, the old theological power, bound themselves firmly to the royal power, thus prolonging their influence "beyond its natural term." [10] This was not, to be sure, an unmitigated good for the royal power, because it thus became tied to discredited superannuated doctrines, and the French monarchy paid dearly for the alliance in 1789.

The open warfare of the commons against the feudal temporal power was a development more or less contemporaneous with the spiritual war between science and theology — in the philosophy of history a century or two of priority does not make much difference. After the religious wars of the sixteenth and early seventeenth centuries, the commons too launched their overt attack. As in the spiritual sphere, the tactics of the commons varied in different countries, though the basic pattern of action was similar throughout Europe: in both England and France the commons split the feudal military power into two parts and united themselves with one against the other. While in England it was commons and nobles against the feudal king, in France it was commons and king against the feudal nobles. In England, when the battle was over, the royal power found its prerogatives limited, although the feudal system was in part preserved; in France Richelieu and Louis XIV humbled the nobility and advanced the political fortunes of artists, scholars, and even artisans like Colbert. In both nations the temporal power of the commons was enhanced at the expense of feudalism.

Saint-Simon called for a reinterpretation of the history of Europe since the Reformation, a shift of emphasis from the internecine wars among the chiefs of the ancient system — popes against kings, kings against nobles, and royal dynasts against one another, to the growing power of the commons, who were steadily accumulating victories, even though at the time they were generally regarded as mere instruments in the conflict of rival feudatories. The commons in Saint-Simon's history emerge as a canny lot, for they always managed to select as allies those elements in the feudal system who would grant them most freedom of action. Far from being mere agents themselves, it was they who used other classes; they were the protagonists who made others their dupes.

In the sixteenth and seventeenth centuries the attacks on the medieval spiritual power had been piecemeal, divided, not a clash, a *choc* between two systems; by the eighteenth century the war was full-scale, directed, under a single command; trenchant criticism of theological beliefs permeated everywhere, and the religious leaders of society were rendered ridiculous even in the eyes of the uneducated masses. Saint-Simon was cautious and circumspect; he knew that the eighteenth-century *philosophes* had acted imprudently, too precipitously, with little regard for the desirable gradualism of mankind's development; but despite their reprehensible technique, he had to confess that the all-out attack was effective. Saint-Simon's ideas were often best expressed as analogies. The eighteenth-century *philosophes* were described laying siege to the old theological edifice as in a contemporary battle scene.

"I picture that old system as a vast building crowned with a lofty structure like a bell-tower dominating a church. The physical scientists had begun by demolishing the bell-tower; but in 1750 the entire lower part of the old system was still intact. It is that lower part which was filled with the masses; it is to the lower part that the clergy descended and there continued to exercize its dominion over the common people. It was to demolish that part that the physical scientists labored under the guidance of Diderot and d'Alembert." [11]

As for the temporal force of the ancient system, in the eighteenth century it not only lost its political power, but it was stripped of public esteem, primarily because of the libertinism of its standard-bearers.

Throughout the pages of *L'Industrie* and *L'Organisateur* the rival systems and the rival powers were dramatized with anthropomorphic images. The old ones were dying, after a long period of decadence; they were no longer capable of carrying their social responsibilities by themselves; they were impotent and decrepit.[12] The new system was young, virile, strong. While the old orders might enjoy the trappings of power, the new industrial scientific capacities were the authentic powers, the *"force civile."* [13]

The triadic periodization of European history which Saint-Simon developed in the Restoration writings made it possible for him to refurbish his earlier versions of the theory of perfectibility. The alternativity of organic and critical epochs was not another form of the ancient circular theory; each new organic epoch was not repetitive of but superior to its predecessor in well-defined excellences. The *Opinions littéraires, philosophiques et industrielles* spelled out in detail four specific virtues in which the successive organic epochs were "perfections" of each other. In this late work his definitive, mature doctrine of perfectibility was contained. He abandoned the bizarre conjectures about future biological evolution and dealt exclusively with changes which had been effected in historic times by altering man's immediate social environment. Systems were more progressive as they approached nearer his concrete ideals of social organization. He set up the value system and then demonstrated perfectibility by his own yardsticks.[14]

The first criterion required of the social organization was that it make the majority of men in society as happy as possible "by procuring for them the greatest means and facilities for the satisfaction of their elementary needs," given the scientific and technological potentialities of the epoch. This was hardly a novel definition: it had antecedents among the *philosophes* and was akin to Bentham's utilitarian principle of the greatest good for the greatest number, which Saint-Simon often quoted. Emphasis upon the satisfaction of primary necessities of life for ordinary people was in the philanthropic spirit; earlier in the century he would not have erected this as his first principle. Implicit is the precept that a society should utilize all its facilities to their maximum capacity. A society which left resources unexploited, such as the fallow lands of the nobility, was less progressive than one which turned them to productive use. The concentration on elementary material progress for the "poorest and most numerous class" was the basis of most later attempts to categorize Saint-Simon as a socialist. This philanthropic aspect of his system did not loom significant until the last years of his life, but at that point it became the pivot around which his whole set of social values revolved.

His second criterion required that the road be open to talent in all spheres of human endeavor. Whatever the chance of birth, those whose intrinsic worth was greatest should be given the full opportunity of advancing in the social hierarchy. The ideal of the Napoleonic army, a marshal's baton in every knapsack, influenced his conception and made it appear eminently feasible. This was the core idea of the hierarchy of talents developed by the Saint-Simonian school; it was also the basis of their formula: *"A chacun selon sa capacité; à chaque capacité selon ses oeuvres,"* which became one of the key slogans of international socialism.[15]

The third criterion is bluntly anti-Malthusian. An increase in the population as an objective measure of progress, a sign that the social organization has advanced, had been one of the standards accepted by most eighteenth-century economists and government officials to judge a state's health and prosperity. In the physiocratic system of nature, the happiness of mankind and the multiplication of the species were one and the same. Condorcet foretold great increases in human population in his Tenth Epoch, though he at least indicated an awareness of the Malthusian problem before Malthus.[16] Saint-Simon had mentioned it indirectly in a Restoration manuscript,[17] but he threw no bright light upon the Malthusian controversy which was absorbing many of his English contemporaries in the first decades of the nineteenth century.

A final criterion for evaluating a social organization was the extent to which it supported scientific research and thus furthered the development of civilization and enlightenment. Saint-Simon used the word civilization primarily to connote a high degree of technological and scientific achievement, even though he was not completely blind to the arts as auxiliary instruments for promoting the welfare of mankind.

With these four criteria as measuring rods, Saint-Simon was able to demonstrate that there had been absolute progress in the passage from the ancient to the medieval and from the medieval to the modern systems. In thus evaluating the three states of mankind, he adopted a position sharply at variance with Condorcet as well as with the traditionalists. Condorcet and the *philosophes*, who had viewed the medieval world as a temporary retrogression, had by contrast idealized the ancients. The traditionalists were examining the whole history of man since the introduction of modern science in the fifteenth century as a retrogression from the medieval ideal. Saint-Simon saw unilinear progress, provable in terms of his four objective criteria, throughout all history. The transition periods between one organic system and another, for all the human misery they entailed, were not really set-backs; they were intrinsic parts of the process of progress. The superiority of the moderns over the medievals seemed too obvious to warrant elucidation, especially in the light of his secular utilitarian value judgments. The part of the thesis hard to demonstrate to men only a generation removed from the *philosophes* was the virtue of the medievals over the ancients, but Saint-Simon defended his position vigorously. In a series of comparisons between the ancient and medieval organizations, the medieval superiority was "incontrovertibly" established by every one of his value standards. To arrive at this conclusion Saint-Simon had to swallow uncritically the current idealizations of the middle ages and often enough he twisted simple fact in a manner beyond the usual license of the philosopher of history; but his central arguments are not easy to refute.

By yardstick one, the Benthamite principle, he only needed to extol the superiority of serfdom over the tyranny of ancient slavery. This milder form of authority over human beings, coupled with the existence, at least in theory, of a Christian moral principle of brotherly love, seemed to clinch the argument. His final judgment was that "the lot of men comprising the majority of society was much less unfortunate" under the theological and feudal régime than it had been under the Greeks and the Romans.[18] Measuring by the second yardstick, advancement in accordance with capacity, he again found the medieval system superior. His contentions were often highly conjectural, if not downright absurd, for his catalogue of medieval social virtues was in the spirit of full-blown romanticism. The medievals established the predominance of the spiritual power, while the ancients had subordinated the spiritual to the temporal. In the middle ages the clergy was usually plebeian, hence open to talent, while in Rome it had always been patrician. As a consequence the state of civilization achieved by the sixteenth century was "loftier" than the most brilliant ages of Greece and Rome. The medieval clergy, recruited on the basis of merit, had directed road and bridge building and the clearing of the forests, had established school systems. They performed useful works, in contrast with the ancient priests who had devoted themselves solely to their auguries. The Catholic clergy preserved the writings and monuments of antiquity in the face of the barbarian invasions, they bridled the warrior instincts of the nobles with a Peace of God, they safeguarded the rights of the individual in judicial procedures. They and they alone carried on intellectual activity. Thus "men of merit, whatever their birth, had greater opportunity to rise to the first rank of society among the Europeans of the middle ages, than among the Greeks and the Romans." [19]

By the third criterion, the quantitative one of a large population capable of warding off potential enemies, he further defined the superiority of the medieval system of organization over the ancient. Rome had succumbed before the barbarians, while the medieval system had assimilated them. The sixty million inhabitants of western Europe in the middle ages was a far greater number, Saint-Simon affirmed *ex cathedra*, than had ever been united in a single system at any time in the ancient world. In summary the medieval system "was much more numerous, possessed greater means of resistance to enemies than all the societies which had preceded it and it finally became preponderant in an absolute sense with respect to the whole rest of the human species." [20]

As for progress in the arts of the imagination, Saint-Simon in the year of his death remained consistent with the position he had upheld under the Empire. The aging noble of the old régime did not succumb to the romantic fashion of preferring the artistic expressions of medieval Europe to the works of Greek genius. Aesthetic patterns of his early upbringing retained a firm hold throughout his life. This was the one field in which he could not admit perfectibility.[21] But except for the fine arts the ancients were inferior in all other manifestations of civilization, and his theory was sustained by the fourth test of progress. Science among them had remained in its infancy, ethics had not been applied to politics, and the ancients believed that peoples were irreconcilable enemies. It had never occurred to them that men might join together in association for the exploitation of nature. They elevated the military class to the apex of society and looked down upon industrial occupations as humiliating. On all these scores, the medieval system was manifestly more advanced.[22]

The three states of mankind, the three successive organic epochs, were thus irrefutable testimony to the steady perfectibility of the species. In the very process of the titanic conflict of systems there was an underlying tendency in universal history which made the alternating epochs of the organic and the critical spiral ever upwards towards perfection expressed in humanitarian values.

Though both movements of the historical process, the critical, transitional period and the period of organized system, were equally natural, complementary in a sense, indispensable for the rhythm of progress, the impression is inescapable in the writings of Saint-Simon that the organized epoch and its creative geniuses have a marked superiority over the men of the critical epoch. He even called these critical epochs "decadent," the term which became current in later nineteenth-century rhythm theories of history. He had a clear predilection for the organized society, as for the synthetic method in science, and there was great pride and self-satisfaction in the thought that he was one of the initiators of a new organic age.

Saint-Simon's ages of synthesis, of the organic, or the organized systems, were the good periods in mankind's history. An age of synthesis had one ideal, developed by its intellectual élite; it was a time when men were not tormented by doubt. The medieval society had been the last good society. Saint-Simon's admiration for the middle ages, however, was not nostalgic like that of the traditionalists, for it was neither possible nor desirable for mankind to return to feudalism and a theocratic society. He was constantly exhorting his fellow men to move forward more rapidly to another organic epoch, the age of industrialism and scientificism.

The period of criticism, of destruction or analysis, was a necessary transitional evil between one good society and another. Its character was determined by history and its dismal role in the process was preordained; but as in the case of the analytic method of science, Saint-Simon could not avoid depicting the critical periods with a certain negativism. It was best for mankind that the transitional period be abbreviated as much as possible, for when old ideas were being dismantled and new ones had not yet emerged, there was an imbalance between the spiritual and temporal forces in society. Spiritual chaos reigned, as the dying and the newborn ideologies engaged in struggles for supremacy. Bitter class conflicts broke out between the men committed to the old temporal order and those who espoused the new. Transitional epochs in history were ages of war and revolution, when men were obsessed by a general sense of crisis.

Saint-Simon remained a "crisis philosopher" even when he preached gradualism. Though major social developments spanned the centuries, they always reached a boiling point, a moment of critical change. These crises were inevitable, at least they had always occurred in the past, but they were not periods to which Saint-Simon looked forward with the unabashed delight of Marxism in the apocalypse of the "revolutionary moment." The crisis was nothing to be jubilant about; it was to be endured and passed through as quickly as possible under the guidance of wise social physiologists. The historic patient was assailed by these crises as a result of a long accumulation of "contradictions," ailments of the body social. To hasten recovery benign historic antibodies, the new classes, had to be roused to perform their function. Saint-Simon had a clear understanding of his own transcendent role in this crisis. He was the social physician, "indicating in a clear and precise manner what course one should follow to effect [the social reorganization] with calm, with certainty, and with promptness, despite the real obstacles; in a word, to contribute, as much as philosophy has it in its power, in determining the formation of the industrial and scientific system, whose establishment can alone put an end to the present social agony."[23] The cure of societies, not the cure of souls, was the philosopher's mission.

In the state of civilization which followed the crisis, in contrast with transitional periods, the various organs of society functioned in orderly relationship with one another. They behaved as if they were parts of a single living organism. Integration was the characteristic attribute of the "good epochs" of history, and only those social or political institutions which were "in harmony with the state of civilization" could long endure.[24] The problem of politics was to make the system of social organization "correspond" to the state civilization.[25]

Up to 1819 Saint-Simon conceived of a "state of civilization" as a dualism of spiritual and temporal parts, a direct carryover of the Christian dualism. In later works he carved a trinity out of the dualism, dividing the spiritual into a rational scientific and a passionate part. This modification expressed a growing awareness of the existence of distinct spiritual forces in society, the artistic and the religious, which appealed to men's emotions and roused them to action. A comparatively late intrusion into his system, the "passionate" part does not figure significantly in his treatment of the relations between the spiritual and the temporal in his philosophy of history. In the main body of his writings the organized system was essentially a dualism of spirit and matter manifest in separate powers, forces, capacities, or orders — terms which he employed to highlight its different aspects.

The recognition that spiritual and temporal powers should be autonomous was the great achievement of the medieval synthesis, "the most significant improvement in social organization achieved by the moderns."[26] The Romans had not understood the separation of the powers, and among them spiritual and temporal functions in society were confused. The medieval dichotomy rendered it possible for an independent power — the Papacy — to devote itself exclusively to the spiritual and the theoretical. It was a momentous intellectual victory for mankind when theory and practice were thus distinguished from each other. Ultimately the cleavage fostered the creation of the modern science of politics separate from political action, a vital innovation in the Science of Man which was basic to the future reorganization of society.

The particular forms assumed in a state of civilization by the spiritual and temporal powers answered to a direct utilitarian purpose. They served the civilization well; they fulfilled rational functions, making due allowance for the level of progress which had been attained. An infallible Papacy was a functional institution at the height of medieval civilization, although in the nineteenth century it had been rendered obsolete by the advancement of scientific knowledge. By definition there were no loose ends in an ideal "organized society." All the parts met the test of rational utility, and each civilization at its zenith was the best of all possible civilizations for its moment in history. When Saint-Simon was confronted by forces which did not seem to contribute to the smooth functioning of the total organism, elements apparently out of harmony with the whole, he concluded that they were either insignificant vestiges of a previous epoch which had decayed or they were the early blossoms of a new civilization destined to burgeon at a later epoch. With this ingenious hypothesis to take care of what was coming into being as well as what was passing away, it was hard to conceive of any phenomenon in the social world which could not be "explained" by the philosophy of history.

In an organized system there were perfectly functional élites at the apex of each of the two major orders of civilization. The spiritual élite in a "good society" was that body of men who were endowed with superior spiritual capacities and were the actual repositories of the scientific knowledge accumulated through the ages. In medieval Europe, an organized system, the Catholic clergy, who enjoyed status as the recognized spiritual power, were in fact the authentic, unchallenged intellectual and scientific élite of their society. Whenever the qualified intellectuals had not constituted a social élite, society was unorganized, it was in a state of transition, of anarchy, of revolution. Such calamitous historical moments might last for centuries. They were the ages of suffering for mankind and it was the duty of true philosophy to find a way of drawing them to a close.

In Saint-Simon's writings the idea of revolution was a recurrent theme in many different contexts. In general he distinguished between political or social revolution and scientific, philosophical, or religious revolution. The two types of revolution corresponded to the two powers, temporal and spiritual. From the very outbreak of the French Revolution, major European thinkers had been debating the relationship between revolutions in ideas and political revolutions. The effect of the doctrines of the *philosophes* on the destruction of the French monarchy had dramatically posed the whole issue of the interconnection between ideas and the temporal world of politics. Throughout most of his philosophy of history Saint-Simon affirmed that political or temporal revolutions invariably followed and indeed were a direct consequence of philosophical or spiritual revolutions. He hammered the point again and again that a novel theory was the real key to a new political order: "[E]very social régime is an application of a philosophic system, and . . . consequently it is impossible to institute a new régime, without having first established the new philosophical system to which it should correspond." [27] The political revolutions of the ancient world were dated in a manner which left no doubt about the chronological antecedence of the spiritual synthesis.[28] But there are contradictory passages, written under the Empire, in which he strayed from the conception that scientific or philosophical revolutions came first. In his eagerness to demonstrate conclusively that nineteenth-century humanity was on the verge of discovering a new synthesis for all science he was capable of reversing his thesis. Institutional and socio-political revolutions became the progenitors of scientific and spiritual innovations. "The spirit of mankind was still vibrating with the shock it had received from Luther, when Descartes organized his system. The revolutionary turmoil was hardly over in England when they saw Locke and Newton appear. What a prodigious scientific development must be expected to derive from the ferment caused by the French Revolution." [29] On occasion he reconciled the antithetical conceptions in a chain theory of cause and effect which explained the continuous alternativity of intellectual and political revolutions.[30] Clearly it is difficult to fit Saint-Simon into a rigid materialist or intellectualist school.[31]

Fundamentally, he took the position of his predecessors Turgot and Condorcet that the great transformations had been wrought by the spiritual forces in society. The geniuses, the scientists, the religious leaders, the intellectual élite brought novelty into the world. They made the discoveries and they evolved the theory for the new system. What they added to the total body of knowledge was an absolute acquisition for the human spirit. The history of mankind could best be set forth in terms of the great idea systems of Socrates, Christ, Aquinas, Copernicus, Descartes, Newton. Since these spiritual leaders, however, were often inept in converting society to their conceptions, the temporal forces, either social classes or a great monarch, had to serve as trail blazers for the introduction of a new ideology. These temporal classes or their leaders did not determine the substance of the doctrine, the "system" of the new age, for that was the creation of philosophic or religious genius, but when they had the good sense to comprehend it they were capable of giving it institutional embodiment.

Discord between the spiritual and the temporal powers in all past civilizations had been one of the symptoms of eventual breakdown of an organized society. As long as the material and spiritual manifestations of civilization were in harmony the social system was maintained and the total "force" of humanity was "organic" and unified. But when the development of human knowledge outstripped the institutions of the social system to which it was bound, disharmony resulted between the two aspects of the force. The spiritual power of science or knowledge, having progressed beyond what was sanctioned by the temporal power of its day, was therefore constrained to inaugurate a period of violent criticism of the social order to which it was tied. Ultimately the backward social system was overthrown and a new temporal order, attuned to the advancement of human knowledge, was established.

This formulation of the historic relations between the spiritual and the temporal presupposed a certain tension between them. As parts of one system both had entered the lists against the old order which they replaced; nevertheless, the spiritual had been stationed in the vanguard of history, and in the past there had always been an element of rivalry between the two powers even within an organized state of civilization. The separation of the powers in the middle ages was not an unmitigated evil, however. Since the temporal and the spiritual forces were of equal strength and their viewpoints divergent, the contest bred a profound and fecund discussion of questions of social organization. The two forces had to seek partisans and this involved them in an appeal to the peoples of Europe, with a consequent popularization of knowledge. In the future industrial scientific society, any tension between the spiritual and temporal would be eliminated, even as the Christian conception of an antagonism of mind and body was destined to yield to a new harmonious image of man.

Would the rhythm of the organic and the critical continue forever throughout all time? Would man have to pass through an infinite number of cycles and crises? Saint-Simon's reply was explicit: the new organic industrial scientific system would be the "final system." With its inauguration the cycles would end and man would enter the Golden Age when history as it was known in the past ceased to exist. The millennium having arrived, there could be no further development in the sense of a new cycle of growth, maturity, and decline. The goal and purpose of history towards which the cycles had been spiraling had been achieved. The critical transition period of Saint-Simon's lifetime was the final age of struggle. The Golden Age would have no life cycle, for it was a veritable heaven on earth.[32]

In the early writings of the Empire Saint-Simon had formulated the primary mission of the nineteenth century as the elaboration of a new universal scientific synthesis. With the Restoration the mission was redefined as the closing of the transitional epoch and the institution of a new organic age. Up to 1814 he had concentrated on the scientific synthesis; thereafter he turned his attention to the whole system, both spiritual and temporal. But the key idea had not changed. Man had to end criticism, analysis, the destruction of the old. A historic duty devolved upon him to expend his energies on the synthesis of the new, on the creation of an organized society. The "state of civilization" came to represent the ideal potential of the world; the "system of social organization" the actualization of the potential; political action the tactics leading to the adoption of the "system of social organization" appropriate for the "state of civilization."

The appeal for a new synthesis, for the inauguration of the new age, were the central aspects of Saint-Simon's thought which attracted young men of talent in his last years. They were all longing for an organismic culture, an end to the contemporary period of transition. Under the spell of an "uncritical" ideology which promised to appease at once their intellectual and their emotional needs, a brilliant group rallied around the doctrine after Saint-Simon's death: the Pereires, the Rodrigues, Michel Chevalier, Bazard, d'Eichthal. Even the young John Stuart Mill, though he was repelled by much of the Saint-Simonian verbiage, had more than a mild flirtation with this system in the early eighteen-thirties. A craving for the protective warmth of the "organic" was the profound source of the doctrine's fascination for scores of artists and writers in the eighteen-thirties and forties, men more sensitive than most of their contemporaries to the disquietudes, the uneasiness, the contradictions of their society.

The most glaring limitation of Saint-Simon's philosophy of history was its exclusively European frame of reference. Saint-Simon had little of Herder's curiosity about the life of primitive peoples or the higher Asiatic and American cultures. His Europocentrism was relieved only by a special interest in the future role of the United States, in whose War for Independence he had participated. Within Europe itself he was so preoccupied with the history of his native France that he sometimes forgot the very existence of other parts of the continent. Most of his sweeping generalizations about the evolution of social systems and the conflict of classes were illustrated primarily with French materials. He partially justified the concentration upon France by a theory of the parallel development of all European nations, at least those in the west, the area which had once been a part of the Roman world. In one passage he drew a line through Europe and referred with approval to the writings of a contemporary commentator on international affairs, the ex-Bishop de Pradt, who had sharply distinguished in 1821 between the spirit of the political systems of the west and the east of Europe.[33] In specific instances it is often difficult to know, when he addressed himself to a "society" or discussed a "social system" or a "social organization," precisely which geographic unit he had in mind — the whole world, the European continent, western Europe, or France alone. Generally he seems to have thought in terms of continental western Europe, with the addition of England and the United States, as constituting civilized society.

His great admiration for the new North American experiment deserves further comment. There he saw white Europeans erecting a "society of industrials" based on production, and the road wide open to talent. The *Lettres à un Américain* contrasted the American nation of free workers with Europe's feudalism-ridden society. Under the Empire he had already reflected on the possibility that the center of world civilization in the industrial scientific epoch might ultimately shift from Europe to America.

"Will Europe always remain the mother-country of the globe? When America shall have been totally peopled, when the Americans have a navy superior to that of the Europeans, will not the new continent become the metropolitan continent?" [34] Olinde Rodrigues reports that in his last period Saint-Simon sometimes wondered whether the "implementation of the European theory would not actually take place in America first." [35]

As for the dark continents of Asia and Africa, Saint-Simon, at least in the *Lettres d'un habitant de Genève*, preached a new crusade, a forced imposition through conquest of European scientific conceptions upon their religious superstitions — a sort of cultural imperialism, the white man's burden. He was a believer in the racial inferiority of the negroes on "physiological" grounds." [36] The fate of the Africans and Asiatics under the religion of Newton would not have been an enviable one, had the prophecy revealed to Saint-Simon in a dream been realized.[37] Napoleon's Egyptian campaign with its prospect of converting the descendants of Cain to the religion of science fired his imagination. When the disciples, under the leadership of Père Enfantin, turned to the East in search of a Female Messiah, Olinde Rodrigues refused to follow them, remaining true to Saint-Simon's Europocentrism. Europe was always his first society; ultimately Europe's system would become a model for the rest of the globe. If Europe failed to fulfill its historic destiny, white America would take over in its stead.

20

Societies Military and Civil

A FAVORITE SUBJECT among eighteenth-century English and French moralists was the antithesis between the character of a military and of a commercial society. The discussion invariably became enmeshed in a parallel controversy over the merits of luxury and the intrinsic worth of the arts and the sciences. Rousseau's slashing attack on the refinements of civilization in his epochal discourses was reinforced by a utopian depiction of the frugal, simple, hardy, well-armed and -exercised military peoples of all ages and by a condemnation of the softness of the commercial nations, their riches, their cheats, the essential effeminacy which doomed them. In 1766 the Scottish philosopher Adam Ferguson challenged this identification of luxury and corruption and in a subtle analysis of historic and contemporary civilizations reflected that the military societies of antiquity had been subject to the decay of "national spirit" as often as the polished, commercial nations, that with proper preventives commercial societies could be preserved.[1] Benjamin Constant, on the morrow of Napoleon's defeat by the nation of shopkeepers, completely reversed the Rousseauist thesis in his tract *De l'esprit de conquête* (1814) and extolled the superior virtues of the modern civil over the military society both in war and in peace.[2] Charles Comte, the liberal publicist of the Restoration, featured the contrast between the two societies as the central argument of his attack against the *émigrés*.

Saint-Simon, who was acquainted with the writings of Ferguson, Constant, and Charles Comte, drew liberally upon their works for illustration, and devoted a substantial portion of *L'Industrie* to an exposition of the opposite natures of the military and the commercial civilizations. In conscious refutation of Rousseau, he eulogized the commercial virtues of work, economy, enterprise, the creation of riches, and above all, peace. A polarity between the military and the commercial civilization became another way of presenting the conflict between the feudal and the industrial systems. The military state in modern times, apart from its sheer destructiveness, was not only immoral but was less powerful than the commercial state. He rejected the idea that national spirit was an attribute reserved uniquely for the warrior nation which lived in continence and dedicated its total strength to defense against a potential enemy, and that when a nation forsook the battlefield and absorbed itself in the arts of peace it grew cowardly, lost its national valor, disintegrated, and was ultimately enslaved.

Saint-Simon set up a series of antinomic characteristics inherent in the two types of civilization. The *bourgeois* state organized around the principle of utility had only friends in other nations; the warrior state could maintain its position only by conquering other nations. The industrial nation, when attacked, found allies in the very bosom of the enemy; the warrior nation, once invaded, was confronted by a solid phalanx of all its adversaries. The superiority of the commercial over the military state was not a phenomenon out of time, but the climax of historical development. In antiquity, Saint-Simon conceded, the predominantly warrior states living in a civilization which was military were naturally victorious; but since the period of the crusades, supremacy had depended far more on the preponderance of economic resources than upon military prowess. Contemporary France and England owed their strength in the world primarily to their economic vitality, not to their armies.

The character of man was changing in modern times: he was evolving into an industrious peaceful creature. While this did not mean that lust for power had been entirely wiped out, there was every prospect that in the future violent military ambitions could be channelized into emulation in the performance of good offices. Man was destined to shed his brutish warlike habits, because utilitarian motives of necessity and self-interest which had so altered his nature in the past that murder and theft were no longer sanctioned by the mass of mankind would continue to be operative in further transforming his aggressive nature. There might be a spasmodic resurgence of the ancient, bloody passion, but it would be punished or educated out of existence.

The whole relationship between military and industrial occupations had been reversed since antiquity; once commerce had been a mere dependent, a supplier of equipment for the soldiery; in modern times it was the soldiers who were the obedient machines while the productive elements in society directed and controlled state action — a rather extravagant proposition to maintain a few years after Napoleon's abdication, at the close of a quarter of a century of devastating mass warfare which had embroiled the whole continent.

To justify this strange contention Saint-Simon in *L'Industrie* reinterpreted the wars of the Revolution and the Empire in a highly original manner, explaining them away as temporary aberrations of the peaceful, commercial spirit of the new Europe. The French Revolution of 1789 represented the triumph of the commercial interests who, in consonance with their real natures, had at the outset denounced warfare in a formal public act. And all would have gone well if not for the provocative attack of the remnants of the military powers which had gathered at Pilnitz. In self-defense France counterattacked and in the process this peaceful nation, drunk with early success, became aggressive and altered its basic character, transforming itself into a military government under a military chieftain who made the sons of France his soldiers, the state his camp, and all Frenchmen the brigands of Europe. In the ensuing confusion the peace-loving spirit of modern times was submerged as an alien barbaric will possessed men on both sides of the Napoleonic battlefields. The true will of the European peoples remained dormant until it finally was able to raise its head again in the coalitions of 1814 and 1815, when an uprising of the nations expressed the interests of pacific civilization against the French emperor. This ingenious dialectical analysis led Saint-Simon to conclude that at the inception of the revolutionary wars France was fighting for industry, liberty, and peace; in the end the nations of Europe were fighting against France in the name of the principles which she had herself first proclaimed.[3] During the Napoleonic wars there had been a temporary recrudescence of the military spirit, but since this was contrary to the essential nature of modern civil society, the pacific interest of commercial, industrial nations ultimately prevailed.

The military society was the idle, decadent society, while the commercial society was a beehive of restless activity. The basic drives of civil man made it inevitable that he would transform the whole world into one great productive and peaceful society. Modern man had a zest for work. To him work was not a biblical punishment or a burden, but an expression of free creativity. Productive labor was now an intense passion beyond the pleasure principle, and it would save society from sinking into the lazy, refined self-indulgence which Rousseau had associated with commercial peoples.

"What we call pleasure, what we call pain, only occupy a very small space in life. To invent, to execute, to direct, to pursue, to wait, to reflect — that is how the largest part of our time is spent. Movement is far more important for us than the pleasure which is its object, and idleness an evil far more real than the pain which it pretends to flee. To be happy, for man, is first of all to act, and then to enjoy."[4]

Men wanted to extend their activities over an ever widening plane. This expansionism was salutary when it manifested itself in an identification of personal, immediate interests with a broadening circle. To the poet, the philosopher, and the artist who were highly conscious of their influence upon mankind, the whole world had always been the orbit of interest. Thus far European statesmen, unlike the artists, had felt that their personal involvement and interest should be severely limited to a single nation. The age of peaceful industrialism was destined to create new universal values when the politicians of industrial states realized that interests could not be restricted to the boundaries of their own country, because in commercial society the welfare of one people and the welfare of the world were indistinguishable. "All the riches and the liberty that are created within a country are gains for those who surround her. All that is produced about her is gained for her. Citizens, work for the world, and the world works for you." [5]

Whereas the military spirit led one people to subjugate another, the new industrial society, from the very nature of its commercial relations, had to bring about universal interdependence and amity and a common crusade for enlightenment.

"Your arms are the arts and commerce. Your victories are their progress. Your patriotism is good-will and not hatred. Do you seek to join to these gentle virtues the strong and masculine virtues which the Spartans developed in battle? O citizens! You have more bitter enemies than the Persians. Ignorance and those whom it nourishes." [6]

For Saint-Simon in 1817 there was one guiding light in the ceaseless struggle against ignorance, which could keep the industrial society from ever becoming effete even though bloody war were abolished as a stimulant of the national spirit. The beacon whose illumination so dazzled him was political economy as revealed by Jean-Baptiste Say, a science for which Saint-Simon planned a far more ambitious role than even its author envisioned. The whole art of government in civil society would become the application on a universal scale of the truths of political economy. Economics was more than a compilation of precepts for the accumulation of private wealth or the enrichment of individual nations; it was the morality of the temporal order in civil society. [7]

From the laws of political economy Saint-Simon deduced a series of axioms or principles for the governance of the pacifist expansive industrial society of the future. Here was a succinct declaration of the emancipation of the industrial society from any remnant of military feudalism, drafted in the spirit of his epigraph *Tout pour l'industrie, tout par elle*. The doctrines of work and progress were the driving ethical concepts of the new society, far more effective in appeasing man's deep-rooted desire for activity than the military society had been. Production was the one positive end of society and the maxim "Respect for property and for property owners" had to be superseded by "Respect for production and for producers." All government interference in industry was injurious, even when it presumed to be helpful; the state should be permitted to do nothing more than protect industry from hostile forces. Producers of useful objects were the sole legitimate directors of society. They alone paid taxes and they alone deserved the vote. Since men could not direct armies against one another without mutual harm to the production of all nations, it was imperative that war be outlawed. The desire of a part of the people to exercise a monopoly at the expense of others was ill-conceived, because a monopoly could only be maintained by force and the monopoly itself diminished the productive capacity of the people who enjoyed it. Man progressed ethically to the degree that industry became perfected. It was therefore "moral" to spread and inculcate ideas which tended to increase the productive activity of one's own nation and fostered respect for the production of others. The whole of the human species having a common goal and common interests, each man ought to consider himself in his social relations as if he were engaged in a world company of workers.[8]

The view of a national society as one vast workshop of productive activity had been expressed often enough in the eighteenth century. Saint-Simon's conception of the whole world as an arena for constantly increasing production and of man as primarily a "working" animal was a further amplification of the theme. The ordering of this great workshop was described not as the art of government but as the *"science of production,* that is to say, the science which has as its object the arrangement of things in a manner most favorable to all kinds of production."[9] Production was the heart of modern civil society, as distinguished from the destructive military society of the ancients.

In *L'Industrie* Saint-Simon argued for a set of practical measures aimed at the increase of productive forces in a national civil society. In France he would favor the actual cultivator of land over the man from whom tenancy was held. He would eradicate the last vestiges of feudal law which still rendered landed property transactions complicated and thus tended to stabilize landowner-ship rather than to throw it open to the stimulus of competition. The right of property was a cornerstone of civil society, but the specific practices governing this right were by no means immutable. Though in 1817 Saint-Simon posed as the popularizer of extreme *laissez-faire* liberalism, the absolute enemy of state interference in economic relationships, almost in the same breath he insisted upon subordinating property to the principle of production and general utility through the action of the laws. Intervention was justified as a defensive measure against the rapacious share of the unproductive *rentier* in the total product at the expense of the direct working cultivator. The land reform laws proposed in *L'Industrie* were expected to have two immediate consequences: to destroy the political power of the feudal landowning class and to increase agricultural production. To industrialize French agriculture was his ultimate goal. If vast credits — thirty milliards — were made available to the new "industrial" farmers by land banks, the total wealth of France would be doubled. This was good state policy, in contrast with the wasteful governmental action of the Bourbons, planning to expend a milliard on *émigré* nobles who would consume their indemnity fast enough without producing anything.

Saint-Simon ran down the list of generally accepted arguments against any form of state intervention in the free play of international economic relations — high tariffs, bounties, trade restrictions, monopolies, or colonial regulations which impeded free competition. The whole world was a mammoth industrial society in which capital investment and productive industry would each receive its due proportion of the total if the "two natural organs for the creation of riches" were allowed to develop freely, unmolested by extraneous forces. Only war could constrain the rest of the world to yield to a national society more than its natural share of the world's goods, and war was a waste of capital and industry. "Commerce develops by itself and by an internal force like the bodies of nature. To force the development by an alien action means to stop it and to kill the body." [10] Competition was the lifeblood of industry and commerce. The enrichment of one man redounded to the benefit of all. To administer colonies cost more to the mother country than the net revenue obtained; hence only that colonization which increased demand for goods in backward areas profited world industry and world production.

Liberty to Saint-Simon meant economic liberty, not constitutional liberty. "Liberty, the liberty to use his hands, his industry, his goods. Make everybody as free as you wish to be. This is the whole of morality." [11] The concepts of liberty and of work had changed fundamentally since the ancients. To Aristotle, Plutarch, and Cicero, work was associated with slavery and liberty was synonymous with leisure. For Saint-Simon the converse had become true. If a man were deprived of his industry and his arts, the normal pursuits in a commercial nation, he had only one other channel of action open to him — he was driven to seek glory, to become a soldier, a slave to military regimen. Only those who worked could be free in the modern world, and least of all the grand warriors. The change of civilization had altered the very nature of the military occupation so that a profession of arms, once the identity mark of a free man, had become the stigma of the slave; it was now a way of life in which a man actually enjoyed less freedom than in any other. Liberty allowed participation in accordance with a man's productive capacity in the work of a world industrial society. The Graeco-Roman contempt for manual labor or the direction of labor and the medieval suspicion of profits resulting from commerce and industry were both wiped out. Work was the cardinal virtue of modern civil society.

If the military nobles had a sense of humanity and historic destiny they would quit the stage, allowing the new industrials full freedom of action, instead of lingering on, impeding the industrial class from assuming the direction of society. The military nobles could act only as a retrogressive force against the mainstream of history, which in an ultimate sense they were impotent to dam up, though they could create temporary confusion and disorder.[12] The chaos of contemporary society was not the consequence of the zeal of the nascent industrial class but the direct result of the rearguard action of the former ruling class, the military nobles still in possession of political offices to which they clung with tenacity.

21

The Physiology of Social Classes

WHEN SAINT-SIMON'S WRITINGS are divested of their polemical character as Restoration political pamphlets and of the pseudo-scientific twaddle into which he lapsed on occasion, there remains a theory of man and society based on professional or occupational class stratification. Underlying the theory were a number of simple preconceptions which he never stopped to analyze, perhaps because they were the cornerstones of his system, and like most fundamental assumptions, they were blithely taken for granted. The most important single postulate implicit in the doctrine is that class defined the nature of a man, his social action, his whole destiny. Of all that could be said of a man, the definition of his class personality was the most revelatory description. There were conditions under which an individual might slough off the skin of his class, but such an emancipation was the exception, not the norm in human behavior.

Class membership meant acting out a social role in terms of an occupation or profession. In a crisis society, the one in which Saint-Simon was living, class membership was influenced by a variety of unnatural extraneous factors such as birth status and inherited wealth. In the good society of the future, unlike this chaotic transitional epoch, class would be determined overwhelmingly by innate capacity or aptitude, which in the language of the day he considered "physiological" in origin.

Classes had histories: in the past they had experienced life cycles from birth through death. In the course of these histories classes had acquired characteristic natures which could be described and analyzed. These class natures were not absolutely static; they had undergone some modification with time; they were altered as they passed through the various stages of the life cycle; but in their innermost being they remained essentially the same. At the height of their maturity and dominion classes defined an organic civilization, since the ruling class set its imprint upon the whole of society. To know the character of a society it was necessary only to inquire into the basic drives of its ruling class. And these basic drives were readily discernible because historic man had formulated idea systems which expressed what the classes in power desired in the world.

Individual men passed their lives defending the interests of the classes to which they belonged by accident of birth, wealth, or capacity. The unit for the expression of self-interest was not the ego, as the eighteenth-century moralists had claimed, but was some kind of corps or class endowed with a complete set of anthropomorphic characteristics. The class sought its own aggrandizement and expansion, for that was in the nature of things. The class fought, was victorious, was defeated, rebelled, was duped, deceived others, plotted, organized, taught, produced. Not all classes employed the same weapons; since classes had different natures and came into being at different periods of civilization, their combat techniques varied accordingly.

Classes were the key to Saint-Simon's philosophy of history. In its very fabric history was the conflict of classes, and the historical process could be explained solely in these terms.[1] Other factors were subsidiary phenomena, events merely affecting and modifying the class conflict which remained the central thread.

Class conflict was not, however, an eternal struggle without meaning or direction, resolving itself in a mere succession of victorious classes of different natures imposing themselves on the world. The whole history of class wars was a process leading towards an ultimate goal, a golden age, the triumph of the industrial scientific society, a timeless world of terrestrial happiness, brotherly love, and ever more production of the goods which would give pleasure to all members of society. In the final stage of history class conflicts as they had been understood in the past would disappear. Class natures and therefore individual natures would change. The human attributes associated with classes fallen into desuetude would atrophy and wither away like a useless part of an animal's body in Lamarckian zoology. If there were no lawyer class there would be no cunning; with the passing of the military, warlike instincts would disappear; with the elimination of metaphysicians, the passion for abstraction would die.

The age of the Revolution was an ideal historical locus for the development of a class theory of this character. During the Terror the French nobility had been proscribed as a class. The laws against *émigrés*, the suspicion of the "aristo," foretold a new kind of overt conflict in European history — not religious war, not dynastic state or national war, but class war. The *émigrés* who returned with the Bourbons were marked as a class, and they presented straightforward class demands, a restoration of their noble privileges and their property. The existence of a class-conscious nobility helped to stimulate the class-consciousness of the *bourgeoisie*. The class conflicts of the period were visible, palpable. On every issue there was a noble interest and a nonnoble interest, embedded in total thought systems which reflected class desires.

The class theories propounded by Montlosier for the nobles or by Saint-Simon for the *bourgeois* were manifestations of a new realism — but they were not the doctrines which won adherents easily on either side of the political barrier, among the ultramontane theocrats or among the liberals, for they were too absolute an expression of the class conflicts of existing society. Run of the mill liberals who dealt in adaptations of eighteenth-century philosophism were in many ways more palatable because they disguised the conflict rather than laid it bare. Saint-Simon never found widespread support among the industrialists whose ambitions his theory nurtured; but for the very reason that his slogans were too naked to be paraded in the political arena, they are far more revelatory of social reality than the sonorous pronouncements of nineteenth-century doctrinaire liberalism. Saint-Simon can now be read with the feeling that this is what the industrialists were driving at all along, while the liberals of the period — who were the chosen mouthpiece of the *bourgeois* — ring false and hollow.

Class as the central concept in Saint-Simon's analysis of contemporary political society stripped off the façade of parties and bared the genuine framework beneath. He signaled out the creative political elements in the nation, condemned those who were attempting to divert the course of history, discerned the real class interests behind the barrage of party verbiage, and demonstrated the urgency of social action. Saint-Simon's depiction of Restoration France as a class society and his categorization of the classes and subclasses was a novel type of stratification that was not mirrored in the relationships and noisy antagonisms of the political arena. His effort to disassociate the apparent from the real, the superficial from the fundamental, the permanent from the transitory, led him to a profound understanding of the inner workings and movements of modern European industrial society.

Finally, Saint-Simon's class theory provided him with an ideology and an organizational plan for the new leading — he would no longer say ruling — classes of the industrial scientific régime, the new organic epoch. He envisioned the society of the future not as a classless society, but as an ideal order based on natural classes, determined by capacity, with each capacity finding its proper and essential place in the great national workshop. This much in the class doctrine of Saint-Simon is fairly constant throughout his life.

In its detail, as contrasted with its generality, Saint-Simon's theory of social classes is annoyingly fluid. He juggled his specific class categories every few years and switched his nomenclature almost at random. Many of the confusing misinterpretations of his doctrine have their origins in his own writings. There is no single theory or terminology to unify the works spanning a quarter of a century and any attempt to fashion a monolithic construct out of them — which scores of commentators have tried — must end in failure. His variant theories of social classes have a history of their own which must be recognized to make sense out of his writings.

During the Consulate and the Empire Saint-Simon envisaged contemporary society as an interplay among three major classes: the property owners, the propertyless, and the savants. The nobility were treated as defunct or the bearers of meaningless titles, the clergy as a dying spiritual power with some residual strength but of no major significance. He warned that there was real danger of a full-scale class war between the property owners and the propertyless, driven into action by their passion for equality. Though he did not mention the Babeuf conspiracy by name, the doctrine of the "equals," he feared, was a potent ideology with explosive possibilities once it possessed the masses. He deplored the revolutionary mob violence and the blind fury of the *sans-culottes* who had destroyed property and plunged society into chaos, and memory sharpened his apprehension that the propertyless would again be highly susceptible to egalitarian preachments, unless some counterforce attracted them. The men of property were small in number and could easily be defeated by the rabble, unless, and it was their only recourse, they won as allies the savants. Even though they were mere intellectuals, they were the real latent power in society. By savants he meant in the first instance the physical scientists, though the term as used in the *Lettres d'un habitant de Genève* included all laymen of the spirit, publicists, social philosophers, and artists as well as positive scientists. If the property owners were so obtuse or apathetic as to allow these scientists to fall in with the rabble, as they had during the Terror, then property owners were doomed and society along with them. Even the propertyless would not gain from the chaos which they helped engender; they would suffer in the general confusion and be sacrificed in the bloody wars of the property-holders, who could not alone bestow unified direction upon society, and would spend themselves in suicidal fights for the possession of material things.

There was only one solution for society: to move this floating class of savants to the front ranks and to subordinate the other classes to it. Under the Consulate Saint-Simon declared for the primacy of the intellectuals; he would put them in control of education and morals and would grant them absolute freedom of research with virtually limitless facilities. As they made new scientific discoveries the benefits of their findings would be diffused through the whole of society. The scientists would render each of their disciplines positive, coördinating their researches on a vast international scale until they arrived at a supreme Science of Man, a social physiology. This Science of Man would be the crowning achievement of centuries of scientific development, and in accordance with its laws all social evils, including the terrible scourge of war, would be eradicated.

The scientists would be imposing their class ideal (we might now say ethos) upon the whole of society. A scientist by nature existed to discover positive truths and to utilize the truths for human betterment. If his were the primary class, society would abandon superstition and conflict and would become a great workshop in which talents vied for universal approbation expressed in terms of rank in the hierarchy of science. To labor for humanity would become the way to fame. At times Saint-Simon regarded the scientists as a new priesthood and called their one fundamental law, the law of gravity, a central unifying religious principle, but this sanctification was not essential to his class theory. The crucial point was that scientists were in the forefront and set the values of intellectual progress, utility, work, humanity, benevolence as the goals of the whole society.

This new more perfect order, whose constituent elements were already present in society, could be achieved in a number of ways. Preferably by universal consent of all classes, the conversion both of the property owners and the propertyless to the belief that in their own class interest they should award supremacy to the scientists. As an alternative, he urged the scientists to seize the initiative themselves and to organize their own ranks around a scientific papacy. Or again, he called upon a great temporal power, Napoleon, to act as the new Constantine and adopt the religion of science which would bestow social supremacy upon its high priests. But the techniques for installing the scientists at the apex of society occupied Saint-Simon's attention less than demonstrating that their ascendancy as a class was urgent and in the long run inevitable. This new spiritual capacity would ultimately organize Europe even as the church once had. Mankind had been moving in that direction through the ages. The only problem was: would men march with history or would they be dragged along wearily after ages of suffering and bloody strife.

Saint-Simon's psychological analysis of the scientists, or savants, reveals an understanding of the complexities of the intellectual personality. Though as a class they were the most important in the whole social organism because they knew the secret of progress, these creative geniuses were by nature a troublesome group. The men who held the future of mankind in their hands through their scientific capacity were capable of great evil as well as great good. They had a demonic quality which it behooved other classes in society to be wary of. In 1802 Saint-Simon arraigned the savants as a class with an accusation of direct blood-guilt in the excesses of the Revolution, for they had acted in a purely destructive — a century later he would have said nihilistic — manner. Their tragic flaw was an itching eagerness to thrust themselves into the temporal world, to join the battles of the political arena, to dominate social affairs, when their positive talents lay in a completely different sphere, in the discovery and proclamation of scientific truth divorced from the passing struggles of the marketplace. During the French Revolution the savants had directed the overthrow of the *ancien régime* without leaving anything in its place. They had abandoned themselves to an orgy of invective against the stable forces without generating any new social conceptions to replace them. Often enough they were innocents in the temporal world, not conscious of the historic role they were destined to play. And sometimes they could be seduced, swerving the course of history from the path of progress. Yet, despite his recognition of their manifold psychological weaknesses and deficiencies, in his first writings Saint-Simon elevated them to the pinnacle of society.

During the wars of the Empire and after his own futile attempts to gain admittance into the official bodies of Napoleonic scientists, Saint-Simon became thoroughly disenchanted with them and remodeled for the first time his theory of social classes. He began to see in the leaders of contemporary science the indifferentists, men blind to the catastrophe of the European continent and the chaos of society, proceeding with their trifling experiments unconcerned for the consequences. They held the clue to the salvation of the continent — the integration of scientific thought and the imposition of a uniform system of knowledge and morality upon society, but they shirked their duty, letting the full weight of the burden fall upon his shoulders alone. In his rage at beholding the egotist scientists, each pursuing petty experiments while the world which needed their spiritual leadership was bleeding itself to death, Saint-Simon drove them from the eminence to which they had been raised in his ideal society a few years before. First he denounced the physical-mathematical scientists, then the physiologists. They had refused to formulate a general scientific theory which would lead to the Science of Man, they were unwilling to abandon the individualist studies which were trapping them in blind alleys and to coöperate in his great scientific revolution, in his "system" which would bring peace and universal happiness to mankind. He cursed them roundly and turned elsewhere.

With the Restoration Saint-Simon began to woo the industrialists, who held material power in their hands. While they by no means constituted an enthusiastic or generous following for his doctrine, at least they supported his works with occasional subsidies and subscriptions and they seriously debated the merits of his projects even when they rejected them. They seemed to be concerned with the social order, they were willing to subject it to searching criticism, they were interested in modifying it — albeit their steps were not as firm and their pace was not as lively as Saint-Simon would have wished.

Once he found some response among the wealthy merchants, bankers, and entrepreneurs, Saint-Simon in a calmer state began to regard the scientists rather more charitably again. He excused their supine attitude since as government placemen they could not afford to attack the state, to venture alone on new conceptions, lest they be ousted from their jobs. Men were generally not farsighted, and although the scientists were destined to supplant the theological classes with the coming of the industrial régime, it was utopian to expect them to jeopardize their immediate interests by boldly announcing their opposition to the contemporary social order. The chief industrial entrepreneurs, however, who had independent incomes, were in a far more favorable position to act as heralds of the new society, and they now became his minions.

Saint-Simon did not again revert to his original pattern of a society virtually directed by men of scientific genius, the idea he had once derived from Condorcet and Bacon. During the Restoration he hinted at newborn misgivings that the corps of physical scientists, if placed in absolute, sole control of society, might rigidify into a sacerdotal power as unprogressive as the Egyptian priesthood. His realization that the scientists, in the light of their subordinate class situation under the Bourbons, could not be more militant in the struggle against theological conceptions did not, however, warp Saint-Simon's judgment of their growing real power in contemporary society. In the eighteen-twenties he was impressed with the new popular esteem for scientists. He observed how profoundly the scientific temper had taken hold in France, banishing superstition, and this despite the overt political triumph of the ultramontane theocrats. Ordinary people had come to accept the conclusions of the scientists on their mere authority, a sign of instinctive recognition of the new spiritual power of science. To Saint-Simon this popular acceptance of science — a provisional credence dependent on proof and subject to change upon presentation of new evidence — was far sounder than the old absolutist belief in religious superstitions and submission to the spiritual authority of the Catholic clergy.[2] The spread of this positivist spirit among the mass of the people was a demonstration that scientists as a class were ultimately destined to triumph over the priests. Though the common people nominally still worshipped in Catholic churches, an ever greater proportion of their everyday beliefs was positive scientific truth. Beneath the crust of the religious Bourbon régime scientists were already assuming and practising their future class functions as a new spiritual élite.

In his writings of the Consulate and the Empire, Saint-Simon had concentrated upon easing the tension among the classes dividing French society, demonstrating how the property owners and propertyless could act together for their mutual benefit by elevating the scientists and following their lead. With the Restoration he focused on an entirely different class struggle; with the resurgence of the aristocrats and the churchmen after 1815 he saw society bisected into two vast hostile orders, the industrials and the idlers. A reconciliation of interests between these two classes he considered neither desirable nor possible. The conflict was bitter, a war to the death in which the historical process assured the triumph of the industrials and the vanquishment of the idlers. The idlers, principally the nobility and the clergy, were retrogressive. They were intent upon a restoration of the medieval image of society, an impossible ideal since the current of history did not run backwards. As a class they were dying and could not be resuscitated. Saint-Simon urged the industrials of the Restoration to give them the *coup de grâce* by taking active and aggressive steps to promote their own interests. They had an obligation not only to themselves but to all humanity. ". . . their particular interests are perfectly in accord with the common interest. It is because we felt this to be true that we have loftily embraced the cause of the industrials, since we consider their cause to be the real center and the hearth of civilization." [3]

Although Saint-Simon sometimes used the term industrial to mean industrialists in the narrow sense, that is, entrepreneurs of manufactures, in writings from 1815 through 1817 treating of the contemporary class conflict he applied it to the whole class of those who worked as distinguished from the idlers. (In some of his early circulars and prospectuses he had used *industrieux* along with *industriels*, until he settled on *industriels* as the collective name for the productive groups.) All industrials, the propertied and the propertyless, the entrepreneurs and the workers, the scientists and the businessmen, were joined by a common desire to produce and by a mutual dependence upon one another's production. Though there were differences in wealth and status among them, these inequalities would not generate conflict as long as men were enlightened about their true class interests. Saint-Simon had not forgotten the mobs who pillaged and wantonly destroyed industrial property during the Revolution, nor was he unaware of the contemporary Luddite uprisings, but in these blind outbursts he saw workers acting not as industrials in accordance with their real class nature but as "ignorant proletarians." [4] When taught the rudiments of political economy, workers would quickly perceive that in the long run their prosperity was bound up with that of their industrial chiefs.

In his Restoration writings, the core of the industrial class were the leading businessmen, the chiefs of industry, whose interests he identified with the progress of mankind. Diderot's *Encyclopédie* had already counterattacked against the prejudice of the physiocrats, who had implied that industrialists and merchants were "sterile" classes, essentially unproductive, mere derivative occupations by contrast with the true source of wealth in agriculture. Saint-Simon, in the Diderot tradition, reversed the hierarchic order of the physiocrats to the point of eulogizing the businessmen as the most useful class, the seminal element who would fructify the whole society.

Among the entrepreneurs, Saint-Simon recognized four major branch chiefs — the leaders in agriculture, commerce, manufacturing, and banking. In 1817 he realized that divisive attempts were being made by the *émigré* nobles to exacerbate the antagonisms between productive agricultural interests and manufacturing; by contrast he minimized the intramural conflicts among entrepreneurs as more apparent than real, of only passing importance. Of the four major branches, he grew to appreciate more and more the central position of the bankers and capitalists, not those who merely drew income from capital invested in government bonds and safe securities (the *capitaliste oisif* [5] was like the vicious landowner who let his estates lie fallow) but the bold spirits who risked their money in novel productive enterprises. Saint-Simon wished to involve the bankers more deeply in productive industrial activity, to wean them away from reliance for their business upon state loans to the creation of land banks which would serve as a stimulant to agricultural production. The banks and the credit system were the lifeblood of industrialism. The bankers were the ideal group for making "combinations" among other industrials; in their operations they continually gave fresh impetus to the expansion of production. "The science of banking or of finance (for it is one and the same thing) is still in its infancy. Bankers have not yet realized that there is more for them to gain in dealing with peoples than with kings. . . ." [6] The doctrine of the Saint-Simonian cult later designated the credit institution as the pulsating heart of modern society — a flattering conception to the young Pereires, future founders of the *Crédit Mobilier,* and to other nineteenth-century European bankers for whom Saint-Simonism became an ideological stimulant during the first great expansion of finance capitalism. [7]

At times Saint-Simon's patience with the Restoration industrialists of all branches was sorely tried, for they seemed almost as reluctant to embrace his philosophy as the scientists of the Empire had been. The tenth letter of *L'Organisateur* complained bitterly that the industrialists of France had neglected to take advantage of current conditions favorable to the immediate institution of the industrial scientific system, had failed to grasp the opportune historic moment, and had thus retarded progress. The whole of history had been leading up to this climax, and at the crucial instant the industrialists were defaulting. Like a prophet chastising the chosen people he upbraided them, for they were the class ordained by history to fulfill a mission, and they were turning deaf ears to him. Despite his vehemence, these castigations of the favorite class were but temporary outbursts, for he always returned to them with new arguments, new hortatory devices, new appeals.

Saint-Simon believed that the whole industrial class, both spiritual and temporal, had to be made conscious of a common set of values which he variously called a theory, a doctrine, a system, or a philosophy. A correct theory was an indispensable element in successful action. He had not invented the theory for the industrial society in accordance with some ideal blueprint, but had found it in a positive manner by observing and studying historical and contemporary class behavior. [8] Whenever the industrial class acted in harmony with its pure historic nature, uncontaminated by the alien habits of the feudal and theological classes and unfettered by the false and misleading doctrines of legist and metaphysical classes, it wrote its own theory; Saint-Simon was merely describing the values he found in operation. These were utility, production, a maximum of socially useful knowledge, terrestrial happiness, humanity, the improvement of the moral and physical conditions of existence for all men, first and foremost the most numerous and the poorest. The industrial class sought the attainment of a society without conflict, an organic society in which natural aptitudes were allowed free expression and men labored in accordance with their capacities, brought to full fruition by a reformed educational system; careers open to talent, violence replaced by conciliation, and man's inner drives seeking an outlet in the exploitation of nature, in the imposition of human will on nonhuman objects; a society become truly Christian, moved by love, not egotism, suffused with a spirit of association and coöperation; esteem and consideration for those who did good works, making the golden age a reality.

The values of the idlers — the class enemies — were by definition the negation of all the industrial class virtues extolled in the theory. Their conduct was warlike, luxury-loving, ostentatious, arrogant. The nobles resisted the course of history. Descendants of warrior barbarians, they had lost their virility, vigor, organizing capacity. Yet they sought to maintain their power by force and conquest. They were decadent, useless, an impediment to the expansion of production. Ignorant nobles encouraged the deceptions of the theological purveyors of superstition. Though the idler classes produced nothing, they expected to be supported and to exercise the prerogatives of dominion. They struggled to maintain privileges, monopolies, any political forms which would prevent the free movement of talent and the reward of industry and genius. They were responsible for prolonging the crisis of civilization because they were dead but would not remain quiet in their graves. They were in disharmony with the status of knowledge, they were supreme examples of egotism, they were un-Christian.

In his Restoration polemics Saint-Simon sometimes called the two orders national and antinational,[9] a crude appeal to French patriotism which would not lack imitators in the next century. He also labeled them bees and drones, producers and nonproducing consumers,[10] moral and immoral,[11] supporting his austere verdict by interpreting Christ's admonition about brotherly love with a highly original bit of exegesis: the industrials produced for others as well as for themselves, hence they obeyed Christ's moral law, which bade them do unto others as they would have others do unto them; the idlers were immoral because they produced nothing for others.

The Parable of *L'Organisateur* had emphasized the easy expendability of the existing governing class as contrasted with the indispensability of the productive class. Written at the height of the conflict between the *émigrés* and the *bourgeois*, it was far more revolutionary in its implications than Saint-Simon was prepared to admit. Apart from its political innuendoes, which in the surcharged atmosphere of the day almost lost Saint-Simon his liberty, the Parable reaffirmed Saint-Simon's belief that work was the cornerstone of progress and the only justification for man's existence. The desire to work was the outstanding characteristic of the industrial class and of industrial man. In the *Lettres d'un habitant de Genève*, Providence had proclaimed as a rule of conduct of the Religion of Newton: "All men shall work." The commandment was repeated in the *Introduction aux travaux scientifiques du xixᵉ siècle*, where "Man must work" became the highest moral principle of society. In his Restoration writings work, which the Reformation theologians had declared a prerequisite for individual salvation, became the central dogma of the Saint-Simonian ethic. It was the basis for distinguishing between the good and evil classes; the class which did not labor was damned. The demand for such spiritualization of labor was more acute in nineteenth-century Catholic than in Protestant countries, a reason for the widespread influence of the Saint-Simonian doctrine in France. It was an ideal *bourgeois* credo for a culture that required something more positive than an affirmation of the Rights of Man. The concept of labor as a psychic and not a mere material force has prevailed.

In Saint-Simon's social theory the class conflict between industrials and idlers dividing France into two nations was a phenomenon of the transitional epoch of civilization. He looked forward to the day when one of the antagonists would be totally eliminated, and when society would consist only of the productive or industrial classes. Since the idlers were superannuated, destined to enfeeblement and death, he could dismiss them with a few sharp characterizations. More and more he turned his attention to the classes of the future, and to the ideal relationships among the constituent elements of the new society. The writings of his last years were thus devoted to an analysis of the functions of the various classes, not in the chaotic present, but in the blue heaven of the future.

Saint-Simon recognized that the industrial chiefs were a minority of the whole industrial class, that by far the greatest number of industrials both in contemporary society and in the ideal régime of the future would remain the manual workers in manufacturing, agriculture, and trade. Towards this class of workers — the most numerous class — his attitude changed profoundly in the course of his philosophical career.

In his first tract, the *Lettres d'un habitant de Genève*, when he was trying to convert the world to the Religion of Newton with solid propositions anchored in class interest, he had plied the proletariat or the propertyless class with ingenious arguments, promising them prosperity if they accepted a religion which gave the scientists free play in the development of the world's resources. What was more important to the common people, he offered them peace. Once scientists and artists and philosophers were elevated to the top rung of society, the rich and powerful would also strive to gain entrance into the preferred circle of the elect of the new religion and they would thus be deflected from wars. Saint-Simon expressed understanding of the indifference of the propertyless classes to the political consequences of contemporary wars, which revolved around the issue of how many of them should be under the yoke of one master and how many under another. Since the propertyless workers suffered more than any other class from the wantonness of power conflicts, it was clearly to their interest that the spirit of competition among the mighty of the earth be directed into scientific emulation rather than wars. He therefore took it for granted that the proletariat would subscribe to the Religion of Newton. Throughout his argument sounded like a dialectical exercise, unwarmed by any love or pity for the plight of the workers.

In his Empire and early Restoration writings, Saint-Simon used the term *prolétaires* as synonymous with "the ignorant." He betrayed the characteristic animus of the early nineteenth-century bankers and industrialists against the laborers who had swelled the mobs of the Revolution. The proletarians were irresponsible, untrustworthy elements, driven by a passion for equality.

After 1820 Saint-Simon's sentiments towards the French proletariat underwent a complete metamorphosis, and working-class humanitarianism became a dominant motif in his writings. His announced purpose was now to improve the lot of the class which had no other means of existence than the labor of its hands, "to ameliorate the lot of this class not only in France, but in England, in Belgium, in Portugal, in Spain, in Italy, in the rest of Europe and in the whole world." [12] Always sensitive to the intimation that his system was premature, "utopian," he dealt explicitly with this point, taking great pains to demonstrate that the masses of western Europe in the eighteen-twenties were morally and intellectually prepared to enter the organic industrial society as responsible participants. The worker "has acquired the requisite capacity to become an associate under the new system, where governmental action will be reduced to what is necessary for establishing a hierarchy of functions in the general action of man on nature. . . ." [13] As proof that workers had already developed sufficient habits of self-restraint, orderliness, and foresight to make the final step, he cited the capacity of French peasants to go hungry during periods of famine without eating seeds, in contrast with the Russians, who were still unable to exercise a checkrein upon their appetites and who were therefore not yet prepared to embrace the new doctrine. The bulk of western Europe's inhabitants had acquired enough education to live under the new system of capacities in which the command function would be severely restricted. They no longer believed in witchcraft; they owned some form of property, at least personal property. In effect, western Europe had no more "real proletarians" in the old sense of the term.

Saint-Simon's eye turned more and more towards the workers of France. He reconsidered the events of the Revolution, reëvaluating the potential capacity of the laboring classes to direct both industrial and agricultural enterprises. He recollected instances of proletarian "association" from his own experience in the Cateau-Cambrésis area where he had speculated in national lands during the Revolution. When inhabitants of local communes had joined together to buy the expropriated lands of an abbey and had then tilled them in common, instead of ruining the lands, as had been widely forecast, the "proletarians" had demonstrated enough ability to increase the annual yield. Even though many of the industrialists of the *ancien régime* went bankrupt during the crises of the Revolution, the total productive capacity of the country did not suffer, for new men arose from the ranks of the proletariat to take the place of the old entrepreneurs. He therefore revised his whole estimate of the "proletarian class," adjudging them quite capable of participating in public affairs and of helping to assure the stability of society.[14] With the general acceptance of the new morality the motive forces behind any internecine strife among the industrials, the conflict of property owners and propertyless workers, would be eliminated because the amelioration of the condition of the poorest class would become the very goal of social organization.

His address to *"Messieurs les ouvriers"* in 1821 — the dignity of the salutation merits note — was one of his characteristic attempts to enlist their support for the doctrine, an appeal in which it is hard to determine where whimsy breaks off and hard-headed realistic argument begins. His idea was to use the workers as agents of conversion in persuading their employers of the worth of his system. For this purpose he composed a model speech which the workers were to address to their "chiefs" — a statement in the hierarchic spirit of the doctrine. "You are rich and we are poor. You work with your heads and we with our hands. From these two facts there result fundamental differences between us, so that we are and should be your subordinates."[15] Saint-Simon was clearly not the herald of a proletarian revolution, whatever else he was.

"The workers" had ingenious arguments at their disposal; with their "bluff good sense" they knew how to make France prosperous, an idea expressed in precise economic terms: doubling the real value of the land of France in the course of a ten-year period, a sort of ten-year plan. There was plenty of capital available. As for an ample labor supply, they not only pointed to the current unemployment, but identified what would now be called underemployment. "The workers" drew their chiefs' attention to the fact that a vast number of agricultural laborers were idle a great part of the year. Six million, they estimated, could be added to the French labor force between harvests. Projects were not lacking: they could drain the swamp-lands of France, cut new roadways, build canals and bridges. This additional employment would both improve the condition of agricultural workers and — Saint-Simon had an almost Keynesian view — act as a general economic stimulant. "The workers" estimated that these projects would increase the annual wages of Frenchmen by 1500 to 1800 millions a year, resulting in an equivalent rise in the consumption and hence the production of industrial goods. What a boon to the French economy, a benefit both for workers and entrepreneurs. If Saint-Simon's system were adopted, productive industry could save an additional two hundred millions a year which were now devoured through taxation by wasteful governmental administrative costs. Dispensing with a military, legist, and noble bureaucracy would yield millions more in capital to invest in productive industry. This was the kind of prosperity the workers comprehended. For the fulfillment of their natures manual laborers wanted and needed more work.

"The workers" were acutely conscious of the maladjustment of the French economy, because in the final analysis they bore the brunt of the taxes. While manufacturers were deprived of capital by the *émigré* administration, the workers were robbed of primary necessities. Therefore they took the initiative in support of Saint-Simon's system, which would at once alleviate their misery, making Henry IV's chicken in every pot a reality, and enrich France by three milliards. In conclusion "the workers" in this imaginary address authorized their employers to speak in their name, twenty-five million men strong. These proletarians of 1821 were no longer considered a blind social force by Saint-Simon; they were now respected associates whom he enlisted as ideal proponents of the industrial system, men with sharp native insight into its workings and productive stimuli.

Perhaps the most striking symbolic act in illustration of the natural unity of all the industrials as Saint-Simon conceived it, the commonalty of workers and entrepreneurial chiefs, was the recital of Rouget de Lisle's *Chant des industriels*, especially composed for the occasion, before Saint-Simon and Ternaux by the assembled workers of St. Ouen in 1821.[16] Joined in a mass public demonstration were the artist, the industrial and his workers, and the philosopher "founder of the industrial doctrine."

Under the Restoration the role of the scientists as a class was subjected to as drastic a redefinition as that of the proletarians.[17] In 1817 Saint-Simon thought of the industrials as composed of practical workers and theoretical workers, a way of grouping them which highlighted their community of interests instead of their parochial antagonisms. "The industrial corps. . . ," he wrote, "consists of two great families: scientists or 'industrials' of theory, and direct producers or applied scientists."[18] To promote the intimacy of the scientists and the entrepreneurs, he dedicated *L'Industrie* to the creation of an effective working relationship between these two symbiotic subclasses.

As placemen in institutes and universities, the scientists were dependent on a feudal theological class government. It was Saint-Simon's design to show the scientists that the nature of their profession required them instead to form an alliance with the industrial enterpreneurs. In *L'Industrie* he advised the scientists to become direct employees of the industrial chiefs, to accept their utilitarian evaluation of scientific discoveries as final judgment and — as a *quid pro quo* — to be rewarded with high salaries like other producers and purveyors of useful objects in an industrial society. It was better to be subject to the abstract principle of utility than subordinate to the whims of a government bureaucrat. He assured the scientists that they would enjoy greater freedom as paid employees of the entrepreneurs — a sharp departure from his 1802 position — than as hirelings of a state which was controlled by feudal theological classes inimical to their positive productive nature. The existing relationship between science and government was a betrayal of the true interests of the scientists and a deterrent to the advancement of mankind. Industrialists and the scientists had an obligation to extend a mutual welcome to each other. More than a century before the widespread establishment of industrial research laboratories by individual entrepreneurs Saint-Simon warned the industrialists that the expansion of their business enterprises was dependent upon scientific discovery and invention. The government, which through its institutes acted as a middle man between the industrials and the scientists, was a wasteful and often a pernicious inter-mediary. The most effective means for the industrialists to win the scientists to their side would be to rid themselves of the fiction that scientists labored only for the love of glory and to resign themselves to paying them large emoluments.

As a result of the influence of a remnant of ancient custom, people long imagined, we still imagine, that the occupation of a scientist is of a completely different nature from the job of a banker, of a manufacturer, etc. One admits that it would be ridiculous for a manufacturer to give away his products for nothing, but one thinks that a scientist is sufficiently recompensed for his by the glory which he derives from them, by the advantage of getting a few columns in a newspaper. In good faith, is not all this quite ridiculous? What! You think that there should be people in society who work for nothing?

Let us leave aside poetic ideas. Let us consider scientists as entrepreneurs of industry; let us look at their works as upon products analogous to others, as upon products which we shall purchase if it is convenient for us to consume them, which we shall reject if we do not consider them useful.[19]

Throughout the Restoration Saint-Simon was occupied with drafting projects for voluntary organizations in which industrialists and scientists, joined in a common purpose, might cement their natural alliance with practical works. A typical proposal involved the founding of a private "society" under whose aegis a periodical devoted to science, technology, and industry would be published — a concrete manifestation of the common interests of the industrial classes which would at the same time serve as an instrument of propaganda.[20] Another project was concerned with one of Saint-Simon's major philosophical fixations, the need of formulating a theory for the ideal industrial system, a task of such magnitude that it could only be accomplished through a collaborative effort. The chief scientists were to contribute an organic encyclopedia of positive knowledge; the entrepreneurs, a body of practical knowledge, a sort of total political economy,[21] and the responsibility of coördinating both of these "enterprises" would devolve upon Saint-Simon and the philosophers who came to his aid. In the course of preparing their parts, the scientists and entrepreneurs would form two cohesive units, in readiness for their ultimate mission, the direction of the industrial society. Thus in the very process of fashioning the theory of the industrial society they would be mobilizing and consolidating the new administrative leadership.

Although Saint-Simon continued to recognize the scientists as an integral but distinctive element of the producing classes, his nomenclature for the industrial subgroups changed, revealing a shifting conception of the role he assigned them in the contemporary world as well as in the ideal society of the future. In *L'Organisateur* of 1819 the binary division of theoretical and practical industrials was replaced by a trinary classification, the most common designations being artists, savants, and artisans. In a footnote Saint-Simon explained that by "artisans" he meant farmers, manufacturers, merchants, bankers, their workers and their clerks, whatever position they might occupy in the hierarchy of wealth and status.[22] The artisans were thus essentially the men whom he had previously called practical "industrials" in *L'Industrie*, a terminology to which he reverted in *Du système industriel*, the *Catéchisme des industriels*, the *Opinions littéraires, philosophiques et industrielles*, and the *Nouveau Christianisme*. The real innovation in 1819 was his recognition of two separate categories within the spiritual force of the new society, the artists and the savants, here made explicit for the first time, although the full implications of the dichotomy were not drawn until later.

Artists had figured in the *Lettres d'un habitant de Genève*, but primarily as stage decorators for the Religion of Science. Beginning with *L'Organisateur* Saint-Simon elevated them to the level of the scientists, considering the two as complementary forces. In the artists — the poets, playwrights, musicians, painters, sculptors, men of eloquence — he came to recognize an intellectual capacity distinct from the physical and mathematical scientists and on a par with them. Unlike the scientists, the artists were not blind or indifferent to the crisis of the times. They were acutely sensitive to the havoc it had raised with man's moral being, and they were troubled by the prevailing chaos, rootlessness, and lack of belief in any system of general values. At this period the romantic agony was at its height in France, and a new generation of poets came forth as the modern seers, the divine sufferers, the true priests of mankind. In the young geniuses of the romantic movement who felt the travail of the civilization in their flesh, who in an egotistic age were capable of passion, of deep despair and of exalted enthusiasm, Saint-Simon saw the new moralists, chosen propagators of his doctrine. No cold scientific rationalists, the artists were men of sentiment who could rouse mankind to an appreciation and understanding of its destiny. Though he never alluded to the romantic movement directly or referred to any of the budding poets by name, he accepted the romantic credo that the poet was the modern counterpart of the true prophet. He admired the zeal of the new writers far more than their political opinions, which were almost without exception theocratic; but he could pass over their intellectual orientation, for he was persuaded it would change with knowledge of his doctrine. It was their passion which he found a moving force.

Du système industriel (1821) and the Catéchisme des industriels (1823–1824) settled upon a definitive trisection of the producing classes of society and a final nomenclature. The first cahier of the Catéchisme des industriels of 1823 started with a definition of an industriel:

"An industrial is a man who works to produce or to put at the disposition of various members of society one or more material means of satisfying their needs and their physical tastes. Thus a farmer who sows wheat, who raises chickens, breeds animals, is an industrial; a wheelwright, a blacksmith, a locksmith, a cabinetmaker are industrials; a manufacturer of shoes, of hats, of linen, of cloth, of cashmeres is likewise an industrial; a merchant, a wagoner, a sailor employed on merchant ships are industrials. All the industrials taken together labor to produce and to place at the disposition of all members of society all the material means of satisfying their needs and their physical tastes. . . ." [23] In this definition all men who participate directly in the economic process, insofar as it deals with the production and distribution of material things are industrials. The term ceased to include the spiritual capacities in society as it had earlier in the Restoration, but it still united both manual laborers and the administrators of enterprise. If there is a division in the general body of the "material" industrials it is based upon the nature of the industrial occupation, not upon status within the occupation such as worker or owner.

This industrial class — as newly defined — was to be placed in the first rank of society, and all others were to work for it and be subordinate to it in the administration of the social order, because it alone was the indispensable class for the continuation of life. The contemporary social reality was precisely the converse, since under the Bourbon monarchy in effect all other classes, even those which did nothing, were given a position superior to the industrials. Saint-Simon's *Catéchisme* was a guide to the industrials written for the purpose of explaining why the topsy-turvy social hierarchy prevailed and of directing them in setting the structure aright.

In the ideal society each branch of industry would have mobility within it, and though the leading industrials — the chiefs (*chefs*) or entrepreneurs — would ordinarily receive a better education than the workers, the difference would not be so great as to prevent the rise of real industrial talent. Of course, gradations in capacity among the various levels would not be wiped out, and those of the highest capacity, the chiefs, would be the natural leaders of society. With their assumption of administrative control in the state, the artificial division between political authority and civil workshop leadership would, however, be abolished. The industrial chiefs would direct in both spheres as they had at the height of the middle ages, the last society of organic unity. In his mid-Restoration view of the world, productive industrialists were the ideal rulers of men, and the Saint-Simonians who followed him continued to stress his apotheosis of the businessman, undisturbed by the witty sallies of some of their great rationalist contemporaries like Stendhal.

For his analysis of the spiritual classes in the last years of his life Saint-Simon reverted to an idea which can be found in his own manuscripts of the year 1813, a distinction between the Platonic and the Aristotelian elements in the progress of the human spirit. In the past twenty-four hundred years mankind had been spiritually dominated by one or the other element, Platonism having controlled the human spirit until the rise of Arab science, from which point on Aristotelianism had been ascendant. In the new industrial society the antagonism between the Platonic and the Aristotelian spirit would cease. Both the Platonic force, in other words the poetic, religious class, and the Aristotelian force, the physical and mathematical scientists, would enjoy equal rank, status, and utility as parts of the total spiritual power. The system of the future was thus envisaged as an amalgam of three classes, the industrials, the scientists, and the artists. If there was to be one supreme class, Saint-Simon in the *Catéchisme des industriels* opted for the industrials, making them the final arbiters of the merits both of the savants and the artists.

In his last work, the *Nouveau Christianisme*, Saint-Simon devoted himself almost exclusively to the elucidation of the sentimental, moralist, religious aspect of his system, even as his *cahiers* of the *Catéchisme des industriels* had emphasized the material and Comte's had expounded the scientific. The fact that the *Nouveau Christianisme*, which was concerned with the acute emotional crisis of the age and the need to replace the existing religious power of the clergy, was his last testament, overweighted the spiritual aspect of his thought and left the impression among disciples that his doctrine was essentially a religious, moral creed. Actually the text itself continued to make reference to the new society in trinary class terms — a combination of the industrials, the savants, and the artists. As a religious doctrine it refused either to deny or to exalt the material, symbolized by the interests of the industrials. It insisted upon the coexistence in the good society of all three elements — body, reason, and passion. The physiology of the healthy body social required the industrialists to hold the reins in economic and administrative life, but of equal importance were the inventions and projects proposed by the scientists, and the emotional inspiration furnished by the artist-priests, constantly rousing men to greater exertions for the benefit of all humanity. Each natural class — the industrials, the scientists, and the artists — were gods in their own realms, but unlike the violent, bickering trespassers of Mt. Olympus, the new élites were coöperative, gently respectful of one another's bounds. If the industrials are allotted primacy on occasion, their role is still that of the first among equals.

22

The Lost Revolution of 1789

THE THEOCRATIC SCHOOL IN FRANCE, illustrated by the works of de Bonald and de Maistre, undertook to effect an intellectual counterrevolution in Europe. Burke's *Reflections on the French Revolution* had fired the signal for the conservative counterattack in 1791 and had probed many of the vulnerable spots in the spiritual armor of the eighteenth-century *philosophes*.[1] The French Catholic traditionalists in exile were profoundly influenced by this Protestant's diatribe against the revolutionaries, and from his arsenal they drew powerful weapons. In the course of elaborating their doctrine they went far beyond his assault on the *philosophes* as the "literary cabal" which had sparked the French Revolution. They took issue with the most general intellectual preconceptions and the dominant political spirit of modern times. In the *Théorie du pouvoir* and *Du Pape* they erected great Catholic thought systems comprehending all major questions of politics and theology. De Bonald and de Maistre had studied deeply their Bacon and Locke, their Voltaire, Montesquieu, and Rousseau. To the false teachings of these great heretics they traced the Revolution. Men had to turn away from the vicious ideas of philosophism and scientificism introduced after the Reformation before the European polity could be restored to its senses.[2] Back to the medieval papacy as the unifying spirit and force in Christendom — it was the only path to salvation.

Saint-Simon assimilated the traditionalist charges against the *philosophes*. His very first work was concerned with redirecting the energies of the European intellectuals, who had joined the *sans-culottes* rabble during the Revolution, to nondestructive, nonrevolutionary scientific endeavor. The causal relationship between the ideology of the eighteenth century and the Revolution was as basic a preoccupation with him as it was with the theocratic school. Only he drew substantially different conclusions from the same evidence.

In his Empire writings, Saint-Simon centered his attack against the

Encyclopedists on the general spirit of their work, because it had been wantonly critical and not "inventive" (we would now say creative). They had been so totally absorbed in skirmishes against theology that their much-vaunted attempt at a scientific synthesis of modern knowledge in the *Encyclopédie* was a dismal failure. Had Saint-Simon been consistent in his determinist history of science he would have dealt less harshly with the eighteenth-century *philosophes*, for they were only performing their historic critical role in destroying the ancient theological system, but like most philosophers of history, however lofty the eminence from which they view the world, he could not refrain from hissing at his villains, and the *philosophes* were among the progenitors of the French Revolution.

During the Restoration Saint-Simon shifted the main emphasis of his attack on the *philosophes* from scientific to political grounds. He censured them less for their scientific method than for their bungling political techniques. To disabuse the world about theology was well and good, but they should have been mindful of the appropriateness of their tactics.[3] The *philosophes* had envenomed the revolutionary battles by spreading the false idea that nobles and priests had always been wicked classes, instead of viewing them dispassionately, calmly, and scientifically as forces destined to grow steadily weaker after having outlived their usefulness in the course of a long historic process. The blood of the Terror was on their philosophical heads.[4]

In a personal sense the French Revolution was the great trauma in Saint-Simon's life. The months in the prisons of the Terror had soured him for the rest of his years on those grandiloquent eighteenth-century generalities which he had taught in the assemblies of his ancestral Picardy in the early part of the Revolution. From one viewpoint his whole system was an impassioned attempt to prevent a repetition of the violence of the Revolution and the Napoleonic wars which he linked up directly with the initial outburst. In retrospect he always prided himself on his abstention from political activities during the Revolution because it was not "honorable" to engage in a work of demolition.

His fullest treatment of the French Revolution appeared in the Restoration polemics. The *ultras* were charging all the men of the third estate, not the *philosophes* alone, with responsibility for the horrors of the Terror, and by extension they attainted the liberal industrialists and bankers who were their class heirs. A good part of Saint-Simon's pamphleteering was a vindication of the productive Restoration industrialists from an accusation which identified them for all time with the revolutionary spirit. He argued ingeniously to exculpate his industrials from the grave indictment that they were men subversive of law, order, and good morals, in secret alliance with Jacobin plotters.

One of his forensic techniques was to maintain — in line with his philosophy of history — that the French Revolution in fact had been no revolution at all but only the final political crisis in a centuries-long process in European civilization. The authentic revolution, the real change, had begun in the eleventh century and had been going on for at least six hundred years before 1789. Little by little the real revolution had been achieving its great purpose, the overthrow of the medieval system. "If someone should absolutely insist upon assigning an origin to the French Revolution it should be dated from the day when the emancipation of the communes and the study of the sciences of observation began in western Europe." [5]

One analysis of the French Revolution in *L'Industrie* rested on a distinction between long-term and immediate causes. The immediate provocations were of a relatively minor nature: the character of the queen, her extravagance and ill-repute, and the economic crisis resulting from the poor harvests which had plunged the people into despair. These finite problems, he believed, could have been handled by prompt governmental action, practical measures such as repudiation of the queen, a declaration of bankruptcy, and the adoption of English state forms. The long-term causes, the more general factors in the revolutionary complex, pushed the nation beyond the point where specific remedies were effective. The *philosophes* had demanded a total reorganization of society to bring it into harmony with the new state of scientific knowledge. Without providing a plan, they aroused in men an acute consciousness of the need for change. Once the insurrection began it could therefore not be stopped until a new social organization had been evolved and the means of embodying it in institutional forms had been devised.

The general causes of the Revolution were not in the French national character but were common to all of *Franche Europe*, by which Saint-Simon meant the area of western Europe dominated by the Romans. A uniform civilization had been imposed upon this whole area by Roman law. The territory had been conquered by the same invading barbarians, and during the subsequent feudal organization of Europe the states had undergone the same experiences. Their essential unity had been further emphasized by their wars at the uncivilized frontiers, their battles with Saracens, Turks, Poles. In the process of emerging from feudalism they had all witnessed the same consolidation of royal power and now they were all confronted with the same revolutionary problem of liquidating the vestiges of feudalism.

This broad-gauged grasp of the French Revolution was unique in the early Restoration. After 1815, with the birth of political parties in France, there was a tendency to reinterpret the Revolution in limited national political terms revolving around the rise and fall of factions. Saint-Simon's thesis preserved the spirit of the earlier philosophical views of Burke, Madame de Staël, Chateaubriand, and those *émigrés* who, in their forced wanderings over the continent, began to sense its unity.

The idea that the French Revolution was the culmination of a gradual evolution in European civilization was one of the central propositions which the French theocratic school had propounded with great intellectual vigor. In the loneliness of exile the *émigré* thinkers grappling with the why and the wherefore of the Revolutionary cataclysm, remote from the dramatic party politics and the revolutionary personalities, had sought for underlying causes. As a group they were the first to conclude that the Revolution was no accident, no chance concatenation of political events, no series of blunders on the part of virtuous men or individual crimes perpetrated by revolutionary monsters, but the slow unraveling of history. In early nineteenth-century French thought the influence of the theocratic school was pervasive beyond the confines of devout Catholics. They had analyzed a complicated series of contemporary political events — the upheaval of a monarchical government in the largest European state — not in terms of the actions of individual men like Louis XVI, Mirabeau, Danton, and Robespierre, but in the light of centuries of history. Causes were profound and often hidden. Their Revolution could be understood only in the context of a world philosophy of history.

The theocrats placed the origins of the French Revolution in the fifteenth century, at the beginning of the breakdown of the medieval papal system. The spirit of science and free inquiry was the foul source of revolutionary licence. Saint-Simon, strongly influenced by their historical approach to the Revolution, merely inverted their system. Both associated the French Revolution with the progress of science, only their great evil was to him the great good. Both agreed that the Revolution was a misfortune, but while for the theocrats it was a divine scourge, a sign from God that men should turn away from the evils of the Baconian spirit, to Saint-Simon the Revolution was primarily a tactical failure in execution; its original avowed objectives, the triumph of industry and science, had been salutary.

The French Revolution, which had been initiated under most favorable auspices, was turned into a fiasco as a consequence of the political miscalculations of the industrials. This was *L'Industrie*'s thesis. The king had awarded the third estate (which for purposes of his exposition Saint-Simon assimilated with the industrials) double representation, a reasonable recognition of the realities of temporal power for they were actually the most important class. And if not for gross bungling on the part of the industrials, events might have flowed along smoothly, the political system of France might have been slowly altered to fit the growing real power of the industrials, the remnants of feudal privilege might have been liquidated by orderly purchase from the nobles, as the industrials had been buying "liberties" and nobles' estates for centuries. In other words there might have been no violent revolution at all, because the feudal classes of 1789 were vested with only a small fraction of their quondam power, their great wealth and force having been gradually dissipated under the kings of France. What happened after 1789 was accident, a fatal error in practical political reckoning on the part of the commons. In 1789 the industrials of France neglected to act in accordance with the dictates of the true laws governing the historical process and they unwittingly led history astray. They called upon two "bastard classes" to represent them: the lawyers and the metaphysicians. The real villains in the historical drama which was subsequently enacted in France were thus less the feudal-theological classes, who by the end of the eighteenth century had become so feeble as to be an insignificant opposition, than the intermediary "bastard classes" who stood in between the feudal theological and the industrial scientific classes.

In Saint-Simon's writings there are two separate analyses of the role of these intermediary classes. The first one, in *L'Industrie* and *Du système industriel,* defines them as lawyers and metaphysicians. The lawyers of eighteenth-century France are considered the heirs of the medieval jurists who, when the new industrial classes first made their appearance in Europe, gave them protective covering.[6] Beneath the shield of the jurists' Roman law, the industrial concept of private property ownership as opposed to feudal property was allowed to develop. Similarly, the metaphysicians, by distracting the theologians into labyrinthine arguments on abstract problems, had made it possible for the physical scientists to pursue their researches relatively unmolested without engaging in open warfare with the theologians at a time when scientists were still a weak spiritual force in society. Thus the role of the intermediaries, of the lawyers and metaphysicians, had been that of benign protectors of the progressive classes during the early stages of their growth. When the Revolution broke out, the climax of eight centuries of increasing industrial strength, it was the moment for the industrials themselves to assume personal direction of political society in addition to their control of civil society. The assemblies should have been peopled with industrials, who, if they had understood their mission, would have proceeded without further ado to the constructive organization of the industrial scientific society. If the industrials felt they needed aid and advice from theorists they should have summoned positive scientists to their side.

Instead of following this appropriate historical course, the industrials early in the Revolution made the fatal tactical blunder of inviting the metaphysicians and the lawyers, particularly the lawyers, to fill up the assemblies as their representatives. The mistake was comprehensible enough, since for centuries the industrials had grown accustomed to the practice of availing themselves of the services of lawyers as their phrase-makers and their public defenders, and it was natural to continue the relationship even during the crucial Revolutionary days, long after the industrials were able to stand on their own feet independent of the support of the lawyers. The industrials, unaware of the degree of their own maturity, allowed the Revolution to fall into the hands of classes who proceeded to organize society in their own image, in terms of metaphysical abstractions like the rights of man and lawyers' constitutions, which were more concerned with political forms and mechanisms than with the establishment of a new social order based on the real forces in society. It was the great tragedy of the Revolution that it was metamorphosed into a lawyers' and a metaphysicians' utopia instead of being the consummation of the industrial scientific civilization.[7]

The total destructiveness of the Revolution was thus in the final analysis to be blamed on the lawyers and the metaphysicians of 1789. Not purged of their guilt, the lawyers were still in control, for the industrials were continuing to hire them as their spokesmen. Under the Restoration the essential character of the lawyers and metaphysicans was becoming more nakedly obvious than ever before, since as classes which in themselves represented no tangible interests in society they were now the willing hirelings of the feudal theological classes as well as of the industrials. Saint-Simon's irrepressible venom against the lawyers sprang less from a desire to pass an unfavorable historic verdict upon them than from his keen realization that in his day they were still in office in the bureaucracy and in the Chamber of Deputies. Bastard classes were prepared to sing anyone's tune as long as they were allowed to retain the trappings of power. The transitional stage in which civilization found itself and the mixed character of the social régime, part feudal, part industrial, was entirely to their liking, since it was expressive of their dual class nature, and as long as there was no definitive settlement on an organic society they would continue to exercise influence. Saint-Simon beseeched the industrials to rid themselves of these false agents who, serving their own ends, were impeding the establishment of a new régime. He urged the industrials to summon in their place positive scientists, industrial publicists, theoreticians of industrialism like himself.

If Saint-Simon has any historical demons, they are the lawyers and metaphysicians, whose full significance in modern history he spelled out in Du système industriel of 1821. The whole conception of the psychology of a social class was novel, and his aperçus on the behavior of a "middle" class in between two major historical protagonists were meaty additions to the class theory of society. Burke had already pronounced himself with vehemence on the role of the lawyers in the French Revolution; Saint-Simon's psychological analysis of the character of this profession and its relationship to the ideology of the French Revolution continued in the same spirit. He devoted whole essays to the analysis of the "Political Importance of the Lawyers in France," [8] and the public calamity of their enduring influence, because the interests of a society of producers were precisely the converse of those of the lawyers. What motivated the actions of lawyers as a class? "They must have power at any price; and to obtain as much as possible, these new 'proteans' know how to assume every shape according to circumstance." [9] The power lust of the legist class has rarely been described with deeper animus. "It is a boundless thirst for *power* — so strong that when they cannot be absolute masters themselves, holding power as subalterns becomes the object of their desires and their efforts. This will cease to arouse wonderment if one reflects on the fact that it was the *Roman Emperors*, the greatest despots who ever lived, who were the inventors of the *science* practiced by the *legists*, as well as the *principles of justice* which the legists charge themselves with applying." [10] They obfuscated the real conflict of the day with words. Society had to have a goal; and this could be either military or industrial. The social ends which the lawyers and metaphysicians talked about, concepts like liberty, were nonsense. "Liberty, considered from the correct viewpoint, is a consequence of the state of civilization, and it is also progressive, but it cannot be the end of civilization." [11] If the leading representatives of the two hostile class systems — the feudal and the industrial — could only face each other openly and squarely, without the interference of the lawyers and metaphysicians, the old would resign and the new would indemnify them. Unfortunately, the lawyers were everywhere; they ran the governors and the governed, and yet they themselves were nothing. They had no productive capacity. They were parasites living on other classes. The productive industrial and the lawyer had nothing in common, for their whole manner of thinking was basically different. The lawyer's mind was always at play with subtleties; the industrialist had straightforward good sense. The industrial had a feeling for "reality and objects"; the lawyer always treated of "other people's affairs" in "abstractions." [12] And yet the industrial continued to rely on lawyers and metaphysicians who mistook "form for substance and words for things." [13]

In the *Catéchisme des industriels* there is a final version of Saint-Simon's theory of the "bastard classes" in the Revolution, one more developed and even more bitter in its vituperation against these stumbling blocks on the path of progress. This second version depicts the intermediary groups as direct historical offshoots of the feudal theological classes, blackening their class character by identifying their origins with feudal rather than industrial society. The jurists at first had been aids in the administration of feudal justice. They sat themselves at the feet of the lords who, finding the job tedious, turned it over to the new class which was thus literally born "between the legs" of the feudal barons. Another class, nonnoble military men, grew out of transformations in the art of war resulting from the introduction of the canon, after which the noble mounted warrior was no longer the unique military figure. Similarly, nonnoble landowners as a class came into being when nobles on crusade or in pursuit of luxury were constrained to sell a part of their estates. These groups taken together were by the end of the eighteenth century intermediary classes since they belonged neither to the feudal theological classes from which they had sprung, nor to the industrial scientific classes. If nonnoble rentiers were added to them they formed an agglomeration which in the pyramidal structure of eighteenth-century society was a second major social stratum below the nobles and the theologians. Beneath both of them was a third stratum, a class composed of the real productive industrials.

According to this novel pattern the society of the old régime was not fundamentally a hierarchy of three estates; it consisted rather of three strata, one of which, the combination of nobles and clergy, was supported by the other two. What happened during the Revolution was that the second stratum ousted the first and seized power for itself, an insurrection it engineered by duping the industrials, the third stratum, into believing that they had common interests and should join in the elimination of the top stratum. The industrials, according to this account, played no role at all in the initiation of the Revolution; at most they were used as pawns by nonnoble military men, rentiers, landowners, lawyers, and members of "honorable professions" — another minor category — who wanted to control the state in their own class interests. The industrials were either fools or spectators, not protagonists of the Revolution. For the aggressive second stratum of the prerevolutionary period he had a separate label, *bourgeois*, which in this context he differentiated significantly from productive industrials (though earlier in the Restoration he had loosely used bourgeois, liberals, and industrials to identify more or less the same people).[14] Thus the French Revolution was a bourgeois, not an industrial's revolution; it was launched not for the purpose of creating a new social order commensurate with humanity's scientific knowledge but solely as part of a struggle for power of the second social stratum of eighteenth-century society against the first.

The bourgeois succeeded, especially since in the early stages they enjoyed the support of the king. When the bourgeois came to power they guillotined the Bourbon monarch and expelled the nobles and the clergy, superseding them as the top stratum in society. Ultimately they chose themselves Napoleon, a bourgeois king who solidified their power by creating a new bourgeois nobility in which military men, state officials, rentiers, and landowners were awarded titles. When Napoleon was finally defeated by the union of the expelled French feudal theological classes with the rest of the feudal theological forces on the continent, the Bourbons were restored and the three old strata were brought back into French society. There was one vital change, however: the new Napoleonic nobility was not dissolved, but was allowed to coexist with the old feudal theological classes. This second stratum of society became part of the ruling classes of the Restoration, even though enmity persisted between the two nobilities. The intolerable result was that the industrials now had to bear on their shoulders the weight of two unproductive strata whereas before the Revolution they had only supported one. Thus they had gained nothing from the whole revolutionary process initiated in 1789 — a generalization supported by statistics, for the nation's budget, to which the industrials alone contributed through the payment of taxes, was now greater than it had been before the Revolution.

As the two rival top strata in society continued their hostilities, the old nobility demanded restitution of its lands and reëstablishment of its unique status; the new Napoleonic nobility wanted to oust the Bourbons and their feudal theological classes in order to restore to the throne the son of their bourgeois emperor and to enjoy unchallenged power at the head of the state. The industrials, the innocents in this drama, were again the victims and now once more, as in 1789, they were in danger of becoming the unwitting tools of the second stratum of society, the rentiers, the lawyers, the Napoleonic soldiers and landowners. These bastard classes again gave the appearance of espousing the industrial cause when in fact they were merely engaging in a class struggle for power.

By their consistent conduct since the emancipation of the communes the industrials had shown that they were in their innermost class nature opposed to violent social change and to the extension of the governing power. This exonerated them from any complicity in Robespierre's tyrannical rule. The industrials may have been lax in not assuming the direction of the Revolution from the outset, but having stepped aside they should not have had to bear the onus of the Terror. Their record during the French Revolution had been the clean slate of nonparticipants.[15] It was they who suffered from the Law of the Maximum and Napoleon's confiscations.

The lost revolution of 1789 had one salutary effect: a clean sweep of the feudal theological system had been attempted and progress had been given real direction throughout the continent. But the job had been botched and left incomplete. The Revolution had not adequately fulfilled its historic mission — "the formation of a new political system" — and a temporary resurgence of the old order had again become possible. "It was because the goal was not achieved that the Revolution is not yet over." [16]

There had been a prolongation rather than a solution of the crisis of the times. Backed by the predictions derived from his philosophy of history, Saint-Simon was come to his day and generation to end the crisis which had been unduly extended into the nineteenth century. Thus the Revolution was for Saint-Simon, as it was for Fourier, de Bonald, de Maistre and scores of other systematizers, the great tragedy of the age, as well as a terrible personal shock. To avoid another revolution, to settle the old conflicts, to bring order out of the social chaos, to recreate society which had seemingly dissolved before their eyes under the Terror became their central purpose. The malady of the age was deep rooted, they all preached, and the political revolution was but a symptom. The dread of another revolutionary outburst haunted the men both of the theocratic and the utopian schools with a persistence which members of another postrevolutionary generation can well comprehend.

Both Saint-Simon and the theocratic school saw in a reconstituted "system" the end of the revolution and the salvation of man. They differed profoundly as to the nature of the system: the traditionalists wanted to return to the medieval papacy and to wipe out from the memory of Europe the intervening centuries of science and irreligion; Saint-Simon was eager to move ahead to the establishment of a society founded on science and industry.

23

Tactics for a Peaceful Revolution

SAINT-SIMON EXAMINED AND EVALUATED the major social classes of France in a series of tests. First, the historical one. It yielded proof positive that the nobility and the clergy had been on the decline for centuries while the industrials were progressively acquiring power and status in the realm. The Count de Montlosier had propounded a similar thesis in a three-volume work which influenced both traditionalists and liberals, *De la monarchie française* (1815); only he had amassed voluminous historical evidence on the undermining of the position of the aristocracy in order to sound the clarion call of counterrevolution, to reverse the trend which was destroying the noblest elements in France and battening the third estate.[1] Saint-Simon also judged the classes of France by the touchstone principle of utility, under the assumption that ruling classes serving the whole of society ought to be preserved, while those no longer fulfilling functions of utility — even though they had been useful in their prime — should be abolished. This automatically eliminated the nobles and the clerics and the lawyers and the metaphysicians, the same nonutilitarian classes which had already been condemned by the verdict of history. Finally, the useful classes were also the ones which triumphed in a third test: they had forward-looking attitudes, they favored peace, material prosperity, scientific advance, free opportunity for the expression of talent, widespread scientific and technical education, a humanitarian morality. The nobles and the clerics of the Bourbon reaction were aligned against science and invention; they clung to status fixed by birth and religion dependent upon revelation; they restricted education; and they preached a holy war in defense of the antiquated Catholic faith wherever "heresy" and "revolution" reared their heads in Europe.

The useless, historically doomed classes with pernicious, anti-progressive ideologies were still in power in 1820, and mankind suffered from their lingering presence. It was a consummation devoutly to be wished by all good men that they be hurried off the stage of history, for they were encumbrances to a new society. But how was their removal to be effected? Violent revolution had been tried in 1789 with horrendous consequences which Saint-Simon dreaded to see repeated. Like so many of his contemporaries, after 1815 he was overwhelmed by the realization that a whole social order had been destroyed during the previous twenty-five years of revolution and international wars. No universally accepted new institutions had replaced the old régime and the chaos which confronted men of his generation made them tremble lest the very bonds which held society together would be loosened. At the same time Saint-Simon could not accept the traditionalist position which aimed at resurrecting the outworn institutions of the pre-revolutionary period and would thus prolong Europe's painful state of transition before the emergence of the new industrial society. He kept asking himself whether there was not another way out of the dilemma, a course which would avoid the choice between the preservation of clerical obscurantism and the reign of barbarism, between what he recognized as the death clutch of the old order and the sheer destructiveness of the revolutionary process. There was only one solution — his system, a philosophy which could reconstitute and reorganize the body politic, sealing off the revolutionary era without falling back upon the mere revival of the old régime. He set himself the task of winning adherents to the new philosophy and teaching his contemporaries how to make their views prevail, how to effect that peaceful revolution which would enthrone the positive spirit and establish the scientific industrial society.

Saint-Simon's political advice, to which much of his journalistic activity was devoted, was at first addressed both to the king and to the industrialists. His king he always preserved above the battle, partly because he was prudent, partly because he hoped to use the Bourbon monarchy, if it could be converted to a comprehension of its own true interests, to usher in the industrial society with one grand royal gesture.[2] The king needed only to effect a rupture with the nobles and the priests and to resurrect what Saint-Simon believed to be the age-long alliance between the Bourbon dynasty and the industrials. To the industrials he proffered more detailed and specific political counsel, because they were marked as direct agents for the realization of the peaceful revolution. For them he acted as self-appointed chief tactician.

Applying his philosophy of history to the contemporary crisis, Saint-Simon prescribed a course of political and social action for the men of the Restoration. At no time did he counsel violence against the temporal rulers obtusely clinging to an antiquated theological feudal system of society. In complete accord with the *émigré* traditionalists, his opponents, who considered revolution the greatest of all evils because it unleashed man's bestiality, he would never preach violence, not even to hasten the dawn of the golden age. Revolutions and nationalist wars were avoidable waste of men and of substance. Throughout the Directorate, the Napoleonic period, and the

Restoration, in politics he was consistently a member of the party of peace and conciliation, whatever the specific international issues. He was pacifist and antirevolutionary, in part because wars and civil strife were an affront to human dignity, accidental and uncontrollable in their effects, irrational; in part because he felt that the purposes of history might be better served without upheavals.

Great wars and revolutions were always conflicts of two systems of ideas, during which temporal forces were aligned as proponents of one or the other side. But since only one of the ideological systems could be historically true, progressive, ultimately triumphant, and the other was false, regressive, doomed to extinction, as long as there was a state of peace among nations or social classes there was at least a remote chance that men would somehow comprehend the two alternatives and would rally to the banner of the progressive idea. Revolutions and wars solved nothing. They engendered only anarchy and chaos, a temporary but widespread confusion of values, as men become too bewildered to differentiate between the progressive and the regressive historic forces. At such times revolutionary leaders grew pretentious and propounded bold new social doctrines prematurely, long before humanity had evolved to a point where it could assimilate them. Such exaggerated expectations did not lead to authentic progress, but to collective madness. The French Revolution, with its sanguine legislative utopias and bloody party strife, was the laboratory which provided Saint-Simon with numerous specimens of wild and visionary social experimentation ending in disaster.

The condition of man in 1820 was different. Since men of the nineteenth century were fortunate enough to have the guidance of Saint-Simon's "science of politics" or "social physiology" or "positive science" or the "New Christianity" (which was its later moral expression), they would not have to endure the prolonged travail, the centuries of horror, which had preceded the introduction of that earlier organic system, medieval Christianity. The protracted crisis of the ancient world, his philosophy of history had shown, would not have to be repeated by the moderns before the maturation of the positivist age. Men of the nineteenth century, who could learn from history about the nature of transitional, revolutionary periods, were capable of acting intelligently to alleviate the birth-pangs of a new society. The optimistic reflection that historical experience had become rich enough to control social action lay at the very heart of his progressist theory of history. If all went well, these sudden starts and plunges of history known as revolutions were destined in the future to become smoothed out into an undulating curve with an ever upward trend.

The validity of Saint-Simon's theory is not destroyed by pointing up a logical contradiction between his broadly determinist philosophy of history and a summons to social action. Mankind, Saint-Simon would argue, had by

1815 reached a level of social progress and scientific knowledge which for the first time in history made conscious, rational, organized action possible. Hence it was worth rousing the progressive forces in society to battle, because the new historical awareness achieved through propaganda was in itself a factor in speedier victory.

Despite this pervasive optimism, Saint-Simon was alert to the danger that many of his contemporaries, though living in the aurora of the new times, might in their benighted ignorance commit either of two major errors which would prolong the crisis of society. Two forms of extremism could jeopardize the peaceful revolution. Among the rival absolutists in the social conflict lay the gravest threat to man's advancement. The "innovators" — some intellectuals and liberals — with their burning impatience might, he feared, attempt to upheave the stagnating theological or religious system of morals through force and violence. Such rashness could only call forth a bloody response from the controllers of the existing spiritual power, the priests of all nations — the reprisal of a bitter reactionary movement. Even if the intellectual revolutionaries were held in check, there was an equally vicious potential to be feared at the other pole, among the reactionaries. The classes in power might blindly and stubbornly combat every manifestation of progress, which in turn would goad into violence the innovators chafing at the bit. The explosive character of long suppressed vital social forces was the favorite topic of his political sermons to the ruling classes. In practical affairs Saint-Simon was consistently the reformer-philosopher of the middle of the road, for only along this path could progress proceed in a rectilinear direction and at a safe tempo.

Liberty was the popular cry of the revolutionaries, but Saint-Simon refused to translate what he considered a hollow slogan into the ultimate moral goal of human action. He cautioned against such a confusion of means and ends. Propaganda for liberty had once been an effective weapon in the struggle of public opinion against the dominant feudal-clerical society which the productive men, the scientists and the industrials, were united to overthrow. Since the revolutionary period of humanity was, however, by now nearly over, this eternal harping on the idea of liberty had become a futile indulgence in a new form of "metaphysics" — a term with distinctly pejorative overtones for the positivist Saint-Simon. The preservation of liberty was not the final purpose for which men had joined in a state of society. If liberty had been their principal concern, instead of entering into a social contract they would have done better to remain in a state of nature which permitted far more freedom than did society.[3] Liberty was a phrase, libertarianism a tactic during the transition from the theological to the scientific society, but it could never become the inspiration of a new epoch of civilization. Saint-Simon and his disciples after him flatly rejected the Jacobin catchwords of the French Revolution as vapid, empty of all positive content.

In commonsense terms they found the natural rights ideology of the Revolution wanting because it afforded mankind no reasonable substantive guidance for action after the old values had been subverted. Men of the nineteenth century were athirst for a new belief and a new program of concrete works, not for the reiteration of destructive revolutionary slogans. Thus in the writing of one of the very first theoreticians of the "organized society," the idea of liberty was presented as essentially devoid of meaning as the description of a condition desired by man. The ideology of liberty was set down not as a universal truth but as a trick, a party shibboleth which the industrials had used when they were underdogs and which had since ceased to serve any creative purpose.

On the other side of the ideological conflict of the day the traditionalists, the conservatives, and the reactionaries of various stripe were ranged beneath the banner of Order, an all-embracing party slogan of the same general character as Liberty. This exaltation of Order as the beacon light of social action was as likely to lead humanity astray as the Jacobin Liberty. Order was a sound enough principle to help preserve the social organism, but it was not an end in itself. That society must preserve order was as axiomatic as the precept that society should afford liberty, but it failed to lay out a positive course of social action.

A third group — whom Saint-Simon might have called the nationalists — were those who preached that the general welfare of the nation was the aim of society. These theorists were in his judgment closer to the true path than either the lovers of liberty or the lovers of order, but their program was equally inadequate because they too argued in metaphysical generalities and failed to specify precisely of what this "general welfare" should consist. Only he, Saint-Simon, offered humanity valid general directives for social behavior when he defined and spelled out the character of a progressive social organization appropriate for the nineteenth century. Those who accepted his standards of progress would solve the critical problems of the age in the everyday process of promulgating practical measures — pragmatically, we might now say. The good society would evolve through peaceful revolution, and the pitfalls of Jacobins, reactionaries, and nationalists would be avoided.

Since Saint-Simon eschewed violence, he had at his disposal but one means of convincing mankind to follow his doctrine of progress and the social good — propaganda. The right tactic was to demonstrate to everybody that the scientific age had dawned, that the theological sun had set, and that all men should proceed to make the necessary adjustments in their individual lives. With a genuine faith in the effectiveness of propaganda and the power of public opinion, Saint-Simon was always starting periodicals, initiating a new project as soon as an old one folded. In 1815, when he wrote his pamphlet *De la réorganisation de la société européenne* in collaboration with the young historian Augustin Thierry, he was a staunch believer in the power of publicists like himself to mold general opinion, which "ruled the world." On the morrow of the Revolution the power of the intellectuals was not underestimated in Europe. Ever since 1802, when Saint-Simon wrote his first pamphlet, he conceived of himself as a *philosophe* who instead of destroying the social order, in imitation of the wrecking job of Voltaire and Rousseau, wanted to reconstruct it through his sway over the minds of men.

In the final weeks of his life, Saint-Simon was busily planning another journal, *Le Producteur*, which after his death appeared under the direction of his disciples. The conception of a "movement," directed by men with a set doctrine embraced with religious zeal, was born in his last years and reached maturity after his suicide attempt of 1823. The Saint-Simonian "movement" implied a world outlook which penetrated every aspect of human existence, and allegiance to a body of fixed beliefs and to the orders of the hierarchic leadership was absolute. This idea of "the movement" was a political creation of modern times; it syncretized characteristics of the philosophical crusade led by "King Voltaire" and the discipline of the extremist political factions of the Revolutionary period with the emotionalism of the *illuminati*. The sole technique allowed by Saint-Simon for the propagation of the new faith was the word alone. The Saint-Simonians launched a whole series of official journals and public lectures and let loose over Europe a flood of brochures; emulating the early Christians they sent preachers and missionaries to proselytize the nations. Like the master, they steadfastly condemned force and violence as legitimate weapons in spreading the new gospel. The doctrine of Saint-Simon would conquer by capturing men's hearts. They were in favor of social change but of eternal change, evolution, development. Their ideal of social transformation involved an endless chain of innovations, never a culmination in one apocalyptic revolutionary outburst — usually the consequence of a long period of immobility during which the innovators had been suppressed by the reactionaries. At one point they even employed a curious phrase, "permanent revolution," to express their approval of progressive, peaceful evolution characterized by a series of minor explosions which avoided the great cataclysm. In their method the cultists were loyal to the master's tactics for a peaceful revolution.

Years before the cult achieved European notoriety, Saint-Simon in his practical advice to the industrialists of the Restoration had already identified the major elements which later Marxism considered prerequisites for the success of a full-blooded social revolutionary "movement." He had a theory for the movement, the positive scientificism which he had been exploring since 1802, and he had a class, the "industrials," whom he considered eminently capable of bearing the standard of history. All that was needed was a fusion of the two elements to assure victory for the industrial society. If the industrialists were not to flounder about aimlessly, they would have to accept the theory and move into action. "Gentlemen, let us look at things as they are. You must absolutely have a theory," he wrote in *Du système industriel*.[4]

As the self-appointed leader of the embryonic "movement," Saint-Simon not only had a scientific theory, he even outlined a political tactic corresponding to it. If the industrialists could be persuaded to adopt his plan of action, all would run smoothly and perhaps within a year the industrial era would be inaugurated under a Bourbon monarchy. If they failed to see the virtues of his plan, if they listened to the martial airs of Napoleonic military glory, then — and here one might have expected a bewildering vision of horror — "the success of the industrial cause will be retarded by several years perhaps." [5] On tactics Saint-Simon was not an absolute determinist. He presented the most "probable series . . . of events," and he did "not consider it impossible that events might happen otherwise." [6] Whatever the minor deviations of the historical process, however, it could not be swerved from a main channel.

In *Du système industriel* (1821) he spelled out rules of conduct to help the industrialists steer a straight course on day-to-day problems amid the confusing political currents of the Bourbon Restoration. The close connection between broad theory and particular political practice, destined to become one of the fundamental Marxist theses, was developed by Saint-Simon with complete self-consciousness in the service of his industrials. His tone was hortatory and didactic, for though the entrepreneurs supported him with money, in his own eyes he was their master. What follows is an abbreviated compendium of his brilliant counsel. The whole section cannot be read without recalling similar tactical advice transmitted by Marx to his proletarian class some three decades later. The context of the conflict changed, but the underlying lessons of effective class war bear a striking resemblance to each other in Saint-Simon and in Marx.

Reassure the Bourbons, Saint-Simon told the industrials, that you are an enemy of the nobles, not of the dynasty. This will make the transition to the industrial society easier, more peaceful. Rid yourselves of lawyers as mouthpieces, for they will lead you into diversionist metaphysical controversies. Either appear in public in your own behalf or hire and support real philosophical publicists (Saint-Simon, for example). Assume the leadership of all creative and productive forces in the nation — workers, farmers, artists, bankers, anybody but lawyers, priests, and nobles. (The conception of a social coalition is too obvious to require comment.) Demand that the national budget be prepared by active industrialists, your first practical proposal in statecraft, your sharp entering wedge. Disassociate yourself from the literary anticlericals (the encyclopedists) and all the metaphysicians of the rights of man theory. That road ends only in bloody revolution, whereas you want peace and a new system instead of mere destructive criticism of the old. Keep away from formal controversies over whether sovereignty derives

from God or from the people, and think in terms of the realities of administration and organization, not the lawyers' or the metaphysicians' formulae.
Rid yourselves of feelings of inferiority with respect to other social classes,
for you are the real repositories of power. You have remained passive too
long. Activate yourselves as a class. "Nothing can free you from doing
the job yourselves; you alone can have both the indispensable will and
capacity." [7]

Divest yourselves of any semblance of alliance with the Napoleonic
nobility, for this can only increase the fears of the Bourbons and make them
seek refuge in the arms of the ancient aristocracy. Avoid the seductive idea
of the Bonapartist nobility that a dynastic change means a social change.
The return of the Bonapartists will bring war and an inevitable strengthening of regressive military force over industrial influence in society. You
should prefer an old monarchy accustomed to the exercise of power to a new
grasping Napoleonic nobility. Beware of the passion of national pride which
the Bonapartists are trying to arouse in you. This is illusory. No one more
than you, whose nature is eminently pacific, suffered under Napoleon.
Beware of connivance with the lieutenants of Bonaparte as you would of
an alliance with the cohorts of Robespierre. Your real brothers, you will feel
in your minds and souls, are your fellow industrialists in other lands. Do
not blame the Bourbons for the invasion of France. This was an inevitable
result of the "antisocial foreign policy which we allowed to be imposed upon
us by Bonaparte and his adherents." [8]

Abandon your supposed "liberal" alliance with the "interests of the
Revolution." These abstractions are meaningless. The only part of the
Revolution you should defend is the distribution of the land, and you
should regret that it did not take place peaceably, *à la manière industrielle*.
Beware of the revolutionary doctrines of equality — *égalité turque*, "the
opposite of true equality, of industrial equality, which consists in having
each one draw from society benefits in exact proportion to his social investment, that is to say, his positive capacity, the useful employment of his
means, among which one must include of course his capital." [9] The revolutionary doctrine of equality could again let the mobs loose and you should
take heed before espousing it.

Beware of the false analogy between the French and the English revolutions which draws in its wake a comparison between the Stuarts and the
Bourbons. More than a century of time has fundamentally changed the
issues from those of merely winning concessions for the industrialists to
establishing an industrial régime. Refrain from violence. Convince the
Bourbon king that it is to his dynastic interest to ally himself with the commons by sending him a petition signed by all productive persons in France,
a number which will be overwhelming. Do not be disheartened by the
victory of the *ultras* in the elections of 1821. This triumph of the ancient

nobility will drive them to foolhardy attempts to recoup their properties, a plan which will ricochet because it will organize the owners of national property in opposition, and in a country-wide upsurge the industrialists will be catapulted into power.

In *Du système industriel* he emphasized the "international," by which he meant the European or at least western European character of the struggle of the "industrials" for the institution of their system.[10] He denied the feasibility of industrialism in one country alone. There was, however, uneven development; the precise moment when the industrial system would triumph was likely to vary in different countries, and the primary role of France might, under certain circumstances, even be eclipsed by other nations.

"To make the full importance of this great European combination felt, I propose to show: 1. that the complete establishment of the industrial régime would be impossible in any nation separately if all the peoples of western Europe were not engaged in this task simultaneously; 2. that if in truth the course of civilization has reserved to France the exclusive honor of beginning the organization of the industrial régime, it is nonetheless true that once the first impulse has been given, certain portions of this great enterprise must naturally be executed by that industrialist class among the other western nations which happens to be the most advanced, France exercising on that portion of the common task only a subsidiary action." [11]

The class conflict which Saint-Simon had described in Restoration periodicals almost exclusively with examples from French history was not a national phenomenon peculiar to his own society. In manuscripts of the period he reviewed the political, intellectual, and social status of the major civilized countries in the light of his ideal of the perfect industrial scientific society. His unpublished *Examen de la capacité politique des différents peuples* analyzed how close each nation was to effecting the transition to the good society, what were the positive factors favoring the industrials in each country, how serious were the impediments to their triumph, what were the identifiable local hostile elements. The world industrial revolution was evaluated in terms of the two rival camps in each major nation. The world, of course, was restricted to western Europe and the United States: he had notes on England, France, Germany, Spain, Italy, Scandinavia, and America; other nations were peripheral, still more or less beyond the immediate ken of the industrial society.

The brief analysis of the politics and potentialities of the United States contradicts dominant European opinion at the time. The early enthusiasm of the *philosophes* and French revolutionaries for the independent colonies had given way in the nineteenth century to denigration and, among the leaders of the Catholic reaction and the skeptics, to a certain contempt: De Maistre's mockery of the "infant in swaddling clothes," Stendhal's repugnance for the intellectual crabbedness of the American small town. In contrast, Saint-

Simon always had an expansive, optimist conception of the American future.

> Of all known peoples the Americans have the greatest political capacity and they enjoy the most favorable situation. They are also the people whose government exercises the least arbitrary action. . . . The Americans on the one hand enjoy the advantage of being able to expand indefinitely and consequently not to fear an increase in population, while on the other hand they have nothing to fear from their neighbors, which dispenses with the need for a standing army. In addition they have the advantage of very long coastlines with many ports so that they can devote themselves equally to agriculture and to commerce. . . . The Americans who came from England to establish a colony brought along the political knowledge which the English had acquired after long labors and at the same time found themselves emancipated from the habits which were bound up with the social organization which the English had before their revolution and with the remnants of the old institutions — all this results in the fact that their political capacity is superior to that of the English.

Saint-Simon was fascinated by the sharp contrast between the peoples and régimes of North and South America, the former the most "liberal that ever existed," the latter "living under the most despotic which exists. . . . The causes and effects of the moral situation of the Europeans inhabiting America merit all our attention because this population exercises a great influence on Europe," — an idea which few continentals entertained at the time. Saint-Simon favored the inclusion of the United States in the concert of powers. "This population may be regarded like a child which has grown up and which from now on ought to be listened to in the council which deliberates on the general interests of the great family. . . ." [12]

During the course of the Restoration Saint-Simon changed his designation of the particular national political society which would serve as a vanguard for the rest. In 1814, along with other Anglophile liberals on the continent, he had looked to England as the most progressive country, by which he meant the state which had first experienced the political and intellectual revolutions which all other societies in due time and in proper succession would have to undergo. To be in the forefront of continental advancement involved in the first instance imitating English institutions. France, he believed, was the political society closest behind the English, and if the progressive classes on both sides of the channel would only join forces, they would accelerate the triumph of the industrial society, for together they represented an invincible force. By the eighteen-twenties he was less sanguine about the industrial class in Britain, and after a reëvaluation of the class prospects in both countries, he reached the conclusion that France, because her revolution was more recent, had outstripped England in the formation of an industrial class. It was harder to change the English peerage into industrials than to transform the Bourbon king. [13] The new society would most likely be organized first in France, since the English industrials had been infected with the attitudes of the reactionary feudal theological classes. Consequently the French liberals who clung to English constitutional monarchy instead of industrial monarchy as an ideal were no longer forerunners but imitators of a confused, regressive form of society. The French industrialists not only had a mission to establish the industrial society in France, but they had to post themselves in the vanguard of a European struggle of industrialism against the remnants of feudalism.

In a period when many industrialists were trying to use the state to protect them from foreign competition, Saint-Simon preached that all the industrial classes of Europe had the same interests, irrespective of the nation to which they belonged. One of the reasons for his sense of urgency in addressing the French industrialists was his conviction that the revolutionary temper of Europe was forcing upon them leadership in the continental movement of the industrial classes. If the French industrial classes were successful, behaved in accordance with the interests of the new society, others would follow suit and the various national industrial classes would lend one another aid and succor. But if the French industrial classes defaulted, the other industrial classes on the continent might resort to revolution and turn the course of history awry.

While his mission was world-wide and not French, at that moment in history, in the eighteen-twenties, France was the avant-garde. The industrialists of Spain and Portugal and Italy, in the throes of revolution, were looking towards France. The destiny of the world was in the hands of the French industrials. The same system had to be introduced into all the western European nations in order to establish a uniform political basis for the international industrial régime. New nations were in the process of instituting the forms which could facilitate the organization of a common western European industrial system. Contemporary revolutions made immediate bold action by the French industrialists in their own country all the more urgent, for they had to provide leadership and a prototype for Europe by moving towards the actual inauguration of industrialism, away from a fixation on political forms. Without guidance by a vanguard of French industrialists the historic opportunity might be wasted, a vacuum of power created, and the revolutionary period prolonged by the strife of classes and parties. With France in the forefront the English industrials would soon seize control of their state without an insurrection and then the combined forces of industrial France and England, overwhelmingly powerful, would reduce to nothingness all opposition from forces of the old régime anywhere in the world.[14]

The tactical formulae proposed to the French industrials were later made applicable to the proletariat, with minor alterations, by Marx and Engels. This does not imply direct adaptation; it indicates that a class theory based on a philosophy of history leading to a worldly millenium can result in similar tactical procedures, irrespective of the identity of the class. The sense of international class solidarity of the industrials which Saint-Simon tried to instill among his French bourgeois found a particularly striking analogue in Marx's later manifesto to the world proletariat.

In separate sections of *Du système industriel* (1821), the Bourbon monarchy was addressed with an equally subtle and circumstantial set of appeals to self-interest, which were intended to convince the king that he should abandon his old nobles, avoid the Bonapartists, and ally himself solely with the industrialists proceeding to the construction of the new system. In the *Postscript to the Address to the King* of 1821, Saint-Simon prepared for the royal signature a set of ordinances which would proclaim the industrial scientific system without further ado.[15] He was, he imagined, writing the laws for his Constantine. Saint-Simon's ideal constitution for promulgation by the king would have as its first article a terse definition of national purpose: "The object of the political association of the French is to prosper by means of peaceful work of a positive utility." Every word in this article is pregnant with meaning: the polity is an association and it has a common goal in which the ideals of peace and work and positivism (as distinguished from religion) and utility are basic pillars of the social structure. The emphasis of the fundamental law has veered completely away from the preservation of the rights of man to the substantive objectives of common social action.

Saint-Simon was eloquent in portraying to the king the distraction of the times resulting from the decrepitude of the old system and the moral agony, the "profound anarchy which society has had to endure in the period from the decadence of the old political system to the final constitution of a new doctrine."[16] The old order was dead beyond resurrection and the king was pursuing a futile task if he aimed to effect the counterrevolution of the theocratic school. Repeatedly Saint-Simon denounced false revivals of antiquated systems ("archaistic utopias," Toynbee called them in his diagnosis of civilizations in a state of disintegration). The theocratic nostalgia of the Restoration recalled the attempt of the French revolutionaries to institute a Roman Republic in France and Bonaparte's abortive military feudalism.

"Sire, a system which centuries had built up and which centuries have destroyed cannot be reëstablished. The destruction of the ancient doctrines is complete, radical, and irrevocable."[17]

But the void left by the old moral system had to be filled or society would continue to teeter on the brink of revolutionary disaster. "A society cannot survive without common moral ideas. . . ."[18] And these moral values had to be derived from a general philosophic system which was universally accepted by all members of the society. If these conditions were not fulfilled, society would be in danger of disintegrating into the general warfare of the state of nature. "Society cannot live on negative ideas, but requires positive ideas. Society is today in a state of extreme moral disorder; egotism is making terrible progress, everything tends towards isolation." [19] Unless the new system were established, the violent revolutionary crisis would continue unabated and in the process the Bourbons might lose their throne.

Both the king and the industrialists were admonished against the fatal fascination of political forms. What counted was the organization of the producers and the system of ideas they believed in; the framework of the political structure was almost a matter of indifference. Governmental institutions were epiphenomena of a state of society; Saint-Simon was not interested in the mechanics of the parliamentary system which absorbed contemporary doctrinaire liberals. He would have been perfectly content to have Louis XVIII proclaim the industrial scientific society. "Sire, the general conclusion of this work is therefore that Your Majesty should invest himself with the character of king-founder of the industrial and scientific system, and should put into action as promptly as possible the theoretical and practical work necessary for the development of the political constitution of this system. . . ." [20]

Saint-Simon's appeal to the king to assume leadership of the new society as "first of the industrials of France and the whole world" [21] was no publicist subterfuge to avoid involvement with the Restoration police. The king would serve the purposes of the new society in a crucial phase of the transition, making it possible, through the publication of royal ordinances, to institute the "system" without a revolution. If the monarchy would sever relations both with the old French nobility and the parvenu Napoleonic nobility the whole feudal-theological structure would collapse overnight and the industrial society would come into being without a political ripple.

Of two ways of bringing about the dawn of the new society, either insurrection or royal dictatorship, the latter method was infinitely preferable. Insurrection, a step in the dark, could entrain a series of consequences similar to 1789, another round of political transformations which in the end solved nothing as far as class relationships were concerned. A royal dictatorship divorced from the two decadent nobilities and the clergy would not be dangerous because it would be able to operate only within prescribed limits, for the specific purpose of establishing the industrial society, a goal so concretely defined that if the royal dictator ever swerved off in another direction his false course would instantaneously be recognized by the majority of the industrials, who would forthwith restrain him. The advantage of the dictatorship of the king on behalf of the industrials lay in the overwhelming strength which would thus be concentrated on one side of the class conflict, so great a preponderance that the nonindustrial classes, faced by a massing of power "perhaps a thousand times weightier" than their's, would not even presume to offer resistance.[22] If the king were dictator, he might even convince the industrials further to ease the transition for the nobility by offering them an indemnity for the loss of their privileges, a method quite in harmony with the historic practices of the industrials in their avoidance of open conflict. Bankers like Laffitte could be relied upon to devise the appropriate financial combinations.[23]

The six ordinances which Saint-Simon drafted for a dictator-king resolved upon accepting the historic mission were not pallid. They amounted to a total reorganization of the educational system of France as well as a transfer of control over finances and administration to the industrials.[24]

First he proposed an order to all classes of the Institute to draft a national catechism which would cover the basic principles of the social organization and the main laws governing the material world. The catechism was to be drafted in such form as to make it teachable by the mutual system (of Bell and Lancaster). There would thus be uniform education under the direction of the Institute to create a real bond among the citizenry. Nothing would be allowed in the school curriculum contrary to the principles established in the national catechism. The ministers of the various cults would be subject to surveillance by the Institute in their preaching as well as in their teaching of children. "No Frenchman will be able to exercise his rights of citizenship before having submitted to an examination on the national catechism. The Institute will regulate the method and the conditions of the examination." [25]

In the temporal realm, Saint-Simon would order the preparation of the budget placed in the hands of a council composed of the Chamber of Commerce, the General Council of Manufactures, the Council of the Regents of the Bank of France, and twelve of the most important agriculturalists from the Council of Agriculture. The budget would have two guiding principles: 1. rapid amelioration of the lot of the people; 2. stimulating the progress of all types of industry. Its first two items of expenditure would be the popular school system and provision for employment of all those who had no other means of subsistence.

Saint-Simon envisioned the abolition of all feudal titles and privileges, and also the dissolution of the royal guard and the army and the institution of a national guard in which company officers would be chosen by the men — captains naming battalion chiefs, battalion chiefs the head of the legion, legion chiefs the commanding general of the national guard of Paris. Officers of the national guard of Paris would be restricted to "patented" citizens. Saint-Simon did not hesitate to recommend dissolution of the Parliament because it was composed of nonindustrials, and to call for a new election in accord with the law of February 5, 1817; citizens would be invited to choose industrials as their representatives. The king's proclamation with one sweep would reduce to nullity the metaphysics of rights of man, of separation of powers, of legitimacy, the worth of the many legal codes which had been promulgated, and the eight constitutions which had governed France in thirty-two years. No new system could be instituted by a representative assembly. "The conception of a new system must be unitary, that is to say, this conception must be formed in a single head." [26]

The king's proclamation would explain the *raison d'être* of the new ordinances. "Europeans are dominated at this moment by philosophical ideas which are false and vague. The political system which they want to establish and which they variously give the names of constitutional, representative, or parliamentary régime, is a bastard system which tends uselessly to prolong the antiscientific and anti-industrial existence of the theological and the feudal powers." [27] It was Saint-Simon's thesis that in political discussions false issues had been posed as basic. The real issues were not separation of powers or metaphysical rights; they were positive questions which should be solved by the state: "Let us ask what are the means of increasing as promptly as possible the value of the territory of France.

"Let us ask, what are the means of accelerating the progress of the sciences of observation?

"How should one go about procuring for the children of the people a broader and more solid education than they have received up to now?

"What are the measures which should be taken to procure to the workers the greatest amount of work possible?

"What are the means of increasing the public esteem of men devoted to useful works, and of decreasing the public esteem of idlers and those whose labors are harmful or useless to society?

"What social organization would assure most completely public tranquillity and would cost least to the nation?" [28]

The temporary abolition of political forms prescribed in the Charter did not bother Saint-Simon because he did not consider the document a real constitution reflecting authentic forces in society. His reflections on the nature of a constitution are interesting, particularly since they were written at the dawn of Europe-wide constitutional movements. A constitution could not be created. It was the expression of or the legitimization of the preponderance of certain forces in society. An authentic constitution mirrored social and spiritual realities, while the French Charter was merely an embodiment of metaphysical generalities. When he issued his sovereign ordinances the king would not be violating a constitution, for none really existed; he would be "constituting" a society in which political power corresponded to present civil realities instead of civil alignments of past centuries.

Through his last years Saint-Simon's means of propaganda and persuasion varied, his historical agents were changed, but his basic technique of peaceful revolution remained the same. He was conscious of his own repetitiveness. Any argument was worthy of exploration as long as it helped convince men to effect a pacific transition. He viewed his system historically, politically, scientifically, morally. He appealed to truth, to utility, to history, to the passion for glory, to virtue, to love of humanity, and in the end to the idea of God. *Mirabile dictu*, all roads led to the industrial scientific system. All the sciences bespoke the need for the system; all his soul-tortured contemporaries were crying out for it.

When he labored his propaganda over and over again from different angles, it was inevitable that inconsistencies should spring up between one method of attack and another. But they were mere contradictions in arguments for the propagation of the doctrine, not errors in the system. The system, though absolute, could be entered by many doors. There was no one path to conversion. Early in the Restoration Saint-Simon had expected a more resounding response from the industrials fighting for their own interests. He thought that rational persuasion with arguments rooted in class interest and history would suffice to solidify their will. Surely by 1821 he had begun to doubt the cogency of the appeal to class interest alone to bring about the peaceful transition to the industrial society. To those who could be moved by these arguments he continued to address his forensic platitudes, but he came to rely more and more upon the emotional religious appeal of Christian morality as the force which would see humanity through the chaos of the crisis period. In his last years the idea of an act of conversion to the new system assumed a greater place in his tactics. Who knows, he mused, if the most ardent new Christians might not come from the gory ranks of Jacobins and Bonapartists.[29] There was the example of Saint Paul, persecutor of Christians. Classes were doomed to historical extinction after they had passed through their life cycle. Individuals could shuffle off their class coils and act like men.

24

Industrialism Against Liberalism

IN THE LAST YEARS OF HIS LIFE Saint-Simon the theoretician of political parties uncovered an insidious rival force in his proximity. The liberal parties of the continent had hardly assumed concrete shape when Saint-Simon leveled against them a barrage of trenchant criticism in the name of the economic and social realities of European society. He was distressed at the ease with which his industrials had allowed themselves to be seduced by politicians, particularly the new liberals. The time had arrived for the industrials to awaken to a consciousness of their own strength as a class and to a realization of their historic destiny. Pusillanimity on their part was prolonging the social crisis. He, Saint-Simon, was striving with all his meagre resources to imbue the industrialists with a class spirit, a true party spirit, to rally them around a class doctrine which would win them total victory. Instead, they were betraying themselves into the hands of the liberals. Later Marxism demonstrated an analogous fixation on proletarian party purity.

In the early Restoration, Saint-Simon had used the neologism liberal in a positive sense, coupling it with industrial in opposition to theological and feudal. Liberals were those who fought the theocratic reaction. Saint-Simon himself contributed articles to the liberal periodicals, the liberal deputies figured on his subscription lists, and to all intents and purposes the cause of the new industrial scientific society and the political aspirations of the liberals were identical. In everyday politics this meant introducing the British parliamentary system into France, making of the Charter a British constitution, broadening the franchise to include the commercial and industrial elements of the nation.

By the eighteen-twenties Saint-Simon turned upon the liberals and in his writings the epithet liberal ceased to be a term of praise and became one of opprobrium. A class analysis of the liberal chieftains active in the political arena had startled him into the realization that the party was not composed primarily of industrialists and their intellectual supporters, but was a heterogeneous lot in which former Jacobins, former Bonapartists, rentiers, lawyers, and military men predominated. The industrialists who belonged to this conglomerate party were pushed into a subordinate position, with the result that in practice the party represented not the goals of a new scientific industrial society, but merely the lust for power of politicians out of office agitating to replace the "ministerials." The industrialists were giving financial support to the liberal lawyers and intellectuals in the belief that they were voicing industrial interests, when in reality the liberals were only conspiring for their own advancement. Saint-Simon did not mince his words: these Restoration liberals were repeating the deceptions of the traducers of 1789, who had similarly ensnared the industrialists into the revolutionary cauldron.

The liberals were a sham political party, devoid of the basic characteristic of a legitimate organization for political action — a common class character and class interest. Liberalism was a metaphysical party slogan, an "order of feelings," a revolutionary idea system, anything but what the industrialists needed, a constructive program for the reorganization of society on a positive foundation. Liberals were captivated by mere political forms and enchanted by the prospect of governing the state through the forms. In the process they were pulling the opposition to the feudal theological classes in a wrong direction, along the road to revolution. This false course of action was being pursued by liberals not only in France, but in other parts of Europe, in Portugal, Spain, and Naples, where they were hatching political revolutions. Saint-Simon again cautioned the industrialists to be wary of the glib phrase-makers and their impostures.

The true cause of the industrialists was best expressed by a new philosophy, *industrialism*, which was concrete and antirevolutionary, implied the establishment of a specific social order, and grew out of the solid class base of the industrialists. To distinguish the political adherents of the new movement, Saint-Simon coined the name industrialist (*industrialiste*), contrasting the term with liberal, which suffered from revolutionary overtones and vagueness. Saint-Simon was profoundly disturbed that liberalism had thrown such confusion into the ranks of the industrialists that Ternaux, the textile manufacturer, merchant, and deputy, his friend, the archetype of the class-conscious businessman, a man who had disdained a noble title, still considered himself a liberal and wrote a profession of liberal faith which was a compilation of sentiments as blurred and indistinct as the other liberal credos.

To differentiate industrialism from liberalism became a major preoccupation with Saint-Simon at the very end of his life. Among the liberals he saw his most dangerous political enemies, for they were misleading his historic agents, the industrialists. The liberals were a greater threat to his cause than were the feudal theological classes, for these declining groups were visibly impotent and held no attraction for the industrialists. In vexation at the rising strength of liberalism, Saint-Simon even wrote words of praise for the Holy Alliance — which he would earlier have condemned as retrogressive — because, unlike the liberal politicians, the monarchs at least recognized the central importance of an organized spiritual force in society, misguided though they were in their choice. The vehemence of Saint-Simon against the liberals is characteristic of a doctrine which, in its anxiety for self-definition, is most hostile to those competitors who make their appeal to the same class.

Saint-Simon's admiration for the British social organization changed with his alienation from the liberal party.[1] England's structure now appeared antiquated even for a transitional period, for it incorporated too many dead feudal elements. Its mixed character, which the liberals, following Montesquieu, prized so highly, was not a virtue but a shortcoming. This "bastard constitution" had organic contradictions and its imitation in France was reactionary.[2] "The human species has entered upon its crisis of puberty," and the English, far from being worthy of emulation, were suffering from "chlorosis," [3] was his social physiological verdict.

Political parties were meaningful organizations, fulfilling a historical destiny — and that was their sole and essential function — only insofar as they represented and gave form to real class interests. This was in line with his conception of any social organization as a biological organism with an essential unitary nature and character. Any political party which was an amalgam or a common meeting ground of a variety of different class interests was by definition an artificial grouping for purposes of historical action. Political parties should be activist expressions of what classes would articulate if they were self-conscious enough to voice their natural wants.

The liberal party was a typical example of a false political agglomeration for it joined under a single rubric such disparate class interests as those of the Napoleonic nobility, the rentiers, the leading Napoleonic soldiers, lawyers, metaphysicians and the chiefs among the industrials. In the Restoration the industrials had aligned themselves with this amorphous party, an act which expressed their vague realization that the liberals were a lesser evil than the *ultras*, but this was no manifestation of conscious choice on their part. The industrials, instead of running this party, in which they were the only real force and in which they represented a large, powerful, and cohesive class, had become dupes of the Bonapartists and Jacobins. The divergent elements in the liberal party were pursuing not only different but contradictory ends, for while the industrials, in conformity with their class nature, really wanted a totally new organization of society on the basis of production, the rest of the liberal politicians were aiming at placing themselves in positions of dominance in the existing political mechanism and enjoying the fruits of power irrespective of any new social goals. Thus political party lines of the Restoration instead of clarifying the social conflicts of the times had only succeeded in obfuscating them.

In March 1824 in the *Deuxième appendice* of the *Deuxième cahier* of the *Catéchisme des industriels* he confronted the two movements without equivocation in the essay entitled *"Sur le libéralisme et sur l'industrialisme,"* [4] not to show their similarities as he had early in the Restoration but to heighten their differences. Liberals, believers in what he designated as "an order of feelings" known as *liberalism*, were engaged in attempts to seize state power in order to enforce those sentiments and to institute constitutional changes in harmony with them.[5] Industrialism was different: it stood for something positive, the establishment of the industrial society, the only scientific system of human organization. Industrialism did not derive its strength from appeals to nebulous liberal ideas which were in their essence negative and destructive; industrialism was rooted in the interests of the industrials and it therefore had a solid foundation; it could become a "meaningful theory of a political party." Liberalism was metaphysical, an epithet as derogatory as theological.

"We invite all the industrials who are zealous for the public good and who know the relations between the general interests of society and those of industry, not to tolerate any longer the designation *liberals*. We invite them to unfurl a new flag and to inscribe on their banner the device: *Industrialism."* [6] Saint-Simon was demanding more than a change of nomenclature. He was hypersensitive to the association of the word liberal with the doctrines of the *philosophes* and the practices of the revolutionary lawyers, two groups with whom he wanted to break sharply before they besmirched his whole industrial mission with their metaphysical phrasemongering. Industrial monarchy, as distinguished from constitutional monarchy, signified a denial of the scribblers and the *avocasserie* of the legists who had lorded it over French politics for decades.[7]

Industrialism was antirevolutionary, anti-egalitarian. It stood for a society directed by industrial chiefs and bankers for the benefit of the workers. If there was solidarity in this society it consisted in every part of the organic body politic recognizing its capacities and not seeking an inappropriate share either in awards or in the administrative direction of the whole.

The tempo at which the contemporary class conflict would be resolved became a perennial problem of his new industrialism as it had been for revolutionary liberalism. During the Consulate and the Empire, when societal relations appeared fluid, Saint-Simon had tried to peddle his doctrine as a fast-working specific which, once swallowed by society, would cure its critical illness. The issue of a slow or rapid institution of the new social order did not loom significant, since European society was visibly in a state of war and revolution, and the novel system would not create an upheaval but, on the contrary, would tend to settle and organize a world which had become chaotic.

With the Restoration there was an apparent pacification of France and the burden of proof was on the innovator that he was not a revolutionary intent upon plunging society into turmoil again. After 1814 Saint-Simon's class theory became gradualist in all his public formulations, at least through 1820. While he took the position that the régime of the Charter was not a definitive solution to the social conflicts in France but a mere cover which disguised the continuing class war beneath the surface, his doctrine was aimed at effectuating the inevitable transfer of leadership from the feudal theological classes to the industrial scientific with a minimum of disturbance. If revolution occurred it would not stem from the character of the industrials, by their very class nature peace-loving, but would be a consequence of provocations on the part of the feudal theological classes intent upon a resurrection of their ancient political powers, when patently they no longer exercized important civil functions or enjoyed real civil authority in society, as contrasted with their inflated role in government. Since Saint-Simon's doctrine was gradualist, in the early Restoration he was continually on the lookout for transitional constitutional forms which would make the transfer of power less painful to society. His defense lawyer at the trial, where he was virtually charged with subversion, emphasized that the development prognosticated by Saint-Simon was one which might take ages before its final fulfillment. While this no doubt was an exaggeration for the purposes of a judicial proceeding, it was a fair statement of Saint-Simon's antirevolutionary faith. To be sure most constitutionalists would consider as rather radical measures the royal ordinances drafted for the king in *L'Organisateur*, decrees whose issuance was meant to facilitate the transition to the new society. To Saint-Simon they were a minimal program.

In the twenties and particularly towards the close of his life he again abandoned the gradualist approach to the introduction of the new society. In his writings of this period there is a new sense of terrible crisis, a feeling which reflected the intensification of the political struggle against the *ultramontanism* and *ultraroyalism* of the mid-twenties in France. While he never advocated revolution, the *Opinions littéraires, philosophiques et industrielles* presented for the first time justifications for what he called a "brusque" change. "Should this change take place brusquely, and by direct measures, or should it be effectuated slowly and in a series of successive measures?

"It is our opinion that the change should occur *brusquely* and by direct measures." [8]

He derived support for this new position primarily from a reconsideration of the events of the last great transitional epoch in human history, the decline of the Roman Empire and the birth of medieval Christianity. The change from polytheism to monotheism, from Roman consuls to Gothic chieftains, from slavery to serfdom had been sudden, he now believed, and carrying out the parallel, he maintained that the modern transition to "industrialism," in the nature of the historical process, would have to be equally "brusque."

Most perceptive as an argument was his reconsideration for the last time of the meaning of the French Revolution. Despite its bloodletting the Revolution, which he identified with liberalism, had not really entailed a fundamental change of system because under Napoleon France had been refeudalized. The thoroughness of a revolution was not to be measured by its violence or cruelty but by the profundity of the transformations in social structure. The liberal French Revolution was only a half-measure; while powers changed hands the nature of the powers did not, and society remained under governmental rather than administrative regimen. If there was to be a deep-going change a new social doctrine had to be accepted with one fell swoop; this involved an abrupt announcement of new principles. To the timid, Saint-Simon addressed himself with a series of propositions half-rationalist, half mystical.

The time for half-measures is obviously over. We must proceed directly for the public good. Under the present circumstances the whole and the naked truth must be presented: the moment of the crisis has arrived.

This crisis is the one which was predicted by several of the sacred writings which comprise the Old Testament.

This is the crisis for which, for many years, the Bible societies have been preparing with great activity.

This is the crisis whose present existence is demonstrated by the institution of the Holy Alliance, whose union is founded upon the most general principles in morality and in religion.

This is the crisis which the Jews have been awaiting since, driven from their country, they have been wanderers and persecuted, without ever renouncing the hope of seeing that epoch arrive when all men treat one another like brothers.

This crisis, finally, tends directly towards the establishment of a truly universal religion and to make all the peoples adopt an essentially pacific social organization.[9]

But although Saint-Simon decided in the last months of his life that the transformation would have to be sudden, he nevertheless continued to believe, paradoxically enough, that it would take place without violence. His confidence was founded on the nature of the new administrative classes of the industrial society, all of which were pacific in character. The truth of his old political axiom was untarnished: a class could not normally act contrary to its nature, hence fear of violent revolution under the aegis of the industrialists was unwarranted. Since the moment of crisis had arrived, a moral conflict between the old and the new social classes had broken into the open, yet there was no danger that this would develop into a conflict of physical force. No one entered such a war, Saint-Simon reasoned, without some prospect of success, and the feudal theological classes recognized that in physical terms they represented no more than an insignificant part of the total society.

Thus towards the close of his career Saint-Simon saw the problem of social change solved only by an abrupt and thorough (as contrasted with gradual), and a peaceful (as contrasted with violent) revolution leading to the immediate introduction of the new system. He condemned liberalism for employing means incommensurate with its ends, for its readiness to drench France in blood for the sake of superficial modifications in political forms. His own industrialism, peaceful and fundamental, could alone effect a rapid transformation of the whole structure and composition of French society.

25

The Natural Elite

ONE OF THE CRUCIAL DEVELOPMENTS in modern intellectual history is the reversal from the eighteenth-century view of men as more or less equal, or at least similar in nature and hence in rights to Saint-Simon's emphasis upon human uniqueness, diversity, dissimilarity, culminating in a theory of inequality and organicism.

The majority of eighteenth-century moralists derived from the Lockian postulate that differences among mature men observable in society were the direct consequence of early education and the play of individual circumstance and experience. While conceding that gross physical defects at birth might account for cases of monstrous intellectual deformity, it was an article of faith that apart from such exceptions all men were born free and equal and were molded into somewhat different shapes by their environment.

All men were equal in their natural faculties, hence in their capacity to receive impressions of the external world; and if they were given identical educations they would all have the same rational concepts.[1] Essentially the capacity to receive impressions was, had been, and was likely to be about the same in all times and in all places among all men. On the problem of whether men were really identical — not merely similar — in the strength of their organs, there were divergences: the French followers of Locke, Helvétius and Condillac, came pretty close to a theory of absolute equivalence at birth, while Rousseau's distinction between natural and unnatural inequalities early in the *Second Discourse* implied that in the state of nature there were inequalities based on health, bodily strength, and powers of the intellect and the soul.[2]

All *philosophes* were agreed in allowing men equality of natural civil rights, though they might differ about their precise definition. Few went so far as to posit equality in wealth and property as a natural and necessary form of equality. While Morelly, Brissot de Warville, and a minority of radicals adopted the extreme view that since property did not exist in the state of nature, it was theft and had to be abolished in society,[3] the over-whelming body of opinion took the position that the maintenance of civili-zation required the preservation of inequalities of wealth and perhaps even of social status in order to force man, who was by nature indolent, to submit to the discomforts of work. This was Voltaire's viewpoint in his paradoxical article on Equality in the *Philosophical Dictionary*; and this was the attitude of the economists who wrote about the new laws of true political economy. Even Voltaire, however, who was no sufferer of the pretensions of cooks and lackeys, held to the theory that "all men are equal in the possession of their natural faculties" and agreed that inequalities of wealth had probably been exaggerated in contemporary society.[4]

Condorcet made the establishment and preservation of "absolute equality," by which he meant equality in law, the heart of his *Déclaration des droits* pamphlet published in 1789;[5] moreover, he was fully aware that his constitution might ultimately result in juridical "inequality in fact" unless society instituted measures to render men more or less equal in other respects. This is the dominant spirit of his final testament, which exalted equality as the primary aspiration of the human spirit, a goal to which man-kind was inevitably progressing. Though absolute equality might never be attained, the essence of progress was the movement towards a social state in which all nations on earth and all individuals within these nations ap-proached as near as possible to a status of equality, material, moral, and intellectual.[6] If the universal "social art" properly fulfilled its function, all men would really become capable of enjoying a more or less equivalent level of prosperity, for there was no basis in nature for such extreme varia-tions of man's estate as the condition of barbarism, of a colonial master's opulence, and of the pauperized lower classes of European civilized society. Strangely enough, the *volte face* from an emphasis on man's potential, if not actual, equality, both of knowledge and of condition to the acceptance of human inequality as the cornerstone of the good society, was executed in the very heat of the revolutionary turmoil.

A cogent expression of the idea of inequality can be found in a passage of a National Assembly committee report prepared by Talleyrand, in which the analogy is drawn between a well-organized state and a great national workshop.[7] The image, which he could well have derived from any number of economists of the seventeenth and the eighteenth centuries, was doubtless nourished by the realities of English and French industrialization. The novelty lies in its incorporation into a government report on education. Men are born with a variety of different faculties, Talleyrand asserted — the Lockian concept is banished — and these diverse faculties lie dormant until the national system of education comes along and arouses them. A wise educational system takes cognizance of the differences among men and fosters the development of special faculties. The real secret of the social art is the placement of individual men in the most appropriate positions in the national workshop in accordance with their native talents.[8] The analogy of the workshop, which presumed acceptance of the Smithian idea of the division of labor, involved a new emphasis on the dissimilarities among individual men and an affirmation of their natural inequalities, which it became salutary to preserve.

Within a few years after the publication of Talleyrand's report with its stress on the creation of schools and institutes for the education of specialists in all branches of knowledge, the *idéologue* scientists who took possession of French thought under the Directorate drew attention to another aspect of inequality, the broad physiological and psychological divergences among men. Their ultimate goal remained the egalitarian society unveiled by Condorcet, but the new medicine was leading the *idéologues* to momentous philosophical conclusions about the nature of man. The intellectual revolution was generated not so much by the discovery of hitherto unknown scientific data as by a new apperception of empirical facts which doctors and life scientists had been accumulating over the century. In the Years IV and V Doctor Cabanis read before the Class of Moral and Political Sciences of the Institute a series of papers on the interrelations between man's physical and moral being, in the course of which he developed a complete typology of character, as well as a series of generalizations on how men were affected by differences in sex, age, temperament, states of morbidity, regimen, and climate. He concluded that even rational men did not behave the same way at all stages of life, that their minds showed not minor but substantial differences in performance when assailed by crisis in their sexual nature, by illness, by senescence. Different men seemed to react differently to crucial transformations in human nature during the course of the life cycle. The emphasis throughout was on the physiological and psychological variations among men, not their similarities, which the legislator would have to take into consideration.[9]

Cabanis here modified the sensationalism of Locke, Helvétius, and Condillac at its very source, their presupposition that in general all human beings received identical impressions from nature. This simply was not in accord with his experience, the doctor found. The differences in sensory perception among men were greater than their similarities and gave rise to "different turns of mind and soul." [10] The subject of inquiry was not a Condillac statue which was endowed with the capacity to feel, but men living in different climates, men with different native temperaments, obeying different patterns of conduct, men subject to the exigencies of sexual change, age, and sickness. There was no "type common to the whole human species."

The doctors whom Cabanis quoted were dwelling upon the fact that men were born physiologically unequal, that the organs of their patients were far from being equally strong, that different patients reacted in diverse ways to the same doses of drug. The scientific study of pathological conditions of the body and Pinel's pioneer inquiries into the nature of madness, free from religious prejudice, were revealing wide disparities in human reactivity and capacity. Cabanis's psychology, anchored in the accumulation of physiological data and medical experience, cast a powerful light upon the dissimilarities among men and broke with the philosophical psychology of Helvétius and Condillac which in the previous generation had served as "scientific" underpinning for the doctrine of equality.[11]

Since the Condorcet ideal of equality was still dominant, his friend Cabanis was studying human distinctions with the lodestar of a perfected Man before his mind's eye. The purpose of medicine as he conceived it was not restricted to curing individual ailments; its higher objective was the perfection of the species.[12] The study of natural human frailties or inferiorities should lead to their elimination through time, a feasible prospect since he firmly believed that acquired characteristics were inherited.[13] Cabanis still had an eighteenth-century faith in the extraordinary malleability of human nature and his aim in focusing upon congenital and environmental differences was not to utilize distinctions as Talleyrand wished but to narrow their range. He studied human pathology in order to make men equally healthy and rational and he trusted in the power of science to achieve the general perfection of the human species. Nonetheless, *idéologue* psychology was turning sharply away from Master Locke when it took to observing distinctions — it was a momentous departure.

The same interest in the investigation of disparities was reinforced by numerous lesser eighteenth- and early nineteenth-century researches in physiognomy and phrenology, divergent as were the hypotheses of Lavater [14] and Gall.[15] Men were distinct from one another and their differences were written on their faces or in the convolutions of their brains. The mystical and astrological elements which sometimes were intermingled with these character studies only served to widen the breach between them and the common sense interpretation of human differences upon which Helvétius had insisted to the rigid exclusion of occult influences and vague concepts such as humors and tempers.

A key figure expressive of the new scientific attitude towards human nature was the physiologist Bichat, whose works were known throughout the civilized world at the turn of the century. In his *Recherches physiologiques sur la vie et sur la mort,* he divided men into three physiological categories. While classifications had been made often enough before in antiquity and in early modern times on the basis of dominant humors and temperaments, the importance of Bichat lies in the fact that his writings were picked up and read by Saint-Simon. And it was in the form expounded by Bichat that the physiological doctrine of inequality penetrated his social theory and became part of a new general conception of man and society.

Bichat distinguishes among three major types — a trinary division has always communicated itself most readily in western society — a brain man, a sensory man, and a motor man. In each type one particular dominant faculty was capable of great development, while the other two were destined to remain feeble.[16] Bichat's vitalist theory allowed for only a given quantum of energy in each individual; and no man, with the rarest of exceptions, could develop all three major faculties to an equivalent degree. Physiologically men were born limited and restricted — either brain, or sensory, or motor — and vital energy invariably tended to channel itself into one receptacle rather than the two others.[17]

The consequences of this theory for education and human progress, if accepted as a new definition of human nature, are manifold. Cabanis had still concentrated upon the flexibility and easy educability of any human trait through laws and medicine; Bichat's iron law of physiology dictated that only one of the major capacities could and should be trained. It was the responsibility of society to identify a man's major faculty and to develop it to the uttermost limits of his capacity, to the neglect of the other two faculties, since it was futile to attempt to fashion what was not by nature educable. Perfectibility lay not in an identical Spartan education for all men, but in the stimulation of uniqueness, in specialization. This led to the conception of an organic society based upon differentiated functions.

The impact of the French Revolution upon the philosophical minds of Europe was a most potent political factor in the repudiation of the concept of equality. Egalitarianism had been a central proposition in the armory of the "literary cabal"; the revolutionaries had paraded *Egalité* upon their banners, the *enragés* among the *sans-culotte* had propounded doctrines and suggested conduct in the name of equality which profoundly shocked the sensibilities of Christian Europe. Equality was an explosive idea which had inflamed the Paris mobs with a violent passion and had implanted illusory hopes in the breasts of "ignorant proletarians." Equality had brought European society to the brink of annihilation. To consider the idea of equality — however it was interpreted — as a dangerous heresy was the instinctive reaction of the conservative thinkers of the continent, and its extirpation became a spiritual necessity for antirevolutionary theorists of every stripe. Burke's invective against the leveling spirit had sounded the call to battle against the "barbarous philosophy" of the equals. In 1793, when Necker in exile sat down to contemplate the meaning of the Revolution in which he had been a major actor, one of his first projects was the writing of *Réflexions philosophiques sur l'Egalité*.[18] If man wished to associate himself with the spirit of the Divine Creation, he had to mirror in the social order he established the diversities of the natural order. "Inequalities in a state of harmony, that is the rule of the universe." [19]

The concept of inequality as translated into political-religious terms by de Bonald and de Maistre, was a major new intellectual force in European thought in the early nineteenth century. They created the image of an anthropomorphic medieval society as the last good society, in contrast with the conflict-ridden, atomistic, egalitarian eighteenth-century world whose bloody climax was the Terror. They revalued status, the virtues of the nobility, the corporations and the *jurandes*, and they conceived of the social order as an organic unity. These men were polemicists of stature and they knew how to excoriate the preachers of equality with a vehemence, a subtlety, and a philosophic universality which no Christian apologist had achieved in more than a century. The theocratic school was less absorbed in attacking the scientific validity of the idea of natural equality than in contrasting this "sterile" political conception with the Christian moral rules of behavior imposed upon one man in his relations with his "neighbor," his "fellow man," his "likeness." De Bonald stripped the idea of equality of that sense of human dignity which it had acquired among the *philosophes* and revealed it as a naked political relationship in contradiction of the Christian commandment of brotherly love.[20]

Thus, paradoxically enough, in the weakening of the ideal of equality there was a confluence of pressures from opposite directions, both from the atheistic doctors of the Institute — the *idéologue* scientists who were the official philosophers of the state until they were ousted by Napoleon — and from the *émigré* theocrats.

Henri de Saint-Simon was influenced by all these waves of doctrine, perhaps most of all by Condorcet, Cabanis, Bichat, and the traditionalists — an odd assortment of antecedents for his organismic view of society rooted in the concept of natural inequalities. In Saint-Simon's doctrine the scientific élite of Condorcet, the findings of the new physiology of Bichat, the new psychology of Cabanis coalesced with an appreciation of the organic social order of the theocrats.

Saint-Simon has one underlying preconception which is identical with the outlook of the philosophical egalitarians, the conviction that the ideal forms of the good society must be congruent with what is natural in man. From a cursory reading of the physiologists, however, Saint-Simon came away with a different version of the natural: the natural was inequality. He inveighed against philosophism for its ignorance of the simple physiological facts, positive scientific facts, which had since been set forth by Cabanis and Bichat. Confirmed in the belief that physiology was the only sound foundation upon which to construct a social theory, after numerous experiments with variant schemes of social classification, the plan he devised in the final phase of his thinking was a direct adaptation of the Bichat typology. His three social functions and three mutually exclusive social classes corresponded to the physiologist's three human types.[21] First society needed scientists to discover positive laws which in turn could be translated into guides for social action. This scientific capacity — the brain type, which he sometimes called the Aristotelian capacity — if given free play would fulfill the mission which Condorcet had proposed for the leading scientific intellects. Bichat's motor capacity was transformed by Saint-Simon into the industrial class. Most of mankind, whose primary aptitude was the motor capacity, were destined to remain manual laborers, though a small élite of this class with essentially the same kind of talent would become the administrators of the temporal affairs of society — the men who organized states and directed public works and engineered vast projects for the exploitation of nature. Saint-Simon's third class, which corresponded to Bichat's sensory man, were the artists, poets, religious leaders, ethical teachers, whom he sometimes identified with the Platonic capacity. In the last years of his life, when he emphasized the religious character of his doctrine, he endowed the sensory aptitude with special worth since he considered it capable of overcoming the atomist, egotist, egalitarian propensities of the contemporary world in crisis. The men of sentiment would give the new industrial society its quality and cohesive humanitarian spirit.

The good society thus represented a harmonious association or coöperation of men fundamentally dissimilar in their most essential natures, organized in three natural classes. Together they embodied the total needs of mankind — rational scientific, manual administrative, sensory religious. The eighteenth-century *philosophes*, even when they admitted human inequalities, had still insisted upon organizing the state and society around those elements which men had in common, their natural equalities and relatively equal capacity for governance and the holding of public office. Saint-Simon and all later organicist doctrines which derived from him may have taken for granted some of the equal rights of the *philosophes*, but they then proceeded to fashion society out of the different clays which were the raw materials of human nature. All men were not equally capable of participating in the administration of society. The new philosopher of society approached the whole problem with the initial preconception that the physiological and psychological differences of men were the very brick and mortar of his perfect social edifice. Independently, Fourier's theory of the passions, developed with an almost compulsive detail and a mania for the multiplication of psychological types, is only an exaggeration of the same tendency. The order of the phalanstery is a harmony of properly distributed human beings who perform social functions in accordance with the requirements of their personality types.

The presumption is overwhelming that each man seeks to express his own and not an alien nature, that he desires to live and work in the classification where he has natural endowments, be they Saint-Simon's scientific, administrative, and poetic capacities, or any one of Fourier's multifarious dominant passion types. Saint-Simon here adapted one of the major contentions of the theocrats, who steadfastly maintained that men were not driven by a passion for equality with other men of higher status or greater wealth, but really had a profound desire to remain in their own traditional occupations and to continue to express themselves in the traditional roles into which they were cast at birth. They wanted not equality but the expression of their true social natures. Saint-Simon merely translated this conception into "scientific" terms: men by nature desired not equality with others but the expression of their true social natures based upon intrinsic and immutable physiological aptitudes. The Aristotelian idea that every being seeks a fulfillment of its essential character or nature has found an echo both in the theocratic and in the Saint-Simonian theories. It is a dogma that no man would be so monstrous as to desire to exercise administrative functions if he were born with a scientific capacity. At least, no good social order would allow such an anarchic misplacement of human talent. In the Saint-Simonian world outlook, organic inequality among men, inequality in the social hierarchy, and difference of social function were natural and beneficent, wholly superior to the *égalité turque* of the Jacobin revolutionaries which was an equality of slavery beneath an omnipotent state authority.[22] Born unequal in their faculties, men required a society in which each was allotted a function "according to his capacity" — this is the true meaning of the famous slogan of the Saint-Simonian cult. If a man operated in a social class to which he did not naturally belong, performing functions for which he was not naturally equipped, he would be wasting his own talents and reducing the total creative potential of humanity. Among Saint-Simon's last words to his favorite disciple was a definition of the quintessential goal of his doctrine and his life's work: "to afford all members of society the greatest possible opportunity for the development of their faculties." [23]

Talleyrand's image of the national workshop survives in Saint-Simon's writings, where the goal of the new society is maximum production through maximum utilization of individual capacities. In Saint-Simon's vision of the golden age of plenty, the emphasis is placed upon ever more production and creation, rather than upon consumption and distribution. The banquet spread before mankind is so sumptuous that dwelling upon material rewards, so characteristic of a world of scarcity, seems to be beside the point. Saint-Simon's humanitarian doctrine thus incorporated the Condorcet principle that society could be organized so that misery and ignorance became accidents rather than the norm of human experience; [24] his theory had none of the crushing pessimism associated with later Social Darwinism, even though he too was inspired by biological analogies.

Perhaps the difference between the Saint-Simon and the eighteenth-century conception has its crux in a new view of humanity. Instead of the man of reason as the most perfect expression of humanity towards which all men are striving, Saint-Simon thinks of man now and in the future as at once rational, activist, and religious, at once mind, will, and feeling. His ends are moral, intellectual, and physical, three major areas of human effort corresponding to the aptitudes of the artist, the scientist, and the industrialist. This is the whole man, whose being is paralleled in the organization of the healthy body social. If man is primarily a rational animal and the highest form of reason is mathematics, the Turgot-Condorcet egalitarian ideal of rational units behaving in accordance with mathematicized social rules is comprehensible. But if humanity is a composite whose various manifestations include the predominantly activist or religious as well as rationalist, the social structure, reflecting and embracing the variety and diversity of men, will be organismic, a harmony of complex, different, and essential parts.

The organismic society, unlike the atomist egalitarian society, which functions like inanimate clockwork, requires a "vitalist" element — some pervasive emotion, feeling, or belief to give life to the body. Though the eighteenth century had developed the concepts of benevolence and humanity as characteristics of natural men of virtue, Saint-Simon in the romantic temper infused the idea of the love of humanity with an emotional drive which it had lacked in the minds of the *philosophes*. Love was the fluid which coursed through the body social, gave it movement and energy. In Saint-Simon's judgment the equal atoms of the eighteenth-century world view were always on the verge of strife; his ideal of love created an organic harmonious whole out of society's vital parts. Men hungered for this comfort on the morrow of a quarter of a century of world revolution which had loosened the very bonds of the social fabric. The need for the emotionalization of relationships if society was not to fall apart and disintegrate into its discrete elements had been dramatized by Burke and de Bonald and de Maistre. Saint-Simon by his own testimony was communicating the same urgent longing of men for a society in which they could feel themselves integral parts, an organic society, as contrasted with a state in which isolated units competed and fought with one another. Egalitarianism had come to represent the eternal struggle of equals in a world of cold and brutal competition.

Saint-Simon's formula for the organization of society aimed to eliminate the sources of social waste, maladjustment, and friction not only through a class division based on function and capacity. Within each class of aptitudes provision is made for the emergence of a natural élite — an élite of real capacity — through keeping the course open to talent. There is a presumption in Saint-Simon that among men with similar or identical aptitudes, superiority and excellence will automatically be recognized without jealousy or conflict. He generalized to all fields of endeavor the apparent unanimity with which the foremost mathematicians, physicists, and biologists seemed to be appreciated by men of science.

In the good society this natural élite corps (he was directly influenced by the contemporary analogy of Napoleon's *troupes d'élite*), one with authentic, proved capacities, directed the various classes. Leadership was not, as the doctrine of popular sovereignty held, a generalized capacity in which all men were more or less equal and which made it feasible and natural for offices to be elective. In the organic society, workers instinctively rendered obedience to their natural superiors, their "chiefs," in their own class.[25] The idealized image of the Napoleonic army, in which ordinary soldiers had risen to be marshals, in which rank was at least in theory the reward of talent and merit, was a prototype for Saint-Simon's civilian class society.

Since it was in the very order of the universe that men should be unequal, instead of attempting to level these differences, Saint-Simon in the spirit of Bichat's physiological doctrines held that it would be beneficial to the whole of society to emphasize them, to nurture and develop the uncommon and extraordinary capacities in individual men. Saint-Simon denied that negroes were equal to Europeans.[26] Among Europeans themselves there were professional and class distinctions which he called "anomalies." The corps of the nobility and the clergy in European society had originally been founded upon just such organic "anomalies" in the human species. Though these "anomalies" had become attenuated through the centuries, the egalitarian *philosophes* had made a fatal error when they proclaimed the abolition of all specialized corps simply because the existing élites in name had ceased to be élites in fact. True scientists of society would not try to minimize unique excellences, but would devote themselves to the regeneration of specialized corps, confining their membership to the men who were patently superior, those who had the most marked "anomalies." In the industrial régime of the future, the real nobles would be industrial chiefs and the real priests would be scientists.[27]

26

The Twilight of Power

SAINT-SIMON, in the *Introduction aux travaux scientifiques du XIXᵉ siècle*, had shown his awareness of the universality of the power drive. "Every man, every grouping of men, whatever its character, tends towards the increase of power. The warrior with the sabre, the diplomat with his wiles, the geometer with his compass, the chemist with his retorts, the physiologist with his scalpel, the hero by his deeds, the philosopher by his combinations all struggle to achieve command. From different sides they scale the plateau on whose height stands the fantastic being who rules all of nature and whom every man who has a strong constitution tries to replace."[1]

The Restoration works established a sharp distinction between the exercise of power by ruling classes in the past and direction of the future industrial society which would become the function of entrepreneurial and scientific chiefs. The prospect of the survival of power, with its dread military and psychological consequences, into the golden age, seemed to poison the benign placidity of free labor in association in the ideal state of mankind. Struck by the ubiquity of the power lust, Saint-Simon in his later works squarely met the challenge which it represented to his entire system. In a significant passage in the ninth letter of *L'Organisateur* he dismissed as irrelevant to the discussion furious madmen like Napoleon who revelled in the exercise of arbitrary power for its own sake, for such men were monstrosities. This was a typical eighteenth-century way of dealing with the abnormal: it was eliminated from consideration. As for the rest of mankind, there was a happy way out of the contradictions with which persistent and omnipresent human aggressiveness confronted the good society: the civilizing process tended to transfer the object of the power lust from men to nature.

By power Saint-Simon meant the exercise of any force by one human being upon another, an act of dominion essentially vicious. Power would not be necessary in the future industrial society composed of men freely utilizing their capacities. The energy which had previously been wasted upon the exercise of power over men would be channeled in another direction, towards the ever more intensive exploitation of nature. ". . . the only useful action that man can perform is the action of man on things. The action of man on man is always in itself harmful to the species because of the two-fold waste of energy which it entails. It can only be useful if it is subsidiary and if it supplements the performance of a greater action on nature." [2] Power injured both the man over whom it was wielded and the man who carried the rod. Men whose capacities were devoted to nothing more creative than action on other men were members of Saint-Simon's do-nothing classes. This succinct expression of a new moral ideal for the industrial society captured the imagination of later socialist theorists and found an echo in their writings.

The historic substitution of nature for man as the object of aggression, so provocatively reminiscent of both Marx and Freud, nurtured Saint-Simon's optimistic belief that with time not only intellectual but moral progress was feasible. Despite the fact that the most recent embodiment of the great demon of passion for power was still alive on the rock of Saint Helena, Saint-Simon forecast the ultimate quiescence of the evil:

This love of dominion, which is certainly indestructible in man, has nevertheless been eradicated in large part by the progress of civilization, or, at least its disadvantages have almost disappeared under the new system. In fact, the development of action against nature has changed the direction of this sentiment by leveling it against objects. The desire to command men has slowly transformed itself into the desire to make and remake nature in accordance with our will.

From this time on the desire to dominate which is innate in all men has ceased to be pernicious, or at least we can foresee an epoch when it will not be harmful any longer, but will become useful. Thus civilization has perfected human morality not only in the animal sense by improving intelligence, but also in the organic sense by curbing the passions.

Though, according to the laws of man's physiology, this second order of vital functions [his organic being] is not by itself perfectible, it can be improved by the exercise of the first order of functions [the intelligence] on the second.[3]

Along with his teachings that man's body influenced his mind, Cabanis had dwelt upon the reciprocal influence of the *moral* on the *physique*, an idea Saint-Simon had always found congenial. This doctrine allowed for the possibility that with a great development of man's scientific knowledge, his passions might be bridled. Society had already given promise of the eventual pacification of the power lust. Saint-Simon proved by homely example that the seductions of industrial civilization were becoming so potent that most men would sacrifice even the exercise of absolute power to enjoy their pleasures in the peace of the new society — *vide* the English nabob who after years of service in India preferred the simple comforts of rural England to arbitrary dominion in Bengal.

Since the natural élite of the industrial scientific society was based upon sheer capacity, talents which presumably all men could instantaneously recognize, there was no room in the society of the future for class and power conflict. Men found their way into the élite because their natural aptitudes drew them there. The prospect of jealousies and internal struggles within scientific élites did not disturb Saint-Simon. The act of appreciation of superior genius appeared to be miraculously free from the baser passions. As for conflicts among coequal bodies of the élite, such as the scientists and the industrial entrepreneurs, they were beyond the realm of possibility. The innermost desire of each member of an élite was the exercise of those aptitudes and functions in which he excelled. It would therefore be contrary to nature for a scientist, for example, a theoretician, to covet administrative powers, or for an industrialist to presume to seek membership in a scientific corps. Such capacities, Bichat had taught, were mutually exclusive, and in the good society each man would find his proper place. In the new moral order, "know thyself" read "know thy capacity."

In past epochs of civilization there had been internecine strife among the ruling classes because these classes were constituted as agencies for the exercise of superior power over all men. The medieval nobles were inflamed by a desire to control the inhabitants of ever more extensive territories, the clergy to enjoy absolute mastery over the minds of their parishioners. Such corps ambitions had to clash because they vied for exclusive power. In the industrial scientific society, basic drives would be turned outwards towards the world of objects. The scientist was discovering the deepest truths of nature and the industrialist was harnessing the refractory forces of nature, two different, noncompetitive functions. The direction of men in the new society was only an ancillary phenomenon to the exploitation of nature, both in the spiritual realm and in the temporal. Dominion over men was indivisible, whereas the management of nature could be separated into specialized functions, eliminating power conflicts.

In the industrial scientific society all capacities were given free play. Saint-Simon himself did not overstress the hierarchic nature of this society, nor did he attribute values of inferiority or superiority to one or another of the major capacities which together constituted the social organism. He was, of course, not completely emancipated from a classical denigration of manual labor; the scientists and the industrial chiefs were endowed with special excellence. But for all that, no working function in society was disdained in and of itself. "All men shall work" was still the commandment of the new order. Men's labors varied with their capacities. As for their rewards, Saint-Simon was not an egalitarian. He dismissed the problem with the assurance that each member of the body politic would be recompensed in accordance with his investment, a vague formula which left room for differentials in material emoluments. Saint-Simon always focused on production, impediments to production, methods for increasing productivity; the rules governing the distribution of rewards were reduced to issues of a secondary nature, for amid the great superfluities of the society of producers there would surely be enough for the needs of all men. The social organism was guided by the lodestar of an ideological absolute which discouraged too wide a disparity between the rewards of one man and another. The primary goal was to raise the physical and moral well-being of the poorest and most numerous classes. While he rejected Condorcet's equality as an ideal, he never raised the incentive of class divergences as the motive drive animating the social body. "Each person enjoys a measure of importance and benefits proportionate to his capacity and to his investment. This constitutes the highest degree of equality possible and desirable." [4]

The only sound system was a functioning class society in which the roles of the men who administered were mere extensions of their social occupations. The "high administration of society," that clumsy phrase which he preferred both to state and government, required no special aptitudes or talents and no specialized personnel beyond those occupied in directing normal social functions. There was no need for a government expert or a man trained in administration. Before the triumph of the industrial society men had been governed, in the order of the future they would be administered. The old and the new leadership were different because they reflected this underlying transformation in the nature of human relationships. Saint-Simon was emphasizing the distinction between the exercise of power based on physical force and of direction founded on a recognition of superior capacity in the élite, between the command function and the organization of an association for the common welfare. At first sight it might seem utopian to turn society over to a group of administrators after men for centuries had accustomed themselves to the absolutes of governance, power, and dominion. Saint-Simon pointed out, however, that in his day many pivotal economic institutions already in operation had dispensed with the command function and were voluntary associations — the banks, insurance companies, savings societies, and canal construction companies. These administered societies were models for the total society of the future, and he anticipated no special difficulties incident to the enlargement of the unit of administration. Society itself was one large national workshop with more varied activities, though none essentially different from those of a canal construction company.

The transfer of political power from the noble class to the chiefs of the industrial class — "professors in administration" — who in their factories and banks and companies had already been virtually exercising civil administration, would not be perplexing to the mass of the workers, since they had

long since grown accustomed on the job to an appreciation of these entrepreneurs as their natural leaders. In the new order entrepreneurial leadership would simply be extended from individual factories to the requirements
of the "high administration of society." For the proletariat such a scheme of
things would involve a return to a more normal relationship in which they
would no longer have to deal with two leaderships, one political and one
civil; the chiefs of daily work would be at the same time the chiefs of the
total society. Thus there would eventually be created an organic integrated
society in which men would cease to be pulled in two opposite directions by
rival forces. Similarly, the unification of the spiritual power in society, ending
the present division between the clergy and the scientists, would not be a
disturbing novelty for the mass of the people but would represent a desirable
amalgamation replacing the confusion which had hitherto bedeviled them.

Saint-Simon drew up a catalogue of distinctions governing the relations
of people and their chiefs under the old feudal order and the new industrial
society. Under the old the people were regimented by superiors; under the
new, they were related to one another by occupational ties. Under the old
they were commanded, under the new they were directed. Under the old
they were subjects, under the new they were members. Above all, the great
virtue of the industrial society consisted in the fact that all its members, from
the simple worker to the rich manufacturer, were "collaborators." [5] In the
old society there was force, in the new a "coöperation" of capacities, a true
"association."

Class conflicts would be banished from the new society. Since the capacities of real classes could not overlap, what could they fight about? Since men
of a class would seek to excel in their natural aptitudes there could be only
rivalry in good works, not a struggle for power. [6] When class chiefs owed
their prestige to their control of men, they could fight over one another's
"governed," but since there would be no governors and no subjects, from
what source would class antagonism be derived? Within a class men of the
same capacity would be striving to excel one another with creations whose
merits all members of the class would be able to evaluate. Between classes
there could only be mutual aid. There was no basis for hostility, and no
occasion for invading one another's territory.

In a few key paragraphs of his tract *Suite à la brochure des Bourbons et
des Stuarts*, published on January 24, 1822, he expressed in capsule form his
whole concept of the natural élite in a society without power. "All privileges
will be abolished and never reappear since the most complete system of
equality which can possibly exist will be constituted. The men who show
the greatest capacity in positive sciences, in the fine arts, and in industry will
be called by the new system to enter the top echelon of social prestige and
will be placed in charge of public affairs — a fundamental disposition which
destines all men possessing a transcendent talent to rise to the first rank, no

matter in what position the chance of birth may have placed them." [7] The whole social structure thus constituted would have as its goal the implementation of a *révolution régénératrice* throughout the European continent.

The regenerated society of the future would be emancipated from the shackles and burdens of government which weighed upon his contemporaries. During the early years of the Restoration his periodicals gave a prominent place to meticulous analyses of the inflated national budget and directed harassing attacks against excessive government expenditures in all branches of the Bourbon administration. Saint-Simon laid down the principle that a government was best when it governed least and most cheaply.[8] The productive industrials were paying the rising tax levies of the Bourbon state, most of whose operations appeared to them supernumerary. The Bourbons were doling out pensions to returned *émigrés*, compensating them with billions of francs for their losses during the Revolution, creating new offices and sinecures after the manner of the *ancien régime*. To the industrials and their mouthpiece Saint-Simon, this was prodigious waste. France needed no army for national defense since nobody was threatening to strike at the Bourbons, whom a coalition of European powers had just set upon the throne. The vast judicial system was overloaded with judges, a large part of whose work could have been accomplished more quickly, wisely, and economically by arbitration tribunals of industrials. If the state were run like a national workshop it would consume but a fraction of current expenditures. Only businessmen, not bureaucrats, were capable of drawing up an economical budget for the state and administering it effectively. *L'Industrie* included essays which were as thoroughgoing statements against government regulation as could be found anywhere on the continent.[9]

The more Saint-Simon analyzed the governmental functions of the state, the less use he found for its existence in such swollen dimensions. His industrial society could operate with administrative and scientific capacities alone, without men adept at wielding force. The existing governmental system, which he hoped to replace in the near future, had raised men to office not because they demonstrated special talents, but because they had cunning and knew how to acquire and to manipulate power.[10] Their evil genius would be thwarted in the productive society of the future.

In the modern world the only useful work was scientific, artistic, technological, industrial (in the broad sense of the term); everything else was parasitic. Hitherto despite the fact that society had had to squander a large proportion of its energies on struggles for power, it had nevertheless managed to achieve a high level of prosperity. *A fortiori*, what great accomplishments was humanity capable of if men ceased to spend themselves in power conflicts and devoted themselves solely to coöperative labor?

After Saint-Simon surveyed the various branches of the Bourbon government, he came to the conclusion that only the police power had some justification for existence. Though he made this grudging admission, he assigned the police a subordinate position in the industrial society, severely reducing the exalted status it enjoyed under the Bourbons. At times he even eliminated the maintenance of order as a formal attribute of the state. "This function . . ." he wrote, "can easily become almost in its entirety a duty common to all citizens. . . ."[11] His state virtually "withered away," though he did not use the phrase.

In the good society, governmental action — by which Saint-Simon understood the command function — would be "reduced to nothing, or almost nothing." Since the goal of society was general happiness and happiness was defined as the development of the arts and sciences and the diffusion of their benefits through technology and industry, only managerial action would be required. Inevitably the progress of industry would reduce poverty, idleness, and ignorance, the chief sources of public disorder, and thus the need for most governmental functions, even the police, would dissolve. The industrial society, by eradicating the causes of disorder, made it possible virtually to eliminate the state. Granted a thoroughgoing economic liberalism — free trade, no domestic governmental regulation of industry and commerce, an inevitable reduction in crime, a foreign policy committed to peace — it seemed difficult to discover any broad areas in which the state could operate. Ultimately decisions affecting the body social would be impersonal and would be reached like other positivist scientific conclusions. "Decisions can only be the result of scientific demonstrations, absolutely independent of any human will. . . ."[12]

However much Marx differed from Saint-Simon in analyzing the historical process there was agreement between them that the new society emerging from the last conflict of systems or classes would witness the twilight of power and the cessation of power conflicts among men. Both saw power and aggressiveness not as ineradicable characteristics of man, but as transient historical manifestations generated by previous, imperfect social systems and destined to perish with them. Their optimism was a corollary to their analysis of the classes designated as the agents of the last revolution. The "industrials" were by definition productive entrepreneurs to whom the spirit of war and conflict was alien; it would be contrary to their nature to become intoxicated with power. The proletarians were in their nature men who worked, not men who exploited, hence they could not engineer a proletarian revolution and thereafter exploit others. The simplicity with which socialist theory turned its head away from the realities of power was the great blind spot of its outlook.

27

The High Administration of Society

URING THE EARLY YEARS OF THE RESTORATION, when Saint-Simon espoused the straight economic liberalism of the English and the French economists who reduced the whole mechanism of the state to a minor police power, he tended to ignore the planning of large-scale economic ventures.[1] The entrepreneurs, he expected, would generate universal well-being through the free, untrammeled operation of their respective egotisms. In the writings of his last years, when he evoked the vision of a new industrial society, the individual freedom of action of entrepreneurs who participated in the coöperative projects was no longer absolute. His new world society was to undertake great public works through "association," building highways and canals, founding credit institutions, developing techniques to increase the yield of agriculture and the output of industry, multiplying the discoveries of scientists. Saint-Simon provided for the guidance of the productive forces of society in a manner which would hardly have enjoyed the full approval of Adam Smith and Jean-Baptiste Say.[2]

The character of the vast international enterprises he dreamed about is sufficiently clear to place him in the ranks of the great social, though not necessarily socialist[3] planners, since the channeling of productive efforts into grand projects takes place without the elimination of the traditional incentives of profit. He still sanctioned rewards for the risk of the speculator, a name which had a positive connotation in his writings, and he warned against stifling the spirit of the entrepreneur by restricting his profits. This early theoretician of the industrial society did not envisage social planning and profit-making as mutually exclusive. He also preserved a hierarchy of classes, though it had changed its character since the days when an aristocracy was its crowning glory. At the apex of the social pyramid loomed the great industrialists and scientists and artists, at the base the proletarians, and between them the ladder of advancement remained free and open to talent. All men were equal only in the sense that all, in accordance with their individual capacities, were joined in productive labor whose end was the advancement of social progress. There was equality of status insofar as nobody was permitted to live as a parasite on the produce of others.

L'Organisateur included a neat plan for the administration of a progressive French monarchy — no longer a power state — in the spirit of the new industrial society. It is not clear whether this was merely a program for a transitional government form, introducing elements of the industrial society into the bosom of the old system, or whether it was a schema for the organization of the new society itself. Whatever its real purpose, it represented a sharp break with the British parliamentary institutions and practices which the Restoration Chamber of Deputies was attempting to imitate, in accordance with the Charter. Like the representative system in operation, Saint-Simon's plan provided for chambers, but the electoral procedures, the qualifications for office, and the functions of the deputies bore no resemblance to any contemporary constitutional régime. Barred from the deliberations would be nobles, politicians, lawyers, and metaphysicians. Men were not to be selected as representatives of a body of voters, but were to be chosen solely for their professional competences. These experts would assemble in the chambers to plan and direct public works, rather than to deliberate about abstract principles. The various managerial devices which Saint-Simon described define the temper of his new industrial society. The similarity of the chamber organization with recent fascist corporate practice as well as technocratic proposals is patent.

Parliament was to consist of three professional houses. First there was a Chamber of Inventions composed of three hundred members divided into three sections. The first had two hundred engineers; the second fifty poets or other literary "inventors"; and the third twenty-five painters, fifteen sculptors or architects, and ten musicians. Clearly the engineers could outvote the artists whenever they met for final decisions. Saint-Simon was acutely perceptive about the ascendancy of the new class of engineers in European industrial society. The crucial character of their military role in the Napoleonic army had been generally recognized; but Saint-Simon was one of the first social theorists who sensed their potential central importance in modern civil society. These engineers, with many of whom he was personally acquainted (he frequented the area of the Ecole Polytechnique and had discovered Auguste Comte when he was a student there) fitted neatly into his chain of capacities. They were a sort of hybrid group with half industrial and half scientific capacities, an ideal combination. They were, he realized, beginning to earn the respect of two of the chief classes of the industrial society — the entrepreneurs and the scientists. In this synthesis of two capacities, the new society would attain its quintessential expression. If the overriding purpose of all the arts and the sciences was to modify nature, these engineers were society's noblest animals, for they were the primary agents in the application of scientific research.

The Chamber of Inventions was to be a central planning agency for France. In the performance of its august functions it was to derive inspiration from two practical ideals both of which seemed to Saint-Simon to be in complete harmony with each other: to increase the total wealth of France and at the same time to ameliorate the lot of its inhabitants, by which he explicitly meant increasing the consumption of objects which were useful and would give pleasure.

The first Chamber of Inventions would be allowed a year in which to draft and promulgate its basic plan. It would, of course, not intrude into fields already preëmpted by individual entrepreneurs; they would continue to run their private manufacturing establishments unmolested. The public engineers and their artistic colleagues would concentrate on a grand works plan which would be revised and extended annually. Saint-Simon went into great detail about the type of projects which would fall within the province of the Chamber of Inventions. Somehow they all seemed to center around the improvement of the transportation system. A number of projects which Saint-Simon sponsored in his activist years had involved travel and transport — the canal across Nicaragua, the canal from Madrid to the sea, the stagecoach network of the Directorate. He was returning to the dreams of his youth. He now had a vision of the great turnpike roads and parkways of the future. Transportation lanes were the arteries of the body of humanity. They would create one world.

Draining, clearing, cutting new roads, opening canals will be considered the most important part of this project: the roads and the canals should not only be conceived as means of easier transportation; their construction should be so devised that they are rendered as pleasant as possible to the travelers. Fifty thousand acres of land (and more if it is considered appropriate) will be chosen among the most picturesque sites which the roads or the canals will cross. These lands will be set aside as resting places for the travelers and pleasure resorts for the inhabitants of the neighborhood.

Each of these gardens will contain a museum of the natural as well as the industrial products of the surrounding areas. They will also include hostels for the artists who might wish to stop there, and a certain number of musicians will always be supported there whose function it will be to inflame the inhabitants of the canton with whatever passion circumstances may require for the greater good of the nation.[4]

In *Du système industriel* there were also plans for a positivist national system of education, plans for increasing agricultural production, plans to assure workers full employment while multiplying the pleasures of the rich, plans for colonization to receive the excess population which would result from the increased prosperity of France.[5]

The conception of art as an instrument to arouse the passions for the public welfare — reminiscent of Plato — was already developed in his 1802 pamphlet. Work projects for humanity had there been designated as one of the benefits of the Religion of Newton. In *Du système industriel* the popularization of artistic culture becomes one of the ways of narrowing the gap between the upper and the lower classes.

The whole of the French soil should become a superb English park, embellished with everything that the fine arts can add to the beauties of nature. For a long time luxury has been concentrated in the palaces of kings, in the dwellings of princes, in the mansions and the châteaux of a few powerful men. This concentration is very harmful to the general interests of society, because it tends to establish two distinct levels of civilization, two different classes of men, that of persons whose intelligence is developed by the habitual sight of works of art and that of men whose imaginative faculties receive no development, since the physical labors with which they are exclusively occupied do not stimulate their intelligence at all.

Conditions today are favorable for making luxury national. Luxury will become useful and moral when the whole nation enjoys it. Our century has been vouchsafed the honor and the advantage of utilizing in a direct manner in political combinations the progress made by the exact sciences and by the fine arts since the brilliant epoch of their regeneration.[6]

This utopia became a partial reality under the self-consciously Saint-Simonian Empire of Napoleon III. It is now so generally diffused an aspect of all peacetime government that its originality in 1820 is hard to appreciate.

In Saint-Simon's scheme, these planned public works would give rise to a series of celebrations: holidays of hope during which orators would stimulate productive effort and greater application to labor by painting a vision of the benefits conferred upon society by the new public works; and holidays of recollection in which the present state of happiness was compared favorably with the past. These festivals are familiar enough to twentieth-century men, who have added to the performances an element which Saint-Simon would have banished — the display of military strength.

Saint-Simon worked out the mechanics for choosing the members of his pivotal Chamber of Inventions. He was willing to start with the technical and artist members of existing governmental bodies: the engineers of the departmental Offices of Bridges and Roads, the members of the Academy, and the artists of the Institute. By 1819–1820 he abandoned the earlier scheme of 1802 under which similar experts were to be elected popularly by all subscribers to a fund for the promotion of science. Despite his misgivings about official bodies, he was prepared to use their members in the initial establishment of the Chamber. Subsequent vacancies were to be filled by coöption.

This Chamber of Inventions would not be allowed to remake the face of France without some control. There was to be a second chamber, known as the Chamber of Review (*examen*), for the deliberations of the pure scientists — the mathematicians, the physicists, and the life scientists in equal numbers, a hundred each. They would examine the projects of the Chamber of Inventions; elaborate a complete system of public education on three levels for each of three unequal economic classes; and conduct another series of fêtes in honor of various sex, age, and productive class groupings (there would be Men's Days, Women's Days, Boys' Days, Girls' Days, Fathers' and Mothers' Days, Children's Days, Managers' Days, Workers' Days). During these holidays the social duties of each classification would be honored. The most important function of the Chamber of Review would be supervision of the system of public education (religious education remained a family matter in the 1819 version of the plan). As a start, the Chamber of Review would be recruited from members of the Institute.

As soon as the Chamber of Inventions and the Chamber of Review were formally constituted, the Chamber of Deputies, composed of operating industrialists, would be established as an executive body. It would be the duty of the members to levy taxes and to execute the grand projects which they too would have an opportunity to pass upon after action by the other two Chambers.

Any Chamber could summon parliament. Ordinarily the first Chamber drafted a project, the second reviewed it, and the third implemented it. The three Chambers together would thus exercise all the functions ordinarily vested in different branches of government under liberal constitutions: they would have sovereign power, they would be at once constitutional and legislative and executive.

Saint-Simon helpfully outlined the first acts of the new parliament. For a professed antirevolutionary, his initial proposals entailed a social upheaval: he would immediately promulgate new civil and criminal laws in consonance with the changed political system. Recognizing that the law of property was the crux of any juridical reform, he issued a clear-cut directive: the new government was to reformulate the law of property so that productive enterprise was always favored. Idle property, nonproductive property would be disadvantaged, while productive property was actively encouraged. Saint-Simon's utopia contained bright little details. All proposed projects were to be brought out for public edification as leaflets never longer than one printed page.[7] The first military project of the Chambers was the protection of the national territory with the least possible number of troops. The whole process of social reorganization would be effected without recourse to any law of confiscation, since those persons whose interests had been hurt by the new system could be indemnified from a sum of two milliard francs allotted for this purpose.[8]

In *Du système industriel*, Saint-Simon faced the argument that his industrial managers would cease to be industrialists once they were put in control of the state budget and other key administrative branches. Would they too then become "officials," nonproductive idlers? He answered that government administration if handled efficiently was not all-absorbing. He had industrialist and banker friends in the existing Chamber of Deputies and the French chambers of commerce and industry were staffed with operating industrialists. These men, who had demonstrated administrative capacity in their own enterprises, would be quite capable of running functions in government on a part-time basis. The industrials would not have to be great parliamentary orators to fill government posts. "The role of the talkers is approaching its end, that of the doers will not be long delayed in making its appearance." [9]

Five years later, in the fourth *cahier* of the *Catéchisme des industriels*, Saint-Simon described a variant schema for the future society, with a new set of names for its principal institutions. The most striking feature of this society was its class character. Classes, not individuals, were the great blocks with which society was structured; with the establishment of ideal relations among classes and the distribution of functions among them, the main problems of social organization were solved. The king was retained as a mere symbol of the principle of unity. Saint-Simon then vested the direction of administrative and financial affairs in the hands of the most important industrialists. Their primacy was made explicit. The intellectuals were considered a "secondary class" on the ground that they were less indispensable than the industrialists. The industrialists would therefore require the savants to organize themselves so as "to employ in a manner most useful to the industrialists the existence which they receive from them." [10]

Saint-Simon's new blueprint failed to spell out precisely what this secondary position of the savants implied, a flagrant weakness in the whole edifice. On the internal organization of the chief savants, however, the fourth *cahier* of the *Catéchisme des industriels* was quite circumstantial. The savants were divided into two classes roughly corresponding to the areas of knowledge covered by the Institute before the Napoleonic reorganization of 1803, an Academy of Physical Sciences and an Academy of Moral and Political Sciences, or, in Saint-Simon's nomenclature, an Academy of Reasoning and an Academy of Sentiment, one branch to perfect a code of physical laws and one to perfect a code of sentiments, one for the continuators of Aristotle and one for the continuators of Plato and the Church Fathers. The Academy of Reasoning included, in addition to the expected complement of physical and mathematical scientists, a subclass of savants devoted to political economy and a substantial number of practical technicians, mechanics, inventors, and engineers. The Academy of Sentiment would be composed of moralists, theologians, poets, painters, sculptors, and musicians. The legists on whom he had heaped vituperation in *L'Organisateur* and *Du système industriel* managed to survive and to carve out a place for themselves in the new industrial society, a position not as inflated as the one they enjoyed in the contemporary world, but tolerable nevertheless. Saint-Simon grudgingly acknowledged that they too had a unique capacity, an aptitude for drafting regulations, and he introduced their representatives into both academies to draw up internal orders governing the relationships among the various groups of savants. Even theologians, their natures transfigured by the moral doctrine of a new Christianity, were accorded a chair in the Academy of Sentiment. Saint-Simon did not destroy the persons of individual human beings who were members of antiquated, decadent classes; he only wiped out the classes, transforming the men who once belonged to them into productive participants in the new society. In the end he even found minor posts in the industrial society for the practical *politiques* of the existing state bureaucracy, whom he had once denounced as useless do-nothings in *L'Organisateur*.

Finally, to make sure that the two Academies developed their projects in harmony, there was to be a top coördinating body of savants, called the Supreme Scientific College, which would draw upon personnel in the existing ministries for advice on the drafting of administrative regulations for the spiritual order of society. The functions of the Supreme Scientific College embraced all those activities which from the earliest period of his philosophical career he had considered necessary for the spiritual guidance of an organic order: the formulation of general laws of knowledge based upon the findings both of the Academy of Reasoning and the Academy of Sentiment; the drawing up of an educational program in accord with the doctrine of Saint-Simon; the compilation of a legal code acceptable to the majority of men in society. The educational system would not be absolutely egalitarian, since distinctions of wealth were preserved in the new society and the rich would naturally be in a position to devote more time to their intellectual improvement, but, he added in a footnote of the *Catéchisme des industriels*, "the education of the poorest class will be extended far enough so that the rich will not be able to abuse them through a superiority of knowledge." [11]

In the fourth *cahier* of the *Catéchisme des industriels* Saint-Simon demonstrated the whole mechanism of the new society, each component part discharging the duties appropriate to it. Nominally he preserved parliamentary institutions, although he superimposed upon them a complex structure of appointive officials who were the administrative brain of society. His governmental machinery is puerile and not worthy of criticism except insofar as it sheds light on the development of his class theory. He had little comprehension of the complexities inherent in formulating legislation, if he expected a workable project to emerge after an initial proposal had been mangled by five or six separate and independent bodies. There is the possibility that he retained the parliamentary system in addition to his new administrative structure based on class capacities only in order to avoid prosecution as a subversive attacking the constitutional régime of the Charter. From the general spirit of his writings, it is apparent that he did not envisage a long life for parliamentarism within the framework of an administered industrial society.

In a fragment of the *Opinions littéraires, philosophiques et industrielles* entitled *Sur l'administration et sur le gouvernement des affaires publiques* he ventured a further characterization of his triadic élite. The "high administration of society" embraced three functions, the invention, review, and execution of projects useful for the mass of the people. Three classes or three capacities naturally dovetailed with the three vital functions — artists, savants, and industrials. The category "artists" in Saint-Simon's terminology of this period was not restricted to the fine arts; it included all "men of imagination"; it embodied the inventive, the expressive, the creative capacity. Artists would reveal to society the glorious future which awaited it, exciting men with the prospect of the new civilization, its riches, its prosperity, its distribution of goods to all members instead of a few; they would ready men for exertion in the vast common enterprise; they would employ all the techniques of all the fine arts — eloquence, poetry, painting, music — to inspire men with a passionate desire for the works of civilization. The artists were the poetic part of the system. Saint-Simon again identified them with the Platonic and the sentimental (a word he used not in a pejorative sense, but as the romantics were employing the adjective). The artists gave the society its drive.

The savants represented the rational element. They would occupy themselves in the accepted manner of scientists with the observation of facts and reasoning on their observations. They would demonstrate the possibility of harmonizing the interests of all the economic strata among the industrials, the rich few as well as the proletarian mass, by increasing the well-being of everybody at the same time. They outlined methods for full continuous employment of all industrials without the temporary economic crises to which Restoration society had become accustomed. They laid the foundations of a system of public education. They solved social problems through the establishment of laws of social hygiene or laws of politics, which became parts of the positive Science of Man.

Projects for the new society were proposed by the inventive artists and by the scientists who observed realities, but before they could be undertaken, they had to be submitted to the judgment of the practical industrialists, who would pass upon their immediate feasibility. The industrials conceived of administrative techniques for putting desirable projects into execution, and they delegated the actual direction of such enterprises to those of their number who were bankers.

The ideal social pattern was thus a coöperative of three classes, each with unique capacities corresponding to the three unique functions which the administration of society required. The social organism under such an exemplary division of labor could operate smoothly, assuring general calm and stability.

What a contrast with the existing mechanism of Bourbon France! There were great administrative staffs and agencies for the maintenance of order, but since there were no common social goals and no division of functions based on natural capacities, government was devoted primarily to levying and collecting taxes to finance worthless projects. All the efforts of the president of the council, M. de Villèle, had operated in a direction precisely opposed to the real interests of good administration; he had filled the Chamber of Deputies with idle, useless nobles, had driven out the industrials, the artists, and the savants, and had established a minimum age of forty as a qualification for holding office, thus reducing the total energy of the body. Villèle allowed his ministries to be run by lawyers; he put education into the hands of the Jesuits who taught vague ideas instead of positive knowledge. When he created a supreme council of commerce he filled it with men who had never engaged in industry, letting only a few retired industrials slip through. "Here are the sad remains of the governmental capacity. Dragged along by the torrent of civilization, it vainly tries, in attaching itself to the past, to continue to play the preponderant role which was once attributed to it in previous forms of society." [12]

Strange as it may seem, the most important intellectual antecedent for this conception of the high administration of an organic society was the theoretician of the contemporary Catholic reaction in France, the Count de Bonald. The ethic Saint-Simon formulated for the entrepreneurs of the nineteenth century was as anti-individualist and social as the precepts of the theocratic philosophers. The degree of socialism or collectivism which Saint-Simon proposed is less determinative of the tenor of his system than the simple fact that the basic unit of consideration ceased to be an individual and the focus shifted to society, an organic association. Historically, modern socialism has derived far more from the traditionalist denial of eighteenth-century liberalism than has been realized. Saint-Simon, who forthrightly ackowledged de Bonald's influence, was one of the most significant vehicles of transmission for this social theory.

In de Bonald, society's central problem was administration, the proper allocation of service duties, not the rights of man. Except for a brief period in the early years of the Restoration, when at least in his public doctrine Saint-Simon adopted Jean-Baptiste Say's *laissez-faire* principles, he was moving fundamentally in the direction of de Bonald's view rather than along the "anarchic" road of economic liberalism. In this sense his relations with the liberal economists were only a marriage of convenience. In the *Théorie du pouvoir* de Bonald had written — and Saint-Simon would agree:

"Man only exists for society and society only educates him for itself. He should therefore employ in the service of society everything which he has received from nature and everything which he has received from society, everything which he is and everything which he has." [13]

In his revival of the medieval conception of the two powers, the spiritual and the temporal, de Bonald had introduced a terminology which profoundly influenced Saint-Simon. All matters political had a religious aspect; all matters religious had a political aspect. The true civil society was the "union of the political and the religious society." Such a society was a "constituted society," as contrasted with a "non-constituted society," a state in which one of these two elements was absent or in which the political and the religious were not harmoniously intertwined with each other. De Bonald's "constituted society" became the organic society of Saint-Simon's system. "Society is not a simple agglomeration of living beings whose independent actions . . . had no cause but arbitrary individual wills, nor any result but accidents ephemeral or trivial," wrote Saint-Simon in a fragment entitled *De la physiologie appliquée à l'amélioration des institutions sociales.* "On the contrary, society is above all a veritable organic machine whose every part contributes in different manner to the movement of the whole."

De Bonald was consciously recognized as a predecessor; but even beyond the great traditionalist another figure is lurking in the background of Saint-Simon's thought, a writer enigmatic, unavowed, a man whose name was tainted yet whose influence was all-pervasive in nineteenth-century social theory — none other than Jean-Jacques himself, discoverer of the General Will.

PART V

THE LAST YEARS

28

The Suicide Attempt

OVER SIXTY, Saint-Simon still had the verve of a far younger man. He had known riches and poverty, war and prison. He could narrate piquant anecdotes about the changing galaxy of political leaders who had attempted to govern France since the outbreak of the Revolution. The man was intoxicated with the future, with new systems, new religions, plans for social reconstruction. Though aging, he did not live among the shadows of the dead, and he was not prone to muse about the glories of the old régime, fantasies which possessed so many of his contemporaries whose noble titles had become meaningless parchment. He was of the declassed nobility, but no victim of nostalgia.

It is hard to know what he lived on during the last years. Manufacturers and bankers still gave him money from time to time, even after they had stopped their regular subvention to his periodicals which were considered dangerous, too radical in their attacks on the Bourbon régime. The only records available, a few stray letters, indicate that in 1822–1823 Saint-Simon had spent many months away from Paris soliciting funds from manufacturers in provincial towns. A propagandist for the industrial society, he could never quite understand why the very men whose cause he was espousing refused to support him.

Debonairly he borrowed money from anyone who would lend, and the debts he accumulated through the years did not weigh heavily upon him. When broke, he sought out the scientists and doctors to whom he had opened his purse in prosperous days — a fair number of them like the surgeon Dupuytren had become famous — and he asked for reimbursement. The old fellow became a nuisance with his seemingly endless brochures, his importunate touches, requests for subscriptions to his journals, and extravagant pretensions. He asked for a thousand francs at a time, not for alms. Often as not he found the door of a former *protégé* closed in his face.

Saint-Simon spawned many more projects than ever reached maturity.

The organizational formula had become stereotyped. A proposal for a new periodical served as the focus of his propaganda for the cause of the industrial society, and he solicited donations as well as subscriptions. Buying a subscription was no mere economic act devoid of ideological significance. More and more it was conceived as spiritual initiation into the system. The total body of subscribers and donors became in his mind members of a "society" and at various times he proposed to grant them certain rights over the content of the periodicals they supported in order to draw them closer to the doctrine. Here was an ideal meeting place for the diverse social classes joined in the common effort. A periodical afforded a particularly good opportunity for industrialists and intellectuals to work together for the triumph of industrialism.

Among his manuscripts there is a *Plan d'une première association entre les industriels et les publicistes*.[1] The project called for the publication of a periodical to be named *L'Industriel*, dedicated to the propagation of the *doctrine industrielle* as defined in "M. St. Simon's *Catéchisme*." (This would tend to date it sometime in 1824, after the publication of the *Catéchisme des industriels*.) In contradistinction to his periodicals of 1817–1818 he now promised to avoid the petty controversies of daily politics, to rise above parties, to eschew partisan appeals to passion and to nonpacific action. The outline of the contents of a sample issue indicates the degree to which in his last years Saint-Simon's theories had begun to harden into a *doctrine*. The manuscripts bear witness that there was probably less abrupt a break than has sometimes been supposed between the system taught by the master to his last disciples and the exposition of the early Saint-Simonians in the formal lectures of the cult. A copy of *L'Industriel* was to begin with an article on the doctrine, to be followed by an impartial analysis of current governmental action, by an examination of great works on the history of legislation and literature as they bore on the doctrine, by an announcement of important discoveries in science and industry and of outstanding creations in the fine arts, and finally by a "short notice" on great industrial operations and on financial, agricultural, commercial, or industrial legislation, as well as on the achievements of distinguished industrials. In the plan Saint-Simon described himself as the "Founder of the Industrial Doctrine, chief of the nascent philosophical school of the nineteenth century."

In addition to his own publications, Saint-Simon combed the Paris newspaper offices seeking organs for the propagation of his doctrine. There is record of an interview with Dubois and Pierre Leroux, directors of *Le Globe*. The discussion led to no agreement, but one of them caught the spark. Pierre Leroux, a future Saint-Simonian, reports the master's parting words: "The other one [Leroux] understood me."[2]

Even Jacques Laffitte — perhaps the boldest and most forthright among the new generation of financiers — did not always receive Saint-Simon's

exertions on behalf of the industrialists with enthusiasm, though he did take
the time to formulate his objections in writing. In a letter composed in 1823
he dictated his criticism of one of Saint-Simon's manuscripts which had been
sent him for forty-eight hours (typical of Saint-Simon's sense of urgency)
in a logical, clear-cut, brutally frank manner.[3] As for Saint-Simon's idea that
since the industrials constituted twenty-four twenty-fifths of the total population they should control and direct everything in France, he considered the
principle "too absolute." Laffitte, the successful banker and tactician for the
liberal deputies in the Chamber, thought that Saint-Simon's distinction
between theoretical and practical capacities had been drawn too sharply;
both could be lodged in one person. He was not against the proposal that
the *chefs des industriels* (he adopted Saint-Simon's terminology) should
frame the national budget, but only when they had learned how; moreover,
he was worried about the implied abolition of the Chamber of Deputies
and the Ministers in the new plan for social reorganization.

Saint-Simon's proposed techniques were for Laffitte hardly adequate
in meeting the real problems of industry, persecuted by the Bourbon régime.
"Industry has fought for fourteen centuries. It is still fighting. That is
evident. But apart from your impossible Commission what do you propose
to do to make it achieve recognition as sovereign by those who wish to keep
it enslaved? Nothing." Neither were the blandishments with which Saint-
Simon hoped to win the approval of the Bourbon monarch at all to Laffitte's
taste. "I do not think that the concession of the idea of divine right [of
kings], with which you say the industrials will be able to accommodate
themselves, is a proposition any more proved than what you contend elsewhere — that the king is the First Industrial." In summary, he neither approved completely of Saint-Simon's principles nor of his mechanics of operation. He was by no means ready to engage in a fight which would lead people
to say that all he was interested in was the replacement of the men in power
by himself. He could only support projects with which he was in full accord
— and this was not one of them.

A long four-page letter from the busy M. Laffitte, though it won Saint-
Simon no immediate aid, is evidence that some of the most prominent of
the industrials considered it worthwhile at least to discuss his ideas seriously.
There was even a specific hint of the conspiratorial in the relationship between Saint-Simon and Laffitte. In the twenties the forces of the *bourgeois*
and the *ultras* were being drawn up for battle and the sentiments expressed
by the financier-politician bordered on treason. Before Laffitte signed the
letter with his powerful flourish he added a note that as a precaution Saint-
Simon should burn it.

In the twenties Saint-Simon had acquired a housekeeper or mistress
named Julie Juliand and a dog called Presto. He had somehow discovered a
natural daughter of one of his early loves and in his final years he lavished

affection upon her. The letters he sent to this Madame Caroline Bouraiche are among the few clues to his fund-raising activities among the business-men of the provinces. One written from Rouen on February 16, 1822, is rather optimistic. "My affairs are going well, though they are not progressing as fast as I expected. I think I shall need about another week. This city is worth infinitely more than Saint-Quentin. Here I have found many very intelligent merchants who take a lively interest in my work." [4]

Madame Bouraiche had young ones to care for and she needed his finan-cial support. Along with Julie and Presto these were heavy responsibilities for the old man. As soon as he detected a glimmer of interest among the provincial businessmen, he would enthuse about his prospects and write with all the fresh confidence of youth. "We shall succeed," he announced to his daughter on March 9, 1822, "What joy it will give me to dispel all your worries for yourself and for our dear children." [5] When Saint-Simon gushed with paternal love he could vie with any of the stage romantics: "The letter you wrote me was charming. I reread it twenty times. Your soul is loving. It is generous. It is moving. Your affection is my most wonderful reward. I shall soon have the joy of pressing you to my heart. . . ." [6]

Momentary elation over a few new subscriptions to his publications soon subsided. Back in Paris he lived in his old quarter, near the Palais Royal, the haunt of his Directory days. He had rooms above the Passage Hulot at 34 Rue de Richelieu. A rather unsympathetic visitor, Dr. Poumiès de la Siboutie, has left a description of the place. "His apartment was a perfect model of the most complete disorder. There was not an unencumbered seat or chair. . . . On his desk the most varied objects were piled up: books, papers, crusts of bread, dirty linen, bottles of various shapes." [7]

Men with all sorts of freakish notions gravitated to Saint-Simon's apartment. No conception was too queer or outlandish as long as it bore the stamp of novelty. Among his friends was a Captain Montgéry, who would call when he returned from the high seas. He contributed to learned journals articles on industry, commerce, and naval matters, and he entertained strange ideas about floating mines and submarine warfare. Though not all the guests were starry-eyed — there was Jean-Baptiste Duvergier de Hauranne, the sober jurisconsult who in his long life compiled volume upon volume of laws, constitutions, decrees, and ordinances, and wrote numerous learned treatises on legislation.

Among the intimates who frequented his flat, the most assiduous were a group of doctors. [8] None of them were run of the mill medical men — they all had some quirk, a quixotic interest, or a fixed idea. Saint-Simon was now attached to the life-scientists and they to him; the great mathematicians and physicists of his days of prosperity had definitely dropped out of his orbit. Doctors Gall and Broussais, the phrenologists, continued a friendship which they had formed earlier in the century. From a few chance remarks it appears that they had a professional interest in his cranium, and as a matter of fact Gall performed an autopsy on him after his death, at which time he found supporting evidence for his own theories in the structure and convolutions of Saint-Simon's brain. The physiologist Blainville, probably the most reputable scientist among his acquaintances, had been well-disposed towards Saint-Simon since his reading of the *Mémoire sur la science de l'homme* in 1813; though he refrained from getting involved in Saint-Simon's "scientific" projects, he assisted him financially from time to time, and respected him as an enthusiast capable of correct intuitions.[9] Dr. Etienne-Marin Bailly was in many ways the most bizarre member of the circle; in addition to his professional practice, he had a militant interest in the French Philhellenic Society which agitated for Greek independence, and he dabbled in astronomy as well as in Dr. Gall's phrenology. He was the author of an imaginative treatise proving the existence of God and of free will on the basis of Gall's system. Auguste Comte, then in the full flush of his anticlericalism, was amused by this ingenious demonstration, which actually aroused some public notice. When Saint-Simon died, it was Dr. Bailly who delivered the funeral oration in the grand manner. To him at least Saint-Simon was an authentic prophet, though he did not figure among the Saint-Simonian disciples when the School was established.

The pittances sent to Saint-Simon by the bankers and the stray subscriptions he managed to collect for his periodicals were not enough to keep him going. A decade later the Saint-Simonian Lerminier, who compiled the traditions of the cult, wrote a moving description of the philosopher's deep despair over the general indifference to his system.

Saint-Simon was not even heard by his contemporaries. The noise of constitutional debates drowned his voice, which was lost amid the strife of parties. Disdain, mockery, oblivion, and poverty were the reward of his labors. He ardently loved glory and humanity. Humanity turned a deaf ear to him. Glory delayed in coming and was to appear only at his grave. Oh! what a frightful smile must move the lips of a man of genius who bears the ingratitude of his age in his heart. The struggle in the soul of Saint-Simon must have been terrible, for he succumbed to it, and casting away life with an overpowering disgust, he resolved to give himself to death.[10]

In the fragmentary *Lettre aux Européens* written at the turn of the century Saint-Simon had already expressed himself on the subject of the suicide of the great man ignored by his contemporaries. "Men of genius should always be in combat. A man of genius who is beaten and cannot hope to be victorious in a new battle should kill himself. In this corps there can be no invalids. Men of genius are veritable gods. They should leave humanity when they can no longer govern it." [11]

On Sunday March 9, 1823, the philosopher of progress and humanity,

of the triumph of science and a reorganized industrial society, was resolved
to die. To Ternaux, the leading textile manufacturer of France and one of
his intermittent supporters, he wrote a last letter:

Sir, after having reflected deeply, I have become convinced that you were
right in telling me that it would take longer than I imagined before public
interest would be aroused by the works which have long been my sole occupation. Hence I have decided to bid you adieu. My last sentiments are those of
profound esteem for your person and an exalted attachment to your noble and
philanthropic character. Permit me to offer you my heart for the last time. I bear
away with me a great sorrow — leaving behind in a frightful position the woman
who has stood by me. This woman has given me great proof of devotion and
disinterestedness. I beg you, with all possible insistence, to grant her your protection. She is not a servant. She is a worker who has a fine intelligence and a
delicacy which makes her capable of filling any confidential position. I conclude
with the hope that you may live long for the happiness of all who have ties with
you.[12]

There is a theory that the final crushing blow fell when Auguste Comte
failed to deliver the promised text, long since overdue, for one of their
periodicals — a terrible defeat since Saint-Simon had already spent the money
collected for this purpose from his industrialist friends.

Two days before, sacks of his manuscripts had been sent off to someone,[13] it is not clear why, perhaps as security for a petty loan. Having
despatched Julie on an errand, Saint-Simon loaded his pistol with seven
bullets and placed it on his customary work table. Then, according to the
tradition handed down to the Saint-Simonians, he took out his watch and
proceeded to think once more about the reorganization of society, determined
to continue the exercise of his intellectual faculties up until the very moment
which he had fixed for the final act. He pulled the trigger and fired the shots
at his head. But he did not die. After a while he was able to gather up enough
strength to call on Dr. Sarlandière, who lived on the same floor. When he
found nobody at home, he made his way back to his own apartment, got
a basin, sat down on the bed, and let the blood flow. Julie found him there
and summoned the doctor. "Explain this, my dear Sarlandière," were Saint-
Simon's words of greeting, "a man with seven bullets in his head can still
live and think."

Without entering into a physiological discussion, the doctor made a
hurried inspection of the room in search of the bullet shells. When he found
only six of them, he inferred that the seventh had lodged in Saint-Simon's
brain and he considered him doomed. Upon the philosopher's demand for
a straightforward prognosis, Sarlandière expressed the opinion that Saint-
Simon would probably die in the night from hemorrhage.

In the meantime Auguste Comte, who had heard of the incident, made
his appearance.[14] "Come then," Saint-Simon urged his disciple, "let us use

to good purpose the hours which remain. Let us talk about our work." Night brought on such searing pains that Saint-Simon pleaded with those who stood around him to cut his jugular vein. Death seemed inevitable. Next morning the seventh bullet was discovered in the ashes of the hearth, and in a few weeks he recovered. The bullets had grazed the skull and pierced an eye, which was lost.[15] Saint-Simon's friends made an effort to hush up the story of the suicide attempt and gave out a stock explanation to the effect that he shot himself accidentally while toying with his pistol. The police were incredulous when they discovered the letter to Ternaux, a note to Julie Juliand, and an affectionate adieu to his old friend Coutte, begging forgiveness for the grief he would cause him.[16]

His industrialist and banker friends were somewhat shaken, and Basterrèche, Ardoin, Ternaux, and Laffitte sent him enough money to proceed with the publication of the *Catéchisme des industriels*. His letters to his daughter once more struck a jubilant note, and he began to attract public attention again.

29

The Master Denied

EVEN BEFORE THE SUICIDE ATTEMPT, Saint-Simon's relations with Auguste Comte had become strained. In the spring of 1824 a quarrel which had long been smoldering flared up. The final rupture ended a collaboration between two of the most extraordinary thinkers in modern times. Their friendship degenerated into a fishwives' squabble which, as might be expected among philosophers, had overtones of profound theoretical dispute and psychological conflict.

During the trial of Saint-Simon in 1820 Auguste Comte had still identified himself with his master's doctrine, even though both of them were aware by that time that their ideas on specific issues had begun to diverge.[1] Comte was delighted over the public vindication of Saint-Simon and jubilantly reported to his friend Valat the success of "our defense." The king's prosecutor could fulminate against a few censorable brochures and win cases against their subversive authors, but never, wrote Comte, could he triumph over doctrines like theirs that were solid thought structures.[2]

During the early years of their relationship Auguste Comte had played it safe. He avoided signing his articles, and Saint-Simon assumed complete legal responsibility for the opinions expressed in the periodicals which in effect they had edited together. This arrangement seemed to be one of common consent. It would have been no consolation for Saint-Simon to have his "pupil" hanged along with him. As for young Comte, he would have been delighted to proclaim his authorship of various articles, if only for reasons of amour-propre, and the public trials did not scare him, but he was afraid lest his parents down in Montpellier learn that he was getting himself enmeshed in subversive politics.

In the twenties, however, Auguste Comte reached the point of philosophical maturity where he was no longer able to endure Saint-Simon's tutelage, and he became less concerned about shocking his family than about his subordinate position with respect to the old philosopher. When the break finally occurred, Comte announced it in long, analytical letters to his friends, for he had to retract his old enthusiasm for his master. At first the young man was calm and perceptive enough to view his relationship with Saint-Simon with a certain detachment, as he would a historical process. Like metropolitan countries towards their colonies, Comte explained, Saint-Simon revealed a fundamental "physiological" — we would now say "psychological" — fault; since Comte had once been his pupil he expected him to remain his pupil indefinitely, even after his "beard had begun to grow." As long as Comte needed to complete his education, he had been able to tolerate Saint-Simon's "regulation" of his works, but as he matured, the imposition became unbearable. By 1824 Comte had come to believe that for the past four years not only had Saint-Simon taught him virtually nothing new, but, what was more serious, the supervision of the master had tended to fetter and to stifle his philosophical talents.[3]

After a long period of disturbed, vexatious relationships, during which they had tried to conceal their mounting mutual annoyance with each other, the issue came to a head in the spring of 1824 over the publication of Comte's *Système de politique positive* as a cahier in Saint-Simon's *Catéchisme des industriels*. They had protracted arguments about this work, during which Comte became convinced that Saint-Simon was madly jealous of his rising fame, that he wanted to "hold him under cover," to make a mere instrument of him. In one climactic outburst Comte bluntly told Saint-Simon that only dullards could endure such a status. The dispute with Augustin Thierry was being reënacted. It had previously been decided that Saint-Simon should sponsor a work by Comte which was to appear in two parts, one a systematic presentation of their common doctrine and the other a history of civilization illustrating the doctrine. After months of delay it was agreed to publish the theoretical part separately, and they were about to go to press when Saint-Simon came forward with the proposal that the treatise should appear anonymously in the *Catéchisme des industriels*, which to Comte meant assigning the authorship to Saint-Simon. Moreover, Saint-Simon, who disagreed with some of the principles enunciated by Comte, wanted to prefix an introduction in his own manner. Comte flatly refused, belaboring Saint-Simon with grievances which he had long borne secretly in his heart. Saint-Simon conceded with reluctance to a separate title page for Comte, and to the omission of any alien introduction; their understanding was formalized in a written agreement. After the bitter wrangling Saint-Simon curtly informed his pupil that their association was at an end.

Disinheritance was a crushing blow to Auguste Comte, because it was only through Saint-Simon that he maintained contact with the liberal Paris journals which could afford to pay honoraria to their contributors. This source of income would now be drying up, and he would have to seek other means of subsistence. Incensed, he wrote his friend Tabarié on April 5: "I shall never pardon M. de Saint-Simon for this, because it is pure vengeance, motivated by nothing and leading to nothing. . . ." [4] Comte now felt that his part in their collaboration had always been at least as fruitful as Saint-Simon's, that for seven years he had been strung along with promises of financial independence once their publications succeeded, and now, abruptly, he had been cut off. Saint-Simon had agreed to send the *Système de politique positive* to the subscribers of the *Catéchisme des industriels* and to give Comte a hundred copies for his own distribution; but for the rest, there was to be nothing further between them. To Comte this meant that he would be obliged to toady to "influential people" in order to earn a living, an odious prospect.

Despite the apparent finality with which he had been dismissed, the ultimate disposition of the second part of his work on the history of civilization remained a problem. It was not clear whether a contractual commitment existed for its publication by that same group of industrialists who were financing the *Catéchisme des industriels*. Comte had no illusions about the popular appeal of his writing, and he realized that in this group lay his main chance to secure patrons for his work, but under no circumstances was he prepared to compromise his "intellectual independence." He had chafed long enough under the journalistic hand of Saint-Simon, who was always intent upon swaying mass opinion and altering his work with that in mind. Comte was writing for an élite of scientists and philosophers, not for the mob. For the future, he was resolved to be more wary and circumspect; he was determined not to surrender any new manuscript unless he were assured equality of status with Saint-Simon vis-à-vis the industrialists who backed the *Catéchisme des industriels*. Comte had become quite cocky and he thought he could win his point. "This is a plan to which he will accede, I believe, because he definitely has far more need of me than I of him." [5]

When it was finally published, the complicated introductory material of the *Catéchisme des industriels, troisième cahier*, was eloquent printed testimony that no real agreement had been effected between Saint-Simon and Auguste Comte. First, there was a title page bearing the description *Catéchisme des industriels IIIe cahier*, followed by two pages of prefatory material written by Saint-Simon, though unsigned, in which he treated the work as the fulfillment of a project he had announced in his first issue, "the task of expounding the generalities of our system." [6] Praise of the final achievement was mingled in equal proportions with criticism: the work was "very good" but it had failed to expound all the generalities of the system and had erred in its emphasis. "In the system which we have conceived the industrial capacity is the one which must be placed in the front rank. It is the one which should judge the value of all the other capacities and make them all work for its greatest advantage." [7] While in Saint-Simon's plan the industrials would grant equivalent rank and esteem to the secondary capacities, which he had symbolically identified with Plato and with Aristotle, Comte had made the "error" of opting for the primacy of the Aristotelian capacity of the members of the Academy of Physical and Mathematical sciences, in short the scientists, and subordinating the spiritual or Platonic and the industrial capacities. Viewed philosophically, Comte's deviation highlighted the "scientific part" of the system and neglected the "sentimental and religious" part. Saint-Simon promised to right this imbalance himself in later *cahiers* of the periodical.[8] But despite its "imperfections" he concluded "formally" that the work appeared to him "the best writing which had ever been published on general politics."[9]

Saint-Simon's introductory material was followed by another title page which read *Système de Politique Positive par Auguste Comte, ancien élève de l'Ecole Polytechnique, élève de Henri Saint-Simon, Tome Premier. Première Partie.* There was no publisher, merely the announcement *"A Paris, Chez les principaux libraires."* After the title page there was inserted a four-page *Avertissement de l'auteur*, by Auguste Comte, announcing that this was the first of a series of works in which he proposed to establish that "politics [*politique*] should today be raised to the rank of the sciences of observation," and to apply politics in this sense to the "spiritual reorganization of society."[10] He then proceeded to outline the structure of the first two volumes as a philosophical prospectus of his total philosophy, at once an exposition of the plan of scientific works which were necessary for the establishment of a *politique* and a first attempt to execute the plan. Volume I was intended to dispose of two fundamental problems: the methodology of *physique sociale* and its application, or "a scientific bird's-eye view of the laws which have governed the general course of civilization, and as a result, a first *aperçu* of the social system which the natural development of the human species should today render dominant."[11] Then he launched into an equivocal description of his relations with Saint-Simon, making obeisance to his master at the same time that he declared his independence. Though he liked to call himself "the pupil of M. de Saint-Simon" he had been led to adopt an approach distinct from that of his master. He hesitated to make the break definitive, and in print he glossed over their dispute as "two different paths towards the establishment of the same political system."[12]

In the spirit of Saint-Simon's introductory remarks, Comte subscribed completely to the philosophical principle that the reorganization of society in its spiritual aspect required two types of works of equal importance though of opposite character. His definitions were somewhat different from Saint-Simon's Platonic and Aristotelian capacities: "The first, which require the use of the scientific capacity, have as their object the remaking of general doctrines; the others, which have to put into play the literary and artistic capacity, consist of the renewal of social sentiments."[13] Saint-Simon's mission, he wrote, had been the discovery of the principal conceptions in both branches of this "great philosophical operation." He, Comte, had meditated on M. de Saint-Simon's seminal ideas for a long time and had then devoted himself to the perfection of "that part of the insights of this philosopher which related to the scientific direction." [14]

Comte's *avertissement* attempted to place his own thinking more or less in harmony with Saint-Simon's. He agreed that there were two spiritual capacities of equal importance — directly contradicting the criticism in Saint-Simon's introduction — and admitted that he was considering only one of them. As for the role of the industrialists he said nothing, thus avoiding a frontal clash with Saint-Simon. The conclusion reciprocated Saint-Simon's flattery and tried to strengthen the now tenuous link of their association. "I thought I ought to make public the preceding declaration, so that if my works appear to merit some approval, it should redound to the founder of the philosophical school of which I am honored to form a part." [15]

After this ponderous prefatory material came the text, with a new pagination and a title, *Plan des travaux scientifiques nécessaires pour réorganiser la société, par Auguste Comte, ancien élève de l'Ecole Polytecnique* [*sic*], *élève de Henri Saint-Simon*, with still another *Introduction*, and finally an *Exposé général*.

According to Comte's version of what had happened to produce this editorial mess — and though it is the only explanation available it is quite plausible — Saint-Simon broke his word. He did publish a hundred copies in the agreed manner, with a separate title page bearing Comte's name and without reference to the *Catéchisme des industriels*; these copies were delivered to Comte for his private distribution. But in addition, Saint-Simon had printed a thousand copies with only *Catéchisme des industriels* on the flyleaf and with his own special introduction, which were distributed to the regular subscribers of the periodical. None were on sale in the bookstores. In retaliation, before Comte sent around his allotment of copies of the *Système de politique positive*, he tore off his own fulsome acknowledgement of discipleship. As far as Comte was concerned, there had been a clear breach of faith, and he took the position that no formal publication of the work had occurred. Whenever Saint-Simon had questioned him about the second part, he had lied, on his own admission, pretending that he was occupying himself with revisions. Now he was planning a one-volume edition of both parts under his own title and with his own name, a format which never appeared.[16]

In a letter to young Gustave d'Eichthal on May first, Comte, outraged by Saint-Simon's deception, gave full vent to his bitter anger. He no longer explained the enmity between them on grounds of simple envy and jealousy alone. His earlier psychological theory, which proved that the fight was inevitable, inherent in the very nature of their physiological "organizations," was now barbed with contempt and sometimes with hate. The trouble with Saint-Simon was that no real collaboration with him was possible unless one resigned oneself to being his tool, since Saint-Simon was convinced that only he was the discoverer of great new ideas and that at most others could contribute to the perfection of his original insights in some minor respect. Saint-Simon considered himself an exception to the ordinary rules of physiology, immune to the deterioration of age. He believed that his mind was sharper than it had ever been. Comte, with the brutality of youth, wrote his friend that Saint-Simon had grown senile and ought to retire forthwith from the philosophical profession.

Comte dwelled on Saint-Simon's terrible passion to dominate, a passion he recognized well because it was also one of the most powerful drives of his own nature, a passion he would in later years exercise in a merciless tyranny over his own friends and disciples. He had come to suspect that Saint-Simon planned to appropriate for himself the major part of whatever glory their joint works might win. His final analysis of Saint-Simon makes the philosopher out to be a publicity-mad monster, prepared to resort to any device in achieving his purpose.

I had been warned seven years ago, when I entered into relations with him, by people who I now realize knew him well, that his morality reduces itself at bottom to the Machiavellianism of a man who has a determined end, to cause a sensation in the world. For him all means are valid as long as they lead to this goal. As a result he is capable of great acts of generosity, but only on condition that one become a willing tool. I had once indignantly refused to share this opinion, but today I am forced to admit that it sums up my relationship with him. The fact is, that as long as I did not desire a separate and independent existence in the eyes of the world (and in effect as long as I simply remained a pupil, that is to say in the first two or three years, I did not look for that), I pleased him completely. But as soon as I wanted to be and appear myself there was nothing but wrangling in our relations.[17]

By mid-July Auguste Comte was determined that in future editions of his work the title page would no longer bear the legend "pupil of Saint-Simon" after his name. At most he would acknowledge his intellectual obligations to his former teacher in a few lines in the preface and he would be more precise in defining his debt than the vague word pupil connoted.

When the *Système de politique positive* proved to be a substantial success, Comte felt that his declaration of independence from Saint-Simon had been eminently justified. He was so elated by the general acclaim that he wanted to eradicate the name of Saint-Simon from his mind. He wrote his confidant Tabarié:

"Now you may rest assured that henceforward I shall behave as if this man had never existed. He has done me so much harm that I shall be rendering him a service if I do nothing more than forget him." [18]

When late in 1824 Saint-Simon put out the volume entitled *Opinions littéraires, philosophiques et industrielles,* Comte, who was then working on the first drafts of the system of positive philosophy, regarded the diffuse miscellany as nothing more than a hash. As usual, it appeared without attribution of authorship. Saint-Simon was operating as the head of a "school" with a doctrine to which individuals were subordinate. According to Comte's information, Saint-Simon wrote half of the *Opinions* himself and significantly influenced the essays of the other collaborators. Comte's estimate of their performance, spun out in a long letter to d'Eichthal, was devastating.[19] Léon Halévy's piece was "bad political literature," Duvergier on "legislation" was weak, Bailly's article on the relationship of physiology and politics would have been miserable even for a *littérateur*, Rodrigues' composition on the political importance of industrialists and bankers was "not exactly bad," but had only a remote connection with the subject. Saint-Simon's sections he dismissed as an endless, wearisome repetition of the same old ideas. What Comte found especially absurd was that Saint-Simon, forthrightly posing the question as to whether the reorganization of society should be effected suddenly or slowly, had made an abrupt volte-face and elected the first alternative. To Comte this smacked of the revolutionary Jacobinism which together they had inveighed against so frequently. He was irritated by the inclusion of a ready-made little constitution for the new society.

Saint-Simon had announced a forthcoming second volume of *Opinions*. All this was preparatory to the issuing of a journal which was to propagate their ideas, for they were already a "school," this little group. Comte mocked them. He did not believe in the reorganization of society through schools of propaganda and clubs. That was again the time-worn method of the Jesuits and the Jacobins, of which the Saint-Simon group was nothing but a tawdry imitation. The only community he recognized was an élite of scientists and philosophers, who needed no formal organization and whose discoveries were not meant for the mob. For the nonce he knew only two persons who were members of that true school of positive philosophers — himself and his correspondent Gustave d'Eichthal.

Comte denigrated the whole new Saint-Simonian enterprise, and predicted that the bankers would abandon it before it was even started. They had invited his collaboration, but anything in which Saint-Simon had a part repelled him (though in an early letter he said he would coöperate simply to earn some money) and was doomed to failure. Comte deplored the fact that bankers and industrialists who had a genuine interest in the public welfare should have fallen into the hands of Saint-Simon.

Comte's envy of Saint-Simon's success among the businessmen was transparent. If the journal should possibly have any success, it would immediately be seized by the government because of Saint-Simon's "revolutionary extravagance"; but it was pointless even to speculate about such an eventuality, for the journal could not succeed. The age was not ripe for philosophical coteries and doctrines, and in this period of anarchy, none could take hold and dominate. The present state of society was best characterized as a "government of money"; that was the only passion which possessed his contemporaries. He expected the social disintegration to become far worse before it could be remedied. Some terrible disorder, he prophesied, would have to shake society before men would be morally prepared to turn to a spiritual doctrine which would regenerate them.

Comte never shared Saint-Simon's admiration for the industrialists or his boundless confidence in their patronage of science. In a letter to Gustave d'Eichthal on November 24, 1825, he warned against the dangers to science of their prospective ascendancy. "Today those people think they are coming into the sole possession of power and they are growing impertinent like nobles, perhaps even more so. If they were given free play they would make mere engineers out of scientists who would be put on bread and water if they failed to invent a new gadget a week." [20]

The new journal heralded by the *Opinions — Le Producteur —* finally appeared after Saint Simon's death. Though at first Comte disdained any part of it, his need for money induced him to become a collaborator — *à contre-coeur*, because he anticipated the irksome censorship of *"Rodrigues et compagnie."* Comte's association with the disciples was short-lived. He could not stomach their deification of the master, and by the end of 1828 he was already poking fun at their plan to found a new religion, a "sort of incarnation of the divinity in Saint-Simon." [21] How bitter was his disillusionment when he found that Gustave d'Eichthal, his one disciple, to whom he had freely unburdened himself of all his grievances against Saint-Simon, to whom he had confided his most intimate philosophical and psychological reflections, was swept along by the religious wave of the Saint-Simonian school. On December 7, 1829, he sent d'Eichthal a biting, sarcastic letter, enclosing an admission card to the opening of his course on positive philosophy: "Since the change of direction which your mind has just taken, I must admit to you that I no longer count on you for anything. You are on so sublime a summit that you must, even against your will, pity our wretched positive studies, which you no longer need and which on the contrary would trouble your theological labors." [22]

When the Saint-Simonians actually transformed themselves into a religious cult and their meetings became a public scandal which ultimately brought them before the King's Bench, Auguste Comte took himself off. His erstwhile colleagues charged that he had stolen all his doctrines from them, a contention which drew from Comte a nasty letter to Michel Chevalier, editor of their new organ *Le Globe.*

For a number of years, Sir, I had a very intimate association with Saint-Simon, and this was a good deal earlier than the relations which any of the chiefs of your society could have had with him. This relationship had entirely ceased about two years [sic] before the death of the philosopher, consequently at a time when there was not yet the slightest question in the world of Saint-Simonians. I must, moreover, have you take note that M. de Saint-Simon had not as yet adopted a theological coloration and that our rupture might even be attributed in part to the fact that I began to discern in him a theological tendency profoundly incompatible with the philosophical direction which is characteristic of my thought.[23]

Chevalier was not daunted by Comte's testiness. With an admixture of acrimony and apostolic zeal, he exhorted him to return to the master's teachings. "For seven years you were by Saint-Simon's side and you were loved as a son. While under his fruitful influence you wrote the *Système de politique positive* which assures you a high rank among the thinkers of our time. All that you have since written is only a commentary on this work, even as the *Système* itself is the elaboration of a work written by Saint-Simon while you were still in the cradle, under the title *Lettre d'un habitant de Genève à ses contemporains.*" With passionate irony the young Chevalier attacked the ingrate: "Tell me, sir, ever since you carefully struck from the third pamphlet of the *Catéchisme des industriels* the name of the master of all of us . . . have you been happier?" [24]

The Saint-Simonians soon despaired of Comte's conversion, for he himself became a Messiah and a High Priest of Humanity, the founder of a rival positivist religion.

For almost twenty years Comte abided by his resolution never again to refer to his relationship with Saint-Simon, but attention was finally drawn to it by other men. When in the fifties some notice was given to Comte's works, both critics and disciples began to question him about the influence of Saint-Simon. Comte was sensitive on the point and believed that his enemies had resurrected his old friend only to plague him and to accuse him of having plagiarized his major ideas. With the publication of George Lewes's *Comte's Philosophy of the Sciences*, which casually noted the connection of the two men, the whole problem became known to Comte's American correspondents and followers.[25] In answer to the charges of his adversaries, Comte fought furiously for his claim to originality in all the ideas which he had developed, and in his letters of this period the repudiation of Saint-Simon's effect upon his doctrine became an *idée fixe*. He freely admitted their association during a brief period, but he always sought to prove that he had learned nothing from him because the old philosopher had been confused and befuddled. Far from attributing any dominant role to the obfuscated ideas of Saint-Simon, Comte maintained that any one of the other friends of his youth — such as Jean-Baptiste Say and Charles Dunoyer — had been of far greater importance to him.[26] His spiritual antecedents were Hume, Kant, Condorcet, and de Maistre, Gall and Bichat, not the venal and corrupt Saint-Simon. When, in order to torment him, Comte's detractors revived the idea that his profound law of the three states had been borrowed, he could find no epithet violent enough to hurl at them. In the introduction to the *Système de politique positive* he mentioned the foolish old philosopher of the Restoration with disdain, and in one of his last letters he called him a "depraved juggler." [27]

Comte's attempt to minimize the significance of Saint-Simon led him to search deeply in his own soul for memories of even earlier teachers, and he ended by discovering Daniel Encontre, a professor of dogma in the Faculty of Protestant Theology at Montauban. In 1850 Comte made elaborate inquiries about Encontre, and after a resuscitation, in a "subjective positivist" sense, had been achieved, he dedicated *La synthèse subjective* to him. Encontre, primarily a mathematician, had prepared Comte at the lycée of Montpellier for the entrance examination to the Ecole Polytechnique, and to this professor's view of the sciences Comte attributed his first intellectual awakening. Encontre apparently was an inspiring teacher, but in extolling him Comte was chiefly interested in belittling the "unworthy Saint-Simon." [28]

After Comte's death, friends and disciples of both positivist messiahs aligned themselves into two forces, proclaiming or denying the influence of Saint-Simon on Comte.[29] Of those who have written on the problem, Deroisin, a rather heretical Positivist, who heard Comte harangue against Saint-Simon in the fifties, had keen insight into how the hostility felt by the High Priest of Humanity towards the founder of the New Christianity was translated into dogma. "Comte had become possessed by hatred for the memory of Saint-Simon. I always heard him speak of him without restraint. Even in his courses he treated him severely. . . .

"Comte's hostility against the Jesus Christ type has been explained by his assimiliating Christ's usurpation of St. Paul's title of founder of the new religion with the attempt to usurp his own brevet as the initiator of the positive philosophy in favor of Saint-Simon." [30]

A reëxamination of the manuscripts and published works both of Saint-Simon and Auguste Comte during the early twenties cannot settle the controversy, but it helps to understand it. The key work is Comte's *Prospectus des travaux scientifiques nécessaires pour réorganiser la société*, which appeared in April 1822 in conjunction with Saint-Simon's inconsequential little essay *Du Contrat social*. This *Prospectus* which was issued in only fifty copies marked *Epreuve* Comte himself considered the first draft of his positive philosophy and positive polity. Begun when he was twenty-four and still a close collaborator of Saint-Simon, it already included the law of the three states and adumbrated the basic positive classification of the sciences. The act of composition for Comte was a momentous one. He was so self-conscious about its significance that he noted the precise hour and minute of writing at the head of each section. The draft did not flow smoothly and there was much writing and rewriting. One half a page is filled with a doodle of his name and his first initial. The young man was asserting himself.[31] A reworking of this opuscule became the controversial April 1824 pamphlet entitled *Système de politique positive, t. I, première partie*. With some changes Comte later reprinted it as the *Plan des travaux scientifiques nécessaires pour réorganiser la société*, an appendix to volume IV of the *Système de politique positive*.

Comte was preparing for the April 1822 essay during the time that he participated in the writing and editing of *L'Organisateur* and *Du système industriel* from 1819 through the first half of 1822. The cover of Comte's 1822 manuscript bore the title *Suite des travaux ayant pour objet le système industriel*; thus he proclaimed that his work was part of the general theory of the *"système industriel."* A textual analysis reveals many parallel passages and ideas in the cahiers of *Du système industriel* and Comte's essay. Does this indicate that Comte was merely utilizing his own contributions, that he was borrowing from Saint-Simon, or, what is more probable, that he was combining his own ideas with those of Saint-Simon? During this formative period it is no more possible to separate the proprietary rights of Saint-Simon or Comte from their common store of ideas than it would be to perform the same task for Marx and Engels. Manuscript notes of Comte and Saint-Simon are therefore not conclusive. Saint-Simon was the man of the spoken word and his writing was far inferior to Comte's in its structural organization. The flashes of insight, however, were Saint-Simon's surely as often as they were Comte's.

Comte believed that he was making revolutionary discoveries in *physique sociale*, that he was laying down fundamental laws of social science. No doubt he experienced sudden moments of scientific illumination when the facts ordered themselves in a pattern which he called a law. Saint-Simon had these moments of intuitive ecstasy under the Empire. It is impossible to deny that both of Comte's fundamental conceptions, the law of the three states and the hierarchic classification of the sciences, were present in embryonic form in Saint-Simon's writings long before he knew Comte and in more developed form during the years of their collaboration. To maintain that all the original ideas of *L'Industrie, L'Organisateur*, and *Du système industriel* were the products of Comte's genius and to dismiss Saint-Simon as nothing more than a "magnetic personality" is to ignore the facts. Such a thesis must gloss over the writings of the Empire and reduce to nullity Saint-Simon's part in the works of the Restoration.[32]

Undoubtedly Saint-Simon felt rancor towards the fledglings who drifted off on their own. On the other hand he was among the first to announce Comte's part in their common work — he advertised Comte's talent in the salons, introduced him to the journalists of Paris, enthused about him to his own patron Ternaux, granted him status on their editorial boards. After Comte had assimilated Saint-Simon's insights he realized the intrinsic superiority of his own organizational powers, he chafed at the bit, he wanted to break loose, to realize his own potentialities. He saw only the weakness of the old philosopher, particularly after the suicide attempt, and he rebelled against his domination.

For Saint-Simon Comte's defection was a personal tragedy. He knew that he had neither the solid scientific training nor the capacity to formulate grand conceptions with which his young assistant was gifted. But Comte not only deprived his master of the use of his talents. When he proceeded to write in an independent direction he was challenging the essential nature of Saint-Simon's "system," which was unitary. The whole purpose of the industrial philosophy was to call a halt to the battle of systems, to achieve integral unanimity in the spiritual and in the temporal world. The young man who left to work in isolation was not simply producing a variant on the truth which might be tolerated; he was a traitor to the unity of the system, an egotist whose vile deed would protract the chaos of contemporary society. Saint-Simon could no more endure this subversion of his monist principle, though garbed in the magic word positivist, than he could brook the false and misleading ideologies of theologians and metaphysicians. In his relations with Comte the inevitable counterpart of his philosophical monism had to be personal absolutism.

30

True Disciples

SIMULTANEOUSLY WITH THE COMTE QUARREL, a group of young enthusiasts made their way into Saint-Simon's circle of friends. As the relations with Comte grew cooler, Saint-Simon's ties with the newcomers became more intimate. It was in their arms that he died. These disciples were young Jewish intellectuals, sons of assimilated Paris banking families and leaders of the religious community. Saint-Simon founded the New Christianity in association with these Jewish neophytes.

At the home of the banker Ardoin, Benjamin Olinde Rodrigues was presented to Saint-Simon. Rodrigues was captivated by this "most curious man," and he talked about him to his two cousins, Emile and Isaac Pereire, who were living in his father's house.[1] They too were drawn to the philosopher, along with Olinde Rodrigues's brother Eugène. At a later date they were joined by Gustave d'Eichthal,[2] whose family, like the Rodrigues and the Pereires, were private Jewish bankers and speculators on the Bourse. This is the young d'Eichthal whose famous correspondence with John Stuart Mill is eloquent testimony of the soul-searching among youthful intellectuals on both sides of the channel. For a number of years d'Eichthal considered himself a disciple of Auguste Comte, but when the Saint-Simonian cult was organized he was swept into the movement along with his friends, to the accompaniment of his young master's sardonic jeers.

Under the Bourbon Restoration the Jews lost many of the civil rights which had been bestowed upon them by the Revolution and Napoleon. With the reimposition of Catholic religious tests, Jews were expelled from the universities and successful careers cut short. The fate of Olinde Rodrigues, a brilliant mathematician, is typical of Jewish intellectuals under the Restoration.[3] Unable to pursue his academic studies, he got himself a job at the *Caisse Hypothécaire* and eventually became one of its directors. Promising young scientists had no choice but to retreat to the stock exchange and the financial world where Jews by this time were solidly entrenched. While the liberal professions were barred to them, their role in the economy was strengthened. The French branch of the Rothschild family who originally hailed from the Rhineland had emerged after the Empire as a secret power in the state. Emile and Isaac Pereire, whose family had migrated to Paris from Portugal via Bordeaux, were destined to become their rivals for the control of the banking and credit system of France under the Second Empire.

This return to the stock exchange made restless malcontents of the young Jews before whom new horizons had been opened under Napoleon. They were confused and bewildered by the recrudescence of a religious intolerance from which they had believed themselves secure. Alfred de Musset and Stendhal have described the trauma produced by the clerical reaction on other young Frenchmen — not Jews — who, nurtured on visions of military glory, suddenly found the black cassocks in command. While Julien Sorel could switch allegiance with conscious hypocrisy and play along with the clerics for his own advancement, the young Jews who were thrown out of the universities had no such alternative. Traditional Judaism had ceased to have spiritual meaning for them. The Jewish religion as practiced in Paris had been "reformed," watered down to a few holiday observances and the acceptance of a morality that was vaguely theist. *Limude Dat U-musar*, a brief compendium of moral teachings published by Elie Halévy, the secretary of the Jewish community in Paris, is characteristic of this denatured Judaism which expressed itself in the formula of the Alliance Israélite which he founded: *Tiens au pays, conserve ta foi.*[4]

There was religious enthusiasm among the young Paris Jews, but in the emotional chaos of the post-revolutionary age they knew not where to pour forth their fervor.[5] Conversions of Jews to Catholicism during the period were not mere devices to win social acceptance. In one branch of the Pereire family six sisters entered a nunnery. Their religious longing was romantic, after the manner of Chateaubriand, but they were also heirs to a rationalist tradition. They yearned for a religious system, a unity of emotive and rationalist moral values which could be embraced with devotion. Small stockbrokers in the twenties, they felt revulsion for a life wasted upon the petty pursuit of personal gain. Though their ancestors, too, had been merchants and moneylenders, they had suffered no spiritual crisis because they had had an absolute religious faith and a family morality which completely filled their emotional needs. From this faith the young Jews had been set adrift. Outcasts in Catholic France of the Restoration, they belonged to neither world. Their souls were empty, until the doctrine of Saint-Simon came to fill the void. In the meeting of Saint-Simon with the young Jewish intellectuals a perfect symbiotic relationship was established.[6]

Olinde Rodrigues became the central figure in the group, the favorite, the constant companion. After Saint-Simon's death, Rodrigues believed that he was the true heir to the doctrine, the interpreter of the mature philosophy of Saint-Simon's last years. He was by right the chief propagator of the new faith because he had heard the living word preached by the master himself. Others could interpret and reinterpret the writings, but he knew their secret meaning. It was a cruel cut for Rodrigues when a young engineer named Enfantin who had seen Saint-Simon alone but once — and had been barked at by his dog — was accepted as *Le Père* by the Saint-Simonians.[7] According to his own testimony, Rodrigues wrote the introduction and helped edit the text of the *Nouveau Christianisme*. In a universal religion of humanity the stigma which the Jews bore, they knew not why, would be erased. Once more the road would be open to talent and the universities would admit them. Religious faith would be expressed in brotherly love for all men, not in burning crosses on the countryside erected by the fanatics of the White Terror.

One day while walking with the philosopher in the Palais-Royal, Olinde Rodrigues introduced to Saint-Simon his friend Léon Halévy, son of the Elie Halévy who was cantor in the largest synagogue in Paris and secretary of the Jewish community.[8] Under Napoleon Léon Halévy had been a prize student at the Lycée Charlemagne; in his twenties he became an instructor in rhetoric and translated Horace into French verse. Daru lavished his praises upon him and Raynouard devoted an article to him in the *Journal des savants*.[9] But since Jews could not hold university posts under the Restoration, Léon Halévy had to await the July Revolution of 1830 before blossoming out as a professor of French literature and a bureaucrat in the Ministry of Public Education, a facile writer of poetry, verse translations, comedies, and tragedies.

In the eighteen-twenties Léon Halévy was another lost Jew in search of an absolute. There was a skeptical humanist streak in this translator of Horace and he could not follow the later extravaganzas of the Saint-Simonians, but as a youth he shared with the rest of his generation the sense of moral vacuity and he hungered for a new revelation. Along with Olinde Rodrigues he was among those closest to Saint-Simon when the doctrine was being clothed in the vestments of a new religion.

Léon Halévy was the last of Saint-Simon's aides and amanuenses. With his assistance Saint-Simon published the *Opinions littéraires, philosophiques et industrielles*. Halévy lacked the genius either of Augustin Thierry or of Auguste Comte, but he had a literary flair and drew a rather convincing portrait of the old philosopher in his recollections and in a poem he published in 1831 in vindication of the "true" theories of Saint-Simon, free from the corruptions of the cult. His ode, *Saint-Simon*, mocked the presumptuous sectaries who read "Gothic mysteries" into Saint-Simon's writings. For two years Halévy had listened to the long colloquies of the "man of ardent speech." He had observed him in the intimacy of his apartment, "his faithful dog and his frugal table, his stick, that sad support of his halting gait." He had been pierced by his "fiery look." [10]

When Léon Halévy called he would find Saint-Simon reading from a heap of cheap contemporary novelists like Madame de Genlis and Paul de Kock. This pile of mediocrity and bad taste did not embarrass Saint-Simon. The "physiologist of society" explained to his young secretary: "The history of the human heart, well or ill-narrated, can only be found there." One day Saint-Simon confessed that he actually preferred the stupidest novels, and Halévy noted that "his library served him well in that respect." Saint-Simon still worked at night. In the morning he would point to his desk smiling, "Open that drawer. Read the night's work. It is quite hot. It comes right out of the oven." It was not his custom to discuss his theories with many people at a time — one favorite sufficed. "Mankind has not yet advanced far enough for three persons to be able to converse together," he told Halévy.[11]

The effect of the Saint-Simonian ideology upon the Jews who joined the cult is one of the most curious phenomena of nineteenth-century intellectual and social history. It seems hardly credible that acute and forceful individuals like the Rodrigues brothers, the Pereire brothers, d'Eichthal, and Halévy, could ever swallow the romantic nonsense of the cult. Yet it would be unwarranted skepticism to doubt the sincerity of their religious conversion to this rather synthetic set of dogmas held together with pantheist emotionalism. Gustave d'Eichthal, one of the most brilliant of the circle, was so entranced by the mysteries of the cult that he even joined the Enfantin group in its search for the Female Messiah.[12]

Halévy left before the doctrines became too theological; Rodrigues was the center of the first schism; the Pereires endured in the faith somewhat longer. By 1832 the Pereires and Rodrigues had awakened from the dream world of the cult, but they carried over into the business ventures on which they embarked most of its basic ideology — the idea that the credit system was the heart of the social mechanism, that the bank was a modern temple, that their "combinations" did not serve primarily the ends of personal enrichmen, but social ideals — the exploitation of nature and the amelioration of man's lot in this world. Their railroad building and their initiation of intricate credit schemes were the fulfillment of a religious mission. God was using their *Crédit Mobilier* as an instrument through which the earth was made to prosper. They were dedicated to the expansion of the banking system as a pious Jew once consecrated himself to the worship of God. The credit system, the canals, the railroads would bring happiness to mankind, and they were the creative agents in this development. In their persons the spiritual and the temporal powers had once more been merged. It is hard to harmonize this ideology with the known business methods of the Pereires, their terrible claws in a showdown struggle for financial power with the rival Rothschilds, but the service of God never eliminated zealous warriors whose battle manners were not those of the drawing room.

31

The New Christianity

D URING THE FIRST TWO YEARS of the Restoration Saint-Simon, who now fancied himself a popular journalist and no longer a closeted philosopher writing in secret for a scientific élite, avoided doctrinal religious issues pretty completely. While he continued to treat the church as an institution, he never again leveled a direct attack on the idea of God in the crude manner of his Empire works. This decision was in part dictated by expediency, since the *bourgeois* who in the eighteenth century had relished Voltairean sallies against revealed religion would never have exposed themselves to charges of irreligion and atheism under the *émigré* government of the Bourbons. A single passing reference in his 1814 plan for European reorganization allowed for religious toleration, with a proviso however — the acceptance by all creeds of common moral principles.

Saint-Simon's demand in 1817 that the industrials adopt a new terrestrial and positive morality was a sudden departure. Industrials, he argued, were confronted by a dangerous dilemma. On the one hand, they could not support the traditional religious system of Catholicism unreformed because its other-worldly morality, the disdain of the church philosophers for business and productive activity, was an ever present affront to the ideals of the industrial society. Industrials were looked down upon as men whose rebellious efforts tended to establish on earth a happiness which God had prohibited to fallen man. The religious morality of the church and industrial civilization were in a deep sense incompatible with each other. The industrials lived by increasing the production and consumption of goods; the church had never been able to look upon consumption which gratified men's desires as anything but sinful indulgence, a distraction from preoccupation with the salvation of the soul. On the other hand, the destruction of Catholic morality before another was adopted to take its place could be catastrophic for the industrials. The French Revolution had demonstrated the hazards of leaving society without a unified set of generally accepted moral principles, and

Saint-Simon warned the industrials that stripping the proletariat of their morality would break the dike which held back their mad desire for equality. Industrials who controlled movable property had more to lose through pillage during a revolutionary outburst than did the noble owners of far-flung estates. Hence there was no escape from the dilemma but to embrace Saint-Simon's new terrestrial morality and labor for its universal acceptance.

The industrial society had to effect a transition from the old religious morality, which was anti-industrial and in any event could no longer contain men's passions, to a terrestrial morality which would be industrial in character, harmonious with the new science, and capable of holding ordinary men and dissuading them from egalitarian revolution. In *L'Industrie* Saint-Simon did not venture to call this positive morality a religion, but its substantive content was not dissimilar from the Physicism of the Empire. He was still thinking in terms of transforming the traditional religious institutions of Christianity through the infusion of new ideas — to him the perfect solution. In religion as in all societal forms he was opposed to an abrupt break between one historic organizational pattern and another. His ideal process of change envisaged one state of being merging into another without the leap of revolutionary action. It was preferable to have the same institutional personnel adopt a new ideology rather than face the monumental and perilous task of cashiering a social class. If priests would only become scientists the religious crisis could be successfully passed without violence. "All one asks is that present-day priests should be up to the standard of their century as their brothers in the middle ages were. Can one fear that the clergy will obstinately desire to have only idiots as its members?"[1] But the priesthood of the Bourbon Restoration was not eager to grasp the new scientific mission so flatteringly proffered to it. The *bourgeois* were terrified by his proposals for a terrestrial morality and dropped him cold.

In 1821 Saint-Simon gave up buffeting the current and tried a new tack. If conformity to Christian belief was the order of the day, he could hoist his religious sails as loftily as Chateaubriand. Instead of appearing as the enemy of Christianity, his system would proclaim itself as the only true Christianity. The device was not unique with Saint-Simon. After the anticlerical bouts of the previous age, a whole group of nineteenth-century reformers caught hold of the idea that attacking Christianity by name was a waste of moral capital. Why not invoke the spirit of Christianity against its institutional chiefs as Luther had once done with signal success? The tactic was destined to have a long history among utopians and revolutionaries in modern times, from Cabet's "*Le communisme c'est le vrai Christianisme*" to recent identical slogans paraded by world communism in Catholic countries.

By the eighteen-twenties Saint-Simon was fully conscious that the day of the antireligious *philosophe* was over. The very manners of polite Restoration society bore witness to a religious revival, however superficial.

"The present generation has caused to vanish from our books and our society that tone of frivolity and of pleasantry in matters of religious belief which the past generation flaunted. It is today almost universally disapproved, and even in the salons of our idlers it is reputed to be in bad taste. It has been replaced by a general feeling of respect for religious ideas which is based on a conviction of their present need."[2] Nevertheless he warned his readers not to confuse this vague "sentiment" with orthodox Catholic belief or to entertain any illusion that it was possible to reëstablish the old theological system as the doctrinaires of the theocratic school hoped. A great spiritual rebirth was about to take place, and he was not averse to calling it Christian, but it would be fundamentally different in character from what the *ultras* anticipated.

Chateaubriand and de Bonald had sufficiently exploited the idea that religion was sentiment and not opinion to make it almost commonplace.[3] The traditionalists had backed out of the *cul de sac* into which eighteenth-century apologists of the Church had landed them. They now bluntly refused to debate religious opinion with skeptics and atheists. If religion was a universal sentiment, proved by travel literature and man's experience throughout all time, then the rationalist acumen of the *philosophes* was irrelevant. The innovation of Saint-Simon was to muster all these traditionalist romantic conceptions of religion into the service of a New Christianity which was soon to label Roman Catholicism the teachings of Antichrist.

In *Du système industriel* Saint-Simon began to attach the term "Christian" to his industrial society and to refer to the morality of the New Testament with increasing frequency and approval.[4] He abandoned nothing of his basic Restoration philosophy of history, except that he now grafted upon it a religious ideal. The industrial society was still the great social reform which he hoped to see realized in his lifetime, but history itself had again become Christian. He retained his old conception of the organized period alternating with an epoch of transition, only now the four historical stages since Christ became four ages in the progress of Christianity. In prophetic tones he foretold an age of peace and plenty on earth as the culmination of Christian history.

I believe that during this fourth epoch [of Christianity] a new temporal and a new spiritual power will be organized.

I believe that the new spiritual power will in the beginning be composed of all the Academies of Science in Europe and of all persons who deserve to be admitted into these scientific corporations. I believe that once this nucleus is formed, those who compose it will organize themselves. I believe that the direction of education, as well as of public instruction, will be entrusted to this new spiritual power. I believe that the pure morality of the New Testament will serve as the foundation for the new system of public education, and that this education will be pushed as far as possible in the direction of positive knowledge, taking into account the different periods of time which the children of parents with various degrees of wealth will spend in school. Finally, I believe that the new spiritual power will settle a substantial number of its members throughout the communes, and these detached scholars will have as their principal mission to enflame their spiritual charges with a passion for the public weal.[5]

Beginning in 1821 he dwelt extensively upon religious and moral sentiment as the drive behind the final surge of humanity into the golden age of the industrial society. In *Du système industriel* he wrote a special address to philanthropists, the lovers of humanity, whom he described as modern counterparts of the propagators of the faith in early Christian times. Neither the Christian fathers nor the contemporary philanthropists were motivated by selfish personal interests or class interests. In both historic epochs they were direct agents of God, and they were inspired by a pure, religious zeal. The early Christians, whom Saint-Simon, inverting his analogy, called the first philanthropists, were able to convert the mighty of the earth to the principles of divine morality by the exercise of their spiritual force alone. In another groundswell of religious enthusiasm, modern philanthropists would force the nobles and ecclesiastics to accept the new manifestation of the Eternal One. The early organizers of the Christian Church were prototypes of the kind of philanthropic propagandists he hoped to enlist in the spread of his doctrine. In drawing the portrait of the church fathers he set up an ideal for his disciples which also served as a rebuke to the existing clergy of Europe who had fallen so far short of this image. The early Christian leaders were revered because they had in a superior measure the virtues required for propagating the faith — a greater capacity for courage, presence of mind, sagacity, strength of soul, disdain for life, and other heroic qualities. The power bestowed upon them did not give them the right to dominate, but was used in the exercise of administrative leadership and was revocable at the will of the early Christian communities.[6]

In reviewing the passages on religion in *Du système industriel*, one is struck with the contradictions to Saint-Simon's previous psychology of human motivation. Throughout most of his writings he had subscribed to a straightforward utilitarian doctrine, as developed by Hume, Adam Smith, and Bentham. Men were moved by two basic forces: self-love, self-interest, self-aggrandizement, and at the same time a sentiment of benevolence, *bienfaisance*, brotherly love, sympathy, humanity. Saint-Simon was more in the Scottish moralist tradition than in the French. A study of his writings leads to the conclusion that from 1802 to 1825 there was a shift in emphasis as to the relative potency of the two drives. In the *Lettres d'un habitant de Genève à ses contemporains*, when he was trying to convert humanity to a project for the advancement of science, his appeals were based almost exclusively on self-interest. Like most intellectuals of the age, he had an underlying belief in the harmony of individual self-interests if allowed free rein. To the Saint-Simon of this period an argument for a course of action based on the self-interest of an individual or class was well nigh irrefutable. If it could be proved that the establishment of an independent scientific priesthood was to the interest of the property-owning and the propertyless classes, it hardly seemed conceivable that men, their eyes once opened to their "interests," would fail to approve. At this period the "interests" of individuals and classes were defined in the common sense terms of ordinary usage. Men of property wanted security from revolution to enjoy their wealth and they sought its increase. Men without property wanted peace so that they would not be used as cannon fodder, and they hoped for greater material prosperity. Intellectuals had an interest in scientific achievement because it gave them an opportunity to exercise their faculties. All these interests, if correctly comprehended, were in harmony with one another. Men in each of these classes pursuing their own interests as they instinctively or rationally understood them would arrive at the same conclusion — in this case the Religion of Newton.

Throughout most of his life Saint-Simon continued to invoke the interests of individuals, often their economic interests. But towards the end he came to believe in the equal if not superior potency of an appeal to man's love for his fellows, his humanity, irrespective of his individual economic or class interest. *Du système industriel* (1821) bore the epigraph "God has commanded: Love and succor each other." His pleas became more generalized, based on the assumption that this humanity in man transcended class and individual interest, that once this passion were afire it would not be confined by considerations of immediate class or personal advantage. The vision of future happiness for all mankind could be translated into a drive for action which might even run counter to considerations of self-interest. It was obviously a highly desirable confluence of circumstances that the immediate selfish interest and the vision of brotherly love should be mutually sustaining drives for action, and Saint-Simon often believed that they were, but he was prepared to face a contradiction between them.

Though individual and class interests existed, they lost their overriding power to effect the transition to a new society. Saint-Simon discovered that men could be moved by a classless "passion for the general welfare" — witness the upper-class martyrs of primitive Christianity. Henceforth he laid great weight upon the individual act of conversion to the gospel of brotherly love in its new form — belief in the religious industrial scientific system.

Self-interest, which in previous writing he had analyzed without prejudice as the natural expression of men and of classes, he now stigmatized as *egotism*. Once he had appealed solely to self-interest to propagate his system; henceforth he would revile egotism. The basic division among men was no longer one of social classes, but of psychological classes: there were philan-

thropists and there were egotists. He lamented that in his own epoch the
egotists in all social ranks were increasing in number (a moral reality brilliantly diagnosed by his contemporaries Stendhal and Balzac) but fortunately the philanthropists were growing more energetic, he consoled himself.
Parenthetically he observed that those who lived far away from the people,
in isolation among the rich, tended to become egotists.

What course of action did he prescribe for the philanthropists, the lovers
of man, not of themselves? They were to preach, by word of mouth and in
writing. They were to convince the kings of the earth that "they should use
the powers authorized them by the people in order to effect the political
changes which have become necessary."[7] The words "new Christianity" appeared for the first time in 1821. Thereafter the doctrine became a full-
fledged religion, and he adapted traditional Christian religious terminology
to aid in its dissemination. He summoned the modern heretics — the warriors
and the clergy — to abjure their false Christianity and to transform themselves into philanthropists. God took the place formerly occupied by history.
It was now God who "condemns to annihilation those social institutions
which are harmful to the human species."[8] History was God and God was
history.

Saint-Simon's various religious posturings froze in a final attitude in the
Nouveau Christianisme, published shortly before his death. The work was
originally intended as an essay in the second volume of the *Opinions littéraires, philosophiques et industrielles*, his most recent collaborative publication. But the urgency of the political and moral crisis moved him to issue
it separately, and it appeared early in 1825, preceded by an unsigned introduction from the pen of Olinde Rodrigues which was an effort to smooth
the transition between his earlier philosophical works and the religious proclamation. The favorite disciple was only partially successful, for there is a
chasm between the two careers which cannot readily be bridged in a few
pages.[9]

As a manifesto of the New Christians, this last work of Saint-Simon's is
not a very pungent piece of writing. In many respects it is his dullest and
most turgid work. The tract has no clear plan; it is verbose and repetitive
and its occasional flights of fancy invariably fall flat. Nevertheless it was
revered by his disciples as the final testament of Saint-Simon and they strove
to discover in it a hidden sense. Unfortunately for his reputation as a
theorist, his name has been identified with this work above all others.[10] It
is the one most frequently translated.

Even in this tract the break with past doctrine is not absolute. Saint-
Simon is still the philosopher of an industrial scientific artistic society organized as an "aristocracy of talent." He still is the enemy of the warrior nobility
and the do-nothings. He still indulges in dialectical turns of thought, contrasts of epochs, of moral systems, of emotional drives. The heart of his whole

system, however, has changed, for it is now first and foremost a religion.

The *Nouveau Christianisme* is cast as a dialogue between an innovator (a New Christian) and a conservative, during the course of which the conservative is converted rather effortlessly. The opening lines announce the innovator's credo, his belief in the existence of God, in straightforward catechismic affirmations. The dialogue ends with a proof that Christianity is a religion which must have been inspired by divine revelation. Forgotten are the Physicism of the Empire and the sacrilegious Dupuis theory. In the New Christianity religion was no longer the mere expression of general science, even though scientific knowledge was a major prerequisite for the priesthood. The essence of Christianity was its moral content. Dogma and ritual in great religions were only utilitarian addenda, handmaidens of the moral principles, which were timeless and not subject to change; the philosopher who once used the phrase "nineteenth-century morality" had recanted his heretical, relativist doctrine. Only the physical sciences have had a history and there has been progress in the accumulation of their data. Morality since the revelation of Christ has had one principle and only one. The absolute perfection of this abstract moral truth could not be altered in time, even though the appropriate application of Christian morality would still be subject to the law of change and progress. In brief, the Christian moral principle was eternal; only its historical embodiment was relativist.[11]

The Christian religion, said Saint-Simon, was summed up in one sublime commandment, the Golden Rule: men should behave toward one another like brothers.[12] When the conservative expressed incredulity at this succinct reduction of Christianity, he was silenced with Saint-Simon's monist dogma: "It would be blasphemy to presume that the All-Powerful One founded his religion on several principles."[13] The Christian apostles had taught this principle of brotherly love in its original simple form in the primitive catechism.[14] Preached to a society that was still divided into two classes, the Roman masters and their slaves, it was a lofty, revolutionary principle. The early Christians were thus daring moral reformers whose principles were to dominate the medieval system. In the heyday of its power, Christian papal society went a long way towards the practical application of the Christian catechism in the abolition of slavery. But the injunction of the primitive catechism — to love one another as brothers — was not the ultimate formulation of the Christian principle.

By the fifteenth century the primitive form of the Christian principle had already become outmoded and urgently needed rejuvenation, but unfortunately the Catholic clergy, secure in their institutional powers, opposed any changes in the original expression of the moral principle. What is worse, they became inveterate enemies of its practical application, unlike their medieval predecessors, and they had remained so ever since. In the *Nouveau Christianisme* Saint-Simon threw caution to he winds. He arraigned the Papacy and the Catholic hierarchy before the bar of primitive Christianity and accused them of heresy. His language and tone were no longer circumspect: he labeled them Antichrists. They were heretics because for four hundred years the Christian principle had needed new raiment, and they refused to recognize its plight. It was no longer sufficient to preach brotherly love, for with the progress of science and the discovery of new worlds it was incumbent upon the church to recast Christianity into a morality which taught that to labor for the amelioration of the lot of the poorest and most numerous classes in society was man's goal on earth. ". . . [T]he vast majority of the population could enjoy a moral and physical existence which is far more satisfactory than what they have enjoyed thus far; and . . . the rich, by increasing the happiness of the poor, would ameliorate their own existence." [15]

The Papacy of the fifteenth century had not only been in a position to preach the new morality, it had actually been potent enough to implement it with positive action. A rational exploitation of world resources could have been organized by the Papacy as a practical way of affording the poor work and plenty. The Papacy at the time of the Reformation was in a far more favorable worldly situation for the practice of brotherly love than the primitive church fathers, who had been outcasts from temporal society. Instead, the papal power not only refrained from extending the enforcement of true Christian principle; in a spirit of negation it organized society to its detriment. The degenerate Papacy was symbolized by Leo X, who not only was uninterested in sponsoring projects for the benefit of the poor but publicly announced that the profits of indulgences would be spent on his own establishments and on his sister. "Leo X was of the dough that kings are made of and consequently he was not the proper man to be pope. . . ." [16]

The Papacy, moreover, sanctioned the creation of two of the most heretical institutions in Christendom, the Inquisition and the Society of Jesus. If Christianity was love, then the force, cruelty, violence, treachery, and deception practised by these institutions were overwhelming testimony to their heresy. Instead of converting the temporal princes to the Christian moral ideal, the Papacy entered into a corrupt bargain with them. It promulgated the false doctrine of the divine right of kings in order to keep the people in subjection and in exchange received from the monarchs a guarantee that the church would continue to enjoy unmolested its secular power, its lands and emoluments. As a result the church became transformed into a secular not a spiritual force. "The spiritual force, the force of morality, the Christian force, the one which bestows frankness and loyalty, is entirely absent. In a word, the Catholic, apostolic, and Roman religion is nothing else but a Christian heresy. It is only a segment of a degenerate Christianity." [17] If his conservative interlocutor needed further proof of the Papacy's violation of the Christian moral principle, Saint-Simon pointed to the administration of the Papal states, the most venal and oppressive in the world, worse than the rule of the Grand Turk.

The modern Catholic Church, by combatting science, by restricting the seminaries to theology, by refusing to educate, was intentionally hampering the progress of science, whose application would ultimately provide the necessary material conditions for alleviating the sufferings of the poor. This was proof of still another Papal heresy. In short, the most numerous religious association in the world, the Catholic Church, was anti-Christian. In his *Nouveau Christianisme* Saint-Simon attacked it with a vituperation and a scorn which he had once reserved for the lawyers and the metaphysicians. This was his last message to humanity. He was no longer counting on the timid *bourgeois*, but on his fiery young men to propagate the faith.

Luther and the Protestant sects fared no better at his hands than had the Catholic hierarchy. Luther had pretended to effect a reformation and insofar as he had castigated the vices of Catholicism he had labored well in the vineyard of the Lord. When it came to rejuvenating the church, however, he lapsed into heresy himself. Luther had appeared fifteen hundred years after Christ and of all men he should have been conscious of the progressive formula of the moral Christian principle. Instead he tried to revive the primitive Christian doctrine and the Old Testament, a work which contained many erroneous and immoral conceptions. He failed to encourage the participation of the artists in the worship of Christianity and he made religion prosaic by eliminating sculpture, painting, and music (*sic!*). Luther failed to realize that the religious principle had to progress in order to survive. His interpretation of the moral principle of Christianity was not in harmony with the level of civilization which had been attained in Christian Europe. By the sixteenth century the formulation of the Christian principle as set forth in the primitive catechism, which Protestantism revived, was regressive, for in the first centuries of the Christian era the "dimensions of the planet were not yet known, so that no general plan of amelioration could be conceived for the territorial property of the human species." [18]

Though Saint-Simon's attack on Protestantism was not as venomous as his anti-Catholic tirades, this was not to be interpreted as a sign of the superiority of the Lutheran doctrine. He was less interested in demonstrating which sect was more heretical than the other than in the fact that both were heretical. The apostles had accepted Caesar because they were still too weak to combat him, but Luther should at least have attempted to subjugate the temporal power of warlike princes who were devastating the world. If Luther had fulfilled his mission he would have called upon the Pope to issue a world plan of public works in these words:

"To ameliorate as rapidly as possible the existence of the poorest class, the most favorable condition would be presented if there were a vast number of public works to execute and if these works would require the greatest development of human intelligence. You can create this condition. Now the dimensions of our planet are known. Have the scientists, the artists, and the industrialists prepare a general plan of works to render the territorial possession of the human species the most productive possible, and the most agreeable for habitation in every respect." [19]

To oust heretical Catholic and Protestant Christians Saint-Simon was launching a movement for the propagation of the New Christianity, which would preach only one principle, the amelioration of the lot of the poorest and most numerous class as rapidly and as effectively as possible. The services of the cult would not be concerned with disputations about dogma but would concentrate on extolling those who upheld the new Christian principle and condemning those who opposed it. What would worship consist of in the New Christianity? A prolix passage at once defines the new religion and conveys the spirit of the cult.

"Today worship should be envisaged only as a means, during days of rest, of calling the attention of men to philanthropic considerations and sentiments, and the dogma should be conceived only as a collection of commentaries having as their object general applications of these considerations and sentiments to the great political events which may arise, or having as their object to facilitate among the faithful the applications of morality in the daily relations which exist among them." [20]

Saint-Simon repeated his earlier strictures against violence and his absolute belief in the powers of persuasion. Propagation of the Christian doctrine by force was contrary to Christianity itself. With this principle he hoped to reassure the rich, who might otherwise be terrified lest the poor, having most to gain from the New Christianity, resort to revolution to inaugurate it speedily. As he explained, he had long delayed the promulgation of the religious cult of his system because he wanted the rich first to become familiar with his scientific and industrial doctrine, to be convinced that he was not an egalitarian subversive preaching against them. His earlier works had demonstrated the real character of the industrial society. The rich had nothing to fear from the New Christianity because the grand projects he planned, the universal exploitation of world resources, affording full employment, could be undertaken only under their direction and to their incidental enrichment. The industrial society with the New Christianity as its moral principle was a capitalist society working under a profit system. Saint-Simon saw no inconsistency between entrepreneurial activity and the moral ideal of the New Christianity. In this sense he was one of the great ideologists of modern philanthropic capitalism.

The treatment of the spiritual power of the old order of society always posed a troublesome problem for Saint-Simon. The old Christian clergy of Europe had failed in their function as an intellectual élite and they had to disappear. But the fate of this class was more disturbing than was the destiny of the military rulers of society. There was no conceivable continuity between the functions of a warrior noble class and a new industrial class, so that the framework of the former could not be preserved to house the latter. The spiritual power seemed to have greater continuity from the middle ages to modern times, since in medieval Europe the Christian clergy were the repositories of whatever scientific knowledge was available and they were also the protagonists of the only moral principle in society. It would perhaps have been desirable, in the name of an orderly transition, if the Christian clergy had assimilated the new science and the new version of the humanitarian principle of early Christianity rather than to have the class of scientists develop outside the Church. Saint-Simon was not intent on destroying the clergy, but on transforming their nature. Indeed, at one time he played with the conceit of a papal decree forcing all priests, before they were ordained, to pass examinations in positive science, to become in effect scientists, as their medieval predecessors had been. Unfortunately the European clergy, having failed to keep abreast of scientific knowledge, had forfeited its right to function as society's intellectual élite. They had become a corps stronghold of superstition and false ideas which they were defending against the new scientists merely out of a desire to maintain themselves in a position of power.

The failure of the clergy to preach the moral law of Christian brotherly love was fatal to their continuance as a spiritual force. Whereas the medieval clergy as the spiritual power had pretended to supremacy over the feudal classes or at least to a status of equality with the feudal-temporal force, the modern religious leaders had resigned themselves to complete dependence upon Caesar and his heirs in all the European political societies. The need for moralists, scientists, teachers of the newly-discovered truths, even theologians as formulators of the truth into religious principles, still existed, but the clergies of the formal European religious faiths were no longer capable of filling this spiritual role and therefore they had to vanish as classes in their existing role. Perhaps a few of them would be assimilated among the leaders of the new Academy of Reasoning or the Academy of Sentiment, but the old religious organizational structures, mere shells of their former selves, would have to be divested of their spiritual power. If the Christian churches persisted in trying to hold the minds and the passions of men in their grip they would have to be destroyed after a few individuals were integrated with the new spiritual bodies. Saint-Simon did not expect this process to be a very profound shock to the European spirit since for a number of hundreds of years the scientists had been slowly absorbing the prestige which was being lost by the clergy. Most people, even those in the lowest ranks of the industrials, no longer gave credence to the clergy's superstition-laden explanations of natural phenomena so that the abolition of the clergy as a class involved nothing more than the continuation of a process which was already far advanced. The acceptance of the New Christianity as the religion of the scientific industrial society would be the climax of this development. The old clergy having betrayed their trust as professors of morals and guides of sentiment and teachers of progressive scientific truth, their duties would be assumed by new classes composed of artists, poets, moralists, scientists, new theologians.

In his last work Saint-Simon wrote about the "church" of the New Christianity, his "mission," and the "voice of God" speaking "through his mouth." He referred to the "revelation of Christianity" and to its "superhuman character." [21] By this time the religious phrases had probably ceased to be mere literary artifices with him as he had truly come to believe that Christianity was a unique historical experience and that he was the messiah of the new creed. In an early passage of the *Nouveau Christianisme* he made explicit reference to the messianic belief of the Jews, and implied that he was its fulfillment. But despite the grandiloquent phrases, nowhere in the whole work is there an iota of what has traditionally been described as religious sentiment or expression. The word "mystical" has a negative connotation whenever he uses it, for his New Christianity is founded upon the truths of positive science and the one absolute moral principle of all time — brotherly love. It is even difficult to identify this religion with romantic pantheism and the romantic religious posturing which was in vogue in Europe during the period. Saint-Simon took occasion to condemn in passing the tendencies towards the "vague" in contemporary German literature, where romantic religiosity had struck deepest roots. His use of the arts in the propagation of the faith is a far cry from Chateaubriand's revelation of the beauties of Christianity. Chateaubriand tried to illustrate the genius of Christianity by pointing to the sublime creations its spirit had inspired; Saint-Simon would employ the artists as mere agents, to rouse men to action in harmony with the New Christianity's philanthropic moral principles. The final rewards of his new religion were not dissimilar from the promise which Diderot extended to the moral man who by his services to science and by his philanthropy had deserved well of humanity — the preservation of his memory among posterity. This positivist terrestrial immortality was later elaborated with freakish detail in Auguste Comte's calendar for the Religion of Humanity. The gulf between Saint-Simon and traditional faiths is so unbridgeable it seems presumptuous to embrace his humanitarian creed and the Judeo-Christian revelations under the same rubric of religion, were it not for the fact that the actual practice of many Jewish and Christian modernists is far closer to Saint-Simon's morality religion than to orthodox belief.[22]

At the outbreak of the French Revolution Saint-Simon was already twenty-nine years old, and the basic emotional pattern of his own personal life had been set in the sensuous irreligious climate of the later eighteenth century.[23] But with the Restoration he revealed a remarkable sensitivity to the temper of the new generation born at the turn of the century and to its peculiar emotional needs. The religious and moral vacuum of post-Napoleonic France, so poignantly described by de Musset in *La Confession d'un enfant du siècle*, [24] and by Stendhal in *Le Rouge et le Noir*, was unbearable for many young men — the legion of Julien Sorels who had inwardly broken with traditional revealed religions, yet had found nothing to fill the emptiness. Olinde Rodrigues, the tense, emotional, mathematician who became the constant companion of Saint-Simon's last days, no doubt strengthened his early intuition that a new morality and a new organic age had to assume a religious form. The Catholic revival in the romantic manner ushered in by the works of men like Chateaubriand was one of the officially approved religious solutions proffered to these young men. The *Génie du Christianisme* was an attempt to make the old religion palatable by embellishing it with the aesthetics of romanticism. But this religion of "sentiment" which passed for the revived Catholicism was rejected by many young intellectuals. Saint-Simon's New Christianity was more eclectic: in many ways it provided an ideal moral and religious syncretism. He praised the rationalist creations of the scientists and the speculations of the entrepreneurs; he dipped their ethics into a bath of moral sentiment, the love for humanity, and called it religion. Saint-Simon himself could not quite improvise the requisite romantic style and imagery for this new religion, which in his hands remained simple, amystical, at times crudely rationalist. Within a few years after his death, the young men who formed a cult in his name unabashedly drank in the metaphors and poetic conceptions of contemporary Catholic thinkers and emerged with a special cult jargon and ritual. Eugène Rodrigues, brother of Olinde, probably introduced the romanticized Spinozaic pantheism of their religious preaching, while Enfantin drew upon Ballanche. It was a feat of exegesis to use the trite doctrinaire text of the *Nouveau Christianisme* in a public evangelism. There is none of the Saint-Simonian mysticism in the master's own written works, though he might conceivably have been swept along with his young men had he lived. Saint-Simon actually had in preparation a third dialogue which was to cover the morality, the worship, and the dogma of the new religion as well as a credo for New Christians. But he died before it was completed.

Enfantin in his Teaching of November 28, 1831, publicly confessed that for long the disciples had not fully comprehended the *Nouveau Christianisme*, particularly the profound dogmas for the cult which it contained, for the simple reason that all was not explicit in this last testament.

"When Eugène and I were laying the first bases of the trinitarian dogma in its theological form, we had not yet understood how profoundly this dogma had been sensed by Saint-Simon in the *Nouveau Christianisme*. Your father Rodrigues was the only one who constantly repeated to us that this book had enclosed within it the most lofty teaching which was ever given man to receive." [25]

Intent upon effecting a fusion between Saint-Simon's theory and Catholicism Enfantin reread the last work in the light of a trinitarian principle and so assiduous were his researches that he found the principle of three everywhere. The good society had three capacities, fine arts, science, and industry and three classes to exercize them; the true religion had three aspects, morality, dogma, ritual.[26]

If read in the spirit of Enfantin the whole history of Christianity as set forth in the *Nouveau Christianisme* was a triad of eras whose character was dialectical. In Saint-Simon's Empire writings the history of scientific development had been established as an alternativity of epochs of synthesis and generalization and epochs of analysis and particularization. The *Nouveau Christianisme* revived this terminology extending it far beyond the limits of a scientific method, adapting it to describe the whole social and moral order. First, there was an age of generalization:

> From the establishment of Christianity until the fifteenth century the human species has principally been occupied with the coördination of its general feelings and the establishment of a universal and unique principle and with the foundation of a general institution having as its goal the superimposition of an aristocracy of talents over an aristocracy of birth, and thus of submitting all particular interests to the general interest. During this whole period direct observations on private interests, on particular facts, and on secondary principles were neglected. They were denigrated in the minds of most people and a preponderance of opinion was agreed on this point, that secondary principles should be deduced from general facts and from one universal principle. This opinion was a truth of a purely speculative character, given that the human intelligence has not the means of establishing generalities of so precise a nature that it would be possible to derive from them as direct consequences all the particulars.[27]

This was the medieval outlook with its monist absolute, one is tempted to say the "thesis." Then followed the second stage, the contrary movement of this trinity — the history of Christianity from the Reformation to the present. During this second era, a new spirit of particularization, specialization, individuation, replaced generalization. This next epoch is clearly the antithesis, the contradiction of the first.

> Since the dissolution of the European spiritual power, a consequence of the insurrection of Luther, since the fifteenth century, the human spirit has detached itself from the most general views and has given itself over to specialization. It has occupied itself with the analysis of particular facts, with the private interests of various classes of society. It has labored to establish the secondary principles which might serve as foundations for the various branches of knowledge. And during this second period the opinion prevailed that reflections on the general facts, on the general principles and on the general interests of the human species

were nothing but vague metaphysical reflections, incapable of contributing effectively to the progress of knowledge and to the perfection of civilization.[28]

Though Saint-Simon does not use any of the Hegelian dialectical language he does express the concept: "Thus the human spirit has followed, since the fifteenth century, a direction opposed to what it had followed up to this period. And surely the important and positive progress which resulted in all our fields of knowledge proves irrevocably how much our ancestors in the middle ages were deceived in judging the study of particular facts, of secondary principles, and the analysis of private interests to be of little utility." [29]

This second antithetic movement of Christian history bore with it spiritual evils of its own, particular to its specializing, individualizing nature. Saint-Simon described again the malady of the modern age of self-centered, egotistic, isolated units, the moral parallel to the dominant trend of scientific particularization.

But it is equally true that a very great evil resulted for society from the state of abandonment in which since the fifteenth century the works relative to the study of general facts, of general principles, and of general interests have been left. This abandonment has given birth to a feeling of egotism which has become dominant among all classes and in all individuals. This sentiment has facilitated for Caesar the means of recovering a large part of the political power which he had lost before the fifteenth century. It is to this egotism that we should attribute the political malady of our age, a malady which makes all the workers useful to society suffer, a malady which makes the kings absorb a very large part of the wages of the poor for their personal expenditure, for that of their courtiers and of their soldiers; a malady which makes royalty and the aristocracy of birth usurp an enormous part of the esteem which is due the scientists, the artists, and the chiefs of industrial works for their services of direct and positive utility which they render to the body social.[30]

Moral deficiencies of the second movement of Christian history necessitated another reversal of the trend away from particularization, individuation, egotism, but in this Saint-Simon's last formula for the alternativity principle he did not call for a complete turning back to the general. He ended with an appeal for the coexistence of both the elements of individuation and of generalization, not quite a new synthesis, but a civilization in which both antithetical elements were present. "It is therefore very desirable that the works which have as their object the perfection of our knowledge relative to general facts, general principles, and general interests, should promptly be activated and should henceforth be protected by society on a basis of equality with those works which have as their object the study of particular facts, of secondary principles, and of private interests." [31] A simultaneous advance on both fronts, the synthetic and the particularistic, was the ideal road for the new religious society.

With less warrant Enfantin and Eugène Rodrigues later read into Saint-Simon's works other trinitarian formulas such as God, Man, and World, or the Infinite, the Ego, and the Non-Ego. Their doctrine moved further and further away from his positivism and shot off into a world of sensual mysticism alien to Saint-Simon's thought. On the other hand, it would be difficult to reduce Saint-Simon to a matter-of-fact *philosophe* of the simple, *idéologue* persuasion.

Eight days before his death Saint-Simon by word of mouth communicated to Olinde Rodrigues his faith that the *Nouveau Christianisme* was the very heart of his system, despite the fact that it would at first be misconstrued.

"Our last work will be the last to be understood. It is generally believed that men are not susceptible of becoming passionate in a religious direction, but this is a grave error. The Catholic system was in contradiction with the system of the sciences and modern industry, and therefore its fall was inevitable. It took place, and this fall is the signal for a new belief which is going to fill with its enthusiasm the void which criticism has left in the souls of men, for it is a belief which will draw its strength from everything that belongs to the ancient belief. . . . *The whole doctrine is there.* . . ." [32]

At another time, while conversing of their future triumph, Saint-Simon prophesied, "A passing sleep followed by a perpetual awakening." [33]

32

Death and Apotheosis

IN THE SPRING OF 1825 Saint-Simon, Rodrigues and Halévy set about planning their new periodical, *Le Producteur*. Realizing that his strength was failing, Saint-Simon prepared the younger men of the group to carry on. "I will be only your adviser," he said, "I will be a consulting philosopher." [1] During the final months of his life he heard from almost all his old friends and former pupils. Augustin Thierry sent him his *Histoire de la conquête de l'Angleterre par les Normands*. Though he was pleased with the work, Saint-Simon disagreed with Thierry's emphasis upon the racial conflict instead of upon the great social progress which the Norman Conquest had brought to England — the sole Saint-Simonian criterion for historical judgment.

On the last Sunday in March his friends gathering for their weekly meal found the master ill with a violent cough. He was chilled and his teeth were chattering, but the old aristocrat made light of his discomfort. Though he could not partake of the food with his disciples, he made a gallant effort to continue the conversation in his spritely manner as he stood against the fireplace. When Dr. Bailly arrived he put him to bed and applied leeches. The master never recovered. After a while, in the hope of rousing his spirits, they moved him to another flat, in Montmartre, but nothing availed. There were no more walks in the Palais-Royal. Too weak to dictate his ideas even to disciples hanging on his every word, he waned.

On the night of May 18 Saint-Simon ran a high fever and he grew delirious. Olinde Rodrigues appeared the next morning. By then Saint-Simon's pulse was strong again and he was fully conscious, even gay. Dr. Gall found his lungs congested and gave him three days to live. The banker Ardoin paid him a visit. When his condition suddenly deteriorated the whole group of his medical friends were summoned and they all attended him — Doctors Burdin, Bailly, Broussais. "The diagnosis is quite clear. The patient is dying," was the verdict.

When they kept asking him questions about his symptoms, he replied in the spirit of the new age of positive science: "Gentlemen, I am happy to provide you with a new subject of observation. You see a man suffering a terrible crisis which no one could overcome, but whose mind is so pre-occupied with his life's work that he cannot converse with you about his illness. Well, do what you think proper. I have complete confidence and am disposed to help you." [2] Dr. Broussais exclaimed with admiration, "What a mind! What a vigorous spirit!" He was dying as he had lived, *la vie expérimentale*.

They inquired about his last wishes, whether he wanted to summon any member of his family, perhaps his nephew General Victor Saint-Simon, whose early education he had directed.[3] The philosopher insisted on devoting his last moments to reflection and he persevered in his resolution to the end, betraying no sign of weakness. At six o'clock Dr. Bailly asked whether he were suffering. "It would be an exaggeration to say that I am not in pain. But what does that matter? Let us talk of other things." [4] He asked Rodrigues, Bailly, and Léon Halévy to draw near. With a voice broken by the death rattle he delivered his last message:

For the past twelve days, Gentlemen, I have been busy explaining how you can best unite your efforts for your enterprise. For the last three hours I have been trying to summarize my thoughts on this subject. At this moment all I can say is that you are entering upon an epoch when united efforts must yield the greatest success. The pear is ripe. You must pluck it. The last part of our work will perhaps be misunderstood. By attacking the religious system of the middle ages only one thing has been proved: that it was no longer in harmony with the progress of positive science. But it was wrong to conclude that religion itself has tended to disappear. Religion only has to bring itself into harmony with the progress of the sciences. I repeat to you, the pear is ripe. You should pluck it. Forty-eight hours after the appearance of our next publication, we shall be a party.

The image of the pear had recurred for the last time. To Rodrigues he had said a few moments before, "Remember that to accomplish something great one must have passion. The essence of my life's work is to afford all members of society the greatest possible opportunity for the development of their faculties." [5]

His voice grew softer. His final words, which he accompanied with an expressive gesture, were: "Our business is well in hand."

The deathbed scene of a man entertaining his disciples with hopes for the future of humanity, whose peaceful reorganization and happiness his doctrines had prepared, became a moving symbol for members of the Saint-Simonian cult. A few years later one of them wrote, "The death of Socrates was less beautiful." [6]

When Dr. Gall performed an autopsy on Saint-Simon's skull he found a brain with a large surface. He thought he could discern signs of a total absence of any quality of circumspection joined to an indefatigable spirit of perseverance.

Olinde Rodrigues and Pierre-Isidore Rouen, a lawyer, went to the second district bureau to fill out the Act of Decease and to get the burial plot.[7] On May 22, 1825, the funeral procession made its way to the cemetery of Père Lachaise.

"Where are his relatives?" asked the porter at the cemetery gates. No one answered. "Where are his friends?" Everyone pressed forward. The curious who were attracted by the crowd were told they were burying a M. Henry de Saint-Simon, one of the "most ardent philanthropists of the epoch."[8] Dr. Bailly's funeral oration, turgid and clumsy though it is, conveyed the strange fascination which this man exerted on his disciples and his friends.

In recent years major discoveries have been made in the physiology of individuals, but not even the greatest of geniuses has been capable of rising beyond this point. It remained for M. de Saint-Simon to open a new road for literature, history, legislation, industry, science, and the fine arts, to lay the foundations for a hitherto unknown science, to draw the attention of scholars to the true nature of the organic forces of society, in a word, to become the founder of a *physiology of the human species.* . . .

Let us leave to history the task of making known a man whose whole life was marked by events that defy comprehension, events for which there are a thousand variant explanations, none of which, however, is adequate for an understanding of this most inexplicable moral phenomenon ever presented to the human intellect. . . .

We who have been instilled with the prejudices of our society have often regretted being born in this old continent of Europe which has appeared to us a mass of ruins incapable of stimulating our imagination. Consumed by the need for action, which made a torment of an existence whose futility wearied us, we arraigned nature for having endowed us with sentiments that set us in conflict with our situation.

But today, gentlemen, formed in the school of this great man, you have embarked on a career for which he showed the way. Today, your sense of living has been heightened by the impulse with which he awakened your faculties, by the delights born of an imagination passionate for the general good. Today, finally, when the conviction of belonging to a society full of energy and vitality has replaced the inertia to which you believed yourselves condemned, you are indebted to him for a new moral existence whose worth you alone can appreciate. . . . The melancholy illness of which he cured you is the same one of which you must in turn cure society. As a result of your efforts the changes which have been wrought in your morale will be effected in the human species. Worthy successors of a man to whom you owe such keen joys, the finest testimony of your gratitude will be the continuation of his work in developing the intelligence of man. . . .[9]

They had all gathered at the grave, including Auguste Comte and Augustin Thierry, who, now almost blind, was led to the cemetery.[10] After the funeral a group met in Olinde Rodrigues' office and *Le Producteur* was officially founded. The Saint-Simonian movement had been launched.

The day of his death Julie Juliand wrote to Saint-Simon's daughter Caroline: "This morning they sketched him. The resemblance is striking. They are also going to make a mask. It will at least be a consolation for us, my dear Caroline. If he could talk he would advise you to be courageous. It was one of his virtues. Conform to his wishes, and by having this virtue be worthy of being the daughter of a great man. His pupils and his friends have religious feelings, enthusiasm for him. His life will be written. His deeds will not be forgotten. They will be revealed." [11]

Julie Juliand could find no work. For two months the personal effects of Saint-Simon were kept under seal because he had been in debt. Presto was almost carried off by the dog-catcher, but Julie saved him. She wrote: "If you knew how much he mourned his master you would love him as much as I do. In my house I have the bust. I wish you could have seen his surprise at the sight of his master, for it is indeed a striking resemblance, even though made twenty hours after his death." [12]

When Julie went to place a wreath on Saint-Simon's grave she was surprised to find that there was no epitaph on the tombstone. But she soon consoled herself. "It seems to be the custom, since the tombs of Molière, of La Fontaine, and of other men of genius bear no further inscription." [13]

At the end of the century, the aged Gustave d'Eichthal, remembering the days of his youth, and Jenny Rebecca Rodrigues Pereire provided for the perpetual upkeep of the grave by making a grant to the municipality of Paris.

NOTES

NOTES

Introduction

1. P. Enfantin and H. Saint-Simon, *Science de l'homme: Physiologie religieuse* (Paris, 1858), Note C, "Lettre à Charles Duveyrier sur la vie éternelle, juin, 1830," p. 207.

2. Friedrich Engels, *Herrn Eugen Dühring's Umwälzung der Wissenschaft*, 2nd ed. (Göttingen-Zürich, 1886), p. 245. One of the fullest treatments of Saint-Simon by Marx occurs in his section of the fourth part of *Die Deutsche Ideologie* (written in 1845–46). This was not a direct discussion of Saint-Simon, but a blistering attack on Karl Grün's *Die soziale Bewegung in Frankreich und Belgien: Briefe und Studien* (Darmstadt, 1845), with the purpose of demonstrating that Grün's account of Saint-Simon's theory had been plagiarized from Lorenz von Stein's *Der Socialismus und Communismus des heutigen Frankreichs* (Leipzig, 1842) and Louis Reybaud's *Etudes sur les réformateurs ou socialistes modernes*, 3 vols. (Brussels, 1844), that Grün had never read a single work of Saint-Simon's in the original, and that even his copying from secondary sources was replete with gross errors and misinterpretations. Marx was incensed by Grün's thesis that Saint-Simon already contained "in the germ" the whole of scientific socialism. Very little was left of Grün's account after Marx had ploughed through it line by line. But in his demolition of Grün he occasionally went astray himself, as when he insisted that the contrast between organic and critical epochs was the Saint-Simonian Bazard's conception and that "at no time and in no place did Saint-Simon ever oppose organic and critical periods of history." In this instance his customary sledge-hammer criticism ("M. Grün lies freely") missed its mark, since this concept is central to Saint-Simon's whole philosophy. *Die Deutsche Ideologie*, in *Marx-Engels Gesamtausgabe* (Berlin, 1927–1935), First Part, V, 479–495. Engels maintained that Marx later changed his original evaluation of Saint-Simon and spoke with admiration of his "genius and encyclopedic brain." Karl Marx, *Capital, A Critique of Political Economy*, edited by F. Engels, trans. by Ernest Untermann (Chicago, 1906–1909), III, 710–711 fn.

3. V. I. Lenin, *Imperialism, the Highest Stage of Capitalism*, in *Collected Works* (New York, 1927–1942), XIX, 196.

4. Henri Gouhier, *La Jeunesse d'Auguste Comte*, 3 vols. (Paris, 1933–1941).

5. Gouhier, II, 2.

6. Auguste Comte, *Correspondance inédite*, 4 vols. (Paris, 1903–1904), II, 255: Auguste Comte to M. Hadéry, August 18, 1853.

7. John Stuart Mill, *Autobiography* (New York, 1948), p. 43.

8. Carlyle's translation of the *Nouveau Christianisme*, with an introductory note, has been lost. Hill Shine, *Carlyle and the Saint-Simonians, The Concept of Historical Periodicity* (Baltimore, 1941), p. 68.

9. Friedrich Nietzsche, *Complete Works*, edited by Dr. Oscar Levy (Edinburgh and London, 1909–1913), XVI, 211.

10. E. Durkheim, "Saint-Simon, fondateur du positivisme et de la sociologie," *Revue philosophique*, Part 1 (1925), XCIX, 321–341.

11. He considered him, along with Comte and the Saint-Simonians, as a case study of a thinker who put "a scientific veneer on ethico-religious conceptions." Vilfredo Pareto, *Les systèmes socialistes*, 2nd ed. (Paris, 1926), II, 194.

12. Gaetano Mosca, *Elementi di scienza politica*, 2nd ed. (Turin, 1923), pp. 282, 462.

13. Arnold J. Toynbee, *A Study of History*, I (London, 1933), pp. 198–199.

14. Joseph Alois Schumpeter, *History of Economic Analysis*, ed. by Elizabeth Boody Schumpeter (New York, 1954), p. 462.

15. *Oeuvres complètes de Saint-Simon* (Paris: Naquet, 1832), 2 parts in 1 vol., xxxviii– 201 pp. and 364 pp.); *Oeuvres de Saint-Simon* (Paris: Capelle, 1841, 201 pp.).

16. N. G. Hubbard, *Saint-Simon, sa vie et ses travaux; suivi de fragments des plus célèbres écrits de Saint-Simon* (Paris, 1857).

17. *Oeuvres choisies de C. H. Saint-Simon, précédées d'un essai sur sa doctrine*, by Lemonnier, 3 vols. (Brussels: Van Meenen, 1859).

18. *Oeuvres de Saint-Simon et d'Enfantin, précédées de deux notices historiques et publiées par les membres du conseil institué par Enfantin pour l'exécution de ses dernières volontés*, 47 vols. (Paris: Dentu, 1865–1876; E. Leroux, 1877–1878). Saint-Simon's writings are in volumes XV, XVIII, XIX, XX, XXI, XXII, XXIII, XXXVII, XXXVIII, XXXIX, XL.

19. C. Bouglé, *L'Oeuvre d'Henri de Saint-Simon; textes choisis avec une introduction* (Paris, 1925).

20. *Saint-Simon, Textes choisis. Préface, commentaires et notes explicatives par Jean Dautry* (Paris, 1951, 183 pp.).

21. *Saint-Simon, Izbrannye sochineniia*, edited by V. Volgin, 2 vols. (Moscow, Academy of Sciences of the USSR, 1948).

22. *Henri, Comte de Saint-Simon. Selected Writings*. Edited and Translated with an introduction by F. M. H. Markham (Oxford, 1952, 116 pp.).

23. *Introduction aux travaux scientifiques du xixᵉ siècle*, in *Oeuvres choisies*, I, 68fn.

24. *Doctrine de Saint-Simon. Exposition. Première année, 1829*, new ed. published with introduction and notes by C. Bouglé and Elie Halévy (Paris, 1924), p. 113.

PART I

THE PHILOSOPHICAL APPRENTICESHIP

1. Hero of the American Revolution

1. *Mémoires de Saint-Simon*, new ed. by A. de Boislisle (Paris, 1879), I, 202.

2. Boislisle, *Mémoires*, I, appendix I, second part, gives a complete genealogy of the various branches of the House of Saint-Simon.

3. D. Juan Verdier de Portdeguy, *Genealogia de la antigua familia y casa de San Simon*, cited by Boislisle, *Mémoires de Saint-Simon*, I, Appendix I, 405.

4. Boislisle, XXIX, 186.

5. C. P. d'Albert, Duc de Luynes, *Mémoires sur la cour de Louis XV (1735–1758)* (Paris, 1860–1865), XIV, 42, considered Jean-François de Gourgue the dean of the *maîtres-des-requêtes*.

6. *Mémoires de Saint-Simon*, XXIX, 186–194; E. Bertin, *Les Mariages dans l'ancienne société Française* (Paris, 1879), pp. 451–455. Saint-Simon's autobiography garbled consequences of the incident beyond recognition: "I was the nearest relative of a famous

author, the Duke de Saint-Simon. His *duché-pairie*, his grandeeship of Spain, and the five-hundred-thousand-franc income which he enjoyed should have passed on to me. He quarreled with my father, whom he disinherited. I thus lost the titles and fortune of the Duke de Saint-Simon; but I inherited his passion for glory." *Histoire de ma vie*, in *Oeuvres*, XV, 71. Lorenz von Stein, *Geschichte der socialen Bewegung in Frankreich* (Leipzig, 1850), II, 133, made the famous Duke de Saint-Simon a grandfather of Claude-Henri.

7. *Mémoires de Saint-Simon*, XXIX, 194.

8. Mathieu Marais, *Journal et mémoires. . . sur la régence et le règne de Louis XV (1715–1737)* (Paris, 1863–1868), II, 274.

9. Duc de Luynes, *Mémoires sur la cour de Louis XV*, XIII, 159; XIV, 42.

10. "Lettre de l'évêque de Metz au Maréchal de Noailles," *L'Athenaeum Français*, II (1853), 1090. M. L. Lalanne, who published the letter, erroneously calls Henri de Rouvroy the Duke's son.

11. Maxime Leroy, *La Vie véritable du Comte Henri de Saint-Simon* (Paris, 1925), p. 43.

12. Among his works are *Histoire de la guerre des Alpes* (Amsterdam, 1769); *Histoire de la guerre des Bataves et des Romains* (Amsterdam, 1770); *Essai de traduction littérale et énergique* (Haarlem, 1771); *Témora, poème épique d'Ossian traduit d'après l'édition anglaise de Macpherson* (Amsterdam, 1774); *Les Nyctologues de Platon* (Utrecht, 1784). See article on him in *Biographie universelle* (1825), XL, 103–104.

13. *Mémoires de Saint-Simon*, I, 404.

14. Jules Michelet, *Histoire du xixe siècle*, 3 vols. (Paris, 1875), I, 17, dwells upon his Picard character; Leroy, *La Vie véritable*, p. 19, calls the family "lacustrine"; the fogs of Picardy were said to be conducive to introspection. Among fellow Picards were Peter the Hermit, Calvin, Babeuf, Saint-Just, Camille Desmoulins, Condorcet, and Lamarck.

15. *Lettre à Boissy d'Anglas, November 2, 1807*, in *Oeuvres*, XV, 69fn.

16. Hubbard, *Saint-Simon*, pp. 10–11.

17. *Notice historique*, in *Oeuvres*, I, 1–129, is the "official biography" prepared by members of the council appointed by Enfantin.

18. The manuscript of an unknown secretary, "Notice sur Saint-Simon," published by Alfred Pereire, *Autour de Saint-Simon* (Paris, 1912), p. 189.

19. Hubbard, *Saint-Simon*, pp. 9, 10.

20. Bibliothèque Nationale. MSS. N.A.F. 24607.

21. Henri Gouhier published fragments of a manuscript from the Archives Nationales, F⁷ 4.233, entitled "Projet d'encyclopédie. Second prospectus," in his "Henri de Saint-Simon et l'alliance franco-anglaise," *La Nef*, III, part 2, No. 20 (July, 1946), 59–73; quotation is from the "avertissement," p. 64. There is a glimpse of Saint-Simon's parents and sister visiting the nobility in the country and participating in their theatricals and other amusements in the Duc de Croÿ, *Journal inédit*, published by the Vicomte de Grouchy and Paul Cottin, 4 vols. (Paris, 1906–1907), II, 385; III, 10. The family was open to the influences of the new science; Madame de Saint-Simon followed a course in experimental physics at the Duc de Croÿ's in the winter of 1772.

22. Leroy, *La Vie véritable*, p. 66.

23. See the account of Saint-Simon's military career in America in H. A. Larrabee, "The Philosophical Foundations of the Social Theory of Saint-Simon," unpublished thesis (Harvard University, 1925), Appendix I, pp. 373–403; also Larrabee's "Henri de Saint-Simon at Yorktown. A French Prophet of Modern Industrialism in America," *Franco-American Review*, II (1937–1938), 96–109. In Thomas Balch, *The French in America*, tr. from the French, 2 vols. (Philadelphia, 1891–1895), I, 187; II, 223–224,

Claude-Henri de Saint-Simon is confused with his relative, the Baron Claude, who commanded a group of volunteers known as "Saint-Simon's Hussars."

24. J. J. Jusserand, *En Amérique jadis et maintenant* (Paris, 1918), p. 39.

25. The incident on the Cormorant in the Bay of Chisapecak (*sic*) is described in *Le Politique* (1819), "Premier article de politique générale," pp. 15–16.

26. Claude Blanchard, *Guerre d'Amérique (1780–1783); Journal de campagne* (Paris, 1881), pp. 100–101.

27. Hubbard, *Saint-Simon*, p. 15; Leroy, *La Vie véritable*, pp. 62–63. This did not prevent him from quoting what Franklin said in his presence. *Du système industriel*, in *Oeuvres*, XXIII, 30.

28. Bibliothèque Nationale. MSS. N.A.F. 24605. Copies of the letters are in the Fonds Enfantin (7855) of the Bibliothèque de l'Arsenal.

29. Hubbard, *Saint-Simon*, p. 10; Michelet, *Histoire du XIXᵉ siècle*, I, 17.

30. Saint-Simon wrote Brimsthon-hille.

31. See G. Lacour-Gayet, *La Marine militaire de la France sous le règne de Louis XVI* (Paris, 1905).

32. The letter, signed "Henry," was received on January 24, 1783.

33. Bibliothèque de l'Arsenal. Fonds Enfantin (7855) contains a note by Gustave d'Eichthal describing the incident; Hubbard, *Saint-Simon*, p. 13.

34. *L'Industrie. Correspondance Politique et Philosophique. Lettres de Henri de Saint-Simon à un Américain*, in *Oeuvres*, XVIII, 133, 149.

35. *Oeuvres*, XVIII, 140. He described the United States as the "finest and most simple social order which has ever existed," XVIII, 141.

36. W. F. Johnson, *Four Centuries of the Panama Canal* (New York, 1906), p. 36.

37. Don Domingo Juarros, *A Statistical and Commercial History of the Kingdom of Guatemala in Spanish America*, translated by J. Baily, Lieutenant, R.M. (London, 1823), with two maps.

38. Account based on autobiography of 1808, *Histoire de ma vie*, in *Oeuvres*, XV, 64. He apparently was in France by 1783, for the records of gentlemen presented at court in that year include his name. See lists appended to R. C. de Fourlay, Marquise de Créquy, *Souvenirs*, new ed. (Paris, 1842), X, 105.

39. Leroy, *La Vie véritable*, p. 98.

40. F. C. A. Marquis de Bouillé, *Mémoires*, 2nd ed. (Paris, 1822), pp. 34–37.

41. *Mémoire introductif de M. de Saint-Simon sur sa contestation avec M. de Redern* (Alençon, 1812), p. 22; the biographical portions of this *Mémoire introductif* were reprinted by Gouhier, *La Jeunesse d'Auguste Comte*, II, 352–355. See also *Histoire de ma vie*, in *Oeuvres*, I, 65, where the clumsiness of M. de Vérac is blamed for the expedition's foundering.

42. De Bouillé, *Mémoires*, p. 37.

43. *Mémoire intoductif*, pp. 22–23.

44. Leroy, *La Vie véritable*, p. 100, letter to the Duc de la Vauguyon, July 26, 1788. Saint-Simon's autobiography mistakenly has him a colonel in 1782. *Histoire de ma vie*, in *Oeuvres*, XV, 64.

45. The account of his Spanish adventure is based upon the autobiographical sketch in the *Mémoire introductif*, p. 23, and the *Histoire de ma vie*, in *Oeuvres*, XV, 65–66.

46. Archivo Histórico Nacional. Estado, leg. 3000, n° 13: *Plan de Sr. Francisco Cabarrús sobre el Banco Nacional*. See also Francisco Cabarrús, *Cartas sobre los obstáculos que la naturaleza, la opinión y las leyes oponen á la felicidad pública* (Vitoria, 1808).

47. Archivo Histórico Nacional. Estado, leg. 3219: *Compte rendu de la Banque*

St. Charles, à la quatrième Assemblée générale de ses actionnaires, le 29 Décembre 1785 (Amsterdam, 1786), p. xviii.

48. Archivo Histórico Nacional. Estado, leg. 2846, n° 8: Copy of letter from Count de Aranda to Floridablanca, May 15, 1788.

49. Archivo Histórico Nacional. Consejos, leg. 17728: *Resumen General de las obras hechas en el Canal de Guadarrama* (Madrid, 1788).

2. Victim of the Terror

1. *Mémoires de Saint-Simon*, I, 420; *Biographie universelle* (1847), LXXX, 404–405; *Le Moniteur*, II, 312, 331.

2. *Le Moniteur*, V, 5.

3. The list of sequestered papers is in the Archives Nationales, T 1666 (1–54).

4. *Mémoires de Saint-Simon*, I, 422; Jean Dautry, *Saint-Simon*, p. 15, refers to letters witten by Claude-Henri's mother on behalf of her sons to officials of the department of the Somme, denying that they were *émigrés*.

5. Archives Nationales. Archives de Police Générale, F^7 4775^{12}: Dossier of Adélaïde-Blanche de Saint-Simon.

6. Archives Nationales F^7 2507: Record of the Section de l'Unité. The Baron Claude de Saint-Simon is confused with Claude-Henri de Saint-Simon in *Le Curieux* (1883), I, 175; and in Claude-Henri's dossier in the Archives Nationales, Archives de Police Générale, F^7 4775^{12}; Albert Mathiez in his review of Leroy's biography, *Annales historiques de la révolution française*, new series (1925), II, 403, cites a number of documents as possibly referring to Claude-Henri de Saint-Simon which in fact belong to the dossier of his relative the baron.

7. Archives Nationales. Archives de Police Générale, F^7 4775^{12}.

8. *Le Moniteur*, XXI, 508.

9. Abbé Charles Mariès, *Oraison funèbre de Monseigneur Charles-François-Siméon Vermandois de Saint-Simon Rouvroy Sandricourt* (Montpellier, 1894), p. 82; Anon., *Articles pour la cause de Mgr. de Saint-Simon* (Paris, 1920), pp. 3–5.

10. Archives Nationales. Archives de Police Générale, F^7 4775^{12}.

11. Antoine Guillois, *Le Salon de Madame Helvétius. Cabanis et les idéologues* (Paris, 1894), pp. 97-98.

12. The account which follows is based upon Claude-Henri de Saint-Simon's dossier, Archives Nationales. Archives de Police Générale, F^7 4775^{12}, supplemented by documents in the Bibliothèque Nationale. MSS. N.A.F. 24605. Many of the facts in Saint-Simon's *apologia* are substantiated in the Péronne archives summarized by Gustave Ramon, *La Révolution à Péronne* (Péronne, 1886); see, for example, first series, pp. 58, 59.

13. Record of the concierge of Sainte-Pélagie on "Claude-Henry ci-devant St. Simon, de présent bonhomme," Bibliothèque Nationale. MSS. N.A.F. 24605.

14. Nevertheless, in 1790 he had twice solicited the Minister of War for the award of this cross. Leroy, *La Vie véritable*, pp. 90–91, 123.

15. On "21 frimaire an III" (December 11, 1794) the same tiny commune of Bussu issued a certificate setting forth that Claude Henry Simon and Jean Baptiste Combis were yarn and linen merchants, an occupation which favored local industry. The variant of the patronym is significant; it indicates that it was not unusual for him to drop the 'Saint' in the Péronne district. Bibliothèque Nationale. MSS. N.A.F. 24605.

16. The best documentary account of his investments can be found in Maxime Leroy, "Les spéculations foncières de Saint-Simon et ses querelles d'affaires avec son

associé, le Comte de Redern," *Revue d'histoire économique et sociale*, XIII (1925), 133–163.

17. *Réponse de M. de Saint-Simon à M. de Redern. Première lettre. Alençon, 12 août 1812* (n.p., n.d.), pp. 3–4.

18. Ramon, *La Révolution à Péronne*, fifth series, p. 66.

19. Bibliothèque Nationale. MSS. N.A.F. 1308.

20. Marquise de Créquy, *Souvenirs*, VII, 157, refers to letters soliciting her participation in a manufactory of earthenware. According to O. Lorenz, *Catalogue Général de la librairie française* (Paris, 1892), I, 616, this work is apocryphal; its real author was an impostor called Causes de Saint-Malo.

21. Marquise de Créquy, *Souvenirs*, VII, 156.

22. Bibliothèque Nationale. MSS. N.A.F. 24605: "Au citoyen St. Simon à Péronne, 17 mars an 2 de la République."

23. Dautry, *Saint-Simon*, p. 14, on the basis of Archives Nationales DXXIX bis/15, and p. 15 on the basis of Archives Nationales A.F. I [/232] and Archives Départementales de la Somme L / 2371.

24. Ramon, *La Révolution*, fifth series, pp. 4, 5–6.

25. Ramon, fifth series, pp. 42–44.

26. Ramon, sixth series, p. 329.

27. Ramon, fifth series, p. 182.

28. The order of arrest is printed *in extenso* in Albert Mathiez, *Un procès de corruption sous la Terreur. L'affaire de la Compagnie des Indes* (Paris, 1920), p. 110. See also "Le banquier Boyd et ses amis," *Annales révolutionnaires*, XII (1920), 218–231; and "Notes sur les frères Simon, banquiers et négociants," *Annales révolutionnaires*, XV (1923), 322–329.

29. See Albert Mathiez, "Vonck et Proli," *Annales historiques de la révolution française*, new series, II (1925), 58; and his *La Révolution et les étrangers* (Paris, 1918), pp. 138–181.

30. A Michel Simons of the same group was the financial backer of a famous brothel. J. Bouchary, *Les Manieurs d'argent à la fin du xviiie siècle*, 3 vols. (Paris, 1939–1949), III, 159.

31. See Albert Mathiez, *François Chabot, représentant du peuple à ses concitoyens qui sont les juges de sa vie politique* (Paris, 1914).

32. A. Mathiez, "L'arrestation de Saint-Simon," *Annales historiques de la révolution française*, new series, II (1925), 571–575. Desfieux wrote a protocol of the search for Simon which is in Archives Nationales. Archives de Police Générale, F[7] 4607.

33. C. Libert, *Les Contemporains: Saint-Simon (1760–1825)* (Paris, 1899), p. 2.

34. Suzanne Tassier, "Un agent belge de Fouquier-Tinville: Charles Jaubert," *La Révolution française*, new series, No. 4 (1935), pp. 326–336.

35. Alexandre Tuetey, *Répertoire général des sources manuscrites de l'histoire de Paris pendant la révolution française*, 11 vols. (Paris, 1890–1914), X, 518, 521, 526. See also A. Mathiez, "Saint-Simon et Ronsin," *Annales historiques de la révolution française*, new series, III (1926), 493–494.

36. *Epître dédicatoire à mon neveu Victor de Saint-Simon* (at the head of *Nouvelle Encyclopédie. Première livraison servant de prospectus*), in *Oeuvres*, XV, 101.

37. See, for example, Ramon, *La Révolution*, first series, p. 60.

3. Masquerade of the Directorate and the Consulate

1. *Papiers de Barthélemy, ambassadeur de France en Suisse, 1792–1797*, 5 vols. (Paris, 1886–1894), IV, 213: letter on Redern's behalf from Barthélemy to Buchot, 10 thermidor (July 28), 1794.

2. The precipitous drop in the value of the assignats is traced in S. E. Harris, *The Assignats* (Cambridge, Massachusetts, 1930), pp. 166–205.

3. Leroy, "Les spéculations foncières de Saint-Simon," *Revue d'histoire économique et sociale*, XIII, 140.

4. E. and J. Goncourt, *Histoire de la société française pendant le directoire*, 2nd ed. (Paris, 1855), p. 4.

5. Marquise de Créquy, *Souvenirs*, VIII, 227–234.

6. Bibliothèque Nationale. MSS. N.A.F. 24605.

7. Hubbard, *Saint-Simon*, p. 31; in 1857 Hubbard still saw remnants of structures which had been started. See also C. Leroux-Cesbron, "Un Allemand propriétaire en France pendant la Révolution," *Revue des études historiques* (1922), pp. 353–362.

8. G. Vauthier, in "Notes et glanes," *Annales historiques de la révolution française*, new series, II (1925), 492–493, published the prospectus for "Berlines with six seats."

9. *Mémoire introductif*, p. 25.

10. Albert Mathiez, "Le faux bruit de l'arrestation de Saint-Simon en fructidor an V," *Annales historiques de la révolution française*, new series, V (1928), 576. The report about a Marquis de Saint-Simon had been published in the *Journal des hommes libres*, 30 fructidor, an V.

11. *Journal de Paris*, September 19, 1797.

12. Dautry, *Saint-Simon*, pp. 18–19, on basis of Archives Nationales F⁷ 6218 (September–October, 1799).

13. MS. letter to Boissy d'Anglas, November 2, 1807, in *Correspondance entre M. de Saint-Simon et M. de Redern* (n.p., n.d. [1808]); *Réponse de M!. de Saint-Simon à M!. de Redern* [Alençon, July 25, 1812], MS. Bibliothèque Nationale Rés.m.Z 187 (4).

14. J. E. de Redern, *Mémoire sur mes anciennes relations d'affaires avec M. de Saint-Simon* (Caen, n.d. [July 8, 1812]), p. 36. Bibliothèque Nationale. Rés.m.Z 187 (3).

15. MS. letter to Boissy d'Anglas, November 2, 1807, in *Correspondance*.

16. *Réponse de M!. de Saint-Simon* . . . . [Alençon, July 25, 1812], MS.

17. Letter from Saint-Simon, May 21, 1807, in *Correspondance entre M. de Saint-Simon et M. de Redern*, p. 6.

18. Redern, *Mémoire sur mes anciennes relations d'affaires avec M. de Saint-Simon*, p. 10.

19. Ramon, *La Révolution*, fifth series, p. 50, refers to an Irishwoman named Thillay, a servant who was arrested in Saint-Simon's house in Péronne in 1793. According to Leroy, *La Vie véritable*, p. 334, a Caroline-Charlotte Thillays, his natural daughter, was born at Paris on 10 prairial, an III (May 29, 1795). This may well be the Madame Caroline Bouraiche to whom he wrote letters of paternal affection in his last years.

20. Redern, *Mémoire sur mes anciennes relations d'affaires*, p. 21.

21. De Lépine, *Le Dieu malgré lui ou le club sous un clocher* (Paris, 1832), p. 19.

22. De Lépine, pp. 8–9.

23. *Biographie universelle*, LXXX, 409.

24. It is in the Collection André Le Mallier, at Le Charnay, near Nevers.

25. Michelet, *Histoire du XIXe siècle*, I, 19.

26. Georges Weill, *Un Précurseur du socialisme, Saint-Simon et son oeuvre* (Paris,

1894), pp. 12–13fn.; Weill saw the manuscript memoirs of Fourcy in Gustave d'Eichthal's collection.

27. See A. de Monzie, "Saint-Simon et l'instruction publique," *Revue d'histoire économique et sociale*, XIII (1925), 177–180.

28. Michelet, *Histoire*, I, 132–133.

29. Arago refers to the eccentrics in the Saint-Simon circle — Clouet, Ferry, Champy — in his *éloge* of Poisson. He calls them "socialists" because "their studies, their systems, tended to nothing less than a radical transformation of society," — perhaps prematurely. Dominique François Jean Arago, *Poisson. Biographie lue par extraits* in *Oeuvres complètes*, 2nd ed. (Paris, 1858–1865), II, 665.

30. *Biographie universelle* (1813), IX, 128–131; Michelet, *Histoire*, I, 20.

31. See G. Pinet, "L'Ecole Polytechnique et les Saint-Simoniens," *Revue de Paris*, III (1894), 73–96; also *Histoire de ma vie*, in *Oeuvres*, XV, 68.

32. *Mémoire introductif*, cited in *Oeuvres*, XV, 69fn.

33. MS. letter to Boissy d'Anglas, November 2, 1807, in *Correspondance*. He was always self-conscious about how laboriously he had learned to think. He was even aware that his style was not attractive. Dautry, *Saint-Simon*, pp. 61–62, on basis of manuscripts in La Sicotière Collection. See also *Mémoire sur la science de l'homme*, in *Oeuvres*, XL, 11.

34. *Histoire de ma vie*, in *Oeuvres*, XV, 69. There are anecdotes about Saint-Simon's benefactions to the future Baron Guillaume Dupuytren, the famous surgeon, when he was an impoverished student, in Pierre Leroux, *La Grève de Samarez, poème philosophique*, 2 vols. (Paris, 1863), I, 260–265.

35. On Saint-Simon in the Lille negotiations, see H. A. Larrabee, "Un chapitre peu connu de la vie d'Henri de Saint-Simon," *La Révolution française* (1929), LXXII, pp. 193–216; R. Guyot, *Le Directoire et la paix de l'Europe* (Paris, 1911), p. 453.

36. Lord Malmesbury tried to protect the identity of his informant: "I could wish you would be so good (unless it be absolutely necessary) not to mention M. Saint-Simon's name to anyone but Mr. Pitt." James Harris, First Earl of Malmesbury, *Diaries and Correspondence*, edited by his grandson, the Third Earl, 2nd ed. (London, 1845), III, 445. In a manuscript prepared under the Empire, Saint-Simon noted that his conclusions about the ineptitude of Pitt in foreign policy were based on the opinion of M. Georges Elis (*sic*) whom he had often met in Paris at the home of Madame —— when he was in France with Lord Malmesbury. "Projet d'encyclopédie. Fragments," *La Nef*, III, part 2, no. 20 (July, 1946), 71fn.

37. Pitt to Malmesbury, August 19, 1797, quoted from Foreign Office Records by Markham, *Henri, Comte de Saint-Simon*, p. xiii.

38. Malmesbury, *Diaries*, III, 445.

39. See Albert Mathiez, "Saint-Simon, Lauraguais, Barras, Benjamin Constant, etc., et la réforme de la Constitution de l'an III," *Annales historiques de la révolution française*, new series, VI (1929), 6; also A. C. Thibaudeau, *Mémoires*, 2 vols. (Paris, 1824), II, 338.

40. For a drawing by Crespy le Prince, see H. Bouchot, *Le Luxe français: La Restauration, illustration documentaire* (Paris, 1893), p. 108.

41. His daughter wrote touching letters on his behalf to the revolutionary committees: He was the eighth man to enter the Bastille and he waved a handkerchief to the people on August 10. Archives Nationales, F⁷ 4638.

42. For the details of Sophie's life before her marriage to Saint-Simon, see G. Vauthier, "Le Premier mariage de Mme. de Bawr," *Nouvelle Revue*, IV, Third series (1908), 355–369.

43. Sophie de Bawr, *Mes souvenirs*, 2nd ed. (Paris, 1853), pp. 170, 192.

44. Sophie de Bawr, pp. 212–218, 226–228, 241–243, 307.

45. The Saint-Simonian account in Weill, *Un précurseur*, pp. 17, 18 and fn., 19fn., is based on notes by Gustave d'Eichthal who received the story from Olinde Rodrigues who had heard it from the lips of the master in the last years of his life.

46. Elise Gagne, *Madame de Bawr* (Paris, 1861), p. 22.

47. Madame Marguerite Louise Virginie Ancelot, *Un Salon de Paris, 1824 à 1864* (Paris, 1866), p. 52.

48. Léon Halévy, "Souvenirs de Saint-Simon," *Revue d'histoire économique et sociale*, XIII (1925), 168.

49. De Lépine, *Le Dieu malgré lui*, p. 5. Jean-Louis Laya (1761–1833), a dramatist and *littérateur*, wrote a satire against the Jacobins in 1793 entitled *Ami des Lois*.

50. *Biographie universelle*, LXXX, 409.

51. Biographical notice of Madame de Bawr, in J. M. Quérard, *La Littérature française contemporaine*, 6 vols. (Paris, 1842–1857), I, 199.

52. Gagne, *Madame de Bawr*, pp. 22–23.

53. Quérard, *La Littérature*, I, 199.

54. Vauthier, "Le Premier mariage de Madame de Bawr," *Nouvelle Revue*, p. 369 and fn.

55. According to Rodrigues, who told the story to d'Eichthal, Sophie and her husband tried to help Saint-Simon in his poverty, but he refused their assistance. Weill, *Un Précurseur*, p. 18, fn. 1. Saint-Simon spoke of her rarely, but always with respect. Léon Halévy, "Souvenirs de Saint-Simon," *Revue d'histoire économique et sociale*, XIII, p. 168.

56. *Oeuvres complètes de Saint-Simon* (Rodrigues edition of 1832), p. xxiii.

57. *Biographie universelle*, LXXX, 409.

58. Weill, *Un Précurseur*, p. 19fn.

59. The letter is reproduced in Hippolyte Auger, *Mémoires inédits*, ed. by P. Cottin (Paris, 1891), pp. 396–398. Auger claims to have received the letter from a Saint-Simonian and to have checked on the authenticity of the handwriting.

60. *Notice historique*, in *Oeuvres*, I, 25–26; *Histoire de ma vie*, in *Oeuvres*, XV, 69–70.

4. Leaflets to Humanity

1. On the relations between Napoleon and the *idéologues*, see R. G. Carey, *The Liberals of France and their Relation to the Development of Bonaparte's Dictatorship, 1799–1804* (Chicago, 1947).

2. Mme. la Baronne de Staël, *De la littérature considérée dans ses rapports avec les institutions sociales*, in *Oeuvres complètes*, 2nd ed. (Paris, 1820), IV, 60.

3. Mme. de Staël, IV, 494.

4. Mme. de Staël, IV, 500–501.

5. Mme. de Staël, IV, 20–21.

6. Mme. de Staël, IV, 47–49.

7. Paul Gautier, *Madame de Staël et Napoléon* (Paris, 1903), p. 65.

8. The Geneva text was discovered by Paul E. Martin, "Saint-Simon et sa Lettre d'un habitant de Genève à l'humanité (1802–1803)," *Revue d'histoire suisse*, V (1925), 477–497.

9. The *Journal typographique et bibliographique* of 24 vendémiaire, an XII (October 17, 1803), announced the *Lettre* (sic) *d'un habitant de Genève à ses contemporains*, "un petit volume in-12 (103 p.), prix: 0 fr. 75 et un franc de port, Paris, Surosne,

Libraire, palais du Tribunat, deuxième galerie de bois, et chez les marchands de nouveautés."

10. *Lettres d'un habitant de Genève à ses contemporains (1803) réimprimées conformément à l'édition originale et suivies de deux documents inédits. Lettre aux Européens. [Essai sur l'organisation sociale. Extrait d'une ouvrage sur l'organisation sociale.]* Ed. with an introduction by Alfred Pereire (Paris, 1925). For the *Essai* Pereire used the text in the Bibliothèque Nationale. MSS. N.A.F. (Van Praët) 873 f.234. In N.A.F. 1308, Lefebvre collection, there is a copy of the same *Essai.* Parts of it had previously been published by Georges and Hubert Bourgin, *Le Socialisme français de 1789 à 1848* (Paris, 1912), pp. 26–27, on the basis of Archives Nationales F^{17} 4317, a copy sent to Fourcroy. On 29 thermidor, an XII (August 16, 1804), Fourcroy sent a curt note of acknowledgment. *Lettres d'un habitant de Genève . . . .* (1925), pp. xiv, 95. The *Lettre aux Européens* was in the Archives Pereire and is now in the Bibliothèque Nationale. MSS. N.A.F. 24606.

11. Jean Dautry, "Sur un imprimé retrouvé du Comte de Saint-Simon," *Annales historiques de la révolution française*, new series, XX (1948), 289.

12. Dautry, *Annales historiques*, 302, on basis of the minutes of the Lycée's Administrative Committee, January 29, 1802, in the Bibliothèque historique de la Ville de Paris. MS. 14.754 A Fol°.

13. *A la société du lycée* (Paris, s.d.), pp. 4–5.

14. *A la société*, pp. 6–7.

15. *A la société*, p. 8.

16. Bibliothèque de l'Arsenal. Fonds Enfantin 7855. The letter was reprinted in the *Oeuvres*, XV, 8–9, and in Pereire's ed. of the *Lettres d'un habitant de Genève*, pp. lix–lx. Weill, *Un Précurseur*, p. 19fn., refers to a letter sent along with the brochure to a M. de Billy, Professor of Mathematics at the Ecole Militaire. The letter (included in the Collection Charavay) asks the professor's opinion and apologizes for not being able to pay at the moment debts left at Fontainebleau. The Genevan edition of the *Lettres* included a special appeal to the local mathematician Louis Bertrand, offering him the glory of being the first scientist to set his foot on the path of perfectibility, and a general call to all Genevans to be the first nation to heed his words since they had contributed more to the progress of knowledge than "any other fraction of humanity." Copy in the Bibliothèque de la société d'histoire et d'archéologie, Geneva, pp. 23, 47. The *variantes* between the Genevan and the Paris editions have been discussed in detail by Martin, "Saint-Simon et sa Lettre d'un habitant de Genève à l'humanité," *Revue d'histoire suisse*, pp. 492–497.

17. *Lettres d'un habitant de Genève*, in *Oeuvres*, XV, 50. Condorcet had also allowed women to participate in the "most important scientific discoveries." *Fragment sur l'Atlantide*, in *Oeuvres*, ed. by A. Condorcet O'Connor and M. F. Arago (Paris, 1847), VI, 633.

18. *Lettres d'un habitant de Genève à ses contemporains*, in *Oeuvres*, XV, 14.

19. *Oeuvres*, XV, 25.

20. *Oeuvres*, XV, 30 fn. 1.

21. "The temporal power will naturally descend to the second rank of esteem when the spiritual power will come into the hands of the scientists." Olinde Rodrigues dropped this footnote in his 1832 edition of the work. It was restored in *Oeuvres*, XV, 59. The tyrannical propensities of this sacerdocy of scientists have often been remarked upon. See Charles Renouvier, *Philosophie analytique de l'histoire* (Paris, 1897), IV, 153.

22. *Lettres d'un habitant de Genève*, in *Oeuvres*, XV, 31–32.

23. *Oeuvres*, XV, 32.

24. *Oeuvres*, XV, 46.

25. *Oeuvres*, XV, 47.

26. *Oeuvres*, XV, 23fn.

27. *Oeuvres*, XV, 22.

28. *Oeuvres*, XV, 48.

29. *Oeuvres*, XV, 48.

30. *Oeuvres*, XV, 55.

31. *Oeuvres*, XV, 51–53.

32. *Oeuvres*, XV, 55.

33. *Lettre aux Européens*, p. ˮ79.

34. *Lettre*, p. 80.

35. *Lettre*, p. 80.

36. A. Aulard, *The French Revolution*, transl. by Bernard Miall, 4 vols. (London, 1910), IV, 258fn., referred to the *Esquisse d'un nouveau plan d'organisation sociale* on the basis of a police report and analysis of 9 prairial, an XII (May 27, 1804), Archives Nationales F⁷ 3832. He reproduced the document in *Paris sous le premier Empire*, 3 vols. (Paris, 1912–1923), I, 21–22. It was also reprinted in Gouhier, *La Jeunesse d'Auguste Comte*, II, 358–359. Bazin, summoned by the police, contradicted Saint-Simon's story and said that since permission to publish in France would be refused, he would have the manuscript printed in Hamburg, and was to start out that very day for the purpose.

37. The *Lettres d'un habitant de Genève* had already accepted the central position of mathematics: "I shall add that mathematics has the only materials which can be used in the construction of a general system. . . ." *Oeuvres*, XV, 40, note 1.

38. Saint-Simon on occasion referred to actual meetings with Condorcet, the aristocratic fellow Picard, in 1791–1792. Dautry, *Saint-Simon*, p. 15fn., on the basis of the papers in the La Sicotière Collection.

39. *Histoire naturelle de Mʳᵉ François Bacon suivie de l'Atlas nouveau et traduite par Pierre Amboise, sieur de La Magdelaine* (Paris, 1631); *La Nouvelle Atlantide de François Bacon traduite en françois, et continuée, avec des réflexions sur l'institution et les occupations des académies françoise, des sciences et des inscriptions, par M. R. Raguet* (Paris, 1702).

40. Antoine Lasalle's fifteen-volume translation of Bacon, *Oeuvres*, appeared in Dijon an VIII–an XI. See also Alexandre Deleyre, *Analyse de la philosophie du chancelier François Bacon avec sa vie, traduite de l'anglais*, 3 vols. (Amsterdam and Paris, 1755).

41. "The love of truth assembles there the men whom the suppression of ordinary passions has rendered worthy of participation; and the enlightened nations, realizing all that truth can accomplish for the happiness of the human species, lavishly endow genius with the means of showing its activity and its strength." *Fragment sur l'Atlantide*, in *Oeuvres*, VI, 598.

42. All peoples on the same intellectual level would participate in a "general subscription of all members" of an international society. *Oeuvres*, VI, 653, 660.

5. The Savant in Arms

1. De Lépine, *La Dieu malgré lui*, pp. 9–10.

2. *Histoire de ma vie*, in *Oeuvres*, XV, 74.

3. Bibliothèque Nationale, Rés. V. 1132. The work was forgotten until Olinde Rodrigues published an analysis in *Le Producteur* (1826), III, 92–109, 281–304.

4. *Le Producteur*, III, 105.

5. Destutt de Tracy's paper reviewing a work on Kant, "De la métaphysique de

Kant, ou Observations sur un ouvrage intitulé *Essai d'une exposition succincte de la Critique de la Raison Pure*, par J. Kinker, traduit du hollandais par J. le F., en 1 vol. in –8°, à Amsterdam, 1801," read before the Institute on 7 floréal, an X (see Institut de France, Académie des sciences morales et politiques, *Mémoires*, first series, IV, 544–606), emphasized the contrast between the metaphysical character of German philosophy and the rigorous nonmetaphysical character of the French school which continued to follow Condillac:

"[In Germany] one is a Kantian as one was a Christian, a Mohammedan, a Brahmin, as one was once a Platonist, a Stoic, an Academician, and as one was later a Scotist or a Thomist, and as finally in the seventeenth century we were all Cartesians. . . . [In France] in the ideological, moral, and political sciences . . . there is no head of a sect. One does not follow anybody's banner. Each one has his personal and completely independent opinions; and if there is agreement on several points, it always takes place without people making a plan for agreement, often without knowing it. . . .

"The Germans so little understand this that they consider us in metaphysics disciples of Condillac in the same sense that they are Kantians or Leibnitzians. They forget that Condillac neither dogmatized, nor created, nor pretended to create, a new philosophical system; nor did he undertake to resolve any of these famous questions of psychology, of cosmology, and of theology which for the Germans comprise metaphysics; they forget that he practically limited himself to an examination of our ideas and their symbols, to seeking for their properties, to drawing from them a few consequences. Moreover, they do not know that among those Frenchmen who like him confine themselves to the same speculations, there is perhaps not one who adopts unqualifiedly Condillac's principles of grammar, or who is fully satisfied with his analysis of the intellectual faculties or who finds no objection to his theories on reasoning. In short, the foreigners do not know that what we esteem in Condillac is not his conclusions but his method.

". . . This method guides us with a slow but certain pace towards truth in all branches of human knowledge. . . .

"It consists in scrupulously observing the facts, in deducing consequences when they are completely certain, in not giving to simple suppositions the quality of facts, in trying to bind together only such truths as are linked naturally with one another and without lacunae, in admitting ignorance and always preferring it to any assertion which lacks verisimilitude (547–555)."

Citoyen Villers published a *Philosophie de Kant ou principes fondamentaux de la philosophie transcendantale, première partie*, in Metz in 1801. Kant was noticed, but he was generally considered too "metaphysical," hence unscientific.

6. G. Lacour-Gayet, *Bonaparte, membre de l'Institut* (Paris, 1921), pp. 33–34.

7. Dr. P. J. G. Cabanis had a prophetic insight into the fate of his class in an IV: "The instinct of despots, who encourage the mathematical and physical sciences, literature and the arts, had always made them fear the moral and political sciences." *Considérations générales sur l'étude de l'homme et les rapports de son organisation physique avec ses facultés intellectuelles et morales*, in Institut de France, Académie des sciences morales et politiques, *Mémoires*, first series, I, 95.

8. F. Picavet, in *Les Idéologues* (Paris, 1891), p. 453, recognized in Saint-Simon's system an attempt to do what Destutt de Tracy, Cabanis, Draparnaud, and other *idéologues* had either "realized or proposed."

9. "Avertissement et le plan de travail," *Introduction aux travaux scientifiques du xixe siècle* (1807), in *Oeuvres choisies*, I, 47–52. There was a limited edition of this work in 1807 in which the work plan appears. The first volume of the two-volume edition of 1808 which was distributed by Saint-Simon and reprinted in the *Oeuvres*

choisies differed only in minor details from the 1807 version. Quotations which follow are from the 1808 edition, accepted as his definitive text.

10. On the title page of volume I of the 1808 edition in the Bibliothèque Nationale (from Fournel's library), there is a manuscript note by Enfantin, "sorti non coupé de la bibliothèque de M. de Lacépède en juillet 1826." A letter attached to this copy, signed by de Lacépède, June 11, 1808, promised to read the work "avec tout l'empressement qu'inspiraient la grandeur du sujet et le nom de l'auteur."

11. Letter from Bouvard, June 20, 1808, cited in *Lettres de C.-H. de Saint-Simon* (Paris, 1808), pp. 3–4.

12. Georges Dumas, *Psychologie de deux messies positivistes* (Paris, 1905), pp. 38–50, first used these works in drawing a psychological profile of Saint-Simon.

13. The Bibliothèque Nationale copy (4° Z 3522, 3–5) consists of three pamphlets separately paged, 75 pp., 23 pp., and 137 pp., with an introductory preface, pp. i–xvi, entitled *Histoire de la vie de Saint-Simon*, an autobiography, and *Esquisse du plan de mon ouvrage*. The three parts are called *Première correspondance, seconde livraison*, and *Troisième livraison*, the last reprinting the work plan of part one, plus volume II of the *Introduction aux travaux scientifiques du xixe siècle*. This copy bears the imprint of Scherff, Paris, 1808. Other copies have only the *1re correspondance* and autobiography, or the full preface, *première correspondance*, and *seconde livraison*. Rodrigues republished the autobiography in his edition of 1832. It was also reprinted in the *Oeuvres*, XV, 64–74.

14. *Lettres de C.-H. de Saint-Simon, 1re correspondance*, p. 13.

15. *Lettres*, p. xii.

16. *Lettres*, pp. 46–47, 49.

17. *Lettres*, p. 65.

18. *Lettres*, p. 70.

19. *Lettres*, p. 72. Bouvard's reply was reprinted in the *Oeuvres*, XV, 75.

20. *Lettres de C.-H. de Saint-Simon, 1re correspondance*, p. 74.

21. MS. of *Histoire de l'homme*, in the Bibliothèque de l'Arsenal, Fonds Enfantin, 7802 (132), 8.

22. See *Histoire de l'homme. Premier brouillon* (n.p., n.d.), Bibliothèque Nationale Rés. R. 967, for a copy with the interpolated pages. Another edition, Bibliothèque Nationale Rés. m.Z. 187 (7), entitled *Histoire de l'homme. 1er brouillon. Introduction. Deuxième cahier* (n.p., n.d.), apparently was issued subsequently. The editors of the *Oeuvres* probably erred in stating that the *Nouvelle encyclopédie prospectus* published in 1810 was the first cahier (*Oeuvres*, XV, 103fn.).

23. *Histoire de l'homme, premier brouillon*, p. 10. Quotation is from the *avertissement*, which was reprinted in *Oeuvres*, XV, 104–105.

24. *Histoire de l'homme*, p. 10.

25. *Histoire de l'homme, Deuxième cahier*, pp. 10–11.

26. *Histoire*, pp. 16–18.

27. *Histoire, premier brouillon*, p. 7.

28. *Histoire*, p. 21.

29. *Histoire*, pp. 9, 11, 15–16.

30. *Histoire*, pp. 21–22.

31. *Histoire*, p. 13.

32. *Histoire, Deuxième cahier*, pp. 21, 53–54, 56.

33. *Esquisse d'une nouvelle encyclopédie ou introduction à la philosophie du xixe siècle, ouvrage dédié aux penseurs. Premier aperçu* (Paris, n.d.), p. 8. This brochure is reproduced in the *Oeuvres*, XV, 89–96.

34. *Esquisse d'une nouvelle encyclopédie*, p. 5.

35. *Nouvelle encyclopédie. Première livraison servant de prospectus* (Paris, impr. de J.-L. Scherff, 1810), pp. 25–27.

36. There are a number of versions with this title in the Bibliothèque Nationale. MSS. N.A.F. 24605; among them is a *Projet d'encyclopédie, second prospectus*, which also appears in the Archives Nationales. Archives de Police Générale, F⁷ 4233; fragments of this sketch were published by Henri Gouhier in *La Nef*, III, Part 2, no. 20 (July 1946), 64–73. Portions of the same encyclopedic project were published by Nauroy, "Un Manuscrit inédit de Saint-Simon, Projet d'encyclopédie, second prospectus, première partie," *Revue socialiste*, XXIX (1899), 452–470. To the same period probably belongs a *Mémoire sur l'encyclopédie*, the original manuscript of which is now lost; the editors of the *Oeuvres* published what they believed to be a fragment (XV, 147ff.).

37. *Projet d'encyclopédie, second prospectus. Fragments*, in *La Nef*, p. 67.

38. *Nouvelle Encyclopédie*, p. 22.

39. *Esquisse d'une nouvelle encyclopédie*, p. 4 and plate at end of book, where he juxtaposed a diagram of Bacon's and his own encyclopedic project to illustrate the obvious superiority of his conception. (See copy in the Bibliothèque Nationale, 4° Z 3522, 6.)

40. *Nouvelle Encyclopédie*, pp. 23–24.

41. *Courrier de l'Europe et des spectacles*, October 8, 1808.

42. Hyacinthe Azaïs to Saint-Simon, July 2, 1809 and July 9, 1809. Bibliothèque Nationale. MSS. N.A.F. 24605. See appendix on Azaïs in George Boas, *French Philosophies of the Romantic Period* (Baltimore, 1925), pp. 310–319.

43. Coëssin to Saint-Simon, November 3, 1808. Bibliothèque Nationale. MSS. N.A.F. 24605. François Guillaume Coëssin's *Neuf livres suivis de la théorie de l'envahissement et d'un aperçu général de la théorie des formes sociales*, which became the Bible of his cult, was published the following year, in 1809. This letter answers Gouhier's query, *La Jeunesse d'Auguste Comte*, II, 359, as to whether they had any relationship in the post-Directorate period.

6. A Psychological Self-Portrait

1. *Epître dédicatoire à mon neveu*, in *Oeuvres*, XV, 96.

2. *Notice historique*, in *Oeuvres*, I, 37.

3. *Epître dédicatoire à mon neveu*, in *Oeuvres*, XV, 97–98. He had already expressed this sentiment in the *Introduction aux travaux scientifiques du xixᵉ siècle*, in *Oeuvres choisies*, I, 60.

4. *Epître dédicatoire à mon neveu*, in *Nouvelle Encyclopédie* (Paris, 1810), p. 7. This paragraph was omitted when the editors reprinted the *Epître* in the *Oeuvres*.

5. *Epître dédicatoire à mon neveu*, in *Oeuvres*, XV, 98–99.

6. *Notice historique*, in *Oeuvres*, I, 41.

7. *Oeuvres*, I, 42.

8. *Oeuvres*, I, 43.

9. *Oeuvres*, I, 43.

10. *Oeuvres*, I, 44.

11. *Oeuvres*, I, 44–45.

12. *Oeuvres*, I, 46–47.

13. *Oeuvres*, I, 47.

14. *Oeuvres*, I, 47. See also a fragmentary autobiographical sketch written in 1809 and first published in 1868 in *Oeuvres*, XV, 77–88.

7. The Climacteric

1. *Réponse de M. de Saint-Simon à M. de Redern. Première lettre. Alençon, 12 août, 1812.*

2. Letter from Saint-Simon, May 21, 1807, in *Correspondance entre M. de Saint-Simon et M. de Redern*, pp. 8–9. A letter to Rihouet, Redern's agent, written 16 ventôse, 1805, used the same image. Bibliothèque Nationale. MSS. N.A.F. 24605.

3. Letter from Saint-Simon, June 22, 1807, in *Correspondance entre M. de Saint-Simon et M. de Redern.*

4. Letters from Redern, July 29 and August 6, 1807, *Correspondance.*

5. *Correspondance*, 2 pages preceding the correspondence in copy in Bibliothèque Nationale, Rés. m.Z. 187 (1).

6. MS. letter to Boissy d'Anglas (a copy, not in Saint-Simon's hand), November 2, 1807, which with prefatory material was titled "Affaire entre M. de Saint-Simon et M. de Redern." It forms part two of the *Correspondance*, the first part consisting of the five letters exchanged between Saint-Simon and Redern.

7. *Correspondance*, November 2, 1807.

8. Archives Nationales. Justice BB^{11}3, no. 7269: Redern's dossier.

9. Hector de La Ferrière-Percy, *Histoire de Flers, ses seigneurs, son industrie* (Paris, 1855), p. 299. See also J. Rombault, "Redern et Saint-Simon," *Bulletin de la société historique de l'Orne*, XL (1895), 359–369.

10. A. Surville, *Le Comte de Redern d'après sa correspondance avec la Ctesse sa femme (1808–1822)* (Flers-de-l'Orne, 1909), p. 5.

11. *Oeuvres*, XV, 112–113. An incomplete manuscript in Saint-Simon's hand was acquired in 1867 by the Saint Simonians and dated 1811 when they reproduced it in *Oeuvres*, XV, 104–118. It contains a "troisième partie" and a "quatrième partie," entitled respectively "Cause de leur future réconciliation," and "Objet d'utilité vers lequel leurs efforts communs se dirigeront," plus a section which the editors labeled "Lettres philosophiques et sentimentales," headed Alençon and consisting of two letters and a critique of Condorcet, "Histoire du passé et de l'avenir de l'espèce humaine."

12. Redern, *Mémoire sur mes anciennes relations d'affaires avec M. de Saint-Simon*, Appendix reproducing five letters from Saint-Simon, October 14, 1811 through June 20, 1812. Redern's *Mémoire* was printed July 8, 1812. Quotation is from pp. 118–119 of the *Oeuvres*, XV, where the five letters were also reproduced.

13. *Oeuvres*, XV, 119–120.

14. *Oeuvres*, XV, 120.

15. *Oeuvres*, XV, 120–121.

16. *Oeuvres*, XV, 121.

17. Surville, *Le Comte de Redern*, pp. 14–15.

18. *Réponse de M. de Saint-Simon à M. de Redern* [Alençon, July 25, 1812], MS., excerpt quoted in *Oeuvres*, XV, 133.

19. *Mémoire introductif de M. de Saint-Simon sur sa contestation avec M. de Redern* (Alençon, impr. de Malassis jeune, 1812, 25 pages), p. 2.

20. *Mémoire introductif*, p. 3.

21. *Mémoire introductif*, pp. 5–7.

22. *Mémoire introductif*, p. 12.

23. *Mémoire introductif*, p. 13.

24. *Mémoire introductif*, p. 14.

25. *Mémoire introductif*, p. 18.

26. *Mémoire introductif*, p. 21.

27. Surville, *Le Comte de Redern*, p. 16.

28. Redern, *Mémoire sur mes anciennes relations d'affaires*, p. 35.

29. *Mémoire*, pp. 36–38.

30. *Mémoire*, p. 41.

31. *Réponse de M. de Saint-Simon à M. de Redern* [Alençon, July 25, 1812], MS. Bibliothèque Nationale, Rés. m.Z. 187 (4), has the signed refusal, dated July 28, 1812, on the text.

32. *Réponse de M. de Saint-Simon à M. de Redern. Seconde lettre. Alençon, 18 août, 1812* (n.p., n.d.), a hand-written postscript. This postscript was published in the *Oeuvres*, XV, 135.

33. Surville, *Le Comte de Redern*, p. 16.

34. *Le Comte de Redern*, pp. 18–19.

35. *Considérations sur la nature de l'homme*, 2 vols. (Paris, 1835). He had known the great Mesmer and had written a work on psychology in 1815 in which a definition of insanity clearly harks back to his estimate of Saint-Simon's strange behavior. "Insanity is an evil rather than an illness; the madmen often feel very good, almost to the point of madness. Whatever the various types may be, the main characteristic is always the same. It is a disproportion between the degree of vivacity with which exterior objects and their resulting sensations are experienced and the fictions of the imagination and recollections which memory reproduces. This occurs either when strong passions have given to chimerical ideas by which they nourish themselves enough liveliness to have a complete reality in our eyes, or when there is a general defect of equilibrium." *Des modes accidentels de nos perceptions, ou examen sommaire des modifications que des circonstances particulières apportent à l'exercice de nos facultés et à la perception des objets extérieurs*, 2nd ed. (Paris, 1818), p. 30. A book entitled *Emigration des peuples barbares* (Paris, 1817) is also ascribed to him. See C. Leroux-Cesbron, "Un Allemand propriétaire en France pendant la Révolution," *Revue des études historiques*, pp. 352–362; *Biographie nouvelle des contemporains* (Paris, 1827), XVII, 295–296; P. Larousse, *Grand Dictionnaire universel du xixᵉ siècle*, XIII, 810; *Biographie universelle*, XXXV; Gouhier, *La Jeunesse d'Auguste Comte*, II, 128–130.

36. The details of his illness were narrated in a letter to his sister Adélaïde, February 8, 1813. Bibliothèque Nationale. MSS. N.A.F. 24605. The Saint-Simonians who edited the *Oeuvres* glossed over the episode of Saint-Simon's nervous collapse, printing only fragments of the letter and creating the impression that after leaving Péronne Saint-Simon took up residence near the Palais Royal (*Oeuvres*, XV, 137). Dumas, following a stray reference in P. Leroux's *Livre de Job* (Paris, 1866), p. 4, searched records at Belhomme's but found no trace of Saint-Simon, who may well have used a false name (*Psychologie de deux messies positivistes*, p. 68). Gouhier, following Dumas, erroneously places the dates of the illness and stay at Belhomme's in 1814 (*La Jeunesse*, II, 268–270), and accepts Hubbard's confusion between the Belhomme who was the proprietor of the establishment in Saint-Simon's day, and the Dr. Belhomme, his son, who became an alienist.

37. In a manuscript draft, *Projet d'encyclopédie. Second Prospectus. Première Partie*, Saint-Simon had shown an acquaintance with Pinel's work and had expressed the opinion that his studies of madness had considerably advanced our knowledge of the "moral man." Bibliothèque Nationale. MSS. N.A.F. 24605.

38. For details on Belhomme's establishment, see R. Semelaigne, *Les Pionniers de la psychiatrie française avant et après Pinel*, 2 vols. (Paris, 1930), I, 12ff.

39. Letter of February 8, 1813, to his sister Adélaïde. Bibliothèque Nationale. MSS. N.A.F. 24605.

40. Letter of February 12, 1813, to his sister Adélaïde. Bibliothèque Nationale. MSS. N.A.F. 24605.

41. Letter of February 13, 1813, to his sister Adélaïde. Bibliothèque Nationale. MSS. N.A.F. 24605.

42. Memorandum entitled "A M. Danicourt." Bibliothèque Nationale. MSS. N.A.F. 24605.

43. Memorandum of proposals for presentation to a family council. Bibliothèque Nationale. MSS. N.A.F. 24605.

44. *Mémoire sur la science de l'homme*, in *Oeuvres*, XL, 40.

45. *Travail sur la gravitation universelle*, in *Oeuvres*, XL, 311–312.

46. Letter quoted in *Oeuvres*, XV, 140–141.

47. See the list of scientists, *Oeuvres*, XV, 139–140.

48. *Oeuvres*, XV, 141–142.

49. *Oeuvres*, XV, 143.

50. *Oeuvres*, XV, 145–146.

PART II

THE UNIVERSAL SYSTEM

8. In Search of a Monist Principle

1. *Introduction aux travaux scientifiques du xixe siècle* (1808), in *Oeuvres choisies*, I, 148. This is an accurate quotation from the Abbé de Condillac, *Traité des systèmes, où l'on en démêle les inconvénients et les avantages* (Amsterdam, 1771), pp. 1–2.

2. Cabanis also believed that he was building a new system. He was as conscious as Saint-Simon that "After having overturned the monstrous temple of *error* and of *tyranny* the time has come for the new edifice to free itself from the ruins which obscure it and to reveal itself poised on an unshakable foundation." *Considérations générales sur l'étude de l'homme et les rapports de son organisation physique avec ses facultés intellectuelles et morales*, pp. 94–95.

3. Charles Fourier, *Théorie des quatre mouvements et des destinées générales*, 3rd ed., in *Oeuvres complètes* (1846), I, 12. The first edition of Fourier's work was published in 1808. There is no reason to believe that either Saint-Simon or Fourier was aware of the other's existence under the Empire. Their works appeared in limited editions and were hardly noticed at the time. In Fourier's system the four movements are material, organic, animal, and social, and they all have one law — passionate attraction.

4. Most of the universal systems were constructed around a first principle other than the Deity. Citoyen Bresson, a *cultivateur*, wrote in five parts a treatise on *La Vérité, découverte en physique, métaphysique et morale* (an V and IX). There is an *Exposition du tableau philosophique des connaissances humaines* by the Citoyen Thiébault (Paris, an X). Volume II of the *Mémoires* of the Institute's Académie des sciences morales et politiques included a notice of Dupont de Nemours's *Philosophie de l'univers;* volume V, a notice of Draparnaud, *Discours sur la philosophie des sciences* (Montpellier, an X), a *Discours sur l'histoire universelle depuis Charlemagne jusqu'à nos jours*, in two volumes by the Citoyen Gin (Paris, 1802). In an VII there was published in Paris a *Nouvelle organisation des sociétés* by a Citoyen Lefèvre; in an II and an III four volumes of Citoyen Lejoyand's *Principes naturels et applicables à toutes les branches de physique et de morale, et spécialement à la médecine*. Two volumes of a universal system by Antoine Lasalle, the translator of Bacon, had appeared in London in 1788 under the title *La Balance naturelle, ou essai sur une loi universelle appliquée*

aux lettres, aux sciences, arts, métiers et aux moindres détails de la vie commune; two more volumes had appeared in Geneva in 1789 under the title *De la mécanique morale ou essai sur l'art de perfectionner et d'employer ses organes propres, acquis et conquis.* In an VII at Paris also appeared a *Science de l'organisation sociale, démontrée dans ses premiers élémens,* by Citoyen Brun; in an IX, a *Théorie des institutions sociales,* by a Citoyen Berthier, and *De l'économie publique réduite à un principe,* by the Citoyen Eugène-Arnaud Vitrolles. H. Azaïs, *Cours de philosophie générale ou explication simple et graduelle de tous les faits de l'ordre physique, de l'ordre physiologique, et de l'ordre intellectuel, moral, et politique* (Paris, 1824) and *Explication universelle,* 2 vols. (Paris, 1826) were continuations of the same tendency.

Robert Flint caught the full significance of Saint-Simon's monism in its historical environment:

"He regarded the science of history as a physical science; in other words, refused to recognize the distinctions which exist between the physical and moral worlds, or at least that any of these distinctions necessitate essentially different explanations of physical and moral phenomena. He had consequently to attempt to bring physical law over into the moral world, and into history a province of the moral world. His attempt was a very curious one, and he himself came to acknowledge that it was unsuccessful. Fancying that the unity of the system of nature and the unity of science implied that there was one all-pervasive law from which every other law and fact in existence might be derived, he was led by obvious and superficial considerations to believe gravitation that law, and to maintain that it accounted for chemical and biological, and even mental and historical, phenomena; that gravitation was, in fact, the law of the universe, of the solar system, of the earth, of man, of society, or, generally, of the whole and all its parts; and that if other laws had the appearance of independence, it was only because they had not yet been reduced under or deduced from it. The social atmosphere seems to have been full of ideas of this kind when he wrote; and although he was one of the least likely of men to escape their influence, it is only fair to remember that his rival Fourier was at the same time insisting with much greater emphasis that the central social law was what he called the law of passional attraction, which he believed to be a rigorous deduction from Newton's law; and M. Azaïs, with copious speech and too facile pen, was explaining everything in the material, mental, and social worlds by expansion." *The Philosophy of History in France and Germany* (Edinburgh, 1874), pp. 160–161.

5. *Introduction aux travaux scientifiques du xixe siècle* (1808), in *Oeuvres choisies,* I, 165fn.

6. *Travail sur la gravitation universelle* (1813), in *Oeuvres,* XL, 217 .

7. *Oeuvres,* XL, 239–241.

8. *Mémoire sur la science de l'homme* (1813), in *Oeuvres,* XL, 161.

9. In the *Travail sur la gravitation universelle* (1813) he imagined that he had actually discovered the proper adaptation of the law of gravity which would make it directly applicable to all the sciences. "Every molecule has a constitutional tendency to move in the direction which offers the least resistance." *Oeuvres,* XL, 271–272. From this law he proceeded as follows:

"A general comparison will be established, on the one hand, between the action of molecules which adhere to one another and on the other hand, the action of molecules in a state of fluidity. Natural philosophy will divide itself into two parts, namely: the natural philosophy of inorganic and of organic bodies. We shall find that in inorganic bodies, the action of the solids prevails over that of the fluids and that in organic bodies, the action of the fluids prevails over the solids. We shall stop looking at the universe as if it were composed of two distinct natures, namely: moral nature and physical nature. We shall consider phenomena which are today looked upon as having supernatural or divine causes as the effects of the action of imponderable fluids." *Oeuvres*, XL, 272. This was Saint-Simon writing in strangely Ionian pre-Socratic language, though he put the words into the mouth of Socrates.

9. The Religion of Science

1. Archives Nationales. Archives de Police Générale, F^7 4775^{12}: Saint-Simon's dossier.

2. Robespierre's police spies were quick to report the superficiality of the ordinary man's anti-Catholicism: "But once he has returned home, having nothing to substitute for the religion which he has just overthrown, if some accident happens to him, if some misfortune occurs, he believes that it is punishment from Heaven. Remorse assails him. He begs pardon from the idol which he has just struck down." "Rapport de Siret, 11 décembre, 1793," in *Paris pendant la Terreur. Rapports des agents secrets du Ministre de l'Intérieur*, 4 vols., published by Pierre Caron (Paris, 1910–1949), I, 257.

3. "Is there any legislator since the beginning of the world who has dared to nationalize atheism?" was asked in a sermon of Chénier and Dusausoir's *Office des décades, ou discours, hymnes et prières en usage dans les temples de la raison*, 2nd ed. (Paris, 1794), p. 175.

4. "A republic of atheists cannot endure; and France is the proof of it." Louis-Gabriel-Ambroise, Vicomte de Bonald, *Théorie du pouvoir*, in *Oeuvres* (Paris, 1880), II, 33.

5. *Introduction aux travaux scientifiques du xix᷉ siècle* (1808), in *Oeuvres choisies*, I, 211–212. Saint-Simon praised de Bonald's works enthusiastically; "His writings . . . seem to me to be the most worthy productions which have appeared for many a year. . . . They are fitting works to rejuvenate science and literature.

"Reading and meditating over the works of M. de Bonald have convinced me that there was an author who profoundly sensed the utility of systematic unity, for he set himself as a goal the task of demonstrating to his countrymen that, given the present state of knowledge, such unity must serve as a basis for scientific and literary work.

"On that point, I am entirely of M. de Bonald's opinion. But I do not share his transports of enthusiasm for deism."

6. "For our ordinances and rites, we have two very long and fair galleries: in one of these we place patterns and samples of all manner of the more rare and excellent inventions: in the other we place the statues of all principal inventors. . . . We have certain hymns and services, which we say daily, of laud and thanks to God for His marvellous works. And forms of prayer, imploring His aid and blessing for the illumination of our labours, and the turning of them into good and holy uses." *The New Atlantis* was first published in 1627, after Bacon's death; the quotation is from the Oxford edition, reset in 1951, pp. 297–298.

7. In 1794 Dupuis presented his work (3 vols. –in 4°, with atlas; 12 vols. –in 8°) to the Convention. In 1798, about the time Saint-Simon was entering upon his philosophical apprenticeship, Dupuis published an abridgement of his work. Picavet, *Les Idéologues*, p. 141.

8. Dupuis, V, vii.

9. Dupuis, V, x–xi.

10. Cabanis in 1795 had ventured the snide hypothesis that religions were the ancient equivalents of a modern metaphysical system like Descartes's. "The theogonies

were for them nothing more than physical or metaphysical systems, like the system of vortices and preëstablished harmony among us, which would without doubt also have become divinities, if the place had not already been preëmpted." *Considérations générales sur l'étude de l'homme*, p. 45.

11. *Travail sur la gravitation universelle* (1813), in *Oeuvres*, XL, 236–237.

12. This position had already been adopted in one passage of the *Lettres d'un habitant de Genève*. "I expect to write you a letter in which I shall envisage religion as a human invention. I shall consider it the only kind of political institution which tends towards the general organization of humanity." *Oeuvres*, XV, 58.

13. *Introduction aux travaux scientifiques du xixe siècle*, in *Oeuvres choisies*, I, 219.

14. *Oeuvres choisies*, I, 213.

15. *Oeuvres choisies*, I, 213.

16. *Oeuvres choisies*, I, 244.

17. *Oeuvres choisies*, I, 212, 214.

18. *Oeuvres choisies*, I, 215.

19. *Nouvelle Encyclopédie*, p. 26.

20. *Notice historique*, in *Oeuvres*, I, 38–39.

21. *Epître dédicatoire à mon neveu*, in *Oeuvres*, XV, 102.

22. *Introduction aux travaux scientifiques du xixe siècle*, in *Oeuvres choisies*, I, 216–218. Saint-Simon's rejection of the idea of God as a fundamental human conception was fortified by the findings of Dr. Itard after experimenting with a "wild child." His report, *De l'éducation d'un homme sauvage ou des premiers développemens physiques et moraux du jeune sauvage de l'Aveyron*, by Citizen Itard, doctor of the National Institute of Deaf Mutes (Paris, an X), was for Saint-Simon proof positive that there were no innate ideas, and none of God. In praising Itard's work (*Mémoire sur la science de l'homme*, in *Oeuvres*, XL, 123–124) Saint-Simon took occasion to criticize violently the brutal treatment which the Abbé Sicard, first guardian of the child, was supposed to have meted out (*Oeuvres*, XL, 122). Itard had received a copy of the manuscript *Science de l'homme*. In his acknowledgement to Saint-Simon he denied the facts about the Abbé Sicard's conduct and called upon Saint-Simon to withdraw his calumnies. Bibliothèque Nationale. MSS. N.A.F. 24605, Itard to Saint-Simon, October 26, 1813.

23. *Mémoire sur la science de l'homme* (1813), in *Oeuvres choisies*, II, 41. When Enfantin first published this work in 1858 he expurgated many such atheistic passages which Lemonnier restored; for example, see *Oeuvres choisies*, II, 103.

24. *Travail sur la gravitation universelle*, in *Oeuvres*, XL, 313.

10. Towards a Positive Science of Man

1. Pierre-Simon de Laplace, *Exposition du système du monde*, 4th ed. (Paris, 1813), p. 5.

2. The law of 3 brumaire, an IV, divided the Institut National des Sciences et des Arts as follows: *1re classe. Sciences physiques et mathématiques:* 1. Mathématiques. 2. Arts mécaniques. 3. Astronomie. 4. Physique expérimentale. 5. Chimie. 6. Histoire naturelle et minéralogie. 7. Botanique et physique végétale. 8. Anatomie et zoologie. 9. Médecine et chirurgie. 10. Economie rurale et art vétérinaire. *2e classe. Sciences morales et politiques:* 1. Analyse des sensations et des idées. 2. Morale. 3. Science sociale et législation. 4. Economie politique. 5. Histoire. 6. Géographie. *3e classe. Littérature et beaux arts:* 1. Grammaire. 2. Langues anciennes. 3. Poésie. 4. Antiq-

uités et monuments. 5. Peinture. 6. Sculpture. 7. Architecture. 8. Musique et déclama-tion. L'Institut de France. *Lois, statuts et règlements* (Paris, 1889), pp. 6–7.

During the reorganization of 3 pluviôse, an XI, the Second Class, Moral and Political Sciences, were dispersed among other classes. The new plan instituted a four-class division: 1. Classe des sciences physiques et mathématiques; 2. Classe de la langue et de la littérature françaises; 3. Classe d'histoire et de littérature ancienne; 4. Classe des beaux arts. *Lois, statuts, et règlements*, p. 72.

The intent of this overhauling of the Institute was made obvious in Article XI of a decree promulgated on 27 ventôse, an XI: "The moral and political sciences in their relations to history constitute one of the subjects of the work of that class. Those of its members who are occupied with researches relative to these sciences should avoid in their treatises any historical, religious, or political discussions which, because of their subject matter or because of the proximity of events, might alter the harmony which should reign among members of the class." *Organisation et règlemens de l'Institut National* (Paris, vendémiaire an XIII), p. 89.

3. J. B. Lamarck, *Système des animaux sans vertèbres, précédé du Discours d'ouver-ture du cours de Zoologie donné dans le Muséum d'Histoire Naturelle l'an 8 de la République* (Paris, 1801). The more complete exposition of the theory appeared in *Philosophie zoologique* (Paris, 1809).

4. Psychology was a term quite current in German metaphysics of the eighteenth century: see Christian Wolff, *Psychologie ou traité de l'âme* (Amsterdam, 1745).

Aristotle's term ἀνθρωπολόγος was general — it meant treating of man. In sixteenth-century English anthropology was used in the broad sense of a science of man or mankind; during the next two hundred and fifty years the sense became somewhat more restricted to a "science of the nature of man embracing Human Physiology and Psychology and their mutual bearing." After about 1860 the term reverted to its more generalized meaning. *The Oxford English Dictionary* (Oxford, 1933), I, 361. At the close of the eighteenth century the Germans tended to use *Anthropologie* to embrace both physiology and psychology. Immanuel Kant wrote a study called *Anthropologie in pragmatischer Hinsicht* (Königsberg, 1798). In France *Anthropologie* still had an anthropomorphic connotation in the 1814 edition of the Dictionary of the French Academy.

Aristotle's φυσιολογία comprehended all of natural science. This sense of physi-ology persisted in English until the end of the eighteenth century when the term came to be restricted to the "science of the normal functions and phenomena of living things." *The Oxford Dictionary*, VII, 811. In his report to the emperor in 1808 Cuvier defined *physiologie* as the "general theory" of the "natural history of living bodies." *Discours sur les progrès des sciences, lettres et arts*, p. 63. Saint-Simon used the term in his own unique way and sometimes in combination as in *physiologie sociale*. *Sciences sociales* and *art social* were common eighteenth-century terms; Condorcet used them both regularly. *Science de l'homme* was used by Cabanis in the *Considérations générales sur l'étude de l'homme*, p. 41.

In 1796 appeared Lagrange's *Essai d'arithmétique politique*.

The early nineteenth century saw the invention of many neologisms, such as the English physianthropy. Comte's *sociology*, coined in 1838, is one of the few new terms which survived.

5. Saint-Simon's image of the sciences as branches growing out of a common trunk can be found in the treatise read by Cabanis before the Institute's Class of Moral and Political Sciences on 7 pluviôse, an IV, *Considérations générales sur l'étude de l'homme* (p. 37): "It is beyond doubt a fine and great idea to consider all the sciences and all the arts as forming an ensemble, an indivisible whole, or like the branches of the

same trunk, united by a common origin, and even more united by the fruit which they are all equally destined to produce, the perfection and the happiness of man." It can of course also be found in Francis Bacon's *The Advancement of Learning* (Oxford University Press, London, 1951), p. 100: "But because the distributions and partitions of knowledge are not like several lines that meet in one angle, and so touch but in a point; but are like branches of a tree, that meet in a stem, which hath a dimension and quantity of entireness and continuance, before it come to discontinue and break itself into arms and boughs: therefore it is good, before we enter into the former distribution, to erect and constitute one universal science. . . ."

The origin of all these images in Genesis is obvious.

6. "We have stated in a number of places of the *Prospectus* that we are chiefly indebted for our encyclopedic tree to Chancellor Bacon. The eulogy of this great man which was read in the *Prospectus* even seems to have contributed to making the works of the English philosopher known to various people. Thus, after such a formal acknowledgment, it is inadmissible either to accuse us of plagiarism, or to look for grounds to render us suspect of it." Jean Le Rond d'Alembert, *Observations sur la division des sciences du Chancelier Bacon*, in *Oeuvres philosophiques, historiques et littéraires*, 18 vols. (Paris, 1805), I, 345.

7. *Organique* was defined in the Dictionary of the French Academy, 1814 edition, as "Terme de physique. Il n'est guère d'usage qu'en cette phrase, Corps organique." Saint-Simon broadened the sense of the word substantially.

8. Johann Gottfried Herder, *Outlines of a Philosophy of the History of Man*, transl. by T. Churchill, 2nd ed. (London, 1803), I, 319, 321–322. "Angebohren, organisch, genetisch ist dies Vermögen: es ist der Grund meiner Naturkräfte, der innere Genius meines Daseyns." Herder, *Sämmtliche Werke*, ed. by Bernhard Suphan (Berlin, 1877–1913), XIII, 276.

9. Condorcet had already emphasized the essential interdependence of all the sciences, including the social sciences, in many passages of the *Fragment sur l'Atlantide, ou efforts combinés de l'espèce humaine pour le progrès des sciences:*

"One might still fear the sort of rivalry which reigns among the sciences. It is in the interest of truth that they should all be united, for there is not a single science which is not more or less immediately dependent upon all the other parts of the scientific system. There is not one science where one could break the chain, without hurting the two portions which have been separated. . . .

"The social sciences, are they not dependent upon the mathematical and physical sciences, since there is no science which does not present truths susceptible of being applied to the needs of men, to the well-being of societies, since without the aid of these sciences it would be impossible either completely to resolve a great number of the questions which social sciences pose or to obtain the facts necessary for their solution?" *Oeuvres*, VI, 607–608.

10. The feeling that a positive social science was still to be created permeated the deliberations of the Institute's Class of Moral and Political Sciences. On 7 ventôse, an VI, Jean-Jacques Régis Cambacérès of the Section of *Science sociale et législation* delivered a *Discours sur la science sociale* in which he said: "No science more than social science is in need of being . . . perfected. This science has to be created almost anew. Most of its principles are still uncertain, undetermined." Institut de France. Académie des sciences morales et politiques, *Mémoires*, 1re série, III, 12. The treatises presented by this Class included many specific studies in problems of social science as well as methodology. Volume I of the *Mémoires*, published thermidor, an VI, included the first of the famous Cabanis treatises which were later assembled to form his *Rapports du physique et du moral* (pp. 37–208) and Baudin des Ardennes's study, *Des clubs*

et de leurs rapports avec l'organisation sociale (pp. 504–542). On 2 fructidor, an V, François Emmanuel Toulongeon read a paper entitled *De l'influence du régime diététique d'une nation sur son état politique* (*Mémoires*, III, 102); on 17 ventôse, an VIII, an associate member, Véron-Fortbonnais, read a *Mémoire sur le genre des questions dont la science de l'économie politique comporte la solution exacte* (*Mémoires*, III, 481 ff.); on 7 prairial, an VIII, Destutt de Tracy read his *Dissertation sur quelques questions d'idéologie* (*Mémoires*, III, 491ff.). In Volume V (p. 67) of the *Mémoires* there was acknowledgement of the receipt of Citoyen Itard's *De l'éducation d'un homme sauvage, ou des premiers développemens physiques et moraux du jeune sauvage de l'Aveyron*. A member of the Class, Baron Degérando, wrote *Considérations sur les différentes méthodes à suivre dans l'observation des peuples sauvages* (an IX), considered a minor classic on anthropological method later in the century. There were also studies on the origin of venereal diseases and their introduction into Alsace, on the habits of American savages, on the semantics of the word "nature," on ancient legislation. Dupont de Nemours presented a treatise on the sociability and morality of dogs, foxes, and wolves. Such works constitute a typical rather than an exhaustive list of the kind of social studies which were undertaken during the period. Social science was becoming positive, but it still lacked a general theory — that was Saint-Simon's main contention.

Simultaneously the enemies of the *idéologues*, the traditionalists, were also focusing their attention on the science of society in revolt against excessive absorption in the sciences of nature. In the *Théorie du pouvoir*, which first appeared from an *émigré* press in Constance in 1795, de Bonald wrote: "What, indeed, are all the sciences in comparison with the science of society? And what is the universe itself if one compares it to man?" *Oeuvres*, I, 101.

11. *Lettres d'un habitant de Genève*, in *Oeuvres*, XV, 39–40 and fn.

12. *Mémoire sur la science de l'homme*, in *Oeuvres*, XL, 25–36.

13. Picavet, *Les Idéologues*, p. 454, has collated contemporary references to Dr. Burdin: "The *Décade* gives us a few details about him. In the year VIII Moreau cites him when discussing the works of Cabanis. In the year XI he announces the *Cours d'études médicales*, in five volumes, by M. Burdin, 'a doctor already known through several works,' who is about to embark upon galvanic experiments in his pneumatic chamber, while the *Décade* inserts a letter of his about hydrophobia."

14. Dr. Jean Burdin, *Essai sur la gangrène humide des hôpitaux* (1796), in collaboration with J. L. Moreau; *Réflexions et observations sur la médecine pneumatique* (1801); *Cours d'études médicales ou exposition de la structure de l'homme*, 5 vols. (1803). The last work was translated into German by F. F. Reuss (Tübingen, 1803); it also had an English translation (London, 1803).

15. *Mémoire sur la science de l'homme*, in *Oeuvres*, XL, 25–26.

16. *Oeuvres*, XL, 26–27.

17. Arthur O. Lovejoy, *The Great Chain of Being* (Cambridge, Mass., 1950), Chapter VIII, pp. 227–241.

18. Lovejoy, Chapter IX, pp. 242–287; Emile Guyénot, *Les Sciences de la vie aux xviie et xviiie siècles. L'Idée d'évolution* (Paris, 1941), pp. 380–439. Saint-Simon had accepted the contemporary notion of a hierarchy of complexity and of perfection from the lowest animal form up to man. "Man is the best organized, that is to say, the most organized of all bodies known to us. . . . The more highly organized an animal is, the more intelligent it is." *Mémoire sur la science de l'homme*, in *Oeuvres*, XL, 188.

19. *Oeuvres*, XL, 27–28. Saint-Simon took seriously the integration of the works of these four scientists. The *Mémoire sur la science de l'homme* purported to present a critical examination of Vicq-d'Azyr's work. *Oeuvres*, XL, 71–81ff. When he claimed

to be quoting from Vicq-d'Azyr he was really "interpreting" the anatomist after his own manner. See Vicq-d'Azyr's *Discours sur l'anatomie*, in *Oeuvres, recueillies et publiées avec des notes et un discours sur sa vie et ses ouvrages par Jacq. L. Moreau*, 6 vols. (Paris, 1805), IV, 5–8. In the *Introduction aux travaux scientifiques du xixe siècle*, in *Oeuvres choisies*, I, 98–110, Saint-Simon had already extracted long passages from Condorcet's *Esquisse d'un tableau historique des progrès de l'esprit humain* and commented upon them. Cabanis's influence permeated all his writings up to 1815. F. X. Bichat (1771–1802), whose *Recherches physiologiques sur la vie et sur la mort* (Paris, an VIII) was widely known, also had a pervasive effect on his thought, particularly his analysis of human aptitudes.

20. *Mémoire sur la science de l'homme*, in *Oeuvres*, XL, 28. The phrase "science positive de l'homme" appeared in the *Mémoire*, 190.

21. *Oeuvres*, XL, 28–31.

22. *Oeuvres*, XL, 17–18.

23. He had already used the phrase "la philosophie positive" in the *Introduction aux travaux scientifiques du xixe siècle*, in *Oeuvres choisies*, I, 198. According to *The Oxford English Dictionary*, this was the original use of the term; actually Madame de Staël's *De la littérature. . . .* (1800) was filled with variations such as "philosophie des sciences positives."

24. *Mémoire sur la science de l'homme*, in *Oeuvres*, XL, 18.

25. *Oeuvres*, XL, 18.

26. *Oeuvres*, XL, 39–40.

27. There are a few passages even in his first tract in which this new attitude is foreshadowed, but the generalization on the over-all shift in emphasis is valid. "My friends, we are organic bodies and I conceived of [this] project by considering our social relations as if they were physiological phenomena. . . ." *Lettres d'un habitant de Genève*, in *Oeuvres*, XV, 40.

11. The Law of Alternativity

1. On 13 ventôse, an XI, the consuls of the Republic (Bonaparte signed as First Consul) ordered the Institute to present a series of reports:

"Article One: The National Institute of France will prepare a general survey of the state and progress of the sciences, of letters and of arts, from 1789 to the first of vendémiaire, an X. This survey, divided into three parts corresponding to each of the classes of the Institute, will be presented to the Government in the month of fructidor, an XI. . . . Article Three: At the same time the National Institute will propose to the government its views concerning the discoveries whose application it deems useful to the public service, concerning the aid and encouragement which the sciences, arts, and letters need, and concerning the perfection of the methods used in various branches of public education." *Organisation et règlemens de l'Institut National* (Paris, vendémiaire an XIII), pp. 169–171. The reports apparently were not presented until 1808, after the reorganization both of the Institute and the government. Saint-Simon's "quotation" of Napoleon's request was an adaptation of this order, *Introduction aux travaux scientifiques du xixe siècle*, in *Oeuvres choisies*, I, 61.

2. On February 6, 1808, a deputation of the Class of Physical and Mathematical Sciences presented their report to Napoleon on the progress of their special fields since 1789. Bougainville introduced his report with sycophancy; the sole merit of the scientists was adding rays to the nation's glory. Cuvier for the physical sciences surpassed Bougainville in his adulation of the Hero who deigned to "crown all sorts of glories with his hands, to encourage every talent, to order the execution of all manner of

useful works." The reports in themselves are really not interesting or provocative. Saint-Simon's judgment of them is correct. G. Cuvier et al., *Discours sur les progrès des sciences, lettres et arts depuis 1789 jusqu'à ce jour ou compte rendu par l'Institut de France à S.M. l'Empereur et roi* (Paris, 1809), pp. 3, 46–47.

Napoleon replied to the scientists after they had delivered their reports: "I wanted to hear you on the progress of the human spirit in recent times in order that what you had to say should be heard by all the peoples and should silence the detractors of our century who, seeking to cause the human spirit to retrogress, seem to have as their goal its extinction.

"I wanted to know what I had to do to encourage your labors, to console me for not otherwise participating in their success. The good of my peoples and the glory of my throne have an equal interest in the prosperity of the sciences.

"My Minister of the Interior will give me a report on your requests. You can always count on my protection." *Discours,* p. 80.

3. *Introduction aux travaux scientifiques du xix⁰ siècle,* in *Oeuvres choisies,* I, 61. Saint-Simon was as unrestrained in his worship of the emperor as were the official scientists of the reorganized Institute: "I feel for the Emperor that tender affection and that lively gratitude with which the soul of a good student feels itself pleasurably agitated for the transcendent professor whose lesson he has understood." *Oeuvres,* I, 224. And again, "The strongest man, after the Emperor, is incontestably the one who admires him most profoundly." *Oeuvres,* I, 231. "The Emperor will conquer the world and will give it laws. . . . Universal monarchy will not be hereditary. It will exist only once in the whole duration of the planet and it is Napoleon who will be its chief. In order to give laws to humanity it was necessary that he unite all powers in his hands." *Oeuvres,* I, 243. "To present to the Emperor a monument worthy of him it would be necessary to carve Mount St. Bernard into his statue, whose base would be the earth itself." *Oeuvres,* I, 246.

4. On Konrad Engelbert Oelsner (1764–1828) see Ludmilla Assing, editor, *Briefwechsel zwischen Varnhagen von Ense und Oelsner, nebst Briefen von Rahel,* 3 vols. (Stuttgart, 1865). During the early part of the Revolution he lived by his pen, sending reports from the battlefield to German newspapers. Later he became the commercial agent of Frankfurt in Paris. He was prodigal with his works. Assing maintains: "In the writings of the Comte de Saint-Simon whole pieces are his." *Briefwechsel,* I, vii.

Des effets de la religion de Mohammed pendant les trois premiers siècles de sa fondation (Paris, 1810) won the prize for Ancient History and Literature at the Institute in 1809. Among other works by Oelsner are *Notice sur la vie de Sièyes* [Anon.] (Switzerland, 1795); *Notice sur la vie et les écrits de M. Joël Barlow, ministre plénipotentiaire des Etats-Unis d'Amérique auprès de S.M. l'Empereur des Français* [Anon.] (Paris, 1813).

5. *Mémoire sur la science de l'homme,* in *Oeuvres,* XL, 68.

6. *Travail sur la gravitation universelle* (1813), in *Oeuvres,* XL, 232–233. Saint-Simon made an interesting observation on Bacon's intellectual fate: "In France everybody talks about this author and very few have read his works." *Oeuvres,* XL, 230–231.

7. F. Bouillier, *Histoire de la philosophie cartésienne,* 2 vols. (Paris, 1868), II, 632–640.

8. Saint-Simon's contrast between Newton and Descartes derived from Fontenelle. *Introduction aux travaux scientifiques du xix⁰ siècle,* in *Oeuvres choisies,* I, 164–165. It is also in the same spirit as the Père Antoine Guénard eulogy, *Discours sur l'esprit philosophique* (crowned by the French Academy in 1755), which Saint-Simon quoted in his *Introduction aux travaux scientifiques,* 236–239. There are also striking textual parallels in Turgot's *Ebauche du second discours dont l'objet sera les progrès de l'esprit*

humain, in *Oeuvres* (1808), II, 278–279: "Descartes envisaged nature like a man who, casting upon it one broad look, embraces it all and with a bird's-eye view makes a plan of it.

"Newton examined it more in detail. He described the country which the other had discovered.

"An attempt has been made to sacrifice Descartes's reputation to Newton. . . .

"Between these two powerful geniuses there has occurred what always happens in all branches of knowledge. A great man opens up new avenues for the human spirit. For a while all men are still no more than his students. Slowly they level the routes which he traced. They unify all the parts of his discoveries. They assemble and they inventory their riches and their strength, until a new great man arises who launches forth from the point where his predecessor had led mankind, even as this predecessor had done. . . ."

9. *Introduction aux travaux scientifiques du xixᵉ siècle*, in *Oeuvres choisies*, I, 164.

10. *Oeuvres choisies*, I, 72.

11. *Oeuvres choisies*, I, 78.

12. *Oeuvres choisies*, I, 73.

13. *Oeuvres choisies*, I, 77.

14. *Oeuvres choisies*, I, 90–91.

15. *Oeuvres choisies*, I, 70.

16. *Mémoire sur la science de l'homme*, in *Oeuvres*, XL, 145–146.

17. *Travail sur la gravitation universelle*, in *Oeuvres*, XL, 256.

18. *Oeuvres*, XL, 228–229.

19. *Oeuvres*, XL, 226–228.

20. *Oeuvres*, XL, 267.

21. *Introduction aux travaux scientifiques du xixᵉ siècle*, in *Oeuvres choisies*, I, 74.

22. *Oeuvres choisies*, I, 141.

23. *Oeuvres choisies*, I, 242.

24. *Mémoire sur la science de l'homme*, in *Oeuvres*, XL, 11.

25. *Oeuvres*, XL, 11–12, 24; *Introduction aux travaux scientifiques du xixᵉ siècle*, in *Oeuvres choisies*, I, 59.

26. "de prendre celle absolument opposée. . . ." *Mémoire sur la science de l'homme*, in *Oeuvres*, XL, 146.

12. Man Before History

1. The members of the Saint-Simonian cult, in their proselytizing, were aware that history was the only portal through which one could enter the doctrine. "If I did not believe that you were already fatigued by so long a letter, I would have tried to trace for you a rapid summary of the history of humanity from its infancy until our times. It would be the best means, I believe, of making you accept the views of the doctrine." Letter from Mme. Bazard to Mme. Le Breton, Bibliothèque de l'Arsenal. Fonds Enfantin 7824 (138).

2. *Introduction aux travaux scientifiques du xixᵉ siècle*, in *Oeuvres choisies*, I, 248.

3. G. W. F. Hegel, *Lectures on the Philosophy of History*, transl. by J. Sibree (London, 1902), p. 34.

4. At times in later years the spirit of his historical determinism was intransigent. In *Du système industriel* (*Oeuvres*, XXI, 28), he dogmatized: "It is not in the power

of any human force to cause this natural movement to retrogress, nor is it in its power to render only partial obedience. . . ."

5. Saint-Simon put these words into Socrates's mouth in an imaginary discourse to his pupils. *Travail sur la gravitation universelle,* in *Oeuvres,* XL, 254.

6. Dautry, *Saint-Simon,* p. 69, from the manuscripts in the La Sicotière Collection.

7. Portions of this text were used by Saint-Simon in *L'Organisateur,* in *Oeuvres,* XX, 118–119.

8. Of the French Revolution he wrote in *Du système industriel* (1821) (*Oeuvres,* XXI, 78): "Events have burdened it with purely accidental elements which tend to disguise its true character."

9. *Introduction aux travaux scientifiques du xixe siècle,* in *Oeuvres choisies,* I, 191.

10. *Travail sur la gravitation universelle,* in *Oeuvres,* XL, 246.

11. *L'Organisateur,* in *Oeuvres,* XX, 70.

12. He called Hume the greatest modern historian (*Du système industriel,* in *Oeuvres,* XXI, 169), though on the surface it would appear that nothing could be further from the spirit of Saint-Simon's philosophical history than Hume's *History of England.*

13. *L'Organisateur,* in *Oeuvres,* XX, 75. In the *Introduction aux travaux scientifiques du xixe siècle,* in *Oeuvres choisies,* I, 196–197, he had attacked Volney's conception of Arab civilization.

14. Cuvier et al., *Discours sur les progrès des sciences,* pp. 83–101.

15. *Discours,* p. 83.

16. Even a decade later Stendhal expressed similar contempt for French historical writing. Henri Beyle, Letter to ———, April 30, 1824, in *Correspondance inédite,* 2 vols. (Paris, 1855), I, 260–264.

17. There is little likelihood that Vico penetrated through his influence on Herder. He was not mentioned by Herder until 1797, when most of his *History of Man* was already published. Alexander Gillies, *Herder* (Oxford, 1944), p. 5. There is, moreover, no indication that Saint-Simon knew anything of Herder. The Italian professor was not well known in France until he was discovered by Michelet and a selection of his works published in translation in 1826. Auguste Comte was the first in Saint-Simon's circle to know of Herder. H. Tronchon, *La Fortune intellectuelle de Herder en France* (Paris, 1920), pp. 512–516.

18. In 1750 Turgot, Prieur de Sorbonne, delivered two discourses in Latin at the opening and the closing of the Sorboniques. They were first published in French in volume II of the 1808 edition of the *Oeuvres: Sur les avantages que l'établissement du Christianisme a procurés au Genre-humain, prononcé le 3 juillet 1750* (19–51); *Sur les progrès successifs de l'esprit humain, prononcé le 11 décembre 1750* (52–92). His outlook on universal history was a conciliation of dominant eighteenth-century conceptions of happiness, progress, and utility, with a Christian outlook — a feat accomplished by diluting the more pessimist expressions of theology. The influence of Turgot upon Condorcet, who wrote his biography, was direct. It is hard to establish any textual filiation between Turgot and Saint-Simon because the *discours* were not mentioned by him. Many passages in his philosophy of history nevertheless parallel Turgot in remarkable ways and will be referred to in the text. Saint-Simon's outlook in some respects was closer to Turgot than to Condorcet in that he too combined an ardent belief in progress with an appreciation of the historical contributions of Christianity.

19. Quotations are labeled either *idée à employer* or *idée à réfuter.* Bibliothèque Nationale. MSS. N.A.F. 24605. In the *Introduction aux travaux scientifiques du xixe*

siècle he wrote paradoxically: "This work, though it is defective in all its details, is one of the finest productions of the human mind." *Oeuvres choisies*, I, 109. He inserted page after page of the *Esquisse* into his own text. *Oeuvres choisies*, I, 99–107. Condorcet's debt to his English predecessors he expressed in a striking image: "I consider Locke the man who discovered the mine, Price and Priestley the men who smelted the metal, and Condorcet the man who forged with the metal the work tools necessary to make new diggings and thus to discover new veins." *Oeuvres choisies*, I, 110. He mingled criticism with his praise: "Condorcet is the first writer who ever undertook to draw up a history of the human spirit, but the philanthropic passion which dominated him bewitched his eyes. He gave us no history, he sketched a novel. He did not see things as they are but as he wished they were." *Oeuvres choisies*, I, 191. In *Du système industriel* he called Condorcet "the most capable philosopher of the second half of the eighteenth century"; of the impact on human thought of the *Esquisse* he wrote that Condorcet "made more true politics after he was proscribed by the Convention than when he was an influential member of the body." *Oeuvres*, XXII, 188fn.

20. Cabanis had expressed a similar disdain for the study of any history prior to the Greeks. "History hardly goes further back than the establishment of the free peoples in Greece (beyond that one finds nothing but ridiculous impostures or allegorical tales)." *Considérations générales sur l'étude de l'homme*, p. 44.

21. Turgot had used the analogy in *Sur les progrès successifs de l'esprit humain*, p. 53. The traditionalist revival of Saint Augustine with his comparison between the upbringing of an individual and the education of the chosen people through a historic process could be a more recent source for this conception.

22. Bibliothèque Nationale. MSS. N.A.F. 24605.

23. The idea had also been presented in the *Esquisse d'une nouvelle encyclopédie*, p. 6. The *Mémoire sur la science de l'homme* listed four successive civilizations, each with its characteristic innovation: 1. the Egyptians, who first conceived of cause and effect and originated religious ideas; 2. the Greeks, who organized polytheism; 3. the Romans, who organized deism; 4. the Saracens who discovered the idea that laws governed the universe. *Oeuvres*, XL, 171–172. According to this periodization the "moderns" had not yet made a major discovery which warranted naming a period after them. Thus far they were only building on the original insight of the Arabs. For the modern contribution equal in scope to the innovations of past civilizations he singled out as a prospect his own monist system which would unify the laws. *Oeuvres*, XL, 172.

24. Bibliothèque Nationale. MSS. N.A.F. 24605: Saint-Simon to Konrad Oelsner, November 10, 1807. The letter indicates that Oelsner sometimes teased Saint-Simon about bold ideas which for him were a matter of deadly earnest. "I do not like the levity of the Gauls. I like that of the Germans still less."

25. A triadic division of the historical process was almost an intellectual reflex in a trinitarian religious society. The variations were numerous. De Bonald too had three states: "the imperfect, the perfect or the natural, and the corrupted or that which was contrary to nature." *Du divorce considéré au xixe siècle relativement à l'état domestique et à l'état public de société*, in *Oeuvres*, III, 188.

26. *Travail sur la gravitation universelle*, in *Oeuvres*, XL, 265.

27. *Du système industriel*, in *Oeuvres*, XXI, 192. He treated the idea most fully in the *Catéchisme des industriels*.

28. The idea of class struggle was by no means a novelty in French social thought, particularly in Turgot and Linguet. See L. Cahen, "L'idée de lutte de classes au xviiie siècle," *Revue de synthèse historique* (1906), XII, 44–56; R. Picard, "Die Klassenkampftheorie am Vorabend der französischen Revolution," *Archiv für die Geschichte des Sozialismus und der Arbeiterbewegung*, I (1910), 435–448.

29. Kant's "Idee zu einer allgemeinen Geschichte in weltbürgerlicher Absicht," *Berlinische Monatsschrift* (1784) was not quoted by Saint-Simon, although available in French in volume II of N.-L. François de Neufchâteau, *Le Conservateur ou recueil de morceaux inédits d'histoire, de politique, de littérature et de philosophie*, 2 vols. (Paris, an VIII). There is no basis for P. J. Buchez's notion of direct influence; see his *Introduction à la science de l'histoire*, 2 vols. (Paris, 1842), I, 135–136. General references to Kant's philosophy were available in Ch. Fr. D. de Villers, *Philosophie de Kant ou principes fondamentaux de la philosophie transcendantale* (Metz, 1801); J. M. de Gérando, *Histoire comparée des systèmes de philosophie, considérés relativement aux principes des connaissances humaines*, 4 T. in 8 vols. (Paris, 1804), IV, 2. See Karl Rosenkranz, *Geschichte der Kant'schen Philosophie* (vol. XII in Kant's *Sämmtliche Werke* [Leipzig, 1840]), pp. 341–343. See also the forward of François Picavet's translation of Kant's *Critique de la raison pratique*, 2nd ed. (Paris, 1902).

30. *Introduction aux travaux scientifiques du xixᵉ siècle*, in *Oeuvres choisies*, I, 234.

31. *Oeuvres choisies*, I, 210fn.

32. For special treatments of Saint-Simon's philosophy of history, see Charles Renouvier, "La question du progrès — Burdin, Saint-Simon et Comte: La théorie des époques organiques," *La Critique philosophique* (1881), Xᵉ année, I, 337–346, 353–368; P. Barth, *Die Philosophie der Geschichte als Soziologie* (Leipzig, 1922), I, 160ff.; V. Volgin, "Über die historische Stellung St. Simons," *Marx-Engels Archiv. Zeitschrift des Marx-Engels Institut*, II (1929), 82–119; E. Troeltsch, *Die Dynamik der Geschichte nach der Geschichtsphilosophie des Positivismus* (Berlin, 1919); R. Flint, *History of the Philosophy of History* (Edinburgh, 1893), pp. 395–408; R. Mathis, *La Loi des trois états* (Nancy, 1924); F. Muckle, *Saint-Simon und die ökonomische Geschichtstheorie* (Jena, 1906).

13. The General Nature of Perfectibility

1. X. Bichat, *Physiological Researches upon Life and Death*, transl. by Tobias Watkins (Philadelphia, 1809), pp. 109–113.

2. *Introduction aux travaux scientifiques du xixᵉ siècle*, in *Oeuvres choisies*, I, 184–185. There are other fragments in which he tried, through his analogy with the life cycle of an individual, to prove that his moment in history was the most perfect moment of all time — that point at which the faculties of human imagination, though diminished, had not yet entirely disappeared, while the powers of reason were approaching full development. *Oeuvres choisies*, I, 185; *Travail sur la gravitation universelle*, in *Oeuvres*, XL, 297.

The *Introduction aux travaux scientifiques* is interspersed with stray reflections about the imaginative insights of the ancients into the great truths of all time. Later generations seemed only to have demonstrated rationally those truths which mankind in the imaginative period perceived directly. "In its youth, Humanity glimpsed all the truths which it has seen demonstrated since it arrived at maturity; it even perceived, in that period when its imagination was bold and vigorous, all those truths which still remain to be demonstrated." *Oeuvres choisies*, I, 110.

3. Cabanis, *De l'influence des ages sur les idées et les affections morales*, in Institut de France. Académie des sciences morales et politiques, *Mémoires*, first series, II, 141, 145, 155.

4. Mme. de Staël, *De la littérature*, in *Oeuvres complètes*, IV, 65.

5. Mme. de Staël, *Oeuvres*, IV, 480–481.

6. There is a characteristic formulation by Condorcet of his idea of progress in

the *Esquisse d'un tableau historique des progrès de l'esprit humain*, in *Oeuvres*, VI, 13: "the result [of my work] will be to show . . . that nature has marked no end to the perfection of the human faculties; that the perfectibility of man is really infinite; that the progress of this perfectibility, henceforth independent of every power which may seek to arrest it, has no other limit but the duration of the world in which nature has thrust us."

7. *Mémoire sur la science de l'homme*, in *Oeuvres*, XL, 131fn.

8. Carl L. Becker, *The Heavenly City of the Eighteenth-Century Philosophers* (New Haven, 1932).

9. *Mémoire sur la science de l'homme*, in *Oeuvres*, XL, 115–117, 127–129.

10. *Oeuvres*, XL, 130–131 fn.

11. *Travail sur la gravitation universelle*, in *Oeuvres*, XL, 294–296.

12. Condorcet had hazarded the hypothesis that moral and intellectual characteristics acquired in one generation could be transmitted to the next. *Fragment sur l'Atlantide*, in *Oeuvres*, VI, 628.

13. *Introduction aux travaux scientifiques du xixe siècle*, in *Oeuvres choisies*, I, 172–174.

14. *Oeuvres choisies*, I, 173.

15. *Oeuvres choisies*, I, 170–171.

16. *Oeuvres choisies*, I, 172.

17. *Oeuvres choisies*, I, 173–174.

18. Bibliothèque Nationale. MSS. N.A.F. 24605: Blainville to Saint-Simon, 1813.

19. Condorcet felt that mankind was on the verge of one of the historic leaps in the perfectibility of the species. *Esquisse*, in *Oeuvres*, VI, 23.

20. Immanuel Kant, *Idea for a Universal History with Cosmopolitan Intent* (1784), transl. by Carl J. Friedrich, in *The Philosophy of Kant* (New York, 1949), p. 117.

21. Herder, *Outlines of a Philosophy of the History of Man*, I, 219.

22. Herder, *Outlines*, I, 219.

23. Herder, *Outlines*, I, 81.

24. Herder, *Outlines*, I, 224.

PART III

IN THE SERVICE OF THE GOOD BOURGEOIS

14. The Reorganization of Europe

1. See Ch. Ballot, *L'Introduction du machinisme dans l'industrie française* (Paris, 1923).

2. Saint-Simon had wooed him with a copy of the *Mémoire sur la science de l'homme*. A. Augustin-Thierry, *Augustin Thierry (1795–1856) d'après sa correspondance et ses papiers de famille* (Paris, 1922), p. 23. Augustin Thierry was nineteen at the time of their meeting. His biographers testify to the stimulating effect of this encounter. *Augustin Thierry*, pp. 39–40.

3. Alfred Pereire published a new edition in 1925 when there was revived interest in peace projects: *De la réorganisation de la société européenne*, ed. with introd. and notes by A. Pereire, preface by Henri de Jouvenel (Paris, 1925).

4. *De la réorganisation de la société européenne*, in *Oeuvres choisies*, II, 261.

5. Saint-Simon consistently mocked the social contract theory with its presupposition of a state of nature in which individual isolated men debated their interests before accepting the burden of society. There was no such state. Man had always been a social and political animal. "In all times, in all places, in all states, active or at rest, wandering or stationary, man always shows himself linked with other men." *L'Industrie*, in *Oeuvres*, XVIII, 20. This is completely in the spirit of Joseph de Maistre's caricature of primitive man standing alone like a chessman in his block, pondering the hardships of his isolated position and finally deciding to enter the pact of society. See Joseph de Maistre, *Cinq paradoxes à Madame la Marquise de Navarre*, in *Oeuvres complètes* (Paris, 1884–1887), VII, 283–284.

6. *De la réorganisation de la société européenne*, in *Oeuvres choisies*, II, 268.

7. Saint-Simon's view of the medieval Papacy was deeply colored by the image of pre-Reformation civil society drawn by de Bonald: "Up to that time Europe could be considered like a single family, troubled sometimes, it is true, by the passions of its members, for there can no more be men without passions than societies without men, but a society joined by a common interest, I mean to say by the same public religion and the same sentiments of respect and of deference for a common chief, whose secular dignity rendered him the equal of kings, whose spiritual character and whose religious functions rendered him superior to all Christians." *Théorie du pouvoir*, in *Oeuvres*, II, 178.

8. *De la réorganisation de la société européenne*, in *Oeuvres choisies*, II, 259.

9. In other works he resumed the attack on the impracticability of the Abbé de Saint-Pierre's projects. See, for example, *L'Industrie*, in *Oeuvres*, XIX, 62.

10. *De la réorganisation de la société européenne*, in *Oeuvres choisies*, II, 273–274.

11. A parallel to Saint-Simon's view of the crusades as a unified European action against the outside world which put a stop to the internecine conflicts of feudal chieftains on the continent can be found in de Bonald's *Théorie du pouvoir*, in *Oeuvres*, II, 160, 161: "A general war undertaken in defense of religion and oppressed humanity extinguished this mad ardor. Europe about faced. And one can from this period on date the development of the political and religious constitution of societies. . . . Thus the general will of self-preservation of civil society then cured Europe of the fury of [internal] combats through the calamities of a general war."

12. *De la réorganisation de la société européenne*, in *Oeuvres choisies*, II, 293.

13. Alfred Pereire, "Saint-Simon, précurseur de l'entente cordiale," in his *Autour de Saint-Simon*, pp. 71–83.

14. *De la réorganisation de la société européenne*, in *Oeuvres choisies*, II, 289.

15. See J. L. Puech, "La société des nations et ses précurseurs socialistes: Le Comte C.-H. de Saint-Simon," *Revue politique et littéraire* (1921), 59th year, 82–85, 147–151; Eugène d'Eichthal, "Les idées de Henri de Saint-Simon sur la paix européenne," in Académie des sciences morales et politiques, *Séances et travaux. Compte-rendu*, new series (1925), Part 2, 85th year, 350–361; Maxime Leroy, "La société professionnelle des nations. Un projet d'Henri de Saint-Simon," *Europe*, V (1924), 207–213; Henry de Jouvenel, "Le Comte de Saint-Simon et la réorganisation de la société européenne," *Revue de Paris* (1925), Part 2, 32nd year, 37–45; F. García Calderón, *La Herencia de Lenín y otros artículos. Saint-Simon y nuestro tempo* (Paris, 1929), pp. 67–68.

16. *De la réorganisation de la société européenne*, in *Oeuvres choisies*, II, 328.

17. *Le Lynx*, I (1815), 228–253.

18. *Le Censeur*, IV (1815), 65.

19. *Le Censeur*, III (1815), 28, 30.

15. The Baconian Society

1. *Le Censeur*, III (1815), 334–356. "In national politics we are only imitators of England. . . ." (p. 344). The letter included a copy of a letter which he had addressed to Louis XVIII, reminding the king that he was now the eldest of the Sandricourts and proclaiming his sole purpose to be the strengthening of the scepter in the hands of the Bourbons.

2. *Le Censeur*, IV, 10–31.

3. *Le Censeur*, IV, 352–364.

4. The great Carnot's opinion of Saint-Simon was equivocal: "I knew M. de Saint-Simon. This is an unusual man. He is wrong to consider himself a savant, but no one has ideas that are as novel and as bold." Quoted in an article by his son, H. Carnot, "Mémoire sur le Saint-Simonisme," in Académie des sciences morales et politiques, *Séances et travaux. Compte-rendu* (1887), CXXVIII, 128.

5. The manuscript from the Archives Nationales AA 66.779 was first published as "Lettre inédite de Henri de Saint-Simon sur l'organisation du droit public," *Revue d'histoire économique et sociale*, XIII (1925), 129–132.

6. It received a brief notice in *Le Censeur*, VI (1815), 322.

7. H. Martin, *Histoire de la Bibliothèque de l'Arsenal* (Paris, 1900), p. 554.

8. Dautry, *Saint-Simon*, p. 29.

9. *Nouveau dictionnaire de pédagogie et d'instruction primaire* (Paris, 1911), pp. 1907–1911: article on "Société pour l'instruction élémentaire."

10. "We are not rich enough to pay endlessly for the education of ministers. Those who, without experience, have the unfortunate ambition to move themselves into the control of affairs of state should be discouraged," said Casimir Périer. J. Lucas-Dubreton, *La Manière forte. Casimir Périer et la Révolution de 1830* (Paris, 1929), p. 20.

11. E. Halévy, "La doctrine économique de Saint-Simon," *La Revue du mois*, VI (1907).

12. See M. Palyi, *Introduction of Adam Smith on the Continent* (Chicago, 1928); E. Allix, "L'oeuvre économique de Germain Garnier, traducteur d' Adam Smith et disciple de Cantillon," *Revue d'histoire des doctrines économiques et sociales*, V (1912), 317–342. On Jean-Baptiste Say's relations with the English economists during his travels in 1814, E. Jones, *Les Voyageurs français en Angleterre de 1815 à 1830* (Paris, 1930), pp. 126–127; Say himself wrote *De l'Angleterre et des Anglais* (Paris, 1815).

13. Bibliothèque Nationale. MSS. N.A.F. 24605. Jean-Baptiste Say delivered public lectures at the Athénée in 1815; later he transferred to the Conservatoire des Arts et Métiers.

14. Bibliothèque Nationale. MSS. N.A.F. 24605, Letter from J.-B. Say to Saint-Simon, August 1, 1815. Say published the *Catéchisme d'économie politique qui montre de quelle façon les richesses sont produites, distribuées et consommées dans la société*, referred to in this letter, later in 1815. The six volumes of his *Cours complet d'économie politique pratique* were published in 1828–1829 (the first edition of a 2 volume *Traité d'économie politique* was in 1803).

15. Bibliothèque Nationale. MSS. N.A.F. 24607.

16. MSS. N.A.F. 24607.

17. *Industriels* is translated industrials throughout because its meaning is not always the same as industrialists in Saint-Simon's writings. This neologism made its appearance in his work about 1817.

18. MSS. N.A.F. 24607.

16. "All For Industry"

1. John Stuart Mill, *Autobiography* (New York, edition of 1948), p. 43.

2. "M. Saint-Simon published his first ideas on this subject only in 1817, at a time when *Le Censeur européen* began to develop the same doctrine, and two years after the publication of the writings of MM. Benjamin Constant, Montlosier, and J.-B. Say. . . . No one can doubt that these writings, which he knew and from which more than others he was in a position to profit, greatly influenced the direction which his ideas took and the formation of the doctrines which he adopted. . . ." C. Dunoyer, *Notice historique sur l'industrialisme*, in *Oeuvres* (Paris, 1870), II, 184.

3. Enfantin reports the claim in *Le Producteur*, V, 98.

4. Bibliothèque Nationale. MSS., N.A.F. 24605, Letter of November 30, 1830, signed Ch. de V . . . (rest of signature illegible) to a Paris doctor who was a Saint-Simonian.

5. Hippolyte Auger, *Mémoires*, pp. 127–130.

6. Bibliothèque Nationale. MSS. N.A.F. 24605, Letter from Eugène Péclet, October 1, 1816. Eugène Péclet (1793–1857), a young physicist, had accepted a post at the Collège de Marseille. In later years he returned to Paris and became a prominent official in the French educational system. Jósef Marja Hoëné-Wrónski was a Polish mathematician and messianist whose mystical philosophy of history culminated in a third and final era of "absolute philosophy."

7. Pereire, *Autour de Saint-Simon*, pp. 173–203, published the account from the manuscript listed in *Catalogue des manuscrits de la ville de Paris*, edited by Fernand Bournon (Paris, 1894), no. 214: "Notice sur Saint-Simon et sa doctrine et sur quelques autres ouvrages qui en seraient le développement (sans nom d'auteur), xixe siècle; in-fol de 21 feuillets."

8. Pereire, *Autour de Saint-Simon*, pp. 188, 189.

9. Bibliothèque Nationale. MSS. N.A.F. 24607.

10. *Prospectus. L'Industrie ou discussions politiques, morales et philosophiques, dans l'intérêt de tous les hommes livrés à des travaux utiles et indépendans*, 4 vols. (Paris, impr. C. L. F. Panckoucke, 1817). Bibliothèque Nationale, Rés. m. Z. 187 (8). Quoted also in *Oeuvres*, XVIII, 12–14.

11. Circular issued in connection with *L'Industrie* (n.p., n.d.), addressed "à toutes celles qui désirent franchement la prospérité de l'industrie," p. 4. Bibliothèque Nationale, Rés. m. Z. 187 (13).

12. A. Augustin-Thierry, pp. 36–39; F. Valentin, *Augustin Thierry* (Paris, 1895), pp. 13–14. Thierry did not mention Saint-Simon's name in the autobiographical preface of his *Dix ans d'études historiques*, 9th ed. (Paris, 1856).

13. Saint-Aubin, who attacked the regulatory economic measures of the Terror with violence, became the subject of a bitter polemic between Albert Mathiez and M. Marion. See M. Marion, "Un historien des finances révolutionnaires: Saint-Aubin," *Revue des études historiques* (1922), pp. 90–94.

14. *L'Industrie* in *Oeuvres*, XVIII, 130.

15. *Oeuvres*, XVIII, 151.

16. *Oeuvres*, XVIII, 168.

17. A. J. Mahul, *Notice historique et bibliographique des journaux et ouvrages publiés en 1818* (Paris, 1819), p. 31.

18. *Le Censeur européen*, III (1817), 205.

19. *Le Censeur européen*, III (1817), 206.

20. *Le Censeur européen*, I (1817), 380–381.

21. Bibliothèque Nationale. MSS. N.A.F. 24605, Letter from Benjamin Constant.

22. Pereire, *Autour de Saint-Simon*, p. 111.

23. Bibliothèque Nationale. MS. N.A.F. 24606. Fragments of "De l'organisation sociale" were published in the *Oeuvres*, XXXIX, 109–172.

17. Revolt of the Subscribers

1. Pereire, *Autour de Saint-Simon*, pp. 13–14. *Lettre de Henry Saint-Simon à MM. les publicistes [au sujet d'une opinion qui sera émise dans le 3ᵉ volume de l'industrie]* (Paris, n.d.) Bibliothèque Nationale. Rés. R. 2644. Also quoted in *L'Industrie*, in *Oeuvres*, XVIII, 214, 218 and fn.

2. *Le Constitutionnel*, June 24, June 29, and July 2, 1817.

3. *L'Industrie* (1817), III, cahier 1, p. 9. According to the editors of the *Oeuvres* (XIX, 8fn.), Auguste Comte edited cahiers 1–3 of this volume of *L'Industrie*.

4. *L'Industrie*, III, *cahier* 2, pp. 6–7.

5. *L'Industrie*, III, *cahier* 2, pp. 5–6.

6. *L'Industrie*, III, *cahier* 2, pp. 8–9.

7. *L'Industrie*, III, *cahier* 2, p. 10.

8. *L'Industrie*, III, *cahier* 2, p. 10.

9. *L'Industrie*, III, *cahier* 3, pp. 2–4.

10. *L'Industrie*, III, *cahier* 4, p. 13.

11. *L'Industrie*, III, *cahier* 4, p. 14.

12. *L'Industrie*, III, *cahier* 4, p. 17.

13. *L'Industrie*, III, *cahier* 4, pp. 18–19.

14. The positivist *Revue Occidentale* published Comte's manuscript drafts of what are labeled the four cahiers of volume III and the first cahier of volume IV of *L'Industrie* (see fn. 17 below), under the titles: *Programmes des travaux qui seront employés dans l'ouvrage qui a pour titre L'Industrie*, and *Programmes etc. . . . , comparaison entre l'état politique de l'industrie en France et l'état politique de l'industrie en Angleterre* (*Revue Occidentale* [1884, 1885], XII, 155–192, 327–335; XIII, 167–182; XIV, 12–45).

15. The letter was inserted in the *Journal des débats*, October 31, 1817.

16. Quoted from F. Dreyfus, *Un philanthrope d'autrefois, La Rochefoucauld-Liancourt* (Paris, 1903), pp. 489–490. The violence of the industrialists' reaction was due less to Saint-Simon's moral ideas than to the radical nature of his terminology. Propagating the moral doctrines on which all Christians, irrespective of denomination, were in agreement, was the central ideology of the *Société de morale chrétienne*, an organization in which the outstanding liberal philanthropists of the Restoration were members — de Lasteyrie, La Rochefoucauld-Liancourt, de la Borde, Delessert, Périer, de Gérando, Guizot, Oberlin. "The purpose of the society is to gather from Christianity all the moral parts about which all the Christian communions are in accord and which one might call Reason itself at its highest degree of perfection. The society proposes to expound and to recall the precepts of Christianity in all their purity and to make manifest the fortunate influence which these precepts exercise on the happiness of the human species, to cause to be born and to revive more and more the sentiments of charity and of common benevolence, so fitting to cause peace to reign on earth," — this was the statement of principle set forth in the *Discours de la première assemblée générale*, December 19, 1821; quoted from Dreyfus, *Un philanthrope d'autrefois*, p. 493.

17. The *Journal général de France* (June 14, 1818) refers to a volume IV in–8° which dates the publication in that format around May–June 1818. A volume IV, première partie, premier cahier, 19 pages in–4° had already appeared in October 1817

(*Oeuvres* XIX, 42) and may have been the work of Comte. It was so considered by Laffitte when he reprinted it (see fn. 14 above). The editors of the *Oeuvres* refer to the 1818 work as a Seconde Partie, to differentiate it from the earlier, briefer issue.

18. *L'Industrie*, IV, Seconde Partie, preface, in *Oeuvres*, XIX, 75.

19. *Histoire de ma vie politique*, in *Lettres de Henri Saint-Simon à MM. les Jurés qui doivent prononcer sur l'accusation intentée contre lui* (Paris, Corréard et Pélicier, March 1820, in-8°, 42 p.), Bibliothèque Nationale 8° Z. 8093 (2). Reprinted in *Oeuvres choisies*, II, 416.

18. The Trial

1. Auguste Comte, *Lettres à M. Valat, 1815–1844* (Paris, 1870), p. 36: April 17, 1818.

2. Auguste Comte, pp. 37, 53: April 17, 1818 and May 15, 1818.

3. E. Corra, *La Naissance du génie d'Auguste Comte* (Paris, 1919), pp. 19–21, 24–25. Comte, *Lettres à M. Valat*, pp. 22–31: February 12 and February 25, 1817.

4. Comte, p. 7: April 17, 1818; p. 53: May 15, 1818.

5. Pereire, *Autour de Saint-Simon*, pp. 41–46. A comparison of facsimiles of the letters in Pereire and of Comte's writing of the period in *Six lettres inédites à Roméo Pouzin* (Paris, 1914) leaves no doubt as to their authorship. The letters were first published by Pierre Laffitte, *Revue occidentale* (1882), VIII, 328–329, 344–358, in accordance with copies (made in 1861) communicated to him by Gustave d'Eichthal.

6. Pereire, *Autour de Saint-Simon*, pp. 148–149.

7. Pereire, p. 160. Saint-Simon in fact had often revealed an acute awareness of the longevity and tenacity of accepted systems of ideas. "To rise suddenly against a dominant opinion, even though it be baneful and absurd, almost always results in a scandal that is at once dangerous and useless; truth has a very difficult enemy to conquer in the habits of the mind. When one has lived with certain ideas for a long time and when these ideas are being combatted, one feels that one is oneself being threatened, and men of the most facile credulity for everything else become those who resist the new evidence most obstinately." *L'Industrie*, in *Oeuvres*, XVIII, 205–206.

8. E. Littré, *Auguste Comte et la philosophie positive*, 2nd ed. (Paris, 1864), p. 13, cites Madame Comte's testimony to the intense mutual affection of master and pupil.

9. A copy of the contract signed by all participants February 22, 1819, is in the archives of the Société Positiviste, Paris. It was published in Pereire, *Autour de Saint-Simon*, pp. 60–65.

10. *Le Politique* (1819), p. 233.

11. *Le Politique*, pp. 467–482.

12. *Le Politique*, p. 40. The first *livraison* of January 1819 had an article signed S.S. An erratum on p. 190 indicates that it should have been A.

13. *Le Politique*, p. 115.

14. *Le Politique*, p. 101.

15. *Considérations relatives à une pétition pour demander l'addition d'un article à la loi des finances.* See *Le Moniteur*, June 10, 1819, on this petition.

16. *L'Organisateur*, in *Oeuvres*, XX, 17–26. Olinde Rodrigues called it the *Parabole de Saint-Simon* when he reprinted it in 1832. It was again reprinted in 1848 as *Paroles d'un mort*.

17. *L'Organisateur*, in *Oeuvres*, XX, 20–22.

18. A review in the *Renommée* on February 6, 1820, could find nothing criminal

in *L'Organisateur*; the reviewer called it "a system like other systems, one that is not even new." Saint-Simon reprinted the review at the end of the twelfth letter of *L'Organisateur*, in *Oeuvres*, XX, 221–225.

19. *Lettres de Henri Saint-Simon à MM. les Jurés qui doivent prononcer sur l'accusation intentée contre lui* (Paris, March 1820).

20. *Plaidoyer de Me Legouix pour M. Henry de Saint-Simon. Cour d'Assises de Paris. Audience du 20 mars 1820. Procès de L'Organisateur*, p. 3. Bibliothèque Nationale Rés. m. Z. 187 (8).

21. *Plaidoyer*, pp. 9–10.

22. *Plaidoyer*, p. 34.

23. *Plaidoyer*, p. 54.

24. Joseph Girard, "Saint-Simon en cour d'assises," *La Revue hebdomadaire*, August 10, 1929, pp. 144–172.

25. See *Le Constitutionnel*, March 21, 1820, p. 4; *Journal de Paris*, March 21, 1820, pp. 2–3.

26. *Le Censeur européen*, March 20, 1820, p. 3.

27. *Circulaire relative à L'Organisateur, 26 mars, 1820*. Bibliothèque Nationale, Rés. m. Z. 187 (19), pp. 1–2.

28. *Lettre d'envoi aux électeurs*, November 20, 1820, in *Oeuvres*, XXI, xi.

29. *Des Bourbons et des Stuarts* of January 1822 was seized by the police.

30. *Du système industriel*, in *Oeuvres*, XXI, 167.

31. *Opinions littéraires, philosophiques et industrielles*, in *Oeuvres choisies*, III, 217–218.

PART IV

A NEW THEORY OF SOCIETY

19. Epochs Organic and Critical

1. *L'Industrie*, in *Oeuvres*, XIX, 25–26.

2. *Oeuvres*, XIX, 24.

3. *Oeuvres*, XIX, 24–25. The *Opinions littéraires, philosophiques et industrielles* saw progressive virtues even in the barbarians. "The barbarian peoples rendered an immense service to the human species by destroying completely the social organization which had been established by the Greeks and the Romans." *Oeuvres choisies*, III, 232fn.

4. *L'Industrie*, in *Oeuvres*, XIX, 26.

5. *Oeuvres*, XIX, 27.

6. Letters eight through fourteen of *L'Organisateur*, in *Oeuvres*, XX, 77–240, an integrated sketch of a philosophy of history, show Comte's collaboration.

7. *Oeuvres*, XX, 80.

8. *Oeuvres*, XX, 94.

9. *Oeuvres*, XX, 97.

10. *Oeuvres*, XX, 90.

11. *Introduction aux travaux scientifiques du xixe siècle*, in *Oeuvres choisies*, I, 146.

12. *L'Organisateur*, in *Oeuvres*, XX, 165.

13. *Oeuvres*, XX, 160.

14. *Opinions littéraires, philosophiques et industrielles* (1825), in *Oeuvres choisies,* III, 221.

15. *Doctrine de Saint-Simon. Exposition. Première Année. 1829,* 2nd ed. (Paris, 1830), p. 70.

16. "In casting one's eye over the general economy of societies one soon realizes that the natural limits of their progress are those of the production of substances which men need and that among these substances the foods and the fuels are those which are in danger of reaching this boundary soonest." *Fragment sur l'Atlantide,* in *Oeuvres de Condorcet,* VI, 645.

17. Bibliothèque Nationale. MSS. N.A.F. 24607, folio 138. He raised the question as to whether the general increase in agricultural production which he was arguing for would result in a geometric increase in population. Since he had no solution for the problem he suggested a prize essay contest on the subject.

18. *Opinions littéraires, philosophiques et industrielles* (1825), in *Oeuvres choisies,* III, 223.

19. *Oeuvres choisies,* III, 227. The manuscripts include a curious explanation of the generally accepted belief among historians that the Greeks were superior to the medievals: "It is one of the consequences of human weakness that in general men judge matters of public interest in accordance with their private interest and classes judge them in accordance with their class interest. Now it is obvious that the existence of historians and of other writers was far more agreeable among the Greeks than in the seventh century, from which it follows that men of letters should naturally give preference to the age of the Greeks over the middle ages. But any person who will take the pains to fix his attention on the veritable general interests of the human species, that is to say, on those of the majority, will be obliged to agree with us that the productive class, that is to say the workers, were infinitely less unfortunate in the middle ages than in the age of the helots among the Lacedemonians." Hence his conclusion that "the human species found itself in a far more advanced state of civilization in the seventh century than in the age of Pericles." Bibliothèque Nationale. MSS. N.A.F. 24606.

20. *Opinions littéraires,* in *Oeuvres choisies,* III, 230.

21. *Oeuvres choisies,* III, 230: "The peoples of antiquity created the fine arts; they raised them to the highest level of perfection which they have ever attained.

"As for direct invention, for imagination working immediately on the senses, the peoples of antiquity have remained the masters.

"We are constrained to admit that the works of the people of antiquity in this area have remained superior to all those which have been produced by their successors."

22. *Oeuvres choisies,* III, 231.

23. *Du système industriel,* in *Oeuvres,* XXI, 5.

24. *Oeuvres,* XXI, 72.

25. A *Prospectus,* dated March 1, 1823. Bibliothèque Nationale. MSS. N.A.F. 24606.

26. *Travail sur la gravitation universelle,* in *Oeuvres,* XL, 247–249; *L'Organisateur,* in *Oeuvres,* XX, 85fn. In the text "moderns" included the medievals, in contrast with the ancients.

27. *L'Industrie,* in *Oeuvres,* XIX, 23.

28. "The philosophical revolution goes back to Socrates and ends with the syntheses of the Platonic philosophers of the Alexandrian school who had embraced Christianity; then the political revolution begins and it ends in the days of Charlemagne, when theism received the most widespread application of which it was capable, all the peoples of civilized Europe having become Christian as a result of the conquests of Charlemagne." *Oeuvres,* XIX, 23–24.

29. *Introduction aux travaux scientifiques du xixe siècle,* in *Oeuvres choisies,* I, 201.

30. "History proves that scientific and political revolutions have alternated, that they have successively acted with respect to each other like causes and effects." *Mémoire sur la science de l'homme,* in *Oeuvres,* XL, 191.

31. For an idealist text (or perhaps a scientific determinism) in the sense that the industrial system is related to modern science as effect to cause, see *L'Organisateur,* in *Oeuvres,* XX, 219–220; elsewhere he expressed the idea that the political and juridical systems of an epoch were the expressions of the scientific level attained at that epoch. *Catéchisme des industriels* and *Nouveau Christianisme,* in *Oeuvres choisies,* III, 105, 378. "Materialist" interpretations of history can also be isolated: "For the advances of industry are the most positive of all." *Catéchisme des industriels,* in *Oeuvres,* XXXVII, 17.

Minor German Marxists have differed in their estimates of Saint-Simon, depending upon whether they emphasized his materialism or idealism. Friedrich Muckle, *Henri de Saint-Simon. Die Persönlichkeit und ihr Werk* (Jena, 1908); *Saint-Simon und die ökonomische Geschichtstheorie* (Jena, 1906) emphasized Saint-Simon's influence on Marx. Gustav Eckstein, "Der alte und der neue Saint-Simon," *Archiv für die Geschichte des Sozialismus und der Arbeiterbewegung,* II (1912), 423–440, was rather balanced in his praise. The real attack came in Heinrich Cunow's essay, "Saint-Simon als Geschichts-theoretiker," *Neue Zeit,* XXXVIII (1919), 281–287, and in his *Die Marxsche Geschichts-, Gesellschafts-, und Staatstheorie* (Berlin, 1920–1921). He denounced Saint-Simon's ideal-ist conception of history and maintained that Marx had far more to learn from Raynal, who, he says without evidence, fashioned Saint-Simon's thought, as well as from Turgot, Necker, and Marat. In the end he dismissed Saint-Simon as a follower of Jean-Baptiste Say. See also W. Berg, "Saint-Simon und seine Schule. Ein Blatt aus der Kindheits-geschichte des modernen Sozialismus," *Neue Zeit,* XXXIX (1920), 211–218, 230–236, 259–264, whose attitude is evident in the title of his study; S. Bauer, "Henri de Saint-Simon nach hundert Jahren," *Archiv für die Geschichte des Sozialismus und der Arbeiterbewegung,* XII (1926), 156–174.

32. *Du système industriel,* in *Oeuvres,* XXI, 166.

33. Abbé Dominique Dufour de Pradt, *L'Europe et l'Amérique en 1821* (Paris, 1822), I, 115–117. A manuscript of Saint-Simon's refers to western Europe as *Franche Europe* and explains the institutional similarity of the nations upon the basis of their common historical experience. They had been shaped by the Roman legists, had been overrun by the barbarians, and they had fought together against the Turk. Bibliothèque Nationale. MSS. N.A.F. 24606.

34. *Introduction aux travaux scientifiques du xixe siècle,* in *Oeuvres choisies,* I, 190.

35. Bibliothèque de l'Arsenal. Fonds d'Eichthal. Olinde Rodrigues to Gustave d'Eichthal, July 11, 1835. MSS. 13748/87.

36. "The revolutionaries applied the principles of equality to negroes. If they had consulted the physiologists they would have learned that the negro, because of his basic physical structure, is not susceptible, even with the same education, of rising to the intellectual level of Europeans." This note in the original edition of the *Lettres d'un habitant de Genève à ses contemporains* was suppressed both in the Rodrigues edition and in the *Oeuvres,* XV, 46.

37. "Know that Europeans are the sons of Abel. Know that Asia and Africa are inhabited by the descendants of Cain. See how bloodthirsty Africans are. Note the indolence of Asiatics. These impure men have not followed through their early efforts to draw near to my Divine Providence. The Europeans will unite their forces and they will deliver their Greek brothers from the domination of the Turks. The founder of the religion will be the commander-in-chief of the army of the faithful [he meant

Napoleon]. These armies will submit the sons of Cain to religion and will erect throughout the world those establishments which may be necessary for the security of the members of the councils of Newton, when they undertake voyages they consider useful for the progress of the human spirit." *Oeuvres*, XV, 56–57.

20. Societies Military and Civil

1. Adam Ferguson, *An Essay on the History of Civil Society*, 6th ed. (London, 1793), pp. 358–387.

2. Benjamin Constant, *De l'esprit de conquête et de l'usurpation, dans leurs rapports avec la civilisation européenne*, 3rd ed. (Paris, 1814), pp. 8, 11: "Among moderns a successful war inevitably costs more than it brings. . . . Our century, which appreciates everything for its utility and . . . opposes irony to real or factitious enthusiasm, would not consent to be fed by a sterile glory, which it is no longer our habit to prefer to everything else."

3. *L'Industrie*, in *Oeuvres*, XVIII, 109–110. Thierry drafted this section.

4. *Oeuvres*, XVIII, 120–121.

5. *Oeuvres*, XVIII, 126.

6. *Oeuvres*, XVIII, 127.

7. *Oeuvres*, XVIII, 185–186.

8. *Oeuvres*, XVIII, 187–188.

9. *Oeuvres*, XVIII, 188.

10. *Oeuvres*, XVIII, 77.

11. *Oeuvres*, XVIII, 81.

12. "Institutions, like individuals, have their youth, their maturity, and their old age. Like individuals they are destined to become extinct and to be replaced by new ones which were born and acquired strength under the tutelage of those which preceded them. The old nobility is a superannuated institution; it no longer renders any services to society, it is a burden on society, and therefore it should be destroyed. . . . Its existence can only be prolonged by a few moments. The progress of knowldge and the tendency of the people to rid themselves of what is harmful to them will inevitably terminate its languishing existence before long." *Du système industriel*, in *Oeuvres*, XXIII, 35.

21. The Physiology of Social Classes

1. Saint-Simon normally used the words *lutte* and *conflit* to describe this process. The cult adopted the milder word *antagonisme*.

2. *L'Organisateur*, in *Oeuvres*, XX, 156.

3. *L'Industrie* (1817), in *Oeuvres*, XIX, 169. Saint-Simon was continually appealing to the class-consciousness of the industrials. "Before the revolution, industry did not possess enough self-confidence to assume the role which was its due, to raise its own banner and to march at the head of civilization. Once the revolutionary crisis was declared, there was no longer time, and spirits were too agitated, too giddy, for calm and tranquil ideas to be developed.

"Today, when none of these obstacles any longer exists and when industry, having gained entrance into the constitution, exercises there the most powerful right of action, a favorable opportunity presents itself. The only thing which industry has to fear is remaining too timid and permitting herself to be led by banners other than her own.

Let industry consult only herself and let her act. The constitution will not be alarmed by her efforts because nothing is more constitutional than industry and the constitution itself is only good because it is industrial." *Oeuvres*, XVIII, 208.

It was Saint-Simon's hope that a "few energetic men, possessing great fortunes or great talents, would employ their means to make it [industry] *want* what it has so much interest in desiring." *Oeuvres*, XVIII, 220.

"[Historical considerations] have as an end to prove to the industrial class, that is to the nation, that the position which it has gradually attained, should naturally invite it to adopt the proposed measure; that its past progress and its present needs unite in determining it; in other words, that the adoption of this measure is the step which the natural order of things reserves to industry in the nineteenth century, and that this step is the only one which remains for industry in order to seize the direction of society, a constant goal towards which all the progress which the industrial class has made since its origin has been moving." *Oeuvres*, XIX, 140–141.

4. The substantive *prolétaire* is frequent in Saint-Simon; he does not use the collective *prolétariat*.

5. *L'Organisateur*, in *Oeuvres*, XX, 149; Saint-Simon employed the terms *capital* and *capitaliste*, but not *capitalisme*.

6. *L'Industrie*, in *Oeuvres*, XIX, 113.

7. Johann Plenge, *Gründung und Geschichte des Crédit Mobilier* (Tübingen, 1903), pp. 39–80.

8. "One does not create a system of social organization. One perceives the new relationships which have developed among ideas and interests and one reveals them. That is all. A social system is a reality or it is nothing. It is not I who drew up the constitutional project whose basis I have expounded. It is the mass of the population of Europe who labored to fashion it during the past eight centuries. If the whole world has not yet become aware of its existence the reason lies in the fact that it is hidden behind the façade of the old social edifice which still stands." *L'Organisateur*, in *Oeuvres*, XX, 179–180.

9. *Le Parti national ou industriel comparé au parti anti-national*. Offprint of the tenth issue of *Le Politique*. Bibliothèque Nationale 8° Z 8092 (2). Reprinted in *Oeuvres*, XIX, 195–209.

10. *Sur la querelle des abeilles et des frelons, ou Sur la situation respective des producteurs et des consommateurs non producteurs* (Paris, n.d.). Offprint of the 11th issue of *Le Politique*. Bibliothèque Nationale 8° Z 8092 (3). Reprinted in *Oeuvres*, XIX, 211–234.

11. "The conduct of the industrials is moral, that of the partisans of arbitrary government is immoral. Thus the industrial party has on its side moral force, which is the greatest of all forces. It also has physical force, since it is at least fifty times more numerous than the party of the idlers." *Le Parti national ou industriel comparé au parti anti-national*, in *Oeuvres*, XIX, 205.

12. *Du système industriel*, in *Oeuvres*, XXII, 81.

13. *L'Organisateur*, in *Oeuvres*, XX, 146, 147.

14. *Opinions littéraires, philosophiques et industrielles*, in *Oeuvres choisies*, III, 267–268.

15. *Henry Saint-Simon à MM. les ouvriers* (n.p., n.d.), pp. 1–2. Bibliothèque Nationale Rés. R 2652. A former industrial reduced to working-class status by ill-fortune, Antoine Nantua, ridiculed Saint-Simon's concern for the proletariat in a published *Réponse à une lettre adressée par M. Henry Saint-Simon à Messieurs les ouvriers* (Paris, 1821). Nantua was the printer Crapelet playing a private joke.

16. S. Leroy, "Ternaux, Rouget de Lisle et Saint-Simon," *Bulletin de la Société*

Grayloise d'émulation, VI (1903), 17–40. *Le premier chant des industriels* was printed in *Du système industriel. Deuxième partie* (Paris, 1821), pp. 209–212. Stanza 4 follows:

> "Laissons dans sa lâche mollesse
> Le sybarite végéter.
> Laissons le noble nous vanter
> Ce qu'il appelle sa noblesse.
> Ternaux! Le vrai noble, c'est toi.
> C'est le sage à la vie active ·
> Qui créa des biens qu'il cultive
> Pour les répandre autour de soi."

Final refrain:

> "Honneur à toi, soutien de l'Industrie!
> Honneur, honneur à tes nobles travaux!
> Dans la carrière enflamme tes rivaux
> Et vis longtemps pour eux, pour la patrie!"

17. *Opinions littéraires*, in *Oeuvres choisies*, III, 239fn.

18. *L'Industrie*, in *Oeuvres*, XIX, 60. In the *Troisième circulaire de l'auteur de L'Industrie* (Bibliothèque Nationale Rés. m. Z. 187 [13]), p. 1, he had another version of the same slogan: "How inexact are those useful expressions industrial class, scientific class, for the scientists are *industrieux* and the *industrieux* are scientists, not in theory but in application."

19. *Troisième circulaire*, p. 2.

20. The workings of such a society, named the *Union générale des capacités industrielles et scientifiques* are described in the *Catéchisme des industriels*, second *cahier*, pp. 137–138.

21. *L'Industrie. Première circulaire de l'auteur*, pp. 2–3. Bibliothèque Nationale Rés. m. Z. 187 (9).

22. *L'Organisateur*, in *Oeuvres*, XX, 19.

23. *Catéchisme des industriels*, first *cahier*, p. 1.

22. The Lost Revolution of 1789

1. Saint-Simon mentioned Burke and the parliamentary debates on the French Revolution in *De la réorganisation de la société européenne*, in *Oeuvres choisies*, II, 300–301 and fn.

2. "A few more years of philosophism and Europe would have been finished." De Bonald, *Théorie du pouvoir*, in *Oeuvres*, II, 161.

3. "*Philosophes* more bold than wise aimed at this antiquated outlook premature blows, blows which were easy to deliver and which were decisive; the system of general ideas crashed completely and society was dissolved." *L'Industrie*, in *Oeuvres*, XVIII, 206.

4. "It is chiefly to the vicious direction followed by the Encyclopedists in their works that one should attribute the insurrection which broke out in 1789, as well as the bloody character which the Revolution assumed from its beginning." *Du système industriel*, in *Oeuvres*, XXI, 182.

5. *Oeuvres*, XXI, 78.

6. "The industrial and scientific system was born and developed under the domination of the feudal and theological system. Now this simple relationship suffices to explain why between two systems as absolutely antipathetic as these there had to

exist a sort of vague intermediary system, destined solely for the task of modifying the ancient system in such a manner as to permit the development of the new system and later to operate a transition. . . . Every change can take place only by degrees both in the temporal and in the spiritual spheres. Here the change was so great and, on the other hand, the feudal and theological system by nature found all modifications so repugnant that it was necessary . . . to have for many centuries the special continuous action of certain classes derived from the old system but distinct and up to a certain point independent of it, classes which, by the very nature of their political existence, had to constitute in the bosom of society what I call abstractly an intermediary and transitional system. These classes were in the temporal sphere the lawyers and in the spiritual sphere the metaphysicians who joined each other in their political action, like the feudal lords and theology, like industry and the sciences of observation." *Oeuvres,* XXI, 6–7.

7. "When the French Revolution broke out it was no longer a question of modifying the feudal and theological system which had already lost almost all of its real strength. It was a question of organizing the industrial and scientific system, which the state of civilization demanded as a replacement. It was, consequently, the industrialists and the scientists who should have occupied the political scene, each in their natural roles. Instead the lawyers put themselves at the head of the Revolution. They directed it with the doctrines of the metaphysicians. It is superfluous to recall what strange aberrations were the result and what misfortunes followed from the aberrations. But one must note with care that despite this great experience, the lawyers and the metaphysicians have without interruption remained in control of public affairs and even today they alone direct all political discussions." *Oeuvres,* XXI, 10–11.

8. *L'Industrie* in *Oeuvres,* XIX, 120–127.

9. *Oeuvres,* XIX, 163.

10. *Oeuvres,* XIX, 165.

11. *Du système industriel,* in *Oeuvres,* XXI, 15fn.

12. *L'Industrie,* in *Oeuvres,* XVIII, 199.

13. *Du système industriel,* in *Oeuvres,* XXI, 12.

14. *Bourgeois* was already a pejorative word in *Du système industriel,* in *Oeuvres,* XXIII, 71.

15. "The industrials played no active role during the course of the Revolution; they neither governed nor administered any public affairs; in no respect did they attempt to seize power. None of the arbitrary acts which have rendered this epoch memorable for its horrors was committed by them. . . ." *L'Industrie,* in *Oeuvres,* XIX, 166. In the period after 1814 liberal pamphleteers went to extravagant lengths to disassociate the industrialists and bankers from Robespierre. An article entitled "Des causes secrètes des excès attribués à la Révolution Française," in *Le Censeur,* VI (1815), 1–140, tried to make him out an *agent provocateur* in the pay of the *émigrés.*

16. *Du système industriel,* in *Oeuvres,* XXI, 89.

23. Tactics for a Peaceful Revolution

1. Saint-Simon could hardly have missed this dramatic description of the consequences of the rise of the third estate quoted by the reviewer of Montlosier's work in *Le Censeur,* VI (1815), 224–225: "We shall see arise in the midst of the old state a new state; in the midst of the old people a new people; in the midst of old customs, old institutions and old laws, new customs, new institutions, new laws. We shall see a double state, a double people, a double social order, marching side by side for a long

time, finally attacking each other and fighting bitterly. Such is this great revolution which has been in itself the source of a multitude of revolutions, a revolution which, spreading through Europe, has covered it with wars and disorders, has filled the German Empire with imperial cities, Italy with republics, has everywhere left a multitude of new rights, new states, doctrines, and constitutions."

2. If the Bourbons instituted the industrial-scientific system he promised them that "the stability of their throne would be assured forever." *Du système industriel,* in *Oeuvres,* XXI, 101.

3. "Besides, under no circumstances can the maintenance of individual liberties be considered the goal of the social contract. . . . People do not associate together in order to be free. Savages associate among themselves to hunt, to make war, but surely not in order to secure liberty, for in this respect, they would have done better to remain in a state of isolation. Activity must have a goal, I repeat, and liberty could not be a goal since it presupposes one. True liberty does not consist of sitting with folded arms, if one wishes, in a state of association. Such an inclination should be severely repressed everywhere that it exists. Liberty, on the contrary, consists in developing, without impediments and to the greatest extent possible, a temporal or a spiritual capacity useful to the association.

"Let us moreover make the observation that to the extent that civilization progresses, the division of labor, considered both from a spiritual and a temporal viewpoint and from the most general viewpoint, increases proportionately. As a result men necessarily depend less on each other individually but each one of them depends more on the mass. . . . Now the vague and metaphysical idea of liberty as it is current today, if we should continue to accept it as the basis of political doctrines, would tend significantly to impede the action of the mass on individuals. From this viewpoint it would be contrary to the development of civilization and the organization of a well-ordered system, which requires that the parts should be strongly bound to the whole and dependent upon it." *Oeuvres,* XXI, 15–16fn.

4. *Oeuvres,* XXII, 74.
5. *Oeuvres,* XXII, 75.
6. *Oeuvres,* XXII, 76.
7. *Oeuvres,* XXI, 233.
8. *Oeuvres,* XXII, 12.
9. *Oeuvres,* XXII, 17fn.
10. *Oeuvres,* XXII, 22.
11. *Oeuvres,* XXII, 23–24fn.
12. Bibliothèque Nationale. MSS. N.A.F. 24607.
13. *Catéchisme des industriels,* second *cahier,* p. 101.
14. *Catéchisme,* second *cahier,* p. 130.
15. *Du système industriel,* in *Oeuvres,* XXII, 236–246.
16. *Oeuvres,* XXII, 214.
17. *Oeuvres,* XXII, 50.
18. *Oeuvres,* XXII, 51.
19. *Oeuvres,* XXII, 51.
20. *Oeuvres,* XXII, 223.
21. *Oeuvres,* XXIII, 56.
22. *Catéchisme des industriels,* first *cahier,* p. 64.
23. *Du système industriel,* in *Oeuvres,* XXIII, 53.
24. *Oeuvres,* XXII, 236–246.
25. *Oeuvres,* XXII, 239.
26. *Oeuvres,* XXII, 249.

27. *Oeuvres*, XXII, 248.
28. *Oeuvres*, XXII, 250–251.
29. *Oeuvres*, XXII, 132.

24. Industrialism Against Liberalism

1. He now called it "radically vicious." *Catéchisme des industriels*, second *cahier*, p. 83.
2. *Catéchisme*, second *cahier*, pp. 74–75, 82.
3. *Catéchisme*, second *cahier*, p. 88.
4. *Catéchisme*, second *cahier*, pp. 163–186.
5. "The word liberalism designates an order of feelings; it does not at all indicate a class of interests. Whence it results that this designation is vague and that consequently it is vicious." *Catéchisme*, second *cahier*, p. 164.
6. *Catéchisme*, second *cahier*, p. 163.
7. *Catéchisme*, second *cahier*, p. 120.
8. *Opinions littéraires, philosophiques et industrielles*, in *Oeuvres choisies*, III, 298.
9. *Oeuvres choisies*, III, 305.

25. The Natural Elite

1. "Quintilian, Locke, and I say: Inequality among intellects is the result of a known cause and this cause is the difference in education." C. A. Helvétius, *De l'homme* (1772), in *Oeuvres complètes* (Paris, 1818), II, 71.
2. Jean-Jacques Rousseau, *The Social Contract and Discourses*, transl. by G. D. H. Cole (London, 1949), p. 160.
3. See especially Morelly's *Code de la nature*, and Brissot de Warville's *Recherches philosophiques sur le droit de propriété et sur le vol considérés dans la nature et dans la société*. André Lichtenberger, *Le socialisme au* xviii*e siècle* (Paris, 1895) is still the classical work on this group.
4. F. M. A. de Voltaire, *Dictionnaire philosophique*, in *Oeuvres* (Paris, 1835), VII, 473–475.
5. Condorcet, *Déclaration des droits*, in *Oeuvres*, IX, 179–211.
6. Condorcet, *Esquisse d'un tableau historique des progrès de l'esprit humain*, in *Oeuvres*, VI, 238.
7. M. Talleyrand-Périgord, *Rapport sur l'instruction publique fait au nom du comité de constitution de l'Assemblée Nationale, les 10, 11, et 19 septembre 1791* (Paris, 1791), pp. 7–8.
8. Talleyrand-Périgord, p. 7.
9. "When one compares one man with another, one sees that nature has set up among individuals differences which are analogous to and correspond in a certain sense to those which can be recognized among species." Cabanis, *De l'influence des tempéramens sur la formation des idées et des affections morales*, in Institut de France, Académie des sciences morales et politiques, *Mémoires*, first series, II, 230.
10. "But the impressions which the same objects make on us do not always have the same degree of intensity and are not always of the same duration; sometimes they glide by hardly exciting our attention; sometimes they captivate it with an irresistible force and leave behind profound traces. Surely men do not resemble each other in their

manner of feeling." Cabanis, *Considérations générales sur l'étude de l'homme* in *Mémoires*, pp. 65–66.

11. Cabanis wrote that his admiration for Helvétius and Condillac did not prevent him from recognizing that "both of them lacked physiological knowledge, from which their works could have significantly profited." If Helvétius had known the "animal economy" better, he could not have "maintained his system of the equality of intellects." *Mémoires*, p. 63.

12. Cabanis, *De l'influence des tempéramens*, in *Mémoires*, pp. 283–284. In the same spirit Condorcet had said: "A well-directed system of education corrects the natural inequality of the faculties instead of strengthening them. . . ." *Esquisse d'un tableau historique* in *Oeuvres*, VI, 251.

13. Cabanis believed that the inheritance of acquired characteristics applied both to "physical dispositions" and to "dispositions of the mind and propensities of the soul." *Considérations générales sur l'étude de l'homme* in *Mémoires*, p. 93.

14. The classical work of Johann Caspar Lavater (1741–1801) was his *Physiognomische Fragmente zur Befoerderung der Menschenkenntniss und Menschenliebe*, 4 vols. (Leipzig, 1775–1778).

15. Franz Joseph Gall (1758–1828) wrote *Recherches sur l'anatomie du système nerveux en général et du cerveau en particulier* (Paris, 1809).

16. Xavier Bichat, *Physiological Researches upon Life and Death*, transl. by Tobias Watkins (Philadelphia, 1809), pp. 112–113. The work was originally published in France in the Year VIII (1799–1800).

17. "You will seldom or never see the perfection of action in the locomotive organs coincident with those of the brain or senses, and on the other hand it is extremely rare to find the former very apt in their respective functions when the latter possess considerable energy in theirs." Bichat, p. 109.

18. These reflections were later appended to his *De la révolution françoise*, 2 vols. (Paris, 1797).

19. *De la Révolution*, II, 116.

20. De Bonald, *Théorie du pouvoir*, 3rd ed. (Paris, 1838), pp. 214–215 and fn.

21. The "immortal physiologist" Bichat was by Saint-Simon's own testimony the source of his conception of mutually exclusive capacities, a theory which in *Du système industriel* he called a law of human organization. *Oeuvres*, XXII, 56.

22. *Oeuvres*, XXII, 17fn.

23. *Notice historique*, in *Oeuvres*, I, 122.

24. Condorcet, *Esquisse d'un tableau historique* in *Oeuvres*, VI, 238.

25. The idea of the natural *élite* was developed by Saint-Simon in *L'Industrie*, in *Oeuvres*, XVIII, 142–145. The same conception had been adumbrated earlier in the fragment entitled "Sur la capacité de l'Empereur," in the *Introduction aux travaux scientifiques du xixe siècle*.

26. *Oeuvres choisies*, I, 173.

27. *Oeuvres choisies*, I, 173fn.

26. The Twilight of Power

1. *Introduction aux travaux scientifiques du xixe siècle*, in *Oeuvres choisies*, I, 143.
2. *L'Organisateur*, in *Oeuvres*, XX, 192.
3. *Oeuvres*, XX, 126–127 fn.
4. *Oeuvres*, XX, 151.
5. *Oeuvres*, XX, 150.
6. Saint-Simon's solution of the problem of internecine conflict within the élite

is reminiscent of Condorcet's treatment of jealousy among the scientists called upon to collaborate on grand international projects. "Once the true methods for studying the sciences, for making progress in them are known, there cannot fail to exist among those who cultivate some one science with success a common opinion, accepted principles which they would not be able to transgress without violating an inner feeling, without giving themselves either a reputation for ignorance or for bad faith.

"These men are doubtless not exempt from the pettinesses of self-love. They are not alien to jealousy. But they will not sacrifice to the impulses of these wretched passions the very object which inspires them." *Fragment sur l'Atlantide*, in *Oeuvres*, VI, 604.

7. *Suite à la brochure des Bourbons et des Stuarts*, in *Oeuvres choisies*, II, 444–445.

8. "Governments will no longer lead men. Their functions will be limited to preventing useful labors from being disturbed. They will have at their disposal but few powers and little money, because limited powers and little money should suffice to attain this end." *L'Industrie*, in *Oeuvres*, XVIII, 168.

9. The function of government was "to protect the men who work from the unproductive action of the idle, to maintain security and liberty in production." *Oeuvres*, XIX, 36.

10. *L'Organisateur*, in *Oeuvres*, XX, 200.

11. *Oeuvres*, XX, 202.

12. *Oeuvres*, XX, 199.

27. The High Administration of Society

1. Works of general utility were to be undertaken by "subscriptions"; the projects would be supervised by the subscribers. *L'Industrie*, in *Oeuvres*, XVIII, 168.

2. The future industrial society is characterized as an "association" in *L'Organisateur*, in *Oeuvres choisies*, III, 375. In the same work (III, 370) he set forth positive goals for society: ". . . the social organization should have as its sole and permanent object to apply itself in the best possible manner to the satisfaction of human needs, to the knowledge acquired in the sciences, in the fine arts and in the practical arts, to the spread of this knowledge, to its perfection, and to its greatest possible increase, in a word to combine as usefully as possible all the particular works in the sciences, the fine arts, and the practical arts."

3. The word *socialisme* was not current in France during Saint-Simon's lifetime; it seems to have come into general usage only about 1831. Alexandre Zévaès, "De l'origine du mot 'socialisme,'" *Revue politique et parlementaire*, CCVI (1952), 142–145.

4. *L'Organisateur*, in *Oeuvres*, XX, 51–52 and fn.

5. *Du système industriel*, in *Oeuvres*, XXI, 161–162.

6. *L'Organisateur*, in *Oeuvres*, XX, 52–53fn.

7. *Oeuvres*, XX, 59fn.

8. *Oeuvres*, XX, 61.

9. *Du système industriel*, in *Oeuvres*, XXI, 150–151.

10. *Catéchisme des industriels*, fourth *cahier*, in *Oeuvres choisies*, III, 198.

11. *Oeuvres choisies*, III, 201fn.

12. *Opinions littéraires, philosophiques et industrielles*, in *Oeuvres choisies*, III, 291.

13. De Bonald, *Théorie du pouvoir*, in *Oeuvres*, I, 101.

PART V

THE LAST YEARS

28. The Suicide Attempt

1. Bibliothèque Nationale. MSS. N.A.F. 24606.
2. P. Félix Thomas, *Pierre Leroux, sa vie, son oeuvre, sa doctrine* (Paris, 1904), p. 18.
3. Bibliothèque Nationale. MSS. N.A.F. 24605.
4. *Notice historique*, in *Oeuvres*, I, 95.
5. *Oeuvres*, I, 96.
6. *Oeuvres*, I, 96.
7. Dr. Poumiès de la Siboutie, "Souvenirs d'un médecin de Paris," *Revue hebdomadaire* (1910), I, 236.
8. The manuscripts include an interesting excursus on the role of doctors in modern society. "As for us we declare positively that doctors appear to us to be the savants most capable of judging our system, which is [essentially] the system of Socrates perfected by means of the knowledge acquired in the two separate directions which that philosopher opened up for the human spirit. Moreover we announce that we place our works under the immediate protection of the doctors. We announce finally that we are profoundly convinced, as the celebrated Vicq-d'Azyr was, that the most important forward step which can be made intellectually to activate the progress of civilization would be the introduction of the study of observations on moral and physical man into public education. It is understood that we did not mean to apply what we said above to doctors who consider the business of curing as the most useful part of their occupation. We only had in view that small number of doctors who rise to the heights of Hippocratic thoughts and feelings and who consider the study of pathology as a means of better knowing man in a state of health. We only had in view that small number of doctors whose principal and direct purpose it is to study the needs of man and the best means of satisfying them, to study his faculties and the best means of developing them. Finally we had in view the doctors in whose eyes politics is nothing but general hygiene and who conceive of social organization as capable of reaching such a degree of perfection that all men participate by their works in the amelioration of the lot of the whole species." Bibliothèque Nationale. MSS. N.A.F. 24606, folio number 315.
9. See H. Gouhier, "La philosophie 'positiviste' et 'chrétienne' de D. de Blainville," *Revue philosophique de la France et de l'étranger*, CXXXI (1941), 38–69; also Pierre Laffitte, "Matériaux pour servir à la biographie d'Auguste Comte," *Revue Occidentale*, 2nd series, VIII (1893), 325. The *Archives positivistes* contain eleven notes from Saint-Simon to Blainville, mostly appeals for help or social communications about visits and appointments. They have been published by Gouhier, "Lettres inédites de Saint-Simon à Blainville," *Revue philosophique*, CXXXI (1941), 70–80. Only one communication is dated, a humble letter of thanks for Blainville's favorable reception of the *Mémoire sur la science de l'homme*, October 8, 1813.
10. J. L. E. Lerminier, *Philosophie du droit* (Paris, 1831), II, 198.
11. *Lettre aux Européens*, p. 76.
12. *Notice historique*, in *Oeuvres*, I, 102–103.
13. Lambert noted that Enfantin recounted this detail to the disciples on May 9, 1835. Bibliothèque de l'Arsenal. Fonds Enfantin, 7804–138.
14. In Comte's *Correspondance inédite*, I, 29, there is a note to Blainville, in-

correctly dated April 11, 1826: ". . . our unfortunate friend has tried to destroy himself but fortunately has not succeeded, and there is every hope that we shall save him." The original note in the Archives Positivistes is dated only "Ce mardi, 11"; Comte had gone around to Blainville's house to ask him to pay a visit, at Saint-Simon's request.

15. The account of the suicide is based on the Saint-Simonion tradition as recorded in the *Notice historique*, in *Oeuvres*, I, 104–106, and in Hubbard, *Saint-Simon, sa vie et ses travaux*.

16. A. des Etangs, *Du suicide politique en France* (Paris, 1860), pp. 445–446.

29. The Master Denied

1. In the April 1820 issue of *L'Organisateur* appeared Comte's *Sommaire appréciation de l'ensemble du passé moderne*. A letter to Valat hinted at intellectual differences. "I shall take care to indicate to you exactly what is in my manner and what is Saint-Simon's." *Lettres à Valat*, p. 106, September 6, 1820.

2. Comte's jubilation at the outcome of the trial was expressed to his friend, *Lettres*, pp. 106–107, September 6, 1820. Throughout he refers to himself and Saint-Simon as a corporate *we*. "We have just had appear yesterday a brochure of about a hundred pages entitled *Considérations sur les mesures à prendre pour terminer la Révolution*."

3. The long letter to M. Emile Tabarié *fils* of April 5, 1824 contains Comte's fullest account of his quarrel with Saint-Simon. Comte, *Lettres à divers* (Paris, 1905), II, 3–7. The same story was repeated with variants to Gustave d'Eichthal on May 1, 1824. *Lettres à divers*, II, 31–41. Comte announced the success of his tract to Tabarié *fils* on July 17, 1824. *Lettres à divers*, II, 11.

4. *Lettres*, II, 6: Comte to Tabarié *fils*, April 5, 1824.

5. *Lettres*, II, 7: Comte to Tabarié *fils*, April 5, 1824.

6. "We shall join to the third *cahier* of the *Catéchisme* a volume on the scientific system and on the system of education.

"This work, for which we have laid the bases, and whose execution we have confided to our pupil Auguste Comte, will expound the industrial system *a priori*, while we shall continue in this catechism its exposition *a posteriori*." *Catéchisme des industriels*, first *cahier*, p. 46.

7. *Catéchisme*, third *cahier*, p. 1.

8. The fourth and last *cahier* of the *Catéchisme des industriels* was nothing but a recapitulation of the first two *cahiers*.

9. *Catéchisme*, third *cahier*, p. 2.

10. *Catéchisme*, third *cahier*, p. 5.

11. *Catéchisme*, third *cahier*, p. 6.

12. *Catéchisme*, third *cahier*, pp. 6–7.

13. *Catéchisme*, third *cahier*, p. 7.

14. *Catéchisme*, third *cahier*, p. 7.

15. *Catéchisme*, third *cahier*, p. 8.

16. Comte, *Lettres à divers*, II, 35–36: Comte to Gustave d'Eichthal, May 1, 1824.

17. *Lettres*, II, 34–35: Comte to Gustave d'Eichthal, May 1, 1824.

18. *Lettres*, II, 12: Comte to Tabarié, July 17, 1824.

19. *Lettres*, II, 80–82: Comte to Gustave d'Eichthal, December 10, 1824.

20. *Lettres*, II, 93: Comte to Gustave d'Eichthal, November 24, 1825.

21. *Lettres*, II, 104: Comte to Gustave d'Eichthal, December 9, 1828.

22. *Lettres*, II, 107: Comte to Gustave d'Eichthal, December 7, 1829.

23. *Lettres*, II, 169–170: Comte to Michel Chevalier, January 5, 1832.

24. *Notice historique*, in *Oeuvres*, V, 115, 117: Michel Chevalier to Comte.

25. Richmond L. Hawkins, *Auguste Comte and the United States* (Cambridge, 1936), pp. 81–82.

26. Auguste Comte to George F. Holmes, September 18, 1852: "It would be strange indeed if his influence had been more profound since he was extremely superficial although ingenious and seductive. Stranger to all knowledge of the sciences, in spite of his affectations in this respect, he could be intellectually defined as a *littérateur très peu lettré*, spending the better part of his days reading bad novels. . . . In my next preface I shall conclude my judgment on him by pronouncing twenty-eight years after his death this verdict of posterity, 'The famous Count Henri de Saint-Simon was a superficial and depraved charlatan very inferior to Cagliostro in every respect.' " Hawkins, *Auguste Comte*, pp. 115–116.

27. Comte, *Correspondance inédite*, II, 255: Comte to M. Hadéry, August 18, 1853.

28. For further material on Encontre, see Henri Gouhier, "Le premier maître d'Auguste Comte, Daniel Encontre," *Revue d'histoire de la philosophie*, I (1933), 76–93.

29. The controversy among disciples and later commentators has ebbed and flowed for more than a century. In general it has tended to revolve about the originality of the law of three states. R. Flint, *The History of the Philosophy of History* (Edinburgh, 1893), pp. 398–399, believes that Comte should have acknowledged his intellectual debt towards his master; Hubbard naturally held that the law of three states was directly borrowed from Saint-Simon. Littré argued that since the *Mémoire sur la science de l'homme* was not published until 1858 it could not have exerted any influence on Comte; to which Flint countered that in 1813 sixty manuscript copies were made, not all of which had been distributed, and therefore the text was available to Comte. Littré had carried his zeal to the point of inverting their influences: "At no moment was Saint-Simon the philosophic teacher of Auguste Comte; at more than one moment Auguste Comte influenced the wavering thought of Saint-Simon." E. Littré, *Auguste Comte*, p. 92. M. Uta, *La Loi des trois états dans la philosophie d'Auguste Comte* (Bourg, 1928), adopted an eclectic attitude, counting Turgot, Condorcet, de Bonald, de Maistre, and Saint-Simon as predecessors.

In 1875 there was a polemic on the subject in Charles Renouvier's *La Critique Philosophique*. F. Pillon stripped Comte of any originality in his article, "Une question de priorité à propos de la loi des trois états," *La Critique Philosophique* (1875), IVe année. E. Sémérie, *La loi des trois états. Réponse à M. Renouvier* (Paris, 1875), answered for the Comtists. His opinion was supported by the next generation: R. Teixeira Mendes, *Une Funeste liaison de la vingtième année d'Auguste Comte* (Rio de Janeiro, 1906); Paul Dubuisson, *Comte et Saint-Simon, Comte n'est-il que le disciple de Saint-Simon?* (Paris, 1906); Georges Deherme, *Un maître: Auguste Comte; une direction: Le positivisme* (Paris, 1921). Henry Maréchal, *Les Conceptions économiques d'Auguste Comte* (Paris, 1919), p. 40, contrasted Comte's method and logic with Saint-Simon's confusion: "Saint-Simon had no scientific culture, he was profound by chance." Ernest Seillière, on the other hand, in *Auguste Comte* (Paris, 1924), p. 14, believed that all the essential ideas in Comtism came from Saint-Simon. George Boas does not credit Saint-Simon with the law of three states: "Saint-Simon's version of the law of the three states is not so clearly defined as Turgot's and it is doubtful that Comte could have derived his formulation from his master." *French Philosophies of the Romantic Period* (Baltimore, 1925), p. 270. But as for the general theory he holds: "I am somewhat inclined towards the position of M. Dumas, that there is little in Comte that was not previously in Saint-Simon." *French Philosophies*, p. 276fn.

30. H.-P. Deroisin, *Notes sur Auguste Comte par un de ses disciples* (Paris, 1909), pp. 20–21.

31. The manuscripts of the *Prospectus* in the Archives Positivistes, Paris. See also Laffitte, "Matériaux pour servir à la biographie d'Auguste Comte," *Revue Occidentale*, pp. 315–334.

32. Passages of the *Prospectus*, April 1822 (p. 77, for example) are such obvious parallels to Saint-Simon's hierarchy of the sciences, developed in his Empire writings, that Gouhier's complete dismissal of Saint-Simon is unwarranted, even granting his architectonic inadequacies.

30. True Disciples

1. Pereire, *Autour de Saint-Simon*, pp. 103–104.

2. In the Bibliothèque de l'Arsenal, Fonds Enfantin 7865, there is a receipt from Saint-Simon to Gustave d'Eichthal in acknowledgment of a subscription to the *Catéchisme des industriels*.

3. Olinde Rodrigues is described in C. Coignet, "Saint-Simon et le Saint-Simonisme," *La Nouvelle Revue*, XX (1883), 125–173: "Belonging to a financial family, Rodrigues had a great capacity for business; at the same time, in matters of religion, he could be a believer to the point of fanaticism and an enthusiast to the point of ecstasy. Small in stature, bony without being thin, his regular features, his hair and his reddish beard recall the traditional type. His gait was uneven and rapid, his speech curt and jerky, sometimes as if marked with a prophetic accent," p. 131.

4. *Limude Dat U-musar* (Metz, 1820).

5. On the religious life of the Pereire and Rodrigues families, see J. Plenge, *Gründung und Geschichte des Crédit Mobilier*, pp. 38–39.

6. An undated fragment, *Naissance du Christianisme*, by Saint-Simon, published in Hubbard, *Saint-Simon*, pp. 256–263, and reprinted in the *Oeuvres*, XIX, 174–187, dwelt on the perseverance and pride of the Jews.

7. Upon leaving the direction of the school, Rodrigues in a speech at the Caisse hypothécaire December 31, 1829, told the disciples: "I shall begin by recalling that among the small number of those who surrounded Saint-Simon on his deathbed, the only one who has not abandoned the memory of the master, the only one who has continued his works, the only one, finally, who today professes and propagates the doctrine in his name, *is I*. The others have fled, have denied the master. It is then through me that there has been preserved a sort of filiation between the dead Saint-Simon and the disciples whom I have been able to win to his doctrine." Bibliothèque de l'Arsenal. Fonds Enfantin 7644, II. Also, *Notice historique*, in *Oeuvres*, II, 114–115.

8. Elie Halphen Halévy was known outside the Jewish community. A Hebrew hymn he composed in praise of the Peace of Amiens, *Ha-shalom*, was translated into French and German and won for its author a Latin eulogy by the Protestant pastor Marron, *Eliae Halévy Hebraice carmine pacis reditum egregie celebranti*. See Léon Halévy, *F. Halévy, sa vie et ses oeuvres* (Paris, 1862).

9. The article on Léon Halévy in the *Grande Encyclopédie*, XIX, 755.

10. Léon Halévy, *Saint-Simon, Ode* (Paris, 1831).

11. Hubbard, *Saint-Simon*, p. 109; Léon Halévy, "Souvenirs de Saint-Simon," *Revue d'histoire économique et sociale*, XIII (1925), 171–173fn. This article (166–176), edited by G. Brunet, consisted of excerpts from the *Souvenirs* published in *La France littéraire* in March 1832.

12. For strange relations between the Saint-Simonians in search of the Female

Messiah and the Jews of Constantinople, also possible relations with a Jewish messianic movement of the late thirties, see Abraham G. Duker, "The Tarniks," *The Joshua Starr Memorial Volume* (New York, 1953), pp. 194–195.

31. The New Christianity

1. *L'Industrie*, in *Oeuvres*, XIX, 41.
2. *Du système industriel*, in *Oeuvres*, XXI, 96.
3. For example, see de Bonald, *Théorie du pouvoir*, in *Oeuvres*, II, 14–15.
4. *Du système industriel*, in *Oeuvres*, XXII, 231–235.
5. *Oeuvres*, XXII, 115–116.
6. Bibliothèque Nationale. MSS. N.A.F. 24607.
7. *Du système industriel*, in *Oeuvres*, XXII, 124.
8. *Oeuvres*, XXII, 112.
9. The belief that Olinde Rodrigues wrote the introduction is based upon a manuscript note in a copy of the *Nouveau Christianisme* in the Bibliothèque de l'Arsenal, Fonds Enfantin 7802 (132) 8. Hoëné-Wrónski once told Frédéric de Rougemont that the *Nouveau Christianisme* was not written by Saint-Simon. Frédéric de Rougemont, *Les Deux cités. La philosophie de l'histoire aux différents ages de l'humanité*, 2 vols. (Paris, 1874), II, 439. This evidence by a rival Messiah is naturally suspect.
10. In a letter to John Stuart Mill on December 1, 1829, Gustave d'Eichthal, who was a close friend of Olinde Rodrigues, thus described the new religious orientation of Saint-Simon's last period: "Saint-Simon, after having in his early writings tried to reorganize society in the name of Science, after having later renewed the same attempt in the name of Industry, realized that he had mistaken the *means* for the *end*; that it is in the name of their *sympathies* that one must speak to men, and above all, in the name of their *religious sympathies* which should summarize all others." J. S. Mill, *Correspondance inédite avec Gustave d'Eichthal* (Paris, 1898), pp. 75–76. D'Eichthal had written in his letter of November 23, 1829 that for two years none of the disciples was able to grasp the full meaning of the *Nouveau Christianisme*. *Correspondance*, p. 57fn. By December 1, 1829, the key had been discovered and the religion of Saint-Simon had been clothed in the language of romanticized Spinozism: "The religious doctrine of Saint-Simon has this *unitary* character which should gather about it all the men of the future. It puts neither *spirit* above *matter*, nor *matter* above *spirit*. It considers them as intimately united one with another, as being the condition one of the other, as being the two modes in which *being* is manifest, *living* being, *sympathetic* being." *Correspondance*, p. 74.
11. "But there is a science which is more important for society than physical and mathematical knowledge. It is the science which constitutes society, which serves as its base. It is morals. Now morals have followed a path absolutely contrary to that of the physical and mathematical sciences. More than eighteen hundred years have elapsed since its fundamental principle was produced, and since that time, all the researches of men of the greatest genius have not been able to discover a principle superior in its generality or in its precision to the one formulated at that epoch by the founder of Christianity." *Nouveau Christianisme*, in *Oeuvres choisies*, III, 378–379.
12. "Les hommes doivent se conduire en frères à l'égard les uns des autres." *Oeuvres choisies*, III, 322. It is not absolutely clear to which New Testament text he refers. It could be the King James version equivalent in Romans, XII: "In love of the brethren be tenderly affectioned one to another." The epigraph of the *Nouveau Christianisme* was derived from passages in the French version of Romans XIII: "for

he that loveth his neighbor hath fulfilled the law . . . and if there be any other commandment, it is summed up in this word, namely, Thou shalt love thy neighbor as thyself."

13. *Nouveau Christianisme*, in *Oeuvres choisies*, III, 322.

14. The primitive catechism to which Saint-Simon referred expressed the Golden Rule in a negative rather than a positive form.

15. *Oeuvres choisies*, III, 332.

16. *Oeuvres choisies*, III, 343.

17. *Oeuvres choisies*, III, 330.

18. *Oeuvres choisies*, III, 348.

19. *Oeuvres choisies*, III, 353.

20. *Oeuvres choisies*, III, 363–364.

21. *Oeuvres choisies*, III, 379.

22. Saint-Simon's limitation of Christianity to a set of moral principles, discarding all its dogmas, never sat well with religious thinkers. J. Régnier, "Les idées morales et religieuses de Saint-Simon," *Nouvelle Revue*, new series, XX (1903), 229–238; Rudolf Stammler, *Sozialismus und Christentum* (Leipzig, 1920), p. 83. De Lépine, *Le Dieu malgré lui*, p. 24, says that Saint-Simon sent a copy of the *Nouveau Christianisme* to the Pope. The romantic Catholic K. W. Schiebler, one of the first Germans to write about the new morality of Saint-Simon sympathetically, was of course repelled by the religious heresies; see his *Der Saint-Simonismus oder die Lehre Saint-Simon's und seiner Anhänger* (Leipzig, 1831).

23. C. Lemonnier, *Revue des cours littéraires* (1876), XXI, 383, was of the opinion that a total view of Saint-Simon's works could, despite the contradictions, only lead to the conclusion that "he died as he lived, that he remained to the end in the ranks of the free-thinkers." Professor Henri Gouhier's judgment is categoric: "The Saint-Simonism of Saint-Simon is not a religion, but a social philosophy disguised as a religion." *La Jeunesse d'Auguste Comte* (Paris, 1933–1941), III, 231.

24. Alfred de Musset's description of his generation in *La Confession d'un enfant du siècle* (Paris, 1937), pp. 19, 24: "Alas! Alas! Religion is vanishing. . . . We no longer have either hope or expectation, not even two little pieces of black wood in a cross before which to wring our hands. . . . Everything that was is no more. All that will be is not yet."

25. *Enseignements d'Enfantin*, in *Oeuvres*, XIV, 4. Rodrigues's speech of December 31, 1829, confirms this. "The *Christianisme*, thanks to my perseverance, was read, reread, and each day more and more understood." Bibliothèque de l'Arsenal, Fonds Enfantin, 7644.

26. *Enseignements d'Enfantin*, in *Oeuvres*, XIV, 5, 9–10.

27. *Nouveau Christianisme*, in *Oeuvres*, XXIII, 182–183.

28. *Oeuvres*, XXIII, 183.

29. *Oeuvres*, XXIII, 184.

30. *Oeuvres*, XXIII, 184–185.

31. *Oeuvres*, XXIII, 185.

32. *Notice historique*, in *Oeuvres*, II, 115, 116. Rodrigues quoted Saint-Simon in a speech delivered on December 31, 1829, when he resigned the direction of the school. Bibliothèque de l'Arsenal, Fonds Enfantin, 7644.

33. *Oeuvres*, XXXVII, xxxvi.

32. Death and Apotheosis

1. *Notice historique,* in *Oeuvres,* I, 118.
2. *Oeuvres,* I, 119.
3. *Oeuvres,* I, 120. ·
4. *Oeuvres,* I, 120.
5. *Oeuvres,* I, 121–122.
6. H. Carnot, "Résumé général de la doctrine saint-simonienne, fait en 1831," *Revue socialiste,* XVII (1893), 316. "Let us remember," wrote *Le Globe* on June 4, 1825, "that the last moments of this extraordinary man were sweet and peaceful, that his religion of human happiness and fraternity was for him the equivalent of the priest's consolation and voice among believers of the Catholic church. He conversed, discoursed with his pupils, talked on with exaltation of his works and of their future, and to use an expression of M. Halévy who rendered him so touching an homage at his tomb, he fell asleep in a dream of public happiness."
7. *Le Curieux* (1885), I, 263–264, published the act of decease.
8. *Le Constitutionnel,* May 22, 1825.
9. *Discours prononcé sur la tombe de M. de Saint-Simon, par le Docteur E. M. Bailly de Blois* (n.p., n.d. [Blois, 1825]). Bibliothèque Nationale 8° Ln²⁷ 18323. Obituaries appeared in *Revue encyclopédique,* XXX (April 1826), 281–283; A. J. Mahul, *Annuaire nécrologique* (1825), VI, 278–289.
10. A. Augustin-Thierry, *Augustin Thierry,* p. 39.
11. *Notice historique,* in *Oeuvres,* I, 127–128.
12. *Oeuvres,* I, 131.
13. *Oeuvres,* I, 132.

Index of Names and Titles

Alcibiades, 13

Alembert, Jean Le Rond d', 13, 51, 64, 81, 131, 139, 140, 145–146, 150, 160, 226, 392

Discours préliminaire, 80, 131, 140, 145–146

Alexander I, Czar of Russia, 172, 179

Allix, E., 402

Ancelot, Madame Marguerite Louise Virginie, 54, 379

Andreä, Johann Valentin, 73

Christianopolis, 73

Aquinas, Saint Thomas, 233

Arago, Dominique François Jean, 192, 378

Aranda, Pedro Pablo Abarca y Bolea, Count de, 22, 375

Ardoin, A., 192, 331, 344, 364

Aristotle, 88, 145, 242, 317, 335, 391

Articles pour la cause de Mgr. de Saint-Simon, 26, 375

Auger, Hippolyte-Nicolas-Just, 190, 379, 403

Mémoires, 190

Augustin-Thierry, A., 400, 403, 423

Augustine, Saint, 398

Aulard, François Victor Alphonse, 381

Avitus, Marcus Maecilius, 9

Azaïs, Pierre-Hyacinthe, 89, 384, 388

Bases du système universel, 89

Babeuf, François-Noël, 47, 373

Bacon, Francis, First Baron Verulam, Viscount St. Albans, 64, 68, 73, 75, 76, 77, 82, 84, 88, 90, 92, 119, 120, 124, 125, 131, 132, 133, 140, 141, 152, 164, 171, 249, 262, 381, 384, 387, 389, 392, 395

New Atlantis, 73, 75, 124, 164

Novum Organum, 131

Bailly, Dr. Etienne-Marin, 329, 338, 364, 365, 366, 423

Balch, Thomas, 373

Ballanche, Pierre-Simon, 360

Ballot, Charles, 400

Balzac, Honoré de, 353

Barras, Paul-François-Jean-Nicolas, Count de, 48, 51, 52, 53

Barth, Paul, 399

Barthélemy, François, Marquis de, 42, 43, 52, 99, 101, 104, 106, 377

Basire, Claude, 37, 39

Basterrèche, Jean-Pierre, 331

Batz, Jean, Baron de, 37, 54

Baudin des Ardennes, Pierre-Charles-Louis, 392

Bauer, Stephan, 408

Bawr, Alexandrine-Sophie Goury de Champgrand, Baroness de, 37, 53, 54–56, 378, 379

Bazard, Saint-Amand, 235, 371

Bazin, Jacques Rigomer, 73, 178, 381

Le Lynx, 178

Becker, Carl Lotus, 160, 400

The Heavenly City of the Eighteenth-Century Philosophers, 160

Béhague, Jean-Pierre-Antoine, Count de, 46

Belhomme, Jacques, 108–109, 111, 386

Belhomme, Dr. Jacques-Etienne, 386

Benaben, (journalist), 200

Benoît ——, 37

Bentham, Jeremy, 118, 227, 228, 351

Berg, W., 408

Bernardin de Saint-Pierre, Jacques-Henri, 49

Bernis, François Joachim de Pierre, Cardinal de, 44

Berry, Charles Ferdinand, Duke de, 211–212

Berthier, Citoyen, 388

Bertin, Ernest, 372

Bertrand, Louis, 380

Beyle, Marie Henri, 91, 260, 280, 345, 353, 360, 397

Le Rouge et le noir, 360

Bichat, Marie-François-Xavier, 49, 51, 134, 159, 194, 298–299, 300, 301, 304, 307, 340, 394, 399, 415

Recherches physiologiques sur la vie et sur la mort, 159, 298–299

Billaud-Varenne, Jacques-Nicolas, 149

Biot, Jean-Baptiste, 49

Blainville, Henri Marie Ducrotay de, 51, 162, 182, 329, 400, 417, 418

Blanchard, Claude, 15, 374

Boas, George, 384, 419

Boislisle, Arthur Michel de, 372

Boissy d'Anglas, François Antoine, Count de, 41, 97, 98, 104, 105, 106, 373, 377, 378, 385